The Linguistic Roots of Ancient Greek

The Linguistic Roots of Ancient Greek

DON RINGE

OXFORD
UNIVERSITY PRESS

OXFORD
UNIVERSITY PRESS

Great Clarendon Street, Oxford, OX2 6DP,
United Kingdom

Oxford University Press is a department of the University of Oxford.
It furthers the University's objective of excellence in research, scholarship,
and education by publishing worldwide. Oxford is a registered trade mark of
Oxford University Press in the UK and in certain other countries

Published in the United States of America by Oxford University Press
198 Madison Avenue, New York, NY 10016, United States of America

British Library Cataloguing in Publication Data
Data available

Library of Congress Control Number: 2023946156

ISBN 9780198879022

DOI: 10.1093/9780191989162.001.0001

Printed and bound by
CPI Group (UK) Ltd, Croydon, CR0 4YY

Contents

Acknowledgments viii
Abbreviations and conventions ix

1. Introduction 1

2. Proto-Indo-European 4
 2.1 Introduction 4
 2.2 PIE phonology 7
  2.2.1 PIE obstruents 8
  2.2.2 PIE sonorants and high vowels 11
  2.2.3 PIE non-high vowels 12
  2.2.4 PIE phonological rules 13
  2.2.5 PIE accent 23
 2.3 PIE inflectional morphology 24
  2.3.1 PIE inflectional categories 24
  2.3.2 Formal expression of inflectional categories 28
  2.3.3 PIE verb inflection 30
  2.3.4 PIE noun inflection 51
  2.3.5 PIE adjective inflection 66
  2.3.6 The inflection of other PIE nominals 69
 2.4 PIE derivational morphology 76
  2.4.1 Compounding 76
  2.4.2 PIE derivational suffixes 77
 2.5 PIE syntax 81
 2.6 The PIE lexicon 87

3. The phonological development of Proto-Greek 88
 3.1 Introduction 88
 3.2 The elimination of laryngeals 88
  3.2.1 The loss of laryngeals next to non-high vowels 89
  3.2.2 Developments of laryngeals preceding high vowels and syllabic sonorants 93
  3.2.3 Developments of tautosyllabic laryngeals following high vowels and syllabic sonorants 99
  3.2.4 Developments of laryngeals not adjacent to a syllabic 106
 3.3 Early developments of nasals 112
 3.4 Early developments of obstruents 116
  3.4.1 'Thorn' clusters 116
  3.4.2 The merger of palatals and velars 116
  3.4.3 Early developments of labiovelars 117

3.4.4 Early developments of stop clusters 121
3.4.5 The devoicing of aspirates 125
3.4.6 Loss of *t and *t^h before final *-i 128
3.5 The origin and development of Proto-Greek *h 131
3.5.1 *s > *h 131
3.5.2 *h-copying ('Hauchumsprung') 141
3.5.3 Osthoff's Law; loss of word-final stops 144
3.5.4 Grassmann's Law 146
3.5.5 Irregularities of aspiration 150
3.6 The development of PIE *y 153
3.6.1 Sievers' Law in Greek 153
3.6.2 Word-initial *y 157
3.6.3 Postconsonantal *y 158
3.7 Other clusters of dental stops 167
3.8 Accent in Proto-Greek 169
3.9 Relative chronology of sound changes 170

4. The development of Proto-Greek inflectional morphology 173
4.1 Introduction 173
4.2 Changes in verb inflection 173
4.2.1 The development of present stems 174
4.2.2 The development of aorist stems 201
4.2.3 Perfect stems 216
4.2.4 Future stems 223
4.2.5 Mood suffixes and the augment 225
4.2.6 Personal endings 227
4.2.7 Participles and infinitives 232
4.2.8 The accent of Greek verb forms 232
4.3 Changes in nominal inflection 233
4.3.1 Cases 233
4.3.2 Accent and ablaut 234
4.3.3 Stem types: Nouns 239
4.3.4 Stem types: Adjectives 250
4.3.5 Noun and adjective endings 254
4.3.6 Pronouns 257
4.3.7 Numerals 260

5. The initial diversification of Greek dialects 262
5.1 Introduction 262
5.2 Aiolic 264
5.2.1 Evidence for an Aiolic group 264
5.2.2 The first compensatory lengthening 266
5.3 South Greek 271
5.3.1 Phonological evidence for South Greek 272
5.3.2 Morphological evidence for South Greek 276
5.3.3 An assessment of South Greek 280

5.4 Other widely shared early innovations 281
5.4.1 Early phonological innovations 281
5.4.2 Early morphological innovations 294

6. The Attic-Ionic dialects 300
6.1 Introduction 300
6.2 Attic and Ionic sound changes 300
6.3 Attic-Ionic morphological innovations 309

7. Widely shared later innovations 312
7.1 Introduction 312
7.2 Later sound changes 312
7.2.1 νσ-clusters 312
7.2.2 Loss of *ϝ 316
7.2.3 Loss of intervocalic *h and *j; contractions of vowels in hiatus 318
7.2.4 Long mid vowels 319
7.2.5 Outcomes of palatalization: σσ ~ ττ 323
7.2.6 Psilosis 324
7.3 Later morphological changes 324
7.3.1 Third-person plural imperatives 324
7.3.2 Subjunctives and optatives 326
7.3.3 Perfect stems 327

8. Syntax 328
8.1 Constituent order 328
8.2 Prohibitions 330
8.3 Moods 332
8.4 Univerbation 333
8.5 Clitics 334
8.6 Prepositions 334
8.7 Reflexives 335

9. Lexicon 336
9.1 Derivational morphology 336
9.2 Sources of the Greek lexicon 338

Bibliography 343
Index 361
1 Greek 361
2 Proto-Indo-European 379
3 Other Indo-European languages 390

Acknowledgments

I am grateful to Philomen Probert, Michael Weiss, Dariusz Piwowarczyk, and Wolfgang de Melo for helpful comments on earlier drafts of this book and several important references; to Joseph F. Eska, Ronald Kim, H. Craig Melchert, Thomas Olander, and Patrick Stiles for commentary on Chapter 2; to Matthew Scarborough for extensive and valuable commentary on Chapter 5 and for alerting me to many recent epigraphical publications; to Jeremy Rau and Georgios Kostopoulos for useful references; and to James Clackson, the late Hans Frede Nielsen, and the late Anthony Kroch for helpful advice. Readers should not assume that any of them agrees with me on any given point.

Abbreviations and conventions

Abbreviations

abl.	ablative
acc.	accusative
act.	active
adv.	adverb
all.	allative
aor.	aorist
Ark.	Arkadian
Arm.	Armenian
Att.	Attic
Av.	Avestan
BL	Bartholomae's Law; Brugmann's Law (*the context will disambiguate*)
Boiot.	Boiotian
Brixhe	Brixhe (1976), *Le dialecte grec de Pamphylie*
Buck	Buck (1955), *The Greek dialects*
C	consonant
Comp	complementizer
CP	complementizer phrase
cpd.	compound
cptv.	comparative
Cret.	Cretan
dat.	dative
deriv.	derivative
DGE	Schwyzer (1923), *Dialectorum graecarum exempla epigraphica potiora*
Dor.	Doric
DP	determiner phrase / noun phrase
du.	dual
fem.	feminine
Frisk	Frisk (1960–1974), *Griechisches etymologisches Wörterbuch*
fut.	future
gen.	genitive
Gk	Greek
GL	Grassmann's Law
Goth.	Gothic
H	laryngeal
Hitt.	Hittite
Hom.	Homeric

Hom. h.	Homeric hymns
IE	Indo-European
IG	*Inscriptiones graecae*
Il.	*Iliad*
indic.	indicative
inf.	infinitive
inj.	injunctive
inst.	instrumental
intr.	intransitive
Ion.	Ionic
ipf.	imperfect
iptv.	imperative
K	dorsal stop
Lat.	Latin
Lesb.	Lesbian
Lith.	Lithuanian
LIV	Rix et al. (2001), *Lexikon der indogermanischen Verben*
loc.	locative
LSJ	Liddell and Scott (1940), *A Greek-English lexicon*, 9th ed.
masc.	masculine
Masson	Masson (1961), *Les inscriptions chypriotes syllabiques*
mid.	middle
mp.	mediopassive
Myc.	Mycenaean
N	nasal sonorant (*in discussions of phonology*); noun (*in discussions of syntax*)
neut.	neuter
NIE	Nuclear Indo-European
nom.	nominative
O	object
OCP	Obligatory Contour Principle
OCS	Old Church Slavonic
Od.	*Odyssey*
OE	Old English
OHG	Old High German
OIr.	Old Irish
OL	Osthoff's Law
ON	Old Norse
OPers.	Old Persian
opt.	optative
pass.	passive
pf.	perfect
PGk	Proto-Greek
PGmc	Proto-Germanic
PIE	Proto-Indo-European

pl.	plural
plup.	pluperfect
pres.	present
pret.	preterite
ptc.	participle
QM	quantitative metathesis
R	sonorant (*in discussions of phonology*); root (*in discussions of morphology*)
RV	*Rigveda*
S	subject
SEG	*Supplementum epigraphicum graecum*
sg.	singular
Skt	Sanskrit
SL	Sievers' Law
subj.	subjunctive
sup.	superlative
T	coronal stop (*in discussions of phonology*); tensed verb (*in discussions of syntax*)
Thess.	Thessalian
Toch.	Tocharian
trans.	transitive
V	vowel (*in discussions of phonology*); lexical verb (*in discussions of syntax*)
voc.	vocative
VP	verb phrase
WGk	West Greek
WH	interrogative and relative
1, 2, 3	first, second, third person
1ary	primary
2ary	secondary
1CL	first compensatory lengthening
2CL	second compensatory lengthening
3CL	third compensatory lengthening

Conventions

I have systematically distinguished the secondary long mid vowels ε̄ and ō ('spurious diphthongs') from the inherited diphthongs ει and ου both because the distinction is etymologically important and because the two pairs were actually pronounced differently in Attic far down into the 5th century BC, as we learn from Attic inscriptions (Threatte 1980: 172–6, 238–42; sociolinguists will recognize the pattern of early 'crossover' spellings as evidence for phonemes with overlapping but distinct variable realizations). In citing specific Homeric passages and epigraphical forms I have given the attested spelling, with a note on what it actually means if the context does not make that clear.

Specific citations of literary works are identified conventionally. I have cited the fragments of lyric poets from David Campbell's Loeb edition, since it is up to date and sufficiently rigorous. For the most part I cite inscriptions from Schwyzer (1923) and Buck (1955), since those collections are easily accessible; they are identified respectively as *DGE* and 'Buck' (with no date). Inscriptions in the Cypriote syllabary, however, are cited from Masson (1961) as 'Masson' (with no date), and Pamphylian inscriptions from Brixhe (1976) as 'Brixhe' (with no date). (Other citations of these works are given with date and page number.) Attestations of Mycenaean forms can be found in Aura Jorro (1999). Hjalmar Frisk's etymological dictionary (Frisk 1960–1974) is cited simply as 'Frisk'. For citation abbreviations see the list above.

In detailing the development of any form from PIE to Ancient Greek, one has to transition from the modified Roman alphabet in which PIE is written to the Greek alphabet. I have tried to follow the principle that whatever is arguably 'Proto-Greek' or later (except for Linear B tablets and inscriptions in the Cypriote syllabary) should be written in the Greek alphabet; complete consistency has been difficult to achieve, but I hope that the result is always clear in context. Additional Roman characters and diacritics have been used for phonemes no longer occurring in attested Greek. In citing epigraphical forms from dialects which have short vowels instead of Attic long vowels in the final syllable, I have applied the usual Greek accent rules instead of assigning the accent of Attic (cf. Hoenigswald 1997: 95 fn. 11) in order to make the length of the final-syllable vowel clear at a glance; for instance, the Thessalian acc. pl. fem. 'thousands' is written χέλλιας rather than χελλίας. I make one systematic exception: in Boiotian forms in which οι has become ῡ and αι has become η I have not adjusted the accent, since there is no reason to believe that those late changes had any effect on the accent.

Forms of other languages are cited in the usual orthography or transcription. Since the few Oscan forms cited are inscribed in the native alphabet, they are given in boldface, as is customary.

1
Introduction

This book is intended to be parallel to *From Proto-Indo-European to Proto-Germanic* (2nd ed., 2017); it traces the development of Ancient Greek from PIE down to roughly the 5th century BC. Experience shows that I need to emphasize the purpose of the book: **it is NOT a comparative and historical grammar of Greek;**[1] it is an attempt to figure out which changes happened when, and to some extent it has to take knowledge of Ancient Greek for granted. For that reason I have not usually transliterated Greek in this volume. Since readers are most likely to be familiar with Classical Attic, I have foregrounded that dialect, but the book is written from the perspective of Ancient Greek as a whole, including the dialects known only from inscriptions. The intended readership of the volume is colleagues, students, and interested amateurs who have learned at least some Greek and internalized the basic concepts of linguistics. Because comprehensive grammars of Ancient Greek are readily available, I have not included a grammatical sketch of the language at the end of the volume.

Since I have tried to present a coherent account of material that is generally agreed on, the overall picture of the grammar of Proto-Indo-European and the development of Greek presented in this volume is relatively conservative. That is partly a practical decision, but there is also an important principle involved. The comparative method is applied mathematics, and its results are exceptionally reliable for just that reason. When we begin to *interpret* the results of the method, trying to push reconstruction further, we are pursuing internal reconstruction—a much less reliable endeavor—of an already reconstructed language, and the farther we push our interpretation, the less and less likely it becomes that our results are correct. It seems to me that some colleagues have lost sight of that basic probabilistic fact, and not only recently. Of course some inferences, such as the 'coloring' of */e/ by adjacent laryngeals in PIE, are so well supported by the evidence that they are practically certain, but others are much less certain; the less straightforward a hypothesis is, the less probable it is. That is why I have taken the decision to write PIE forms in surface-contrastive notation, why I accept the existence of PIE underlying */a/, and so on.

I have included innovative suggestions on a small scale when they seemed necessary or appropriate, giving references to earlier publications; I hope that I have

[1] The most comprehensive historical grammar of Greek is still Schwyzer (1939). Also useful are Chantraine (1963, 1973) (for Homeric Greek), Rix (1976a), and Sihler (1995).

The Linguistic Roots of Ancient Greek. Don Ringe, Oxford University Press.
 DOI: 10.1093/9780191989162.003.0001

not forgotten to reference any distinctive views of previous researchers that I have accepted. Conclusions that are almost universally accepted in the field (such as the reconstruction of three 'laryngeal' consonants for PIE, or—most obviously—sound changes such as Grassmann's Law) have not been referenced. Since this is intended to be a handbook, I have often omitted discussion of alternative opinions; in particular, arguments based on etymologies which I do not accept have mostly been passed over in silence.

Chapter 2, which describes the reconstructed grammar of PIE, is in principle identical with Chapter 2 of Ringe (2017): the two narratives start at the same place, the common ancestor of the languages. However, further work in several relevant fields has prompted various revisions. The discussion of the 'homeland' question has made great progress during the past decade, with the result that the introduction to Chapter 2 deserved to be expanded; Jasanoff (2018) solved the 'thorn problem' so elegantly that all previous discussion has become irrelevant; and it is becoming increasingly clear that subjunctives are an important key to the reconstruction of the PIE verb.

Linguistic point of view

It seems only fair to warn the reader that I have also had to presuppose some prior knowledge of linguistics in order to keep the work within reasonable bounds. In the following paragraphs I will try to spell out the background that I take for granted.

I expect readers to have acquired a basic grounding in MODERN linguistics, without necessarily being familiar with the details of any one theory. In phonology I presuppose an understanding of the principle of phonemic contrast, familiarity with systems of ordered rules, and an understanding of how surface filters differ from the latter (but not, for example, familiarity with Optimality Theory). In morphology I presuppose a general understanding of case, tense, aspect, mood, and the other traditional inflectional categories, as well as the concepts of productivity and defaults. Though I have little to say about syntax in this volume, what I do say presupposes some version of generative syntax.

I also expect readers to have a basic familiarity with the principles of language change. I subscribe to the uniformitarian principle (on which, see Ringe and Eska 2013: 3–4, 30–1), without which scientific historical linguistics is not possible; in addition, I define 'linguistic descent' as an unbroken series of instances of native language acquisition by children, and I hold that apparent cases of linguistic descent in the undocumented past should be taken at face value unless there is convincing evidence to the contrary (see e.g. Ringe et al. 2002: 60–5, Ringe and Eska 2013: 228). Note especially that I take the regularity of sound change seriously; since investigation of historically documented languages shows that sound change is overwhelmingly regular in statistical terms, it is a serious breach of the uniformitarian principle not to assume the same for prehistory. (Sociolinguistic studies have not altered this picture; see e.g. Labov 1994: 419–543.) Readers who want to understand the consequences of the regularity of sound change are urged to read Hoenigswald (1960), the classic exposition of that subject. Finally, I adopt the overwhelmingly likely hypothesis that changes in language structure originate as failures to learn in detail, and that most such learner errors are made by native learners, i.e. small children. It might be supposed that that insight won't contribute much to the investigation of 'deep' prehistory, but in fact it has important practical consequences, especially in dealing with morphological change; an immediate consequence is that we must replace reliance on 'proportional analogy' with a much more interesting question: what would a three-year-old make of this or that pattern of data, and what rules would (s)he be likely to abstract from it? Interested readers should consult Ringe and Eska (2013).

Limitations of space do not permit me to cite full evidence for the standard reconstructions offered here; I often cite only those cognates that support a particular reconstruction most clearly. Examples have also been chosen to illustrate particular points clearly with a minimum of explanation, even though that limits the range of examples that can be used. But I wish to emphasize that everything said in this volume rests on scientific reconstruction from attested languages using the 'comparative method'. In other words, these conclusions are based on observation and logical inference (mathematical inference, in the case of phonology), not on speculation. Readers who are not already familiar with the principles of historical linguistics are urged to read one of the many good elementary textbooks on the subject.

2
Proto-Indo-European

2.1 Introduction

The earliest ancestor of Greek that is scientifically reconstructable is Proto-Indo-European (PIE), the ancestor of all the Indo-European (IE) languages. As is usual with protolanguages of the distant past, we can't say with certainty where and when PIE was spoken; recent work in several disciplines has led to the following fairly complex picture.

For decades the place where PIE was spoken has seemed most likely to be the river valleys of Ukraine in the 5th millennium BC (the 'steppe hypothesis'); it has been accepted that IE languages spread from that area by means of substantial population movements. The archaeological evidence is laid out extensively in Anthony (2007), and the archaeological and linguistic evidence is discussed in Anthony and Ringe (2015). The most prominent alternative, an origin in Anatolia as much as three millennia earlier, was first proposed in Renfrew (1987); in addition, Renfrew proposed a spread of IE languages with the spread of farming, but without much population movement, westward through Greece into the rest of Europe. That alternative has never been accepted by most Indo-Europeanists. Some computational cladistic analyses, beginning with Gray and Atkinson (2003), found dates for PIE that are compatible with Renfrew's hypothesis, but Chang et al. (2015) showed that the addition of unobjectionable 'ancestry constraints' to Gray and Atkinson's model—for instance, the requirement that Latin be the ancestor of the Romance languages in the phylogenetic tree—compressed the calculated time depth so as to yield dates consistent with the steppe hypothesis instead.[1]

The debate just summarized was completely transformed by the advent of ancient DNA analysis. Haak et al. (2015) demonstrated from ancient DNA evidence that there was a massive migration from the steppes into Europe at exactly the time that the steppe hypothesis posits (as well as an earlier migration from the eastern Mediterranean). It is now generally accepted that the non-Anatolian IE languages, at least, radiated from somewhere north of the Black Sea beginning around 3500 BC, the probable date when the ancestors of the Tocharians abruptly moved far to the east (Anthony and Ringe 2015: 208).

[1] This is ultimately a result of technical details of Gray and Atkinson's algorithm. For discussion, see Chang et al. (2015: 217–24, especially fn. 25).

The Linguistic Roots of Ancient Greek. Don Ringe, Oxford University Press.
 DOI: 10.1093/9780191989162.003.0002

However, how the speakers of Anatolian languages reached Anatolia is uncertain. They could have moved from the northern to the southern shore of the Black Sea before the radiation of the non-Anatolian languages, but a movement of the ancestors of 'Nuclear IE' (see below) in the opposite direction is also at least possible. Further DNA evidence will almost certainly be forthcoming in the future, and we can hope that it will resolve that question.

Though there continue to be gaps in our knowledge of PIE, a remarkable proportion of its grammar and vocabulary is securely reconstructable by the comparative method. As might be expected from the way the method works, the phonology of the language is relatively certain. Though syntactic reconstruction is in its infancy, some points of PIE syntax are uncontroversial because the earliest attested daughter languages agree so well. Nominal morphology is also fairly robustly reconstructable, with the exception of the pronouns, which continue to pose interesting problems. Only the inflection of the verb causes serious difficulties for Indo-Europeanists, for the following reason.

From the well-attested subfamilies of IE which were known at the end of the 19th century—Indo-Iranian, Armenian, Greek, Albanian, Italic, Celtic, Germanic, and Balto-Slavic—a coherent ancestral verb system can be reconstructed. The general outlines of the system are already visible in Karl Brugmann's classic *Grundriss der vergleichenden Grammatik der indogermanischen Sprachen* (2nd ed., 1897–1911); in recent decades Warren Cowgill, Helmut Rix, and other scholars have codified and systematized that reconstruction along more modern lines. The result is perhaps the standard reconstruction among more conservative Indo-Europeanists; it is sometimes called the 'Cowgill-Rix' verb, though 'Indo-Greek' might be a more apt designation.[2] Various versions of the Indo-Greek reconstruction can be found in Rix (1976a: 190 ff.), Rix et al. (2001), and the handbooks cited below. Unfortunately it is quite difficult to derive the system of the Hittite verb—by far the best known Anatolian verb system, and fortunately also the most archaic—from the Indo-Greek reconstruction of the PIE verb by natural changes, and even the Tocharian verb system presents us with enough puzzles and anomalies to raise the suspicion that the PIE verb system was somewhat different. A thorough exploration of this question is Jasanoff (2003a); a good summary discussion is Clackson (2007: 114–56). Though Jasanoff's reconstruction as a whole has not won general acceptance, a number of his individual observations must be correct.

Interestingly, there is by now a general consensus among Indo-Europeanists that the Anatolian subfamily is, in effect, one half of the IE family, all the other subgroups together forming the other half; and it is beginning to appear that

[2] In fact Cowgill strongly disagreed with at least one point in the conservative reconstruction, namely the view that the Hittite *ḫi*-conjugation can be descended from a PIE perfect (see especially Cowgill 1979). I therefore follow Clackson (2007: 115) in naming the model after the most conservative daughters on which its reconstruction is based, replacing his term 'Greco-Aryan' with my preferred alternative 'Indo-Greek'.

within the non-Anatolian subgroup, Tocharian is the outlier against all other subgroups (cf. Winter 1998, Ringe et al. 1998, Ringe 2000, Ringe, Warnow, and Taylor 2002 with references, Jasanoff 2003b). A probable cladistic tree of the IE family is roughly as in Figure 2.1.[3]

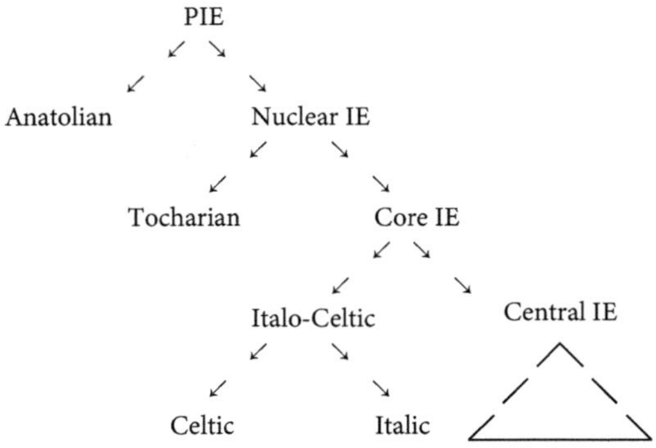

Figure 2.1 A probable cladistic tree of the Indo-European family

(On the Italo-Celtic subgroup, see also Jasanoff 1997 and Weiss 2012, both with references; for an attempt to sort out Proto-Italic and Proto-Italo-Celtic developments, see Schrijver 2006: 48–53.) The 'Central' subgroup includes Germanic, Balto-Slavic, Indo-Iranian, Armenian, Greek, and probably Albanian; its internal subgrouping is still very unclear, though it seems likely that Indo-Iranian, Balto-Slavic, and Germanic were parts of a dialect chain at a very early date.

Note the implications of this phylogeny for the reconstruction of the PIE verb. The Indo-Greek verb is a reasonable reconstruction of the system for 'Core IE', and can even account for most of the 'Nuclear IE' system; it is only for the ancestor of the whole family that it is seriously inadequate.

That is fortunate for anyone proposing to write a prehistory of Greek, because Greek is clearly one of the Central subgroups of the family. Though I will discuss some of the problems to be faced in trying to reconcile the Anatolian, Tocharian, and Core IE verb systems, my discussion of the development of the Greek verb in detail will start roughly from Core IE.

The consequences of this subgrouping for lexical reconstruction are also significant. Because Anatolian is half the family, a word or morpheme cannot strictly be reconstructed for PIE unless it has reflexes in at least one Anatolian language and at least one non-Anatolian language, and since Anatolian is lexically divergent from the other daughters and is not as well attested as some others, the number

[3] Since this cladistic tree is relatively new, there are no generally accepted names for many of the higher order internal nodes. Following Chang et al. (2015), I adopt 'Nuclear IE' for the non-Anatolian clade; the other names are simply stopgaps (though note that Jasanoff 2018 also uses 'Core IE'). For full discussion and some alternative suggestions, see now Olander (2019).

of items which can be reconstructed for PIE with confidence is somewhat limited. On the other hand, the phonologies of Nuclear IE, Core IE, and even Central IE were almost identical to that of their ancestor PIE (so far as we can tell). Since we are dealing with a subgroup of Central IE, it does not matter much how far back an inherited item can be traced, and I will loosely cite as 'PIE' items which are reconstructable for any of the internal nodes in the tree above except those restricted to Italo-Celtic. Words confined to two or three adjacent subgroups of Core and Central IE will be cited as 'post-PIE'.

The rest of this chapter will present a brief sketch of PIE grammar as reconstructed from the grammars of the daughter languages by standard application of the comparative method. In recent years a range of introductions to PIE have become available, and the interested reader should consult them as well. Tichy (2006) provides a concise introduction (mostly standard, though with a few idiosyncracies), including a good bibliography; Meier-Brugger (2010) covers the same material in much more detail. Clackson (2007) focuses instead on points that are still under discussion; his chapter on the verb covers much of the same ground as my discussion in 2.3.3. Beekes (2011), like the older books referenced at the end of this paragraph, discusses historical linguistics in general as well as IE linguistics. Fortson (2010: 53–169) is a brief sketch comparable to this one; both his book and Mallory and Adams (2006) are much broader in scope than the other volumes mentioned, including much information on PIE archaeology and culture. Older treatments of PIE that are still worth consulting include Sihler (1995) and Szemerényi (1996). All the above books, except Clackson's, present some version of the Indo-Greek verb. Beekes' rejection of a PIE phoneme */a/ distances his treatment a bit from the others; Szemerényi's reluctance to accept the PIE 'laryngeals' is by now obsolete, though his discussion of other points is valuable. Further information about particular topics can be found in the references cited below.

2.2 PIE phonology

A complete presentation of what is known about PIE phonology is beyond the scope of this book. Here I present only the main outlines and some of the more interesting quirks. The standard reference is Mayrhofer (1986), to which readers are referred for further information, with references, on every point discussed in this section. A more modern synthesis, making somewhat different judgments of some of the evidence and referring to much recent work in the field, can be found in Byrd (2015: 5–40).[4]

[4] For an interesting hypothesis regarding the origins of the admittedly unusual PIE sound system, see Kümmel (2012).

The phonology of PIE was very unlike that of any modern IE language. The system of surface-contrastive sounds, in which I will cite PIE forms, was as follows:

Obstruents:

bilabial	coronal	palatal	velar	labiovelar	(glottal?)
p	t	ḱ	k	k^w	
(b?)	d	ǵ	g	g^w	
b^h	d^h	$ǵ^h$	g^h	g^{wh}	
	s		h_2	h_3 (?)	h_1

Sonorants:		High vowels:		Non-high vowels:		
y (~ i)	w (~ u)	i	u	e	a	o
r (~ r̥)		ī	ū	ē	ā	ō
l (~ l̥)						
n (~ n̥)						
m (~ m̥)						

There was also a system of pitch accent: one syllable of each phonological word exhibited high pitch on the surface, customarily marked with ´ in reconstructions. Numerous peculiarities of this system call for comment.

2.2.1 PIE obstruents

The palatal, velar, and labiovelar stops are collectively referred to as 'dorsals'. Their exact pronunciation is not reconstructable; all we can say for certain is that the 'palatals' were pronounced further forward in the mouth than the others, and that the 'labiovelars' were pronounced with lip-rounding but were otherwise identical with the 'velars'.[5] That PIE possessed stops of all three types is no longer controversial, since Craig Melchert has demonstrated that the three-way contrast between the voiceless stops *ḱ, *k, and *k^w is preserved in Luvian before front vowels (Melchert 1987, 2012b); for instance, we find Luvian *ziyar* '(s)he is lying down' < PIE *ḱéyor, *kīsa(i)-* 'to comb' < *kes-, and *kui* 'what?' < *k^wíd. A further indication that the triple contrast is not some kind of artifact of the comparative method can be found in a simple constraint on the shape of PIE root-syllables: though a root could not contain oral stops at the same place of articulation both in its

[5] In any case it is most unlikely that the 'palatals' were really palatal stops; in many IE languages they became velars, and as Michael Weiss pointed out to me many years ago, shifts of palatal stops to velars are at best very rare in the attested historical phonologies of natural human languages (so Kümmel 2007: 241–3). The palatals were also clearly the commonest dorsals (though not by a very wide margin), which suggests that they were typologically the unmarked set, i.e. probably really velars. I have retained the traditional terms, instead of replacing them with 'velars, postvelars, labiopostvelars', to avoid confusion. For further discussion, see especially Kümmel (2007: 310–27).

onset and in its coda,[6] there were roots which contained both a palatal and a velar (*ḱenk- 'to hang', *kreḱ- 'to strike', *koḱso- 'joint') or both a palatal and a labiovelar (*k^{w}eḱ- 'to catch sight of'), and perhaps both a velar and a labiovelar (post-PIE *kneyg^{wh}- 'to bow').

The 'voiced aspirate' stops were probably breathy-voiced; their reflexes are still breathy-voiced in many modern Indic languages.

The distribution of PIE stops was in some ways idiosyncratic. The voiced bilabial stop *b might have been absent from the PIE inventory (see especially Olander forthcoming, on which this discussion is based). The only reasonably good example with an Anatolian reflex is *g^{h}rebh$_2$- 'grasp' (Hitt. *karpiezzi* '(s)he lifts', Skt aor. 3sg. *ágrab^{h}īt*, OCS inf. *grabiti*; see the discussion at *LIV* s.v.), since *leb- 'lick' (Hitt. *lilipai* '(s)he licks'; Melchert 1994a: 93, Lat. *labium* 'lip', OE *lippa*) is likely onomatopoeic; the only good example shared by Tocharian and Core IE is *d^{h}ewb- 'deep' (Toch. B *tapre* 'high', Goth. *diups*).[7] Most surprising of all was a series of constraints on the shapes of root-syllables. A root could not contain two voiced stops, nor could it contain both a voiceless stop and a voiced aspirate unless the former occurred in a root-initial cluster with *s. Thus, among potential roots with an initial coronal and a final velar, only the following could have occurred:

*tek-	*dek-	———
*teg-	———	*d^{h}eg-
———	*deg^{h}-	*d^{h}eg^{h}-

(Cf. the actually reconstructable roots *teḱ- 'to produce', *teg- 'to cover', *deḱ- 'to accept', *delǵ^{h}- 'to be firm', *d^{h}yoh$_3$g^{w}- 'to insert, to stab', *d^{h}eg^{wh}- 'to burn'.) The types '*teg^{h}-, *deg-, *d^{h}ek-' did not occur—though the type *steg^{h}- did (cf. at least *spr̥d^{h}- 'contest', *skab^{h}- 'to scrape', *skab^{h}- 'to prop', *sperǵ^{h}- 'to hurry', *stemb^{h}H-[8] 'to prop', *steyg^{h}- 'to step').

6 Apparently this constraint classed *m with the bilabial oral stops; that is, there were no roots like '*pem-' and '*meb^{h}-', including both a bilabial oral stop and *m. However, *n was not classed with the coronal oral stops, since we must reconstruct *nad^{h}- 'to tie', *newd- 'to push', *ten- 'to stretch', etc. Three clear exceptions to the constraint, *tewd- 'to beat', *tend- 'to cut', and *mems- 'meat', are securely reconstructable; it is of course not surprising that they involve coronal stops and *m. Other apparent exceptions, such as *b^{h}rem- 'to make a noise', either appear to be onomatopoeic or are not securely reconstructable for PIE proper, so far as I am aware.

7 'River' is sometimes reconstructed as *h$_2$ábon- < **h$_2$ép-h$_3$en-, presumably *'containing running water', in an attempt to connect it with Skt *ā́pas* 'the waters' (cf. Wodtko et al. 2008: 311–17). But while all the Italic and Celtic cognates are n-stems (or derived from n-stems), some of the Anatolian derivatives are not (Kloekhorst 2008 s.v. *ḫapa-*); therefore a reconstruction *h$_2$áb^{h}o(n)- seems more likely. Germanic river names that might contain a cognate with PGmc *p < PIE *b (Neri 2009: 8 with references) are not a convincing counterargument, because the putative meaning of a name cannot be checked against other evidence.

8 It is customary to write '*H' for a laryngeal the precise identity of which cannot be reconstructed—a problem that recurs fairly often, since most daughter languages merged the laryngeals in many environments.

Both the typological oddity of a system with voiced aspirates but no voiceless aspirates and the apparent dearth of parallels to the constraints just described have led some scholars to propose a 'glottalic hypothesis', according to which the PIE voiced stops were really ejectives, while the other manners of articulation were voiceless and voiced (perhaps with non-contrastive aspiration; see e.g. Gamkrelidze and Ivanov 1973). But a stop system with a similar set of contrasts is actually attested in the Indonesian language Kelabit (first reported in Blust 1974), and Madurese seems to have gone through a similar stage relatively recently; moreover, adopting the glottalic hypothesis makes it very difficult to account for the shapes of the oldest stratum of Iranian loanwords in Armenian, which the traditional reconstruction explains with ease (Meid 1987: 9–11). Most mainstream Indo-Europeanists have therefore rejected the glottalic hypothesis, or at least regard it as unproven (cf. e.g. Vine 1988).[9]

The pronunciation of the three 'laryngeals' (symbolized as *h*'s with subscript numerals) can be reconstructed only approximately, and their position in the chart above should not be taken very seriously; note especially that the third laryngeal did not pattern like a labiovelar consonant. We can at least be confident that all the laryngeals were obstruents of some kind, because they behaved like obstruents with respect to the syllabification rules (see 2.2.4 (ii)). *h_2 was clearly a voiceless fricative pronounced far back in the mouth, to judge from its reflexes in the Anatolian languages (the only subgroup in which it usually survives as a consonant). *h_3 seems to have been voiced and apparently exhibited lip-rounding, to judge from the fact that it rounded adjacent short *e (see 2.2.4 (i)). For recent discussion of the phonetics of those two laryngeals, see Melchert (2011) and Weiss (2016). About the pronunciation of *h_1 nothing can be said with certainty except that it was an obstruent. It should be clear that 'laryngeals' is an anachronistic misnomer, retained only because it has become standard in the field. For comprehensive discussion, see Kümmel (2007: 327–36).

There seem to have been very few constraints on the distribution of *s and the laryngeals, to judge from the reconstructability of such roots as *ses- 'to be asleep', *$h_1$yeh$_1$- 'to make', *$h_1$reh$_1$- 'to row', *$h_3$omh$_3$- 'to swear', *$h_2$weh$_1$- 'to blow', *$h_2$anh$_1$- 'to breathe', *$h_2$arh$_3$- 'to plow', etc., and full words like *$h_2$áwh$_2$o-s 'grandfather', *$h_1$óh$_3$s 'mouth', *h_1nḗh$_3$-mn̥ 'name', and *$h_2$wl̥h$_1$-no- 'wool'. *s was by far the commonest obstruent in the language; *h_2 was perhaps the second most common in a lexical count, though *t may have been commoner in speech because it occurred in so many suffixes and endings.

[9] It might also be observed that although the glottalic hypothesis might yield a less odd system of consonants for PIE, it would force us to posit a large number of sound changes that have few parallels (Wolfgang de Melo, p.c.).

2.2.2 PIE sonorants and high vowels

One of the more unusual features of PIE phonology was the existence of a class of 'sonorants' (or 'resonants') whose syllabicity was determined by rule. They appear to have been underlyingly non-syllabic; in fact, almost all the syllabic sonorants which are reconstructable for PIE can be derived from underlyingly non-syllabic segments by the rules discussed in 2.2.4 (ii).

The one clear exception to that generalization involves the high front vocalics. Though most of the short syllabic high vowels can be derived from underlying */y/ and */w/, there were a few examples of syllabic *i in positions where underlying */y/ should have surfaced as non-syllabic *y; for instance, though non-syllabic sonorants normally occurred in the context VC_V, where the first vowel was short and C indicates any single non-syllabic, *i also occurred in that position. The clearest examples are derivatives from locatives in *-i, e.g. Rigvedic Skt trisyllabic *ápyas* (i.e. *ápias*) 'in the water' (adj.; Mayrhofer 1986: 161) and Gk πεδίον 'plain' ← *'(thing) at the foot (of the mountain)' (Hoenigswald 1985). A possible widely attested example is *néwios 'new' (a derivative of *néwos 'new' with a suffix of unclear function; cf. Rigvedic Skt trisyllabic *návyas*—i.e. *návias*—and Welsh *newydd* < Proto-Celtic *nowi(y)os < *néwios). The syllabic *i of *néwios contrasted with the *y of *ályos 'other' and *sewyós 'left(-hand)' in the same prosodic environment (cf. Rigvedic Skt disyllabic *savyás* 'left(-hand)' and Welsh *eil* 'other' without the additional syllable of *newydd*). It seems that the *i of *néwios can only have been an underlying vowel */i/. (See Mayrhofer 1986: 160–1, 168 for discussion and further examples.)[10]

Though I know of no similar syllabification evidence for an underlying vowel */u/, there is another phenomenon which probably reflects PIE */u/. Though nearly all PIE roots contained a non-high vowel and were subject to the phonological rules collectively called 'ablaut' (see 2.2.4 (i)), there were a handful of non-ablauting roots, and the most securely reconstructable example is $*b^h$uH- ($*b^h uh_2$- ?) 'to become', with invariant *u. Unless we wish to posit a root which never contained a vowel in PIE, we ought to recognize an underlying high vowel */u/ in this root.

If the above analysis is correct, it makes the occurrence of *ī and *ū, which were likewise very rare, somewhat less puzzling: in addition to the (underlyingly non-syllabic) sonorants, PIE had genuine high vowels, both long and short, though they were rare. As we will see in the next section, many other PIE underlying vowels were also surprisingly rare.

[10] For 'new' a reconstruction *néwiHos is phonologically possible; it is not clear to me that it makes sense morphologically. Note that I write *-iV-, *-uV- where some write *-iyV-, *-uwV- (or the equivalent); there is no actual difference.

2.2.3 PIE non-high vowels

The PIE system of non-high vowels, simple as it seems on the surface, was probably even simpler underlyingly. The vowels exhibited extensive alternations in morphologically related forms according to the following patterns:

ē ~ e ~ 0 ~ o ~ ō
ā ~ a ~ 0

It seems clear that */e/,*/a/ were the underlying segments in most cases, and that the other vowels were derived from them by various phonological rules, which had generally been morphologized to a greater or lesser extent (see 2.2.4 (i)). The system is referred to as 'ablaut'; the alternants of each series are called 'ablaut grades', so that it is customary to speak of 'e-grade, o-grade, zero grade', and so on.

Roots and words which appear to exhibit underlying */a/ are few enough that the 'Leiden school' has tried to explain them all away; Lubotsky (1989) and Pronk (2019) are reasoned arguments for that position. It is true that apparent *a following an obstruent might actually reflect underlying */h_2e/, unless the obstruent is an unaspirated stop and the word is attested in Indo-Iranian (in which *h_2 aspirated an immediately preceding stop). But *a following a sonorant is less easy to dispense with, since a sonorant preceding *h_2 ought to have become syllabic unless another syllabic preceded (see 2.2.4 (ii)). Moreover, *h_2 survives as *h*- in Hittite, Palaic, and Luvian and as *x*- in Lycian; thus a PIE word whose reflexes begin with *a*- in Latin and Greek but do not begin with a consonant in the Anatolian languages is most straightforwardly reconstructed with *a-. It is admittedly possible to construct sets of phonological rules and levelings that will account for most of the examples, but the simpler solution seems preferable, other things being equal, because it relies on the mathematics of the comparative method—especially given the known weakness of typological arguments. The following list includes a large proportion of the better examples of */a/ (not all of which would be reconstructed with */a/ by every Indo-Europeanist who accepts its existence): *ar- 'to fit', *ay- 'to give', *ay- 'to be hot', *ayd^h- 'to burn (intr.)', *b^{h}rag- 'to break', *$h_2$wap- 'evil', *Hyaǵ- 'to worship', *kalh_1- 'to call', *kan- 'to sing' (of birds), *karp- 'to pluck', *kaw- 'to hit', *kwas- 'to kiss', *kwath_2- 'to bubble', *ḱad- 'to fall', *ḱas- 'gray', *lab^h- 'to take', *lad- 'beloved', *nad^h- 'to tie', *nas- 'nose', *plak- 'to be pleasing', *sak- 'holy', *sal- 'to jump', *sark- 'to be whole', *skab^h- 'to prop', *skab^h- 'to scrape', *stag- 'to drip', *tag- 'to touch', *war- 'to burn (intr.)', *alb^{h}ós 'white', *ályos 'other', *átta 'dad', *awl- 'tube', *b^{h}ágos 'a share', *dáḱru 'tear (i.e. eye-water)', *dayh_2wḗr 'brother-in-law', *g^{h}eb^{h}al- 'head', *ǵ^{h}áns 'goose', *kápros 'male (animal)', *kátus 'fight', *kawl- 'shaft', *laywós and *skaywós 'left(-hand)', *pláth$_2$us 'wide', *sáls 'salt', *sámh$_2$d^{h}os 'sand', *sasyóm 'grain', *sáwsos 'dry', *smáḱru 'beard', *táwros 'bull', *wástu- 'settlement'. (Cf. Melchert 1994a, Ringe 1996, Rix et al. 2001 *passim*, Wodtko et al. 2008 *passim*; the discussion of *swad- or (more likely) */sweh$_2$d-/ 'pleasant' by Seebold

1967 and Stang 1974 gives a good idea of the problems involved.) A large proportion of the words which exhibit *a* in the daughter languages can be shown to reflect PIE underlying */h_2e/, and many other examples are ambiguous.

Since long vowels and *o which cannot be derived from underlying */e/ and */a/ were even rarer, it is clear that */e/ was overwhelmingly the most common underlying vowel, and the most common underlying segment, in PIE. Like the fairly large obstruent system, this is reminiscent of the situation in Northwest Caucasian languages, though the PIE system was typologically less extreme.

Whether words could begin with vowels in PIE is unclear, since apparent initial vowels might actually have been preceded by *h_1, which was lost word-initially before a vowel in all the daughters (and so can be definitely reconstructed in that position only from related forms beginning with *h_1C-).

2.2.4 PIE phonological rules

A remarkable amount of the phonological rule system of PIE can be reconstructed. Only the most important rules are discussed here.

2.2.4 (i) Ablaut and laryngeals

The default underlying vowel */e/ was replaced by *o in a wide variety of morphological environments. Fuller details will be given in the discussion of PIE inflection and derivation (2.3 and 2.4); here I give only a general outline of the system.

Some ablauting nouns exhibited *o in the root-syllable in the 'strong' cases (the nominative, accusative, and vocative), but *e or 0 in the 'weak' cases (the remaining cases of the paradigm, roughly speaking); typical examples include *pód- ~ *ped- 'foot' and *ḱwón- ~ *ḱun- / *ḱwn̥- 'dog'. The same pattern reappears in the indicative of some ablauting verb stems, in which the singular active had *o in the root, but the rest of the paradigm had *e or 0. In Hittite this pattern is characteristic of the most archaic stratum of the 'hi-conjugation' (e.g. *sākki* '(s)he knows', *sekkanzi* 'they know' < *sók- ~ *sék- (Melchert 1994a: 81, *pace* Kloekhorst 2008 s.v.); *dāi* '(s)he puts', *tiyanzi* 'they put' < *d^hóh_1-i- ~ *$d^h$$h_1$-i-). In Core IE (see above) it had become restricted to the 'perfect' stem; 0 is usual in the weak forms (cf. e.g. *memóne '(s)he has in mind', *memnḗr 'they have in mind'), but see Jasanoff (2003a: 32–3, 40–2) for relics of e-grade weak forms in Indo-Iranian. For PIE we must reconstruct surface *e in other types of noun and verb stems in exactly the same phonological environments in which the above types exhibited *o; thus it is clear that the o-grade rule had already been morphologized in PIE.

Some types of polysyllabic ablauting nouns and adjectives exhibited *o in the final syllable of the stem in the strong cases when that syllable was unaccented and followed by an overt ending (e.g. in acc. sg. *swésor-m̥ 'sister'); it looks as though *o might have replaced 0 in a position in which the latter had become inadmissible, though the phenomenon is not well understood. The pretonic root-syllables of derived causative verbs also appeared in the o-grade (e.g. in *woséyeti '(s)he clothes (someone)'), for reasons that are likewise not understood. A considerable number of derived nominals, especially thematic nouns, also exhibited o-grade roots.

It is clear from the above that the o-grade rule was triggered by a disjunct set of morphological environments that had no apparent connection with one another. It appears that underlying */a/ did not undergo this rule.

In all types of ablauting stems an underlying non-high vowel was often deleted when it was unaccented on the surface; the same zero-grade rule also applied frequently in derivation. The correlation between lack of surface accent and lack of a vowel was still fairly robust in PIE, and it is clear that lack of accent was the original environment in which the rule applied. However, reconstructable exceptions in both directions—i.e. cases in which the rule unexpectedly failed to apply, on the one hand, and zero-grade syllables which unexpectedly bore a surface accent, on the other—are numerous enough to demonstrate that the rule had already been at least partly morphologized in PIE. Instances of unaccented *o have been mentioned above; clear instances of unaccented *e in ablauting nouns include *pedés 'of a foot' (cf. Lat. *pedis*), *nébʰesos 'of a cloud' (cf. Homeric Gk νέφεος; Hitt. *nēpisas* 'of the sky'), etc. Instances of accented zero-grade syllables include *h_2ŕ̥tḱos 'bear' (the animal), *wĺ̥kʷos 'wolf', *septḿ̥ 'seven', *ń̥- 'un-', and instances of regularly syllabified */y/ and */w/ in such forms as *mustís 'fist' and *suh$_3$nús 'offspring, son'; instances of *í and *ú that never alternated with *y and *w can, of course, have been underlying high vowels (see the discussion in 2.2.2).

The ablaut pattern of the 'thematic vowel', a largely functionless morpheme that was the stem-final segment in large numbers of verb, noun, and adjective stems, was unique. It underwent the zero-grade rule only when immediately followed by some derivational suffixes (such as *-yó-, which formed adjectives from nouns). Moreover, the e- and o-grades of the thematic vowel appear to have been conditioned by the segment that followed immediately, but differently in verbs and in nominals. In verb stems the e-grade appeared word-finally (i.e. when there was no ending or a zero-ending, e.g. in imperative 2sg. *wérye 'say!'), before a Core IE e-grade subjunctive suffix (see below), and before coronal obstruents (which were very common in verb endings; cf. e.g. *wéryesi 'you say', *wéryeti '(s)he says', etc.). The o-grade appeared elsewhere, including before *h_2 (cf. e.g. *wéryonti 'they say', *wéryomos 'we say', *wéryowos 'the two of us say', Nuclear IE *wéryoh$_2$ 'I say', Central IE *wéryoyd '(s)he would say'; on the ending of the last, see 2.2.4 (iv)). In nominals the e-grade originally appeared only word-finally and before *h_2 (e.g. in voc. sg. *swéḱure 'father-in-law!' and neut. collective *wergáh$_2$ 'work' (underlyingly /-éh$_2$/, see below)), while the o-grade appeared elsewhere, including before endings beginning with *e (e.g. in nom. sg. *swéḱuros and *wérǵom, and in dat. sg. *swéḱuroey 'to/for (the) father-in-law'). Thus most forms of thematic nominals exhibited the o-grade of the thematic vowel, and for that reason thematic nominal stems are often called 'o-stems'.

There was at least one phonological rule (with morphological triggers) which lengthened vowels directly: in some ablauting nouns and adjectives and in a few types of ablauting verb stems, the root-vowel was lengthened in the strong cases and the indicative singular active respectively. Thus we are able to reconstruct *h_1nḗ$h_3$mn̥ ~ *$h_1$nó$h_3$mn- 'name' (the latter with underlying */-é-/), *Hyḗk^{w}r̥ ~ *Hyék^{w}n- 'liver', *mḗh_1n̥s ~ *méh_1n̥s- 'moon', *mḗms ~ *méms- 'meat', *wḗsu-s ~ *wésu- 'good', *h_1ḗd-s-ti '(s)he's eating' but *$h_1$éd-n̥ti 'they eat', *wḗḱ-ti '(s)he wants' but *wéḱ-n̥ti 'they want', *wḗǵ^h-s-t '(s)he brought it (in a vehicle)' but *wéǵ^h-s-n̥d 'they hauled it', and likewise *nā́s-h_1e ~ *nás- 'nose, nostrils', *wā́stu ~ *wástu- 'settlement' (cf. Narten 1968, Schindler 1975a: 5–6, 1975b: 262, Oettinger 1979: 100, Normier 1980: 254, 262 fn. 42, Strunk 1985, Ringe 1996: 70–1).

Long vowels also arose by contraction of adjacent identical vowels or by compensatory lengthening. The latter process will be discussed in 2.2.4 (iv). Two instances of vowel contraction are worth noting here, and both require some explanation. In athematic verb stems the subjunctive mood reconstructable for Core IE was marked by suffixing the thematic vowel; for instance, to aorist indicative *g^{w}ém-d '(s)he stepped', *g^{w}m-énd 'they stepped' corresponded subjunctive *g^{w}ém-e-ti '(s)he will step', *g^{w}ém-o-nti 'they will step'. (The subjunctive was the only category in which the thematic vowel had a grammatical function.) In the Core IE subjunctive of thematic stems the (functionless) thematic vowel of the stem and the subjunctive vowel contracted into a long vowel; thus to present indicative *g^{w}m̥-sḱé-ti '(s)he's walking (i.e. stepping iteratively)', *g^{w}m̥-sḱó-nti 'they're walking' corresponded subjunctive *g^{w}m̥-sḱḗ-ti (= /-sḱé-e-ti/) '(s)he will walk', *g^{w}m̥-sḱṓ-nti (= /-sḱó-o-nti/) 'they will walk'. The other instance of vowel contraction occurred in the context of a derivational process called 'proto-vr̥ddhi'. The rule seems originally to have worked as follows: an ablauting nominal stem was put in the zero grade, the vowel *e was inserted into it (not necessarily in the same position as its underlying vowel), and an accented thematic vowel was suffixed. For instance, to form a proto-vr̥ddhi derivative from *dyew- 'sky' one took the zero-grade *diw-, inserted *e to give *deyw- (sic), and so derived *deyw-ó-s 'god' (literally 'skyling'). At some point this rule was extended to non-ablauting stems that already contained *e, and the two *e's then contracted into a long vowel; for instance, from *swéḱuros 'father-in-law' was formed *swēḱurós 'male member of father-in-law's household'. This is the historical source of the derivational process called vr̥ddhi in Sanskrit.

The short e-grade vowel *e, but not any of the other vowels in the ablaut system, had distinctive allophones when adjacent to the second and third laryngeals. Next to *h_2 it was *a, apparently indistinguishable from underlying */a/; next to

*h_3 it was *o, apparently indistinguishable from underlying */o/.[11] Thus underlying */$h_2$éwis/ 'bird' must have been pronounced approximately as *[χáwis], and */stéh$_2$t/ '(s)he stood up' approximately as *[stáχt]; and we can't be certain what underlying vowel the first *o of *$h_3$ósdos 'branch' reflects. (But the laryngeal had no effect on the *o of *h_2ḱ-$h_2$ows-iéti '(s)he's sharp-eared', so far as we can tell, nor on the *ē of *ḗh_2g^{wh}-ti '(s)he's drinking'; cf. Beekes 1972, Eichner 1973, Jasanoff 1988a, Kimball 1988, Kim 2000a.) All the daughter languages, even in the Anatolian subfamily, show the effects of these 'vowel-coloring' rules.

As might be expected, the coloring rules complicate the task of reconstruction considerably, and we are often constrained to rely on indirect inference in reconstructing PIE underlying forms. For example, we can be reasonably certain that the etymon of Toch. B *āśäṃ* '(s)he leads', Skt *ájati* '(s)he drives', Gk ἄγει '(s)he leads', and Lat. *agit* '(s)he drives' should be reconstructed as underlying */h_2éǵeti/ because a derived noun *h_2óǵmos 'drive, path of driving' is also reconstructable (cf. Gk ὄγμος 'furrow, swath, path of a heavenly body'), and underlying */a/ is not known to have been subject to the o-grade rule. On the other hand, the first syllable of *mah$_2$tḗr 'mother' participates in no alternations of any kind, and though we are fairly certain that the word contained *h_2 (because of the parallel with *ph$_2$tḗr 'father' and *d^{h}ugh$_2$tḗr 'daughter'), we do not really know whether the vowel immediately preceding it was */e/ or */a/. If it was really somehow derived from a 'nursery word' of the *mama*-type, */a/ is actually more likely, as Michael Weiss observed to me many years ago.

Since I write surface-contrastive segments in PIE forms, readers should remember that every *a next to *h_2 either is or could be underlying */e/. When it is clear that *o next to *h_3 is underlying */e/, that will be noted explicitly unless it is obvious from context.

How much reinterpretation by language learners the coloring rules caused within the PIE period is unclear. But the loss of laryngeals in most daughters certainly caused the outcomes of these rules to be reinterpreted as underlying, and a wholesale restructuring of the ablaut system necessarily resulted in every daughter language.

Finally, it should be noted that laryngeals not adjacent to syllabics were apparently deleted by three different rules. A laryngeal which was separated from an o-grade vowel by a sonorant, but was in the same syllable as the o-grade vowel, was dropped (cf. Beekes 1969: 74–6, 238–42, 254–5, Nussbaum 1997 with references).

[11] I do not believe that the Indo-Iranian sound change called Brugmann's Law (BL) distinguishes the two. Which examples of BL reflect regular sound change and which reflect rule extension is of course a matter of judgment, but it seems to me that BL *as a regular sound change* cannot be shown to have lengthened *o except before a single sonorant followed immediately by a vowel (before the loss of laryngeals occurred); it follows that *pátis* 'master, husband' < *pótis, *áhis* 'serpent' < *$h_3$óg^{wh}is, etc., are not relevant to BL. The short vowel of *ávis* 'sheep' reflects leveling on gen. sg. *ávyas* ← *$h_2$áwis, etc. (see 2.3.4 (ii)).

For instance, whereas the laryngeal of *$d^h eh_1$- 'put' survived in the derived noun *$d^h óh_1$mos 'thing put' (cf. Gk θωμός 'heap' and OE *dōm* 'judgment', both with long vowels that reveal the prior presence of a laryngeal), that of *$terh_1$- 'bore' was dropped in *tórmos 'borehole' (cf. Gk τόρμος 'socket' and OE *þearm* 'intestine'). The most important application of this rule was in the Central IE thematic optative, in which the sequence */-o-yh_1-/ was reduced to *-oy- in most forms. Further, by 'Pinault's Rule' laryngeals were dropped between an underlying non-syllabic and */y/ (in that order) if there was a preceding syllable in the same word (cf. Peters 1980: 81 fn. 38 with references and especially the comprehensive discussion of Pinault 1982); thus, though the present (i.e. imperfective) stem of *$sneh_1$- 'twist, spin' was *$snéh_1$ye/o-, with the laryngeal preserved (cf. Gk νῆι '(s)he's spinning', the η of which can only reflect *ē < *eh_1, and OIr. *sniïd* '(s)he twists', with *i* < *ī < *ē < *eh_1), that of *$werh_1$- 'say' was *wérye/o- (cf. Homeric Gk ἔ̆ρωι 'I say'; a PIE present *$wérh_1$yeti would have given 'ἐρέει' in Homeric Greek). Finally, it seems clear that a laryngeal was dropped if it was the second of four underlying non-syllabics and was followed by a syllable boundary (Hackstein 2002b with references). For example, the oblique stem of */$d^h ugh_2$tér-/ 'daughter', underlyingly */$d^h ugh_2$tr-/, surfaced as *d^hugtr- with the laryngeal dropped (at a point in the derivation before the operation of Sievers' Law; on which, see 2.2.4 (ii)); the daughters have all leveled in one direction or the other.

2.2.4 (ii) Syllabification of sonorants

PIE syllabification is the topic of much ongoing research; recent treatments include Cooper (2015) and Byrd (2015). The former treats selected topics, including the syllabification of sonorants, in depth; the latter attempts a unified explanation for all the (complex) phenomena, including Sievers' Law (see further below). Here only the most essential outline will be sketched.

In a large majority of cases the syllabification of sonorants can be predicted by a simple rule (Schindler 1977b: 56) as follows. Vowels were unalterably syllabic and obstruents (including laryngeals) unalterably non-syllabic. Each sequence of one or more sonorants was syllabified as follows. If the rightmost member of the sequence was adjacent to a syllabic (i.e. a vowel, on the initial application of the rule), it remained non-syllabic, but if not, it was assigned to a syllable peak. The rule then iterated from right to left, the output of each decision providing input to the next. Forms of *ḱwon- 'dog' neatly illustrate the process. The zero grade was underlyingly */ḱwn-/ (since full-grade forms show that the high vocalic was an alternating sonorant, not an underlying syllabic high vowel). The genitive singular */ḱwn-és/ 'dog's, of a dog' was syllabified as follows: the *n was adjacent to a vowel and therefore remained non-syllabic; consequently the *w was not adjacent to a syllabic, and it therefore surfaced as syllabic *u, giving *ḱunés (cf. Skt *śúnas*, Gk κυνός). On the other hand, the locative plural */ḱwn-sú/ 'among dogs' was syllabified as follows: the *n was not adjacent to a vowel and therefore became syllabic *n̥; consequently the *w was adjacent to a syllabic and therefore remained non-syllabic, giving *ḱwn̥sú (cf. Skt *śvásu*).

However, there were systematic exceptions to this rule. Most strikingly, the zero grade of the stem-forming nasal infix *-né- seems to exhibit only non-syllabic reflexes in the daughter languages when a sonorant precedes; for instance, the zero grade of the Core IE present stem *linékʷ- 'be leaving behind' is always a reflex of *linkʷ-, never of the '*l̥yn̥kʷ-' that the syllabification rule predicts. In addition, the i-stem and u-stem accusative endings are always sg. *-im, *-um, pl. *-ins, *-uns, likewise contrary to the general rule. The output of underlying *CRRV- also regularly violates the rule if a sequence *CRR̥C- occurs elsewhere in the paradigm; for instance, gen. pl. *trióHom 'of three' exhibits the same syllabification as loc. pl. *trisú 'among three', though by rule '*tr̥yóHom' would be expected. Of course leveling and/or morphological changes in the daughter languages might have obscured the original situation, but the fact that all attested reflexes of these forms violate the simple right-to-left rule argues strongly that the situation in PIE was more complex. For further discussion, I refer the reader to Byrd (2015).

The output of the basic syllabification rules was input to a further adjustment rule known as 'Sievers' Law' (SL). The correct formulation of SL is still under discussion; see most recently Byrd (2015: 183–207) for an Optimality Theory analysis and Barber (2013) for the Greek evidence (both with full bibliography of earlier treatments, of which the most comprehensive is Seebold 1972). For the purposes of this sketch I will assume that SL was *originally* an exceptionless 'natural' phonological rule that applied to all sonorants in a simply statable environment; the reality in Central IE (as reflected in Rigvedic Sanskrit, for example) was almost certainly more complex. The maximally simple formulation is the following: if a non-syllabic sonorant was immediately preceded by two or more non-syllabics, or by a long vowel and a non-syllabic, it was replaced by the corresponding syllabic sonorant. For instance, the adjective-forming suffix *-yó-[12] appeared with non-syllabic *y in *pedyós 'of feet; on foot' (of which the derivational basis was */ped-/ 'foot'; cf. Gk πεζός 'on foot', with ζ < *dy), but with syllabic *i in *neptiós 'of grandsons/nephews' (basis */nept-/ 'grandson/nephew'; cf. Gk ἀνεψιός 'cousin' (with analogical ἀ-), Av. *naptiiō* 'descendant', late Church Slavonic *netĭjĭ* 'nephew'). There seems likewise to have been a syllabic *i in *(h_2)ōwióm 'egg', possibly (though not certainly) a derivative of *$h_2$áwis 'bird'. Similarly, the present-stem forming suffix *-yé- ~ *-yó- appeared with non-syllabic *y in *wr̥ǵyéti '(s)he's working', but with syllabic *i in *h_2ḱ$h_2$owsiéti '(s)he is sharp-eared'. The other

[12] There were probably two or more suffixes of this shape with different functions; for instance, the *-yó- of *pedyós 'on foot' might have been delocative, while that of *neptiós cannot have been (Barber 2013: 205; I am grateful to Michael Weiss for calling this to my attention). For present purposes what matters is that all were underlyingly *-yó-.

sonorants seem to have behaved in a similar fashion in PIE, to judge from sychronically isolated forms in the daughter languages (though the rule remained productive in the attested daughter languages only in applying to */w/ and—especially—*/y/). For instance, */n/ remained non-syllabic after a light syllable in *Hyaǵnós 'reverend, worshipful' (cf. Gk ἁγνός 'holy, chaste', Skt *yajñás* 'sacrifice') but became syllabic after a heavy syllable in *pl̥th$_2$n̥ós 'broad' (cf. Proto-Celtic *litanos 'broad' > OIr. *lethan*, Welsh *llydan*; superlative substantivized in Homeric Gk πλατάνιστος 'plane tree', lit. 'the broadest one') and apparently in *dh$_2$pn̥óm 'sacrificial meal' (cf. Gk δαπάνη 'expense', originally a collective with shifted accent).

It should be emphasized that there was no 'converse of SL' replacing syllabic sonorants or high vowels with non-syllabic sonorants after light syllables in PIE; the evidence against it (such as the reconstructable adjective *néwios 'new', cited above) is much stronger than the evidence against the glottalic hypothesis, for example (on which, see above). See Barber (2013: 28–30) for discussion and references.

A phenomenon called 'Lindeman's Law' might originally have been a special case of SL affecting word-initial CR-clusters (where C indicates any non-syllabic and R indicates a sonorant; Schindler 1977b: 64). In the case of monosyllabic forms which began underlyingly with /CR-/, we find cognates with reflexes of non-syllabic sonorants and those with reflexes of syllabic sonorants in no particular pattern (Lindeman 1965); for instance, the accusative singular of the word meaning 'sky, day' seems to be reconstructable both as *dyḗm (reflected, e.g., in Doric Gk acc. sg. Ζῆν-α 'Zeus') and as *diḗm (reflected, e.g., in Lat. acc. sg. *diem* 'day'). Both syllabifications of the Sanskrit reflex (*dyā́m*, *diā́m*) are attested in the Rigveda. Lindeman's Law apparently continued to apply to all sonorants at a much later period than SL. It could originally have been the result of SL applying within phrases and thus affecting word-initial CR-clusters, but that is difficult to establish (see the discussion of Barber 2013: 48, 52–65). In particular, the apparent restriction of the alternation to monosyllabic forms is odd and difficult to assess. If Lindeman's Law was really a special case of SL, polysyllabic forms conceivably were affected by yet another PIE rule applying only to words and sensitive to word-length; possibly innovative rules in the daughter languages have obscured the picture; possibly the reflexes of the alternants of underlyingly monosyllabic forms have simply survived better in the daughters.

The labial sonorants exhibited a striking type of exceptional behavior: in the word-initial clusters *mn-, *mr-, *ml-, *my-, *wr-, and (therefore probably) *wl-, both sonorants were non-syllabic; clearly reconstructable examples include *mréǵ^{h}us 'short', *mléwHti '(s)he says', *myewh$_1$- 'move', *wrah$_2$d- 'root', and the extended verb root *mnah$_2$- 'think about' (Neri 2009: 6–7). It is possible that at least some of the unalterably non-syllabic sonorants were obstruents at some pre-PIE period; as Warren Cowgill observed to me more than forty years ago, the fact that */b/ was absent in PIE might imply that pre-PIE **b had become *w.[13] On the other hand, labial sonorants might have been exempt from the basic syllabification rule at some pre-PIE stage, in which case this phenomenon would simply be an archaism.

2.2.4 (iii) Some rules affecting obstruents

The contrast between velar and labiovelar stops is not reconstructable next to *w, *u, or *ū; evidently it was neutralized in that position (cf. Weiss 1993: 153–65 with references, 1995: 137–9). We conventionally write velars (the unmarked member of the opposition). Thus from the 'Caland' root *$h_1$leng^{wh}- 'light (in weight)' (see 2.4.2 (ii)) were formed the adjectives *$h_1$ln̥g^{wh}rós (with the labiovelar preserved between *n̥ and *r; cf. Gk ἐλαφρός) and *$h_1$léng^{h}us (with the corresponding velar next to *u; cf. Gk ἐλαχύς 'little', Skt *rag^{h}ús* 'swift', both reflecting remodeled *$h_1$ln̥g^{h}ús with a zero-grade root).

The sibilant fricative */s/, which was underlyingly voiceless, seems to have been voiced to *[z] before voiced stops (e.g. in *nisdós 'seat, lair, nest'); it probably also had a breathy-voiced allophone before breathy-voiced stops (e.g. in *misd^{h}ó- 'reward').

Underlying */ss/ was simplified to single *s. For instance, the 2sg. pres. indic. of 'be', composed of the stem *$h_1$és- and the personal ending *-si, surfaced as *$h_1$ési 'you are' (cf. Skt *ási*, Gk εἶ < *éhi < *ési). The two */s/'s didn't always belong to different morphemes; some become adjacent in zero-grade formations. For instance, *$h_2$áwses- 'ear' appeared with two zero-grade syllables before the nom.-acc. dual ending, and the underlying form */$h_2$uss-íh_1/ surfaced as *$h_2$usíh_1 'two ears' (cf. Szemerényi 1967a: 67–8).[14]

Geminate coronal stops apparently appeared on the surface only in nursery words (*átta 'dad'; cf. Hitt. *attas* 'father', OCS *otĭcĭ* 'father' (with a diminutive suffix), and Lat. *atta*, Gk ἄττα, respectful terms of address for old men); possibly those were the only lexical items in which they were intramorphemic. Where two coronal stops were brought together by morphological processes, however, an *s was inserted between them. For instance, addition of the verbal adjective suffix *-tó- to the root *yewg- 'join' yielded *yugtós 'joined', but addition of the same suffix to *b^{h}eyd- 'split' yielded *b^{h}idstós 'fissile'. The s-insertion rule still operates in Hittite (cf. e.g. *adwēni* 'we eat' but *aztēni* 'you (pl.) eat', where the ending is *-tēni* and *z* = /ts/); in the non-Anatolian daughters the complex clusters it created were simplified.

[13] So also Schindler (1972b: 3), who however suggests **b > PIE *m. Though the number of examples with *m is considerably larger, there is a greater probability that *m was syllabified differently at some pre-PIE stage; see 2.3.6 (i) for a probable example with references.

[14] Though the final VC-sequences of PIE disyllabic nouns are conventionally treated as suffixes in discussions of ablaut, they typically have no recoverable meanings or functions and must therefore not (or no longer) have been separate morphemes synchronically.

Our understanding of 'thorn clusters' in PIE has evolved over the past several decades. A century ago specialists confronted the following unusual (though not unique) comparative problem. In the position after a dorsal stop, Sanskrit sibilants normally correspond to Greek -σ-, while Sanskrit coronal stops normally correspond to Greek -τ- and -θ-; for instance, Skt *dákṣiṇas* ≈ Gk δεξιός 'right(-hand)' (< *deḱsi-), while Skt *aṣṭáu* = Gk ὀκτώ 'eight' (< *oḱtṓw). But there are also cognate pairs in which Sanskrit sibilants correspond to Greek -τ- or -θ-, e.g. Skt *ŕ̥kṣas* = Gk ἄρκτος 'bear', Skt *kṣam-* = Gk χθον- 'earth'. It appeared that there was some third consonant, neither *s nor a dental stop, that could follow dorsal stops, and Karl Brugmann reconstructed the final segment of such clusters algorithmically as '*þ' (so that 'bear', for example, was '*ŕ̥ḱþos'); but since PIE *þ occurred nowhere else in the language, Brugmann's solution never seemed plausible. The discovery of Hittite and Tocharian provided new evidence suggesting that the thorn clusters were actually clusters of coronal plus dorsal, in that order; for instance, whereas 'earth' had been reconstructed as '*ǵʰþem-', the Hittite nominative and accusative singular *tēkan* instead suggested *dʰ(e)ǵʰem- (cf. Schindler 1967a). The problem then became how clusters of the shape *TK could have evolved into clusters of the shape *KT* or *Ks*.

A complex hypothesis was gradually evolved to accommodate all the comparative evidence (see Merlingen 1957, 1962, Mayrhofer 1983, Pinault 2006b, Ringe 2010 with references). However, Jasanoff (2018) has made a convincing case for a phonetically motivated development of *TK to *TʲKʲ (with palatalization), followed by phonetically motivated metathesis to *KʲTʲ in Core IE.

For the prehistory of Greek what happened to the reduplicated present stem *té-teḱ-ti '(s)he produces' (root *teḱ-) in Core IE is especially instructive. The zero-grade forms were subject to the rules given immediately above; for instance the 3pl., underlyingly */té-tḱ-nti/, surfaced as *téḱʲtʲn̥ti in Core IE. Some daughters extracted *teḱʲtʲ- and treated it as the underlying root.[15] Indo-Iranian treated the form as the zero grade of the root and created a new full-grade *tḗḱʲtʲ- by adding another *e, which of course contracted with the one already present (see 2.2.4 (i)); hence 3pl. *tḗḱʲtʲn̥ti > Skt *tákṣati* but 3sg. *tḗḱʲtʲ-s-ti > *tā́ṣṭi* '(s)he fashions'. Only Gk τίκτει 'she's giving birth' preserves the original reduplicated present, and it has been remodeled in ways typical of Greek: the reduplicating vowel has been replaced by *i, and a thematic stem has been constructed on the old zero grade of the athematic stem (thus *téteḱ- ~ *tétḱ- > *tétek- ~ *tétʲkʲ- (with merger of palatals and velars and thorn-cluster palatalization) → *títek- ~ *tíkʲtʲ- (with replacement of the reduplicating vowel and metathesis) > *títek- ~ *tíkt- → τικτ-ε- ~ τικτ-ο-).

Clusters of obstruents undergo rules of voicing assimilation in all the daughters, but since most such rules are natural and could have arisen repeatedly, it

[15] Latin apparently added the thematic vowel (*téḱʲtʲ-e-ti > *texit* 'she weaves')—if the Latin verb belongs here; for an alternative, see Rix et al. (2001) s.v. 2. **tek*.

is unclear whether they should be reconstructed for PIE. The most interesting example is 'Bartholomae's Law', an Indo-Iranian rule by which breathy-voicing spreads rightward through a cluster of obstruents; for instance, in Sanskrit the addition of the past participial suffix /-tá-/ (< PIE verbal adjective *-tó-, see above) to the root /bud^h-/ 'awaken' (< PIE *b^{h}ewd^h-; Sanskrit roots are traditionally cited in the zero grade) gives _budd^{h}á-_ 'awake'. It is possible, but not certain, that the rule was inherited from PIE. Given the uncertainty surrounding the prehistory of these assimilation rules, I write unassimilated forms for PIE (*yugtós, etc.).

Various simplifications of consonant clusters occurred in PIE. It's clear that *KsK clusters were simplified by loss of the first stop; for instance, the present of *preḱ- 'ask' (cf. Lat. _precēs_ 'prayers'), underlyingly */pr̥ḱ-sḱé/ó-/, surfaced as *pr̥sḱé-ti '(s)he keeps asking' (cf. Lat. _poscit_ '(s)he asks for', Skt _pr̥cc^{h}áti_ 'she asks'). Some word-initial clusters of stops were simplified before some sonorants (syllabic or not); obvious examples are *ḱm̥tóm 'hundred', evidently derived from */déḱm̥t/ 'ten' but lacking the initial *d-, and *ǵ^{h}m- ~ *ǵ^{h}m̥-, the zero-grade alternant of 'earth' (see above). Further details are beyond the scope of this sketch.

2.2.4 (iv) Auslautgesetze

It is likely that word-final */t/ was voiced when a vowel or sonorant preceded (Hale 1994, Ringe 1997); thus the surface form of 'ten', cited immediately above, was probably *déḱm̥d. This relatively unnatural rule still operated in Hittite and in Proto-Italic, and it is more likely that that reflects a common inheritance than a parallel innovation.[16]

The morphologized effects of some pre-PIE phonological rules affecting word-final sequences had a major impact on PIE nominal inflection. The most important of these rules is 'Szemerényi's Law', by which the word-final sequences **-VRs and **-VRh_2 (at least) became *-V:R (where R symbolizes a nonvocalic sonorant, V a vowel, and : vowel length). These rules affected the nom. sg. forms of numerous masculine and feminine nouns, and the nom.-acc. of neuter collectives; for instance, **p$h_2$tér-s 'father' > *ph_2tḗr (the reconstructable form). A word-final *-n that arose by this process was subsequently dropped, at least if the preceding segment was (unaccented) *ō (cf. Jasanoff 2002: 34–5); thus **tétḱons 'craftsman' > **tétḱōn > **tétḱō > *téḱ^{j}t^{j}ō. We know that these rules had already been morphologized in PIE because (a) the resulting long vowel had begun to spread to other nom. sg. forms in which it was not phonologically justified (e.g. *pṓds 'foot'), and (b) word-final sonorants other than *-n were sometimes dropped in nom. sg.

[16] This has been adumbrated repeatedly in the literature; see e.g. Schwyzer (1939: 409), Szemerényi (1973: 60–1). If the first component of the Latin compound _atavos_ 'great-great-great-grandfather' is identical with the adverb *ád (as suggested by Alan Nussbaum, p.c. to Michael Weiss), it is a further piece of supporting evidence. On the function of *ád, see 2.3.4 (i).

forms (only; e.g. *sókʷh₂ō 'companion' was an i-stem, and its nom. sg. ought to have ended in **-oys, as George Cardona reminds me). For up-to-date discussion, see Piwowarczyk (2015).

Also fairly important was a complex of rules called 'Stang's Law', by which word-final */-Vmm/, */-Vwm/, and apparently */-Vh_2m/ surfaced as *-V:m, and */Vyi/ became *V:y in final syllables; for instance, the acc. sg. of *dom- 'house' seems to have been *dṓm instead of expected '**dómm̥', that of *dyew- 'day, sky' was clearly *dyḗm instead of '**dyéwm̥', feminines in *-ah_2 had acc. sg. forms in *-ām, and i-stem loc. sg. */-ey-i/ became *-ēy. The same or similar rules appear to have applied before acc. pl. *-ns, ultimately giving forms in *-V:s, but the details are not completely clear.

In utterance-final position laryngeals were lost, at least if a syllabic immediately preceded. Such a sandhi rule is recoverable from various phenomena in the Rigveda; in addition, vocatives were complete utterances, and it is clear that the final laryngeal of stems in *-ah_2 was lost in the voc. sg. (cf. Kuiper 1947: 210–12, 1961: 18). This rule was ordered after the laryngeal-coloring rules, so that in the vocatives in question the output was short *-a. This is the source of Greek vocatives in -τα to masc. ā-stems in -της (< -τᾱς ← *-τᾱ), of OCS vocatives in *-o* (< *-a) to nouns in *-a* (< *-ā < *-ah_2 = */-eh_2/), and of Umbrian vocatives in *-a* to nouns in *-o* (< *-ā < *-ah_2).

2.2.5 PIE accent

A PIE word could contain at most one accented syllable. It seems clear that the surface instantiation of accent was high pitch (as attested in Vedic Sanskrit and Ancient Greek, both described by native grammarians), though in all the daughter languages this eventually evolved into prominence ('stress'), and in many the system was eventually lost.

The rules by which accent was assigned in PIE are still incompletely understood, but the following facts are fairly clear. In principle any syllable of a word could be accented. Thematic nominals (i.e. those ending in the thematic vowel; see 2.2.4 (i)) had the accent on the same syllable throughout the paradigm; thematic verb stems also have fixed accent in the earliest attested languages and apparently did in PIE as well. Some athematic verb stems and nominals exhibited fixed accent (mostly on the root), but most exhibited alternating accent; there were several patterns, but in all of them the surface accent was to the left in one group of forms (the nominative and accusative cases of nominals, the active singular of verbs) and to the right in the rest. It seems clear that stems and endings could be underlyingly accented or not, that the leftmost underlying accent surfaced, and that words with no underlying accent were assigned accent on the leftmost syllable by default; but not all the details have been worked out satisfactorily.

There was a class of small particles, pronouns, and the like, called 'clitics', that never bore an accent. Much more surprisingly, there were rules applying in sentential contexts—therefore on the phrase level, at the end of the phonology—that deaccented major words. Vocatives were normally deaccented; so were finite verb forms in main clauses, though not in subordinate clauses. When such forms occurred sentence-initially, however, they were accented after all. Sentence-initial vocatives clearly received accent on their leftmost syllables by default. Sentence-initial finite verbs in main clauses apparently received whatever accent they would have borne in subordinate clauses—at least to judge from Vedic Sanskrit, the only daughter that preserves the inherited system more or less intact.

This complex and unusual accent system partly survives in Greek, though it has undergone extensive modifications.

2.3 PIE inflectional morphology

Core IE clearly had a large and complex inflectional system. Most of its inflectional morphology is preserved in Indo-Iranian; its nominal inflection is reasonably well preserved in Balto-Slavic and its verb inflection in Greek, and substantial parts of the system survive in other ancient and mediaeval IE languages, especially in Latin. The morphological history of Core IE languages is characterized for the most part by gradual loss of categories and inflectional classes among nominals and both loss and renewal in verb inflection.

PIE also possessed a fairly large and complex inflectional system, but comparison of the Anatolian languages with Core IE suggests that the development from PIE to Core IE involved some increase in inflectional complexity with little loss. (The Tocharian languages have lost much of the PIE system of nominal inflection, which limits their usefulness in assessing the PIE situation.)

Since the development of PIE into Core IE is a subject of ongoing discussion and the reconstruction of the PIE inflectional system is uncertain in many points, my treatment of those earliest stages in the prehistory of Greek will be fairly brief. I will then lay out the Core IE system in greater detail and use it as the starting point for the separate development of Greek.

2.3.1 PIE inflectional categories

The classes of inflected lexemes in PIE included verbs, nouns, adjectives, pronouns, determiners, and most quantifiers. All except verbs were inflected according to a single system and are therefore grouped together as 'nominals'; verb inflection was considerably more complex than nominal inflection.

All nominals were inflected for number and case. Singular, dual, and plural were distinguished, the dual expressing 'two'. Comparison of IE languages attested early suggests that PIE nominals were inflected for nine cases, as follows.

case	*functions (not lexically governed)*
vocative	direct address
nominative	subject of finite verb; complement of 'be', etc.
accusative	(default) direct object of verb; extent, duration
dative	indirect object; benefactive; possession (at least as predicate of 'be'); purpose
genitive	complement of noun phrase: possession, partitive, measure
instrumental	instrument; accompaniment
ablative	motion from; separation
locative	location, time at or within which
allative	motion to or toward

The allative survives as such only in Old Hittite, but since a few Greek adverbs appear to be fossilized allatives, the case should be reconstructed for PIE. For instance, Homeric Gk χαμαί 'to the ground' evidently reflects the PIE allative *ǵ^{h}máh$_2$ ~ *ǵ^{h}m̥áh$_2$ (by Lindeman's Law) to which the 'hic-et-nunc' particle *-i has been suffixed; the caseform survives in its original function in Old Hitt. *taknā*, whose stem has been remodeled. In Core IE the allative apparently underwent syntactic merger with the accusative.[17] The ablative case poses a different and more intractable kind of problem which will be discussed at length below.

Each noun was arbitrarily assigned to a concord class, called a 'gender'. In Nuclear IE there were three genders, conventionally called masculine, feminine, and neuter. Whether the feminine gender was already present in PIE continues to be debated; see Melchert (2014b) for a summary of the debate with numerous references and Kim (2014) for a recent proposal regarding the origin of the feminine. Anatolian has no feminine gender, and possible relics of an original feminine in the Anatolian languages are sparse and equivocal (see Hoffner and Melchert 2008: 64 with references); possible instances of feminine *concord* are especially uncertain (Melchert 2014b: 259 with references). The existence of a class of Lycian animate nouns in *-a* < *-ah$_2$ that indicate females (*lada* 'wife', *kbatra* 'daughter', and possibly *xawa* 'sheep', *wawa* 'cow'; see Melchert 1994b: 231) suggests that *-h$_2$ might have marked feminine nouns in PIE, but some other such nouns indicate males (Melchert 2014b: 261–2 with references), and many archaic Nuclear IE languages exhibit, in addition to numerous feminines in *-ah$_2$ and *-ih$_2$ ~ *-yáh$_2$-, stems in

[17] As Craig Melchert reminds me, the accusative is also occasionally used for motion to or toward in Old Hittite (Hoffner and Melchert 2008: 248–9), which suggests that it already had that function in PIE; whether there was any functional difference between the two in Old Hittite (or in PIE) is not clear. But the existence of such a fossil as Gk χαμαί seems to me to force the reconstruction of an allative case for the protolanguage.

*-ah$_2$ that are masculine. The suffix *-ser- is an archaic inflectional marker of feminine gender in the Core IE numerals 'three' and 'four' (see 2.3.6 (i)) and must have been inherited from the proximate ancestor of Core IE, but in Anatolian it is a suffix which derives nouns denoting females (Hoffner and Melchert 2008: 59), which suggests that it was still derivational in PIE. The most likely relic of a feminine gender in Anatolian is perhaps Hittite *sia-* 'one', which can have been backformed to the feminine reconstructable for Core IE (see 2.3.6 (i)).

Since adjectives, determiners, and most quantifiers modifying a noun exhibited gender concord with the noun, and concord of number, case, and gender obtained under coreference (see 2.5), nominals other than nouns normally had parallel sets of case-and-number forms, one for each gender. Only in the personal pronouns was gender concord not expressed in the inflectional morphology.

Since there was also concord of person and number (but not gender) between a finite verb and its subject (see 2.5), finite forms of verbs were inflected for three persons and three numbers. Since PIE was a 'null subject' language, the subject was expressed only by the concord marking on the verb in very many clauses, and the hearer was obliged to recover its person and number from the inflection of the verb.

The category of aspect was important in PIE verb inflection, but it appears that aspect was expressed by derivational rather than inflectional morphology, much as in modern Russian (though the Russian system is a much later, purely Slavic creation). In the Anatolian languages aspect is still expressed derivationally; for a good description of the Hittite system, see Hoffner and Melchert (2008: 317–23). The PIE system was based on an opposition between perfective and imperfective stems; apparently most basic verbs were inherently perfective or imperfective—unlike the attested Hittite situation, in which most basic verbs are 'neutral' with respect to aspect—but a verb of either aspect could be derived from a basic verb of the other. A perfective stem denoted an event without reference to its internal structure, if any. The event might in fact have been complex, or repeated, or habitual, or taken a long time to complete; but by using a perfective verb the speaker indicated no interest in (or perhaps knowledge of) those details (cf. Comrie 1976). Since reference to present time includes the time of speaking, which imposes internal structure on the event, a perfective stem could not refer to present time; if it had a 'present tense', that tense would necessarily refer to something other than the actual present (e.g. the immediate future, or actions performed habitually). Though it is not usually remarked, many Modern English verbs actually exhibit this characteristic; we say, 'Tomorrow I go on vacation', or 'I go to the beach once a year', but if we are talking about the actual present we must use an explicitly imperfective form of 'go': 'Vacation is over, so I am going home'. A PIE imperfective verb did focus on the internal structure of an event; the event could extend over time during which something else happened, be repeated, be habitual, be attempted but not completed, be an action performed independently by several subjects or separately upon several objects, and so on. Stative verbs, which indicate a state rather than an action, are a special type of imperfective; there were certainly derived statives in PIE, but basic statives do not seem to have had any special morphological characteristics.[18]

The Nuclear IE languages (i.e. the non-Anatolian half of the family) eventually reorganized the PIE derivational aspect system into a tighter inflectional system, in which a single verb could have two or three stems indicating different aspects. The perfective stem in this inflectional system is traditionally called the 'aorist'; reconstructable examples (cited in 3sg. subject form) include *bʰúHt 'it became', *gʷémd '(s)he took a step', *luktó 'it got light', *mr̥tó '(s)he disappeared/died', *wḗǵʰst '(s)he transported (it)', *wéwked '(s)he said', etc. The imperfective stem is traditionally (but rather unfortunately) called the 'present', even though there were both present and past tenses made from it; reconstructable examples include *gʷm̥sḱéti '(s)he's walking' (i.e. taking repeated steps), *ǵn̥h_3sḱéti '(s)he recognizes (habitually)', *h_2áǵeti '(s)he's driving (them)', *bʰinédst '(s)he tried to split (it)',[19] *bʰoréyeti '(s)he's carrying (it) around', *spéḱyed '(s)he kept looking at (it)', etc. Many 'present' stems were stative in meaning, e.g. *$h_1$ésti '(s)he is', *gʷí$h_3$weti '(s)he's alive', *ḱéyor 'it's lying flat', *wéstor '(s)he's wearing'. But in the Nuclear IE aspect system there was also a third type of stem with exclusively stative meaning,[20] most unfortunately called the 'perfect'; typical examples include *wóyde '(s)he knows', *dedwóye '(s)he's afraid', *stestóh_2a '(s)he's standing upright', etc. While it is often clear which classes of Anatolian verbs correspond to Nuclear IE 'presents' (imperfectives) and 'aorists' (perfectives), the origin of the Nuclear IE 'perfect' (stative) is a problem that we will need to discuss in more detail.

PIE verbs clearly had two 'moods', indicative and imperative; the latter expressed commands. There were two indicative 'tenses', present and past. Nuclear IE, at least, had two further moods, 'subjunctive' and 'optative'; the subjunctive was used to make statements that the speaker wished to regard as less than fully

[18] I remain unconvinced by the assessment of the Homeric evidence suggested by Hollenbaugh (2018). Of course it is true that Homer uses imperfects in narrative, sometimes when aorists might be expected; but the formulaic nature of the Homeric oral tradition, in which formulas must be modified for use in different contexts, could easily have led to many such cases, and it is even possible that the oral poets eventually derived a blanket 'license' to the effect that imperfects in place of aorists (but not vice versa) were permissible.

[19] To judge from the aspect system of Ancient Greek, imperfective verb forms could express attempted but not completed actions. See Comrie (1976) for discussion.

[20] Many treatments of the PIE perfect suggest that it expressed states resulting from prior actions; a typical exposition of this 'stative-resultative' hypothesis is Szemerényi (1996: 293). (See the extensive discussion of Randall and Jones (2015: 141–5; with references), to whom I owe the term just used.) But so far as I can see, any 'resultative' nuance of meaning can be lexical rather than grammatical. A perfect meaning 'be broken' derived from a change-of-state verb such as 'break' cannot avoid implying a prior action; a perfect meaning 'know' or 'remember' is much less likely to have any such implication. Only if we can show that particular perfects developed from pure statives to stative-resultatives do we have good evidence for a grammatical category expressing the latter—assuming that it can be shown to differ from the 'résultatif' of Chantraine (1927). For further discussion of the Indo-Iranian and Greek evidence, see now Kümmel (2020) and Ringe (2022).

realized or certain, including (importantly) future events, while the optative was used to express the wishes of the speaker and potential events. Whether the subjunctive and/or optative should be reconstructed for PIE has long been debated, as they are absent from the Anatolian verb system, but in 2.3.3 (i) I will argue that PIE is likely to have had a subjunctive mood.[21] In any case, since neither of those moods marked tense, the expression of tense was confined to the indicative and was a subordinate detail of the Nuclear IE verb system. PIE also had participles, which were adjectives but could be used to express subordinate clauses as nominalizations; the participial suffixes were attached to aspect stems.

The final morphosyntactic category of the verb was 'voice'. The unmarked voice was the active. The 'mediopassive' voice was used (1) to mark the verb of a passive clause; (2) to mark reflexives and reciprocals;[22] and (3) in certain lexically marked verbs, which are called 'deponent verbs'. The Nuclear IE perfect (i.e. stative) had no mediopassive voice, to judge from the following distributional facts. In Tocharian the only direct reflex of the perfect is the preterite participle; it is indifferent to voice, being used both actively and passively. In Latin and Gothic, where the mediopassive has become largely or entirely passive in meaning, the reflexes of the perfect have no passive forms, which are supplied by phrases; Latin does not even have any (non-periphrastic) deponent perfects. Only in Greek and Indo-Iranian are mediopassive perfects clearly attested, and while the formations are similar in exhibiting reduplication but no suffix, they can easily be parallel innovations.[23]

2.3.2 Formal expression of inflectional categories

In nominals, number and case were expressed by 'fused' endings in which no separate markers of number on the one hand and case on the other could be

[21] Jasanoff (2003a: 182–4) argues that three Hittite 2sg. imperative forms in *-si* reflect haplologized subjunctives in *-s-e-si. Some facts from other IE languages suggest as much: Cardona (1965) established that Vedic 'imperatives' in *-si* actually are subjunctives, since they are occasionally used in subordinate clauses; Szemerényi (1966b) suggested haplology as the source of such forms; Jasanoff (1986) identified similar forms in Old Irish, where they are amenable to Szemerényi's explanation; and Jasanoff (1987) argued for the existence of such a form in Tocharian. On the other hand, the pattern of attestation of indisputable subjunctives in *-e- ~ *-o- suggests that they are Nuclear IE innovations. In Tocharian they are still in competition with an apparently older formation (see the discussion in 2.3.3 (i) with references), examples made directly to roots are fairly few, and the subjunctive vowel *replaces* a stem-final thematic vowel (cf. Ringe 2000: 131–6); only in Core IE is the 'classical' IE subjunctive in place. It seems prudent not to dismiss the possibility that the Hittite 2sg. imperatives in *-si*, and possibly Toch. B *päklyauṣ*, A *päklyoṣ* 'hear!' as well, are of different origin.

[22] In Hittite the reflexives and reciprocals marked by mediopassive verbs are direct (Hoffner and Melchert 2008: 303), though most are accompanied by the innovative particle *-z(a)*. In Indo-Iranian and Greek, which have overt reflexive pronouns, they are usually 'indirect' reflexives, in which the subject is implied to perform the action of the verb for his or her own benefit. It seems likely that the Hittite situation is original, given that the reflexive pronouns of Core IE languages seem to have developed from a PIE 3rd-person pronoun (see 2.3.6 (iii)).

[23] A tiny handful of Old Irish deponent suffixless preterites resemble the Indo-Iranian and Greek mediopassive perfects (Jasanoff 2003a: 31, 44), but since they are made to verbs with deponent presents they can easily be innovations.

distinguished; for instance, gen. sg. *-és ~ *-os ~ *-s and gen. pl. *-óHom shared no distinguishable marker of the case 'genitive', and neither exhibited any distinguishable marker of number (cf. e.g. nom. pl. *-es, dat. pl. *-os, loc. pl. *-sú, etc.; it is reasonable to suppose that the singular was unmarked for number). In those nominals that expressed gender (i.e. all except nouns and personal pronouns), feminine gender was normally expressed in Nuclear IE by a suffix which followed all derivational suffixes but preceded the case-and-number endings. Neuter gender was distinguished from masculine (and, in nouns, feminine) only in the nominative, accusative, and vocative cases, in which it exhibited different case-and-number endings; thus in those cases the endings expressed gender as well. This organization of nominal inflection persisted far down into the individual histories of the attested daughter languages.

In PIE the inflection of verbs seems to have been similar: tense, the imperative mood, voice, and the person and number of the subject were all marked by a single set of fused polyfunctional morphemes called simply 'endings' because they were the final element of a (finite) verb form. The participial suffixes occupied the same position as the finite verb endings. In the Anatolian languages this system persisted without change. In Nuclear IE, however, many of the affixes used to derive verbs from one another in PIE became markers of aspect, eventually adding a new layer to the inflectional template of verbs. In addition, subjunctive and optative moods were marked by suffixes added to the aspect stem but preceding the endings, so that the structure of an inflected verb became root (+ aspect affix) (+ mood suffix) + ending, and the participial suffixes now occupied the same position as the mood suffixes.

Some daughters of Central IE also evolved a prefix *é-, called the 'augment', that marked past tense (in the indicative only). In those daughters there was a three-way opposition in the indicative of the present and aorist stems: (1) forms with primary endings, which marked them for present tense (only in the imperfective, for the reasons given above); (2) forms with secondary endings and the augment, which marked them for past tense; (3) forms with secondary endings but no augment, called 'injunctives', which were apparently unmarked for tense and were used where tense could be inferred from context (see especially Hoffmann 1967a). The augment is clearly attested in Greek, Phrygian, Armenian, and Indo-Iranian. In Greek it not only marks past tense forms but is also affixed to the 'gnomic aorist', which makes statements that are asserted to be always true. From this odd pattern of facts Delfs (2006) argued convincingly that the augment was originally an evidential particle, citing parallels from Wintun languages; De Decker (2018: 24–9) cautiously suggests a similar conclusion on the basis of the distribution of augmented forms in the Homeric poems. The fact that it still has two disjunct functions in Greek—past tense and gnomic aorist—suggests that its incorporation into verb inflection was recent enough that its original evidential function had not yet been lost. Since it cannot be reconstructed as an inflectional affix even for Central IE with any confidence, I will discuss the augment in the context of the individual development of Greek.

2.3.3 PIE verb inflection

This section will sketch those parts of the verb system reconstructable for PIE and describe in detail the verb system that can be reconstructed for Core IE. Since the latter is essentially the Indo-Greek verb, further information can be found in the handbooks cited at the end of 2.1 and in Rix et al. (2001) (though my reconstructions differ from theirs in various details, generally accepting fewer innovative hypotheses than those of Rix et al.). For alternative reconstructions, see Jasanoff (2003a), Mottausch (2003).

2.3.3 (i) Verb stems: From derivation to inflection

PIE verb stems expressed aspect and some other categories. They fell into two purely formal classes, called 'athematic' and 'thematic'. The latter ended in the thematic vowel *-e- ~ *-o- (see 2.2.4 (i)); the former apparently always ended in a non-syllabic. Some stems were affixless, while others were marked by one of a wide variety of affixes. PIE stem-forming affixes were part of the derivational morphology; in Nuclear IE many, but not all, eventually became inflectional markers of aspect.

Comparison of Nuclear IE aspect-marking affixes with Anatolian derivational affixes enables us to infer the PIE system and make further inferences about its development in the daughters. The following equations of suffixes and an infix seem straightforward:

Hittite		*Nuclear IE*	
affix	*function*	*affix*	*function*
-ni(n)- *(infix)*	causative	*-né- ~ *-n- *(infix)*	present (= imperfective)
-nu-	causative, factitive	*-néw- ~ *-nu-	present
-ske/a-	imperfective	*-sḱé/ó-	present
-ahh-	factitive	*-(a)h_2-	factitive present
-āi- < *-ah_2-yé-	denominative	*-yé/ó-	denominative present
-e-	stative, fientive	*-éh_1-	stative, fientive

It is striking that while the affixes have different functions in Hittite, they are almost all used to derive present (i.e. imperfective) stems in Nuclear IE; only *-éh_1- appears also in aorist (i.e. perfective) stems, namely in the Greek intransitive aorist in -ή-, which will be discussed in detail in the appropriate place below. One factitive present derived from a u-stem adjective actually survives in Nuclear IE: Skt *á dab*^{h}*noti* '(s)he damages' < *d(^{h})eb^h-né-w-ti is clearly cognate with Hitt. *tepnuzzi* '(s)he makes (it) small(er)', derived from *tēpus* 'small'. A few other Sanskrit examples, such as *inóti* '(s)he lets go, (s)he drives', derived from *i-* 'go', show that the transitivizing function of the first two Hittite affixes was their original function even in Nuclear IE; so does Gk κριμνάντων 'while weighing (anchor)' (Pindar *Pythian* IV.25) beside ἐκρέμω 'you were hanging' (*Il.* 15.18, 21), Att. intr. κρέμασθαι. How these affixes came to be imperfectivizing in Nuclear IE is not clear. The last three affixes in the table are still derivational in many Nuclear IE languages, but the first three have become inflectional markers of the imperfective aspect.

In addition, the cognates of several imperfective aspect markers of Nuclear IE appear fossilized in various Anatolian verb stems. Reduplicated stems are not uncommon; for instance, Hitt. *mimmai* '(s)he refuses' (< *'(s)he hesitates') appears to be cognate with Gk μίμνει '(s)he's waiting' < *mi-mn-e/o-, while the stem of Hitt. *sissandu* 'let them seal (it)' is cognate with that of Lat. *serit* '(s)he sows', both < *si-sh$_1$-e/o- 'press (things) in (one after another)'. Two Nuclear IE derived causative presents appear to have Hittite cognates: Hitt. *lukkizzi* '(s)he sets fire to' = Skt *rocáyati* '(s)he makes (it) give light' < PIE *lowkéyeti; Hitt. *wassezzi* '(s)he clothes' = Skt *vāsáyati* < PIE *woséyeti. Stems in *-ye/o- corresponding to Nuclear IE presents are also represented; for instance, Hitt. *weriyezzi* '(s)he calls' = Ionic Gk ἔρει '(s)he says' < PIE *wéryeti, and Hitt. *sākizzi* '(s)he gives a sign' = Lat. *sāgit* '(s)he senses keenly'[24] < PIE *sah$_2$giéti. (For possible Hittite and Luvian survivals of the imperfectivizing function of *-ye/o-, see Melchert 1997b.)

The only widespread perfective aspect marker in Nuclear IE was *-s-, the suffix of the 'sigmatic' aorist. Whether any Anatolian verb stems exhibit a cognate of that affix is disputed, but several plausible examples can be cited: Hitt. *ganess-* 'recognize' appears to be cognate with the stem of Toch. A *kñasu* 'I recognized', *kñas-äṣt* 'you recognized' < PIE *ǵnēh$_3$-s- (Schmidt and Winter 1992: 51–2, Hackstein 1993: 151–6); Hitt. *u-lesta* '(s)he hid him/herself' seems to be more or less identical with Skt *ní aleṣṭa* '(s)he has hidden him/herself' < *ley-s-; Hitt. *karszi* '(s)he cuts' might be a stem-cognate of Gk ἔκερσε '(s)he sheared', Hitt. *pāsi* '(s)he swallows' is conceivably a stem-cognate of Skt *ápās* '(s)he has drunk', and so on.

The relation of the Hittite 'hi-conjugation' to the Nuclear IE perfect is much less clear. Hittite active verbs fall into two arbitrary inflectional classes with different endings in the singular, called 'mi-conjugation' and 'hi-conjugation' after their present 1sg. endings. The endings of the mi-conjugation are for the most part clearly cognate with those of the Nuclear IE present and aorist stems. The hi-conjugation resembles the Nuclear IE perfect (i.e. stative), but it is the *past tense* endings of the hi-conjugation that are cognate with the Nuclear IE perfect indicative endings. Many scholars reconstruct the perfect for PIE; it is suggested that it survived as the Anatolian hi-conjugation past, and that a present tense was

[24] Actually attested are Hom. εἴρω 'I say' and Lat. infinitive *sāgīre*, quoted in the meaning '*sentīre acūtē*' (Cicero, *De divinatione* I.65).

backformed from it. But unlike the perfect, the hi-conjugation is not stative in meaning, and stem-cognations between Hittite hi-conjugation verbs and Nuclear IE perfects are few and scattered. Numerous other difficulties with the hypothesis that the perfect gave rise to the hi-conjugation are discussed in Jasanoff (2003a: 7–17), and in my opinion the hypothesis does not survive Jasanoff's examination of it. The alternative is to reconstruct something like the hi-conjugation for PIE. Jasanoff (2003a) reconstructs a very complex verb system for PIE, including 'h_2e-conjugation' presents (i.e. imperfectives) and aorists (perfectives) as well as a perfect and pluperfect, but his reconstruction does not offer a convincing explanation for the pattern of facts just rehearsed. Moreover, he effectively projects the Hittite system of two isofunctional and lexically arbitrary conjugations back into PIE; and while we might settle for such a reconstruction if necessary, we should first try to figure out what the original function of the h_2e-paradigm could have been (cf. Willi 2018: 51).

Surprisingly, two other Core IE categories have a hi-conjugation ending: the active 1sg. of thematic present stems and the active 1sg. of subjunctives. We should expect the ending in the present, at least, to be *-o-mi, and that is in fact the source of Hitt. thematic pres. 1sg. *-a-mi*; but in Nuclear IE we find *-o-h_2 instead, in which *-h_2 is the zero grade of perfect 1sg. *-h_2a, as expected after the thematic vowel. The fact that the same ending shows up in the Nuclear IE thematic *present tense* and the Hittite hi-conjugation *past* strongly suggests that the PIE ancestor of the hi-conjugation also did not mark tense—though in most other ways it did not resemble the Nuclear IE perfect.

Some other peculiarities of the Nuclear IE subjunctive might point in the same direction. Tocharian languages have a separate subjunctive stem, and while a few Tocharian subjunctives appear to be cognate with Core IE subjunctives (Ringe 2000: 131–4), many others cannot be. Among the latter are subjunctives of classes I and V, which must be reconstructed with (post-)PIE *o in the active singular and *e or zero in other forms (Jasanoff 2003a: 161–3 with references). Kim has therefore suggested that those subjunctives, the Nuclear IE perfect, and the hi-conjugation all share an origin in a class of perfective presents (Kim 2007: 188–9, 193–7). But the Tocharian subjunctive is not perfective in any of its uses (Peyrot 2013: 190–3), and the Nuclear IE perfect was a stative imperfective, not necessarily implying any prior action (Kümmel 2020, Ringe 2022).

An obvious alternative is that the PIE h_2e-conjugation was actually a subjunctive, which did not mark tense because it did not primarily refer to present or past events (Ringe 2012). That is congruent with another oddity of the Core IE subjunctive. In Indo-Iranian, and to a lesser extent in Greek, the subjunctive is found with both primary and secondary endings. It is sometimes suggested that the Core IE subjunctive had both sets of endings with different functions; a clear exposition of that hypothesis is Rix (1976a: 259–61). However, the distribution of endings in Vedic suggests a different hypothesis. Not only the active 1sg., but also the 1du.

and 1pl., have secondary endings, and given the use of the subjunctive in exhortations, those are pivotal forms (unlike in the indicative) and likely to be old. The active 3pl. also has a secondary ending, and the 2sg. and 3sg. exhibit both primary and secondary endings. Only the more peripheral members of the paradigm—the active 2pl., 2du., and 3du. and the mediopassive—always have primary endings in Vedic. It seems reasonable to suggest that the subjunctive originally had secondary endings, which makes sense, since it did not refer to present time. The primary endings of Indo-Iranian and Greek, as well as those of daughters attested later—Italic, Tocharian, Armenian, and Celtic, as well as Germanic, in which a few subjunctives became presents (Ringe 2017: 185–6; with references)—must be parallel innovations.

The fact that 1sg. *-o-h_2 also appears in the Core IE thematic present indicative, where it is the only secondary ending in the paradigm, prompts a further inference: the Nuclear IE simple thematic present developed out of the *-e/o-subjunctive.

The foregoing hypothesis can be summed up as follows. The PIE h_2e-paradigm was the subjunctive and had no primary endings. In Anatolian it lost its modal function, acquiring primary endings and becoming an arbitrary conjugation of verbs. In Nuclear IE one class of h_2e-paradigms—probably a small and unimportant one—survived as the perfect, probably with substantial innovations. Otherwise the system underwent a wholesale reorganization. Some other h_2e-paradigms survived as subjunctives in Tocharian. Those that did not end in short vowels became class I and V subjunctives; those that did[25] became subjunctives of the type familiar from Core IE daughters. Some of the latter developed into simple thematic present stems.[26] In the course of that development the stems ending in a short vowel were remodeled so as to exhibit the same endings: all the 1sg. forms, including the preexisting presents in *-sḱé/ó- and *-yé/ó-, wound up with an ending *-o-h_2, but otherwise the preexisting thematic endings 'won out'. Most of these developments had at least begun in Nuclear IE, before Tocharian lost contact with the other daughters.[27]

For Core IE a coherent system of aspect stems is solidly reconstructable, as described in the next few paragraphs.

Present (imperfective) stems exhibited the widest variety of affixes. Basic presents included at least the following types.

[25] It is striking that while unsuffixed mi-verbs ending in etymologically short vowels are probably not attested in Hittite (Hoffner and Melchert 2008: 199, fn. 66), hi-verbs of that shape might be (pp. 224–7).

[26] The connection between vowel-final hi-conjugation verbs and thematic presents goes back to Watkins (1969: 107–8), though in the context of a very different reconstruction of the PIE verb.

[27] This narrative covers some of the same ground as Willi (2018: 197–9), though with different judgments of the evidence; the most important difference is that I have made the subjunctive central to the changes hypothesized instead of trying to derive it from a thematic present.

Athematic presents:

- root-presents (i.e. affixless athematic presents), e.g. *$h_1$és- ~ *h_1s- 'be' (cf. Skt 3sg. *ás-ti*, 3pl. *s-ánti*), *h_1ḗd- ~ *$h_1$éd- 'be eating' (cf. Lat. 3sg. *ēs-t*, 3pl. *ed-unt*);[28]
- athematic presents reduplicated with *Ce-, e.g. *d^hé-d^heh_1- ~ *d^hé-$d^h$$h_1$-[29] 'be putting' (cf. Skt 3sg. *dád^{h}ā-ti*, 3pl. *dád^h-ati*);
- athematic presents reduplicated with *Ci-, e.g. *stí-stah_2- ~ *stí-sth_2- 'be getting up (into a standing position)' (cf. Gk 3sg. ἵστη-σι, 3pl. ἱστᾶσι < *hιστά-ᾱσι);
- nasal-infixed presents (with the infix *-né- ~ *-n-), e.g. *li-né-k^w- ~ *li-n-k^w- 'be leaving behind' (cf. Skt 3sg. *riṇák-ti*, 3pl. *riñc-ánti*), *tl̥-ná-h_2- ~ *tl̥-n-h_2- 'be lifting' (cf. OIr. 3sg. *tlena-id* '(s)he steals');
- presents with suffix *-néw- ~ *-nw- (~ *-nu-), e.g. *tn̥-néw- ~ *tn̥-nw- 'be stretching' (cf. Skt 3sg. *tanó-ti*, 3pl. *tanv-ánti*).

Thematic presents:

- simple (i.e. affixless) thematic presents, e.g. *b^hér-e/o- 'carry' (cf. 3sg. Skt *b^{h}ára-ti*, Gk φέρε-ι, etc.), *su(H)-é/ó- 'push' (?; cf. Skt 3sg. *suváti* '(s)he impels');[30]
- thematic presents reduplicated with *Ci-, e.g. *sí-sd-e/o- 'be sitting down' (cf. 3sg. Gk ἵζε-ται, Lat. *cōn-sīdi-t*, etc.);
- presents in *-sḱé- ~ *-sḱó-, e.g. *pr̥-sḱé/ó- 'keep asking' (root *preḱ-; cf. 3sg. Skt *pr̥cc^{h}á-ti*, Lat. *posci-t* '(s)he asks for');
- presents in *-yé- ~ *-yó-, e.g. *wr̥ǵ-yé/ó- 'be working' (cf. 3sg. Av. *vərəziie-iti*, Goth. *waúrkei-þ*);
- presents in *-ye- ~ *-yo- (with accent on the root), e.g. *g^{wh}éd^h-ye/o- 'keep asking for' (cf. OIr. 3sg. *guidi-d*, OPers. *jadiyā-miy* 'I pray');
- presents in *-se- ~ *-so-, e.g. *$h_2$lék-se/o- 'protect' (cf. 3sg. Skt *rákṣa-ti*, Hom. Gk ἀλέξε-ι; probably originally desiderative *'want to protect', see below).

[28] Many colleagues hold that athematic presents with ablaut *ē ~ *e, often called 'Narten presents', are derived, typically from roots that also make root-aorists; for a comprehensive exposition of that view, see Kümmel (1998) and Melchert (2014a). On the other hand, at least some of the reconstructed present–aorist pairs are questionable (see Ringe 2012).

[29] I remain unconvinced by the arguments of Lühr (1984) that this type of present exhibited o-grade of the root in the active singular. As I pointed out in Ringe (2001), of about fifty such presents reconstructed in Rix et al. (2001) only one—Hitt. *wewakki* '(s)he demands'—is attested with both reduplication and an o-grade root. The distribution of palatals and velars in Skt reduplicated presents is not reliable evidence, since a pattern of initial palatal in the reduplicating syllable and initial velar in the root has been generalized. The second vowel of Old Saxon *dedos* 'you (sg.) did' can reflect OHG influence; on the origin of *ō in the OHG paradigm, see Ringe and Taylor (2014: 76). For my own (tentative) suggestion about the origin of PGmc *dō- 'make, do', see Ringe (2012).

[30] The latter is perhaps the best example with an unaccented zero-grade root, but it is far from certain; the most plausible cognates, Hitt. *suwezzi* '(s)he banishes' and OIr. *im·soí* '(s)he turns it', can reflect a present in *-yé/ó-. Skt *syáti* '(s)he ties' appears to be cognate with Hitt. 3sg. *ishāi*, 3pl. *ishiyanzi*, but Luv. 3pl. *hishiyanti* suggests that the Hittite verb might originally have been reduplicated, its initial *h- lost by dissimilation (Melchert 1994a: 168 with references).

Derived presents included at least the following types.
Athematic derived presents:

- factitives in *-h_2-, formed from adjectives, e.g. *néwa-h_2- 'renew' (cf. Lat. *novā-re*; Gk νεᾶν 'to plow a fallow field') ← *néwo- 'new'.

Thematic derived presents:

- transitives, including some causatives and iteratives, in *-éye- ~ *-éyo- (with o-grade root), formed from basic verbs, e.g. *sod-éye/o- 'seat (someone)' (cf. Skt 3sg. *sādáya-ti*) ← *sed- 'sit down', *b^hor-éye/o- 'be carrying around' (cf. Gk 3sg. φορεῖ < *p^horée-i) ← *b^her- 'carry';
- desideratives in *-(h_1)se- ~ *-(h_1)so-, with and without reduplication *Ci-, formed from basic verbs, e.g. *wéyd-se/o- 'want to see' (cf. Lat. *vīse-re* 'to visit') ← *weyd- 'catch sight of', *ḱí-ḱl̥-$h_1$se/o- 'try to conceal' (cf. OIr. fut. 3sg. *céla-id* '(s)he will hide' < *kexlāti-s ←< *kiklāse-ti) ← *ḱel- 'hide';
- desideratives in *-syé- ~ *-syó-, formed from basic verbs, e.g. *b^huH-syé/ó- 'want to become' (cf. Lith. fut. 1sg. *bū́siu* 'I will be', ptc. *bū́sią̨s*; remodeled in Skt fut. 3sg. *b^haviṣyá-ti*);
- denominatives in *-yé- ~ *-yó-, formed from nominals, e.g. *$h_1$reg^{w}es-yé/ó- 'get dark' ← *$h_1$rég^{w}es- 'darkness' (cf. Skt 3sg. *rajasyá-ti*); *somHe-yé/ó- 'make (things) the same' (cf. Skt 3sg. *samayá-ti* '(s)he puts in order') ← *somHó- 'same' (note the e-grade nominal stem vowel before the present-stem suffix);
- (?) factitives in *-yé- ~ *-yó-, formed from adjectives, e.g. *$h_1$lewd^{h}ero-yé/ó- 'make free' (cf. Gk ἐλευθερõν < *eleut^{h}eróe-en) ← *$h_1$léwd^{h}ero- 'free' (note the o-grade vowel before the suffix).

Whether one inherited formation was present or aorist is uncertain (see Harðarson 1998, but also 4.2.2 (iv)):

- statives/fientives in *-éh_1-, some formed from 'Caland' roots that participated in a wide range of derivational processes, e.g. *ph_2ǵ-éh_1- 'be/become fixed' (cf. Gk παγῆναι), *$h_1$rud^h-éh_1- 'be/become red' (cf. Lat. *rubē-re* 'to blush') ← *$h_1$rewd^h- 'red'; perhaps also from derived adjectives, e.g. *sil-éh_1- 'be/become silent' (cf. Lat. *silē-re* 'to be silent', Goth. *anasilan* 'to become still') ← *si-lo- 'silent'.

There were far fewer types of aorists; the following are reconstructable.
Athematic aorists:

- root-aorists, e.g. *g^{w}ém- ~ *g^{w}m- 'step' (cf. Skt *gam-* 'go'), *b^huH- (*b^huh_2- ?) 'become' (cf. Skt *b^hū-*);

- s-aorists, e.g. *dḗyḱ-s- ~ *déyḱ-s- 'point out' (cf. Gk δεῖξαι 'to show', Gāthā-Av. 2sg. *dāiš* 'you showed'), *wḗǵʰ-s- ~ *wéǵʰ-s- 'transport in a vehicle' (cf. Lat. *vēx-isse* 'to have conveyed').

Thematic aorists:

- simple thematic aorists, e.g. *$h_1$ludʰ-é/ó- 'arrive' (cf. 3sg. Hom. Gk ἤλυθε '(s)he came', OIr. *luid* '(s)he went', Toch. B *lac* '(s)he went out');
- reduplicated thematic aorists, e.g. *wé-wk-e/o- 'say' (root *wekʷ-; cf. 3sg. Skt *á-voca-t*, Hom. Gk ἔ-ειπε).

It appears that a majority of aorists were root-aorists in PIE. Only a modest number of s-aorists are attested in as many as three subfamilies of IE. The simple thematic aorist listed is the only one attested in three subfamilies; moreover, since Cardona (1960) demonstrated that nearly all thematic aorists can be shown to be secondary developments of root-aorists in the individual histories of the daughters, we must reckon with the possibility that this one, too, was actually a root-aorist in PIE (though the fact that it is attested as a relic—and thus comparatively archaic—thematic preterite in Tocharian argues caution). About reduplicated thematic aorists we are even less certain: the example listed is well attested in Indo-Iranian and Greek, the two non-Anatolian daughters that preserve the greatest number of archaisms in the verb system, but it is almost the only one not restricted to a single daughter.[31] There were even fewer types of perfect stems, all of which were athematic; the following are reconstructable:

- root-perfects, e.g. *wóyd- ~ *wid- 'know' (cf. 3sg. Skt *véda*, Gk οἶδε, Goth. *wait*);
- reduplicated perfects, e.g. *me-món- ~ *me-mn- 'have in mind' (cf. 3sg. Hom. Gk μέμονε '(s)he desires', Lat. *meminit* '(s)he remembers', Goth. *man* 'I think so').

The root-perfect listed is the only one reconstructable; so far as we can tell, all other perfects were reduplicated.

Note that almost all reconstructable stems of Core IE derived verbs (factitives, causatives, denominatives) were present (imperfective) stems. There must have been a way of expressing the perfective aspect of those derived verbs in Core IE, but we do not know what it was; probably it was a phrasal construction of some sort.

[31] Hom. ἦραρε '(s)he fit (it)', ptc. ἀραρών is probably cognate with the Armenian aorist 3sg. *arar* '(s)he made' (Bendahman 1993: 83), but the possibility that Greek and Armenian were especially close to one another in prehistory makes this example even less probative than the other.

A final point about the system sketched above should be emphasized. To judge from developments in Greek—the attested daughter of Core IE which best preserved the inherited system of aspect stems—verb stem formation in Core IE had not yet become inflectional. Very surprisingly, there are more than a few 'crossovers' between inherited perfective and imperfective stems in Greek (in both directions); that is difficult to explain in a hard-and-fast inflectional system, but at least somewhat easier if the system was still derivational. Specific examples will be discussed in 4.2.1 and 4.2.2.

2.3.3 (ii) The Nuclear IE mood suffixes

PIE probably had no suffixes indicating mood. Nuclear IE clearly had subjunctive and optative moods marked by suffixes that followed the aspect suffixes (if any) but preceded the endings. The early development of the subjunctive has been outlined in the preceding section; what remains to be said is that in Core IE the subjunctive of thematic stems was made by suffixing the subjunctive vowel to the thematic vowel, with contraction (see 2.2.4 (i)). The source of the optative is completely unclear.

As might be expected, in Tocharian the optative is formed from the subjunctive stem by further suffixation. But if the subjunctive stem ends in the thematic vowel *-e- ~ *-o-, that vowel is deleted before the optative suffix is added—unlike in Central IE, where the final thematic vowel of an aspect stem is not deleted before the optative suffix. Moreover, many Tocharian present stems and subjunctive stems are identical, and it often appears that the subjunctive has been formed from the present; but if the present stem is thematic, the stem-final thematic vowel is deleted before the subjunctive thematic vowel is added—again unlike in Core IE. The reconstructable situation seems to be as follows:

		Tocharian	*Core IE*
subjunctive:	athematic	*-e- ~ *-o-	*-e- ~ *-o-
	thematic	*-e- ~ *-o-	*-ē- ~ *-ō- (see 2.2.4 (i))
optative:	athematic	*-yéh_1- ~ *-ih_1-	*-yéh_1- ~ *-ih_1-
	thematic	*-ih_1- (?)	*-o-y(h_1)- (Central IE; see also below)

Since we know that in nominal derivation the thematic vowel was deleted before the suffix *-yó-, the deletion of the thematic vowel before the subjunctive and optative suffixes in Tocharian is plausibly an archaism, abandoned in the development of Core IE.

In Central IE the stems listed in the preceding section constructed subjunctive and optative stems as follows; I cite forms from some daughters (usually 3sg.) for some of the stems.

indicative/imperative	_subjunctive_	_optative_
*$h_1$és- ~ *h_1s-	*$h_1$és-e/o- (cf. Skt _ásati_, Lat. fut. _erit_)	*h_1s-iéh_1- ~ *h_1s-ih_1- (cf. Skt _syā́t_, Gk εἴη)
*h_1ḗd- ~ *$h_1$éd-	*$h_1$éd-e/o- (cf. Skt _ádat_)	*$h_1$éd-ih_1- (cf. Old Lat. 1sg. _edim_)
*d^hé-d^heh_1- ~ *d^hé-$d^h h_1$-	*d^hé-d^heh_1-e/o-	*d^hé-$d^h h_1$-ih_1- (cf. Skt _dád^{h}īta_)
*stí-stah_2- ~ *stí-sth_2-	*stí-stah_2-e/o-	*stí-sth_2-ih_1- (cf. Gk ἱσταίη)
*li-né-k^w- ~ *li-n-k^w-	*li-né-k^w-e/o- (cf. Skt 1du. _riṇácāva_)	*li-n-k^w-iéh_1- ~ *li-n-k^w-ih_1-
*tl̥-ná-h_2- ~ *tl̥-n-h_2-	*tl̥-ná-h_2-e/o-	*tl̥-n-h_2-iéh_1- ~ *tl̥-n-h_2-ih_1-
*tn̥-néw- ~ *tn̥-nw-	*tn̥-néw-e/o- (cf. Skt 1du. _tanávāvahai_)	*tn̥-nu-yéh_1- ~ *tn̥-nw-ih_1-
*b^hér-e/o-	*b^hér-ē/ō- (cf. Lat. fut. _feret_)	*b^hér-o-y(h_1)- (cf. Skt _b^háret_, Gk φέροι)
*pr̥-sḱé/ó-	*pr̥-sḱḗ/ṓ- (cf. Skt _pr̥cc^{h}ā́t_)	*pr̥-sḱó-y(h_1)-

(etc.: all thematic stems formed the subjunctive by lengthening the thematic vowel and the optative with *-y(h_1)-, which selected the o-grade of the thematic vowel)

*$h_1$rud^h-éh_1-	*$h_1$rud^h-éh_1-e/o-	*$h_1$rud^h-éh_1-ih_1- (?)
*néwa-h_2-	*néwa-h_2-e/o-	*néwa-h_2-ih_1- (?)
*g^wém- ~ *g^wm-	*g^wém-e/o- (cf. Skt _gámat_)	*g^wm̥-yéh_1- ~ *g^wm-ih_1-
*b^huH-	*b^húH-e/o- (cf. Skt _b^húvat_)	*b^huH-yéh_1- ~ *b^huH-ih_1- (cf. Skt _b^hūyā́t_)
*dḗyḱ-s- ~ *déyḱ-s-	*déyḱ-s-e/o-	*déyḱ-s-ih_1-
*wóyd- ~ *wid-	*wéyd-e/o- (cf. Skt _védati_, Hom. Gk 1pl. εἴδομεν)	*wid-yéh_1- ~ *wid-ih_1- (cf. Skt _vidyā́t_)
*me-món- ~ *me-mn-	*me-mén-e/o-	*me-mn̥-yéh_1- ~ *me-mn-ih_1- (cf. Skt _mamanyā́t_)

(Direct evidence for s-aorist optatives is sparse, though archaic-looking examples occur in Cretan Greek;[32] direct evidence for modal forms made to derived

[32] We might expect to find the s-aorist optative robustly attested in Indo-Iranian, but that is not the case. Instead of active s-aorist optatives we find root-aorist optatives in Vedic (Hoffmann 1967b: 32), and a category called the precative seems to have been built on them (p. 32); middle s-aorist optatives and precatives are rare and clearly innovative (Narten 1964: 43–5, 67–8). S-aorist optatives in Avestan are also rare and often doubtful (Kellens 1984: 370, 372). The s-aorist itself clearly underwent considerable expansion in Vedic, demonstrably inherited examples being few (Narten, _op. cit._). Some scholars have drawn the conclusion that the PIE s-aorist was rare and had no optative. But Indo-Iranian is not a basal subgroup in the IE cladistic tree, and the presence of reflexes of s-aorists in Tocharian and (probably) Hittite suggests that the s-aorist underwent a steep decline in Indo-Iranian followed by a re-expansion. The only other daughter in which we might expect to find s-aorist optatives surviving is Greek, in which they are an unproblematic part of the verb system. Further study of this question is needed.

athematic presents is even scantier.) As can be seen, the rules for the construction of these secondary mood stems were straightforward. If the stem was athematic and ablauting, the subjunctive was made by suffixing the thematic vowel to the e-grade of the stem; if it was athematic but non-ablauting (like the derived statives and factitives, and *b^huH- 'become'), the thematic vowel was suffixed to the invariant stem; if the stem was thematic, the subjunctive vowel contracted with the stem-final thematic vowel, producing a long thematic vowel. Optatives were made by suffixing *-yéh_1- ~ *-ih_1- to athematic stems (though if the accent fell consistently to the left only the zero-grade of the optative suffix appeared); when this suffix was added to thematic stems the thematic vowel of the stem appeared in the o-grade and the suffix in the zero grade—with the result that the laryngeal was dropped whenever a non-syllabic followed immediately (see 2.2.4 (i) *ad fin.*), though it was apparently restored in the dialect ancestral to Balto-Slavic.[33]

In the dialects ancestral to Italic and Celtic the system of mood suffixes was the same, except that in place of the analyzable thematic optative complex *-o-y(h_1)- there appeared an unanalyzable *-ā- of unknown origin (Trubetzkoy 1926, Benveniste 1951, Jasanoff 1994).[34] It seems unlikely that this opaque suffix replaced the transparent *-o-y(h_1)- of Central IE (as suggested by Jasanoff 1994: 204–5), but replacement of the equally transparent Tocharian suffix seems almost as unlikely. This is an unsolved problem.

2.3.3 (iii) Endings

The person/number/voice endings, including imperative endings, reconstructable for PIE stems that did *not* follow the h_2e-paradigm are the following. (In general I accept the reconstructions of Warren Cowgill; see also Sihler 1995: 453–80, 570–2.)

[33] See Olander (2015: 323, 337–8, 353). The alternative, namely that the laryngeal-drop rule operated early in the prehistories of most of the daughters but not in Balto-Slavic, seems moderately less likely, considering the relatively close positions of Balto-Slavic and Indo-Iranian in the probable post-PIE dialect map.

[34] It is true that the OIr. subjunctive suffix *-ā- could reflect earlier s-subjunctive *-ase-, which clearly appears in British Celtic, by regular sound change (Rix 1977, McCone 1991: 85–113). But Jasanoff (1994) argues strongly against that possibility on morphological grounds; in addition, he notes that Middle Welsh 3sg. *el* '(s)he may go', which is completely isolated in its paradigm, can reflect a preform *elāt but not *elaset (pp. 200, 205–7). There are also several probable Continental Celtic subjunctives that appear to exhibit a suffix *-ā-*. Though the lexical meaning of Hispano-Celtic *aśeCaTi* is not certainly recoverable, it is probably a subjunctive, since it occurs in a context which appears to be a set of prescriptions including also *CaPiseTi* and *amPiTiśeTi*, which must be either futures or s-subjunctives, and a number of apparent third-person imperatives in *-Tus* (Eska 1989: 20–2); the Gaulish form *axat*, in a healing charm quoted by Marcellus of Bordeaux (*De medicamentis* 8.171), is likewise probably a subjunctive, since a modal form would be expected in a charm and this is the only form in the (very short) charm that could be a verb. Gaulish *lubijas* (Lambert 2002: 131–2) is much less certain because the context is fragmentary, but of the interpretations that have been proposed a 2sg. subjunctive still seems the most plausible. I am grateful to Joseph Eska for calling to my attention the Continental Celtic forms and Jasanoff (1994).

	active			
	primary	*secondary*	*imperative*	*displaced iptv.*[35]
1sg.	*-m-i	*-m	—	
2sg.	*-s-i	*-s	0, *-d^{h}í	*-tṓd
3sg.	*-t-i	*-t (*[-t ~ -d])	*-t-u (*-t-ow?)	*-tṓd
1du.	*-wós	*-wé	—	
2du.	*-tés	*-tóm	*-tóm	
3du.	*-tés	*-tā́m	*-tā́m	
1pl.	*-mós	*-mé	—	
2pl.	*-té	*-té	*-té	
3pl.	*-ént-i ~ *-nt-i	*-ént (*[-énd]) ~ *-nt (*[-nd])	*-ént-u ~ *-nt-u (*-ént-ow ~ *-nt-ow?)	

	mediopassive		
	primary	*secondary*	*imperative*
1sg.	*-h$_{2}$á-r	*-h$_{2}$á	—
2sg.	*-th$_{2}$á-r	*-th$_{2}$á	???
3sg.	*-ó-r / *-t-ó-r	*-ó / *-t-ó	???
1du.	*-wós-d^{h}h$_{2}$	*-wé-d^{h}h$_{2}$	—
2du.	???	???	???
3du.	???	???	???
1pl.	*-mós-d^{h}h$_{2}$	*-mé-d^{h}h$_{2}$	—
2pl.	*-d^{h}h$_{2}$ué[36]	*-d^{h}h$_{2}$ué	*-d^{h}h$_{2}$ué
3pl.	*-ró-r / *-ntó-r	*-ró / *-ntó	???

Some comments are necessary to make this system intelligible.

In PIE the primary endings marked the non-past of imperfective stems, while the secondary endings marked the past tenses of both imperfective and perfective stems. The imperative endings were restricted to that mood. By Core IE, when the aspect system was evolving toward inflectional status and the subjunctive and optative moods were in place, the distribution of endings was more complex. Secondary endings characterized the optative mood, probably the subjunctive mood, and the past tenses of aorist stems (called the 'aorist indicative' because there was no non-past aorist indicative) and present stems (the 'imperfect indicative'). Primary endings marked the non-past tense of present stems (the 'present indicative') and might have begun to spread to the subjunctive mood. However, in Nuclear IE

[35] See Ringe (2007; with references).

[36] This reconstruction is intended to account for the shape of Hitt. *-ttuma:* *-d^{h}h$_{2}$ue > *-dduwe > *-ttuma* by regular sound changes. Skt *-d^{h}va* and (indirectly) Gk -σθε presuppose a form without the laryngeal, but if the PIE ending was *-d^{h}we we have no source for the Hittite *-m-*. The stop-plus-laryngeal cluster accounts simultaneously for Hitt. *-tt-* and *-m-*, and the existence of the latter seems to show that Sievers' Law operated after clusters of two obstruents in PIE, though it ceased to do so at some point in the development of Indo-Iranian (cf. Barber 2013: 30–7 with references).

thematic stems and subjunctives the primary 1sg. ending *-o-mi was replaced by h_2e-paradigm *-o-h_2 (see the discussion in 2.3.3 (i)).

There are obvious similarities between the primary, secondary, and imperative endings. Since the relations were somewhat different in the active and the mediopassive, I discuss them separately in that order.

Except in the 2du. and 3du., which are puzzling, and leaving aside the 2sg. imperative (see below), it is clear that the active secondary endings were the 'basic' members of the paradigm. In the sg. and the 3pl., the primary endings were normally derived from the secondary endings by the addition of the 'hic-et-nunc' particle *-i. In the 3sg. and 3pl., the imperative endings were derived from the secondary endings by the addition of a parallel particle *-u (or *-ow; the daughters disagree). In the 2pl. all three were the same, which may be an archaism or may simply reflect impoverishment in a relatively peripheral inflectional category. In the 2du. and 3du. it appears that the secondary ending was likewise used in the imperative. In the 1du. and 1pl. it looks as though a different particle was added to produce the primary endings, though the details are obscure. The 2sg. imperative was apparently endingless, and was probably the unmarked member of the imperative paradigm; *-d^hí seems to have been some sort of emphatic particle added to originally endingless forms.

The *hic-et-nunc* particle of the mediopassive seems to have been *-r rather than *-i; it survives in Anatolian, Tocharian, and Italo-Celtic—all peripheral subgroups of the family.[37] In the Central daughters, however, including Greek, it was replaced by *-y, apparently reflecting the spread of active *-i to the mediopassive. In the 1du. and 1pl. it looks like the mediopassive endings were derived from the active ones by suffixation of a particle following the (active) *hic-et-nunc* particle. In the 2pl., as in the active, all three endings appear to have been the same. The unreconstructability of mediopassive dual and imperative endings is an artifact of the defective attestation of their reflexes: in effect, only Greek and Indo-Iranian (and, for the imperative, Hittite) provide any evidence, and they disagree.

[37] There are a few late Phrygian examples of αδδακετορ and αββερετορ beside αδδακετ and αββερετ; they are usually taken to be mediopassive forms (Haas 1966: 226, Brixhe 2004: 785 with references). But they are used in exactly the same formulas as the forms without -ορ (Haas 1966: 119, 123–4), so that there is no evidence other than their shape that they are actually mediopassive; it is not impossible that their prehistory is completely different. (For further discussion, see Sowa 2007: 75–7, whose solution presupposes a reconstruction of the PIE verb different from that proposed here.) If they really are mediopassive, they suggest an interesting hypothesis regarding the diversification of Core IE, namely that there was a dialect chain as follows:

Italic – Celtic | Germanic – Balto-Slavic – Indo-Iranian – Greek – Phrygian,

with a significant but incomplete break between Celtic and Germanic, and that the replacement of *-r by *-y in the mediopassive endings failed to occur at either end of the chain. Such a dialect chain would probably have to predate the geographical arrangement suggested in Cowgill (1986: 65).

Reflexes of the third-person mediopassive endings (primary) sg. *-ó-r, pl. *-ró-r, (secondary) sg. *-ó, pl. *-ró appear only in a restricted set of verbs and forms in Anatolian and Indo-Iranian; it is clear that already in PIE they had largely been replaced by the competing endings with sg. *-t-, pl. *-nt-, whose distinctive consonants have evidently been imported from the active. To judge from the situation in Sanskrit, 3pl. *-ró survived longest in the optative.

The underlyingly accented endings of the mediopassive and the non-singular active were accented on the surface if the stem was unaccented; otherwise they, like the endings of the singular active, were unaccented on the surface (i.e. the leftmost underlying accent of a verb form surfaced). The alternative forms of the active 3pl. were distributed as follows. If the stem was athematic and unaccented, the accented full-grade form of the ending surfaced; if the stem was accented or thematic or both, the zero-grade form of the ending surfaced.

The PIE h_2e-paradigm, and the Nuclear IE perfect (stative) that was descended from it, exhibited an almost completely different set of endings in the indicative. Exceptionally, primary and secondary (i.e. non-past and past) were not distinguished, nor were active and mediopassive. The endings can be reconstructed as follows:

1sg.	*-h_2a
2sg.	*-th_2a
3sg.	*-e
1du.	*-wé (*-wéH?; see the 1pl. below)
2du.	???
3du.	???
1pl.	*-mé (*-méH?; see Jasanoff 2003a: 32)
2pl.	*-é
3pl.	*-ḗr < **-érs (cf. Jasanoff 1988b: 71 fn. 3) ~ *-r̥s

The unaccented 3pl. ending must have been employed when the non-singular stem was e-grade and accented, though we do not have enough evidence to reconstruct actual examples of such forms. The similarity between these endings and those of the (secondary) mediopassive is obvious, though specialists are not agreed on what inferences should be drawn from that fact. Once again the dual endings are not reconstructable because Greek and Indo-Iranian disagree.

2.3.3 (iv) Non-finite forms

Most Nuclear IE active participles were made with a hysterokinetic suffix *-ónt- ~ *-nt- (see 2.3.4 (ii)); mediopassive participles ended in a suffix *-m$h_1$nó-.[38] (As Fellner 2021 demonstrates, the Tocharian participles do exhibit a similar

[38] This is the underlying form. It must have surfaced as *-m̥$h_1$nó- after the final non-syllabic of athematic stems and as *-mno- after thematic stems (see 2.2.4. (i) *ad fin.* and 2.2.5), but early leveling in the daughters has disrupted that pattern, yielding e.g. Greek -μενο- and Tocharian B *-mane* < *-m$h_1$no-.

distribution, though Toch. B *-mane*, A *-māṃ* can also be affixed to active intransitive stems.) The former suffix, at least, also appears in Anatolian, though there it exhibits an ergative pattern (passive if affixed to transitive stems, active if to intransitives). The Nuclear IE perfect participle exhibited a different suffix *-wos- ~ *-us-; it has no clear Anatolian cognate. A Core IE infinitive suffix *-d^hyo- (with case endings), suffixed to aspect stems, is reconstructable, but not much is known about its distribution, since it survives only in Indo-Iranian and Italic (see Rix 1976b, Fortson 2012 with references); possibly it was suffixed only to present stems. Most of the infinitives of the daughter languages were clearly caseforms of derived nouns in PIE, and of course those nouns were formed directly from the verb root rather than from aspect stems.

2.3.3 (v) The architecture of Core IE verb paradigms

The system outlined in this section was first codified by the late Warren Cowgill, whose conclusions regarding the Core IE verb still seem to me to be largely correct.[39]

Verb roots appear usually to have constructed aspect stems according to the following pattern. If a basic verb made only one aspect stem, it was unaffixed; thus we find present *$h_1$és-ti '(s)he is', *wés-tor '(s)he is wearing', and *h_2áǵe-ti '(s)he is driving' (none with any aorist or perfect), aorist *b^húH-t '(s)he became' and *$h_1$lud^hé-d '(s)he arrived' (neither with any present or perfect), perfect *wóyd-e '(s)he knows' (with no present or aorist). If a basic verb made two or three stems, either the present or the aorist was unaffixed, and the other of those two stems was affixed, as was the perfect. The following verbs illustrate the system (all forms are given in the 3sg.):

present	*aorist*	*perfect*
*d^hé-d^he$h_1$ti 'is putting'	*d^héh_1-t 'put'	—
*stí-stah_2-ti 'is getting up'	*stáh_2-t 'stood up'	*ste-stóh_2-a (*/-e/) 'is standing'
*tl̥-ná-h_2-ti 'is lifting'	*télh_2-t 'lifted'	*te-tólh_2-a (*/-e/) 'is holding up'
*sí-sd-eti 'is getting seated'	*sédst (= */séd+t/) 'sat down'	—
*g^wm̥-sḱé-ti 'is walking'	*g^wém-d 'stepped'	*g^we-g^wóm-e 'has the feet in place'
*ǵn̥h_1-yé-tor 'is being born'	*ǵn̥h_1-tó 'was born'	*ǵe-ǵónh_1-e 'is ... years old'
*wér-ye-ti 'is saying'	*wérh_1-t 'said'	—

[39] So far as I can discover, Cowgill published this explicitly only in Cowgill (1974b: 435–6; reprinted in Cowgill 2006a: 28–30); he was still of the same opinion in the early 1980s.

*déyḱ-ti 'is pointing out'	*dḗyḱ-s-t 'pointed out'	—
*wéǵ^{h}e-ti 'is transporting'	*wḗǵ^h-s-t 'transported'	—
*wértsti (= */wért+ti/) 'is turning around'	—	*we-wórt-e 'is turned toward'
—	*h$_2$néḱ-t 'reached'	*h$_2$a-h$_2$nóḱ-e 'extends to'

Derived verbs made only present stems, which were always affixed.

The system just outlined appears to be a coherent inflectional system, and it certainly became that in the daughters of Core IE; but there are indications that it was still a derivational system down into the prehistory of Greek—i.e. after Core IE had begun to diversify. Greek has more than twenty verbs that have simple thematic presents with e-grade roots and simple thematic aorists with zero-grade roots, but in every case only one of the two stems can be securely reconstructed for Core IE (Ringe 2012: 125–31). It appears that two aspect stems developed out of one in those cases. The most obvious example is the Greek present λείπε̄ν 'to leave behind (serially), to try to abandon'. Comparison of Skt pres. (3sg.) *riṇákti* and Lat. pres. *linquere* virtually forces us to reconstruct a nasal-infixed present for this verb,[40] and it follows that Greek must have replaced that inherited present with a simple thematic present; but the only possible source for such an innovation is the aorist subjunctive, whose shape the Greek present replicates exactly. The simplest hypothesis is that at least a few aorist subjunctives became present stems in Greek (and then furnished a model for the remodeling of other verbs); but that is most unlikely to have happened in an inflectional system based on the opposition of present and aorist.[41] It appears that the aspect system was still derivational even in Central IE, though at that point it would not continue to be for much longer.

There are other scattered indications in Nuclear IE that the aspect system was still derivational. Most strikingly, two presents and two aorists seem to be reconstructable for the root *ǵnoh$_3$- 'recognize': present *ǵn̥h$_3$-sḱé/ó- (Lat. *nōscere*, Gk γιγνώσκε̄ν (with innovative reduplication), OPers. subj. 3sg. *xšnāsātiy*) and nasal-infixed *ǵn̥-nó-h$_3$- ~ *ǵn̥-n-h$_3$- (Skt 3sg. *jānā́ti*, Toch. A 2sg. *knānat*) and aorist *ǵnóh$_3$- ~ *ǵn̥h$_3$- (Gk γνῶναι, Skt precative 3sg. *jñeyā́s*) and *ǵnḗh$_3$-s- ~ *ǵnóh$_3$-s- (Hitt. pres. *ganeszi*, Toch. A pret. 1sg. *kñasu*, 2sg. *kñasäṣt*). But it does appear that by the Central IE stage the verb system was evolving into a set of fixed inflectional paradigms, more or less in the shape hypothesized by Cowgill.

The following section will illustrate the Core IE verb system more fully with complete paradigms of several reconstructable verbs.

40 From which I remain convinced that Sappho's ἀπυλιμπάνω is not directly descended; see 4.2.1 (ii), 5.4.2 (i) for discussion.

41 The superficially similar development in Germanic is much easier to motivate; see Ringe (2017: 182–6).

2.3.3 (vi) Sample Central IE verb paradigms

In the finite categories of these paradigms the forms are given in the order 1sg., 2sg., 3sg., 1du., 2du., 3du., 1pl., 2pl., 3pl.; participles are given in the masc. nom. sg. and gen. sg., followed by a semicolon, then the fem. nom. sg. and gen. sg., except for o-stem participles, which are given in the masc. nom. sg. only. Infinitives are omitted, as are displaced imperatives. Asterisks have been omitted for typographical clarity.

A consequence of our uncertainty regarding the reconstruction of the thematic optative (see 2.3.3 (ii)) is that even Core IE verb paradigms cannot always be given in full. Since Greek clearly belonged to the Central group, I have given the paradigms ancestral to that group, with thematic optatives in *-oy(h$_1$)- and mediopassive primary endings in *-y, the latter replacing PIE *-r (see 2.3.3 (iii)).

- h$_1$es- 'be' (root present only, active only)

1ary indic.	*2ary indic.*	*subjunctive*	*optative*	*imperative*
h$_1$ésmi	h$_1$ésm̥	h$_1$ésoh$_2$	h$_1$siḗm	—
h$_1$ési	h$_1$és	h$_1$éses	h$_1$siéh$_1$s	h$_1$és, h$_1$sd^{h}í
h$_1$ésti	h$_1$ést	h$_1$ésed	h$_1$siéh$_1$t	h$_1$éstu
h$_1$suós	h$_1$sué	h$_1$ésowe	h$_1$sih$_1$wé	—
h$_1$stés	h$_1$stóm	h$_1$ésetom	h$_1$sih$_1$tóm	h$_1$stóm
h$_1$stés	h$_1$stā́m	h$_1$ésetām	h$_1$sih$_1$tā́m	h$_1$stā́m
h$_1$sm̥ós	h$_1$sm̥é	h$_1$ésome	h$_1$sih$_1$mé	—
h$_1$sté	h$_1$sté	h$_1$ésete	h$_1$sih$_1$té	h$_1$sté
h$_1$sénti	h$_1$sénd	h$_1$ésond	h$_1$sih$_1$énd	h$_1$séntu

participle h$_1$sónts, h$_1$sn̥tés; h$_1$sóntih$_2$, h$_1$sn̥tyáh$_2$s

- leyk^w- 'leave behind' (nasal-infixed present, root-aorist, reduplicated perfect)

present stem, active:

1ary indic.	*2ary indic.*	*subjunctive*	*optative*	*imperative*
linék^{w}mi	linék^{w}m̥	linék^{w}oh$_2$	link^{w}iḗm	—
linék^{w}si	linék^{w}s	linék^{w}es	link^{w}iéh$_1$s	linék^w, link^{w}d^{h}í
linék^{w}ti	linék^{w}t	linék^{w}ed	link^{w}iéh$_1$t	linék^{w}tu
linkuós	linkué	linék^{w}owe	link^{w}ih$_1$wé	—
link^{w}tés	link^{w}tóm	linék^{w}etom	link^{w}ih$_1$tóm	link^{w}tóm
link^{w}tés	link^{w}tā́m	linék^{w}etām	link^{w}ih$_1$tā́m	link^{w}tā́m
link^{w}m̥ós	link^{w}m̥é	linék^{w}ome	link^{w}ih$_1$mé	—
link^{w}té	link^{w}té	linék^{w}ete	link^{w}ih$_1$té	link^{w}té
link^{w}énti	link^{w}énd	linék^{w}ond	link^{w}ih$_1$énd	link^{w}éntu

participle link^{w}ónts, link^{w}n̥tés; link^{w}óntih$_2$, link^{w}n̥tyáh$_2$s present stem, mediopassive:

1ary indic.	*2ary indic.*	*subjunctive*	*optative*	*imperative*
link^{w}h$_2$áy	link^{w}h$_2$á	linék^{w}oh$_2$a	link^{w}ih$_1$h$_2$á	—
link^{w}th$_2$áy	link^{w}th$_2$á	linék^{w}eth$_2$a	link^{w}ih$_1$th$_2$á	???
link^{w}tóy	link^{w}tó	linék^{w}eto	link^{w}ih$_1$tó	???
linkuósd^{h}h$_2$	linkuéd^{h}h$_2$	linék^{w}owed^{h}h$_2$	link^{w}ih$_1$wéd^{h}h$_2$	—
???	???	???	???	???
???	???	???	???	???
link^{w}m̥ósd^{h}h$_2$	link^{w}m̥éd^{h}h$_2$	linék^{w}omed^{h}h$_2$	link^{w}ih$_1$méd^{h}h$_2$	—
link^{w}d^{h}h$_2$ué	link^{w}d^{h}h$_2$ué	linék^{w}ed^{h}h$_2$ue	link^{w}ih$_1$d^{h}h$_2$ué	link^{w}d^{h}h$_2$ué
link^{w}n̥tóy	link^{w}n̥tó	linék^{w}onto	link^{w}ih$_1$ró	???

participle link^{w}m̥h$_1$nós

aorist stem, active:

2ary indic.	*subjunctive*	*optative*	*imperative*
léyk^{w}m̥	léyk^{w}oh$_2$	lik^{w}yḗm	—
léyk^{w}s	léyk^{w}es	lik^{w}yéh$_1$s	léyk^w, lik^{w}d^{h}í
léyk^{w}t	léyk^{w}ed	lik^{w}yéh$_1$t	léyk^{w}tu
likwé	léyk^{w}owe	lik^{w}ih$_1$wé	—
lik^{w}tóm	léyk^{w}etom	lik^{w}ih$_1$tóm	lik^{w}tóm
lik^{w}tā́m	léyk^{w}etām	lik^{w}ih$_1$tā́m	lik^{w}tā́m
lik^{w}mé	léyk^{w}ome	lik^{w}ih$_1$mé	—
lik^{w}té	léyk^{w}ete	lik^{w}ih$_1$té	lik^{w}té
lik^{w}énd	léyk^{w}ond	lik^{w}ih$_1$énd	lik^{w}éntu

participle lik^{w}ónts, lik^{w}n̥tés; lik^{w}óntih$_2$, lik^{w}n̥tyáh$_2$s

aorist stem, mediopassive:

2ary indic.	*subjunctive*	*optative*	*imperative*
lik^{w}h$_2$á	léyk^{w}oh$_2$a	lik^{w}ih$_1$h$_2$á	—
lik^{w}th$_2$á	léyk^{w}eth$_2$a	lik^{w}ih$_1$th$_2$á	???
lik^{w}tó	léyk^{w}eto	lik^{w}ih$_1$tó	???
likwéd^{h}h$_2$	léyk^{w}owed^{h}h$_2$	lik^{w}ih$_1$wéd^{h}h$_2$	—
???	???	???	???
???	???	???	???
lik^{w}méd^{h}h$_2$	léyk^{w}omed^{h}h$_2$	lik^{w}ih$_1$méd^{h}h$_2$	—
lik^{w}d^{h}h$_2$ué	léyk^{w}ed^{h}h$_2$ue	lik^{w}ih$_1$d^{h}h$_2$ué	lik^{w}d^{h}h$_2$ué
lik^{w}n̥tó	léyk^{w}onto	lik^{w}ih$_1$ró	???

participle lik^{w}m̥h$_1$nós

perfect stem (active):

indicative	*subjunctive*	*optative*	*imperative*
lelóyk^{w}h$_2$a	leléyk^{w}oh$_2$	lelik^{w}yḗm	—
lelóyk^{w}th$_2$a	leléyk^{w}es	lelik^{w}yéh$_1$s	???, lelik^{w}d^{h}í
lelóyk^{w}e	leléyk^{w}ed	lelik^{w}yéh$_1$t	???
lelikwé	leléyk^{w}owe	lelik^{w}ih$_1$wé	—
???	leléyk^{w}etom	lelik^{w}ih$_1$tóm	???
???	leléyk^{w}etām	lelik^{w}ih$_1$tā́m	???
lelik^{w}mé	leléyk^{w}ome	lelik^{w}ih$_1$mé	—
lelik^{w}é	leléyk^{w}ete	lelik^{w}ih$_1$té	???
lelik^{w}ḗr	leléyk^{w}ond	lelik^{w}ih$_1$énd	???

participle lelikwṓs, lelikusés; lelikwósih$_2$, lelikusyáh$_2$s

- d^{h}eh$_1$- ‘put’ (reduplicated athematic present, root aorist)

present stem, active:

1ary indic.	*2ary indic.*	*subjunctive*	*optative*	*imperative*
d^{h}éd^{h}eh$_1$mi	d^{h}éd^{h}ēm	d^{h}éd^{h}eh$_1$oh$_2$	d^{h}éd^{h}h$_1$ih$_1$m̥	—
d^{h}éd^{h}eh$_1$si	d^{h}éd^{h}eh$_1$s	d^{h}éd^{h}eh$_1$es	d^{h}éd^{h}h$_1$ih$_1$s	d^{h}éd^{h}eh$_1$, d^{h}éd^{h}h$_1$d^{h}i
d^{h}éd^{h}eh$_1$ti	d^{h}éd^{h}eh$_1$t	d^{h}éd^{h}eh$_1$ed	d^{h}éd^{h}h$_1$ih$_1$t	d^{h}éd^{h}eh$_1$tu
d^{h}éd^{h}h$_1$uos	d^{h}éd^{h}h$_1$ue	d^{h}éd^{h}eh$_1$owe	d^{h}éd^{h}h$_1$ih$_1$we	—
d^{h}éd^{h}h$_1$tes	d^{h}éd^{h}h$_1$tom	d^{h}éd^{h}eh$_1$etom	d^{h}éd^{h}h$_1$ih$_1$tom	d^{h}éd^{h}h$_1$tom
d^{h}éd^{h}h$_1$tes	d^{h}éd^{h}h$_1$tām	d^{h}éd^{h}eh$_1$etām	d^{h}éd^{h}h$_1$ih$_1$tām	d^{h}éd^{h}h$_1$tām
d^{h}éd^{h}h$_1$m̥os	d^{h}éd^{h}h$_1$m̥e	d^{h}éd^{h}eh$_1$ome	d^{h}éd^{h}h$_1$ih$_1$me	—
d^{h}éd^{h}h$_1$te	d^{h}éd^{h}h$_1$te	d^{h}éd^{h}eh$_1$ete	d^{h}éd^{h}h$_1$ih$_1$te	d^{h}éd^{h}h$_1$te
d^{h}éd^{h}h$_1$n̥ti	d^{h}éd^{h}h$_1$n̥d	d^{h}éd^{h}eh$_1$ond	d^{h}éd^{h}h$_1$ih$_1$end	d^{h}éd^{h}h$_1$n̥tu

participle d^{h}éd^{h}h$_1$n̥ts, d^{h}éd^{h}h$_1$n̥tos; d^{h}éd^{h}h$_1$n̥tih$_2$, d^{h}éd^{h}h$_1$n̥tyah$_2$s (?)

present stem, mediopassive:

1ary indic.	*2ary indic.*	*subjunctive*	*optative*
d^{h}éd^{h}h$_1$h$_2$ay	d^{h}éd^{h}h$_1$h$_2$a	d^{h}éd^{h}eh$_1$oh$_2$a	d^{h}éd^{h}h$_1$ih$_1$h$_2$a
d^{h}éd^{h}h$_1$th$_2$ay	d^{h}éd^{h}h$_1$th$_2$a	d^{h}éd^{h}eh$_1$eth$_2$a	d^{h}éd^{h}h$_1$ih$_1$th$_2$a
d^{h}éd^{h}h$_1$toy	d^{h}éd^{h}h$_1$to	d^{h}éd^{h}eh$_1$eto	d^{h}éd^{h}h$_1$ih$_1$to
d^{h}éd^{h}h$_1$uosd^{h}h$_2$	d^{h}éd^{h}h$_1$ued^{h}h$_2$	d^{h}éd^{h}eh$_1$owed^{h}h$_2$	d^{h}éd^{h}h$_1$ih$_1$wed^{h}h$_2$
???	???	???	???
???	???	???	???
d^{h}éd^{h}h$_1$m̥osd^{h}h$_2$	d^{h}éd^{h}h$_1$m̥ed^{h}h$_2$	d^{h}éd^{h}eh$_1$omed^{h}h$_2$	d^{h}éd^{h}h$_1$ih$_1$med^{h}h$_2$
d^{h}éd^{h}h$_1$d^{h}h$_2$ue	d^{h}éd^{h}h$_1$d^{h}h$_2$ue	d^{h}éd^{h}eh$_1$ed^{h}h$_2$ue	d^{h}éd^{h}h$_1$ih$_1$d^{h}h$_2$ue
d^{h}éd^{h}h$_1$n̥toy	d^{h}éd^{h}h$_1$n̥to	d^{h}éd^{h}eh$_1$onto	d^{h}éd^{h}h$_1$ih$_1$ro

(and the only imperative form reconstructable is the 2pl., identical with the 2ary indicative)

participle d^{h}éd^{h}h$_1$m̥h$_1$nos

aorist stem, active:

2ary indic.	*subjunctive*	*optative*	*imperative*
d^{h}ḗm	d^{h}éh$_1$oh$_2$	d^{h}h$_1$iḗm	—
d^{h}éh$_1$s	d^{h}éh$_1$es	d^{h}h$_1$iéh$_1$s	d^{h}éh$_1$, d^{h}h$_1$d^{h}í
d^{h}éh$_1$t	d^{h}éh$_1$ed	d^{h}h$_1$iéh$_1$t	d^{h}éh$_1$tu
d^{h}h$_1$ué	d^{h}éh$_1$owe	d^{h}h$_1$ih$_1$wé	—
d^{h}h$_1$tóm	d^{h}éh$_1$etom	d^{h}h$_1$ih$_1$tóm	d^{h}h$_1$tóm
d^{h}h$_1$tā́m	d^{h}éh$_1$etām	d^{h}h$_1$ih$_1$tā́m	d^{h}h$_1$tā́m
d^{h}h$_1$m̥é	d^{h}éh$_1$ome	d^{h}h$_1$ih$_1$mé	—
d^{h}h$_1$té	d^{h}éh$_1$ete	d^{h}h$_1$ih$_1$té	d^{h}h$_1$té
d^{h}h$_1$énd	d^{h}éh$_1$ond	d^{h}h$_1$ih$_1$énd	d^{h}h$_1$éntu

participle d^{h}h$_1$ónts, d^{h}h$_1$n̥tés; d^{h}h$_1$óntih$_2$, d^{h}h$_1$n̥tyáh$_2$s

aorist stem, mediopassive:

2ary indic.	*subjunctive*	*optative*	*imperative*
d^{h}h$_1$h$_2$á	d^{h}éh$_1$oh$_2$a	d^{h}h$_1$ih$_1$h$_2$á	—
d^{h}h$_1$th$_2$á	d^{h}éh$_1$eth$_2$a	d^{h}h$_1$ih$_1$th$_2$á	???
d^{h}h$_1$tó	d^{h}éh$_1$eto	d^{h}h$_1$ih$_1$tó	???
d^{h}h$_1$uéd^{h}h$_2$	d^{h}éh$_1$owed^{h}h$_2$	d^{h}h$_1$ih$_1$wéd^{h}h$_2$	—
???	???	???	???
???	???	???	???
d^{h}h$_1$m̥éd^{h}h$_2$	d^{h}éh$_1$omed^{h}h$_2$	d^{h}h$_1$ih$_1$méd^{h}h$_2$	—
d^{h}h$_1$d^{h}h$_2$ué	d^{h}éh$_1$ed^{h}h$_2$ue	d^{h}h$_1$ih$_1$d^{h}h$_2$ué	d^{h}h$_1$d^{h}h$_2$ué
d^{h}h$_1$n̥tó	d^{h}éh$_1$onto	d^{h}h$_1$ih$_1$ró	???

participle d^{h}h$_1$m̥h$_1$nós

- b^{h}er- 'carry' (simple thematic present)

present stem, active:

1ary indic.	*2ary indic.*	*subjunctive*	*optative*	*imperative*
b^{h}éroh$_2$	b^{h}érom	b^{h}érōh$_2$	b^{h}éroyh$_1$m̥	—
b^{h}éresi	b^{h}éres	b^{h}érēs	b^{h}éroys	b^{h}ére
b^{h}éreti	b^{h}éred	b^{h}érēd	b^{h}éroyd	b^{h}éretu
b^{h}érowos	b^{h}érowe	b^{h}érōwe	b^{h}éroywe	—
b^{h}éretes	b^{h}éretom	b^{h}érētom	b^{h}éroytom	b^{h}éretom
b^{h}éretes	b^{h}éretām	b^{h}érētām	b^{h}éroytām	b^{h}éretām
b^{h}éromos	b^{h}érome	b^{h}érōme	b^{h}éroyme	—
b^{h}érete	b^{h}érete	b^{h}érēte	b^{h}éroyte	b^{h}érete
b^{h}éronti	b^{h}érond	b^{h}érōnd	b^{h}éroyh$_1$end	b^{h}érontu

participle b^{h}éronts, b^{h}érontos; b^{h}érontih$_2$, b^{h}érontiah$_2$s

present stem, mediopassive:

1ary indic.	*2ary indic.*	*subjunctive*	*optative*	*imperative*
b^{h}éroh$_2$ay	b^{h}éroh$_2$a	b^{h}érōh$_2$a	b^{h}éroyh$_2$a	—
b^{h}éreth$_2$ay	b^{h}éreth$_2$a	b^{h}érēth$_2$a	b^{h}éroyth$_2$a	???
b^{h}éretoy	b^{h}éreto	b^{h}érēto	b^{h}éroyto	???
b^{h}érowosd^{h}h$_2$	b^{h}érowed^{h}h$_2$	b^{h}érōwed^{h}h$_2$	b^{h}éroywed^{h}h$_2$	—
???	???	???	???	???
???	???	???	???	???
b^{h}éromosd^{h}h$_2$	b^{h}éromed^{h}h$_2$	b^{h}érōmed^{h}h$_2$	b^{h}éroymed^{h}h$_2$	—
b^{h}éred^{h}h$_2$ue	b^{h}éred^{h}h$_2$ue	b^{h}érēd^{h}h$_2$ue	b^{h}éroyd^{h}h$_2$ue	b^{h}éred^{h}h$_2$ue
b^{h}érontoy	b^{h}éronto	b^{h}érōnto	b^{h}éroyro	???

participle b^{h}éromnos (← /-o-mh$_1$no-s/)

- g^{w}em- 'step' (sḱé-present, root aorist, reduplicated perfect; active only)

present stem:

1ary indic.	*2ary indic.*	*subjunctive*	*optative*	*imperative*
g^{w}m̥sḱóh$_2$	g^{w}m̥sḱóm	g^{w}m̥sḱṓh$_2$	g^{w}m̥sḱóyh$_1$m̥	—
g^{w}m̥sḱési	g^{w}m̥sḱés	g^{w}m̥sḱḗs	g^{w}m̥sḱóys	g^{w}m̥sḱé
g^{w}m̥sḱéti	g^{w}m̥sḱéd	g^{w}m̥sḱḗd	g^{w}m̥sḱóyd	g^{w}m̥sḱétu
g^{w}m̥sḱówos	g^{w}m̥sḱówe	g^{w}m̥sḱṓwe	g^{w}m̥sḱóywe	—
g^{w}m̥sḱétes	g^{w}m̥sḱétom	g^{w}m̥sḱḗtom	g^{w}m̥sḱóytom	g^{w}m̥sḱétom
g^{w}m̥sḱétes	g^{w}m̥sḱétām	g^{w}m̥sḱḗtām	g^{w}m̥sḱóytām	g^{w}m̥sḱétām
g^{w}m̥sḱómos	g^{w}m̥sḱóme	g^{w}m̥sḱṓme	g^{w}m̥sḱóyme	—
g^{w}m̥sḱéte	g^{w}m̥sḱéte	g^{w}m̥sḱḗte	g^{w}m̥sḱóyte	g^{w}m̥sḱéte
g^{w}m̥sḱónti	g^{w}m̥sḱónd	g^{w}m̥sḱṓnd	g^{w}m̥sḱóyh$_1$end	g^{w}m̥sḱóntu

participle g^{w}m̥sḱónts, g^{w}m̥sḱóntos; g^{w}m̥sḱóntih$_2$, g^{w}m̥sḱóntiah$_2$s

aorist stem:

2ary indic.	*subjunctive*	*optative*	*imperative*
g^{w}ḗm[42]	g^{w}émoh$_2$	g^{w}m̥yḗm	—
g^{w}ḗm[43]	g^{w}émes	g^{w}m̥yéh$_1$s	g^{w}ém, g^{w}m̥d^{h}í
g^{w}émd[44]	g^{w}émed	g^{w}m̥yéh$_1$t	g^{w}émtu
g^{w}m̥wé	g^{w}émowe	g^{w}mih$_1$wé	—
g^{w}m̥tóm	g^{w}émetom	g^{w}mih$_1$tóm	g^{w}m̥tóm
g^{w}m̥tā́m	g^{w}émetām	g^{w}mih$_1$tā́m	g^{w}m̥tā́m
g^{w}m̥(m)é	g^{w}émome	g^{w}mih$_1$mé	—

42 < *g^{w}ém-m̥ by Stang's Law.
43 < * g^{w}ém-s by Szemerényi's Law.
44 Possibly *g^{w}ḗn by assimilation and Szemerényi's Law; cf. Kim (2001).

g^{w}m̥té	g^{w}émete	g^{w}mih$_1$té	g^{w}m̥té
g^{w}ménd	g^{w}émond	g^{w}mih$_1$énd	g^{w}méntu

participle g^{w}mónts, g^{w}mn̥tés; g^{w}móntih$_2$, g^{w}mn̥tyáh$_2$s

perfect stem:

indicative	*subjunctive*	*optative*	*imperative*
g^{w}eg^{w}ómh$_2$a	g^{w}eg^{w}émoh$_2$	g^{w}eg^{w}m̥yḗm	—
g^{w}eg^{w}ómth$_2$a	g^{w}eg^{w}émes	g^{w}eg^{w}m̥yéh$_1$s	???, g^{w}eg^{w}m̥d^{h}í
g^{w}eg^{w}óme	g^{w}eg^{w}émed	g^{w}eg^{w}m̥yéh$_1$t	???
g^{w}eg^{w}m̥wé	g^{w}eg^{w}émowe	g^{w}eg^{w}mih$_1$wé	—
???	g^{w}eg^{w}émetom	g^{w}eg^{w}mih$_1$tóm	???
???	g^{w}eg^{w}émetām	g^{w}eg^{w}mih$_1$tā́m	???
g^{w}eg^{w}m̥(m)é	g^{w}eg^{w}émome	g^{w}eg^{w}mih$_1$mé	—
g^{w}eg^{w}mé	g^{w}eg^{w}émete	g^{w}eg^{w}mih$_1$té	???
g^{w}eg^{w}mḗr	g^{w}eg^{w}émond	g^{w}eg^{w}mih$_1$énd	???

participle g^{w}eg^{w}m̥wṓs, g^{w}eg^{w}musés; g^{w}eg^{w}m̥wósih$_2$, g^{w}eg^{w}musyáh$_2$s

- weǵ^{h}- 'transport (in a vehicle)' (simple thematic present, s-aorist)
  present stem, active and mediopassive: exactly like that of *b^{h}er- (see above)

aorist stem, active:

2ary indic.	*subjunctive*	*optative*	*imperative*
wḗǵ^{h}sm̥	wéǵ^{h}soh$_2$	wéǵ^{h}sih$_1$m̥	—
wḗǵ^{h}s	wéǵ^{h}ses	wéǵ^{h}sih$_1$s	wḗǵ^{h}s
wḗǵ^{h}st	wéǵ^{h}sed	wéǵ^{h}sih$_1$t	wéǵ^{h}stu
wéǵ^{h}sue	wéǵ^{h}sowe	wéǵ^{h}sih$_1$we	—
wéǵ^{h}stom	wéǵ^{h}setom	wéǵ^{h}sih$_1$tom	wéǵ^{h}stom
wéǵ^{h}stām	wéǵ^{h}setām	wéǵ^{h}sih$_1$tām	wéǵ^{h}stām
wéǵ^{h}sm̥e	wéǵ^{h}some	wéǵ^{h}sih$_1$me	—
wéǵ^{h}ste	wéǵ^{h}sete	wéǵ^{h}sih$_1$te	wéǵ^{h}ste
wéǵ^{h}sn̥d	wéǵ^{h}sond	wéǵ^{h}sih$_1$end	wéǵ^{h}sn̥tu

participle wéǵ^{h}sn̥ts, wéǵ^{h}sn̥tos; wéǵ^{h}sn̥tih$_2$, wéǵ^{h}sn̥tyah$_2$s
(The mediopassive of s-aorists has been remodeled everywhere that it survives; presumably it had an accented e-grade root and the expected suffixes and endings.)

Some generalizations about the above paradigms can be made. Thematic stems, including subjunctives, had fixed accent on the stem. In athematic stems the accent usually alternated, falling on the endings in the mediopassive and the non-singular active, but on the preceding syllable in the singular active. However, s-aorists seem to have had fixed accent on the root, and it appears that there were a few root-presents that exhibited a similar pattern; and reduplicated presents (but not perfects) seem to have had fixed accent on the reduplicating syllable. No matter what the accentual pattern was, there was normally a difference in ablaut between the singular active and all other forms of athematic stems; the commoner attested patterns are exemplified in the above paradigms.

Obviously the inflection of thematic stems was simpler and easier to learn. In the development of Greek, athematic presents would become less common, while numerous innovative thematic presents and aorists would be created.

2.3.4 PIE noun inflection

2.3.4 (i) Endings

Like verb stems, nouns fell into two purely formal classes, athematic and thematic, the latter ending in the thematic vowel. The inflection of thematic nouns was already at least slightly different from that of athematic nouns in PIE, but it seems clear that it became much more different in Nuclear IE. Not all the details can be recovered; in addition to gaps in the evidence, we have to reckon with the possibility that the paradigms of thematic and athematic nouns have converged in Anatolian. For a similar reconstruction of the endings (with different judgments on some points), see Kim (2012a).

The athematic endings reconstructable for PIE proper are the following:

	singular	*plural*	*dual*
vocative	-0	*-es	*-h_1e, *neuter* *-ih_1
nominative	*-s ~ -0, *neuter* -0	*-es	*-h_1e, *neuter* *-ih_1
accusative	*-m, *neuter* -0	*-ns < **-ms[45]	*-h_1e, *neuter* *-ih_1
genitive	*-és ~ *-s → *-os	*-óHom (*H ≠ *h_2)	
dative	*-éy	*-ós	
locative	-0´ → *-í	*-sú (?)	
instrumental	*-éh_1 ~ *-h_1 (?)	*-ís (?)	
allative	*-áh_2 (~ *-h_2 ?)	???	

The endings reconstructed without question marks have left reasonably clear reflexes in Anatolian languages, especially Hittite, though the dual has been reduced to a few fossils (see Hoffner and Melchert 2008: 68 fn. 15 with references); note especially Hitt. dat. pl. *-as* = Lycian *-e* < *-os, Old Hitt. gen. pl. *-an* < *-oHom, and endingless locatives like Hitt. *dagān* 'on the ground'. The thematic inst. sg. ending is indirectly attested in Hittite (see below); the loc. pl. ending is not attested in Anatolian, but it is well attested in Core IE and has no obvious source (as an adverbial ending, for example). The allative is attested as a productive case only in Old Hittite, and no plural forms are known. On the inst. pl. see below.

[45] For possible Hittite evidence that *-ms was still the PIE ending, see Kim (2012b).

It is clear that the endings of the direct cases were underlyingly unaccented, while those of the oblique cases were underlyingly accented but lost their accent whenever there was an accent to the left in the form (i.e. the leftmost underlying accent surfaced). One would expect ablaut to correlate with accent, but the directly reconstructable situation was no longer so straightforward. Of the singular oblique endings, the genitive showed extensive ablaut alternations which survive fairly well in the daughters. The instrumental ending ablauted too, but the distribution of the alternants is difficult to reconstruct, largely because most of our evidence comes from a single daughter, Indo-Iranian.[46] For the dative ending only a full-grade form is reconstructable. In the plural the system of ablaut in endings had broken down completely; each ending appeared in only a single form, and there was evidently no longer any relation between ablaut and accent.

Most of the zero-endings of the non-neuter nom. sg. arose by Szemerényi's Law (see 2.2.4 (iv)) or are obviously analogical on those that did, but most stems in *-h_2 lacked an overt nom. sg. ending for reasons that are unclear. On the other hand, the voc. sg. and the neut. sg. direct cases were underlyingly endingless. The loc. sg. was rather different. It seems to have been characterized by an ending which had an underlying accent but no segmental portion to 'carry' it, with the result that the accent had to be linked leftward to the last syllable of the stem. Such a remarkable shape was of course unstable; though endingless locatives are securely attested in Hittite and (especially) in ancient Indo-Iranian languages, the loc. sg. tended to be recharacterized with the *hic-et-nunc* particle *-i, which eventually was reinterpreted as an accented ending *-í. The development of the proterokinetic i-stem loc. sg. **-éy-i > *-ēy by Stang's Law (see 2.2.4 (iv)) shows that that process must have been underway in PIE (as Craig Melchert reminds me).

Strikingly, no distinctive neut. pl. endings can be reconstructed. It appears that collectives derived with a suffix *-h_2, which were grammatically singular, effectively functioned as neut. plurals in PIE.[47] Since Szemerényi's Law affected sequences *-Rh_2 as well as *-Rs, the most archaic reconstructable collectives of r-stems and r/n-stems ended in *-ōr, while those of n-stems ended in *-ō. What happened to collectives in the daughters will be discussed below.

The thematic endings should have been identical to the athematic endings, preceded by the thematic vowel *-o- ~ *-e-. Ablauting endings appeared in the zero grade; so did the non-neut. dual direct ending, according to all the Nuclear IE evidence, though there is no evidence that it ablauted in athematic stems. Not all the

[46] For that reason I hesitate to accept the hypothesis of Kim (2012a) that the unexpected distribution of full-grade *-eh_1 shows that the ending was originally a postposition, though that is still likely on general grounds.

[47] Such collectives can still be formed to non-neuter nouns in Hittite (Hoffner and Melchert 2008: 68–9). Similar phenomena occur in Arabic and Old Georgian, for example. For a comprehensive discussion of number systems, see Corbett (2000).

endings are clearly attested in the daughters; a reasonable reconstruction of those that are is the following:

	singular	*plural*	*dual*
vocative	*-e, *neuter* *-o-m	*-o-es	*-o-h_1, *neuter* *-o-y(h_1)
nominative	*-o-s, *neuter* *-o-m	*-o-es	*-o-h_1, *neuter* *-o-y(h_1)
accusative	*-o-m, *neuter* *-o-m	*-o-ns ← **-ōm[48]	*-o-h_1, *neuter* *-o-y(h_1)
genitive	*-o-s	*-o-oHom (?)	
dative	*-o-ey	*-o-os (?)	
locative	(**-e →) *-e-y	???	
instrumental	*-o-h_1	???	
allative	*-a-h_2 (*-o-h_2?)	???	

The one clear difference from athematic inflection is that the neut. direct case ends in *-m; that is guaranteed by the equation Hitt. *iukan* = Skt *yugám* = Gk ζυγόν = Lat. *iugum* < PIE *yugóm 'yoke', a fossilized derivative of *yewg- 'join' made to a pattern that is not productive in any daughter. The gen. sg. might be expected to end in *-o-s, and in fact the Hitt. ending is *-as* (though that could be an athematic ending that has spread to thematic stems).[49] Inst. sg. *-o-h_1 is probably attested in the Old Hittite connective particle *ta* (Rieken 1999b: 86). Dual *-o-h_1 and *-o-y(h_1) (the latter with loss of the laryngeal when no word-initial syllabic followed) are supported by evidence across Nuclear IE; dat. sg. *-o-ey (with contraction of the vowels in hiatus), and apparently nom.-voc. pl. *-o-es (likewise with contraction) are supported by evidence across Core IE. That the all. sg. ending was *-a-h_2 (with a zero-grade ending) and the gen. and dat. pl. were *-o-oHom and *-o-os (without ablaut) are guesses from the general behavior of sg. and pl. endings; Hitt. all. sg. *-a* and dat. pl. *-as* could reflect forms with or without contraction of vowel sequences, and in the gen. pl. the contraction of two vowels and of three would yield the same outcome in all the daughters. Only the endingless loc. sg. **-e is not securely attested anywhere, though it might survive in Gk τῆλε 'far' (Alan Nussbaum, p.c. to Michael Weiss);[50] but that must have been the original ending, because that is the only way to explain the e-grade vowel of the Oscan thematic loc. sg. **-eí** (in nominal forms the thematic vowel is e-grade when there is no ending, as in the voc. sg.). The high front vocalic in the attested ending must originally have been the *hic-et-nunc* particle *-i (see above). Most daughter languages seem not to have preserved even the extended ending *-ey, regularizing it to *-oy, though Hitt. dat.-loc. sg. *-i* and Indo-Iranian loc. sg. *-ai might reflect the older diphthong.

48 This is the ending expected by Szemerényi's Law < **-oms. For possible evidence of the survival of *ō (at least) in this ending in PIE, see Kim (2012b).

49 An ending *-osyo is also attested in Anatolian (see Melchert 2012a with discussion), but it seems originally to have been the pronominal ending (see further below).

50 Harðarson (1995) instead suggests an athematic loc. sg., the final /-e/ of the Greek form reflecting the first laryngeal.

The ablative case poses unique problems. The Anatolian languages exhibit an ablative suffix reconstructable as *-ti, thematic *-o-ti; it is both sg. and pl. (!) and was almost certainly an adverb-forming suffix. Elsewhere in the IE family such a suffix appears unambiguously only in Tocharian A, whose 'secondary' ablative ending *-äṣ*, suffixed to the oblique caseform of nouns, can reflect *-V-ti (Jasanoff 1987: 109–10).[51] Anatolian also exhibits a suffix *-d, likewise indifferent to number, which marks the instrumental case of nouns and adjectives but also appears in Old Hitt. *kēt* 'on this side of', which might originally have been an ablative (Melchert and Oettinger 2009: 54; but cf. Hoffner and Melchert 2008: 143). Melchert and Oettinger (2009) suggest that this was the original PIE ablative ending, that it appears also in the Sanskrit pronominal ablatives *mát* 'from me', *asmát* 'from us', etc., and that it is also connected with Core IE thematic abl. sg. *-e-ad. But the last is a transparent innovation (see below). The similarity of Old Hitt. *kēt* and the Sanskrit pronominal forms, and the fact that *-d is indifferent to number in both daughters, are much more striking; but the identification of *kēt* as an ablative is not secure, and it is possible that the Sanskrit forms are innovations using the only unambiguous ablative ending that the language possessed. Note also that, except for *-e-ad, reconstructable Core IE has no distinctive ablative endings at all for its nouns or adjectives.[52] Under the circumstances I hesitate to reconstruct any ablative endings for PIE, though it seems probable that the language had an ablative case.

The evidence for inst. pl. *-is is much better. Jasanoff (2009: 141–2) adduces Sanskrit, Greek, and Latin adverbs in *-is* that are plausibly fossilized caseforms; a number of the longer Core IE inst. pl. endings also end in *-is* (see below); and Joshua Katz has plausibly explained the PGmc pronominal dative ending *-iz as an inst. pl. ending (cf. Katz 1998: 118–21). Like inst. sg. *-éh_1 ~ *-h_1, inst. pl. *-is appears to be an inherited case ending, parallel to dat. pl. *-os. Apparently those endings were replaced by *-d, which might originally have been an adverb-forming suffix, in Anatolian. That may seem surprising, but as we will see below, various endings were also replaced by adverbial suffixes in Core IE languages.

Because Tocharian lost much of its inherited case system (before constructing a new system by the accretion of postpositions), it is unclear how much change had occurred in the Nuclear IE system. For the reconstruction of Core IE we have abundant material but widespread disagreement among the daughters on some points. The nature of the problem can be seen by comparing the athematic dat. pl. and inst. pl. endings of various daughters:

[51] The *-ä-* of this ending, like most of the initial vowels of Toch. A secondary case endings, can reflect resegmentation of an originally stem-final vowel; that is why I suggest that only *-ti is inherited (following Jasanoff 2009: 139) rather than connecting the entire ending with PIE *éti 'further, in addition' (with Melchert and Oettinger 2009: 57).

[52] An ending *-im appears in Latin adverbs such as *illim* 'from there' and in the Luvian ablatives of demonstrative pronouns *zin*, *apin* (Melchert and Oettinger 2009: 55–6), but it is not clear whether it became an actual case ending in any language but Luvian. Whether it is the source of the *-m- in Nuclear IE dat.-abl. pl. *-mos (see below) is also unclear.

	dat. pl.		*instr. pl.*	
Latin	-bus	< *-b^hos	—	
Old Irish	-^{i}b	< *-$b^h$is (*originally the inst. pl.*)		
Gothic	-m	< *-mos *and/or**-mis (*the latter inst. pl.*)		
Greek	(*replaced by loc. pl.*)		(*Hom. adv.* -φι,) *Mycenaean* -pi < *-b^hi	
Armenian	(*replaced by gen. pl.*)		-wk^h	< *-b^hi + *particle*
OCS	-mŭ	< *-mos or *-mus	-mi	< *-mī(s)
OLith.	-mus	< *-mus	-mìs	< *-mīs
Sanskrit	-b^hyas	< *-b^hyos	-$b^h$is	< *-$b^h$is
Avestan	-biiō	< *-b^hyos	-biš	< *-$b^h$is

Though the resemblances are obvious, the details differ from subgroup to subgroup. Most of the daughters seem to have preserved dat. pl. *-os and inst. pl. *-is in some form, but they have inserted labial consonants between those endings and the stem. The source of *-b^h- is clearly the adverb-forming suffix *-b^hí (Jasanoff 2009: 139; cf. Melchert and Oettinger 2009: 63–4); the latter has actually been pressed into service as a case ending in Greek and Armenian, and there is a possible Tocharian relic in Toch. B *ṣp* 'and' < *se-b^hi 'with it' (Ringe 2002). The source of *-m- is less clear; Melchert and Oettinger (2009: 62–3) suggest an adverbial ending, while Katz's discussion of Tocharian and Anatolian pronouns suggests that dat. pl. *-mos contains the *-m- of the stressed oblique pronoun suffix *-mé and might actually survive in enclitic plural (all persons) Toch. B *-me*, A *-m* (cf. Katz 1998: 154–66, 243–5, 248–51 with fn. 60). It is also unclear what system should be reconstructed for Core IE. For the sake of concreteness I suggest the following set of athematic nominal endings for Core IE (given in an order which takes account of the syncretisms among them):

	singular	*plural*	*dual*
vocative	-0	*-es, *neuter* *-h_2	*-h_1e, *neuter* *-ih_1
nominative	*-s ~ -0, *neuter* -0	*-es, *neuter* *-h_2	*-h_1e, *neuter* *-ih_1
accusative	*-m, *neuter* -0	*-ns, *neuter* *-h_2	*-h_1e, *neuter* *-ih_1
instrumental	*-éh_1 ~ *-h_1	*-b^hís	*-b^hV́H or *-mV́H
dative	*-éy	*-mós	*-b^hV́H or *-mV́H
ablative	*-és ~ *-s ~ *-os	*-mós	*-b^hV́H or *-mV́H
genitive	*-és ~ *-s ~ *-os	*-óHom	*-ów(s) (*-óHs ?)[53]
locative	-0´	*-sú	*-ów(s)

[53] This reconstruction rests on the Avestan ending *-å*, which (if inherited) would reflect Proto-Indo-Iranian *-ās; Avestan distinguishes the gen. du. from the loc. du. in *-ō*, which might reflect Proto-Indo-Iranian *-au, to judge from Old Lith. *dvíejau* 'in two' (cf. Tichy 2006: 68, Beekes 2011: 217). But Sanskrit has *-os*, apparently < Proto-Indo-Iranian *-aus, for both endings, and OCS has *-u* < Proto-Balto-Slavic

The function of the inherited allative had been taken over by the accusative. If the above reconstruction is correct, it implies that *-b^h- (or, in Indo-Iranian, *-b^hy-) spread at the expense of *-m- in most daughters, but *-m- spread at the expense of *-b^h- in Balto-Slavic and Germanic. The reconstruction of the inst.-dat.-abl. dual ending is indeterminate because the only endings of the daughters that agree even approximately are OCS *-ma* and Av. *-biia* (Skt *-b^hyā́m* with an added particle); the vowel of the ending must have been *o or *a, but any laryngeal could have followed, and it is unclear what the initial consonant of the ending was.

Note the widespread incidence of syncretism in this system.[54] Though reconstruction of the dual endings is difficult, it seems clear that no more than three or four can be reconstructed; of course it is not surprising that syncretism was most extensive in the most 'marked' of the numbers. The nom. pl. and voc. pl. were always identical, as were the dat. pl. and abl. pl.; the abl. sg. and gen. sg. were also identical—so that the ablative did not have a distinctive ending in any number, though the pattern of syncretisms still distinguished it as a separate case. Most strikingly of all, though the neuter exhibited endings in the three direct cases (nom., acc., and voc.) that were largely different from those of the masculine and feminine, there was only one neuter ending for all three cases in each of the numbers. That pattern of syncretism in the neuter persisted in almost all the daughters for as long as each still distinguished a neuter gender and nominative and accusative cases. The other syncretisms also had a significant impact on the development of the case-marking system in the daughters.

The thematic endings diverged from the athematic endings to a greater extent in Core IE than they had in PIE:

	singular	*plural*	*dual*
vocative	*-e, *neuter* *-o-m	*-o-es, *neuter* *-a-h_2	*-o-h_1, *neuter* *-o-y(h_1)
nominative	*-o-s, *neuter* *-o-m	*-o-es, *neuter* *-a-h_2	*-o-h_1, *neuter* *-o-y(h_1)
accusative	*-o-m, *neuter* *-o-m	*-o-ns, *neuter* *-a-h_2	*-o-h_1, *neuter* *-o-y(h_1)
instrumental	*-o-h_1	*-ōys	*-oh_1-b^hVH or *-oh_1-mVH ?
dative	*-o-ey	*-oy-mos	*-oh_1-b^hVH or *-oh_1-mVH ?

*-au(s) for both; so the likelihood of a non-accidental syncretism arising twice independently must be weighed against the likelihood that Avestan has innovated, introducing an ending of unclear origin. Fortunately the question is unimportant for the prehistory of Greek.

[54] Throughout this book I use the term 'syncretism' in a purely descriptive sense: it designates a situation in which forms with different syntactic features exhibit the same inflectional markers. It does not imply that there was ever a time at which different inflectional markers were used. I distinguish syncretism from the syntactic merger of morphosyntactic categories, in which one category takes over all the functions of another, regardless of inflectional marking. For instance, in Latin the instrumental case has undergone syntactic merger with the ablative, and the dative and ablative cases exhibit syncretism in the plural—as they did already in PIE, the earliest reconstructable ancestor of Latin.

ablative	*-e-ad	*-oy-mos	*-oh$_1$-b^{h}VH or *-oh$_1$-mVH ?
genitive	*-o-syo	*-o-oHom	*-oy-ow(s) ? (*-oy-oHs ?)
locative	*-e-y	*-oy-su	*-oy-ow(s) ?

The following especially call for comment:

1) The thematic abl. sg. had a distinctive ending, but it was obviously just the (original) endingless loc. sg. in *-e[55] plus the adverb (postposition?) *ád (> Lat. *ad* 'to, at', OE *æt* 'at'), which clearly did not mean 'to' in pre-PIE (Kim 2012a: 123 fn. 4). This is yet another indication that the case system of PIE and its daughters developed partly by the accretion of postpositions or adverbs.
2) The gen. sg. of thematic nouns is problematic. Proto-Tocharian *-nsë is of obscure origin; Italo-Celtic exhibits an ending *-ī, which appears to be an unanalyzable derivational morpheme (cf. Nussbaum 1975, Melchert 2014b: 268 with references), though Old Latin also exhibits *-osio*, and there are other Continental Celtic endings as well; the Central daughters seem to have generalized *-osyo, which I have therefore entered in the table of endings above. It is clear that *-osyo was originally the pronominal ending, a fact which fits with the following.
3) Before the consonant-initial loc. pl. ending *-su and dat.-abl. pl. *-mos, thematic stems seem to have exhibited an element *-y- which was homonymous with the pronominal masc. nom. pl. ending and was certainly imported from pronominal inflection. Jasanoff (2009: 145–8) argues convincingly that inst. pl. *-ōys reflects earlier **-oy-is (by Stang's Law), and that the ultimate source of the element *-y- was an inherited collective *tóy 'that (group)' which was coopted for the masc. nom. pl. of the distal deictic (see 2.3.6 (ii)).

Whether there was any similar element before the oblique dual endings is not clear. I have reconstructed *-oy- for the gen.-loc. and *-oh$_1$- for the inst.-dat.-abl. because that is what the Indo-Iranian evidence suggests, and it is clear that Indo-Iranian has preserved the distribution of *-oy- in the plural best of all the daughters; but there is no guarantee that any daughter has not innovated in the dual, and my reconstruction should not be taken too seriously.

Note what had happened by the Core IE period to the collectives that had originally functioned as the plurals of neuter nouns. Though their suffix *-h$_2$ was originally derivational, and was thus part of the stem, in neut. pl. function it had

[55] This seems to me more likely than an instrumental plus a postposition (suggested by Melchert and Oettinger 2009: 62). On the possible relation of *ád to other ablative endings, see the discussion above.

become restricted to the nom.-acc.-voc.—that is, it had become an inflectional ending—and the non-neut. pl. endings of the other cases had been extended to cover neut. plurals as well (cf. Jasanoff 2009: 144–5). The same pattern appears in Hittite, but the relatively large number of Hittite neuter a-stem nouns attested only as collectives (Hoffner and Melchert 2008: 82–3) suggests that that was at least partly a parallel development rather than a shared inheritance. However, it seems likely that in some athematic stems—at least in n-, r-, and r/n-stems—the collective suffix had already been reanalyzed as an ending at the PIE stage. Apparently the addition of collective *-h_2 triggered the accent and ablaut pattern typical of the direct cases of amphikinetic nominals (on which see below); for instance, the collective of *wódr̥ 'water' was **wédor-h_2 > PIE *wédōr 'the waters' (Schindler 1975a: 3–4; cf. Nussbaum 2014: 278–80 for possible nuances of meaning), that of *h_1nḗ$h_3$mn̥ 'name' was **$h_1$né$h_3$mon-h_2 > *$h_1$nóh_3mō 'nomenclature' (or perhaps 'pair of names, full name', Nussbaum 2014: 297–8), and so on. It seems clear that a full amphikinetic inflection was constructed to those forms, and since the collective suffix had already become opaque (by Szemerényi's Law, see above) in PIE, it is likely that the reanalysis of collectives as plurals occurred in the protolanguage.

Neuter plural subjects must nevertheless have continued to trigger singular concord with the verb, as their ancestors the collectives had done, because that rule of concord still operates in attested Hittite, Gāthā-Avestan, and Attic Greek (see e.g. Fortson 2010: 158 for some attested examples). For further discussion of this complex of problems, and its possible relationship to feminine gender in IE, see Neri and Schuhmann (2014).

2.3.4 (ii) Accent and ablaut patterns

Like athematic verb stems, athematic nouns exhibited accent and ablaut alternations within the paradigm; but it is clear that the system of alternations was originally more elaborate in noun inflection. A comprehensive summary of the *communis opinio* can be found in Rieken (1999a); I here present only an outline of the system. It is necessary to distinguish between monosyllabic athematic nouns, traditionally called 'root nouns' (even when they are not derived from verb roots), and polysyllabic athematic nouns.

Monosyllables exhibited two types of accent and ablaut alternations. The easier type to reconstruct, because it has survived robustly in Indo-Iranian and Greek (and even become productive in the latter language), exhibited alternating accent: on the root in the direct cases, but on the endings in the oblique cases. Typical examples include (masc.) *$h_2$nér- ~ *$h_2$nr- 'man', (fem.) *wráh$_2$d- ~ *wr̥h_2d- 'root', (neut.) *ḱḗr (< **ḱérd) ~ *ḱr̥d- 'heart'.

But there was also a type which had the accent on the root in all forms, but exhibited an ablaut alternation between the direct and oblique cases; this 'acrostatic' type was recognized only in the 1960s, because it was already being eliminated by morphological change in PIE and has to be reconstructed from relics in the daughters (cf. Schindler 1967c, 1972a). Fairly clear examples of acrostatic monosyllables include (fem.) *dóm- ~ *dém- 'house' (whose archaic gen. sg. is well attested in reflexes of the fossilized phrase *déms pótis 'master of the house'), *nók^{w}t- ~ *nék^{w}t- 'night', (neut.) *h$_2$óst ~ *h$_2$ást- 'bone', *mḗms ~ *méms- 'meat'. Sometimes it is difficult to determine whether a noun was originally acrostatic from the reconstructable pattern of inflection. For instance, from (masc.) nom. sg. *pṓds, acc. sg. *pódm̥, gen. sg. *pedés, etc., 'foot', should we conclude that the original inflection was acrostatic *pód- ~ *péd- and that the noun has been transferred into the alternating type without adjustment of the root-ablaut, or is it likelier that an inconvenient oblique stem *pd- was replaced by *ped- (a process for which probable parallels can be cited)?

Polysyllabic nouns seem originally to have exhibited four different accent patterns (cf. Schindler 1975b: 262–4). Acrostatic polysyllables survive much better than acrostatic monosyllables, though their ablaut alternations are usually leveled in the daughters; representative examples include (masc.) *mḗh$_1$n̥s- ~ *méh$_1$n̥s- 'moon', (fem.) *h$_2$ówi- ~ *h$_2$áwi- 'sheep', (neut.) *h$_1$nḗh$_3$mn̥ ~ *h$_1$nóh$_3$mn- 'name' (*/-é-/), *Hyḗk^{w}r̥ ~ *Hyék^{w}n- 'liver', *ósr̥ ~ *ésn- 'autumn', *wā́stu ~ *wástu- 'settlement'. Moreover, in late PIE there developed a new class of neuter s-stems with root-accent but clearly secondary ablaut (involving multiple full-grade syllables), and that type seems to have become productive; typical examples are *néb^{h}os ~ *néb^{h}es- 'cloud', *ḱléwos ~ *ḱléwes- 'fame', *ǵénh$_1$os ~ *ǵénh$_1$es- 'lineage', etc.

The other three polysyllabic types exhibited alternating accent: on the leftmost syllable of the stem in the direct cases and on the endings in the oblique cases ('amphikinetic' accent); on the rightmost syllable of the stem in the direct cases and on the endings in the oblique cases ('hysterokinetic' accent); or on the penultimate syllable of the stem in the direct cases and on the rightmost syllable of the stem in the oblique cases ('proterokinetic' accent). Note that in every one of these patterns the accent was to the left in the direct cases and to the right in the oblique cases.

The amphikinetic type appears to be the most archaic; isolated examples survive only in Hittite and the Indo-Iranian languages. Securely reconstructable amphikinetic nouns include, for instance, (masc.) *póntoh$_2$- ~ *pn̥th$_2$- 'path',[56] *léymon-

56 I here follow de Vaan (2008) s.v. *pōns*. An alternative reconstruction is *péntoh$_2$-; Neri (2009: 7) suggests that it was an 'individuative' formed to a collective in *-h$_2$, which in turn was formed to a basic acrostatic noun *pónt- ~ *pént- which survives in OCS *pǫtĭ* and in Lat. *pōns* 'bridge'. If that is true, the range of reference of the ultimate derivative and the base noun must have overlapped substantially—both could, in effect, mean 'path'. But in that case the ablaut grade of the basic noun's direct cases could easily have spread to the ultimate derivative by lexical analogy; the latter would then be *póntoh$_2$- ~ *pn̥th$_2$-´. If that is what happened, we cannot be sure that any reflex of the original base noun survives, since all the attested forms (including Old Prussian *pintis*, with a zero-grade root) can reflect *póntoh$_2$- ~ *pn̥th$_2$-´. This is a good example of the tension between theory and evidence, and of the way that the attested evidence can underdetermine a reconstruction.

~ *limn- 'lake', (fem.) *dʰéǵʰōm ~ *ǵʰm- (loc. *dʰǵʰém) 'earth', and neuter collectives such as *wédōr ~ *udn- 'waters' (cf. Schindler 1975a: 3–4). Interestingly, the inflection of masculine n-stems in Germanic appears to have evolved from an originally amphikinetic pattern (cf. Jasanoff 2002: 32–5), which suggests that this type of inflection had not yet been reduced to relics in Central IE.

Hysterokinetic inflection is most familiar from the r-stem kinship terms, e.g. *ph₂tér- ~ *ph₂tr- 'father', *dʰugh₂tér- ~ *dʰugtr- (with laryngeal lost, see 2.2.4 (i)) 'daughter'. But it seems clear that there were also a good many hysterokinetic n-stems, such as *poh₂imén- ~ *poh₂imn- 'shepherd', *uksén- ~ *uksn- 'bull', and other hysterokinetic stems can be reconstructed, e.g. *dn̥ǵʰwáh₂- ~ *dn̥ǵʰuh₂- 'tongue' (Peters 1991).

Proterokinetic inflection may have been the most widespread type among polysyllabic athematic nouns in Core IE. Whole classes of nouns followed this accent paradigm, including, for instance, feminine nouns in */-tey-/[57] (e.g. *dʰéh₁-ti- ~ *dʰh₁-téy- 'act of putting', *gʷém-ti- ~ *gʷm̥-téy- 'step, act of walking', *mén-ti- ~ *mn̥-téy- 'thought'), masculine nouns in */-tew-/ (e.g. *ǵéws-tu- ~ *ǵus-téw- 'taste'), most neuters in */-men-/ (e.g. *séh₁-mn̥ ~ *sh₁-mén- 'seed'), most feminines in *-h₂- that were not derived from o-stems (e.g. *gʷénh₂- ~ *gʷnáh₂- 'woman', *h₁widʰéwh₂- ~ *h₁widʰwáh₂- 'widow'), and a large number of neuter r/n-stems (e.g. *páh₂wr̥ ~ *ph₂uén- 'fire'; cf. Schindler 1975a: 9–10). There was a conspicuous group of basic neuter nouns with o-grade direct cases which were originally acrostatic (Schindler 1975a: 4–8) but are proterokinetic in the daughters of Core IE, e.g. *wódr̥ ~ *udén- 'water' (but cf. Hitt. inst. sg. wedand(a) < *wéd-n̥- (Craig Melchert, p.c.)), *móri ~ *mréy- 'sea', *ǵónu ~ *ǵnéw- 'knee' (but cf. Hitt. gēnu, Lat. genū), *dóru ~ *dréw- 'tree, wood'.

None of this applied to thematic nouns, which had the accent on the same syllable throughout the paradigm, either on the thematic vowel (e.g. in (masc.) *deywós 'god', (fem.) *snusós 'daughter-in-law', (neut.) *yugóm 'yoke') or on the leftmost syllable of the stem (e.g. in (masc.) *éḱwos 'horse', (neut.) *wérǵom 'work'). However, there was a derivational rule by which collectives were formed from o-stem nouns by the addition of the collective suffix *-h₂- and a shift of accent, so that from (masc.) *kʷékʷlo- 'wheel', for example, was formed a collective *kʷekʷlá-h₂- 'set of wheels'; and in the daughter languages these collectives tended to be reinterpreted

---

[57] Lundquist (2015) observes that, though both oxytone and barytone forms of nouns of this class are attested in Vedic, the oxytone forms are almost invariably older; he suggests that the barytone forms are innovations and do not constitute evidence for an alternation of accent in this class of nouns. That might be true (though it needs to be remembered that the subdialects of later Vedic texts are not necessarily direct descendants of Rigvedic or of each other, so that the traditional interpretation of the pattern as leveling in different directions is not certainly false). But the reconstruction of nouns of this class as proterokinetic does not rest solely on the Vedic accent facts; a fossil such as PGmc *dēdiz 'deed', with a full-grade root but oxytone accent (to judge from the voiced Verner's Law alternant of its suffix), is reasonable evidence for proterokinetic accent in Central IE.

as neuter plurals and, in some cases, to be integrated into the paradigms of the nouns from which they had originally been formed. The result was a class of thematic nouns with an alternation of accent between singular and plural, and sometimes also a shift of gender in the plural (as in Lat. masc. *locus* 'place', pl. neut. *loca*). Various daughters leveled the alternations in different ways; for instance, in Greek the accent alternation is normally leveled (cf. Homeric masc. κύκλος 'wheel', pl. neut. κύκλα), while in Slavic languages the gender is normally leveled (cf. e.g. Russian neut. *m'ésto* 'place', pl. *m'está*).

Finally, feminines (some of which were originally collectives) were also formed from o-stem nouns with the suffix *-h$_2$-; these, too, had fixed accent (e.g. *d^{h}oHnáh$_2$- 'grain', *pĺ̥h$_2$mah$_2$- 'flat hand, palm').

2.3.4 (iii) Sample Central IE noun paradigms

These are naturally much smaller than the verb paradigms and require less comment. I omit the oblique cases of the dual, whose reconstruction is shaky in any case. Readers should bear in mind that the plural paradigms given for neuter nouns were innovations that at least partly postdated PIE. The accent given for vocative forms is the *underlying* accent dictated by the accent-and-ablaut paradigm; on the surface vocatives were either accentless or accented on the initial syllable (see 2.2.5).

	night (fem.)	foot (masc.)	root (fem.)	star (masc.)	heart (neut.)
singular					
nom.	nók^{w}ts	pṓds	wráh$_2$ds	h$_2$stḗr	ḱḗr
voc.	nók^{w}t	pód	wráh$_2$d	h$_2$stér	ḱḗr
acc.	nók^{w}tm̥	pódm̥	wráh$_2$dm̥	h$_2$stérm̥	ḱḗr
inst.	nék^{w}teh$_1$	pedéh$_1$	wr̥h$_2$déh$_1$	h$_2$str̥éh$_1$	ḱr̥déh$_1$
dat.	nék^{w}tey	pedéy	wr̥h$_2$déy	h$_2$str̥éy	ḱr̥déy
abl.-gen.	nék^{w}ts	pedés	wr̥h$_2$dés	h$_2$str̥és	ḱr̥dés
loc.	nék^{w}t(i)	péd(i)	wráh$_2$d(i)	h$_2$stér(i)	ḱḗr(i)
dual					
n.-v.-acc.	nók^{w}th$_1$e	pódh$_1$e	wráh$_2$dh$_1$e	h$_2$stérh$_1$e	ḱérdih$_1$
...					
plural					
nom.-voc.	nók^{w}tes	pódes	wráh$_2$des	h$_2$stéres	ḱérdh$_2$ (?)
acc.	nók^{w}tn̥s	pódn̥s	wráh$_2$dn̥s	h$_2$stérn̥s	ḱérdh$_2$ (?)
inst.	nék^{w}tb^{h}is	pedb^{h}ís	wr̥h$_2$db^{h}ís	h$_2$str̥b^{h}ís	ḱr̥db^{h}ís
dat.-abl.	nék^{w}tm̥os	pedmós	wr̥h$_2$dr̥ós	h$_2$str̥mós	ḱr̥dmós
gen.	nék^{w}toHom	pedóHom	wr̥h$_2$dóHom	h$_2$str̥óHom	ḱr̥dóHom
loc.	nék^{w}tsu	pedsú	wr̥h$_2$dsú	h$_2$str̥sú	ḱr̥dsú

	sheep (fem.)	moon, month (masc.)	name (neut.)	(collective:) names (neut.)	lake (masc.)
singular					
nom.	$h_2$ówis	mḗh_1n̥s	h_1nḗ$h_3$mn̥	$h_1$nóh_3mō	léymō
voc.	$h_2$ówey	mḗh_1n̥s	h_1nḗ$h_3$mn̥	$h_1$nóh_3mō	léymon
acc.	$h_2$ówim	mḗh_1n̥sm̥	h_1nḗ$h_3$mn̥	$h_1$nóh_3mō	léymonm̥
inst.	$h_2$áwih_1	méh_1n̥seh_1	$h_1$nó$h_3$mn̥eh_1	h_1n̥$h_3$mnéh_1[58]	limnéh_1
dat.	$h_2$áwyey	méh_1n̥sey	$h_1$nó$h_3$mn̥ey	h_1n̥$h_3$mnéy	limnéy
abl.-gen.	$h_2$áwis (→ -yos)	méh_1n̥sos	$h_1$nó$h_3$mn̥(o)s	h_1n̥$h_3$mnés	limnés
loc.	???	méh_1n̥s(i)	$h_1$nó$h_3$mn̥(i)	h_1n̥$h_3$mén(i)	limén(i)
dual					
n.-v.-acc.	$h_2$ówih_1e	mḗh_1n̥sh_1e	h_1nḗ$h_3$mn̥ih_1 (?)		léymonh_1e
...					
plural					
nom.-voc.	$h_2$óweyes	mḗh_1n̥ses			léymones
acc.	$h_2$ówins	mḗh_1n̥sn̥s			léymonn̥s
inst.	$h_2$áwib^{h}is	méh_1n̥sb^{h}is			limn̥b^{h}ís
dat.-abl.	$h_2$áwimos	méh_1n̥smos			limn̥mós
gen.	$h_2$áwyoHom	méh_1n̥soHom			limnóHom
loc.	$h_2$áwisu	méh_1n̥su			limn̥sú

[58] The evidence of the daughters suggests that *m was non-syllabic in this and the following two forms; see 2.2.4 (ii) *ad fin.*

	earth (fem.)	thought (fem.)	taste (masc.)	sea (neut.)	tree (neut.)
singular					
nom.	dʰéǵʰōm	méntis	ǵéwstus	móri	dóru
voc.	dʰéǵʰom	méntey	ǵéwstew	móri	dóru
acc.	dʰéǵʰōm	méntim	ǵéwstum	móri	dóru
inst.	ǵʰméh₁	mn̩tíh₁ ?[59] (mn̩tyéh₁?)	ǵustúh₁ ?[60] (ǵustuéh₁?)	mriéh₁ ?	druéh₁ ?
dat.	ǵʰméy	mn̩téyey	ǵustéwey	mréyey	dréwey
abl.-gen.	ǵʰmés	mn̩téys	ǵustéws	mréys	dréws
loc.	dʰǵʰém(i)	mn̩téy (-ēy)	ǵustéw(i)	mréy (-ēy)	dréw(i)
dual					
nom.-voc.-acc.	...	méntih₁	ǵéwstuh₁	mórīh₁ (?)	dórwih₁
plural					
nom.-voc.		ménteyes	ǵéwstewes	mórih₂	dóruh₂
acc.		méntins	ǵéwstuns	mórih₂	dóruh₂
inst.		mn̩tíbʰis	ǵustúbʰis	mríbʰis	drúbʰis
dat.-abl.		mn̩tímos	ǵustúmos	mrímos	drúmos
gen.		mn̩téyoHom	ǵustéwoHom	mréyoHom	dréwoHom
loc.		mn̩tísu	ǵustúsu	mrísu	drúsu

---

[59] The expected form is of course *mn̩téyh₁, but no reflex of such a form is attested. Potential Vedic reflexes of both endings suggested here are attested, in fact for this word (*matī́* and *matyā́*). The former is clearly an archaism, appearing in the stereotyped *cvi*-formation (Schindler 1980: 391), though it is unclear how far back the ending goes in proterokinetic stems; it must have originated in acrostatic stems (Schindler 1975a: 4–5, 1975b: 262, Mayrhofer 1989: 15). For similar evidence of the relative antiquity of inst. sg. -*vā́* in proterokinetic u-stems, see e.g. Nussbaum (2010: 271) with references. The productive proterokinetic endings -*yā́*, -*vā́* can have been favored by the obvious parallel with thematic -*ā́* < *-oh₁; for that reason I hesitate to project *-éh₁ back into Core IE proterokinetic i- and u-stems (*pace* Neri 2009: 7). I am grateful to Ronald Kim for helpful discussion of these points and those in the next footnote.

[60] Vedic exhibits only inst. sg. forms in -*vā* ~ -*uā* (and innovative -*unā*) for u-stems, but -*ū* is attested in Gāthā-Avestan in *vohū* 'good', *xratū* '(spiritual) power', the latter replaced in younger Avestan by *xraθβā*; it is reasonable to suspect that i-stems and u-stems developed in a parallel fashion and to reconstruct *-úh₁ (with caution) for Core IE.

	seed (neut.)	(collective:) seed(s) (neut.)	sun (neut.)[61]	woman (fem.)	widow (fem.)
singular					
nom.	séh$_1$mn̥	séh$_1$mō	sáh$_2$wl̥	g^{w}ḗn	h$_1$wid^{h}éwh$_2$
voc.	séh$_1$mn̥	séh$_1$mō	sáh$_2$wl̥	g^{w}ḗn	h$_1$wid^{h}éwh$_2$
acc.	séh$_1$mn̥	séh$_1$mō	sáh$_2$wl̥	g^{w}énh$_2$m̥	h$_1$wid^{h}éwh$_2$m̥
inst.	sh$_1$m̥énh$_1$	sh$_1$m̥néh$_1$	sh$_2$uéneh$_1$	g^{w}náh$_2$h$_1$[62]	h$_1$wid^{h}wáh$_2$h$_1$
dat.	sh$_1$m̥éney	sh$_1$m̥néy	sh$_2$uéney	g^{w}náh$_2$ay	h$_1$wid^{h}wáh$_2$ay
abl.-gen.	sh$_1$m̥éns	sh$_1$m̥nés	sh$_2$uéns	g^{w}náh$_2$s	h$_1$wid^{h}wáh$_2$s
loc.	sh$_1$m̥én(i)	sh$_1$m̥én(i)	sh$_2$uén(i)	g^{w}náh$_2$(i)	h$_1$wid^{h}wáh$_2$(i)
dual					
n.-v.-acc.	séh$_1$mn̥ih$_1$			g^{w}énh$_2$h$_1$e	h$_1$wid^{h}éwh$_2$h$_1$e
...					
plural					
nom.-voc.				g^{w}énh$_2$as	h$_1$wid^{h}éwh$_2$as
acc.				g^{w}énh$_2$n̥s	h$_1$wid^{h}éwh$_2$n̥s
inst.				g^{w}náh$_2$b^{h}is	h$_1$wid^{h}wáh$_2$b^{h}is
dat.-abl.				g^{w}náh$_2$mos	h$_1$wid^{h}wáh$_2$mos
gen.				g^{w}náh$_2$oHom	h$_1$wid^{h}wáh$_2$oHom
loc.				g^{w}náh$_2$su	h$_1$wid^{h}wáh$_2$su

[61] A preform *sóh$_2$wl̥ might be suggested by Lat. *sōl* (masc.), but the latter more likely reflects *sh$_2$uṓl ← derived amphikinetic *sáh$_2$wōl (Neri 2003: 232, Melchert 2014b: 263 fn. 8; I am grateful to Michael Weiss for calling this to my attention). Gatha-Avestan gen. sg. *x^{v}ə̄ṇg* < *sh$_2$uéns virtually guarantees that the basic noun was proterokinetic, and Vedic Skt *súar* guarantees that it was neuter.

[62] Such a form, ending in two laryngeals, seems improbable; but in Germanic a disyllable would have yielded a trimoric vowel which would not have become the *-u which is reconstructable for Northwest Germanic. PGmc *-ō (bimoric), reflected in Early Runic dat. sg. *-u* (Krause 1971: 117) and OHG dat. sg. *-u*, must reflect a single syllable with a syllable-final laryngeal, and if the inst. sg. ending was not simply lost after the suffix *-ah$_2$, we apparently need to reconstruct *-ah$_2$-h$_1$ for this ending.

	father (masc.)	bull (masc.)	dog (masc.)	tooth (masc.)	tongue (masc.)
singular					
nom.	ph$_2$tḗr	uksḗn	ḱwṓ	h$_1$dónts	dn̥ǵ^{h}wáh$_2$s
voc.	ph$_2$tér	uksén	ḱwón	h$_1$dónd	dn̥ǵ^{h}wáh$_2$
acc.	ph$_2$térm̥	uksénm̥	ḱwónm̥	h$_1$dóntm̥	dn̥ǵ^{h}wā́m
inst.	ph$_2$tr̥éh$_1$	uksn̥éh$_1$	ḱunéh$_1$	h$_1$dn̥téh$_1$	dn̥ǵ^{h}uh$_2$áh$_1$
dat.	ph$_2$tr̥éy	uksn̥éy	ḱunéy	h$_1$dn̥téy	dn̥ǵ^{h}uh$_2$áy
abl.-gen.	ph$_2$tr̥és	uksn̥és	ḱunés	h$_1$dn̥tés	dn̥ǵ^{h}uh$_2$ás
loc.	ph$_2$tér(i)	uksén(i)	ḱwén(i) (?)	h$_1$dént(i) (?)	dn̥ǵ^{h}wáh$_2$(i)
dual					
n.-v.-acc.	ph$_2$térh$_1$e	uksénh$_1$e	ḱwónh$_1$e	h$_1$dónth$_1$e	dn̥ǵ^{h}wáh$_2$h$_1$e
…					
plural					
nom.-voc.	ph$_2$téres	uksénes	ḱwónes	h$_1$dóntes	dn̥ǵ^{h}wáh$_2$as
acc.	ph$_2$térn̥s	uksénn̥s	ḱwónn̥s	h$_1$dóntn̥s	dn̥ǵ^{h}wā́s
inst.	ph$_2$tr̥b^{h}ís	uksn̥b^{h}ís	ḱwn̥b^{h}ís	h$_1$dn̥tb^{h}ís	dn̥ǵ^{h}uh$_2$b^{h}ís
dat.-abl.	ph$_2$tr̥mós	uksn̥mós	ḱwn̥mós	h$_1$dn̥tmós	dn̥ǵ^{h}uh$_2$mós
gen.	ph$_2$tr̥óHom	uksn̥óHom	ḱunóHom	h$_1$dn̥tóHom	dn̥ǵ^{h}uh$_2$óHom
loc.	ph$_2$tr̥sú	uksn̥sú	ḱwn̥sú	h$_1$dn̥tsú	dn̥ǵ^{h}uh$_2$sú

	field (masc.)	nest (masc.)	work (neut.)	yoke (neut.)	cloud (neut.)
singular					
nom.	h$_2$áǵros	nisdós	wérǵom	yugóm	néb^{h}os
voc.	h$_2$áǵre	nisdé	wérǵom	yugóm	néb^{h}os
acc.	h$_2$áǵrom	nisdóm	wérǵom	yugóm	néb^{h}os
inst.	h$_2$áǵroh$_1$	nisdóh$_1$	wérǵoh$_1$	yugóh$_1$	néb^{h}eseh$_1$
dat.	h$_2$áǵroey	nisdóey	wérǵoey	yugóey	néb^{h}esey
abl.	h$_2$áǵread	nisdéad	wérǵead	yugéad	néb^{h}esos
gen.	h$_2$áǵrosyo	nisdósyo	wérǵosyo	yugósyo	néb^{h}esos
loc.	h$_2$áǵrey	nisdéy	wérǵey	yugéy	néb^{h}es(i)
dual					
n.-v.-acc.	h$_2$áǵroh$_1$	nisdóh$_1$	wérǵoyh$_1$	yugóyh$_1$	néb^{h}esih$_1$
…					
plural					
nom.-voc.	h$_2$áǵroes	nisdóes	wérǵah$_2$	yugáh$_2$	néb^{h}ōs
acc.	h$_2$áǵrons	nisdóns	wérǵah$_2$	yugáh$_2$	néb^{h}ōs
inst.	h$_2$áǵrōys	nisdṓys	wérǵōys	yugṓys	néb^{h}esb^{h}is
dat.-abl.	h$_2$áǵroymos	nisdóymos	wérǵoymos	yugóymos	néb^{h}esmos
gen.	h$_2$áǵrōHom	nisdṓHom	wérǵōHom	yugṓHom	néb^{h}esoHom
loc.	h$_2$áǵroysu	nisdóysu	wérǵoysu	yugóysu	néb^{h}esu

	palm (fem.)	grain (fem.)		
	singular		*plural*	
nom.	pl̥h$_2$mah$_2$	d^{h}oHnáh$_2$	pĺ̥h$_2$mah$_2$as	d^{h}oHnáh$_2$as
voc.	pĺ̥h$_2$ma	d^{h}oHná	pĺ̥h$_2$mah$_2$as	d^{h}oHnáh$_2$as
acc.	pĺ̥h$_2$mām	d^{h}oHnā́m	pĺ̥h$_2$mās	d^{h}oHnā́s
inst.	pĺ̥h$_2$mah$_2$h$_1$	d^{h}oHnáh$_2$h$_1$	pĺ̥h$_2$mah$_2$b^{h}is	d^{h}oHnáh$_2$b^{h}is
dat.	pĺ̥h$_2$mah$_2$ay	d^{h}oHnáh$_2$ay	pĺ̥h$_2$mah$_2$mos	d^{h}oHnáh$_2$mos
gen.	pĺ̥h$_2$mah$_2$s	d^{h}oHnáh$_2$s	pĺ̥h$_2$mah$_2$oHom	d^{h}oHnáh$_2$oHom
loc.	pĺ̥h$_2$mah$_2$(i)	d^{h}oHnáh$_2$(i)	pĺ̥h$_2$mah$_2$su	d^{h}oHnáh$_2$su

(See 2.2.4 (iv) on the phonology of the vocative and accusative forms.) As usual, the ablative was identical with the genitive in the singular and the dative in the plural. The dual direct cases of these stems seem to have ended in *-ah$_2$-ih$_1$.

2.3.5 PIE adjective inflection

In principle adjectives were inflected like nouns, except that there were forms for each of the three genders. The masculine and neuter case-and-number forms were made directly to the adjective stem (and were therefore identical in the oblique cases). In Nuclear IE the feminine was characterized by a suffix, which was *-h$_2$- for o-stems and apparently */-yeh$_2$-/ (proterokinetic) for all athematic adjectives. The large and productive classes of adjectives were o-stems, u-stems (proterokinetic), active participles in */-ont-/ (hysterokinetic) made to athematic verb stems and in *-o-nt- (with fixed accent) made to thematic verb stems, and perfect participles in */-wos-/ (probably originally amphikinetic, but perhaps mostly hysterokinetic in Core IE).

The following paradigms were typical:

'thin' (u-stem, proterokinetic; the *a's are underlyingly */e/)

	masc.	*neut.*	*fem.*
singular			
nom.	ténh$_2$us	ténh$_2$u	tn̥h$_2$áwih$_2$
voc.	ténh$_2$u	ténh$_2$u	tn̥h$_2$áwi
acc.	ténh$_2$um	ténh$_2$u	tn̥h$_2$áwih$_2$m̥
inst.	tn̥h$_2$uéh$_1$?		tn̥h$_2$wih$_2$áh$_1$?[63]
dat.	tn̥h$_2$áwey		tn̥h$_2$uyáh$_2$ay
abl.-gen.	tn̥h$_2$áws		tn̥h$_2$uyáh$_2$s
loc.	tn̥h$_2$áw(i)		tn̥h$_2$uyáh$_2$(i)
dual			
n.-v.-acc.	ténh$_2$uh$_1$	ténh$_2$uih$_1$	???
...			
plural			
nom.-voc.	ténh$_2$awes	ténh$_2$uh$_2$	tn̥h$_2$áwih$_2$es
acc.	ténh$_2$uns	ténh$_2$uh$_2$	tn̥h$_2$áwih$_2$n̥s
inst.	tn̥h$_2$úb^{h}is		tn̥h$_2$uyáh$_2$b^{h}is
dat.-abl.	tn̥h$_2$úmos		tn̥h$_2$uyáh$_2$mos
gen.	tn̥h$_2$áwoHom		tn̥h$_2$uyáh$_2$oHom
loc.	tn̥h$_2$úsu		tn̥h$_2$uyáh$_2$su

[63] I here follow the suggestion of Jochem Schindler apud Jasanoff (2003a: 102; noted by Neri 2009: 7); it is supported indirectly by the ā-stem endings of Vedic and OCS (see Jasanoff's discussion for details). Of course it is not guaranteed for Core IE, since Indo-Iranian and Balto-Slavic together represent only part of the Central IE subgroup, but we have even less evidence for any alternative.

'being' (active participle, hysterokinetic)[64]

	masc.	*neut.*	*fem.*
singular			
nom.	$h_1$sónts	$h_1$sónd	$h_1$sóntih$_2$
voc.	$h_1$sónd	$h_1$sónd	$h_1$sónti
acc.	$h_1$sóntm̥	$h_1$sónd	$h_1$sóntih$_2$m̥
inst.	$h_1$sn̥téh$_1$		$h_1$sn̥tih$_2$áh$_1$
dat.	$h_1$sn̥téy		$h_1$sn̥tyáh$_2$ay
abl.-gen.	$h_1$sn̥tés		$h_1$sn̥tyáh$_2$s
loc.	$h_1$sónt(i)		$h_1$sn̥tyáh$_2$(i)
dual			
n.-v.-acc.	$h_1$sónth$_1$e	$h_1$sóntih$_1$	$h_1$sóntih$_2$h$_1$e (?)
...			
plural			
nom.-voc.	$h_1$sóntes	h_1sṓnd	$h_1$sóntih$_2$as
acc.	$h_1$sóntn̥s	h_1sṓnd	$h_1$sóntih$_2$n̥s
inst.	$h_1$sn̥tb^{h}ís		$h_1$sn̥tyáh$_2$b^{h}is
dat.-abl.	$h_1$sn̥tmós		$h_1$sn̥tyáh$_2$mos
gen.	$h_1$sn̥tóHom		$h_1$sn̥tyáh$_2$oHom
loc.	$h_1$sn̥tsú		$h_1$sn̥tyáh$_2$su

[64] This is the accent paradigm attested in Vedic and reconstructable for Greek. As Craig Melchert points out (p.c.), o-grade direct cases are unusual in hysterokinetic stems; that suggests that the original inflection was amphikinetic, though it is nowhere attested.

'full' (o-stem)

	masc.	*neut.*	*fem.*
singular			
nom.	pl̥h$_1$nós	pl̥h$_1$nóm	pl̥h$_1$náh$_2$
voc.	pl̥h$_1$né	pl̥h$_1$nóm	pl̥h$_1$ná
acc.	pl̥h$_1$nóm	pl̥h$_1$nóm	pl̥h$_1$nā́m
inst.	pl̥h$_1$nóh$_1$		pl̥h$_1$náh$_2$h$_1$
dat.	pl̥h$_1$nóey		pl̥h$_1$náh$_2$ay
abl.	pl̥h$_1$néad		pl̥h$_1$náh$_2$s
gen.	pl̥h$_1$nósyo		pl̥h$_1$náh$_2$s
loc.	pl̥h$_1$néy		pl̥h$_1$náh$_2$(i)
dual			
n.-v.-acc.	pl̥h$_1$nóh$_1$	pl̥h$_1$nóy(h$_1$)	pl̥h$_1$náh$_2$ih$_1$ (?)
...			
plural			
nom.-voc.	pl̥h$_1$nóes	pl̥h$_1$náh$_2$	pl̥h$_1$náh$_2$es
acc.	pl̥h$_1$nóns	pl̥h$_1$náh$_2$	pl̥h$_1$nā́s
inst.	pl̥h$_1$nṓys		pl̥h$_1$náh$_2$b^{h}is
dat.-abl.	pl̥h$_1$nóymos		pl̥h$_1$náh$_2$mos
gen.	pl̥h$_1$nṓHom		pl̥h$_1$náh$_2$oHom
loc.	pl̥h$_1$nóysu		pl̥h$_1$náh$_2$su

2.3.6 The inflection of other PIE nominals

The remaining classes of nominals that were inflected in PIE included at least personal pronouns, anaphors, determiners, wh-elements (both interrogative and relative), and (most) quantifiers. The membership of that list is given in syntactic terms, but the inflectional system classified these stems differently. At least some quantifiers with relatively general meanings (such as 'all' and 'many') were inflected as ordinary adjectives, but others seem to have exhibited pronominal inflection (see below). Numerals were a more or less distinct inflectional class, many exhibiting formal peculiarities of one sort or another. The personal pronouns had a reduced inflectional system very unlike that of other nominals. The remaining items of the above list largely shared inflectional peculiarities; their system of inflection is usually referred to as 'pronominal inflection' by Indo-Europeanists. In this section I will discuss those inflectional classes.

2.3.6 (i) PIE numerals

It is fairly likely that PIE, like Proto-Algonkian, possessed more than one lexeme translatable by English 'one', though it is not possible to reconstruct the semantics of the words in detail. An obviously archaic m-stem seems likely to have been the basic numeral (I give the Core IE paradigm):

	masc.	*neut.*	*fem.*
nom.	sḗm	sém	sémih$_2$
voc.	sém	sém	sémi
acc.	sḗm	sém	sémih$_2$m̥
inst.	sméh$_1$		syáh$_2$(a)h$_1$? (sih$_2$áh$_1$?)
dat.	sméy		syáh$_2$ay
abl.-gen.	smés		syáh$_2$s
loc.	sém(i)		syáh$_2$(i)

The initial *sy- of the feminine oblique forms appears to reflect underlying */smy-/ (Gippert 2004 with references); the failure of */m/ to syllabify in this environment might be another systematic peculiarity in the syllabification of labial sonorants (as suggested by Gippert; see 2.2.4 (ii)), or it could be a fossilized relic of a pre-PIE phonological system in which the syllabification rules were different. This word survives as the ordinary numeral in Tocharian, Greek, Armenian, and probably Hittite: Hittite *sia-* (Hoffner and Melchert 2008: 153–5) appears to have been back-formed to the inherited feminine.[65] It also obviously underlies the Latin adverb *semel* 'once'. Most of the other languages have instead various derivatives of a stem *oy-, which may originally have meant 'single' or the like:

Skt *ékas* < *óykos;
Av. *aēuuō*, OPers. *aiva* < *óywos (cf. Gk οἶος 'alone');
Lat. *ūnus*, OIr. *óen*, Welsh *un*, Goth. *ains* (and so all the Germanic languages), Old Prussian *ains* < *óynos (cf. Gk οἴνη 'one-spot (on dice)').

It is clear that 'two' was inflected as a dual, and that its direct caseform was masc. *dwóh$_1$, neut. *dwóy(h$_1$); it is not clear whether there was originally a separate feminine stem, though some Central daughters seem to show a fem. direct caseform *dwáh$_2$ih$_1$. The oblique forms are difficult to reconstruct, as is usual for duals. In addition, there was an uninflected form *dwó (Cowgill 1985b), which might have arisen by loss of the direct masc. case ending in pausa (see 2.2.4 (iv) *ad fin.*). It is also clear that there was a parallel stem meaning 'both' (i.e. 'all two'), which either was or ended in *b^{h}ó-. But while Germanic seems to reflect such a monosyllabic stem (cf. Goth. *bai*, etc.), the other languages exhibit compounds of various kinds: the commonest form is compounded with a form of *h$_2$ant- 'forehead' (Jasanoff 1976; cf. Toch. B *antapi*, Toch. A masc. *āmpi*, fem. *āmpuk*, Gk ἄμφω, Lat. *ambō*), but we also find *(H)u- (Skt *ub^{h}áu*) and *(H)o- (OCS *oba*). It seems

[65] Note that Armenian *mi* 'one' also reflects generalization of the feminine, though at a later stage of its development (cf. Gk fem. μία). The connection of the Hittite numeral with Tocharian A *ṣya-* was made by Pinault (2006a: 84), who, however, offers a completely different explanation; Hackstein (2005: 178–9) had already suggested a connection between the Tocharian form and Aiolic Greek fem. ἴα.

mildly implausible that Germanic—not a notably archaic daughter—preserves the original stem, but that might be the case.

With ‘three’ we are on firmer ground. In Core IE this numeral preserved an extraordinarily archaic feminine in */-ser-/, clearly attested in Indo-Iranian and Celtic:

	masc.	*neut.*	*fem.*
nom.-voc.	tréyes	tríh$_2$	tisres (*accent?*)
acc.	tríns	tríh$_2$	tisrn̥s (*accent?*)
inst.	tribʰís		tisr̥bʰís
dat.-abl.	trimós		tisr̥mós
gen.	trióHom		tisróHom
loc.	trisú		tisr̥sú

The accent of the fem. direct forms is doubtful. Sanskrit accents the endings, which is hard to believe for the PIE nom. pl. and almost impossible for the acc. pl.; unfortunately neither Iranian nor Celtic preserves any unambiguous reflex of the original accent.

Core IE ‘four’ had a similarly archaic feminine stem:

	masc.	*neut.*	*fem.*
nom.-voc.	kʷetwóres	kʷetwṓr	kʷétesres
acc.	kʷetwórn̥s	kʷetwṓr	kʷétesrn̥s
inst.	kʷetwr̥bʰís		kʷetesr̥bʰís
dat.-abl.	kʷetwr̥mós		kʷetesr̥mós
gen.	kʷeturóHom		kʷetesróHom
loc.	kʷetwr̥sú		kʷetesr̥sú

The Tocharian forms of ‘four’ obviously reflect the same inherited word: TB *śtwer*, TA *śtwar* < PToch. *śətwḗrə are sound-change reflexes of *kʷetwóres, while the fem. form TB *śtwāra*, TA *śtwār* reflects Proto-Tocharian *śətwërá, the masc. form with the addition of neut. pl. *-a and a-umlaut of the preceding vowel. But the Anatolian languages have a completely different word, Hitt. *mēyawas* and its cognates, which (strictly speaking) renders the PIE form unreconstructable.

The subsequent numerals up through at least ‘nine’ were uninflected: we are able to reconstruct *pénkʷe ‘five’, *swéḱs ‘six’,[66] *septḿ̥ ‘seven’, *oḱtṓw ‘eight’, and (with a bit more uncertainty) *(h$_1$)néwn̥ ‘nine’. Whether *déḱm̥d ‘ten’ was productively inflected is unclear: in the daughters it isn’t, but the reconstructable decads are recognizably inflected forms of ‘ten’. Thus *wī́ḱm̥tih$_1$ ‘twenty’ must be **dwí-dḱm̥t-ih$_1$ ‘two tens’ (cf. the discussion of Szemerényi 1960: 129–40, and note the neuter dual ending), while the higher decads ended in an archaic neuter collective *dḱṓmd (Schindler 1967b: 240). ‘Hundred’, reconstructable as *ḱm̥tóm, was

[66] See now Rothstein-Dowden (2021).

a derivative of 'ten' (Risch 1962; **d- was lost by the same regular sound change that dropped the initial dental stop in oblique cases of 'earth', see 2.2.4 (iii), 2.3.4 (ii, iii)). Higher numerals cannot be securely reconstructed.

2.3.6 (ii) PIE 'pronominal' inflection

The inflection of the determiner 'that' was unusual in a number of ways. I give the Core IE paradigm:

	masc.	*neut.*	*fem.*
singular			
nom.	só	tód	sáh$_2$
acc.	tóm	tód	tā́m
inst.	tóh$_1$ (tónoh$_1$?)[67]		???
dat.	tósmey		tósyah$_2$ay
abl.	tósmead (?)		tósyah$_2$s
gen.	tósyo		tósyah$_2$s
loc.	tósmi		tósyah$_2$(i)
dual			
nom.-acc.	tóh$_1$	tóy(h$_1$)	???
	masc.	*neut.*	*fem.*
plural			
nom.	tóy	táh$_2$	táh$_2$as
acc.	tóns	táh$_2$	tā́s
inst.	tṓys		táh$_2$b^{h}is
dat.-abl.	tóymos		táh$_2$mos
gen.	tóysoHom		táh$_2$soHom
loc.	tóysu		táh$_2$su

The suppletion *só- ~ *tó- was completely unparalleled elsewhere in the inflectional system. It was in place already in Nuclear IE, since it appears in the Tocharian deictics; whether it existed already in PIE is unclear, since this deictic does not appear in Anatolian (Proto-Anatolian 'that' was *obós). Other peculiarities of this paradigm will reappear in various paradigms cited below: the endinglessness of the nom. sg. masc.; the neut. direct case ending *-d; the infixation of *-sm- in most of the masc. and neut. sg. forms (but gen. sg. *-osyo) and of *-sy- in the fem. sg., almost certainly reflecting earlier compounding with the numeral 'one' (Gippert 2004 with references; see the preceding section); the nom. pl. masc. ending *-y, originally a collective suffix (Jasanoff 2009: 145–7); the reappearance of *-y- in the masc. and neut. oblique pl. forms; the infixation of *-s-,

[67] Rieken (1999b) argues convincingly that PIE *tóh1 underlies the Hittite connective *ta*. The longer form, confined to Central IE, is the probable source not only of OE *þon*, Goth. *þana-*, but also of the Old Persian pronominal ending *-anā*; it might also underlie Vedic *ténā* ~ *téna*, if the *e* of that form can have been introduced from inst. pl. *téb^{h}is*.

which might be the zero grade of the gen. sg. ending (Jasanoff 2009: 145 fn. 15), in all the gen. pl. forms. Those are the signature of PIE 'pronominal' inflection.

The relative pronoun *Hyó- was apparently inflected like 'that', except that the nom. sg. masc. was 'normal' *Hyós. It appears that a number of quantifiers and similar lexemes were also inflected in the same way; for instance, a neut. nom.-acc. sg. *ályod 'other' is securely reconstructable from Lat. *aliud*, Gk ἄλλο, Lydian *aλad*. The scope of this phenomenon is unclear, though its existence in the protolanguage is probable. Indo-Iranian and Italic preserve relics of the system especially well; though the lexemes which are inflected according to this 'pronominal' pattern are often not cognate, they typically include the basic words for 'other, other (of two), which (of two)?, every, any, one'—that is, quantifiers which happen to have thematic stems. Various other daughters have eliminated this peculiarity almost completely (including Greek, which makes ἄλλο especially probative).

A number of parallel pairs of stems seem to have existed in PIE, such that the o-stem was used in adnominal function while the i/e-stem was used as a full DP (Warren Cowgill, p.c. ca. 1980; cf. Sihler 1995: 395–400). The distinction between the Latin interrogative pronoun *quis* 'who?' and interrogative adjective *quī* 'which?' apparently preserves the PIE situation, though elsewhere leveling has obscured it. The pairs in question are the following:

	adnominal	*full NP*
weak deictic	*o-	*i/e-
determiner 'this'	*ḱo-	*ḱi/e-
interrogative	*kʷo-	*kʷi/e-

The o-stems were inflected like the relative pronoun (i.e. like the determiner 'that' except that the nom. sg. masc. ended in *-os). But the inflection of the i/e-stems exhibited a type of ablaut otherwise unexampled in PIE. I give the Core IE paradigm of the weak deictic:

	masc.	*neut.*	*fem.*
singular			
nom.	éy	íd	íh_2
acc.	ím	íd	$\text{íh}_2\text{m̥}$
inst.	íh_1		???
dat.	ésmey		$\text{ésyah}_2\text{ay}$
abl.	ésmead (?)		$\text{ésyah}_2\text{s}$
gen.	ésyo		$\text{ésyah}_2\text{s}$
loc.	ésmi		$\text{ésyah}_2\text{(i)}$
dual			
nom.-acc.	???	???	???

	masc.	*neut.*	*fem.*
plural			
nom.	éyes	íh_2	í$h_2$es (?)
acc.	íns	íh_2	íh_2n̥s (?)
inst.	éyb^{h}is		íh_2b^{h}is
dat.-abl.	éymos		í$h_2$mos
gen.	éysoHom		í$h_2$soHom
loc.	éysu		í$h_2$su

This lexical item occurred also as a clitic (i.e. unaccented); the difference seems to have been that the accented form was weakly deictic, while the clitic form referred to an entity already mentioned in the discourse. The interrogative, too, occurred as a clitic; its clitic form was indefinite in meaning (*k^{w}id 'something', etc.). Apparently the 'this'-determiner, like 'that', was always accented.

2.3.6 (iii) PIE personal pronouns

The first- and second-person pronouns and the Core IE reflexive pronoun exhibited a unique type of inflection. It seems best first to give the forms, then to comment. For further information the reader is referred especially to Katz (1998), on which my account is based (though cf. also Sihler 1995: 369–82).

	1st person	2nd person	3rd person → Core IE reflexive
singular			
nom.	éǵh_2	túh_2	
acc.	emé ~ me	twé ~ te	swé ~ se
gen.	méme ~ moy	téwe ~ toy	séwe ~ soy
dat.	méǵ^{h}ye ~ moy	téb^{h}ye ~ toy	séb^{h}ye ~ soy
dual			
nom.	wé	yú	
oblique	n̥$h_3$mé ~ noh_3	u$h_3$wé ~ woh_3	
plural			
nom.	wéy	yū́ (< **yúy ?)	
oblique	n̥smé ~ nos	uswé ~ wos	

Every detail of these paradigms requires further discussion.

The pronoun in the third column was reflexive only in Core IE. It was probably third-person reflexive, since probable cognates are third-person pronouns in Anatolian (Hitt. enclitic *-sse* 'to/from him/her/it', Hoffner and Melchert 2008: 2135–6; *-sis* 'his/her/its', pp. 138–41) and the Toch. B conjunction *ṣp* 'and' plausibly reflects an inst. sg. *se-b^{h}i 'with it'.[68] In Indo-Iranian and Balto-Slavic it became

[68] Anatolian does show traces of the use of this pronoun as a reflexive, but so far as I can see they can be innovations; see Yakubovich (2009: 161–96) for comprehensive exposition and analysis. I am grateful to Craig Melchert for helpful discussion of this point.

a reflexive for all persons, but in the more westerly languages (as probably in Core IE) the reflexives of the first and second persons were the ordinary first- and second-person pronouns. The Core IE reflexive lacked a nominative; that is an indication that it was bound by the subject of the clause (as in very many daughters). It was morphologically singular by impoverishment: though it was bound by dual and plural subjects, the marked number features were deleted in the morphological component of the grammar, so that only singular forms surfaced. (See especially Noyer 1997 for a comprehensive discussion of morphosyntactic feature impoverishment.) It was also subject to gender impoverishment. The use of the reflexive in Latin and of German *sich* appears to have preserved these peculiarities faithfully. The inflection of the reflexive was clearly parallel to that of the second person singular, the only difference being the initial *s- instead of 2sg. *t-.

The inflection of the first- and second-person pronouns seems to have exhibited the following structural features.

1) They were subject to gender impoverishment.
2) Within each number, the nominative was formed from a separate stem. Consequently these were the only PIE nominals in which the acc. du. differed from the nom. du.
3) The singulars were formed from stems completely different from the non-singulars.
4) There was some sort of relation between the dual and plural stems. It looks as though the nom. du. was endingless, and the nom. pl. was formed with the collective suffix *-y. But the relation of the oblique stems was more complex, the duals ending in *-h_3- while the plurals ended in *-s-.
5) The clitic accusative form of each pronoun seems to have been the endingless oblique stem. The stressed accusative was formed by the addition of a suffix, probably originally *-mé in the first person and *-wé in the others, to the zero grade of the stem (see the comprehensive discussion of Katz 1998: 89–99 with numerous references). In the 1sg. **mmé seems to have become *emé, which survives unchanged in Gk ἐμέ.
6) At least in the singular there were special genitive and dative forms that showed little resemblance to the caseforms of other nominals.
7) Most strikingly, the case system was greatly impoverished; only four cases can be reconstructed in the singular, and in the non-singular we cannot even do that.

As Katz observes, this last characteristic is likely to be an extreme archaism, dating to a period when the PIE case system was not so fully developed.

2.4 PIE derivational morphology

The system of PIE word formation was also very elaborate; Brugmann (1906) spends more than 500 pages listing and exemplifying its formal machinery. The following paragraphs discuss only some of the most important derivational types.

2.4.1 Compounding

In the more archaic IE daughter languages one encounters combinations of verbs and adverbs (or 'preverbs') that exhibit meanings which are not transparently compositional. Evidently PIE possessed such 'compound verbs', but it is not clear that any of their idiosyncratic meanings in the daughters should be projected back into PIE. For instance, reflexes of Core IE *pró b^her- exhibit a wide range of derived meanings, some of which are shared by more than one daughter language: 'offer, present' in Sanskrit and Greek, 'reveal, display' in Greek and Latin, 'carry off' in Greek and Gothic, and so on; but since all can be derived straightforwardly from the etymological meaning *'carry forward', the latter could easily have been the only meaning of the phrase in Core IE. In all the daughters at least some of these phrases have become lexemes with idiosyncratic meanings even if they are not yet single phonological words (like Modern English 'get up', 'get out', etc., though the English examples are of much more recent origin). In most attested IE languages these compounds have also undergone univerbation to single phonological words, but in the three that are well attested earliest—Hittite, Vedic Sanskrit, and Homeric Greek—univerbation is still in progress, and the pattern is rather different in each. It therefore seems most likely that these were still phrases in PIE and all its daughters down through Central IE.

By contrast, PIE nominal compounds, including adjectives and nouns that were derived from compound verbs, were typically single phonological words. Adjectives could be preceded by a wide variety of adverbial prefixes, of which the most widely attested are *n̥- 'un-', *$h_1$su- 'good', *dus- 'bad', and *sēmi- 'half'. There seem to have been several types of compound nouns; they are usually classified by meaning according to a system worked out by the Sanskrit grammarians more than two millennia ago. Determinative compounds were one of the most important types. In a determinative the final member of the compound is a noun which refers directly to what the compound denotes; the preceding member can be an adjective, as in the modern English example *blackbird* (a kind of bird which is black), or a noun, as in *werewolf* (a wolf who is also a man; cf. OE *wer* 'man'). Exocentric compounds, often referred to as bahuvrīhi compounds (the Sanskrit term), were the other most important type. In a bahuvrīhi the final noun characterizes, but does not refer to, what the compound denotes; a typical English example is *tenderfoot* (literally, a person whose feet are tender (because (s)he isn't used to backpacking—NOT a tender foot, which would be the case if the compound were a determinative). Few actual PIE examples of these compounds are reconstructable, for the simple reason that nominal compounding remained exuberantly productive in most of the daughters (including Greek), with new compounds steadily replacing older ones. But we can at least reconstruct the Central IE compound adjective *ń̥d^{h}g^{wh}itos 'imperishable' (and even a phrase *ń̥d^{h}g^{wh}itom ḱléwos 'imperishable fame', with reflexes both in the Rigveda and in Homer), and several scholars have seen that Homeric Gk ἰοχέαιρα, an epithet of Artemis, is probably the same word as the Vedic Skt bahuvrīhi *íṣuhastas* 'arrowhand', i.e. 'with arrows in his/her hand(s)'; the PIE word must have been something like (fem.) *ísuǵ^{h}esrih_2 (Heubeck 1956, Peters 1980: 223–8, both with references).

Also important were agentive nominal compounds in which the final element was a verb root and the prior element the object of the verb; this is the type exemplified by Vedic Skt *vr̥tra-hán-* 'slayer of Vr̥tra' and Lat. *au-cep-s* 'bird-catcher'.

2.4.2 PIE derivational suffixes

The suffixes by which verbs were derived from other verbs and nominals are listed in 2.3.3 (i), since the result of such derivation was in every case a distinctive type of aspect stem. Nominal derivation was much more elaborate, as the following sections will show.

2.4.2 (i) PIE noun-forming suffixes

The proto-vr̥ddhi derivational process is described in 2.2.4 (i), since it involved a (very unusual) morphologized phonological rule. The collective suffix *-h_2- is discussed at the end of 2.3.4 (ii), because it was often integrated into noun paradigms as a neuter nom.-acc. pl. ending. In some cases collectives might have been reinterpreted as feminine singulars; in many of the daughters, including Greek, a large proportion of feminine *-ah_2-stems belong to derivational classes that could have originated as collectives.

Large and productive classes of thematic nouns with o-grade roots (which I symbolize as R(o)) were formed from verb stems. The type R(ó)-o- (masc.) and its collective R(o)-áh_2- (fem.) denoted the action of the verb; the type R(o)-ó- (masc.), which was probably restricted to the final element of compounds, denoted the agent. Typical examples include *ǵónh_1-o-s, collective *ǵonh_1-áh_2 'begetting, birth, offspring' (Gk γόνος, γονή 'offspring'; Skt *jánas* 'creature, person', *janā́* 'birth'), *-ǵonh_1-ó-s 'begetter' (Gk compound τεκνογόνος 'begetting children' with typically shifted accent), all derived from *ǵénh_1- 'to beget, to bear (a child)'; *d^{h}róg^{h}os '(act of) running' (Gk τρόχος 'circular course'), *d^{h}rog^{h}ós 'runner, wheel' (apparently decompound; cf. Gk τροχός, OIr. *droch*, both 'wheel'), from *d^hreg^h- 'to run'; *sóng^{wh}os 'chant' (PGmc *sang^{w}az 'song'), collective *song^{wh}áh_2 (Gk ὀμφή 'divine voice') from *seng^{wh}- 'to chant'. Similar collectives were also made with zero-grade roots, e.g. *b^hugáh_2 'flight, escape' (Gk φυγή, Lat. *fuga*) from *b^hewg- 'to run away, to flee'. Other types of nouns derived with the thematic vowel also existed, though they may not have been productive; obvious examples are the neuters *yugóm 'yoke' (Hitt. *iukan*, Skt *yugám*, etc.) from *yewg- 'to join' and *wérǵom 'work' (Gk ἔργον, PGmc *werką) from *werǵ- 'to work'. As can be seen from the cognates cited, nouns denoting actions tend also to denote the results of those actions; there is no clear dividing line between them.

Neuter s-stems with accented e-grade roots were also action/result nouns. Well-attested examples include *ǵén$h_1$os ~ *ǵén$h_1$es- 'family, lineage' (Skt *jánas*, Gk γένος, Lat. *genus*) from *ǵénh_1- 'to beget'; *ḱléwos ~ *ḱléwes- 'fame' (Skt *śrávas*, Gk κλέος) from *ḱlew- 'to hear'; *wék^{w}os ~ *wék^{w}es- 'word' (Skt *vácas*, Gk ἔπος) from *wek^w- 'to say'; etc.

Another class of action/result nouns were proterokinetic neuters in *-men-. Typical examples include *néwm̥n ~ *numén- 'nod' (Gk νεῦμα, Lat. *nūmen*) from *new- 'to nod' and *séh$_1$mn̥ ~ *sh$_1$mén- 'seed' (Lat. *sēmen*, OCS *sěmę*) from *seh$_1$- 'to sow'. This class seems to have made amphikinetic collectives; thus the collective of the latter was *séh$_1$mō ~ *sh$_1$mn- (OHG *sāmo*).

Still another group of these nouns were masculine, with the thematic suffix *-mo-. Two ablaut classes, R(ó)-mo- and R(0)-mó-, were well represented. To the former belonged, e.g., *tórmos 'borehole' (Gk τόρμος 'socket', PGmc *þarmaz 'intestine') from *terh_1- 'to bore'; an example of the latter is *d^hu$h_2$mós 'smoke' (Skt *d^hūmás*, Lat. *fūmus*) from *d^huh_2- 'to smoke'.

Two large and productive groups of action nouns, feminines in *-ti- and masculines in *-tu-, had proterokinetic inflection; caseforms of both developed into infinitives in various daughter languages. Typical examples include *g^{w}ém-ti-s ~ *g^{w}m̥-téy- 'step' (Skt *gátis*, Gk βάσις; cf. Lat. *con-venti-ō*, Goth. *ga-qumþ-s* 'assembly', lit. 'coming together'); *mér-ti-s ~ *mr̥-téy- 'death' (Lat. *mors*, *morti-*, Lith. *mirtìs*); *pér-tu-s ~ *pr̥-téw- 'crossing' (Av. *pərətuš*; Lat. *portus* 'port', PGmc *ferþuz 'fjord' and *furduz 'ford'). Additional examples have been cited in 2.3.4 (ii).

Neuter nouns denoting instruments were formed with four similar suffixes, *-tro-, *-tlo-, *-d^hro-, and *-d^hlo-; the root seems usually to have been accented and e-grade. Typical examples include *$h_2$ár$h_3$trom 'plow' (Gk ἄροτρον, OIr. *arathar*); *póh$_3$tlom 'drinking-cup' (Lat. *pōculum*); *kréyd^hrom 'sieve' (Lat. *crībrum*); *syúHd^hlom 'awl' (OCS *šilo*; the collective appears in Lat. *sūbula*).

Masculine agent nouns were made with a suffix *-ter-; both amphikinetic and hysterokinetic inflection seem to be reconstructable, though the accent and ablaut relations have become confused in the daughters. An example of the former is *ǵénh_1tōr 'parent' (Gk γενέτωρ, Lat. *genitor*); the latter underlies such examples as Gk δοτήρ 'giver'.

Abstract nouns were derived from adjectives with a variety of suffixes. There was a large group in *-tah$_2$, e.g. *h$_2$yuHn̥táh$_2$ 'youth' (Lat. *iuventa*, Goth. *junda*). At least some of these nouns made to o-stem adjectives ended in *-étah$_2$; cf. e.g. Skt *nagnátā* 'nakedness' (to *nagnás* 'naked') and Goth. *hauhiþa* 'height' (to *hauhs* 'high'). Also well attested is a suffix *-tāt- (*-tah$_2$t-?), e.g. in *néwotāt-s 'newness' (Lat. *novitās*; Gk νεότης 'youth').

2.4.2 (ii) PIE adjective-forming suffixes

An extensive derivational system called the Caland system (after the Sanskritist who first noticed some of the connections) can be reconstructed for PIE. At the center of the Caland system were proterokinetic adjectives in *-u-, isofunctional thematic adjectives in *-ró- with zero-grade roots, and adjective stems in *-i- (likewise with zero-grade roots) that appear in compounds. (The system also included, for example, neuter s-stem action nouns (see 2.4.2 (i)) and derived statives/fientives (see 2.3.3 (i)).) Occasionally a complete set of such adjectives can be reconstructed for PIE. For instance, *h$_2$r̥ǵ-ró-s 'white' survives in Vedic Skt *r̥jrás* 'shining, swift' and Homeric Gk ἀργός 'bright'; the synonymous u-stem *h$_2$árǵ-u- ~ *h$_2$r̥ǵ-éw- is attested in Toch. B *ārkwi*; and the compounding stem *h$_2$r̥ǵi- appears in Homeric Gk pl. ἀργίποδες 'swift-footed' (lit. *'sparklingfoots') and Skt *r̥jipyás* 'eagle' (lit. *'white-backed'; the second element is the zero grade of *op- 'back', cf. Aischylos *Agamemnon* 115).[69] (The i-stem may not originally have been confined to compounds, to judge from Hitt. *harkis* 'white'.) For 'deep' we are likewise able to reconstruct both PIE *d^{h}ubrós (cf. Toch. B *tapre* 'high') and *d^{h}éwbus ~ *d^{h}ubéw- (cf. Lith. *dubùs* 'hollow'; apparently transferred into the thematic class in PGmc *deupaz 'deep'). More often one member of a Caland word-family survives especially well; for instance, there are widespread reflexes of *h$_1$rud^{h}rós 'red' (Gk ἐρυθρός, Lat. *ruber*, late Church Slavonic *rŭdrŭ*, Toch. B *ratre*) and of *g^{w}ráh$_2$u-s ~ *g^{w}r̥h$_2$áw- 'heavy' (Skt *gurús*, Gk βαρύς, Lat. *gravis*, Goth. *kaúrus*).

The Caland system was a system of 'primary' derivation, operating on roots. The most important PIE 'secondary' adjective suffix, forming adjectives from nouns, was thematic *-yó-. The thematic vowel of an underlying noun was zeroed before this suffix. For instance, from *kóros 'cutting, section, division' (OPers. *kāra* 'people, army'; Lith. *kãras* 'war') was formed *kóryos 'detached', substantivized in the northern languages to mean 'detachment, war party' (Lith. *kãrias*, PGmc *harjaz 'army'; OIr. *cuire* 'company, host'); from *h$_2$áǵros 'meadow, field' (Skt *ájras*, Gk ἀγρός, Lat. *ager*, PGmc *akraz) was formed *h$_2$áǵrios 'characteristic of meadows/fields' (Skt *ajryás*; Gk ἄγριος 'wild'); and so on. Otherwise the suffix was simply added to the noun stem, e.g. *diwyós 'heavenly' (Skt *divyás*,

69 That PIE *op- ~ *ep- might have meant '(animal's) back' was suggested to me by Warren Cowgill ca. 1980.

Homeric Gk δῖος) from *dyew- 'sky', *ph$_2$triós 'fatherly' (Skt *pítryas*, Gk πάτριος, Lat. *patrius*) from *ph$_2$ter- 'father', etc.

Verbal adjectives with zero-grade roots were derived by means of the thematic suffixes *-tó-, *-nó-, and *-wó-. The last of these seems to have been rare, though an example which survived very widely was *g^{w}ih$_3$wós 'alive' (Skt *jīvás*, Lat. *vīvos*, PGmc *k^{w}ik^{w}az, etc.). By contrast, *-tó- became the suffix of perfect participles in Latin, and both *-tó- and *-nó- acquired a similar function in Indo-Iranian, Balto-Slavic, and Germanic.

There seems to have been a system of contrastive adjective suffixes in PIE. Adjectives in *-ero- apparently meant 'X (as opposed to its antonym)'; those in *-mo- or *-m̥o- meant 'X (as opposed to everything else)'. Typical examples are *éperos 'behind' (Skt *áparas*; neut. in OIr. prep. *íar* 'after') and *pr̥Hmós 'furthest forward' (Lith. *pìrmas*; remodeled in PGmc *frumō 'first'). There were also forms of these suffixes extended with *-t-, namely *-tero-, e.g. in *énteros 'inside' (Skt *ántaras*; Lat. comparative *interior* 'further in'), and *-tm̥o-, e.g. in *éntm̥os 'inmost' (Skt *ántamas*, Lat. *intimus*).

There was an important class of athematic adjectives in *-went- meaning 'having X' (where X is the noun to which the suffix was added); cf. e.g. Skt *putrá-vant-* 'having sons' (*putrá-s* 'son'), Gk χαρί-εντ- 'graceful, lovely' (χάρι-ς 'grace, loveliness'). This class is well represented in Anatolian, Indo-Iranian, Greek, and Tocharian (a distribution which guarantees its antiquity, even though specific examples are hard to reconstruct).

Finally, it is clear that two formally similar but functionally distinct suffixes have been important in the development of the daughter languages. One, apparently underlyingly */-en-/, was used to 'individualize' adjectives; it appears in Latin cognomina (originally nicknames) such as *Catō* 'the Shrewd' (*catus* 'shrewd'). The other, underlyingly */-Hen-/, had a function similar to *-went- (see the preceding paragraph); it is well represented in Indo-Iranian (Hoffmann 1955) and appears in Latin cognomina such as *Nāsō* 'Bignose' (*'having a nose'; cf. *nāsus* 'nose').

2.4.2 (iii) Derivational suffixes that eventually became inflectional

Several PIE derivational suffixes were integrated into the inflectional system in numerous daughter languages. By far the most important were the collective suffix *-h$_2$- (see 2.3.4 (i) *ad fin.*) and the feminine suffixes *-h$_2$-, which formed feminines in *-ah$_2$- from o-stems, and *´-ih$_2$- ~ *-yáh$_2$-, which formed feminines from athematic stems and induced proterokinetic inflection. Numerous examples of fem. *-ah$_2$- can be found among the adjectives of all the more archaic non-Anatolian languages; *-ih$_2$- ~ *-yáh$_2$- survives robustly in Greek, Indo-Iranian, Balto-Slavic, and Germanic, always with some innovations. For examples, see 2.3.5.

In Core IE, at the latest, there was an elative suffix *-yos- ~ *-is- deriving adjectives that meant something like 'exceptionally X', where X was the meaning of the basic adjective. This suffix apparently induced amphikinetic inflection; for example, from *$h_1$wér-u-s ~ *$h_1$ur-éw- 'broad' (Skt *urú́s*, Gk εὐρύς, both with zero grade of the root generalized) was constructed *$h_1$wér-yos- ~ *$h_1$ur-is- 'unusually broad' (Skt *várīyas*- 'broader'). Note that the suffix was added directly to the root; evidently it was part of the Caland system. In all the daughters in which this suffix survives it has become a comparative suffix. Superlatives were subsequently formed from it, in *-is-m̥o- in Italic and Celtic, but in *-is-to- in the other daughters (cf. Skt *váriṣṭʰas* 'broadest').

2.5 PIE syntax

By now it is clear that the syntax of a natural human language is an autonomous system of rules not derived from the language's inflectional morphology.[70] It follows that the Classical tradition, which treats syntax as the interface between inflection and 'meaning', is fundamentally misconceived. In this section I will use a generalized transformational framework which I hope will be familiar from basic introductions to syntax.[71]

Unfortunately the reconstruction of autonomous syntax is very difficult. The best discussion of the reasons for that disappointing state of affairs is Walkden (2014: 47–64), to which the interested reader is referred. Here I will outline the scholarly consensus about the syntax of PIE; it is fragmentary, but a good deal better than nothing. A similar outline, with examples, can be found in Fortson (2010: 152–68); Clackson (2007: 157–86) offers a discussion of selected topics in greater depth, also with examples.

[70] This is easy to demonstrate. For instance, modern standard German, like some other languages, has 'dummy subjects' whose semantic content is zero, e.g.

> *Es* regnet heute. 'It's raining today.' (cf. French: *Il* pleut aujourd'hui.)
> *Es* gibt keine Ausnahmen. 'There are no exceptions.' (cf. French: *Il* n'y a pas d'exceptions.)

We know that they are subjects because when some other constituent is fronted in a main clause the dummy subject appears after the verb:

> Heute regnet *es*.
> Keine Ausnahmen gibt *es*.

But German also has dummy topics, e.g.:

> *Es* wird hier getanzt. 'There's dancing here.' (Literally: 'It is danced here.')

Dummy topics do not appear after the verb:

> Hier wird getanzt.

Either phenomenon is a good argument for autonomous syntax; to differentiate between the two a theory of autonomous syntax is absolutely necessary.

[71] For an introduction to the latest version of generative syntax, 'Minimalism', see e.g. Radford (2004). For current purposes any version since about 1980 will be adequate; a good introduction to the earliest version of generative syntax that can handle all relevant phenomena is Haegeman (1991).

Kiparsky (1995) suggested that, since neither Hittite nor Vedic Sanskrit seems to possess an obvious complementizer,[72] no CP-projection can be reconstructed for PIE. But since it has become clear that phrase structures cannot be projected from lexemes, even from 'functional heads' (as was supposed in the late 1980s), the reconstruction of a CP does not depend on the reconstruction of a particular complementizer (cf. Newton 2005: 97).[73] In fact it is difficult to see what projection in a subordinate clause Old Hittite *takku* 'if' or *mān* 'when' can occupy if it is not Comp (see Hoffner and Melchert 2008: 414–29 for the facts), and the same can be said of Rigvedic *yát* 'if, when'. The same position (which Kiparsky calls 'Focus') is apparently the landing site for WH-elements in most early IE languages: Mark Hale demonstrated that fully 90% of Vedic interrogative and relative pronouns occur clause-initially, and that virtually all of the remaining examples occur immediately following a single constituent that has been topicalized (Hale 1987: 8–24). For instance, in the Vedic clause:

brahmā́ kó vaḥ saparyati? 'Which priest honors you (pl.)?' (*RV* VIII.7.20c, cited by Hale 1987: 10).

the interrogative *kó* 'which?' has been moved into clause-initial CP, and the noun *brahmā́* 'priest' is still further to the left because it is topicalized. It seems clear that we must reconstruct a CP for PIE, optionally dominated by at least a 'Topic Phrase' into which a topic can be moved, so that the topic normally precedes everything else. Whether we can be more specific is not so clear. For one thing, the system might have been more complex, with multiple focus positions (see especially the discussion of Newton 2005: 97–100); for another, it now appears that in Hittite interrogatives, at least, can occupy more than one focus position in the clause (see Goedegebuure 2009), and it is possible that the same was true of PIE. It also appears that both adjoined and embedded relative clauses were present in Old Hittite (see Probert 2006b); the implications of that fact for the reconstruction of PIE syntax are not clear.

It is of course not surprising that topics have been moved to the leftmost position in the clause in ancient IE languages (and almost certainly were in PIE as well), but the position of the Comp node to the left is interesting because it contrasts with the 'headedness' of the rest of the clause. In Hittite, both Tocharian languages, and Vedic prose the unmarked word order of the verb phrase (i.e. the lexical verb and its objects) and of the 'inflection'-phrase is head-final; the basic schema is Comp–S–O–V–T, where T ('Tense') marks the position of the finite verb and V

[72] Hitt. *kuit* is actually used as a complementizer, though there seem to be no Old Hittite examples (Hoffner and Melchert 2008: 414, 426).

[73] In fact this is true under any assumptions about phrase structure, since the recorded history of languages shows that complementizers replace one another fairly frequently with no impact on the structures that host them.

the position of non-finite members of the verb phrase (if any). Typical examples include the following:[74]

Hittite:
n=us LUGAL-*us* … $^{\text{LÚ.MEŠ}}$APIN.LÁ *iyanun.*
ptcl=them-ACC king-NOM … farmers make-PAST-1SG
'I, the king, made them farmers.' (cited in Hoffner and Melchert 2008: 247)

Tocharian B:
$k_u$ce tu pwārntse yarke yamaṣṣeñcañ ṣeyeṃ, tu
what that fire-GEN reverence do-PRES-PTC-NOMPL be-IPF-3PL that
yparwe tuwak kottarcce pelaikne ākṣtsi
at-first that-EMPH family-ADJ-OBL law teach-INF
añmassu kakā-me weñā-meś:
desirous call-PRET-3SG-them say-PRET-3SG-them-ALL
'In as much as they had been doing reverence to fire, he therefore, desiring to teach them this, the family law, called them and said to them:'[75] (Berlin 108b9)

Vedic prose:
téna‿ asmíṃl loké d^hṛtáḥ purástāt prā́yaṇaṃ
that-INST this-LOC world-LOC held-NOM east-from approach-ACC
kuryāt.
make-AOR-OPT-3SG
'For that reason, firmly established in this world, let him make the approach from the east.' (*Maitrāyaṇī-Saṃhitā* 3.6.1)

The same is true of the ostentatiously straightforward Latin of Julius Caesar's *Bellum Gallicum*; by a statistical analysis of double-object clauses Ann Taylor has demonstrated that Homeric Greek was underlyingly verb-final (Taylor 1990: 91–5), and Fortson notes that traditional sayings in Homer, like those of Vedic, are normally verb-final (Fortson 2010: 156–7). It seems clear that the underlying word order of clauses that we must reconstruct for PIE is the one given above.

Surface word order was clearly much more variable, however.[76] We would expect it to have been possible to extrapose heavy constituents to the right, beyond the tensed verb, so as to avoid the parsing problems posed by center embedding; 'dislocation' to the left would also be unsurprising. (See Hoffner and Melchert 2008: 406–9 for Hittite examples of these processes and Fortson 2010: 159–61 for general discussion.) But in addition conservative daughters of PIE exhibit one or

[74] The word-for-word translations employ the Leipzig Glossing Rules (https://www.eva.mpg.de/lingua/pdf/Glossing-Rules.pdf).

[75] The object pronouns attached to the verbs are clitics which do not 'count' as separate phonological words.

[76] I am grateful to Joseph Eska for helpful discussion of this paragraph and for several references.

more 'scrambling' rules, by which constituents of the sentence can be reordered for pragmatic reasons. The result can be an unusual permutation of words even in straightforward prose, e.g. in Cicero's letters:

Ad eōrum	*voluntātem*	*mihī*	*conciliandam*		
to their	will-ACC	me-DAT	win-over-PASS-FUT-PTC-FEM-ACC		
maximō	*mihī*	*tē*	*ūsuī*	*fore*	*videō.*
great-SUP-MASC-DAT	me-DAT	you-ACC	utility-DAT	be-FUT-INF	see-1SG

'I see that you will be of the greatest utility to me for winning their good will for me.' (Cicero, to Atticus 1.2)

in which *maximō* 'greatest', which modifies *ūsuī* 'utility', has been fronted to a position immediately after the participial embedded clause. It is very likely that such rules existed in PIE as well. Ancient Greek exhibits even more extreme movement, routinely separating the constituents of noun phrases and apparently moving sequences that are not constituents even in straightforward prose. Agbayani and Golston (2010) demonstrate that such 'hyperbaton' cannot be syntactic in nature and make a strong argument that it is phonological. Whether similar movement processes operated in PIE is not clear.

The internal word order of noun phrases in PIE was probably also head-final. Tocharian noun phrases are almost as relentlessly head-final as clauses; Clackson (2007: 166) points out that the fossilization of PIE *déms pótis 'head of household', with the genitive preceding the head noun, as δεσπότης in Greek (and of a similar phrase in Lith. *viẽšpats*) likewise suggests underlyingly head-final noun phrases in the protolanguage. But the daughters diverge to a significant degree, and more work on the order of elements in noun phrases will certainly be needed.

Case is assigned to noun phrases in at least three ways in conservative daughters, and the PIE system must have been much the same. 'Structural' case assignment depended on the syntactic environment of the noun phrase. Thus subjects of finite verbs were assigned nominative case; direct objects of verbs were assigned accusative case by their governing verbs in the default instance (see further below); noun phrase complements of noun phrases were assigned genitive case by government by N; and the indirect object of verbs like 'give' was probably assigned dative case structurally (whatever the structure of those verb phrases may have been). It is likely that some verbs assigned case to their objects by lexical rather than structural government; for instance, since verbs meaning 'remember' take genitive objects in many daughter languages, there is a reasonable probability that at least one such verb did so in PIE as well. Adjectives may also have assigned case lexically to the complements of their adjective phrases. Whether PIE possessed adpositions is debated (see below), but if it did, they must have assigned case to their objects. Finally, it seems clear that in many instances case was assigned semantically (i.e. expressed a particular meaning directly). Number and case clearly 'percolated' from a DP node to all constituents of the noun phrase not dominated by intermediate DP nodes; thus adjectives and determiners in a noun phrase, for example, were marked with the same number and case as the head noun. Adjectives, determiners, and most quantifiers modifying a noun exhibited gender concord with the noun. In addition, concord of number and gender obtained under coreference.

One peculiar detail of case assignment seems to be an instance of 'conjunction reduction'. In Vedic a pair of conjoined vocatives is normally replaced by a vocative and a nominative; the paradigm example is *Vā́yav Índraś ca* 'O Vayu and Indra'. Since there is also one Greek example in Homer, Ζεῦ πάτερ ... Ἠέλιός τε 'O Zeus and Helios' (*Il.* 3.277), it seems clear that this construction was inherited at least from Central IE (Fortson 2010: 156); it apparently shows that the nominative was the default case.

Typical of all the more archaic languages are 'absolute' constructions, in which a noun phrase and a participle in an oblique case are the equivalent of a subordinate clause; a stereotyped Latin example is the ablative absolute *hīs rēbus gestīs*, literally 'with these things done', meaning 'when these things had been done'. The attested languages that have undergone relatively little merger of cases use different cases in this way: the ablative in Latin, the locative in Sanskrit, the dative in Old Church Slavonic. It seems likely that PIE used several cases, with different meanings or implications, in absolute constructions.

Whether PIE possessed adpositions has sometimes been questioned. If some of the oblique case endings ultimately reflect adverbs (see 2.3.4 (i)), it is almost certain that the adverbs had first become postpositions, since that is the usual intermediate stage between adverb and inflectional ending (as Patrick Stiles reminds me). The extensive set of adverbs which were used with the oblique cases (Brugmann 1911: 758–930) could have been modifiers of DPs which were assigned case directly, but it seems at least as likely that they were adpositions. Among Anatolianists there appears to be a consensus that some Hittite local adverbs preceded by nouns in some cases are actual postpositions, but there are also areas of disagreement (see Hoffner and Melchert 2008: 297–301, with references p. 294, and Melchert 2009). The situation in Vedic Sanskrit appears to be similar. It seems clear that in all daughters at least some inherited adverbs eventually developed into genuine adpositions. In the Tocharian languages a number of postpositions have become case-marking clitics (the 'secondary' case system), typically appended to entire phrases ('Gruppenflexion'); there are also independent postpositions and a few prepositions. If any adverbs had become adpositions already in PIE, or even in Core IE, they are much more likely to have been postpositions than prepositions; that is in line with the overall head-final syntax of the language and the direct testimony of Hittite and Tocharian. The fact that some case endings appear originally to have been postpositions (see 2.3.4 (i)) points in the same direction.

Many of the same adverbs that eventually became adpositions also appear as particles in verb-plus-particle constructions in the more conservative IE languages. Eventually the particles became lexical prefixes in all the daughters (a process called 'univerbation'), but that was clearly an independent development, since it is still incomplete in Hittite, Vedic, and Homeric Greek. Even the creation of verb-plus-particle lexemes in the first place might have been a parallel development, since it was repeated much later—and independently—in German and English (German verbs with 'separable prefixes' and English constructions of the type *get up*).

Though there were no comparative or superlative forms of adjectives in PIE nor (probably) in Core IE, there must have been a syntactic construction expressing comparison. One might expect the standard of comparison to have been in the ablative, as in Vedic and Latin, but Hittite uses the dative-locative instead (Hoffner and Melchert 2008: 273–6).

Whether PIE had reflexive pronouns is unclear—it seems possible that mediopassive forms of transitive verbs were the only way to express reflexive objects—but Core IE clearly did. To judge from the situation in the attested daughters, binding of reflexive pronouns at that stage occurred only within the clause.

There was concord of person and number (but not gender) between a finite verb and its subject. It seems clear that PIE was a 'null subject' language, like all its earliest attested daughters (and many later descendants, such as modern Spanish); probably unstressed direct and indirect objects could also be null on the surface, as in Hittite (Hoffner and Melchert 2008: 277) and Gothic (Walkden 2014: 164).

Mediopassive forms of transitive verbs were also used in passive clauses, as in Hittite, Tocharian, Vedic, Greek, Latin, etc. It is likely that this was an innovation in PIE, the inherited middle, which was originally reflexive, being used also to express the passive (a process that repeated itself, with other morphological means, much later in Romance and Slavic). The agent of a passive clause was probably in the instrumental case, as argued in Jamison (1979) and Melchert (2016), since that is usual in Vedic Sanskrit and apparently also in Old Hittite (Hoffner and Melchert 2008: 269).

In all the most archaic daughters the present indicative of 'be' can be omitted, resulting in clauses with no overt verb. These are sometimes called 'nominal' clauses. For examples from several languages, see Fortson (2010: 158).

A striking feature of PIE syntax was clitic floating, traditionally called 'Wackernagel's Law', by which clitics, including clitic pronouns, moved to a position immediately to the right of the first constituent in the clause. Recent work on archaic IE languages has shown that more than one movement process is involved, and in fact more than one landing site can be identified structurally; see especially Hale (1987) and Taylor (1990) for extended discussion, and Fortson (2010: 161–3) for a brief summary with examples. Hittite, Vedic, and Ancient Greek preserve Wackernagel's Law particularly well, though it is also observable to some extent in other early-attested daughters.

2.6 The PIE lexicon

In addition to the derivational types discussed in earlier sections of this chapter, at least several hundred underived PIE lexemes can be reconstructed. Unfortunately there is no good, up-to-date comparative dictionary of PIE. Pokorny (1959) is badly out of date; moreover, it errs extravagantly on the side of inclusion, listing every word known to the author that might conceivably reflect a PIE lexeme if one's etymological standards are not too strict. Rix et al. (2001) is a great improvement, but it covers only non-derived verbs; moreover, the authors persist in listing items that are attested in only one daughter, so that a non-specialist must read through the volume to get an accurate idea of what is securely reconstructable for PIE. Wodtko et al. (2008) is comprehensive for what it covers, but it includes only a selection of PIE nouns (admittedly a large and interesting selection). Under the circumstances it is still advisable to consult the best etymological dictionaries of the more archaic daughters as well.

Reconstruction of the PIE lexicon can tell us a good deal about the culture of the protolanguage's speakers; Fortson (2010: 16–47) provides a good introduction. The most difficult problem is assessing the gaps that we inevitably find. For instance, it comes as no surprise that there was no PIE word for 'iron', since there are numerous indications that PIE was spoken before the Iron Age. But what about the fact that there is also no reconstructable word for 'finger'? Obviously speakers of the language had fingers, and they must have had a word for them; the fact that we cannot reconstruct it can only be the result of its loss in all the major subgroups (or all but one). The hard fact is that linguistic evidence relentlessly degrades and disappears over time, and that imposes an inexorable limit on what can be reconstructed.

3
The phonological development of Proto-Greek

3.1 Introduction

This chapter describes in detail the regular sound changes that occurred in the development of Greek roughly down to the time when the attested Greek dialects began to diverge from one another. I say 'roughly' because that time is somewhat indeterminate in two different ways. In terms of real time, we know that the attested Greek dialects had begun to diverge somewhat earlier than the late Mycenaean period when the Linear B documents were written (the 14th and 13th centuries BC), because the dialect of those documents exhibits innovations not shared by some other Greek dialects; but we do not know exactly how much earlier that divergence had begun. In terms of the chronology of changes, it is not always easy to distinguish between changes which occurred before the dialects had begun to diverge significantly, and are therefore shared by all the dialects, and changes which occurred later in one dialect and spread to all the rest, or even occurred independently in already diversified dialects. I will comment on difficult cases as we encounter them.

I group the sound changes in sets, arranged partly thematically and partly chronologically, and I will discuss the chronological relationships of each sound change to others, to the extent that they can be recovered.

3.2 The elimination of laryngeals

The sound changes which eliminated the 'laryngeal' consonants appear to have occurred early in the prehistory of Greek; no sound change can be shown to have occurred earlier. In some positions the laryngeals were lost; in others they are reflected by vowels, or by vowel length. But Greek, unlike most daughters of PIE, preserved the original distinction between the three laryngeals in most positions, because they gave rise to different Greek vowels. Exactly what happened depended on what sounds were adjacent to the laryngeals.

The Linguistic Roots of Ancient Greek. Don Ringe, Oxford University Press.
 DOI: 10.1093/9780191989162.003.0003

3.2.1 The loss of laryngeals next to non-high vowels

When followed immediately by non-high vowels in the same syllable, laryngeals were lost; the allophones of PIE */e/ which the laryngeals had induced (*[a] next to *h_2, *[o] next to *h_3) thereby became fully contrastive. Since the same change occurred in most daughters, it is often difficult to determine whether or not a particular word had a laryngeal in it in PIE (especially in the case of *h_1). The following examples, some with laryngeals and some without, seem reasonably certain:

PIE *$h_1$esti '(s)he is' (Lat. *est*; for the laryngeal cf. Skt *ā́sat-* 'not existing' < *ṇ̥́-h_1s-ṇ̥t-) > ἐστι;
PIE *$h_1$ed- 'eat' (Lat. *edere*; for the laryngeal cf. 'tooth' in 3.2.4) > Hom. inf. ἔδμεναι;
PIE *én 'in', deriv. *éndom 'inside' (Old Lat. *en* > Lat. *in*, Hitt. *andan*; no laryngeal in Vedic Skt *jm-án* 'on the earth'[1]) > ἐν, ἔνδον
PIE *op- ~ *ep- 'back' (Hitt. *āppa* 'back, again', *āppan* 'behind, after'; cf. Skt *ṛjipyás* 'eagle' < *h_2ṛ̥ǵi-p-yó-s 'white-back' with no evidence of laryngeal) > ἐπί, Myc. *o-pi* 'on' (orig. locative *'on the back of');
PIE *$h_2$ánti → *$h_2$antí 'on the surface (lit. 'forehead'), in front of' (Hitt. *hānz* 'in front' and remodeled *hantī* 'apart'; Lat. *ante* 'in front of') > ἀντί 'instead of';
PIE *h_2áǵeti '(s)he is leading/driving', deriv. *h_2óǵmos 'path of driving' (Skt *ájati*, Lat. *agit*, both '(s)he drives') > ἄγει '(s)he is leading', ὄγμος 'furrow';
PIE *$h_2$ank- 'to bend', derivs. (s-stem) *$h_2$ánkos and (o-stem) *$h_2$ónkos '(a) bend' (Skt *áñcati* 'it curves', s-stem *áṅkas* '(a) curve'; Lat. o-stem *uncus* 'hook') > ἀγκύλος 'bent, crooked', ἄγκος 'glen', ὄγκος 'barb';
PIE *átta 'dad' (Lat. *atta*, respectful form of address for old men; cf. Hitt. *attas* 'father') > Hom. ἄττα 'Sir, Father';
PIE *ályos 'other' (Lydian *αλα-*, Lat. *alius*) > ἄλλος;
PIE *$h_2$ówis ~ *$h_2$áwi- 'sheep' (Kimball 1987: 189; Lycian acc. sg. *xawã*, Toch. B *$ā_u$* 'ewe' (Kim 2000b), Skt *ávis*, Lat. *ovis*) > Hom. ὄϊς;
PIE *$h_2$óst ~ *$h_2$ást- 'bone', extended *$h_2$ostey- (Hitt. *hastai*, Lat. *os*, cf. Welsh *asgwrn*) > ὀστέον > Att. ὀστõν;
PIE *$h_3$ósdos 'branch' (Goth. *asts*, cf. Hitt. *hasduēr* 'twigs, brush') > ὄζος;
PIE *$h_3$órō, *$h_3$óron- ~*h_3ṛ̥n- 'eagle' (Hitt. *hāras*, *hāran-*) in deriv. ὄρνῑς 'bird';
PIE *órsos 'arse' (Hitt. *ārras*, OE *ears*) > Att. ὄρρος;
PIE *ǵénh$_1$os, gen. *ǵénh$_1$esos 'lineage' (Skt *jánas*, *jánasas*, Lat. *genus*, *generis*; for the laryngeal cf. 'parent' below and in 3.2.4) > γένος, γένεος > Att. γένος, γένōς;

[1] I am grateful to Michael Weiss for alerting me to this form.

PIE *h_2ḱ-$h_2$ows-iéti '(s)he is sharp-eared' (Goth. *hauseiþ*, OE *hīerþ*, both '(s)he hears') > ἀκούει '(s)he hears';

PIE *somHós 'same' (Skt *samás*, with the first *a* not lengthened by Brugmann's Law) > ὁμός.

One example suggests that not all laryngeals in this position were lost without a trace. It seems clear that the 2sg. ending of the perfect indicative was *-th_2a, unambiguously attested in Skt *vétt^{h}a* 'you know' < *wóydsth_2a because only the second laryngeal aspirates a preceding voiceless stop in Sanskrit. The corresponding Greek form is οἶσθα, likewise with aspiration of the inherited *t. Since this form is an isolated relic, it is difficult to maintain that it does not reflect regular sound change. But though other surviving sequences of voiceless stop plus *h_2 are rare in Greek, the few that can be found do not exhibit aspiration of the stop; for instance, to Skt *pr̥t^{h}ús* 'broad' corresponds Gk πλατύς, with τ rather than θ, and ἀκούε̄ν 'to hear' (see above) likewise exhibits no aspiration. It is conceivable that the ending was remodeled on imperative 2sg. -θι, but there is no positive reason to think so. The θ of 'you know' is an unsolved problem.

Laryngeals immediately preceded by a non-high vowel in the same syllable were likewise lost, and the laryngeal-induced allophones of */e/ likewise became fully contrastive, but in these cases the vowel was also lengthened (if it was not already long). These new long vowels merged with the inherited non-high long vowels. The following examples, some with laryngeals and some without, are typical:[2]

PIE *d^{h}éd^{h}e$h_1$ti '(s)he is putting', deriv. *d^{h}ó$h_1$mos 'thing put' (Skt *dád^{h}āti*; Goth. *doms* 'reputation', OE *dōm* 'judgment') >→ τίθητι > τίθησι, θωμός 'heap';

PIE *snéh$_1$yeti 'she is spinning' (Skt *snā́yati* '(s)he wraps', OIr. *sniïd* '(s)he twists') > *snḗyeti > νῆι;

PIE *$h_1$ger- 'wake up', pf. *$h_1$ge$h_1$góre '(s)he is awake' (Skt *jāgā́ra*) > ἐγερ-, *ἐγήγορε → ἐγρήγορε (Warren Cowgill, p.c. ca. 1978; *LIV* s.v. **$h_1$ger*);

PIE *h_2wḗ$h_1$ti '(wind) blows' (Skt *vā́ti*) > *ἄϝητι > Hom. ἄησι;

PIE *ph_2tḗr 'father' (Skt *pitā́*, Lat. *pater*) > πατήρ;

PIE *Hyḗk^{w}r̥ ~ *Hyék^{w}n- 'liver' (Skt *yákr̥t*, Lat. *iecur* with full grade generalized) > ἧπαρ;

PIE *sēmi- 'half-' (Lat. *sēmi-*; probably a vr̥ddhi derivative of *sem- 'one') > ἡμι-;

[2] For the most part, examples with laryngeals and those without have to be distinguished inferentially. Roots with apparently final long vowels, and words derived from them, must contain a laryngeal because PIE roots had to end in a consonant. Inherited long vowels appear in acrostatic nominals and vr̥ddhi derivatives (see 2.2.4 (i)) and in forms affected by Szemerényi's Law (see 2.2.4 (iv)). Possible Greek examples of inherited *ā with external cognates are all more or less uncertain.

PIE *stáh$_2$t '(s)he stood up' (Skt *ást^{h}āt* with the 'augment' prefix) > ἔστᾱ (also with augment) > Att.-Ion. ἔστη;
PIE *b^{h}ah$_2$ti 'it shines, it illuminates' (Skt *b^{h}āti*) → '(s)he makes clear' → '(s)he says' (cf. Lat. *fātur*) > φᾱτι > Att.-Ion. φησι; post-PIE deriv. *b^{h}oh$_2$náh$_2$ 'voice' (cf. Beekes 1972: 129) > φωνᾱ́ > Att.-Ion. φωνή;
PIE *swáh$_2$dus 'pleasant, sweet' (Skt *svādúṣ*) > ᾁδύς > Att.-Ion. ἡδύς;
PIE *b^{h}āǵ^{h}us 'arm' (*-ah$_2$-?; Skt *bāhúṣ*) > πᾶχυς 'forearm' > Att.-Ion. πῆχυς;
post-PIE *ā́mr̥ 'day' (cf. Arm. *awr* < collective *ā́mōr) > ἆμαρ > Hom. ἦμαρ;
PIE aor. *ǵnóh$_3$t '(s)he recognized' (cf. Lat. *nōvit* '(s)he knows', with the meaning of the perfect) > ἔγνω (with augment);
PIE *dédoh$_3$ti '(s)he is giving' (Skt *dádāti*) >→ δίδωτι > δίδωσι;
PIE *h$_2$áḱmō 'stone' (Skt *áśmā*, Lith. *akmuõ*) >→ ἄκμων 'anvil';
PIE *ǵénh$_1$tōr 'begetter, parent' (Lat. *genitor*) > γενέτωρ.

Note also:

PIE *h$_1$lud^{h}éd '(s)he arrived' (Toch. B *lac* '(s)he went out', OIr. *luid* '(s)he went'), with augment *é h$_1$lud^{h}ed > Hom. ἤλυθε '(s)he came'.

This loss of laryngeals with compensatory lengthening probably preceded the operation of Osthoff's Law; see 3.5.3 for further discussion.

When a laryngeal was lost between two non-high vowels, the vowels thereby brought into hiatus contracted. The clearest examples involve inflectional endings:

PIE gen. pl. *-óHom (where *H ≠ *h$_2$; Old Hitt. *-an*, Skt *-ām* (often scanned as two syllables in the Rigveda), Lith. *-ų̃*, PGmc trimoric *-ǭ̂ > Goth. (fem.) *-o*, OE *-a*) > -ῶν;
PIE ah$_2$-stem dat. sg. *-ah$_2$-ay (Goth. *-ai*) > -ᾱι > Att.-Ion. -ηι.

Note that in the former example the contraction product is a lower mid vowel. There is also at least one example of contraction of vowels in hiatus with no intervening laryngeal:

PIE o-stem dat. sg. *-o-ey (Av. *-āi*) > -ωι.

It can be seen that the result is likewise a lower mid vowel. Contraction of the augment prefix with a following laryngeal-plus-vowel sequence likewise yielded low and lower mid vowels, e.g.:

PIE *é h$_1$est 'it is said that (s)he was' (Skt *ā́s* '(s)he was') > Dor. ἧς '(s)he was';
PIE *é h$_2$aǵed 'it is said that (s)he was leading/driving' (Skt *ā́jat* '(s)he drove') > ἆγε '(s)he was leading' > Att.-Ion. ἦγε.

That shows that the contraction was early, since much later contractions yield higher mid vowels (see 7.2.3); but it is not clear that any further conclusions can be drawn, since the result might have been the same whether or not the laryngeals were still in place when the augment was univerbated with the following verb form.

When a laryngeal between a non-high vowel and a high vowel was lost, contraction likewise occurred:

post-PIE *pléh$_1$-isto- 'fullest' (root *pleh$_1$- 'fill', cf. πλήρης 'full', Lat. *implēre* 'to fill', etc.) > πλεῖστος 'most' (Cowgill 1965: 147);
PIE *stah$_2$urós 'stake, pale' (ON *staurr*) > σταυρός.

Though the formation of the latter word is not especially clear, the root must be *stah$_2$- 'stand', and the Gmc diphthong can only reflect PIE *V(H)u. It is highly likely that *h$_2$ was lost between *o and *i in the word for 'shepherd':

PIE *poh$_2$imḗn 'shepherd' (Lith. *piemuõ*; cf. PGmc deriv. *faimnijōn- 'girl' in OE *fǣmne*) > ποιμήν;

the only grounds for caution are the facts that an extended root *pah$_2$i- 'protect' is otherwise sparsely attested and the o-grade (as opposed to zero grade) in the root of a hysterokinetic noun is unexpected.

It is difficult to find indisputable examples of laryngeals between a non-high vowel and a syllabic sonorant (in that order). Developments of laryngeals between a high vowel or syllabic sonorant and a non-high vowel will be dealt with below.

In one environment the losses of laryngeals next to non-high vowels gave rise to a Greek rule of word formation. The first members of compounds were frequently stems ending in the thematic vowel */-e-/; if the second member began with a laryngeal, or with a sequence of laryngeal plus non-high vowel, loss of the laryngeal yielded a long non-high vowel either by compensatory lengthening or by contraction of the vowels now in hiatus. Inherited examples do not seem to be recoverable, but the process is still clear from some of the Homeric examples. For instance:

κρατερός 'powerful' ends in the thematic vowel; ὄνυξ 'claw, hoof' originally began with the consonant cluster *h$_3$n- (see 3.2.4); in a compound of the two the sequence */ ... e-h$_3$ ... / became *-oh$_3$- and then *-ō-, whence ω in Hom. pl. κρατερώνυχες.

But from a later Greek point of view the compound is divisible as κρατερ-ώνυχες, and it appears that the initial vowel of the second member has been lengthened simply because the word is a compound. Because the trigger for lengthening was no longer obvious, the rule spread to other environments. For instance, there is no *phonological* reason why the second vowel of πρόσωπον or ἐπώνυμος should be long, because neither πρός nor ἐπί ends with a vowel that could be lengthened or contract with a following non-high vowel; the vowels of those compounds have simply been lengthened by the generalized rule, 'lengthen the initial non-high vowel of a second member of a compound'. This rule is called 'Wackernagel's Law' after the philologist who formulated it (or sometimes 'Wackernageldehnung', to distinguish it from the syntactic rule named for the same discoverer). It is responsible for the lengthened vowels of χρῡσήορος, ἀγήνωρ, στρατηγός, Ἱππημολγοί, τετρᾱ́ορος, etc., which could in principle have arisen by the original sound change (though some contain loanwords, or can be shown to have been formed much later, and so on), as well as the length in Πεισήνωρ, γαμψώνυχες, οὐδενόσωρος, etc., which can only be the result of the morphological rule.

3.2.2 Developments of laryngeals preceding high vowels and syllabic sonorants

The development of word-initial laryngeals before high vowels is treated in great detail in Peters (1980: 5–125, with numerous references), on which the first part of this section relies heavily (with a few modestly different judgments).

At least the first laryngeal was lost without a trace when *i immediately followed if the laryngeal was word-initial or was preceded by another *i. There are two certain examples, and a third is probable:

PIE *$h_1$yeh$_1$- 'make' (Hitt. pres. 3sg. *iezzi*, Toch. A *yaṣ*) → 'put' → 'throw', pres. 3sg. *h_1í-$h_1$yeh$_1$-ti > *ῑ̆́ jητι >→ Att. ῑ̆́ησι, with rough breathing leveled in from aor. ἡκ- ~ ἑ- ←< *$h_1$yeh$_1$- (Peters 1976, and see 3.2.4); the anomalous long vowel of the Attic reduplicating syllable shows that there must have been an initial laryngeal, and the absence of *h*- in the Hittite cognate shows that it must have been *h_1, of which the first copy has been lost in the onset of the reduplicating syllable while the second has lengthened that syllable (see 3.2.3);

pre-Greek *ní-$h_1$ih$_1$k-ah$_2$ 'overthrow' (Klingenschmitt 1975: 162 fn. 22 with references) > νῑ́κᾱ 'victory' > Att.-Ion. νῑ́κη; this was originally a compound made to the root of the first example with a root-extension *-k- attested only in Greek and Italic;

PIE *$h_1$ey- 'go' (?; Skt ipf. 3pl. *ā́yan* ?< *é $h_1$yend), pres. 2pl. *$h_1$ité (Skt *it^h á*) > ἴτε (Peters 1980: 103–5 with references).

In the last example the length of the 'augment' in Sanskrit suggests that the root began with a laryngeal, which can only have been *h_1 because it did not color the following vowel in 3sg. εἶσι, etc. Of course it is true that the augment is long by rule before /i/ and /u/ in Sanskrit, but the rule must have arisen by sound change in at least one relevant verb and then spread (at first by lexical analogy), and this very common verb is a good candidate for its point of origin. Nevertheless the example is less than certain (in spite of the supporting arguments enumerated by Peters, *loc. cit.*).

That other laryngeals were also lost before *i is likely but difficult to demonstrate. On the reduplicating syllable of Hom. ἰαύεν 'to pass the night', which should have had an initial *h_2, see below. There probably was an initial laryngeal in the preform of Hom. ἰ̄χανάᾱι 'it desires' (Chantraine 1973: 360), because the cognation with its Sanskrit synonym *ī́hate*, Gāthā-Avestan *iziiā* 'I desire' strongly suggests that a reduplicated stem *Hi-Hǵ^h- or *Hi-Hiǵ^h- underlies both forms, but the laryngeal might have been *h_1, since a connection with Theokritos' ἀ̄χήν 'poor' is far from obvious (Mayrhofer 1986–2001 s.v. *EH*) and there are no other potential cognates. It is conceivable that pl. ἰθαρώτεροι 'more cheerful' (Alkaios 58.18) is derived from the root of αἴθεν 'to kindle', but it is not clear that that root began with *h_2; if it was an extension of the *ay- ~ *i- 'be hot' which appears in Hitt. *āri* 'it is hot' (←< *áy-or), *inuzzi* '(s)he heats (it)' (< *i-néw-ti), it apparently began with a vowel (or with *h_1, which was lost in Hittite). Other iota-initial words also cannot be shown to have been laryngeal-initial; the ones with reliable etymologies that have come to my attention are ἰ̄ός 'arrow' (< *ἰhϝός, cf. Skt *íṣus*), ἰ̄λῦς 'mud' (cf. OCS *ilŭ*), and perhaps ἱερός 'holy', if it is connected with Skt *iṣirás* 'strong', which is doubtful in view of its variation from dialect to dialect (West Greek ἱαρός, Lesbian ἶρος; note also that this word and ἰ̄ός are not obviously derived from *(H)eys- 'look for, seek'). On the other hand, there are no clear counterexamples in which a word-initial laryngeal survives before *i (Peters 1980: 73–98); that οἴᾱξ 'steering-oar, tiller' is connected with Hitt. *hissas*, Skt *īṣā́* 'thill' is conceivable but hardly compelling, and even if it is connected it might exhibit a full-grade root, like Slovene *ojê* 'thill' (Peters 1980: 94–5). A possible example of ι < *h_2i after a consonant is ἱμάντ- 'strap'; the formation is apparently complex and questionable (cf. the discussion of Beekes 2013 s.v. ἱμάς), but it seems likely that the root is zero-grade *sh_2i- 'tie' (pres. 3sg. Hitt. *ishāi*, Skt *syáti*)—unless the word is completely unrelated and the equation is a mirage, which is not impossible in view of the word's peculiar shape.

The development of laryngeals before *u was at least partly different. In at least two clear examples a word-initial laryngeal followed by *u survived as a vowel, yielding a u-diphthong:

PIE *$h_1$wéru- ~ *$h_1$uréw- 'broad' → *$h_1$urús (Skt *urús*) > εὐρύς; that the root was *$h_1$wer- is demonstrated by Skt *várīyān* 'broader', *váriṣṭ^{h}as* 'broadest' (cf. Peters 1980: 52–4);

(post-)PIE *$h_2$udáh$_2$ 'voice, speech' > αὐδή; root *$h_2$wed- 'speak', cf. Skt pres. 3sg. *vádati* (cf. Peters 1980: 14).

The fact that the ablauting vowel did not immediately follow the laryngeal in these PIE roots is what makes these examples convincing; note further that in the first example the generalization of zero-grade roots in u-stem adjectives is normal in Greek, while in the second an e-grade root would not be expected in a derivative of this type and a zero-grade root would be (see 2.4.2 (i)). The fact that the first laryngeal is reflected by ε and the second by α is part of a pattern that we will encounter repeatedly in this and subsequent sections.

A similar root-initial example in a reduplicated present is Hom. ἰαύε̄ν 'to pass the night', which can only reflect *h_2í-$h_2$us-e/o- (with the zero-grade root expected in a reduplicated thematic present, cf. Peters 1980: 34–8). It seems clear that the root-initial *h_2 yielded α in this stem, and it might seem equally clear that the reduplication-initial *h_2 has been lost by regular sound change; but if it had instead become *a, the shape of the reduplicating syllable would be so anomalous that it would probably have been reshaped, and ἰ- would be the most probable result of reshaping. The reduplication could even be a Greek innovation subsequent to the change *$h_2$us- > αὐh- (*LIV* s.v. 2. **h_2u̯es*, Hackstein 1995: 220–1 with references).

Other examples of *Hu- > Vὐ- are unfortunately elusive, because it is often difficult to prove that a word-initial sequence reflects PIE *Hu- rather than */Hew-/. Discussion of two potential examples will show what we are up against. Since the first syllable of Skt *uṣā́s* 'dawn' is consistently zero grade, we might propose for its Greek cognate the following development:

> post-PIE *$h_2$usṓs > *awsṓs > *ἀϝhώς (see 3.5.1) > *hαϝhώς (see 3.5.2) > PGk *hαϝϝώς (see 5.2.2); that preform would then yield αὔως (i.e. ἄϝϝως) in Lesbian, but ᾱ̔ϝώς in the other dialects (see 5.2.2); the latter would survive in most (until its ϝ was lost) but become *ἡώς in Attic-Ionic (see 6.2), whence Hom. ἠώς (with psilosis) but Att. *ἑώς → ἕως.

If the preform given is correct, this noun must have belonged to the hysterokinetic accent paradigm (see 2.3.4 (ii)), as it does in Sanskrit. However, the long ō-vowel in the suffixal syllable is not normal in such a paradigm; it shows that 'dawn' must originally have belonged to the amphikinetic paradigm, with a nom. sg. *$h_2$áwsōs. Greek usually shifts those nouns into the hysterokinetic paradigm, and it sometimes levels the zero-grade initial syllable of the oblique forms into the nom. and acc. (like Sanskrit), but not always; an example that escaped leveling is λειμών 'meadow' (cf. Peters 1980: 31–2). Therefore we cannot be sure that the *aw- of the oldest recoverable Greek form is not an archaism, reflecting *$h_2$aw- rather than *h_2u-. We have a similar problem with the family of Hom. ἀέξειν 'to enlarge, to increase', but for a diametrically opposed reason. The root was clearly PIE *$h_2$weg-s- > ἀϝεξ- —that is demonstrated not only by the Homeric form but by Skt *vakṣáyati* '(s)he makes it grow' and Goth. *wahsjan* 'to grow'—and it might be supposed that the post-Homeric forms αὔξεν, αὐξάνεν and their derivatives could only reflect *$h_2$ug-s-. They probably do, but unfortunately there is another possibility. Though 'Schwebeablaut', in which the full-grade vowel appears in one position in some forms derived from a root and in another position in other forms, was clearly not a feature of PIE phonology, *$h_2$weg- does exhibit derivatives with the full-grade vowel in the 'wrong' position (Anttila 1969: 118); a clear example is Skt *ójas* 'strength' < *$h_2$áwg-es-. Apparently such forms were backformed to zero-grade examples like Skt *ugrás* 'strong' < *$h_2$ug-rós, the full-grade vowel being inserted without reference to where it occurred in related words. We do not know how early that occurred; if it began before the last common ancestor of Greek and Sanskrit began to diversify, it is not impossible that αὔξειν reflects *$h_2$áwg-s-.[3] We will have to be satisfied with the two clear examples of *Hu- > Vυ- that we have.

Once again, however, there are no counterexamples in which a word-initial laryngeal was clearly lost before *u (cf. Peters 1980: 63–72).

Word-internally, on the other hand, loss of laryngeals before *u is the rule if a consonant or a syllabic sonorant precedes. The examples are all u-stem adjectives:

PIE *g^wráh$_2$u- ~ *g^wr̥h$_2$áw- 'heavy' (Lat. *gravis*) → *g^wr̥h$_2$ús (Skt *gurús*, Goth. *kaúrus*) > βαρύς;

PIE *pláth$_2$u- ~ *pl̥th$_2$áw- 'broad' (Lith. *platùs*) → *pl̥th$_2$ús (Skt *pr̥t^{h}ús*) > πλατύς;

post-PIE *pl̥h$_1$ús 'much' (Skt *purús*) > πολύς; on the unexpected o, see 3.2.3 *ad fin.*[4]

However, because the laryngeal immediately precedes the suffix in all the above examples they are not entirely probative. Most adjectives of this class were proterokinetic in PIE, with an alternation between *-u- and */-éw-/ in the suffix; Greek generalized that inflection to all of them, so that -υ- in the nom. and acc. sg. alternates with -εϝ- in most other forms.[5] But the second alternant of the suffix begins with a non-high vowel, before which the laryngeal was regularly lost (see 3.2.1)—and it is possible that that loss was leveled into the forms with zero-grade suffix *-u-.

Before syllabic sonorants laryngeals gave rise to vowels word-initially and probably when preceded by a consonant; the sonorants became non-syllabic. This is called 'Rix's Law' after the colleague who established that it is a regular sound

[3] For a different assessment, based on hypotheses about PIE word-formation that strike me as somewhat speculative, see Ozoliņš (2015: 63–5, 87–98).

[4] Since the superlative of this adjective is πλεῖστος (see above) we might expect the direct cases to reflect *pléh$_1$-u-, yet Goth., OHG *filu* < PGmc *felu 'a lot, much' (noun) and OIr. *il* 'much, many' reflect a preform *pélh$_1$u-. I have no opinion about this oddity; I leave it undiscussed because it is not directly relevant to the history of Greek.

[5] The effects of laryngeal coloring have been leveled out; thus in Attic we find only gen. sg. βαρέος, πλατέος, etc. However, coloring seems to be preserved in the place name Πλάταια (Beekes 2013 s.v. πλατύς).

change. Examples with word-initial *h$_2$R̥- are most numerous (Rix 1970: 84–92; I omit the less certain examples):

PIE *h$_2$n̥tb^{h}í 'on both sides' (Jasanoff 1976: 125–7; root *h$_2$ant- 'forehead, front', see 3.2.1) > *h$_2$m̥b^{h}í (Lat. *amb-*) > ἀμφί;
PIE *h$_2$nḗr 'man' (Skt *nā́*), gen. sg. *h$_2$n̥rés (hysterokinetic accent paradigm) >→ ἀνήρ, *ἀνρός (with the usual Greek generalization of *-os) > ἀνδρός;
PIE *h$_2$lek- 'protect', desiderative pres. 3sg. *h$_2$lékseti '(s)he wants to protect' → '(s)he is protecting' (ἀλέξει, Skt *rákṣati*), zero-grade root-noun *h$_2$l̥k- 'protection' in Hom. dat. ἀλκὶ (πεποιθώς) '(relying on his) defensive capability';
PIE *h$_2$r̥ǵrós 'white' (Skt *r̥jrás* 'flashing; fleeting') > *ἀργρός > ἀργός 'bright'; for the laryngeal cf. Hitt. *harkis* = ἀργι-, probably also with zero-grade root;
PIE *h$_2$ŕ̥tḱos 'bear' (Hitt. *hartaggas*, Skt *ŕ̥kṣas*) > ἄρκτος;
PIE pres. *h$_2$r̥-nu- mid. 'be getting (a share of)' (3sg. Arm. *aṙnow* '(s)he takes', Av. subj. *ərənauuataē-ca* 'and he shall partake') > ἄρνυσθαι 'to gain, to earn, to win'; note that inherited presents in *-néw- ~ -nu- normally exhibit zero-grade roots.

In all these examples a full-grade root can be excluded because the vowel of the full grade was in a different position in the root ('man', 'strength') and/or because a zero grade is actually attested in Indo-Iranian ('white', 'bear', 'gain') and/or is expected on morphological grounds ('on both sides', 'man's', 'strength', 'white', 'gain'). Of course for the examples with αρ and αλ we could propose that the laryngeal was simply lost and the syllabic sonorant developed normally, since it is plausible that syllabic liquids might regularly yield those sequences (rather than ρα and λα) word-initially in most Greek dialects (see 5.4.1 (ii)). But that hypothesis cannot account for the two examples with syllabic nasals, which normally became α word-initially before a consonant (see 3.3).

Moreover, there are three solid examples in which word-initial *h$_3$R̥- yielded ὀR- (even in dialects in which syllabic liquids normally acquired α-vowels; Rix 1970: 92–7):

PIE *h$_3$nób^h- 'navel' (Skt *nā́b^{h}is*, OE *nafela*), zero grade in deriv. *h$_3$n̥b^h-l̥H- > ὀμφαλός (cf. Lat. *umbilīcus*, OIr. *imbliu* with further suffixes);
PIE pres. *h$_3$r̥-néw- ~ *h$_3$r̥-nu- 'cause (things) to rise' (cf. Lat. *orīrī* 'to rise'; also Skt *r̥ṇóti* '(s)he makes it move'?—but there is at least one other root that the Skt verb could reflect; on the other hand, the causative meaning of this suffix is an archaism) > mid. ὄρνυσθαι 'to be rising';
PIE verbal adj. *h$_3$r̥tós 'risen, up' (Lat. *ortus*) in κονι-ορτός 'dust-cloud'.[6]

[6] The alternative to Rix's analysis of these forms of 'rise' involves positing that a full-grade ὀρ-, whatever its etymology might be, has been leveled through the paradigm of the verb, which for early

(The other examples adduced by Rix could involve morphological remodeling or leveling of ablaut grades.)

Finally, there is a probable example with *h_1 (Rix 1970: 97–8), though the facts require some discussion. A PIE athematic present *$h_1$rew- 'ask' probably survives in Hom. ἐρείομεν 'let's ask' at *Il.* 1.62 (with metrical lengthening to ε̄ of the vowel of the midmost of five successive light syllables, Chantraine 1973: 297), and a thematized *$h_1$réw-e/o- is well attested in Hom. ἐρέεσθαι. It follows that the thematic aorist, Att. ἐρέσθαι = Ion. ἐ̓ρέσθαι < *ἐρϝέσθαι[7] (see 7.2.2) must reflect zero-grade *h_1r̥w-é/ó-, with ε as the effective reflex of the laryngeal according to the pattern exemplified above. There are no clear cognates in other IE languages,[8] but the phonological pattern shows that the root was part of the language at a date when laryngeals were still separate phonemes. We will encounter several other such roots below.

Whether Rix's Law operated on laryngeals immediately preceded by consonants is less clear, largely because potential examples are difficult to find. The most plausible examples are the active 3pl. forms of reduplicated athematic presents. That is because they originally exhibited a zero-grade 3pl. ending *-n̥ti, to judge from their reflexes in Sanskrit and Avestan[9]—unlike athematic root presents, most of which had accented endings except in the active singular, and so should have exhibited a full-grade 3pl. ending *-énti, before which root-final laryngeals would simply have been lost (see 3.2.1). That is, the PIE forms were *d^hé-$d^h h_1$-n̥ti 'they are putting' (Skt *dádʰati*), *dé-dh_3-n̥ti 'they are giving' (Skt *dádati*), *stí-sth_2-n̥ti 'they are standing up', yielding Proto-Greek *τίθεντι (see 4.2.1 (i) on the reduplicating syllable), *δίδοντι, *hίσταντι 'they are standing (it/them) up' by Rix's Law. We would expect those forms to survive without change in West Greek, and in fact ἵσταντι is actually attested in Pindar (fr. 70b.8) and τίθεντι 'they are establishing (games)' occurs in an Insular Doric inscription of the 2nd century BC from

Ancient Greek seems implausible. It follows that apparent Anatolian cognates with no reflex of an initial laryngeal (such as *órmos 'moon', cf. Hitt. *armas*) reflect some other root.

[7] The fact that εἴρεσθαι (ει = ε̄) is apparently a present rather than an aorist in Homer—note that εἴρεαι 'you ask' and its compounds are attested more than a dozen times—is striking but has no bearing on the phonology of this example; this is probably another example of the split of a single inherited stem into a present and an aorist in Greek (Ringe 2012: 125–30). For further discussion of the Homeric facts, see Wackernagel (1916: 120–1; who notes that the problematic aorist ἐρέσθαι is attested in Homer only in the *Odyssey*), Chantraine (1973: 394 with references); on iptv. 2sg. ἔρειο *Il.* 11.611, which is difficult under any hypothesis, see Chantraine (1973: 297). For a different judgment on the identity of the PIE root, see *LIV* s.v. 1. *$h_1 reh_1$.

[8] It is possible but not certain that ON *raun* (fem.) 'trial' (potentially < *$h_1$rownah$_2$) is related; if it is, there is no direct connection with ἔρευνα (potentially < *$h_1$réwnih$_2$, see 3.6.3), because the formation is different and the *n cannot be part of the root—PIE roots never end in two sonorants (Anttila 1969: 36–7 with references).

[9] Of course the corresponding imperfect form and the corresponding mediopassive forms also exhibited zero-grade endings beginning with *-n̥-, and the active participial suffix was zero-grade *-n̥t-. However, the imperfect and the participle were vulnerable to remodeling on the root-aorist, which had alternating accent and full-grade endings (in the participle, a full-grade suffix in the direct cases), while the mediopassive was probably vulnerable to leveling from the more basic active.

Nisyros (*IG* XII-3.103.10). The Homeric forms should be *τίθεισι (*ε̄), *δίδουσι (*ō), *ἵστᾱσι, with *-τι > -σι (see 5.3.1) and the second compensatory lengthening (see 7.2.1) and the accent still on the reduplicating syllable. The actually attested forms are τιθεῖσι, διδοῦσι, ἱστᾶσιν, with the accent on the root. It seems clear that the accent has been shifted—possibly by leveling from (Ionic) 3sg. τιθεῖ, etc., in the spoken language of the poet, possibly only graphically during the transmission of the text—and does not actually represent a contraction of vowels (cf. Chantraine 1973: 298); thus the Homeric forms are also reasonable evidence for the operation of Rix's Law word-internally. The only reason these forms are not clinching is that they are integral parts of paradigms within which leveling could have occurred at many points in their development.

It is reasonable to ask how laryngeals between two syllabic sonorants developed. Three potential examples suggest that the outcome was *VRV*, and one is almost certain:

PIE *ń̥h_2l̥tos 'unnourished' (cf. Lat. *altus* 'tall, high', OE *eald* 'old' with leveled ablaut and meanings shifted from *'nourished, grown up') > Hom. ἄναλτος 'insatiable'? —but this compound could have been created within Greek long after laryngeals had been eliminated;
PIE *h_2n̥$h_1$mós 'breath' >→ ἄνεμος 'wind' with shift of accent? — but the preform could just as well have been *$h_2$ónh$_1$mos (cf. Arm. *hołm* 'wind'), and the ablaut of the present stem could have been leveled into the noun before the verb was lost;[10]
PIE *h_1n̥$h_3$mn̥-yé/ó- 'to name' (Goth. *namnjan*, OE *nemnan*) > *ἐνομα̨ν-jε/ο- >→ ὀνομαίνε̄ν.

The last example is the most persuasive; it is even conceivable that the Greek noun, whose ablaut does not match that of any cognate, was backformed to the verb. Alternatively, the original acrostatic noun *h_1nḗ$h_3$mn̥ ~ *$h_1$nó$h_3$mn- could have been remodeled as proterokinetic *$h_1$nó$h_3$mn- ~ *h_1n̥$h_3$mén- on the model of derived n-stems; but the oblique stem would still yield an example of the proposed outcome, which I therefore tentatively accept as a regular sound-change outcome.

3.2.3 Developments of tautosyllabic laryngeals following high vowels and syllabic sonorants

At least the sequence *ih_1, and probably also *ih_3, became ī before a non-syllabic in Greek. Examples are few but convincing:

[10] The same indeterminacy affects the etymology of Lat. *animus*, Oscan **anams**.

post-PIE *h$_1$í-h$_1$yeh$_1$-ti '(s)he is throwing' (see 3.2.2) > *ἴ̄jητι >→ Att. ἵ̄ησι, with rough breathing leveled in from aor. ἡκ- ~ ἑ- ←< *h$_1$yeh$_1$- (Peters 1976);
pre-Greek *ní-h$_1$ih$_1$k-ah$_2$ 'overthrow' (Klingenschmitt 1975: 162 fn. 22 with references) > νί̄κᾱ 'victory' > Att.-Ion. νί̄κη (see 3.2.2);
pre-Gk *opi-h$_3$k^w- 'look at, eye (something)' in *ὀπῑπεύς 'spy', derivational basis of Hom. ὀπῑπεύε̄ν 'to spy on'; cf. also Hom. voc. παρθενοπῖπα 'girl-ogler, voyeur' and Myc. *o-pi*, o-grade of ἐπί (cf. Frisk s.v. ὀπῑπεύω with references).

A further probable example is:

PIE *píHwō, fem. *píHwerih$_2$ 'fat' (Skt *pī́vā*, fem. *pī́varī*) > πί̄ων, fem. πί̄ε̄ρα;

the accented zero-grade root-syllable is surprising enough that one might consider reconstructing the rare PIE vowel *ī instead, but since Av. *paēma* 'milk', etc., are almost certainly related, I (reluctantly) reconstruct the zero grade of an ablauting root in this word (cf. Mayrhofer 1986–2001 s.v. *pī́van-*). These new *ī merged with the (very rare) PIE *ī; a clear example of the latter is

PIE *wīs- ~ *wis- 'poison' (Lat. *vīrus* vs. Skt *viṣám*, Toch. B *wase*) > *ϝῑhός > ἰ̄ός.

Possible alternative outcomes of these sequences can be explained in other ways. For instance, the final laryngeal of Doric ϝί̄κατι 'twenty' < PIE *wī́k̑m̥tih$_1$ has probably been lost in pausa (see 2.2.4 (iv)); ζωός 'alive' apparently reflects not PIE *g^{w}ih$_3$wós directly, but a form into which the full-grade *g^{w}yoh$_3$- has been introduced by lexical analogy with the related verb; Hom. du. ὄσσε 'eyes' might reflect PIE *h$_3$ók^{w}ih$_1$ directly (cf. OCS *oči*), with a development of *ih$_1$ to *jε (Forssman 1969), but its -ε could also have been leveled in later so as to make the form more obviously a dual.

On the other hand, it seems clear that *ih$_2$ yielded *ya after a single consonant preceded by a short vowel but *ia after a consonant cluster, as if the outcome were automatically subject to Sievers' Law (see 3.6.1). Inherited examples with *ya seem all to be nom. and acc. forms of feminines with the suffix *-ih$_2$- ~ *-yáh$_2$-:

PIE *píHwerih$_2$ fem. 'fat' (Skt *pī́varī*) > *πί̄ϝερjα > πί̄ε̄ρα (see 5.2.2);
PIE *stérih$_2$ fem. 'sterile' (Skt *starī́*) > *στέρjα > στεῖρα;
PIE *pl̥th$_2$áwih$_2$ fem. 'broad' (Skt *pr̥thivī́* with ablaut remodeled) > *πλατάϝjα > Πλάταια (with productive recessive accent), >→ πλατεῖα (with laryngeal 'coloring' eliminated by lexical analogy with other fems. of u-stems);
PIE *h$_1$sóntih$_2$ fem. 'being' → *h$_1$sn̥tíh$_2$ (Skt *satī́*) > *ἐhᾳτjα > Arkadian ἔασσα;

(post-)PIE *swah₂déwih₂ fem. 'sweet' (Skt *svādvī́* with ablaut remodeled) > *hϝᾱδέϝjα > ἡδεῖα 'pleasant';
(post-)PIE *widúsih₂ fem. 'knowing' (Skt *vidúṣī*) > Hom. ἰδυῖα.

Inherited forms with the disyllabic reflex are somewhat more varied:

PIE *pótnih₂ 'mistress, lady' (Skt *pátnī*) > Hom. πότνια;
PIE *sémih₂ fem. 'one' → *smíh₂ (Arm. *mi* 'one') > μία;
PIE *-trih₂, fem. nom. sg. derived from the amphikinetic agent suffix *´-tor-, e.g. in *ǵénh₁trih₂ 'birth-mother' (Skt *jánitrī*, Lat. *genetrīx* with extension *-k-) > -τρια, e.g. in δέκτρια 'receiver' ([Arkhilokhos] 331.2), ψάλτρια 'lyre-player';
PIE *tríh₂ neut. 'three' (Skt *trī́*, Toch. B *tarya*) > τρία (Rix 1976a: 75);
PIE *kʷrih₂tó '(s)he bought' (cf. Toch. B *käryāmtte* 'we bought', Skt past ptc. *krītás* 'bought', pres. 3sg. *krīṇā́ti* '(s)he buys') > ἐ-πρίατο.

It is not immediately clear what sequence of changes gave rise to this pattern. The complex analysis of Peters (1980: 127–205), in which he suggests that the disyllabic outcome did not arise by regular sound change alone, seems to be motivated partly by a fairly rigid conception of rule interactions, but especially by the conviction that ἄρουρα 'arable land' < *áro-wr-ya (see 3.6.3) can only have developed by sound change alone. I am not convinced. It is true that τρία could reflect late remodeling (Peters 1980: 145–6), and conceivable that the α of ἐπρίατο first arose in 3pl. ἐ-πρίαντο < *kʷrih₂n̥tó (cf. Risch 1982: 328; not *-énto, *pace* Rix 1976a: 215 and Peters 1980: 192 fn. 149) if Rix's Law operated between *i and a syllabic sonorant. But spread of a stem alternant from the 3pl. (only, since the other endings began with non-syllabics) is not expected, and the clear[11] distribution of outcomes among these inherited examples strongly suggests conditioned sound change. It is true that Greek exhibits numerous examples of *-jα rather than *-ια after heavy syllables. But a large majority are formed from nt-stems, most of those stems are active participles, and the participles made to athematic stems originally exhibited an ablauting suffix *-ont- ~ *-n̥t-, to which the feminine must at first have been *-ónt-ia(-) ~ *-ą̨t-yā́- with an etymologically justified *-y- in the oblique stem—from which *-y- could have been leveled through the paradigm, then to the paradigms of other active participles, and finally through other nt-stems and beyond. It also needs to be remembered that *ἄροϝρjα was created within

[11] That Hom. voc. πότνα θεά is an 'Aiolism', and an innovation, is argued convincingly by Peters (1980: 213–15). We do not know enough about Linear B spelling conventions to say for certain that any one interpretation of potential Mycenaean examples is correct, though the discussion of Peters (1980: 215–17) is eminently sensible. For a different assessment, see Hajnal (2007: 151–2).

the prehistory of Greek, and that Greek has expanded the range of the light Sievers' Law alternant *-y- at the expense of heavy *-i- (see 3.6.1 for discussion with references).

In another daughter, pre-Proto-Germanic, it seems clear that regular sound-change outcomes that violated Sievers' Law were quickly adjusted to conform to it (in both directions, see Ringe 2017: 144–5); could the same thing have happened to these forms early in the prehistory of Greek? It probably depends on how many exceptions to the existing phonological rule the new sound change created. Since linguistic changes normally begin as native-learner errors, it is plausible to suppose that a few apparent exceptions to the rule, perhaps not often encountered by small children, might be misparsed as errors and 'corrected' by applying the rule to them. On the other hand, if a sound change created a 'critical mass' of exceptions to a pre-existing rule, it is much more likely that they would be learned correctly through frequent exposure. Exactly what happened in this particular case is probably beyond recovery, both because the changes in question appear to have occurred very early and because the distribution of Sievers' Law outcomes in Greek was drastically altered at some point, effectively destroying the phonological rule.

The development of *uH before non-syllabics was more straightforward: so far as can be determined, the outcome was always ῡ. There seem to be only three watertight examples, but one clearly contains $*h_2$:

PIE $*d^h uh_2$mós 'smoke' (Skt d^h*ūmás*, Lat. *fūmus*; for the laryngeal cf. Hitt. *tuhhuwais*) > θῡμός 'emotion, spirit (etc.)';
PIE $*b^h$úHt 'it became' (Skt *áb*^{h}*ūt* with augment; for the laryngeal cf. the Skt full-grade b^h*avi-*) > ἔ-φῡ;
PIE $*h_3 b^h$rúH-s 'eyebrow' (Skt b^h*rū́s*) > ὀφρῦς.

At least two other examples of ῡ were inherited from PIE, namely μῦς 'mouse' (Skt *mū́s*, Lat., OE *mūs*, ON *mús*) and ὗς 'pig' (Lat. *sūs*, ON *sýr* 'sow'), but it is not clear whether their PIE ancestors contained *uH or the rare *ū.

If the sequence *iH or *uH was followed by a non-high vowel, the laryngeal was simply lost, as might be expected; thus the gen. sg. of ὀφρῦς is ὀφρύος, with a short υ.

Sequences of the syllabic sonorants *m̥, *n̥, *l̥, *r̥ and laryngeals followed by a non-syllabic developed very differently. If the sonorant was *n̥ and the following non-syllabic was *y, the laryngeal was apparently lost; a plausible example is 'weave' (Warren Cowgill, p.c. ca. 1980):

PIE pres. *u-né-b^h- 'be weaving' (Skt *sám unap* 'you enveloped' *RV* II.13.9) → *ub^h-né-H- (Skt inj. 2sg. *ub*^{h}*nā́s*, 3sg. with augment *aub*^{h}*nāt*) → *ub^h-n̥-H-yé- > *ὐφανjε- > ὑφαίνε̄ν, with the regular outcome of *-n̥y- (see 3.3 and 3.6.3) and no trace of the laryngeal.

The same development reappears in τετραίνε̄ν 'to bore', though that stem has undergone even more remodeling (see 4.2.1 (ii)). I can find no other examples, or counterexamples.

Otherwise these sequences typically developed into sequences of *non*-syllabic sonorant plus long vowel, and the identity of the vowel reflects that of the laryngeal: *Rh$_1$ > Rη, *Rh$_2$ > Rᾱ, *Rh$_3$ > Rω (see especially Beekes 1969: 203–5, 210–16, 218–20). Probative examples are found in inherited formations to roots of the shape *(s)CerH- in which a zero grade would be expected; the verbal adjectives in *-tó- are the most obviously relevant category. Examples of such adjectives are fairly numerous:

PIE *tm̥h$_1$tós 'cut' (for the laryngeal-final root cf. Middle Irish *tamnaid* '(s)he cuts (it) off') > *τμητός in Hom. ἐΰτμητος 'well-cut', cf. full-grade *témh$_1$- in τέμενος 'land reserved for a god';

PIE *ǵn̥h$_1$tós 'born' (Skt *jātás*, Lat. *nātus*, Goth. *aírþa-kunds* 'of earthly origin') > *γνητός in Hom. κασί-γνητος 'brother', lit. 'co-gnātus' (cf. Hitt. *katti-* 'with'), cf. full-grade *ǵénh$_1$- in γενέτωρ 'parent' (see 3.2.4);

PIE *tr̥h$_1$tós 'perforated' (for the root cf. Lat. *terere* 'to rub') > Hom. τρητός, cf. full-grade *térh$_1$- in Hom. τέρετρον 'auger, gimlet';

PIE *wr̥h$_1$tós 'said, sayable' (Goth. neut. *waúrd* 'word') > *ϝρητός > Hom. ῥητός 'stated, specified', cf. full-grade *wérh$_1$- in Hom. ἐρέω 'I will say', Palaic *wērti* '(s)he says';

PIE *g^{w}l̥h$_1$tós 'thrown, throwable' (cf. Skt *udgūrṇas* 'raised, brandished' with alternative suffix *-nó-) > *βλητός in Hom. ἀπόβλητος 'disposable, worthless', cf. full-grade *g^{w}élh$_1$- in Hom. βέλεμνα 'missiles';

PIE *kl̥h$_1$tós 'called' (for the laryngeal-final root cf. Old Lat. *calāre*) > Hom. κλητός 'called, invited, chosen', cf. full-grade *kálh$_1$- in ἐκάλεσε '(s)he called';

PIE *dm̥h$_2$tós 'built' (for the laryngeal-final root cf. Toch. B /t^{s}əma-/ 'grow') > *δμᾱτός in νεόδμᾱτος 'new-built' (Pindar *Isthmian* IV.62) > Att.-Ion. νεόδμητος, cf. full-grade *démh$_2$- in δέμας 'body';

PIE *ḱm̥h$_2$tós 'tired' (remodeled in Skt *śāntás* 'resting, quiet') > *κμᾱτός in Hom. h. ἄκμητος 'tireless', cf. κάματος 'toil, labor', and see further below;

PIE *d^{h}n̥h$_2$tós 'fleeting' (?; Skt *d^{h}ánvat* 'it flows', *LIV* s.v. **d^{h}enh$_2$*) > θνᾱτός 'mortal' > Att. Ion. θνητός, cf. θάνατος 'death', and see further below;

PIE *ḱr̥h$_2$tós 'mixed' (cf. Skt *ā́-śīrtas* 'mixed', *RV* VIII.2.9) > *κρᾱτός in Hom. ἄκρητος, Att. ἄκρᾱτος 'unmixed', cf. full-grade *ḱérh$_2$- in aor. ἐκέρασε '(s)he mixed';

PIE *pr̥h$_2$tós 'sold' (for the laryngeal-final root cf. OIr. *renaid* '(s)he sells') > Att. πρᾱτός 'sold';

PIE *tl̥h$_2$tós 'lifted, liftable' (cf. Lat. *lātus* 'carried, brought') > τλᾱτός > Att.-Ion. τλητός 'bearable, endurable', cf. full-grade *télh$_2$- in τελαμών 'shield-strap';

PIE *str̥h$_3$tós 'spread out, strewn' (cf. Skt *stīrṇás* with alternative suffix *-nó-) > στρωτός, cf. full-grade *stérh$_3$- > *στερο- → στορε- in aor. ἐστόρεσε '(s)he spread' (see 5.4.1 (iii));

PIE *g^{w}r̥h$_3$tós 'swallowed, swallowable' (cf. Skt *gīrṇás* with alternative suffix *-nó-) > βρωτός 'edible'.

There are also a few adjectives in *-ró-, for which zero-grade roots are also expected, though close cognates are difficult to find:

*skl̥h$_1$rós 'hard' > σκληρός, cf. full-grade *skélh$_1$- in σκέλλε̄ν 'to harden', σκελετός 'dried up';

*ǵ^{h}l̥h$_3$rós 'yellow, green' > χλωρός; the full-grade *ǵ^{h}élh$_3$- appears in OCS *zelenŭ* 'green', PGmc *gelwaz 'yellow' (> OE *ġeolu*, OHG *gelo*), Lat. *helvos* 'bay (horse)', etc.

Presents in -σκε/ο- also typically exhibit zero-grade roots, since the suffix was originally accented; thus it is no surprise to find:

θνήσκε̄ν 'to be dying' < *d^{h}n̥h$_2$-sḱé/ó- vs. aor. θανε̄ν 'to die' < *d^{h}n̥h$_2$-é/ó-;

so also βλώσκε̄ν 'to be coming/going' < *ml̥h$_3$-sḱé/ó- (aor. μολε̄ν) and θρώσκε̄ν 'to leap (severally or repeatedly)' < *d^{h}r̥h$_3$-sḱé/ó- (aor. θορε̄ν), though cognates are shaky and the o of the aorists is not easy to explain (see 5.4.1 (iii)).

A present in *-yé/ó- suggests that laryngeals were not lost between *r̥ and *y:

PIE *sr̥h$_3$-yé/ó- 'rush' *vel sim.* (Hitt. *sarhieddu* 'let him attack', *LIV* s.v. **serh$_3$*) > *hρωjε/o- > Hom. ipf. 3pl. ῥώοντο 'they moved swiftly' *Il.* 18.411, 417.

But it is possible that the laryngeal was at first lost in that position, then leveled in from other members of the paradigm at an early date.

Finally, compounds of PIE *n̥- 'un-' and roots beginning with a laryngeal provide examples of this outcome, as demonstrated by Beekes (1969: 98–113). Potentially inherited examples are:

Hom. νήγρετος (ὕπνος) 'unwaking (sleep)' < *n̥-h$_1$gr-, cf. aor. ἐγρ-έσθαι 'to wake up';

Hom. νηκούστησε 'he failed to listen', *Il.* 20.14 < *n̥-h$_2$ḱ-h$_2$ows-, cf. ἀκούε̄ν = PGmc *hauzijaną (OE *hīeran*, etc.) < *h$_2$ḱ-h$_2$ows-ié/ó- 'be sharp-eared'.

A significant number of examples are made to roots or stems that appear to have begun with *HC-sequences but have no certain non-Greek cognates, e.g.:

Hom. νηλεές 'pitiless(ly)' < *n̥-h$_1$lewés-, cpd. of s-stem ἔλεος 'pity' < *h$_1$léwos;

Hom. νημερτής 'unerring' < *n̥-$h_2$mertés-, cpd. of s-stem *ἄμερτος 'missing (a mark), wild shot' < *$h_2$mértos, cf. aor. ἁμαρτε̃ν 'to miss, to err' with zero-grade αρ < *r̥ and apparently /h-/ by some lexical analogy;
νήκεστος 'incurable' < *ń̥-$h_2$kes-to-, cpd. of *$h_2$kes-tó- 'curable', deriv. of s-stem ἄκος 'cure' < *$h_2$ákos;
ἀνωφελής 'useless' ← *νωφελής in Myc. neut. pl. *no-pe-re-a*$_2$ < *n̥-h_3b^{h}elés-, cpd. of s- stem ὄφελος 'use, advantage'< *h_3b^{h}élos.

Though the evidence for these regular outcomes is thus extensive, some care is needed in judging individual examples. For instance, Hom. νώνυμ(ν)ος is an example of the inherited type of negative compound, and 'name' certainly began with an *HC-sequence, but the laryngeal was *h_1 (see 3.2.4); thus this example has at least been adjusted to fit the later shape of its derivational base. Hom. νηνεμίη 'windlessness, calm' is even less probative. The ancestral shape of its base ἄνεμος is itself problematic (see 3.2.2 *ad fin.*), and it is possible that the ἄ- of 'wind' reflects a full-grade vowel; in that case *νήνεμος would reflect the productive rule creating negative compounds in /nV_x:-/ from words beginning with short non-high vowels of any origin. Other examples of these compounds certainly arose by such a rule.

Word-internal examples from roots of the shape */CReH-/ are not probative for the sound change under discussion because the e-grade and zero-grade forms of the roots merged by regular sound change. For instance, the γνω- of γνωτός 'recognizable' and γιγνώσκε̄ν 'to know (someone) on sight' can and probably does reflect zero-grade *ǵn̥h_3-, but since full-grade *ǵnoh_3- also yielded γνω- (as in ἔ-γνω '(s)he recognized' < *ǵnóh_3-t) and since leveling within paradigms is continuously possible, we cannot cite any form of this and similar verbs as a certain example of the sound change under discussion here.

There is some evidence that *R̥H-sequences could yield an alternative outcome under some conditions. The most convincing example is:

Hom. παλάμη '(flat) hand' < *pĺ̥$h_2$mah_2 (Lat. *palma*, OIr. *lám* 'hand', OE *folm* 'hand'(poetic)).

The word is so isolated in Greek that its shape can reflect only regular sound change. The conditioning factor for its divergent outcome of *l̥h_2 can only be the fact that the zero-grade syllable was accented. But we have already seen some accented examples of word-initial *n̥H- which instead yielded the majority outcome; thus a further condition for this disyllabic outcome was probably that the sequence in question was not word-initial. If this reasoning is correct, it is possible that nouns like θάνατος 'death' and κάματος 'toil' do not reflect full-grade *θένατος, *κέματος with assimilation of the short vowels across a sonorant (which did occur sporadically in Greek), but derivation from the preforms of the adjectives *θνᾱτός, *κμᾱτός by a shift of accent (cf. Rix 1976a: 73–4, Nussbaum 1986: 165–7 with references).

If a sequence *R̥H was followed by a non-high vowel, the laryngeal was simply lost, as expected; thus aor. βαλε͂ν 'to throw', for instance, reflects *g^{w}l̥h$_1$-é/ó-, with the usual outcome of syllabic *l̥. On the reflexes of syllabic nasals in this position, see 3.3.

This is also the place to discuss a minor puzzle of Greek sound change. There was a PIE adjective meaning 'long' that is well attested in the core subgroups of the family:

> PIE *dl̥h$_1$g^{h}ós 'long' > Skt *dīrg^{h}ás*, Av. *darəyō*, OCS *dlŭgŭ*; cf. also Lith. *ìlgas* (initial stop lost), Goth. *tulgus* 'firm' (transferred into the u-stems; *'long-lasting', cf. Lat. *dūrus* 'hard' with a similar shift in meaning).

We can be reasonably sure that the laryngeal was *h$_1$ because of a Greek compound:

> ἐνδελεχής 'continual', deriv. of s-stem *δέλεχος 'length' < *délh$_1$g^{h}os.

We would therefore expect the Greek reflex of the adjective to be 'δληχός'; but of course it is (Hom.) δολιχός. The source of the sequence -ολι- is unknown. It seems possible that πολύς 'much' < *pl̥h$_1$ús (see 3.2.2) exhibits the same apparent change of *l̥h$_1$ to ολ, though this additional example does not help to explain it. It has even been suggested that πόλις 'city' is cognate with Skt *pur-* 'citadel', possibly < *pl̥H-; but πόλις is an i-stem with conservative inflection, and it seems incredible that its ι could somehow have arisen from a laryngeal, as the ι of δολιχός apparently did.

3.2.4 Developments of laryngeals not adjacent to a syllabic

In one environment a word-initial laryngeal before a non-syllabic did not survive as a separate segment in Greek. Word-initial *Hy-, apparently with any laryngeal, yields /h-/ in 1st-millennium Ancient Greek; evidently *Hy- > *hy- > *[j̥] > *h*-. There are now three clinching examples, discovered by three different colleagues:

> PIE *h$_1$yeh$_1$- 'make' (Hitt. pres. 3sg. *iezzi*, Toch. A *yaṣ*) → aor. *h$_1$yeh$_1$-k- 'throw' (Lat. pf. *iēcisse*) > ἡκ- (Peters 1976);
>
> PIE *h$_2$yu-gih$_3$- 'having vigorous life' (cpd. of *h$_2$óyu and *g^{w}yoh$_3$- with delabialization next to *u; cf. Lat. *iūgis* 'ever-flowing', Av. *yauuaējī-* 'having eternal life') > ὑγιής 'healthy' (Weiss 1995: 149–51; connection suggested in Schwyzer 1939: 303);

PIE *Hyewh₂- 'graze' (cf. Skt *yávasam* 'pasture', *sūyávasas* 'having good pasture', *gávyūtis* 'cow-pasture') > *ἐϝα- in Hom. εἰαμενή 'water-meadow' (ει = ε̄ by metrical lengthening of the third of five light syllables; Nikolaev 2014, citing unpublished work by Jochem Schindler on the Indo-Iranian forms).

Relying on these three clear examples, I posit *Hy- whenever the Greek rough breathing appears to correspond to a reflex of *y- in other IE languages, including the following (cf. Lejeune 1972: 165–6):

PIE *Hyós rel. 'who, which' (Skt *yás*) > ὅς;
PIE *Hyḗkʷr̥ ~ *Hyékʷn- 'liver' (Skt *yákr̥t*, Lat. *iecur* with full grade generalized) > ἧπαρ;
PIE *Hiǵnós 'holy' (cf. Goth. *swikns* 'pure', compounded with *h₁su- 'good', Heidermanns 1993: 582 with refs.) → *Hyaǵnós (full grade reintroduced from the related verb; Skt *yajñás* 'worship') > ἁγνός 'holy, pure';
PIE *Hyéh₁gʷah₂ 'strength' *vel sim.* (Lith. *jė́ga*) > ἥβᾱ 'youth' > Att.-Ion. ἥβη;
PIE *Hyeh₁-ro- 'period of time' (Goth. *jer* 'year'), o-grade deriv. *Hyoh₁-ro- (cf. Lat. *hōrnus* 'this year's' < *ho-jōr-ino-) > ὥρᾱ;
PIE *Hyewdʰ- ~ *Hyudʰ- 'be excited' (Toch. A *mar yutkatār* 'don't worry', Skt *yúdʰyati* '(s)he fights', Lat. *iubēre* 'to command'), deriv. *Hyudʰ-sm- with further suffixation in Hom. ὑσμῑ́νη 'combat'.

There is also an example attested only in the psilotic dialect of Homer (on which, see further 3.5.1):

PIE *Hyn̥h₂tḗr, voc. *Hyénh₂ter 'husband's brother's wife' (Old Lith. *jentė*, Skt *yātár-*) in Hom. pl. εἰνατέρες (ει = ε̄ by metrical lengthening).

By contrast the reflex of PIE initial *y- is ζ- (see 3.6.2).

In the Linear B documents forms of the relative pronoun are written both as *jo-* and as *o-*. That can only mean either that the regular sound change *j̥- > *h-* was in progress during the period when the Linear B documents were written, or that the sound change had occurred at some time after the Linear B script was adapted for Greek, in which case the spellings with *jo-* would be etymological. In either case the PGk stage must have been *hj- or *j̥-.

Otherwise when no syllabic sound was adjacent the usual outcomes of PIE laryngeals are straightforward: *h₁ > ε, *h₂ > α, *h₃ > ο. Only Greek clearly exhibits this 'triple reflex' of laryngeals, and that fact makes Greek evidence crucial for the reconstruction of these PIE consonants.

Examples of word-initial laryngeals followed by a consonant are numerous. In many cases only Greek offers evidence of the laryngeal. In some the evidence of Greek is corroborated by Anatolian languages or by Armenian; in others it is corroborated by lengthening of the final vowels of first elements of compounds or of reduplicating syllables in Indo-Iranian. There are more than a dozen examples with *h_1:

PIE *$h_1$ger- ~ *$h_1$gr- 'wake up', pf. *$h_1$ge-$h_1$gór-e '(s)he is awake' (Skt *jāgā́ra* '(s)he is awake') > pres. *ἐγερ-jε/ο- > ἐγε̄́ρε̄ν 'to be waking (someone) up', aor. ἐγρέσθαι 'to wake up', pf. *ἐγήγορε → ἐγρήγορε '(s)he is awake' (by contamination with ἐγρέσθαι; Warren Cowgill, p.c. ca. 1978; *LIV* s.v. **$h_1$ger*);

PIE *h_1s-ónt- ~ *h_1s-n̥t- pres. ptc. 'being' (Skt *sánt-* ~ *sat-*; cpd. *ā́sat-* 'not existing' < *ń̥-$h_1$sn̥t-) > *ἐhόντ- ~ *ἐhα̨τ- > Ion. ἐόντ-, Ark. fem. ἔασσα (see 3.2.1);

PIE *$h_1$werǵ- 'shut in, enclose' (Lith. *ver̃žti*) > Hom. ἐέργε̄́ν, cf. also Cyprian aor. 3pl. *ka-te-wo-ro-ko-ne* *κατ-έϝοργον 'they besieged';

PIE *$h_1$wers- 'rain, fall (as dew)' (Skt *várṣati* 'it's raining') > Hom. ἐέρση 'dew';

PIE *$h_1$ln̥g^{wh}rós and *$h_1$léng^{h}u- ~ *$h_1$ln̥g^{wh}éw- 'light(weight)' (OHG *lungar* 'vigorous', Skt *rag^{h}ús* 'swift') >→ ἐλαφρός 'light', ἐλαχύς 'little';

PIE *$h_1$leng^{h}- 'clear oneself under oath' (Hitt. *linkzi* '(s)he swears') > ἐλέγχε̄ν 'to cross-examine, to refute';

PIE *$h_1$léwd^{h}eros 'free' (Lat. *līber*, Venetic dat. pl. *louderobos* 'for (his) children') > ἐλεύθερος;

PIE *$h_1$rég^{w}os 'darkness' (Goth. *riqis*; Skt *rájas* 'empty space', Arm. *erek* 'evening') > ἔρεβος 'the passage to the underworld';

PIE *$h_1$reyp- 'tear down' (ON *rífa* 'to tear') > ἐρείπε̄ν;

PIE *$h_1$rép-ye/o- 'be snatching' (Lat. *rapere* with remodeled root) > Hom. ἐρεπτόμενος 'devouring';

PIE *$h_1$rewg- 'belch' (Lat. *ē-rūgere*) > Hom. ἐρεύγεσθαι;

PIE *$h_1$rud^{h}rós 'red' (Toch. B *ratre*, Lat. *ruber*) > ἐρυθρός;

PIE *$h_1$roHwáh$_2$ 'rest' (OE *rōw*) > Hom. ἐρωή 'lull, pause (in battle)'.

A further example is Hom. ἐρείομεν 'let's ask', adduced in 3.2.2. The large proportion of examples beginning with ἐρ- has led to reservations on the part of some specialists; they point out that, since initial /r-/ is synchronically absent in Greek and Armenian, such an example as ἔρεβος = *erek* might actually reflect a sound change by which word-initial *r- acquired a prothetic vowel in those languages (Rix 1976a: 58, Mayrhofer 1982: 186 fn. 30). It is difficult to prove or disprove that suggestion. A possible example of post-PIE initial *r- which does not exhibit prothesis in Greek is Hom. ῥίμφα 'lightly, swiftly', which might be cognate with OHG *ringi* 'slight', reflecting a preform *ring^{wh}- (Heidermanns 1993: 445–6), but the cognation is uncertain. In any case there is no such alternative for the examples beginning with *h_2:

PIE *$h_2$wes- 'spend the night' (Skt *vásati* '(s)he stays', Goth. *wisan* 'to be'; cf. Toch. B *yṣīye*, A *wṣe* 'night') > Hom. aor. ἀέσαι;

PIE *h_2wḗ$h_1$ti '(wind) is blowing' (Skt *vā́ti*; for the laryngeal cf. Hitt. *hūwanz* 'wind') > Hom. ἄησι;
PIE *h_2ḱ-$h_2$ows-ié/ó- 'be sharp-eared' (PGmc *hauzijaną 'to hear' > Goth. *hausjan*, ON *heyra*, OE *hīeran* 'to hear') > ἀκούε̄ν 'to hear';
PIE *$h_2$leg- 'care (about)' (Lat. *dī-ligere* 'to love') > Hom. (οὐκ) ἀλέγω 'I (don't) care';
PIE *$h_2$lék-se/o- 'protect' (Skt 3sg. *rákṣati*) > ἀλέξε̄ν;
PIE *$h_2$melǵ- 'milk' (verb; OE *melcan*, Lith. *mélžti*) > ἀμέλγε̄ν;
PIE *h_2nḗr, *$h_2$nér- 'man' (Skt *nā́*, Arm. *ayr*; cf. Skt cpd. *sūnára-* 'vigorous') > ἀνήρ, ἀνέρ-;
PIE *$h_2$pélos 'wound' (noun; Toch. B *pīle*, A *päl*) > ἄπελος 'open wound';
PIE *$h_2$reh$_1$g- 'take care of' (intensive ON *rœkja*, OHG *ruohhen* 'to care for') > Hom. ἀρήγε̄ν 'to help';
PIE *$h_2$stḗr, *$h_2$stér- 'star' (Hitt. *hasterz*, Arm. *astł*, Goth. *staírno*) > ἀστήρ, ἀστέρ-;
PIE *$h_2$tug- 'frightful' (Hitt. *hatugis*) in Hom. ἀτύζεσθαι 'to be scared witless' (cf. Benveniste 1937).

Clear examples with *h_3 are fewer, as that laryngeal was less common in PIE:

PIE *h_3b^{h}rúH-s 'eyebrow' (Skt *b^{h}rū́s*) > ὀφρῦς;
PIE *$h_3$ner- 'dream' (Arm. *anowrǰ*) > Hom. ὄναρ and deriv. ὄνε̄ρος;
PIE *$h_3$neyd- 'blame, criticize' (Skt ptc. *nidānás* 'blamed', Av. pres. 1sg. *nāismī* 'I insult', Goth. *ganaitjan* 'to abuse'), s-stem neut. result noun *$h_3$néydos > ὄνειδος 'reproach';
PIE *$h_3$nog^h- 'nail, claw' (OE *næġl*), extended *$h_3$nog^h-w- (cf. Toch. B pl. *mekwa*, Lat. *unguis*) > *ὀνοχ^w- > ὄνυχ-;
PIE *$h_3$reǵ- 'put in a straight line' (Lat. *regere* 'to guide') > ὀρέγε̄ν 'to reach'.

There is also the case of ὀμείχε̄ν 'to urinate' (Lat. *meiere*, OE *mīgan*, pres. 3sg. Skt *méhati*, Av. *maēzaiti*; cf. also Arm. *mêz* 'urine') and ὀμίχλη 'mist' (Lith. *miglà*, OCS *mĭgla*; cf. also Skt *meg^{h}ás* 'cloud', Arm. *mêg* 'fog'). Though the two words have been associated by folk etymology, they are not derived from the same root; the final consonant of 'urinate' was PIE palatal *ǵ^h, as the Iranian and Armenian *z*'s demonstrate, while that of 'cloud, mist' was velar *g^h, according to the unanimous testimony of Indo-Iranian, Balto-Slavic, and Armenian. Probably one of those roots began with *h_3 and the other did not, but we cannot tell which was which, as the reflex of the laryngeal has spread from one to the other in Greek but been eliminated by an opposite lexical analogy in Armenian.

In at least two words the vowel which resulted from the initial laryngeal has been (irregularly) assimilated to the vowel of the following syllable in most Greek dialects; in each case one dialect preserves the vowel which we expect to find:

PIE *$h_1$dónt- ~ *$h_1$dn̥t- 'tooth' (Skt *dánt- ~ dat-*) > ἐδόντ- in Aiolic pl. ἔδοντες (cited by Proklos in his commentary on the *Kratylos*); otherwise assimilated ὀδόντ-;

PIE *h$_1$néh$_3$mn̥ ~ *h$_1$nóh$_3$mn- 'name' (cf. Toch. B *ñem*, Hitt. *lāman*, Lat. *nōmen*) >→ *ἔνομα > *ἔνυμα in Lakonian Ἐνυμακρατίδᾱς; otherwise assimilated (Att.) ὄνομα > (most dialects) ὄνυμα.

On the last example, see also 3.2.2 *ad fin.* The fact that such an assimilation was clearly possible makes a third case exceptionally difficult to assess. There was clearly a PIE root *Hneḱ- meaning 'reach' which had a byform *Hnenḱ- in which the nasal had been copied into the syllable coda; that much is clear from the Sanskrit forms:

Skt aor. *ā́naṭ* '(s)he has reached' < PIE *é Hneḱ-t, pf. *ānā́śa* ~ *ānáṃśa* '(s)he reached' < PIE *He-Hnóḱ-e ~ *He-Hnónḱ-e.

But because all non-high vowels merged as *a* and *ā* in Indo-Iranian, Sanskrit gives us no information about the identity of the root-initial laryngeal. The corresponding Old Irish form suggests that it was *h$_2$ or *h$_3$:

OIr. pret. *t-ánaic* '(s)he came' < *t(o) ānogge < Proto-Celtic *ānonke, in which *ā reflects either *ā < *h$_2$a-h$_2$ ... or *ō < *h$_3$o-h$_3$ ...

An a-vowel is apparently attested for this root in Gk διᾱνεκής 'continual', but the latter is a hyper-Atticism for διηνεκής (attested in Homer and Plato; see Schwyzer 1939: 190); it appears that the root was uniformly ἐνε(γ)κ- in Greek. The balance of probability is that the root was PIE *h$_2$ne(n)ḱ-, and that the initial vowel of aor. ἐνεγκεῖν 'to bring' has been assimilated to the vowel of the following syllable, but certainty is not attainable.[12]

It is possible, but not certain, that word-initial laryngeals before non-syllabics failed to vocalize in highly specific environments. Peters (1980: 23–6 fn. 18), argues that laryngeals were lost in the environment *HCR̥- in Greek when *R̥ was not nasal. Many of his examples can be explained in other ways, but at least one isolated word seems worth mentioning here. Gk λῆνος 'wool' (neut. s-stem) seems to be derived from PIE *h$_2$wl̥h$_1$no- 'wool' (Hitt. dat. *hulani*, Skt *ū́rṇā*, Lat. *lāna*, Goth. *wulla*, Lith. pl. *vìlnos*); if it is, the initial laryngeal must have been dropped very early, so that the pre-Greek shape of the word was *wlēno-. However, there are several problems with this etymology. That it is an s-stem is puzzling, but given

[12] I am not convinced that there are two different roots involved, nor that the Greek aorist was originally reduplicated, *pace LIV* s.vv. **h$_1$neḱ*, **h$_2$neḱ*. It is not clear why the nasal in this root was sporadically copied into the syllable coda, but since such a process has left clear traces in Indo-Iranian, Greek, and Celtic it must be accepted as a descriptive fact. A further example of assimilation across a sonorant might be present in the word-family (Hom.) ὄροφος 'roof': ἐρέφειν 'to roof'; on the other hand, this root might have begun with *r-, in which case the initial vowels would be prothetic (*LIV* s.v. 2.**rebʰ*-).

that it is, its accentuation is expected. But in that case why did accented $^{*}\acute{l}̥h_1$ not yield 'ἐλε' (see 3.2.3 *ad fin.*)? After all, the word would still have begun with *w after the loss of the laryngeal, so it cannot be exempted from that development by arguing that the sequence was word-initial. Under the circumstances it seems best to suspend judgment. An example with a more solid etymology raises other questions. From the fact that Att. νῆττα, Ion. νῆσσα 'duck' appears in *Akharnians* 875 as 'Boiotian'[13] νᾶσσα it seems likely that it reflects the PIE word, usually reconstructed as $^{*}h_2$ánh$_2$t- ~ $^{*}h_2$n̥h$_2$t- (Lat. *anas*, OHG *anut*, Lith. *ántis*, Skt *ātís*, etc.). If the reconstruction is correct, the initial laryngeal must have been lost before the change of *n̥h$_2$ to νᾱ (see 3.2.3). However, it is possible that the PIE word was *ánh$_2$t- ~ *n̥h$_2$t-, with no initial laryngeal; in fact the Greek form might plausibly be adduced as evidence for that hypothesis, and there is no counterevidence. Note that in this word the sonorant-plus-laryngeal sequence was word-initial, so that the absence of a disyllabic reflex is not problematic.

Word-internally and word-finally the regular outcomes of the three laryngeals were also respectively ε, α, and ο. The examples adduced in 3.2.3 are typical, e.g. ε < $^{*}h_1$ in the medial syllables of τέμενος, γενέτωρ, τέρετρον, ἐρέω, and βέλενμα and α < $^{*}h_2$ in the medial syllables of ἐκέρασε and τελαμών. Other examples include:[14]

PIE $^{*}h_2$ónh$_1$mos or $^{*}h_2$n̥h$_1$mós 'breath' (cf. Arm. *hołm* 'wind' and see 3.2.2 *ad fin.*), possibly remodeled on $^{*}h_2$ánh$_1$ti '(s)he breathes' (Skt *ániti*), >→ ἄνεμος 'wind';
PIE *kréwh$_2$s 'raw meat' (Skt *kravís*) > κρέας 'meat';
PIE *méǵh$_2$ neut. 'big' (Skt *máhi*) > μέγα;
PIE *ph$_2$tḗr 'father' (Skt *pitā́*, Lat. *pater*) > πατήρ;
PIE *d^{h}ugh$_2$tḗr 'daughter' (Skt *duhitā́*, Goth. *daúhtar*) > θυγάτηρ;
PIE *sámh$_2$d^{h}os 'sand' (ON *sandr*, Middle High German *sam(b)t*) > ἄμαθος;
PIE $^{*}h_2$árh$_3$trom 'plow' (OIr. *arathar*, ON *arðr*) > ἄροτρον.

A substantial majority of the isolated examples are α < $^{*}h_2$; the first and last examples in this short list are important because their ε and ο cannot be explained by any sort of morphological change. Examples that alternate with full-grade η, ᾱ/η, ω < *eh$_1$, *ah$_2$, *oh$_3$ respectively are of course not hard to find:

[13] Of course a genuine Boiotian form would contain ττ; if the form is correctly transmitted, Aristophanes was presumably making the word as 'foreign' as possible (Colvin 1999: 167, 179). I no longer believe that this Greek word can instead be a participle of 'swim' (Katz 2004: 196–9); note that the apparent Hittite cognate is actually *lahhanzan-* 'shelduck' (see Melchert 2003, especially pp. 136–7, for discussion).

[14] It can be seen that the Sanskrit reflex of laryngeals in these positions is usually *i*, though in some cases the laryngeal simply disappears. This is a good diagnostic for recognizing laryngeal outcomes in Greek.

PIE *d^{h}é-d^{h}eh$_1$-ti '(s)he's putting', *d^{h}é-d^{h}h$_1$-te 'you (pl.) are putting', *d^{h}h$_1$-tós 'placed' (Skt *dá-d^{h}ā-ti, d^{h}a-t-t^{h}á, hi-tás*) >→[15] τίθησι, τίθετε, θετός 'adopted (child)';
PIE *stáh$_3$-t '(s)he stood up', with augment *é stah$_3$-t, verbal adj. *sth$_3$-tós 'standing, stationary' (Skt *á-st^{h}ā-t* '(s)he has stood up', *st^{h}i-tás* 'having stood up') > ἔστᾱ > Att.-Ion. ἔστη, στατός 'standing, stalled (horse)';
PIE *dé-doh$_3$-ti '(s)he's giving', *dé-dh$_3$-te 'you (pl.) are giving', *dh$_3$-tós 'given' (Skt *dá-dā-ti, da-t-t^{h}á*, Lat. *datus*) >→ δίδωσι, δίδοτε, θεό-δοτος 'god-given' (cf. Skt *devá-ttas* with different first member).

Such examples are less probative as evidence for regular sound change, since leveling within paradigms must be reckoned with; but since they are consistent with the regular sound changes of Greek, there is no reason not to accept them as regular sound-change outcomes.

3.3 Early developments of nasals

PIE word-final *-m became -ν in Greek. Like the developments of laryngeals, this sound change could have occurred indefinitely early. Most examples involve inflectional endings:

PIE *yugóm neut. nom.-acc. 'yoke' (Skt *yugám*, Lat. *iugum*) > ζυγόν;
PIE *néwom masc. acc. 'new' (Skt *návam*, Lat. *novom*) > νέον 'young';
PIE *h$_2$ówim acc. 'sheep' (Skt *ávim* with leveled root-ablaut) > Hom. ὄϊν;
PIE *b^{h}āǵ^{h}um acc. 'arm' (Skt *bāhúm*) > πᾶχυν > Att.-Ion. πῆχυν 'forearm';
PIE *pl̥h$_2$mām 'flat hand' (Lat. *palmam*) > *πάλαμᾱν > Hom. παλάμην;
PIE *dyḗm ~ *diḗm acc. 'sky' (Skt *dyā́m ~ diā́m*, Lat. *diem* 'day') > *Zῆν → Dor. Zῆν-a 'Zeus' with added acc. ending;
PIE *b^{h}érom 'I was carrying', with augment *é b^{h}erom (Skt *áb^{h}aram*) > ἔφερον;
PIE *d^{h}éd^{h}ēm 'I was putting, I put (several things)', with augment *é d^{h}ed^{h}ēm (Skt *ádad^{h}ām*) >→ ἐτίθην;
PIE opt. *h$_1$siḗm 'let me be' (Skt *syā́m ~ siā́m*, Old Lat. *siem*) > εἴην;
PIE *b^{h}éretom 'the two of you were carrying', with augment *é b^{h}eretom (Skt *áb^{h}aratam*) > ἐφέρετον;
PIE *b^{h}éretām 'the two of them were carrying', with augment *é b^{h}eretām (Skt *áb^{h}aratām*) > ἐφερέτᾱν > Att.-Ion. ἐφερέτην.

[15] In this present and in διδόναι 'be giving' the reduplicating vowel *e has been replaced by *i so as to conform to the majority type of reduplicated presents. The only present stem reduplicated with *e which survives in Greek is τετραίνε̄ν 'to bore holes in', to which further suffixes have been added.

Of course this sound change also affected endingless forms of the few m-stem nominals that existed in PIE. From those forms the innovative -ν was leveled through the paradigms, but that process took a long time; it was still incomplete in the Mycenaean period. The following forms are relevant:

PIE nom. *d^{h}éǵ^{h}ōm 'earth' (Hitt. *tēkan*), loc. *d^{h}ǵ^{h}ém 'on the ground' (Skt *kṣám-i* with deictic particle *-i) >→ *d^{h}ǵ^{h}ṓm, *d^{h}ǵ^{h}óm > nom. χθών, loc. *χθόν → dat. χθονί, whence by leveling acc. χθόνα, gen. χθονός, but PIE allative *ǵ^{h}m̥áh$_2$ 'to the ground' + deictic *-i > Hom. adv. χαμαί;

PIE neut. nom.-acc. *sém 'one' (cf. Lat. *semel* 'once') > ἕν, whence by leveling gen. ἑνός, dat. ἑνί, but Myc. dat. *e-me* = *ἑμεί, with -μ- not yet leveled and the original dat. ending *-éy;

PIE nom. *ǵ^{h}éyōm 'winter', loc. *ǵ^{h}yém ~ *ǵ^{h}iém 'in winter' (Hitt. *giemi*, Lat. *hieme*, both with deictic *-i) >→ nom. χιών 'snow', whence χιόν- by leveling, but zero-grade oblique stem *ǵ^{h}im- in deriv. χίμετλα 'chilblains'.

In most environments PIE syllabic *m̥ and *n̥ became a vowel, which at first must have been nasalized *[ə̃] but was eventually lowered, for which reason I write it as *ą; it merged with α in all the attested dialects except the Mycenaean of the Linear B tablets, in which it is variably written *a* and *o* word-finally after *m* (the position in which it is by far the most common in the documents), and it is highly probable that it was still [ã] in Mycenaean (Skelton 2022). Relatively isolated examples are numerous, e.g.:

PIE *septḿ̥ 'seven' (Skt *saptá*, Lat. *septem*) > ἑπτά;

PIE *déḱm̥d 'ten' (Goth. *taíhun*, Lith. *dẽšimt*; Skt *dáśa*, Lat. *decem* with final cons. lost by lexical analogy with 'seven') > δέκα;

PIE *ḱm̥tóm 'hundred' (Skt *śatám*, Lat. *centum*, Lith. *šim̃tas*) > ἑ-κατόν (ἑ-, reduced form of ἕν 'one');

PIE *wī́ḱm̥tih$_1$ 'twenty' (Lat. *vīgintī*) > Dor. ϝῑ́κατι;

PIE pres. *g^{w}m̥-sḱé/ó- 'step (repeatedly), walk' (Skt *gácc^{h}ati*) > Hom. βάσκε̄ν 'to go';

PIE *sm̥- 'one, same' (Skt *sa-*; cf. Lat. *sim-plex* 'simple', lit. 'one-fold') > ἁ-, e.g. in ἅπαξ 'once', ἁπλόος > ἁπλõς 'single, simple', lit. 'one-fold', *ἁκόλουθος 'walking the same path (κέλευθος 'path') > ἀκόλουθος 'companion' (by Grassmann's Law, see 3.5.4);

PIE non-neut. acc. sg. *-m̥, e.g. in *pódm̥ 'foot', *nók^{w}tm̥ 'night' (Skt *pā́dam*, with *-m* leveled in from vowel stems; Lat. *noctem*) > -α, e.g. in πόδα, νύκτα;

PIE *n̥- 'un-' (Skt *a-*, Lat. *in-*, Goth., OE *un-*), e.g. in *ń̥d^{h}g^{wh}itom (ḱléwos) 'imperishable (fame)' (Skt *ákṣitaṃ* (*śrávas*)), > ἀ-, e.g. in Hom. (κλέος) ἄφθιτον;

PIE *h₁l̥ŋgʷʰrós and *h₁léngʰu- ~ *h₁l̥ŋgʷʰéw- 'light(weight)' (OHG *lungar* 'vigorous', Skt *ragʰús* 'swift') >→ ἐλαφρός 'light', ἐλαχύς 'little';

PIE *h₁sóntih₂ fem. 'being' → *h₁sn̥tíh₂ (Skt *satī́*) > *ἐhα̨τjα > Arkadian ἔασσα;

PIE *tn̥tós 'stretched, stretchable' (Lat. *tentus* 'stretched') > τατός 'stretchable';

PIE *néwmn̥ 'nod, act of nodding' (Lat. *nūmen* 'will, divine will) > νεῦμα;

pre-Greek *spérmn̥ 'sowing, seed' (cf. σπέ̄ρε̄ν 'to sow') > σπέρμα, Myc. *pe-ma* ~ *pe-mo;*

PIE non-neut. acc. pl. *-n̥s (Skt *-as*, Lat. *-ēs*), e.g. in *nókʷtn̥s 'nights' (Lat. *noctēs*), > -ας, e.g. in νύκτας;

PIE 1ary act. 3pl. *-n̥ti (Skt *-ati*, e.g. in *tákṣati* 'they fashion') > -ατι, e.g. in Northwest Gk pf. (κατάδικοι ...) γεγόνατι 'they have been (convicted)' *IG* IX-1².171.6, > Ark. -ασι, e.g. in pf. [ϝō]φλέ̄ασι 'they owe', *DGE* 661.1;

PIE 2ary mp. 3pl. *-n̥to (Skt *-ata*), e.g. in *wésn̥to 'they were wearing' (Skt *ávasata* with augment), > -ατο, e.g. in εἵατ(ο), *Il.* 18.596 (ει = ε̄, either by contraction with the augment or by lengthening of a line-initial light syllable in the transmission of the text).

If the syllabic nasal was followed immediately by a vowel or *y, the result of this development was not merely *α̨ but a sequence *α̨m or *α̨n, depending on the identity of the syllabic nasal. It seems clear that the various losses of laryngeals preceded this change and gave rise to some of the examples of syllabic nasals before vowels and *y. Examples of various origins include:

PIE allative *ǵʰm̥áh₂ 'to the ground' (with *m̥ by Lindeman's Law; cf. Hitt. *taknā* with leveled ablaut) + deictic *-i > Hom. adv. χαμαί;

PIE *sm̥Hó- 'some' (Goth. *sums*, OE *sum*) > ἁμό- in Hom. ἁμόθεν 'from somewhere';

PIE *sm̥H ... 'same' (cf. OIr. *samail* 'similar') > ἅμα 'at the same time';

PIE *demh₂- 'tame' (verb root; cf. Lat. *domāre*, Goth. *gatamjan*), zero-grade *dm̥h₂- > δαμ- in Hom. intr. aor. δαμήμεναι 'to be overcome';

PIE *dh₂pn̥óm 'sacrifice' (with *n̥ by Sievers' Law; ON *tafn*, Lat. *damnum* 'expense') > *δαπανό- in δαπάνη 'expense' (collective with shifted accent);

PIE *pl̥th₂n̥ós 'broad' (Proto-Celtic *litanos > OIr. *lethan*, Welsh *llydan*) > *πλατανό- in πλατάνιστος 'plane-tree' (substantivized superlative with shifted accent);

PIE *ń̥udros 'waterless' (with syllabic *n̥ before zero-grade *u at compound boundary; Skt *anudrás*) > ἄνυδρος;

PIE *ténh₂u- ~ *tn̥h₂áw- 'stretched, thin' (Skt *tanús*, Lat. *tenuis*) >→ τανaός, compounding form τανυ- 'stretched, long';

PIE *h₁n̥h₃mn̥-yé/ó- 'name' (verb; Goth. *namnjan*, OE *nemnan*) >→ *ὀνομα̨ν-jε/ο- > ὀνομαίνε̄ν 'to name';

PIE *mn̥yétor '(s)he is mentally active' → post-PIE *mn̥yétoy (Skt *mányate* '(s)he thinks') > *μα̥νjετοι >→ μαίνεται '(s)he is raving';
PIE pres. *u-né-bʰ- 'be weaving' (Skt 2sg. *sám unap*) → *ubʰ-né-H- (Skt inj. 2sg. *ubʰnā́s*, 3sg. with augment *aubʰnāt*) → *ubʰ-n̥-H-yé- > *ὐφανjε- > ὑφαίνε̄ν.

Whether the same development occurred before *w is not completely clear, but it is probable. Note especially the following:

PIE *seyk- 'walk' *vel sim.* (cf. Toch. B *siknaṃ* '(s)he steps') in post-PIE pres. *sik-néw- ~ *sik-nu- ~ *sik-n̥w-; the first alternant is thematized in *hικ-νέϝ-ε/ο- > ἱκνέεσθαι 'to come to, to arrive', the third in *hικ-α̥νϝ-ε/ο- > Hom. ἱκά̄νε̄ν (see 7.2.2).

Of course the suffixal ν in the last form cited might have been introduced by leveling within the paradigm before it was split. But the few examples of α (rather than αν) before *w are even more easily susceptible to explanation by leveling, e.g.:

PIE pf. *memóne '(s)he has in mind' (Goth. *ga-man*, Lat. *meminit* '(s)he remembers') ~ *memn̥- > Hom. μέμονε '(s)he desires, (s)he is eager for' ~ μεμα-, e.g. in 1pl. μέμαμεν, etc.—whence ptc. μεμαώς ←< *memn̥-wṓs.

Since μεμα- has even been leveled into position before a vowel in 3pl. μεμάᾱσι, we certainly cannot use μεμαώς as evidence for the regular sound-change outcome of *n̥ before *w. The same is true a fortiori of Hom. ἐκγεγαώς 'born of [+ gen.]', which must have been formed, or perhaps re-formed, after the root-final laryngeal had been lost.

At some point after the resolution of syllabic nasals before vowels and semivowels —possibly long after—the sequence *my > *ny. I can find only two examples:

PIE pres. *gʷm̥-yé/ó- 'step (repeatedly), walk' (Lat. *venīre* 'to come') > *gʷα̥m-yé/ó- > *γʷανjε/ο- > βαίνε̄ν 'to go';
PIE *kóm 'with' (Lat. *cum*) in pre-Gk *kom-yó-s '(held in) common' > *κονjός > κοινός.

Though *kóm does not otherwise survive in Greek, the latter derivation is practically certain, since it is parallel to that of another word meaning 'common':

pre-Gk *ξυνjός 'common' (cf. ξύν 'with') > Ion. ξῡνός.

3.4 Early developments of obstruents

3.4.1 'Thorn' clusters

The reflexes of 'thorn' clusters in Greek are velar + dental or labial + dental, the latter reflecting inherited clusters of labiovelars (see 5.4.1):

PIE *h₂ŕ̥tḱos 'bear' (Hitt. *hartaggas*, Skt *ŕ̥kṣas*, Av. *aršō*, Lat. *ursus*) > ἄρκτος;
PIE *tḱey- 'settle', pres. 3pl. *tḱiénti (Skt 3sg. *kṣéti*, 3pl. *kṣiyánti*, Av. *šaēiti, šiieinti*) > Myc. 3pl. *ki-ti-je-si* *κτιjένσι, Hom. ptc. ἐϋκτίμενος 'well settled';
PIE *tétḱō 'craftsman' (Skt *tákṣā*, Av. *tašā*) > τέκτων 'carpenter';
PIE *tken- ~ *tkn̥- 'hurt' (Skt *mā́ kṣaṇiṣṭʰās* 'do not injure yourself') > Hom. ἔ-κτα-μεν 'we slew' (*LIV* s.v. **tken*);
PIE *h₂adʰgʰ- 'press' (Hitt. *hatki* '(s)he closes') > ἄχθεσθαι 'to be loaded; to be oppressed';
PIE nom. *dʰéǵʰōm 'earth' (Hitt. *tēkan*), loc. *dʰǵʰém 'on the ground' (Skt *kṣám-i* with deictic particle *-i; for the palatal cf. Av. gen. *zəmō*) >→ *dʰǵʰóm, *dʰǵʰóm > nom. χθών, loc. *χθόν → dat. χθονί;
PIE *n̥dʰgʷʰitom (ḱléwos) 'imperishable (fame)' (Skt *ákṣitam* (*śrávas*)) > Hom. (κλέος) ἄφθιτον.

It now seems likely that what produced this outcome was a simple metathesis motivated by misperception; see Jasanoff (2018) for discussion. Metathesis is also the longstanding explanation for the shape of the present stem related to 'carpenter':

PIE *teḱ- 'produce' (cf. aor. τεκεῖν 'to give birth'), pres. *téteḱ- ~ *tétḱ- (the latter in Skt 3pl. *tákṣati*) >→ *τιτεκ- ~ *τιτκ- → *τιτκ-ε/ο- > τίκτεῖν.

3.4.2 The merger of palatals and velars

As in Italo-Celtic, Germanic, Tocharian, and Hittite, the PIE 'palatals' and 'velars' merged as velars. The merger can be demonstrated only with examples that have cognates in languages that did not undergo it, namely Indo-Iranian, Balto-Slavic, and (under some conditions) Armenian, Albanian, and the Luvian subgroup of Anatolian.[16] Moreover, there seem to have been few minimal pairs involving these consonants in PIE, with the result that Greek exhibits no pairs of homonyms with velars of different etymological sources. Nevertheless it is possible to find examples of former palatals and velars in approximately the same phonological environments, e.g.:

[16] On the Armenian facts, see, e.g., Schmitt (1981: 61–5); on Albanian, see Demiraj (1997: 63–6); on the Luvian subgroup, see Melchert (1994a: 251–6, 302–3).

PIE *ḱéyor '(s)he's lying down' (Luv. *ziyar*) → *ḱéytor (Hitt. *kitta*) → *ḱéytoy (Skt *śéte*) >→ κεῖται (see 5.4.2 on the ending);

PIE *kes- 'comb' (verb; Luv. *kīsa(i)-*, OCS pres. 3sg. *češetŭ*) > κεσ- in κέσκεον 'flax- hards';

PIE *ḱerh$_2$- 'mix' (verbal adj. *ḱr̥h$_2$tós in Skt *ā́-śīrtas* 'mixed') > κερα- in aor. κεράσαι;

PIE *ker- 'cut, shear' (pres. 3sg. Arm. *k^{h}erê* '(s)he scrapes', Hitt. *karszi* '(s)he cuts off') > κερ- in pres. *κερ-jε/o- > κε̄́ρε̄ν;

PIE *ḱléwos 'fame' (Skt *śrávas*) > κλέος;

PIE *klep- 'steal' (inf. Toch. B *kälypītsi*, Old Lat. *clepere*; cf. Old Prussian *auklipts* 'hidden') > κλέπτε̄ν;

PIE *peḱ- 'comb' (verb; Lith. *pèšti* 'to pluck'; Lat. *pectere* 'to comb' with t-extension) > πέκε̄ν 'to card (wool)';

PIE *plek- 'plait' (with t-extension Lat. *plectere*, OCS pres. 3sg. *pletetŭ*, the latter with *t* < *kt) > πλέκε̄ν;

PIE *ǵénh$_1$os 'lineage' (Skt *jánas*, Lat. *genus*; for the palatal cf. Av. *zīzanəṇti* 'they beget') > γένος;

PIE *gem- 'squeeze' (Lat. *gemere* 'to sigh, to groan'; for the velar cf. Serbo-Croatian aor. 3sg. *žê* '(s)he squeezed') > γέμε̄ν 'to be loaded full';

PIE *leǵ- 'collect, gather' (Lat. *legere*, Albanian pres. 3sg. *mbledh*) > λέγε̄ν 'to gather; to say';

PIE *(s)teg-[17] 'cover' (Lat. *tegere*; for the velar cf. Lith. *stógas* 'roof') > στέγε̄ν;

PIE *mréǵ^{h}u- ~ *mr̥ǵ^{h}éw- 'short' (Lat. *brevis*) → *mr̥ǵ^{h}ús (Av. *mərəzu-*) > βραχύς;

PIE *h$_1$léng^{h}u- ~ *h$_1$ln̥g^{wh}éw- 'light(weight)' → *h$_1$ln̥g^{h}ús (Skt *rag^{h}ús* 'swift') > ἐλαχύς 'little';

PIE *leyǵ^h- 'lick' (Skt pres. 3sg. *réḍ^{h}i* < *láiẓ^{h}ḍ^{h}i < *léyǵ^{h}ti) > λείχε̄ν;

PIE *steyg^h- 'walk forward' (Skt *stig^h-* in *prá stiṅnoti* 'he makes progress', *Maitrāyaṇī- saṃhitā* 2.1.12, Goth. *steigan* 'to ascend') > στείχε̄ν 'to march'.

3.4.3 Early developments of labiovelars

Sequences of dorsal + *w became rounded dorsals (eventually labiovelars—see below). There are two straightforward examples:

PIE *h$_3$nog^h- 'nail, claw' (OE *næġl*), extended *h$_3$nog^h-w- (cf. Toch. B pl. *mekwa*, Lat. *unguis*) > *ὀνοχ^w- > ὄνυχ-;

PIE *ǵ^{h}wḗr 'wild animal' (Lith. *žvėrìs*) > *χ^{w}ήρ > θήρ.

[17] In this family of words, as in some others, a preconsonantal *s- has been gained or lost by resegmentation of compounds. It is often not clear whether the *s- is original. See especially Southern (1999) for extensive discussion.

Other examples are more involved. PIE *éḱwos 'horse' apparently survives in Greek as ἵππος, but every detail of the Greek word (except its stem class) raises problems. The initial /h-/ must reflect lexical analogy with some other word, since there is no aspiration in fossilized names like Λεύκ-ιππος 'His-horses-are-white', Ἄλκ-ιππος 'His-horses-are-his-defense'; thus Myc. *i-qo* should probably be interpreted as *ἴκʷκʷος. There has never been a convincing explanation for the ι. It has been suggested that *ḱw/*kw might have become geminate *κʷκʷ by regular sound change. Possible support for that hypothesis is found in Boiotian τὰ ππᾱ́ματα 'money lent' or 'money owing' in a transcription of promissory notes (four times in *DGE* 523); Boiotian ἔππᾱσις 'right to own land (as a foreigner)', frequent in proxeny decrees (= Att. ἔγκτησις); a handful of Boiotian names like Γυνόππᾱστος (*DGE* 459(1).2); and ἀππᾱσάμενος 'upon regaining (his own land)', Corinna 654.iii.39, all apparently built to a root ππᾱ- 'inherit, possess' < *ḱwah₂- or the like (Schwyzer 1939: 301, Buck 1955: 64, 127, Frisk s.v. πέπᾱμαι, *LIV* s.v. *$ku̯eh_2$*); the zero-grade *ḱuh₂- might appear in κῦριος 'possessed of power, authoritative', which is plausibly connected with Skt *śū́ras* 'hero' (so Schwyzer, Frisk, *locc. citt.*). Though some of the evidence is open to different interpretations—for instance, ταππαματα might actually reflect crasis with a vowel-initial compound, and the consistent ππ of the compounds might conceivably be an irregular development of μπ—the uniformity of the attestations suggests that we probably should recognize a root ππᾱ- (remodeled as πᾱ- in other dialects, not surprisingly). But the fact that this root is isofunctional with Att.-Ion. κτη- raises the suspicion that both reflect a loanword of unusual shape from some indigenous language.[18] I think it prudent to suspend judgment.

It would be most economical to order the merger of palatals and velars before this development, but it is not quite certain that that is what happened. Since the PIE 'palatals' were almost certainly phonetically velars, while the 'velars' and 'labiovelars' were phonetically postvelars and labiopostvelars, the original system was

[k] [q] [qʷ]
[kw] [qw]

(and so for the other manners of articulation). The development discussed here, if it occurred first, would yield a system

[k] [kʷ] [q] [qʷ]

in which the [kʷ]-series was rare and dorsal + *w no longer occurred. Merger of the places of articulation would then yield the PGk system. We cannot tell in which order rounding and the place merger occurred.

[18] The traditional root-cognation of Hom. aor. κτη-σα- 'acquire', pf. ἐ-κτη- 'possess' with pres. 3sg. Skt *kṣ-áya-ti*, Av. *xšaiieiti* '(s)he rules', reflecting a PIE *tkah₂-, is highly questionable (*LIV* s.v. 1. **tek*, fn. 1); the meanings do not match well, and no stem cognates can be reconstructed.

After the merger of *Kw-sequences with labiovelars, *o became υ when between a nasal and a labiovelar (in either order); this is sometimes called 'Cowgill's Law' (Vine 1999). Two examples seem completely straightforward:

> PIE *nók^{w}ts, *nók^{w}t- ~ *nék^{w}t- 'night' (Lat. *nox*, *noct-*, Skt *nák RV* VII.71.1, adv. *náktam* 'at night'; Hitt. *nekuz mēhur* 'evening time' with gen. sg. *nék^{w}ts) > νύξ, νυκτ-;
> PIE *h$_3$nog^{h}- 'nail, claw' (OE *næġl*), extended *h$_3$nog^{h}-w- (cf. Toch. B pl. *mekwa*, Lat. *unguis*; possibly with an acrostatic paradigm, Vine 1999: 559) > *ὀνοχ^{w}- > ὄνυχ-.

Two other examples exhibit υ for expected *e, which can only mean that there was a chain of sound changes *e > *o > υ in this environment:

> PIE *g^{w}ḗn, *g^{w}énh$_2$- ~ *g^{w}náh$_2$- 'woman' (Jasanoff 1989; for the nom. sg. cf. OIr. *bé*, Goth. *qens* 'wife'; for the ablaut cf. OIr. acc. sg. *bein* vs. gen. sg. *mná*, Skt nom. sg. *jánī* vs. gen. sg. *gnā́s*) >→ *g^{w}enáh$_2$ (OCS *žena*) > *g^{w}onā́ > γυνᾱ́ > Att.-Ion. γυνή;
> PIE *neg^{w}nós 'naked' (Skt *nagnás*; with dissimilation Hitt. *nekuma-nt-*) >→ *mog^{w}nós (with a different dissimilation; Av. *maγnō*) >→ γυμνός (with metathesis).

A further example exhibits the same sequence of sound changes between two labiovelars:

> PIE *k^{w}ék^{w}los 'wheel', collective *k^{w}ek^{w}láh$_2$ (Skt masc. acc. sg. and neut. *cakrám*, Av. acc. *caxrəm*, OE *hwēol* ~ *hweogol*, Toch. B *kokale* 'chariot') > κύκλος, Hom. pl. κύκλα.

To the sound changes as formulated above the most obvious counterexamples are Hom. θε̄νέμεναι 'to slay' < *χ^{w}έν-jε/ο- (cf. pres. 3sg. Hitt. *kuēnzi*, Skt *hánti*), φόνος 'killing, murder' (Vine 1999: 556–7); it is not clear how to account for their apparent failure to undergo the sound change. Rounding of *e to *o did not occur between *w and a labiovelar:

> PIE *wék^{w}os 'word' (Skt *vácas*) > Hom. ἔπος.

Neither did raising of *o to υ:

> PIE *wṓk^{w}s, acc. *wók^{w}m̥ 'voice' (Skt *vā́k*, Lat. *vōx*; for the short vowel cf. Toch. B *wek* < acc. *wók^{w}m̥, Lat. *vocāre* 'to call') > Hom. acc. ὄπα.

There are other υ's in words where ο or even ε might be expected (e.g. ὕπνος 'sleep', non-Att. ὄνυμα 'name'), but it does not seem possible to account for them by regular sound changes (for the former cf. OCS *sŭnŭ* 'sleep', likewise with a zero-grade root); see Vine (1999) for comprehensive discussion (and some alternative judgments).

Labiovelars adjoining these new υ's were delabialized; all five examples of Cowgill's Law listed above exhibit that development. So do compounds in which *u and a labiovelar became adjacent:

pre-Gk *$γ^w$ου-k^wολός 'cow-herd' (for the second element cf. αἰ-πόλος 'goat-herd' with the default reflex of *k^w) > Myc. *qo-u-ko-ro* *$γ^w$ουκολος, Hom. βουκόλος;
pre-Gk *οὔ $κ^w$ιδ 'not at all' > *οὐκι > οὐκ (by apocope of *-ι before vowels; in isolation *$κ^w$ιδ > τι 'something, somewhat').

So does a word which underwent (irregular) metathesis of the buccal features of its first two segments:

PIE *wl̥k^wos 'wolf' (Skt *vŕ̥kas*, Lith. *vil̃kas*, Goth. *wulfs*) → *λύ$κ^w$ος > λύκος.

It is not clear that this was a separate sound change. Delabialization of labiovelars next to *u was a PIE phonological rule (see 2.2.4 (iii)); we have already seen a preexisting compound in which the rule operated, namely

PIE *$h_2$yu-gih_3- 'having vigorous life' (cpd. of *$h_2$óyu and *g^wyoh_3- with delabialization next to *u; cf. Lat. *iūgis* 'ever-flowing', Av. *yauuaējī-* 'having eternal life') > ὑγιής 'healthy' (Weiss 1995: 149–51),

and it is possible that new examples became subject to the existing rule immediately. It might depend on how many new inputs to the old rule were encountered by native language learners: if only a few, not heard frequently, they might assume that they had misheard the labiovelars next to *u and learn them incorrectly as velars; if there were many such sequences, or if at least one was frequent, they were more likely to learn them correctly, in which case unrounding of the labiovelars must have been a subsequent change.

Labiovelars were also delabialized before *y. That sound change must have occurred before the developments of stop + *y discussed in 3.6.3, because in that position inherited labiovelars develop exactly like inherited (palatals and) velars. At least seven examples can be cited:

PIE *pek^w- 'cook' (Lat. *coquere*, Skt pres. 3sg. *pácati*) in pre-Gk pres. *pék^w-ye/o- > *πεκϳε/ο- > πέσσε̄ν, Att. πέττε̄ν; aor. *pék^w-s- > πέψαι with the default reflex of *k^w;

PIE *$h_3$ok^w- 'eye' (Lat. *oculus*, OCS *oko*, both with suffixes) in *$h_3$ok^w-ye/o- > *ὀκjε/o- > Hom. ὄσσεσθαι 'to see'; cf. ὀφθαλμός 'eye' with the labial reflex of a labiovelar regular before other consonants;

PIE du. *$h_3$ók^{w}ih_1 'two eyes' (OCS *oči*) > *ὄκjε > ὄσσε (Forssman 1969), or alternatively > *ὄκ^{w}ι (with utterance-final loss of laryngeal, cf. 2.2.4 (iv)) >→ *ὄκjε (with generalized masc. ending added) > ὄσσε;

PIE *wók^w- 'voice' (see above) + Gk fem. suffix *-ya (see 3.2.3) > *ϝόκjα > Hom. ὄσσα 'rumor';

PIE *sók^w-$h_2$oy- ~ *sk^w-h_2i- 'companion' (Skt *sák^{h}ā*, Lat. *socius* 'ally'; deriv. of *sek^w- 'accompany, follow') in pre-Gk *sm̥-sok^w-yo- 'companion' > *hą̣hoκjo-, denom. verb *hą̣hoκjε-jε/o- 'accompany' > Hom. ἀοσσεῖν 'to help' (*h- lost regularly in East Ionic);

PIE *néyg^w- ~ *nig^w- 'wash' (Skt pres. 3sg. mid. *nenikté*), pres. *nig^w-yé/ó- (OIr. 3sg. *nigid*) > *νιγjε/o- > νίζε͂ν; aor. *nig^w-s- > νίψαι, cf. also Hom. acc. χερνίβα 'basin';

pre-Gk pres. *slag^w-yé/ó- 'seize (severally), be catching' > *hλαγjε/o- > Hom. λάζεσθαι; aor. *slag^w-é/ó- > λαβε͂ν.

Since the root of ἐλαχύς 'little' originally ended in a labiovelar, it might be supposed that the comparative ἐλάσσων 'less' is a further example. But the PIE elative of this adjective was *$h_1$léng^{wh}-ios-, with a full-grade root (cf. Av. *rənjištō* 'swiftest'); clearly the Greek comparative was constructed (or remade) when the zero grade of the root had been leveled through the paradigm, and in that case the velar (resulting from delabialization next to *u already in PIE) might have been leveled through the paradigm too by that point.

3.4.4 Early developments of stop clusters

PIE *Tst clusters lost the first stop in Greek, as in Iranian (but not in Indic). There are a handful of examples that are probably inherited, e.g.:

PIE *úd-s-teros 'farther up/out' (Skt *úttaras*) > ὕστερος 'later';

PIE *ń̥-wid-s-tos 'unseen' (cf. Skt *vittás* 'found' ← *'caught sight of') > ἄϊστος;

PIE *wóyd-s-th_2a 'you (sg.) know' (Skt *vétt^{h}a*) > οἶσθα;

PIE iptv. 2sg, *wid-s-d^{h}í 'know!' (Skt *vidd^{h}í*) > ἴσθι;

PIE *b^{h}id^h-s-tós 'trustworthy' (cf. Lat. *fīsus* 'having trusted') > *φιστός → πιστός (see 3.5.4);

PIE *b^{h}ud^h-s-tós 'observable' *vel sim.* (Skt *budd^{h}ás* 'awake') >→ *πυστός in Hom. ἄπυστος 'unheard-of';

pre-Gk *áyeri-h_1d-s-tom neut. 'eaten in the morning' > ἄ̆ριστον 'breakfast'.

Like most of its relatives, Greek exhibits regressive voicing assimilation in clusters of stops. Examples in which the second stop was voiced are rare, mostly exhibiting suffixes that are difficult to find cognates for, but an example that must be old is ἔπιβδαν acc. 'day after a festival' (Pindar *Pythian* IV.140) < *epi-pd- *'in the footsteps', with zero grade of *pód- ~ *ped- 'foot' (cf. Skt *upabdáis* 'with their (repeated) stamping' *RV* VII.104.17, Av. *frabdō.drājō* 'length of the front of the foot').

Regressive devoicing occurred mostly before suffixes beginning with *-t-, e.g.:

PIE *lugtós 'breakable, broken' (cf. Skt *rugṇás* 'broken' with alternative suffix) > *λυκτός in epic ἀλυκτοπέδῃσι 'with unbreakable fetters', Hesiod *Theogony* 521;
PIE *ń̥-nig^{w}tos 'unwashed' (cf. Skt *niktás* 'washed') > ἄνιπτος;
pre-Gk *ń̥-sl̥h$_1$gtos 'unceasing' (cf. λήγεν 'to cease' < *sléh$_1$g-, Joseph 1982) > Hom. (Aiolic) ἄλληκτος.

Regressive assimilation also occurred before the *-s- of the s-aorist, e.g in aor. ὀρέξαι 'to stretch out' < *h$_3$rég-s-.

Clusters containing aspirate stops raise unresolved issues. In Indo-Iranian voicing and aspiration spread progressively through an obstruent cluster by a phonological rule called Bartholomae's Law (BL); for instance, in Sanskrit the pres. 3sg. act. of *dug^h*- 'milk' is *dógd^{h}i* < *dóg^h*- + *-ti*, the past participle of *bud^h*- 'wake' is *budd^{h}ás* 'awake' < *bud^h*- + *-tá-*, the infinitive of *vah-* 'convey' is *vóḍ^{h}um* < *váh-* + *-tu-m*, and the action noun derived from *vŕ̥̥d^h*- 'grow' is *vŕ̥̥dd^{h}is* 'increase'.[19] It is unclear whether BL reflects an Indo-Iranian sound change or a rule inherited from PIE. The fact that both consonants in *d^{h}g^{wh}ey- 'perish' and *h$_2$ad^{h}g^h- 'press' (see 3.4.1) are aspirates suggests some sort of assimilation; so does the fact that both consonants in *d^{h}ég^{h}ōm 'earth' are aspirates, since one or the other might have been assimilated in loc. sg. *d^{h}g̑^{h}ém and then been leveled through the paradigm. But most IE languages show no trace of BL.

The Greek evidence, however, is ambiguous. Productive formations do not undergo BL; they undergo regressive assimilation of voicing and aspiration, exactly like inherited voiced stops, e.g.:

PIE *lég^{h}trom 'thing to lie down on' (cf. λέχος 'bed', Goth. *ligan* 'to lie down'; for the suffix cf. ἄροτρον 'plow' < PIE *h$_2$árh$_3$trom (3.2.4)) > λέκτρον 'bed';

[19] In Iranian, and probably in Proto-Indo-Iranian, BL applies even to clusters ending in sibilants; for instance, in Avestan the 2sg. (Proto-Indo-Iranian. ending *-sa) of *augh- 'speak solemnly' (Skt *oh-*) is *(pairi-)aoγžā*, and the desiderative of *dab^h- 'deceive' (Skt *dab^h*- 'harm') is (inf.) *diβžaidiiāi*. In Sanskrit all sibilants are voiceless, and regressive devoicing and deaspiration occurs in such clusters; thus the desiderative of *dab^h*- 'harm' is (3sg.) *dípsati*. That is probably a Sanskrit innovation.

PIE *dʰugʰtós 'produced' (Skt *dugdʰás* 'milked') > *θυκτός → *τυκτός 'fashioned' (see 3.5.4) in Hom. εὔτυκτος 'well-made';

PIE *éwgʰtos 'solemnly spoken' (late Av. *aoxtō* with BL cluster remodeled; cf. Skt pres. 3pl. *óhate* 'they praise', which shows that this was a 'Narten' root with full grade for expected zero grade) >→ Hom. neut. pl. εὐκτά 'what is desired', *Il.* 14.98;

pre-Gk *skabʰtḗr 'digger' (cf. σκάφος 'digging', Lat. *scabere* 'to scratch', Goth. *skaban* 'to shave') > σκαπτήρ;

pre-Gk collective *dʰrébʰtrah₂ 'means of upbringing' (cf. τρέφε̄ν 'to raise (a child)') > Hom. pl. θρέπτρα 'recompense for upbringing';

pre-Gk *wr̥bʰtós or *sr̥bʰtós 'stitched' (cf. Hom. ῥαφή 'seam') > Hom. ῥαπτός;

Hom. κρυπτός 'hidden' and κρύβδα 'without the knowledge of', derivs. of κρυφ- 'hide', cf. Hom. κρυφηδόν 'secretly'.

(Note also πιστός and ἄπυστος, cited above, with τ, not θ.) But a few isolated forms suggest that BL did originally operate in Greek. The most isolated of all is 'yesterday':

PIE *ǵʰ-dyés 'yesterday' (with deictic *ǵʰ-, which is the initial consonant of Lat. *hic*, and the form of 'day' attested in Skt *sadyás* 'one day', Brandenstein 1936: 29, Schindler 1977c: 34; Skt *hyás*, Lat. *herī*) > χθές.

A further possible example is

PIE *eǵʰstr̥ós 'external' (?; cf. Lat. *extrā* 'outside') > ἐχθρός 'hated, hostile' (Frisk s.v. ἔχθος);

that ἐξ, Lat. *ex* reflect PIE *éǵʰs is plausible, given that ἔσχατος 'furthest' can be a derivative with metathesis. A remarkable example attested in a paradigm is Hom. πολλὰ πέπασθε 'you (pl.) are long-suffering / have suffered much' (3x), analyzable as pf. πεπαθ- + -τε, cf. 1sg. πέπονθα, 2sg. πέπονθας; a mediopassive ending -σθε is not in question, since this verb is inflected exclusively in the active (with the exception of the future stem). The present stem of this verb also exhibits BL:

πάσχε̄ν 'to be experiencing, to have something happen to one' < παθ- + -σκε/ο- (cf. Rix 1976a: 78).[20]

Though the potential non-Greek cognates of this verb are questionable, its forms probably indicate that BL was once a living rule in Greek. The forms with regressive assimilation must then be the results of reanalysis; a plausible hypothesis is

[20] A similar but less certain example is λέσχη 'place to relax, lounge, meeting-hall', plausibly < *λέχ-σκᾱ, cf. λέχος 'bed, couch' (Rix, *loc. cit.*).

that BL did not affect stop + *s in Greek (as opposed to stop + *s + stop), and that the rule deaspirating stops before *s was extended to other productive formations.

Of course it does not follow that BL was inherited from PIE; parallel development is not completely out of the question. More interestingly, it seems clear that Greek and Indo-Iranian were both dialects in the 'core' of the IE speech area as PIE began to disintegrate, and they may even have been adjacent dialects in a chain (see 2.3.3 (iii) with fn. 37); that BL was a post-PIE sound change that did not spread far through the dialect continuum is therefore a distinct possibility.

An assimilation similar in pattern to that of πάσχε̄ν is exhibited by another σκ-present:

> μίσγε̄ν 'to be mixing' ← μιγ- + -σκε/ο-, cf. Hom. intr. aor. μιγῆναι 'to get mixed, to have sex (with)'.

Whether this is the result of a regular sound change is difficult to determine, as there are no other similar examples.

A handful of Greek words beginning with σφ- and σχ- have apparent cognates in Sanskrit beginning with *sp^{h}-* and *sk^{h}-* and in most other IE languages with *sp-* and *sk-* respectively; it is plausibly suggested (e.g. in *LIV*) that these are PIE words beginning with *sb^{h}-, etc., possibly with devoicing of the stops already in PIE. Not all the examples are convincing, but the following seem to be worth mentioning:

> PIE *sb^{h}r̥h$_{2}$g-éye/o- pres. 'crackle (in a fire)' (Skt ptc. *sp^{h}ūrjáyant-*) > Hom. ipf. 3pl. σφαραγεῦντο *Od.* 9.390, 440;
>
> PIE *sb^{h}er- 'kick' (?; pres. Skt *sp^{h}uráti* '(s)he kicks (it) away', inf. Lat. *spernere* 'to reject', OE *spurnan* 'to kick, to reject') in words for 'heel' and the like (OIr. *seir* 'heel', Welsh *ffêr* 'ankle'), possibly including σφυρόν 'ankle';
>
> PIE *sǵ^{h}eyd- 'cut off', pres. *sǵ^{h}inéd- ~ *sǵ^{h}ind- (?; Skt 3sg. *c^{h}inátti*, Lat. inf. *scindere* 'to split') >→ *sk^{h}id-yé/ó- > σχίζε̄ν;
>
> PIE *sǵ^{h}h$_{2}$-yé/ó- (?; Skt *c^{h}yati* '(s)he skins' *Taittirīya-saṃhitā* 5.2.12) > σχα-ε/ο- in οὐκ ἔσχων 'I failed to cut it open', Aristophanes *Clouds* 409;
>
> PIE *sg^{wh}al- 'stumble' (?; pres. 3sg. Skt *sk^{h}alate*, Arm. *sxalê*) > σφάλλεσθαι 'to be tripped, to topple'.

The first example is impressive (though we must hypothesize that zero-grade αρα was leveled in from some related form in which it was accented), but all the others raise problems of one sort or another. PIE *sḱ > Skt *(c)c^{h}* by regular sound change (cf. Skt *gácc^{h}ati* '(s)he goes' = Hom. βάσκει), so that in the third and fourth examples only Greek suggests anything other than a voiceless stop; in σφυρόν 'ankle' the υ is unexplained, and if the Greek word is removed from the equation only

Sanskrit suggests anything other than a voiceless stop; the last example could be onomatopoeic. I think it prudent to suspend judgment.

3.4.5 The devoicing of aspirates

The PIE breathy-voiced stops ('voiced aspirates') were devoiced, the ultimate outcomes being φ, θ, χ. There are scores of examples; the following are straightforward.[21]

PIE *b^{h} > φ:

PIE pres. *b^{h}ér-e/o- 'be carrying' (Skt 3sg. *b^{h}árati*, Lat. 3pl. *ferunt*, Goth. inf. *baíran*) > φέρε̄ν;

PIE aor. *b^{h}éwg- ~ *b^{h}ug- 'run away from, escape' (Lat. pf. 3sg. *fūgit*) > φυγε̃ν;

PIE *b^{h}ah$_2$ti 'it shines, it illuminates' (Skt *b^{h}āti*) → '(s)he makes clear' → '(s)he says' (cf. Lat. *fātur*) > φᾱτι > Att.-Ion. φησι;

PIE *b^{h}úHt 'it became' (Skt *áb^{h}ūt* with augment; for the laryngeal cf. the Skt full-grade *b^{h}avi-*) > ἔφῡ;

PIE *b^{h}ráh$_2$tēr 'brother' (Skt *b^{h}rā́tā*, Lat. *frāter*, Goth. *broþar*) > Att. φρᾱ́τηρ 'member of a phratry, fellow-clansman';

PIE *h$_3$b^{h}rúH-s 'eyebrow' (Skt *b^{h}rū́s*) > ὀφρῦς;

PIE *néb^{h}os 'cloud' (Skt *náb^{h}as*, OCS *nebo* 'sky'), deriv. *néb^{h}elah$_2$ (Lat. *nebula* 'fog') > νέφος, νεφέλᾱ > Att.-Ion. νεφέλη;

PIE pres. *u-né-b^{h}- 'be weaving' (Skt 2sg. *sám unap*) → *ub^{h}-né-H- (Skt inj. 2sg. *ub^{h}nā́s*, 3sg. with augment *aub^{h}nāt*) → *ub^{h}-n̥-H-yé- > *ὐφανjε- > ὑφαίνε̄ν;

PIE *h$_2$n̥tb^{h}óh$_1$ 'both' (Toch. B *antapi*, Jasanoff 1976: 125–7), *h$_2$n̥tb^{h}í 'on both sides' > *h$_2$m̥b^{h}óh$_1$, *h$_2$m̥b^{h}í (Lat. *ambō*, *amb-*) > ἄμφω (accent remodeled on δύο), ἀμφί;

PIE *h$_3$nób^{h}- 'navel' (Skt *nā́b^{h}is*, OE *nafela*), zero grade in deriv. *h$_3$n̥b^{h}-l̥H- > ὀμφαλός (cf. Lat. *umbilīcus*, OIr. *imbliu* with further suffixes);

PIE *ǵómb^{h}os 'row of teeth' (Skt pl. *jámb^{h}āsas*, OE *camb* 'comb') > γόμφος 'peg';

PIE *alb^{h}ós 'white' (Lat. *albus*, Hitt. *alpās* 'cloud') > ἀλφός 'white skin-lesion';

PIE *orb^{h}o- 'bereaved, orphan' (Lat. *orbus*, Arm. *orb*) >→ ὀρφανός;

PIE *-b^{h}i, adverb suffix (Arm. *-b* ~ *-w*, inst. sg. ending) > -φι, inst. pl. ending, e.g. in Myc. *po-pi* *ποδφί 'with feet', Hom. ῑ̓φι 'with power'.

[21] It may be helpful to observe here that the default outcomes of breathy-voiced stops are *b^{h}*, *d^{h}*, *h*, *g^{h}* in Sanskrit; *f*, *h* word-initially, but *b*, *d*, *h*, *v* word-medially (*g*, *gu* after *n*) in Latin; *b*, *d*, *g*, *w* (*gw* after *g* = [ŋ]) in Gothic; *b* (*w* between vowels), *d*, *j*, *ǰ*, *g* in Armenian. In Iranian, Balto-Slavic, Celtic, and Anatolian the breathy-voiced stops merged with the voiced stops; in Tocharian they merged with the voiceless stops, probably after being devoiced, as in Greek.

PIE $^{*}d^{h}$ > θ:

PIE $^{*}d^{h}uh_{2}$mós 'smoke' (Skt *d^{h}ūmás*, Lat. *fūmus*) > θῡμός 'strong emotion';

PIE aor. $^{*}d^{h}eh_{1}$- 'put' (Skt 3sg. *ád^{h}āt*) → $^{*}d^{h}eh_{1}$-k- with suffix of unclear function (Old Lat. pf. 3sg. *fēced*) > ἔθηκε;

PIE $^{*}d^{h}$óh_{1}mos 'thing put' (Goth. *doms* 'reputation', OE *dōm* 'judgment') > θωμός 'heap';

PIE $^{*}d^{h}$érs- ~ $^{*}d^{h}$r̥s- 'dare, be bold' (pf. 3sg. $^{*}d^{h}ed^{h}$órse > Skt *dad^{h}árṣa*, Goth. *ga-dars*) in $^{*}d^{h}$érsos 'daring, bravery' > Lesbian θέρσος, $^{*}d^{h}$r̥sús 'brave, bold' > θρασύς (the latter with -σ- leveled from the former; the former → Att.-Ion. θάρσος by leveling on the latter);

PIE $^{*}d^{h}$wór- ~ $^{*}d^{h}$ur- 'door' (Lat. pl. *forēs*, OE *duru*) >→ θύρᾱ;

PIE $^{*}d^{h}ugh_{2}$tḗr 'daughter' (Skt *duhitā́* with $^{*}d^{h}$ > *d* by Grassmann's Law, Goth. *daúhtar*, Arm. *dowstr*) > θυγάτηρ (accent remodeled on 'mother');

PIE $^{*}d^{h}$éh_{1}s- ~ $^{*}d^{h}h_{1}$s- (cf. Lat. *diēs fēstus* 'holiday', *fasnom > *fānum* 'temple') > θέσ-φατος 'god-spoken', *θεhός > θεός 'god';

PIE *sám$h_{2}d^{h}$os 'sand' (ON *sandr*, Middle High German *sam(b)t*) > ἄμαθος;

PIE *méd^{h}u neut. 'sweet' (Skt *mád^{h}u*, OE *medu* 'mead') > Hom. μέθυ 'wine';

PIE $^{*}h_{1}$lud^{h}éd '(s)he arrived' (Toch. B *lac* '(s)he went out', OIr. *luid* '(s)he went'), with augment *é h_{1}lud^{h}ed > Hom. ἤλυθε '(s)he came';

PIE $^{*}h_{1}$léwd^{h}eros 'free' (Lat. *līber*, Venetic dat. pl. *louderobos* 'for (his) children') > ἐλεύθερος;

PIE $^{*}h_{2}$ánd^{h}os 'plant' (Skt *ánd^{h}as* 'herb') > ἄνθος 'flower';

PIE $^{*}h_{1}$rud^{h}rós 'red' (Toch. B *ratre*, Lat. *ruber*) > ἐρυθρός;

PIE *misd^{h}ó- 'reward' (Skt *mīḍ^{h}ám* 'prize', Goth. *mizdo*) > μισθός 'pay';

PIE iptv. 2sg, *wid-s-d^{h}í 'know!' (Skt *vidd^{h}í*) > ἴσθι.

PIE $^{*}\acute{g}^{h}$ > χ:

PIE nom. $^{*}\acute{g}^{h}$éyōm 'winter', loc. $^{*}\acute{g}^{h}$yém ~ $^{*}\acute{g}^{h}$iém 'in winter' (Hitt. *giemi*, Lat. *hieme*, both with deictic *-i) >→ χιών 'snow';

PIE allative $^{*}\acute{g}^{h}$m̥áh_{2} 'to the ground' (cf. Av. gen. *zəmō* for the shape of the root) + deictic *-i > Hom. adv. χαμαί;

PIE $^{*}\acute{g}^{h}$áns- 'goose' (Skt *haṃsás* 'swan', OHG *gans*) > χᾱ́ν > Att.-Ion. χήν;

PIE $^{*}\acute{g}^{h}$ésr- 'hand' (Hitt. *kissar*; Skt *hástas* with innovative 2nd syllable) > χέ̄ρ;

PIE $^{*}\acute{g}^{h}$ew- 'pour' (pres. 3sg. Toch. B *kuṣäṃ*, Skt *juhóti* '(s)he sacrifices', both with stem-forming affixes) > *χέϝε̄ν > χε̃ν;

(post-)PIE $^{*}\acute{g}^{h}$éslom 'thousand' (Skt *sa-hásram*), deriv. $^{*}\acute{g}^{h}$éslio- in Ionic gen. pl. χειλίων (ει = ε̄) *DGE* 688.D.12, Thessalian acc. pl. fem. χέλλιας *DGE* 614.29;

PIE *mrég^{h}u- ~ *mr̥$\acute{g}^{h}$éw- 'short' (Lat. *brevis*) → *mr̥$\acute{g}^{h}$ús (Av. *mərəzu-*) > βραχύς;

PIE *ley$\acute{g}^{h}$- 'lick' (Skt pres. 3sg. *réḍ^{h}i* < *láiẓ^{h}ḍ^{h}i < *léy$\acute{g}^{h}$ti) > λείχε̄ν;

PIE pres. $^{*}(h_{3})$méy$\acute{g}^{h}$-e/o- 'be urinating' (Skt 3sg. *méhati*, inf. Lat. *meiere*, OE *mīgan*) > ὀμείχε̄ν Hesiod *Works and Days* 727;

PIE *seǵ^{h}- 'hold' (cf. Skt *sáhas* 'power, dominance') > ἔχε̄ν 'to hold, to have';
PIE pres. *h$_2$ánǵ^{h}-e/o- 'be strangling' (Lat. *angere*) > ἄγχε̄ν;
PIE *spérǵ^{h}- ~ *spr̥ǵ^{h}- 'hurry' (Skt *spr̥háyati* '(s)he craves') > σπέρχεσθαι.
PIE *g^{h} > χ:[22]
PIE *g^{h}eluh$_2$- 'tortoise' (Russian CS *žely*) > χέλῡς;
PIE *g^{h}ay... 'long hair' (Av. *gaēsuš* 'curly-haired') > Hom. χαίτη;
PIE *steyg^{h}- 'walk forward' (Skt *stig^{h}*- in *prá stiṅnoti* 'he makes progress', *Maitrāyaṇī- saṃhitā* 2.1.12, Goth. *steigan* 'to ascend') > στείχε̄ν 'to march';
PIE *ewg^{h}- 'speak solemnly' (Gatha-Av. 3sg. *aogədā* '(s)he said', Skt pres. 3pl. *óhate* 'they praise') > εὔχεσθαι 'to pray', Myc. *e-u-ke-to* 'she declares formally';
PIE *leg^{h}- 'lie down' (Goth. inf. *ligan*, OCS pres. 3sg. *ležitŭ*) in *lég^{h}os 'act of lying down' > λέχος 'bed';
PIE *h$_1$léng^{h}u- ~ *h$_1$ln̥g^{wh}éw- 'light(weight)' (Skt *rag^{h}ús* 'swift') > ἐλαχύς 'little';
PIE *(h$_3$)mig^{h}láh$_2$ (Lith. *miglà*, OCS *mĭgla*; cf. Skt *meg^{h}ás* 'cloud') > ὀμίχλη 'mist'.
PIE *g^{wh} > *χ^{w} > φ ~ θ (~ χ, see 3.4.3):
PIE *g^{wh}en- 'kill' (3sg. Hitt. *kuēnzi*, Skt *hánti*, '(s)he kills') > Hom. pres. θε̄νέμεναι; o-grade action noun *g^{wh}ónos 'killing' (cf. OE *bana* 'slayer') > φόνος; zero-grade *g^{wh}n̥- > φα- in Hom. pf. πέ-φα-ται 'he is slain';
PIE *g^{wh}er- 'be warm' (*g^{wh}órmos 'heat' > Skt *g^{h}armás*) > θέρεσθαι; ε leveled into adj. θερμός 'warm' (≈ Arm. *ǰerm*);
PIE pres. *snéyg^{wh}-e/o- 'to snow' (OHG inf. *snīwan*, Old Lat. 3sg. *nīvit*) > νείφε̄ν; zero-grade noun *snig^{wh}- 'snow' (Lat. *nix*, *niv-*) > Hom. acc. νίφα;
PIE *h$_3$ḗg^{wh}is ~ *h$_3$óg^{wh}i- 'snake' (Arm *iž*, Skt *áhis*) > ὄφις;
PIE *sóng^{wh}os 'chanting' *vel sim.* (Goth. *saggws* 'song'), coll. *song^{wh}áh$_2$ > *hoνχ^{w}ᾱ́ > ὀμφή 'oracular voice';
PIE *h$_1$ln̥g^{wh}rós 'light(weight)' (OHG *lungar* 'vigorous') > ἐλαφρός 'light';
PIE *neg^{wh}rós 'kidney' (Lat. dial. pl. *nefrōnēs*, *nebrundinēs*, OHG *nioro*, all extended as n-stems) > νεφρός.

Further examples will be adduced in the discussion of Grassmann's Law (3.5.4). Miller (1977) has demonstrated convincingly that devoicing preceded Grassmann's Law and that no reordering of rules occurred.

There is a persistent claim that breathy-voiced stops became plain-voiced stops in Greek when immediately preceded by nasals (cf. e.g. Miller 1977: 137–8). But

[22] It is customary to reconstruct with velars words which have no reflexes in the daughters that distinguish palatals from velars (Indo-Iranian, Balto-Slavic, Armenian, Albanian, and the Luvian subgroup of Anatolian). I have avoided such examples here, with the result that few word-initial examples can be cited.

the examples γόμφος, ἄνθος, ἄγχε̄ν, and ὀμφή (among others) show that devoicing occurred regularly after nasals—regardless of accent or any other conditioning factor—since their voiceless aspirates cannot be the result of any kind of leveling or lexical analogy;[23] and positing an irregular ('sporadic') sound change is unacceptable unless the evidence in favor of an etymology is absolutely ineluctable, since the historical record shows that the regularity of sound change is statistically overwhelming. I therefore reject the traditional connection of θάμβος with τάφος, both 'astonishment'; of θρόμβος 'clot, lump' with τρέφεσθαι 'to coagulate', and so on (*pace* Schwyzer 1939: 333)—unless the words with voiced stops were borrowed from some other language, or folk etymology is in question. Worst of all is the attempt to connect θιγγάνε̄ν, aor. θιγε̄ν 'to touch' with Lat. *fingere* 'to make (out of clay)'. The meanings of the words are quite different; the nasal appears only in the present, so leveling of -γ- into the aorist would have to be posited; and finally, the apparently parallel nasal infix of Lat. *fingere* is clearly an innovation, since it is restricted to Italo-Celtic (see *LIV* s.v. **d*^{h}*ei̯ĝ*^{h})[24] and a root-present for this verb is securely reconstructable for PIE (cf. Skt 3sg. *dégd*^{h}*i*, 3pl. *dihánti*, Goth. ptc. dat. *þamma digandin* 'to the one who made (the pot)').

3.4.6 Loss of *t and *t^h before final *-i

In the context of a discussion of PIE thematic verb endings Warren Cowgill proposed an unusual sound change for Greek (Cowgill 1985a: 99–103); a longer version of the same article published posthumously includes a further argument in its favor (Cowgill 2006b: 536–45). Yet another argument in favor of Cowgill's hypothesis can be made from the accent of some of the relevant forms, and for that reason I have come to believe that it is correct. This section is a summary of Cowgill's work, with the additional argument from accent.

The PIE active thematic primary 3sg. ending is solidly reconstructable as *-e-ti (see 2.3.3 (iii), 4.2.6):

PIE *-eti > Hitt. *-ezzi*, Skt *-ati*, Lat. *-it*, OCS *-etŭ*, Goth. *-iþ*;

[23] Miller's suggestion (*loc. cit.*) that this sound change occurred only when the consonant cluster was derived, not underlying, can hardly be correct, as there is no convincing way to analyze any of the consonants as an affix; nouns were not derived with a nasal infix in PIE. Note further that while the claimed examples cited immediately below must have evaded Grassmann' Law (see 3.5.4), the claimed example πύνδαξ has not (cf. πυθμήν 'bottom of a jar', Skt *bud*^{h}*nás* 'bottom'). I remain unconvinced by the reasoning of Miller (2014: 23; with references), which in my opinion goes well beyond what the facts will support; note especially that the laryngeal internal to γόμφος posited by Nikolaev (as cited by Miller) should have been lost already in PIE (see 2.2.4 (i) *ad fin.*), but evidence for deaspiration is even less persuasive for PIE than for Greek.

[24] That Arm. *dizanel* 'to heap up' reflects a nasal-infixed present is possible but cannot be demonstrated.

but the Greek ending is -ει, with no reflex of *t. It is true that Arm. 3sg. -ê also reflects earlier *-ey, but in Armenian *t between vowels normally disappears (see e.g. Schmitt 1981: 59); thus *berê* '(s)he is carrying' < *b^héreti is no different from *hayr* 'father' < *ph_2tḗr or *bay* 'word' < *b^hh_2tís (cf. φάτις 'speech, saying, oracular voice'), and 3sg. -ê does not support a preform of -ει with no *t.

Cowgill's solution is to propose a regular sound change by which word-final *-eti > -ει at an early date, almost certainly in Proto-Greek; but such a proposal must be both supported by further examples and constrained so as not to apply to obvious counterexamples. One other example of a verb ending seems clear, provided that the sound change also applied to *t^h after the devoicing of aspirates (see 3.4.5):

pre-Gk *δίδοθι 'give (several or continuously)!' > δίδοι, attested in Boiotian (*DGE* 538.4), literary Doric (Pindar *Olympian* I.85, etc.), and possibly in Corinthian (cf. Bechtel 1923: 265; not in *DGE*).

Examples from other word classes will be adduced below, since they require more discussion.

But there are also numerous examples of *-ti and *-t^hi which did not lose their stops, and Cowgill's proposed sound change must be formulated so as to exclude them. He notes that they fall into the following categories:

1) the vowel preceding the stop was high, e.g. in ἴθι 'go!' and *πέρυτι 'last year' (cf. Skt *parút*) > Att. πέρυσι;
2) a diphthong preceded the stop, e.g. in εἶτι '(s)he's going';
3) the vowel preceding the stop was long, e.g. in τίθητι, δίδωτι, etc.;
4) the vowel preceding the stop was nasalized, e.g. in pf. 3pl. *-ą̄τι > West Greek -ατι, Arkadian -ασι;
5) the vowel preceding the stop was short, non-high, and not nasalized, but was accented, e.g. in ἔτι 'yet, still' and φάθι 'say!';
6) the relevant sequence was preceded by a consonant, e.g. in ἐστι, ἀντί, 3pl. -ντι, etc.

That is, *t and *t^h were lost only between short non-high non-nasalized unaccented vowels and word-final *-i. Therefore the sound change must have occurred when most finite verb forms were either unaccented or had acquired recessive accent (see 4.2.8).

Cowgill initially expressed 'considerable qualms' about his proposal 'both because of its complex, rather arbitrary-seeming conditioning, and because Greek does not ordinarily lose intervocalic stops' (Cowgill 1985a: 103). But the second reservation can be dismissed out of hand. Loss of *t is widely attested in other languages; as Agnes Korn and Martin Kümmel remind me, within the IE family it occurred not only in French and Armenian, but also in Khotanese and in many Middle and Modern Indic languages. It is even possible to suggest a scenario that would fit into the prehistory of Greek in an interesting way: these stops might have become *s before the change of *s to *h (see 3.5.1), thus participating in that change and the subsequent loss of intervocalic *h (see 7.2.3); in that case the first stage of this sequence of changes could have been the leading edge of the more general change of voiceless dentals to σ which went to completion later, especially but not only in South Greek (see 5.3.1).

The narrow conditioning of the change is indeed more surprising. However, two other distributional facts argue strongly that Cowgill was right.

The first distributional support was adduced in the longer version of Cowgill's article (Cowgill 2006b: 539–41). According to Cowgill's hypothesis, athematic subjunctive 3sg. *-eti should have become -ει (actually attested in early Ionic inscriptions), while thematic subjunctive 3sg. *-ēti should have remained unchanged in Proto-Greek, ultimately yielding Att.-Ion. -ησι. In fact both endings are attested indirectly in our text of Homer. Athematic -ει has of course been replaced mechanically by -ῃ in our text (see 4.2.3 (i), 4.2.5), while -ησι is spelled -ῃσι, but the two alternatives are not evenly distributed. As Cowgill notes, in subjunctives to athematic stems Homer has -ῃ (originally -ει) 272 times and -ῃσι only thirty-five times, while in subjunctives to thematic stems the figures are 171 and 160 (Cowgill 2006b: 540). The former pair of numbers is clearly significant; the parity of the latter pair can easily be attributed to subsequent morphological change in the Ionic dialect (or even in the epic tradition). Cowgill discusses the distribution of these forms in more detail (pp. 540–1), but the raw numbers speak for themselves.

The other distributional support comes from a consideration of the pattern of accent. As is well known, word-final -αι and -οι, though they are heavy for metrical purposes, are normally light for the purposes of assigning accent. The commonest exceptions are optative 3sg. -αι and -οι, and a plausible rationale for their exceptionality is that those endings were *-αιδ and *-οιδ (or *-αιτ and *-οιτ) before the loss of word-final stops in fully accented words (see 3.5.3). But under Cowgill's hypothesis there is also another less salient exception:

pre-PGk *οἴκοθι 'at home' > οἴκοι (n.b. not 'οἶκοι'!).

This allows us to make a generalization: word-final -αι and -οι are light for the assignment of accent *except* when the ending originally included a consonant! Of course that also accounts for the fact that 3sg. -ει, virtually the only word-final -ει relevant to the assignment of accent, is also heavy. So far as I can see, this non-obvious pattern is clinching: Cowgill was right to suggest that 3sg. -ει reflects *-eti and -οι in two very different grammatical forms reflects *-ot^{h}i.

The remaining example of this regular sound change is *sui generis*. PIE apparently had an adverb *káti 'in addition' and/or an adposition *káti 'with'

(Hitt. *katti-*). It survives in Thess. κατίγνειτος, Hom. κασίγνητος 'brother' (lit. *co-gnātus*). But it also survives in the common Greek word for 'and', which is καί in most Greek dialects but κάς in Cyprian and early Arkadian. The latter form can only reflect *katy before vowel-initial words, but the former reflects deaccented *kati under Cowgill's hypothesis.[25]

3.5 The origin and development of Proto-Greek *h

3.5.1 *s > *h

We have already seen (in 3.2.4) that PIE word-initial *Hy- eventually became *h. A much more frequent source of *h was PIE *s.[26] Except when followed immediately by a stop, PIE word-initial *s > *h in Greek. Straightforward examples are numerous. There is a large family of words and compounding forms based on the numeral 'one', e.g.:

PIE neut. nom.-acc. *sém 'one' (cf. Lat. *semel* 'once') > ἕν;
PIE *sm̥- 'one' (Skt *sa-*; cf. Lat. *sim-plex* 'simple', lit. 'one-fold') > ἁ-, e.g. in ἅπαξ 'once', ἁπλόος > ἁπλõς 'single, simple', lit. 'one-fold';
PIE *sēmi- 'half-' (Lat. *sēmi-*) > ἡμι-;
PIE *somHós 'same' (Skt *samás*) > ὁμός;
PIE *sm̥H ... 'same' (cf. OIr. *samail* 'similar') > ἅμα 'at the same time';
PIE *sm̥Hó- 'some' (Goth. *sums*, OE *sum*) > ἁμό- in Hom. ἁμόθεν 'from somewhere'.

Note also the following typical examples:

PIE nom. sg. masc. *só, fem. *sáh$_2$ 'that' (Skt *sá*, *sā́*, Goth. *sa*, *so*) > ὁ, ἁ̄ > Att.-Ion. ἡ Hom. 'that', later 'the';
PIE *septḿ̥ 'seven' (Skt *saptá*, Lat. *septem*) > ἑπτά;
PIE *sédos 'seat' (Skt *sádas*, ON *setr*) > ἕδος;
PIE *sélos 'standing water' *vel sim.* (Skt *sáras* 'pool') > ἕλος 'floodplain';
PIE *sékʷetor '(s)he accompanies' (Lat. *sequitur*) → *sékʷetoy (Skt *sácate*) >→ ἕπεται;

[25] As Tijmen Pronk reminds me, this PIE lexical item is often reconstructed as *km̥t- (see e.g. Melchert 1994a: 126 with references), but there is no positive evidence for such a preform; as Melchert's discussion makes clear, it was prompted by a desire to connect this word with others. For a quite different hypothesis of the development of this conjunction (which does not depend on reconstructing *a), see Lüttel (1981). As Cowgill notes, whereas West Greek ποί can reflect dissimilatory loss before the definite article (*ποτὶ τ ... > ποὶ τ ...), the distribution of καί is completely different (Cowgill 2006b: 543).

[26] For extensive discussion of the origin and development of Proto-Greek *h from a modern phonological point of view, see Jatteau (2016).

PIE *sépti '(s)he handles' (Gāthā-Av. *haptī* '(s)he holds') → *sép-e/o- (cf. Skt *sápati*) in Hom. ptc. acc. ἕποντα 'taking care of';
PIE *selk- 'pull' (Toch. B *sälkāte* '(s)he pulled out') > ἕλκεν;
PIE pres. *sérp-e/o- 'crawl' (Lat. *serpere*) > ἕρπεν;
PIE *sál-s 'salt' (Lat. *sal*) > ἅλς;
PIE *sál-ye/o- 'jump' (Lat. *salīre*) > ἅλλεσθαι;
PIE *sólwos 'whole' (Skt *sárvas*) > ὅλος;
PIE *suH- 'rain' (Toch. B pres. 3sg. *suwaṃ*; possibly *suh$_2$-, cf. Hitt. *suhhai* '(s)he shakes out') > ὗεν;
PIE *sénos 'old' (Skt *sánas*, Lith. *sẽnas*), fem. *sénah$_2$ > Att. ἕνη καὶ νέᾱ 'last day of the (lunar) month', lit. 'old and new (moon)';
PIE *ser- 'to put things on a string' (Lat. *serere* 'put in order, arrange'), action/result nouns *sórmos > ὅρμος 'necklace', *sérmn̥ > *hέρμα̨ in Hom. pl. ἕρματα 'earrings';
PIE *sáh$_2$wl̥ ~ *sh$_2$uén- 'sun' (Skt *súar*, Gāthā-Av. gen. *x*^{v}*ə̄ṇg*), deriv. *sáh$_2$wel- in *hά̄ϝελιος > Hom. ἠέλιος, Att. ἥλιος;
PIE *seyk- 'walk' *vel sim.* (cf. Toch. B *siknaṃ* '(s)he steps') in post-PIE pres. *sik-néw- ~ *sik-nu- ~ *sik-n̥w- → *hικνέϝε/ο- > ἱκνέεσθαι, and *hικα̨νϝε/ο- > Hom. ἱκά̄νεν, both 'to come to, to arrive'.

For one PIE word Greek exhibits doublets, one with *s- > *h- and one with *s- preserved unchanged:

PIE *súH-s or *sū́-s 'pig' (Lat. *sūs*, ON *sýr* 'sow') > ὗς and σῦς.

Since sound changes do not capriciously fail to operate on a lexical basis, we need an explanation for σῦς. Conceivably it was generalized from positions after a word in the same phrase ending in a stop or *s; since *s did not become *h in those positions within a word, it is conceivable that it did not do so within phrases either. But it is difficult to see why the alternant with σ- should have been generalized only in this word. More likely σῦς was borrowed from a closely related language in which PIE *s- survived (so e.g. Lejeune 1972: 92 fn. 2). Unfortunately we know virtually nothing about other IE languages that were in contact with Greek prehistorically.

PIE *s also became Greek *h word-initially before sonorants. There seems to be only one example with *sy-:

PIE *syuHmén- '(piece of) sewing' (cf. Skt neut. *syū́ma* 'strap') > ὑ̆μήν 'membrane'.[27]

27 The quantity of the υ is somewhat shaky. When used as the name of the marriage god the word has a long ῡ, but the υ of the derivative ὑμέναιος is consistently short; in its literal meaning the word seems to appear in verse only in Apollonios of Rhodes' *Argonautica* 4.1648, where it has a short υ. Frisk s.v. 2. ὑμήν suggests metrical lengthening for the instances with long ῡ, though other explanations are possible. If Gk 'membrane' does have a short υ, we must hypothesize that the root's laryngeal was lost

Evidently the *y was lost at some point, though how that happened is not recoverable; it is plausible, but not provable, that *sy- and *Hy- both became *hy-, probably realized phonetically as voiceless *[j̥] (see 3.2.4 *ad init.*), which then became *h-. Examples with *w are more numerous, and both the *h- and the *w survived down into the Hellenistic period in various dialects. Note the following examples:

Nuclear IE *swé acc. 'himself, herself, themselves' (cf. Skt *svayám*) > ϝ̔ε (preserved in Pamphylian ϝhε[28]) > Lesb. ϝε, Att. ἑ;
PIE *swéḱs 'six' (Rothstein-Dowden 2021; Av. *xšuuaš*, Welsh *chwech*) > (*)ϝ̔έξ > Att. ἕξ, Boiotian ϝέξ;
PIE *swéḱuros 'father-in-law' (Skt *śváśuras*, Lat. *socer*) > *ϝ̔έκυρος > Att. ἑκυρός (accent by lexical analogy with ἑκυρᾱ́);
PIE *swáh₂dus 'pleasant, sweet' (Skt *svādús*) > ᾱ̔δύς > Att.-Ion. ἡδύς;
PIE *swéyd- ~ *swid- 'sweat' (Skt pres. 3sg. *svidyati*) > *ϝ̔ιδ- in noun ἱδρώς.

In most dialects the ϝ was eventually lost, but in many the rough breathing persisted through the Hellenistic period.

It should be noted that some words with initial *s- or *sw- are attested only or mainly in 'psilotic' dialects that lost the rough breathing in the prehistoric period (see 7.2.6), especially Lesbian and East Ionic; an example is Hom. ἀοσσε͂ν 'to help', adduced in 3.4.3. Other examples include:

PIE *sn̥tér 'separately' (cf. Goth. *sundro*, ON *sundr* with zero-grade suffix and further endings) > *hατέρ > Hom. ἄτερ 'without';
PIE *sér(i) 'on top' (Hitt. *sēr* 'above') > *hερι- > Hom. ἐρι- 'very' (Willi 1999);
PIE *ser- 'flow' (cf. Skt pres. 3sg. *sísarti*, Lat. deriv. *serum* 'whey') in agent noun *sorós > *hορός > Hom., Ion. ὀρός 'whey';
PIE nom. pl. *swésores 'sisters' (Skt *svásāras*) > *hϝέhορες > ἔορες '(female) relatives' (Hesykhios).

The third word seems to be an Ionic loanword in Plato, Aristotle, and Theophrastos, since the rough breathing is not usually lost in Attic. An example that seems to have lost its *h- in Attic in a different way is

PIE *ser- 'to put things on a string' (Lat. *serere* 'put in order, arrange') → pres. *sér-ye/o- > *ἕ̄ρε͂ν, cpd. συν-έ̄ρε͂ν with regular loss of *h-, whence decompound Att. ἕ̄ρε͂ν (Frisk s.v. 1. εἴρω).

by resegmentation in some related word in which it occurred before a vowel. In any case the etymology, with its initial *sy-, can be allowed to stand.

[28] And in Argolic ϝhεδιέστᾱς 'private citizen' (Buck 83.7), as Philomen Probert reminds me.

As we will see in 3.5.5, there are also irregularities with the breathings that are less easy to explain.

There are also a number of examples of initial *s- > *h- followed by coronal sonorants, for instance:

PIE *snusós 'daughter-in-law' (Arm. *now*, gen. *nowoy*; cf. Skt *snuṣā́*, OE *snoru* with shift of stem class) > *hνυhός > νυός;
PIE pres. *snéh$_1$ye/o- 'be spinning' (Skt *snā́yati* '(s)he wraps', OIr. *sniïd* '(s)he twists') > *hνηjε/ο- > νῆν;
PIE *snéh$_1$wr̥ 'sinew' (Toch. B *ṣñor*, cf. Skt *snā́van-*) >→ *snēwro- (cf. Lat. *nervos*) > *hνεϝρο- > νεῦρον;
PIE *snah$_2$- 'bathe, swim' (Skt pres. 3sg. *snā́ti*) > *hνᾱ- in νᾱ́χε̄ν 'to swim' > Att.-Ion. νήχε̄ν;
PIE pres. *snéyg^{wh}-e/o- 'to snow' (OHG inf. *snīwan*, Old Lat. 3sg. *nīvit*) > νείφε̄ν; zero-grade noun *snig^{wh}- 'snow' (Lat. *nix, niv-*) > Hom. acc. νίφα, cf. also ἀγά-νε̄νιφος 'very snowy' with Aiolic treatment of intervocalic *-sn-;
PIE *sleh$_1$g- 'cease' (cf. Oscan acc. **slaagím** 'boundary', Joseph 1982) > *slēg- > λήγε̄ν, cf. also Hom. (Aiolic) ἄλληκτος;
PIE zero-grade *sl̥ǵ- 'let go' (Skt pres. 3sg. *sr̥játi*) > *hlag- in Cretan aor. λαγάσαι, *DGE* 179.I.5;
pre-Gk aor. *slag^w-é/ó- 'take hold of, grab' >→ hλαβε/ο- (East Argolic ptc. λhαβό̄ν) > λαβε̄ν;
PIE pres. *sréw-e/o- 'be flowing' (Skt 3sg. *srávati*) > *ῥέϝε̄ν > ῥε̄ν;
PIE *srī́gos 'cold(ness)' (Lat. *frīgus*) > ῥῖγος;
PIE *sreb^h- ~ *sr̥b^h- 'slurp, suck up' (zero grade in Lat. *sorbēre*, Arm. aor. *arb* '(s)he drank'), intensive *srob^h-éye/o- > ῥοφε̄ν.

It can be seen that *h- survives before ρ but is eventually lost before the other coronal sonorants in the well-attested dialects. For the most part the same developments are observable before *m:

PIE *smey- 'smile' (pres. Skt 3sg. *smáyate*, Toch. B ptc. *smimane*) → *smey-d- in Hom. aor. 3sg. μείδησε, cf. also φιλο-μμειδὴς Ἀφροδῑ́τη with Aiolic treatment of intervocalic *-sm-;
PIE *sémih$_2$ fem. 'one' → *smíh$_2$ (Arm. *mi* 'one') > μία;
PIE *smer- 'to receive a portion' (Lat. *merērī* 'to deserve'; cf. ἕμαρται 'it is fated' < *hε-hμαρ- < *se-smr̥-) > μέ̄ρεσθαι.

However, there are also plausibly inherited words in which *sm- yields σμ-:

PIE *smerd- 'be painful, hurt' (OE *smeortan*) in Hom. σμερδαλέος, σμερδνός 'terrible';

PIE *smewH ... 'burn, smolder' (OE *smēocan* 'to smoke (intr.)') in Hom. σμῡ́χοιτο '(as if) it were burning' *Il.* 22.411.

In addition there are doublets with σμ- ~ (*hμ- >) μ-; the most conspicuous is σμῑκρός ~ μῑκρός 'little, small' (cf. Lat. *mīca* 'grain, a little'?).

The most plausible hypothesis to account for this constellation of facts is that there was at least one dialect of Greek (not necessarily surviving to be attested) in which the *s of word-initial *sm- did not become *h, and that the attested pattern of outcomes reflects substantial borrowing between dialects at an early date.[29]

PIE *s between vowels also became *h, which persisted until the Mycenaean period (see below) and was then lost. The change *s > *h clearly occurred after the laryngeals, which were obstruents, had been lost, since the vowels to which they gave rise (see 3.2.4) provided part of the environment for this change. As might be expected, examples are easy to find:

PIE $^*d^h$éh$_1$s- ~ $^*d^h$h$_1$s- (cf. Lat. *diēs fēstus* 'holiday', *fasnom > *fānum* 'temple') > $^*t^h$es- in *θεhός > θεός 'god', cf. θέσ-φατος 'god-spoken';

PIE gen. *génh$_1$esos 'of a lineage' (Skt *jánasas*, cf. Lat. *generis* with alternative ending *-es) > *γένεhος > γένεος > Att. γένο̄ς, cf. nom.-acc. γένος < PIE *génh$_1$os (Skt *jánas*, Lat. *genus*); so also the other forms of s-stem nominals with overt endings (see below);

PIE *wīs- ~ *wis- 'poison' (Lat. *vīrus* vs. Skt *viṣám*, Toch. B *wase*) > *ϝῑhός > ῑ̓ός;

PIE *snusós 'daughter-in-law' (Arm. *now*, gen. *nowoy*; cf. Skt *snuṣā́*, OE *snoru* with shift of stem class) > *hνυhός > νυός;

PIE *pésos 'penis' (Skt *pásas*, cf. Lat. *pēnis* < *pesnis) > *πέhος > πέος;

PIE subj. 1sg. *h$_1$ésoh$_2$ 'I will be' (Lat. fut. *erō*, cf. Skt subj. *ásāni*) > *ἔhω > Ion. ἔω;

PIE *h$_1$sónt-, fem. *h$_1$sóntih$_2$ 'being' → *h$_1$sónt-, *h$_1$sn̥tíh$_2$ (Skt *sánt-*, *satī́*) > *esónt-, *esn̥tíh$_2$ (see 3.2.4) > *ἐhόντ- ~ *ἐhą̄τja > Ion. ἐόντ-, Ark. ἔασσα;

PIE *nésontor 'they are returning' (cf. Goth. *ga-nisan* 'to be saved') → *nésontoy (Skt *násante* 'they unite') > *νέhοντοι >→ Hom. νέονται 'they go home';

PIE pres. *trés-e/o- 'be afraid' (Skt 3sg. *trásati*) > *τρέhε-hεν > τρε̃ν;

PIE nom. pl. *swésores 'sisters' (Skt *svásāras*) > *hϝέhορες > ἔορες '(female) relatives' (Hesykhios, evidently from a psilotic dialect).

[29] The existence of (σ)μῑκρός 'small' is probably responsible for an unetymological detail of the shape of μέγας 'big'. The PIE ancestor of the latter clearly began with *m- (cf. Goth. *mikils*, Skt *mahánt-*, Hitt. *mekkis* 'much', Toch. B *māka* 'much', all languages in which *sm- survives), but the Proto-Greek word was apparently *hμεγα(λο)-, to judge from Pamphylian acc. sg. fem. μhε[ι]άλα (Brixhe 1976: 168, 172), Megarian Μhεγαρεύς (*DGE* 152, V c.), and the fact that numerous Homeric examples of this adjective and its derivatives must be scanned with long μ- (e.g. in the frequent phrase ἐνὶ μεγάροισι 'in the long-halls'). Lexical analogy between antonyms is the easiest way to account for this anomaly.

That /h/ was still present in Mycenaean is shown by spellings such as s-stem nom. pl. *pa-we-a₂* *φάρϝεhα 'bolts of cloth', in which *a₂* unambiguously spells /ha/.

Between a vowel and a syllabic nasal the regular development is likewise *h:

PIE*é h₁esm̥ 'I was' (Skt *ā́sam*, recharacterized with postvocalic *-m*) > *ḗsm̥ > *ή̆hα̹ > Hom. ἦα;
PIE *ḗsror 'they are sitting' → *ḗsn̥toy (Skt *ā́sate*) > *ή̆hα̹τοι > *hήhα̹τοι (by 'Hauchumsprung', see 3.5.2) >→ Hom. ἥαται (spelled εἵαται in our text).

When the syllabic nasal precedes, however, the outcome does not seem to be uniform (Schwyzer 1939: 307). There are at least two examples in which *s has become *h:

PIE *dens- 'teach, learn' (Av. inj. 3sg. *didą̊s* '(s)he taught', Gāthā-Av. pres. 1sg. *dīdaŋ́hē* 'I learn') ~ *dn̥s- > *δα̹h- in Hom. aor. 3sg. δέδαε '(s)he taught', δαήμεναι 'to learn';
pre-Gk *sm̥-sokʷ-yo- 'companion' > *hα̹hoκjo-, denom. verb *hα̹hoκjε-jε/o- 'accompany' > Hom. ἀοσσε͂ν 'to help' (psilotic).

Since the latter is a compound it might be suspected of exhibiting the word-initial development at the beginning of its second member, but since it is completely opaque it could exhibit the regular phonological development after a syllabic nasal if it had been constructed early enough. Unfortunately there is also at least one example in which *s apparently survives unchanged:

PIE *dénsus ~ *dn̥séw- 'dense' (Hitt. *dassus* 'powerful'; Lat. *dēnsus* has been shifted into the o-stems) → *dn̥sús > δασύς 'thickly overgrown, shaggy'.

On the other hand, Att. δαυλός 'tangled' *vel sim.* (Aiskhylos *Suppliants* 93) could be a derivative of the same adjective, reflecting *δα̹hυλός with *h < *s. (Much less certain is Hom. ἄσις 'mud', which might or might not be connected with Skt *ásitas* 'dark-colored', reflecting a preform *n̥si-.) It is difficult to give a principled account of this double outcome. Hoenigswald (1953) shows that one can be constructed if we accept two hypotheses: first, that the double outcome of syllabic liquids, e.g. both ρα and αρ < *r̥ (see 5.4.1), reflects a dual pronunciation of *all* non-vocalic syllabic sonorants at an early date, perhaps even in PIE; and second, that the alternation between the two pronunciations was governed by something very similar to Sievers' Law. In that case the syllabic half of the syllabic nasal, so to speak, would be the first half after a heavy syllable in pre-Greek *ḗsm̥ and *ḗsn̥toy, so that the *s would effectively be intervocalic and would become *h; in the preform of δέδαε the syllable preceding the syllabic nasal was light, the syllabic part of the nasal would be at its end, and the *s would again be intervocalic and become *h.

In word-initial syllables one would expect the position of syllabicity within the syllabic sonorant to depend on the shape of the preceding word, leading to doublets like Hom. κρατερός vs. καρτερός, Hom. κραδίη vs. Att. καρδίᾱ—and that is apparently what we find in δαυλός, with *s effectively between vowels, vs. δασύς, with *s effectively following a consonant. We can even account for ἄσις with the suggestion that in word-initial position the syllabic portion of the sonorant came first.[30] As Hoenigswald emphasizes, 'All this is offered with the utmost caution' (Hoenigswald 1953: 291); there is no corroboration of these hypotheses from any other IE language, and in fact sequences *[ən] and *[nə] (or the like) must have passed through a fully syllabic stage *[n̩] to develop into *ą, as they clearly had by the Mycenaean period. But no other explanation of the dual outcome of *s in this position seems workable.

The situation is roughly similar for *s adjacent to syllabic *r̥. When the latter follows, *s > *h, as expected:

(post-)PIE *isu-ǵ^{h}esr- 'with arrows in hand' (cf. Skt *íṣuhastas* with second element remodeled) >→ fem. *iswo-k^{h}esr̥-ya > *ἰhϝο-χεhαρ-jα > Hom. (Ἄρτεμις) ἰοχέαιρα (Heubeck 1956).

When *r̥ precedes, there is no evidence that *s underwent any change when a syllabic followed, but there are only two examples:

PIE *d^{h}érsus ~ *d^{h}r̥séw- 'daring, bold' (cf. Skt pf. *dad^{h}árṣa*, Goth. *ga-dars* '(s)he dares') → *d^{h}r̥sús > Hom. θρασύς with derivs. θαρσῦνε̄ν 'to be bold, to dare', etc.;
post-PIE or substrate *pŕ̥som 'leek' (Lat. *porrum*) > πράσον (Frisk s.v.).

The σ of the former can have been leveled in from inherited θέρσος 'boldness' (preserved in Lesbian, cf. Alkaios 206.2; elsewhere → θάρσος by leveling on the adjective), with regularly surviving σ (see below), while it is not certain when the latter entered the language. However, *s did become *h between *r̥ and a non-syllabic sonorant:

PIE *tres- 'be afraid' (pres. τρε̃ν, Skt 3sg. *trásati*), zero-grade *tr̥s- in adj. *tr̥s-ró- 'afraid' > *trahro- in *τράhρων 'timid' (Hom. τρήρων; see further below).

That suggests that the failure of *s to undergo the change in the preceding two examples resulted from the special circumstances noted above. I can find no examples of inherited *l̥s (nor of non-initial *sl̥).

[30] Hoenigswald proposes (p. 291) that the development of word-initial *r̥ to αρ suggests as much, but it has since become clear that all the relevant examples are or could be laryngeal-initial.

When *s occurred between *y and a vowel (in that order) the outcome must at first have been *jh, which seems to have developed straightforwardly into [jj], written in attested Greek as the second half of an ι-diphthong in hiatus. I can find only one clear example:

PIE *tweys- 'shake' (cf. Skt *atviṣanta* 'they have been inflamed' *RV* VIII.94.7 with zero-grade root) in pres. *twéys-e/o- > *ʦϝέιhε/o- > σείε̄ν.

When *s occurred between a vowel and *y (in that order) we observe a double outcome of the cluster *sy. When a morpheme boundary intervened the result was *hy > [jj], written as the second half of an ι-diphthong. Examples are fairly numerous, though most are (or could be) innovative Greek formations:

PIE opt. 3sg. *$h_1$siéh$_1$t 'let him be' (Skt *syā́t*; cf. Old Lat. *siet*) >→ *esyēd (see 3.2.4; unaccented main-clause form, see 2.2.5) > *ἐhjη (see 3.5.3) > εἴη;
(post-)PIE *widúsih$_2$ fem. 'knowing' (Skt *vidúṣī*) > *ϝιδύhjα (see 3.2.2) > Hom. ἰδυῖα;
PIE *mus- 'fly' (cf. Lat. *musca*) in pre-Gk *músya > *μύhjα > μυῖα;
PIE *kónis ~ *kénis- 'dust, ashes' (cf. Lat. *cinis* 'ashes') in pre-Gk *konis-yé/ó- 'make dusty' > *κονιhjε/ο- > Hom. κονί̄ε̄ν (ῑ = ιι̯);
pre-Gk pres. *nas-ye/o- 'be dwelling, inhabit' (cf. Att. νεώς 'temple' (i.e. 'house (of the god)') < νηός < νᾱϝός < *ναhϝός < *nas-wó-) > Hom. ναίε̄ν;
pre-Gk *aydós-yo- 'respected; respectful' (cf. αἰδώς 'respect') > *αἰδóh-jo-ς > αἰδοῖος.

When there was no morpheme boundary between *h and *j the outcome in most dialects was apparently *h, which of course was eventually lost because it was intervocalic. The only examples are gen. sg. forms in *-syo:

PIE *tósyo 'of that' (Skt *tásya*, OE *þæs*) > *τóho > *τóο > τõ; so also the gen. sg. of o- stem adjectives and nouns;
PIE *kʷésyo 'whose?' (Gāthā-Av. *cahiiā*, Goth. *ƕis*) > *ʧʷέho > Hom. τέο.

However, in Homer the thematic endings are in competition with τοῖο, -οιο; Pelasgiote Thessalian -οι < *-οιο exhibits the same development, and Myc. *-o-jo* probably does. It is conceivable that in a few dialects *sy with no internal morpheme boundary developed like *s+y, but it is also possible that *-osyo was reinterpreted as (nom. sg.) *-os+yo in those dialects—whence the usual development *with* an internal morpheme boundary (Nussbaum 1985).

There is also a chronological problem to be addressed. We should expect the development of *sy with no internal morpheme boundary to be the regular sound change development, since those examples are morphologically isolated, whereas those with an internal morpheme boundary should be more vulnerable to morphologically motivated changes simply because they are morphologically complex. Therefore, in the (probable) chain of changes *sy > *hj > *h, either the morphologically complex examples must have become *h by regular sound change and then been restored to *hj (or the like) by leveling, or else they must have somehow been inhibited from undergoing the final change to *h; or, during the period when the change *hj > *h was in progress, native learners must have sorted the examples out in such a way that the morphologically complex examples retained the more conservative alternative *hj while the isolated examples underwent the change. Of the three alternatives, outright inhibition of a regular change is by far the least likely; alleged examples are all highly doubtful. We are left with the choice between the first and third. Probable cases of the third alternative are known; the most striking is the loss of inflectional *-n* in early Middle English (Moore 1927; cf. Kiparsky 1982: 91–3). But it seems clear that such changes are comparatively rare, probably because they can occur only when a sound change takes several generations to go to completion, giving native learners ample time to manipulate the old and new alternatives in competition. On the other hand, the first alternative—a straightforward sound change followed by a clearly distinct episode of leveling—is almost as unattractive as the second; it strains credulity to suggest that a comparatively isolated word like *μύhα 'fly' (assuming that such a form ever existed) was remodeled to *μύhjα, undoing the sound change *hj > *h, just because all other nouns in short *-ᾰ exhibited *j before the stem vowel. I conclude, with due caution, that the distribution of the outcomes of *hj is the result of morphological influence on a sound change still in progress, of the sort that Kiparsky argues we must posit for the phenomenon discovered by Moore.

*s also became *h word-internally between a vowel and other sonorants and between those sonorants and a vowel, with one notable class of exceptions (to be discussed below). In these instances the subsequent development of the *h-cluster was complex; I will deal with those details in 5.2.2. Here I simply list relevant inherited examples with their eventual outcomes in some alphabetic Greek dialects.

PIE *$h_1$esmi 'I am' (Skt *asmi*, unaccented main-clause form) > *esmi (see 3.2.1) > *ἐhμι (Hom., Att., etc. ἔ̄μι, Lesb. ἐμμι);
PIE *wésmn̥ 'garment' (Skt *vásma*) > *ϝέhμᾳ (Hom., Att. ἕ̄μα);
PIE *n̥smé 'us' (Skt *asmā́n* with added acc. pl. ending) > *ᾳhμέ (Dor. ἅ̄μέ, Ion. ἡμέας);
PIE *ḗs$h_2$ar 'I'm sitting' (Hitt. *ēshari*) → *ḗs$h_2$ay (Skt *ā́se*) >→ *ἥhμαι (Hom. ἧμαι);
post-PIE *wes-nu- 'dress, clothe' (Arm. *z-genow* '(s)he wears') > *ϝεhνυ- (Hom. καταείνυσαν 'they covered', *Il.* 23.135, ει = ε̄);

PIE *$h_1$rég^{w}es- 'darkness' (Goth. *riqis*; Skt *rájas-* 'empty space') in *ἐρεγ^{w}εh-νό- 'dark' (Hom. (Aiolic) ἐρεβεννός);

(post-)PIE *ǵ^{h}éslom 'thousand'(Skt *sa-hásram*), deriv. *ǵ^{h}éslio- > *χέhλιο- (Ion. gen. pl. χειλίων (ει = ē) *DGE* 688.D.12, Thessalian acc. pl. fem. χέλλιας *DGE* 614.29);

PIE *ǵ^{h}ésr-[31] 'hand' (Hitt. *kissar*, Toch. B *ṣar*, Arm *jeṙn*) > *χεhρ- (Hom., Att., etc. χέ̄ρ);

PIE *tres- 'be afraid' (pres. τρε̃ν, Skt 3sg. *trásati*), zero-grade *tr̥s- in adj. *tr̥s-ró- 'afraid' > *trahro- in *τράhρων 'timid' (Hom. τρήρων);

PIE *ísus 'arrow' (Skt *íṣus*) → *iswós > *ῑhϝός (Hom. ῑ̓ός);

PIE *ṓmsos[32] 'shoulder' (Toch. B *āntse*) > *ὤμhος (Hom., Att. ὦμος);

PIE *ǵ^{h}áns- 'goose' (Skt *haṃsás* 'swan', OHG *gans*) > *χάνh- (Hom., Att. χήν);

PIE *méh$_1$n̥s- 'moon' (Skt *mā́s*, Lat. *mēnsis* 'month') > *mēns- > *μηνh- 'month' (Att. μήν);

PIE *(h_2)áns- 'handle' (Lat. *ānsa*), deriv. *(h_2)ansio- 'reins' (Middle Irish pl. *éisi*) > *ἀνhιο- (pl. Hom. ἡνία, Att. ἡνίαι);

PIE *$h_2$áwsōs 'dawn' → *$h_2$usṓs (Skt *uṣā́s*) > *ἀϝhώς (Hom. ἠώς, Att. ἕως);

PIE *$h_2$áwsos 'ear' (OCS *uxo*) >→ *ὄϝhος (by lexical analogy with *ok^w- 'eye'; Hom., Att. ὄ̄ς).

The exceptions to this development involve the clusters *rs and *ls (see especially Wackernagel 1888, Miller 1976, the latter with comprehensive references). It is clear that when the immediately preceding syllabic was accented, *s in those clusters underwent no change:[33]

PIE *órsos 'arse' (Hitt. *ārras*, OE *ears*) > (*)ὄρσος (in Ion. ὀρσοπῦγιον 'part of the rump where the tailfeathers are attached') > Att. ὄρρος;

PIE *d^{h}érsos 'daring, bravery' (cf. Skt *dad^{h}árṣa*, Goth. *ga-dars* '(s)he dares') > Lesbian θέρσος (→ Hom. θάρσος by leveling from the related adj.);

PIE *$h_1$wers- 'rain, fall (as dew)' (Skt *várṣati* 'it's raining') > Hom. ἐέρση 'dew';

PIE *ters- 'dry out' (cf. Skt pres. 3sg. *tŕ̥ṣyati*) > Hom. τέρσεσθαι;

PIE *k^{w}els- 'make a groove' (Hitt. *gulszi* '(s)he engraves') > Hom. τέλσον (ἀρούρης) 'boundary (of the field)'.

[31] In this word and in 'goose' and 'moon' below the consonant cluster that occurred before vowel-initial endings has been leveled into the nom. sg.

[32] Gothic acc. pl. *amsans* could reflect the same preform, but Skt *áṃsas* must reflect a preform with a short vowel in the root, since Osthoff's Law did not operate in Skt (cf. *māṃsám* 'meat'); like the Gothic word, Arm. *ows* is ambiguous, while Lat. *umerus* must reflect yet a third preform. How to reconcile these discrepancies is not immediately obvious, but it is at least clear that the Greek word exhibited intervocalic *ms, and that the Toch. B word is exactly cognate with it. Schulze (1936) suggests plausibly that the form with the long vowel is a vr̥ddhi-formation originally meaning 'shoulder-joint', but that does not account for the medial vowel of Lat. *umerus*.

[33] The additional hypotheses of Forbes (1958a) seem to me unnecessary, especially in view of the fact that Greek verb forms with recessive accent must reflect PIE accentless forms (see 4.2.8).

Yet there are numerous examples of reconstructable PGk *rh and *lh that must reflect earlier *rs and *ls, above all in the s-aorist (see 4.2.2 (iii)). The conditions under which *s became *h in these clusters are elucidated by an old collective with shifted accent formed to PIE *órsos 'arse' (see above):

(post-)PIE *orsáh_2 'backside' > *ὀρhᾱ́ 'rear; tail' (Hom. ὀρή, Att. ὀρᾱ́).

The clear contrast both in accent and in the outcome of *s in this pair of forms establishes that *s > *h immediately following *r if the preceding syllabic was *not* accented (cf. Schwyzer 1939: 285–6). A further probable example that points in the same direction is an old causative made to the PIE root *$h_1$wers- 'rain, fall (as dew)' (see above):

PIE *wors-éye/o- 'make it rain' (Skt 3sg. *varṣáyati*; initial laryngeal lost because separated from *o by a sonorant within the same syllable, see 2.2.4 (i)) > *ϝορhέjε/ο- 'urinate' (Att. ὀρε̃ν).

It is reasonable to posit the same development for *ls. Further examples, some less certain, are adduced by Schwyzer, *loc. cit.* and especially Miller (1976).

3.5.2 *h-copying ('Hauchumsprung')

If a word began with a vowel or *w and exhibited an *h between the first and second syllabics, either intervocalic or as part of a cluster including a sonorant, the *h was copied into the onset of the initial syllable (though see further below on intervocalic examples).[34] That the *h was copied, not simply moved (by metathesis, as the traditional name *Hauchumsprung* implies), is demonstrated by the subsequent development of the sonorant clusters, in which the *h was clearly still present. Clear examples include:

PIE *(h_2)áns- 'handle' (Lat. *ānsa*), deriv. *(h_2)ansio- 'reins' > *ἀνhιο- > *hανhιο- (pl. Hom. ἡνία, Att. ἡνίαι);
PIE *$h_2$áwsōs 'dawn' → *$h_2$usṓs (Skt *uṣā́s*) > *ἀϝhώς > *hαϝhώς (Hom. ἠώς, Att. ἕως);
PIE *n̥smé 'us' (Skt *asmā́n* with added acc. pl. ending) > *ᾳhμέ > *hᾳhμέ (Dor. ἁμέ, Ion. ἡμέας);
PIE *ḗs$h_2$ar 'I'm sitting' (Hitt. *ēshari*) → *ḗs$h_2$ay (Skt *ā́se*) >→ *ἧhμαι > *hῆhμαι (Hom. ἧμαι);

[34] I am grateful to Oliver Sayeed for helpful discussion of this section and for alerting me to several problematic examples. Readers should not assume that he agrees either with my specific judgments or with my conclusions.

PIE *ḗsror 'they are sitting' → *ḗsn̥toy (Skt *ā́sate*) > *ἥh ą̣τοι > *hήhą̣τοι (Hom. ἥαται, spelled εἵαται in our text);
PIE *éws-e/o- pres. 'be burning (trans.)' (Skt 3sg. *óṣati*) > *ἕϝh-ε/o- > *héϝh-ε/o- 'singe, burn off (bristles)' (Hom. εὕε̄ν, Att. ἀφ-εύε̄ν);
PIE *wésmn̥ 'garment' (Skt *vásma*) > *ϝέhμą̣ > *hϝέhμą̣ (Hom., Att. ἕ̄μα).

The rough breathing of augmented forms such as ipf. ἕ̄πετο '(s)he accompanied', plup. ἑ̄στήκε̄ '(s)he was standing' could have arisen by this sound change: the attested forms exhibit /he:-/ plausibly < *hee- < *hehe- < *e-he-.

Recognition of this sound change also allows us to suggest a scenario for at least one non-obvious example:

pre-Gk *ár-smn̥ 'fitting, thing fit together' (cf. Hom. aor. ἀραρε̄ν 'to fit', fossilized ptc. ἄρμενος 'fitting, suitable', substantivized neut. pl. ἄρμενα 'gear' Alkaios 383.2) > *ἄρhμą̣ > *hάρhμą̣ (Hom., Att. ἅρμα 'chariot').

Were it not for the initial /h-/, a preform *ár-mn̥ would be reconstructed; but since suffixes beginning with nasal consonants (except participial *-meno-) have byforms with *-s-, the preform given above is plausible and solves the problem—though see also the end of this section.

A surprising number of words that might be expected to reflect this sound change do not do so, but for many there are plausible explanations. Homeric examples simply reflect the fact that the text of Homer was originally psilotic; as has long been known, rough breathings in Homer reflect partial Atticization of the text, so that (for example) the contracted form ἥλιος 'sun' (/h-/ < *s-, see 3.5.1) has the rough breathing because it coincides with the Attic form, while uncontracted ἠέλιος has the smooth breathing because it is foreign to Attic. (The classic discussion is Wackernagel 1916: 40–52; see also (more briefly) Chantraine 1973: 184–8.) That accounts not only for ἠώς, but also for (Ἄρτεμις) ἰοχέαιρα (< *ihwo-), ἀϋτμή 'breath' (if it is related to OE *sēoþan* 'to boil', plausibly < *$h_2$sewt-), and plausibly for poetic words attested elsewhere, e.g. ἔαρ 'blood' (cf. Hitt. *ēshar*), and words attested only in Hesykhios, e.g. ἤμορος 'without a share' (*ń̥-smoro-) and ἠϊκανός 'rooster' (plausibly 'dawn-singer'). No dialect exhibits a rough breathing in forms of 'be', but that is easily explained by leveling from the pres. indic. 3sg. ἐστι, the 'pivotal' form of the paradigm, which should never have had a rough breathing. (In the presents 'be sitting' and 'wear' leveling worked in the opposite direction.)

Surprisingly, many of the remaining exceptions exhibit o-vowels in the initial syllable: ὦμος 'shoulder', ὄ̄ς 'ear' (which of course could owe its smooth breathing to 'eye', to which it owes its vowel), ὀ̄ρᾱ́ 'tail', ὀ̄ρε̄ν 'urinate' (and ὀ̄ρανός 'sky', if derived from *worso- 'rain'), ὦνος 'price' (< *wṓsnos) with its derivatives. In fact there are no certain examples of h-copying across an o-vowel;[35] that seems like an improbable condition on such a change, but the pattern is regular.

However, there are other counterexamples to h-copying which are less easy to explain. Given that ἰ̄ός 'poison, rust' < *ϝῑhός occurs almost exclusively in poetry, we might suggest that its occasional appearance in Attic prose (e.g. Plato *Timaeus* 59c) reflects borrowing of a poetic—ultimately a Homeric—word; and it is at least conceivable that αὔριον 'tomorrow', reflecting *h₂awsr-, a derivative of 'dawn' (cf. Lith. *aušrà*) has lost its rough breathing by lexical analogy with ἆμαρ 'day'. But such an explanation is not plausible for at least two words:

*h₁ésu- 'good' (Hitt. *assus*), compounding form *h₁su- (Skt *su-*) > Hom. ἐΰς, pan-Greek εὐ-;
*wésr̥ 'spring(time)' (cf. Av. loc. *vaŋri*, Lith. *vasarà* 'summer') > ἔαρ.

Neither of these words has a rough breathing attested in any dialect. Since most examples of h-copying involve word-internal *h next to a sonorant, we might suggest that copying was triggered only by *h-clusters, and that these two words fail to exhibit copying because their *h's were intervocalic; in that case the initial /h/ of ἕπετο, etc., must be the result of morphological change rather than regular sound change, and the initial /h/ of ἧαται is the result of leveling (from a rather small basis, namely those forms in which μ immediately followed the root).

On the other hand, any attempt to explain the initial /h/'s in the first list of this section by leveling or lexical analogy runs into even greater difficulties; ἡνία 'reins' and εὕν 'to singe' are especially difficult to explain because of their isolation. I conclude, with caution, that h-copying was a regular sound change—probably failing to occur over o-vowels, possibly not triggered by intervocalic *h—whose outcomes might have been disturbed by subsequent changes not all of which can be recovered.

The fact that *h is copied into an onset including *w-, but not into an onset including *y-, is striking; it probably indicates that initial *y- was no longer a semivowel at the time when this change occurred. The clear examples are ζεῖν 'to boil' < *ʤέh-ε/ο- (or the like) < *yés-e/o- (cf. OHG *jesan* 'to ferment'), the word-family of ζώνη 'belt' < *ʤώhνᾱ (cf. Av. *yåŋhaiia-* 'gird'), and probably ζῡ́μη 'yeast' < *ʤῡ́hμᾱ (cf. Lat. *iūs* 'broth').

[35] From the fact that a byform οἷμος of οἶμος 'way, course, (Hom.) stripe' is attested, and from the occurrence of φροίμιον 'prelude' in tragedy (beside προοίμιον elsewhere), it has been conjectured that οἶμος and Hom. οἴμη 'song' reflect pre-Gk *óy-smo- '(act of) going' (see Frisk s.vv.). In that case the smooth breathings must reflect psilosis, and the puzzling restriction on h-copying did not apply to the syllable nucleus οι (of which the ο might have been somewhat fronted; note that in Homer *ϝ exhibits its usual metrical effects before οι, but not before other o-vowels). But the given etymologies of these words do not strike me as overwhelmingly convincing.

H-copying must have occurred after the change of *s to *h but before the sound changes that altered *hR- and *Rh-clusters (see 5.2.2). When the latter changes occurred is difficult to say. If the hypothesis of Parker (2008) is correct, all such clusters at first became *RR-clusters in all Greek dialects; the first compensatory lengthening was a subsequent change. If Mycenaean *a-ke-ra₂-te* spells *ἀγέρραντες (Heubeck 1979: 245–54, Aura Jorro 1999 s.v.), h-copying must have occurred earlier. In that case the fact that Mycenaean *a-mo* 'wheel', probably the same word as ἅρμα 'chariot', is never spelled with a_2- /ha-/ (Colvin 2007: 11) requires an explanation. Several are available: possibly in some Greek dialects the suffix did not originally contain *-s-; possibly the rough breathing of ἅρμα should be attributed to some other change, such as lexical analogy; possibly the Mycenaean noun lost its *h- by lexical analogy with ἀρ- 'fit'; it is even possible that *s developed differently between two non-syllabic sonorants in some dialects. That h-copying as a whole was a later change, as Colvin suggests *loc. cit.*, seems less likely.

3.5.3 Osthoff's Law; loss of word-final stops

Osthoff's Law (OL) is a cover term for sound changes that shortened long vowels when they were followed by a sonorant which was in turn followed by another consonant (but not before word-final sonorants, which were presumably extra-metrical). Such sound changes can be shown to have occurred in Latin, Celtic, and Germanic, for example (but no such sound change occurred in Indo-Iranian or Tocharian). The Greek version of OL did not operate before sonorant plus *h, nor before the cluster μν; otherwise its operation seems to have been general. However, probative examples are surprisingly few (cf. Schwyzer 1939: 279–80). 3pl. forms like Hom. βάν 'they went' reflect 3pl. *-énd colored by the laryngeal which preceded it and was then lost; corresponding participles such as (masc. nom. pl.) βάντες typically owe the stem vowels in their direct cases to leveling (note that *$g^w h_2$-ónt-es would have given 'βόντες' by regular sound change), while oblique βαντ-, for instance, could reflect *$g^w h_2$-n̥t- by Rix's Law (see 3.2.2). Since aorist passive -η- does not ablaut, it might be suggested that 3pl. forms such as Hom. μίγεν 'they mingled' and corresponding participles like μιγέντες are reliable examples of OL; but the aorist passive suffix probably reflects PIE stative/fientive *-éh_1- (see 2.3.3 (i) and 4.2.2 (iv)), and we cannot be certain that *-éh_1n̥C- would not have developed into *-énC- directly upon loss of the laryngeal. The same problem might recur in masc. nom. pl. πάντες 'all'; the Tocharian B cognate *poñc* reflects *pā́ntes (Ringe 1996: 97), but in Tocharian *-VHn̥- apparently yields *-V̄n- (cf. TB *yente*, TA *want* 'wind' < *w^yēntos < *$h_2$wéh_1n̥tos > Skt *vā́tas*, 3syll. in the Rigveda), so a preform *páh_2n̥tes is not excluded. The difference in vowel length between Hom. πτέρνη 'heel' and Skt *pā́rṣṇis* could reflect acrostatic ablaut; alternatively, the Sanskrit form could be a vr̥ddhi-derivative (so Frisk s.v. πτέρνη). But when all the examples that can be explained in other ways have been excluded, at least the following remain:

PIE inst. pl. *-ōys (Skt *-ais*) > -οις;
PIE *mḗh_1n̥s 'moon, month', obl. *méh_1n̥s- (Skt *mā́s*, OIr. *mí*, *mís*- 'month', Lat. *mēnsis* 'month') >→ *mēns- 'month', e.g. in gen. sg. *mēnsós > *mēnhós > Lesb. μῆννος, Att.-Ion. μηνός; nom. sg. *mḗns (which might reflect the PIE form directly) > *μένς > Hom. μείς, i.e. με̄́ς;
PIE *sné$h_1$wr̥ 'sinew' (Av. *snāuuarə*, Toch. B *ṣñor*) > *snḗwr̥; thematized *snḗwrom (possibly backformed to the nom.-acc. pl.) > νεῦρον (cf. Lat. *nervos* with metathesis);
PIE displaced iptv. *-tōd → 3sg. iptv.; reanalysis */-t-ō-t/ with 'reduplicated' 3sg. ending leads to the creation of 3pl. *-ntōnd (Ringe 1997: 138–40; see 4.2.6, 7.3.1), which > *-ntond > Lesb. -ντον;
post-PIE *ā́mr̥ 'day' (cf. Arm. *awr* < coll. *ā́mōr) in *μεσ-ᾱμρ-ίᾱ 'midday, south' > Ion. μεσαμβρίη (short α, since it was not fronted); in this case OL must have preceded the fronting reflected in Hom. ἦμαρ;
Gk nom. sg. *γ^{w}ασιλήϝς 'sub-king' *vel sim.* (loanword, see 4.3.3) > βασιλεύς.

Two examples are possible but less certain:

PIE nom. sg. *dyḗws 'sky, day' (?; Skt *dyáus*) > Ζεύς;
PIE nom. sg. *g^{w}ṓws 'bovine' (?; Skt *gáus*) > βοῦς.

The problem is that only Indo-Iranian clearly exhibits long diphthongs in the nom. sg. of these words, and it is at least possible that the long vowel was introduced from acc. sg. *dyḗm, *g^{w}ṓm only in that daughter (see, e.g., Szemerényi 1996: 181–2, Meier-Brügger 2010: 211–12, Fortson 2010: 116; for comprehensive discussion, see Wodtko et al. 2008 s.vv. **dei̯*-, **g$^{u̯}$óu̯*-). That *Rh did not trigger OL is demonstrated not only by the oblique forms of 'month', but also by ὦμος 'shoulder' (see 3.5.1); that OL was not triggered by μν is shown by a range of examples such as πλήμνη 'hub' and κρημνός 'steep bank, cliff'. OL followed the loss of laryngeals (see 3.2.1) and preceded the loss of word-final stops (see immediately below). Later levelings and contractions produced numerous new long vowels before RC-sequences which were not shortened; evidently OL did not remain a phonological rule of Greek.

That inherited word-final *-d and *-t were lost in Greek is immediately obvious from comparison of relevant words with cognates:

PIE *tód neut. 'that' (Skt *tát*, OE *þæt*) > τό;
PIE *ályod neut. 'other' (Lydian *aλad*, Lat. *aliud*) > ἄλλο;
PIE *k^{w}íd 'what?' (Hitt. *kuit*, Lat. *quid*) > τί;

PIE *mélid 'honey' (Hitt. *milit*) > μέλι;
PIE *b^héroyd '(s)he might carry' (Skt *b^háret*) > φέροι;
PIE *b^héretōd 'one must carry' (Skt *b^háratāt*) > φερέτω 'let him/her carry';
PIE *é b^hered '(s)he was (reportedly) carrying' (Skt (narrative) *áb^harat*) > ἔφερε '(s)he was carrying';
PIE *é b^herond 'they were (reportedly) carrying' (cf. Faliscan *fifiqo[n]d* 'they made') > ἔφερον 'they were carrying';
PIE *é stah$_2$t '(s)he (reportedly) stood up' (Skt *ást^{h}āt*) > ἔστᾱ '(s)he stood up' > Att.-Ion. ἔστη;
PIE *é h$_1$est '(s)he (reportedly) was' (Vedic Skt *ā́s*) > ἦς '(s)he was'.

All Greek dialects exhibit the outcome of this change. It definitely followed Osthoff's Law, since the third-person imperative vowel was shortened before *-nd (see above). It might not have been a very early change, since reflexes of *-d survive in fixed constructions. An obvious case is Lesbian ὄττι 'whatever' (e.g. in Sappho 1.15); the ὅτι of most other dialects can have been re-formed after the loss. However, it probably occurred before the creation of the new 3pl. ending -αν in the sigmatic aorist (see 4.2.6 (i)), since an ending *-αδ or *-ατ would have been clearly marked.

Other stops and clusters of stops were also lost word-finally, though examples are rare. At least one was inherited:

PIE *é h$_2$aǵt '(s)he (reportedly) said' (*LIV* s.v. 2. *h$_2$eǵ*; cf. pres. 3sg. Arm. *asê*, Lat. *ait*) > Att.-Ion. ἦ '(s)he said'.

Two examples involve loanwords from unknown sources:

γάλα 'milk' < *γάλακτ, gen. γάλακτος (cf. Lat. *lac*, *lactis*);
voc. sg. ἄνα 'lord!' < *ϝάνακτ, cf. gen. ἄνακτος.

3.5.4 Grassmann's Law

Grassmann's Law (GL) is a cover term for regressive aspirate dissimilation; such a sound change occurred (independently) in Greek, Indic, and Tocharian (Winter 1962: 24–5, Schindler 1977a: 6). In Greek, GL occurred after the devoicing of aspirates and the change of word-initial *s- to *h-. The aspirates were deaspirated and *h- was lost if an aspirated stop followed anywhere in the word. (However, word-internal *h did not trigger GL; see the end of this section for a discussion of that peculiarity.) The following completely isolated examples establish this sound change for Greek:

PIE *b^hāǵ^{h}u- 'arm' (Toch. B obl. *pokai*, Skt *bāhús*) > *φᾱ́χυς > πᾶχυς 'forearm' > Att.- Ion. πῆχυς;

PIE *b^{h}end^{h}- 'tie' (Goth. *bindan*, Skt *band^{h}*-) > *φενθ- > πενθ- in πενθερός 'father-in- law' (cf. Skt *bánd^{h}us* 'kinsman');

PIE *b^{h}ud^{h}- 'bottom' (Skt *bud^{h}nás*) > *φυθ- > πυθ- in πυθμήν 'bottom of a jar';

PIE *g^{wh}ed^{h}- 'ask for' (Goth. *bidjan*, Av. 3sg. *jaδiieiti*), derived noun *g^{wh}ód^{h}os > *χ^{w}όθος > πόθος 'desire' (see also 5.4.1 (i));

PIE *d^{h}eyǵ^{h}- 'make (out of clay)' (Skt 1sg. *déhmi*, Goth. ptc. dat. sg. *digandin*) in result nouns (masc.) *d^{h}óyǵ^{h}os, (neut.) *d^{h}éyǵ^{h}os > *θοῖχος, *θεῖχος > τοῖχος, τεῖχος, both 'wall' (cf. Skt *dehī́* 'rampart');

PIE *d^{h}eg^{wh}- 'burn' (Skt 3sg. *dáhati*) > *θεχ^{w}- > τεφ- in τέφρᾱ 'ashes';

PIE *g^{h}eb^{h}al- 'head' (Toch. A *śpāl*, OHG *gebal* 'skull') > *χεφαλ- > Att.-Ion. κεφαλή;

PIE *seng^{wh}- 'speak solemnly' *vel sim.* (Goth. *siggwan* 'sing'), action noun *sóng^{wh}os (Goth. *saggws* 'song'), whence collective *song^{wh}áh$_2$ > *hονχ^{w}ᾱ́ > Att.-Ion. ὀμφή 'divine voice' (see also 5.4.1);

PIE *sámh$_2$d^{h}os 'sand' (ON *sandr*, Middle High German *sam(b)t*) > *hάμαθος > ἄμαθος;

PIE *sweh$_1$- 'become accustomed' (Lat. *suēscere*), extended as *swēd^{h}- in derived noun *hϝήθος > ἦθος 'accustomed place, custom';

PIE *seh$_1$- sift' (cf. OCS *prosějati*, Welsh *hidl* 'sieve'), extended as *sēd^{h}- in *hηθμός > ἠθμός 'sieve, strainer';

PIE *stemb^{h}H- 'prop' (Skt *stamb^{h}i*-, cf. Toch. B *ścama* '(s)he stood'), action noun *στέμφος 'prop, support' in cpd. *hą-στεμφής 'with a (firm) support' > Hom. ἀστεμφής 'fixed, unmoved'.

In addition, a number of fossilized compounds and derivatives that are still analyzable on a purely Greek basis exhibit the effects of GL. Several involve the prefix *hą- 'same; with' < PIE *sm̥- (Skt *sa*-), like the last isolated example cited above, e.g.:

δελφῦ́ς 'womb': *hα-δελφεϝ-ός '(born of the) same womb, uterine brother' > Ion. ἀδελφεός, Att. ἀδελφός 'brother' (the latter apparently an allegro form);

Hom. λέχος 'bed': *hά-λοχος '(sharing the) same bed' > Hom. ἄλοχος 'wife';

κέλευθος 'path': *hα-κόλουθος '(walking the) same path' > ἀκόλουθος 'companion';

Hom. σπέρχεσθαι 'to hurry', action noun *σπέρχος: *hα-σπερχές 'with haste, hastily' > Hom. ἀσπερχές.

Note also:

PIE *sed- 'sit down', e.g. in *sédos 'seat' (Skt *sádas*) > Hom. ἕδος: innovative Gk deriv. *hέδ-εθλον (cf. γένε-θλον 'descent, ancestry') > ἕδεθλον 'abode; ground, foundation';

*hέχε̄ν 'to hold' (see below), χέ̄ρ 'hand': *hεχε-χε̄ρ-ίᾱ 'hand-holding' > ἐκεχε̄ρίᾱ 'truce' (with double application of GL).

Since GL followed the assimilation of stops to following obstruents (see 3.4.4), which often involved deaspiration, we should find alternations between aspirated and unaspirated stops and between /h/ and zero. In fact such alternations still occur in nine paradigms:[36]

PIE *seǵ^{h}- 'hold' (Skt *sáhate* '(s)he prevails') > pres. *hεχ-ε/ο- > ἔχε̄ν 'to hold, to have', with innovative zero-grade aor. > σχε̄ν 'to get' and desiderative *seǵ^{h}-se/o- > future ἕξε̄ν;
PIE *d^{h}reg^{h}- 'run' (agent noun *d^{h}rog^{h}ós 'runner' > τροχός, OIr. *droch,* both 'wheel') > pres. *θρεχ-ε/ο- > τρέχε̄ν but fut. *θρεχ-σε/ο- > (ἀπο)θρέξεσθαι;
PIE *d^{h}reb^{h}- 'coagulate' (cf. Middle English *draf,* OHG pl. *trebir* 'dregs') > (trans.) pres. *θρεφ-ε/ο- > τρέφε̄ν but aor. *θρεφ-σ- > θρέψαι;
PIE *d^{h}rah$_2$g^{h}- 'disturb' (cf. OCS *raz-dražiti* 'to provoke, to enrage') > pres. *θρᾱχ-jε/ο- > θρᾱ́ττε̄ν, but pf. *θε-θρᾱχ- 'be in a disturbed state' > τετρᾱχ- in Hom. plup. 3sg. τετρήχει 'it was in an uproar';
PIE *d^{h}uh$_2$- 'smoke' (cf. noun *d^{h}uh$_2$mós > Skt *d^{h}ūmás,* Lat *fūmus,* Gk θῡμός 'strong emotion') extended in Gk *θῡφ- 'burn up', e.g. in pres. *ἐπι-θῡφ-ε/ο- > ἐπιτῡ́φεσθαι 'to be consumed by fire' but pf. ptc. *ἐπι-θε-θῡφ-μένο- > ἐπιτεθῡμμένος 'furious';
PIE *d^{h}rub^{h}- 'break up' (?; cf. Latvian pl. *drubazas* 'splinters'?) > *θρυφ- in pres. *θρυφ-jε/ο- > *θρυπʧε/ο- (see 3.6.3) > θρύπτε̄ν but intransitive aor. *θρυφ-ή- > aor. passive τρυφῆναι;
Gk *θαφ- 'bury' (< *d^{h}m̥b^{h}-, cf. Arm. *damban* 'grave'?; so *LIV* s.v. 2.*d^{h}emb^{h}*, but only the zero grade of this root is attested anywhere) in pres. *θαφ-jε/ο- > *θαπʧε/ο- (see 3.6.3) > θάπτε̄ν but intransitive aor. *θαφ-ή- > aor. passive ταφῆναι;
Gk *θαχ- 'swift' in *θαχ-ύ- > ταχύς but cptv. *θαχ-joh- >→ Hom. θάσσων;
Gk *θριχ- 'hair' in nom. sg. θρίξ, dat. pl. θριξί, but acc. sg. τρίχα, gen. sg. τριχός, etc.

On the other hand, at least four paradigms have leveled such alternations in favor of the unaspirated alternant. Three are common verbs:

PIE *b^{h}eyd^{h}- 'trust' (Lat. *fīdere,* Goth. *beidan* 'to wait for') > *φειθ- in pres. πείθεσθαι (with aor. πιθέσθαι and pf. πεποιθέναι), but trans. aor. πεῖσαι 'to persuade' and fut. πείσε̄ν (both already in Homer) in place of expected *φεῖσαι, *φείσε̄ν;

[36] I omit Hom. aor. ptc. ταφών 'thunderstruck', pf. τέθηπεν '(s)he is amazed', since in my opinion the -π- of the latter has not been convincingly explained (*pace* Barton 1993: 2 with fn. 3 and references, 5–7 with references); I also reject the proposed connection of this fragmentary paradigm with θάμβος 'astonishment' (see 3.4.5), which would involve an irregular sound correspondence.

PIE *b^{h}ewd^{h}- 'be alert' *vel sim.* (Skt pres. 3sg. *bód^{h}ati* '(s)he observes', Goth. *ana- biudan* 'to command') > *φευθ- in Hom. pres. πεύθεσθαι 'to try to find out' (with aor. πυθέσθαι), but fut. πεύσεσθαι (already in Homer) in place of expected *φεύσεσθαι;

PIE *d^{h}ewg^{h}- 'produce' (Skt pres. 3sg. *dógd^{h}i* '(s)he milks', Goth. *daug* 'is useful') > *θευχ- in Hom. pres. τεύχε̄ν 'to make, to fashion' (with pf. ptc. τετευχώς 'made, fashioned'; also aor. τυχε̄ν 'to hit (a mark)' by lexical split, with new. pres. τυγχάνε̄ν), but aor. τεῦξαι, fut. τεύξε̄ν (both Hom.) in place of expected *θεῦξαι, *θεύξε̄ν.

Note that all three verbs originally had thematic aorists in Greek. It might therefore be argued that these roots were reanalyzed as πειθ-, πευθ-, τευχ- at an early period when they had no sigmatic stems, and that the future and the sigmatic aorist are later formations. The fourth leveled example is an adjective:

PIE *b^{h}éńg^{h}u- ~ *b^{h}n̥ǵ^{h}éw- 'dense, numerous' (cf. Skt cptv. *báṃhīyas-* 'more') → *b^{h}n̥ǵ^{h}ús (Skt *bahús* 'much, many') > *φαχύς > παχύς 'thick', with Hom. cptv. πάσσων.

It is unclear why θάσσων preserved its aspirate (see above) while πάσσων underwent leveling. But in any case the appearance of πάσσων in Homer offers us valuable evidence for the date of GL. The form cannot be an Atticism in our text, because the Attic comparative was παχύτερος; πάσσων must be a genuine 8th-century form. GL must therefore have occurred as a regular sound change at least a few generations earlier, since time must be allowed for the alternation that it created to be leveled out in this word.[37] On the other hand, it must have followed assimilation in stop clusters, which can have occurred very early (see 3.4.4), and apparently also the developments of stops followed by *j (Janko 1977, Miller 1977: 139; see 3.6.3). Hom. ὄφρα 'while, until' (cf. τόφρα 'for that long, up till then') < *hjóp^{h}r̥ could furnish further evidence if we could be sure that any of the post-Homeric examples (notably in Pindar) are not just psilotic Homericisms.

Whether GL occurred at roughly the same time in all attested dialects is not clear; for discussion, see 3.5.5.

By the 5th century BC, and probably long before, GL had ceased to be a general rule of Greek phonology, at least in the Attic-Ionic dialects (see also section 3.5.5 *ad fin.*). Aside from the alternating roots listed above, it had been fragmented into several rules each of which applied in a morphologically restricted environment, as follows.

[37] This secure inference renders most discussions of the chronology of GL irrelevant.

1) In reduplicating syllables, the root-initial aspirated stops φ, θ, χ were regularly replaced by the corresponding unaspirated stops π, τ, κ. Thus we find pres. τιθέναι 'to put (several), to be putting', κιχράναι 'to lend', Hom. κιχήμεναι 'to find'; aor. (all Homeric) πέφραδε 'he showed', πεφιδέσθαι 'to spare', πέφνε 'he slew', κεχάροντο 'they rejoiced'; and dozens of perfects, e.g. πεφάσθω 'let it be said', πεφυλαχέναι 'to have guarded' and πεφυλάχθαι 'to be on one's guard', τεθνάναι 'to be dead', τεθυκέναι 'to have sacrificed' and τεθύσθαι 'to have been sacrificed', κεχηνέναι 'to gape', κεχρῆσθαι 'to make habitual use of', etc., etc.; there are no exceptions.
2) Roots of the shape θV̆- (only) underwent deaspiration before the aorist passive suffix -θη-; thus τεθῆναι 'to get put', τυθῆναι 'to get sacrificed' (but χυθῆναι 'to get poured', θραυσθῆναι 'to be shattered', etc.).
3) The aorist passive 2sg. imperative -θη-θι was dissimilated to -θητι, e.g. in ἐνθῡμήθητι 'think it through', ἡττήθητι 'yield!'

It is striking that in all these cases GL applies across only one syllable nucleus; evidently such a rule was easier to learn than one that applied anywhere within the word. However, there are also numerous potential cases in which only one syllable nucleus intervenes, yet GL no longer applies: mediopassive verb endings beginning with -σθ- never trigger GL in attested Greek (as can be seen from some of the infinitives cited above), nor do the adverbial endings -φι, -θεν, -θι, though the sound change must originally have applied to such forms. The 'backward' operation of GL in the passive aorist imperative must have resulted from some sort of native-learner error, though the details remain obscure. This is an outstanding example of the restriction and fragmentation of a phonological rule.

It is clear that medial *-h- did not trigger GL from isolated examples like θεός 'god' < *θεhός, cf. θέσ-φατος 'god-spoken' (both < PIE $^*d^hh_1s$-, cf. Lat. *fānum* 'temple' < *fasnom < $^*d^hh_1s$-nó-m; full-grade collective $^*d^h\acute{e}h_1s$-na-h_2 in Oscan acc. **fíísnam** 'temple'). Since intervocalic *h was still being lost in the Mycenaean period (see 3.5.1), we might be tempted to see this as evidence that GL was a post-Mycenaean change. Unfortunately an alternative explanation is possible: even in languages in which initial /h/ is fully voiceless, intervocalic /h/ often is not; prehistoric Greek could have been such a language, and that difference could have been sufficient to prevent non-initial *h from triggering GL (Ives Goddard, p.c. 1983).

3.5.5 Irregularities of aspiration

Though the regular sound changes discussed in 3.2.4 (*ad init.*), 3.5.1, 3.5.2, and 3.5.4 account for the pattern of initial /h-/ and aspirated consonants in Greek, there are notable irregularities in individual words, not all of which can be explained by dialect borrowing or decomposition (as in 3.5.1). This section will discuss some salient cases in Classical Attic, as well as some that are widespread in Greek dialects; for discussion of examples confined (mostly) to individual dialects, see especially Buck (1955: 52–5, 59–61).

Leveling within paradigms is the simplest and most convincing explanation for phonologically unexpected outcomes, but it accounts for only a minority of cases. It seems clear that the *h- which must have arisen by copying (see 3.5.2) in *hε̄μι 'I am', *hεhεντι 'they are', *hήhą 'I was', etc., has been eliminated by leveling on pres. 3sg. ἐστι, ipf. 3sg. ἦς, the 'pivotal' forms of the paradigm (Lejeune 1972: 121); thus we find only ἔ̄μι, ἔ̄σι, ἦα, etc. Conversely, the copied /h-/ has been leveled through the paradigms of ἧσται '(s)he is seated' < PIE *és-, ἕσται '(s)he is wearing' < PIE *wés-; in the latter case such a development might have been encouraged by the derived noun ἓ̄μα 'garment' < *wésmn̥, in the former by lexical analogy with ἑδ- 'sit' < *sed- (Lejeune, *loc. cit.*). The consistent rough breathing of εὕε̄ν 'to singe' must reflect a similar process (which in that case was almost inevitable, since copied /h-/ occurred throughout the present stem). The rough breathing of aor. indic. ἕσπετο '(s)he followed' (stem σπ-έ/ό-, e.g. in inf. σπέσθαι) must likewise have been leveled from pres. indic. ἕπεται, ipf. indic. ἕ̄πετο (see 3.5.2)—possibly except in Homer, where such forms could conceivably reflect an inherited reduplicated stem without augment.

Some other cases can be the result of lexical analogy between words of related meaning. The rough breathing of ἕσπερος 'evening' < *wésperos (cf. Lat. *vesper*) can reflect lexical analogy with *haϝhώς 'dawn' (see 3.5.2, and cf. Att. ἕως; but see Sturm 2018 for an alternative explanation). Those two words are apparently responsible, in turn, for the rough breathing of Att. ἡμέρᾱ 'day' (Schwyzer 1939: 305), a change not reflected in other dialects and apparently incomplete even in early Attic inscriptions (Buck 1955: 54, Threatte 1980: 500). A lexical analogy operating in the other direction might explain the smooth breathing of αὔριον 'tomorrow' < *$h_2$aus-r- (cf. Lith. *aušrà* 'dawn', see 3.5.3; cf. Lejeune 1972: 121, 122 with fn. 2). Various other words, most notably ἵππος 'horse' and ὅρος 'boundary', exhibit an unexpected initial /h-/ (Schwyzer 1939: 306). For several of these puzzles (and some others), see Sturm (2018) for an alternative solution.

A more systematic puzzle is the fact that non-psilotic dialects initial upsilon is always ὑ-, regardless of its etymological origin. To be sure, a substantial proportion of cases can be explained by regular sound change, or by some combination of sound change and lexical analogy. ὗς 'pig', ῡ̔ει 'it's raining', ὕπνος 'sleep', υἱύς 'son' all reflect inherited *s-; ὕ̄μήν 'membrane' reflects *sy- (see 3.5.1); ὑγιής 'healthy' reflects *h_2y- (see 3.2.4), and Hom. ὑσμῑ́νη 'combat' probably reflects *Hy-; Doric acc. ὕ̄μέ 'you (pl.)' reflects *h-copying: *hυhμέ < *ὐhμέ < *usmé (see 3.5.2). The preposition ὑπό 'below' can reflect *supo (cf. Toch. B *spe* 'near'), and its rough breathing can have spread analogically to ὑπέρ 'above' ←< *upér (cf. OHG *obar*, *ubiri*, Skt *upári*), precisely as in Latin (*sub*, *super*), and in contrast to Sanskrit (*úpa*, *upári*, with the reverse analogy). But at least ὕδωρ 'water' ←< coll. *udṓr (cf. Rigvedic Skt *udā́*), ὕστερος 'later' (cf. Skt *úttaras* 'upper'), and ὑφαίνε̄ν 'to weave' (cf. Skt inj. 2sg. *ub*^{h}*nā́s*) exhibit a rough breathing that can only be the result of a phonological rule—one that applied fairly late, to judge from the fact that it ignores GL (as in the last example cited). It used to be supposed that a sequence of regular sound changes *u- > *ju- > *hu-* could account for such an outcome (cf. Schwyzer 1939: 305 with references, rejecting that proposal); but that hypothesis has become untenable, since it now seems clear that only PIE *Hy-, not also *y-, yields Gk /h-/ (see 3.2.4 and 3.6.1), and no alternative is generally accepted.[38]

Especially in inscriptions we encounter regressive *assimilation* of aspiration between stops, apparently undoing GL. Examples are widely distributed in time and space; typical are:

θυφλός 'blind' *DGE* 786 (West Ionic, 7th century BC)
φεφύλαχσο 'guard!' *DGE* 538.4 (Boiotian, early 6th century BC)
τᾶς φαρθένō 'of the girl' *DGE* 661.28 (Arkadian, 5th century BC)
καταθίθεθθαι 'to accept mortgages' *DGE* 179.VI.4–5 (Cretan, mid 5th century BC; = Attic κατατίθεσθαι)

Instances in Attic inscriptions are numerous, and there are also examples of progressive assimilation; see Threatte (1980: 455–68) for examples and discussion. Transposition of aspiration from one stop to another is also occasionally attested; for examples see e.g. Buck (1955: 60) and Threatte, *loc. cit.*

Miller (1977: 143–4) (citing additional examples, with references) argues that at least some of these forms reflect not a reversal of GL, but a state of the language in which GL had not yet occurred. That none of the inscriptions he cites offers counterexamples to that hypothesis can reflect the fact that most are short,[39] but the fact that Boiotian, in particular, seems to offer no examples of GL before the late 5th century BC is more interesting (though one needs to remember that all the longer Boiotian inscriptions date from the 3rd century BC and later). Since Boiotian is conservative in a number of other details, it is possible that GL did not occur in that dialect until the 5th century BC; in that case it must have spread slowly through the Greek dialect continuum, probably beginning in East Ionic around 800 BC at the latest. (Threatte 1980: 456 makes it clear that the situation in Attic is very different; examples in Attic inscriptions do reflect a reversal of GL.)

On the other hand, it is also possible that GL occurred at an early date in all dialects, that it was reversed in Boiotian (and perhaps in other dialects) by assimilation of aspirates, and that the latter was subsequently eliminated under the

[38] For an interesting hypothesis, see Jatteau (2016: 303–18).

[39] Cretan inscriptions are a special case. In the archaic (and archaizing) Cretan alphabet, only /th/ is represented by a distinctive letter θ, /ph/ and /kh/ being represented by π and κ respectively; that substantially reduces the number of potential examples even in very long documents, such as *DGE* 179 (the Gortyn Laws).

influence of those dialects that had not undergone the reversal (the great majority). Such a sequence of changes is reasonably plausible precisely because PIE root constraints ensured that aspiration was non-contrastive in inherited roots after the devoicing of aspirates (Hoenigswald 1965: 59), and Greek acquired few new roots that provided exceptions to that generalization (e.g. κεύθεν 'to conceal'), with the result that relevant learner errors could cause little confusion and would therefore be more likely to be 'acceptable' and to catch on.[40]

On a somewhat more wide-angle view, once GL had occurred the contrast between aspirated and unaspirated voiceless stops was neutralized in many positions (as Philomen Probert reminds me). Subsequent shifts in both directions are perhaps to be expected, and it is not even necessarily clear what particular spellings of stops in neutralized positions mean in structural terms.

3.6 The development of PIE *y

3.6.1 Sievers' Law in Greek

The most comprehensive review of the development of Sievers' Law (SL) in Greek is Barber (2013), on which this section is largely based.[41]

We have seen (in 2.2.4 (ii)) that the Lindeman's Law phenomenon, in which word-initial *CR- varies with *CR̥-, is difficult to assess even for PIE. Examples with *R̥ are not rare in Greek, but many could have arisen, or at least been favored, by paradigmatic leveling. Examples that cannot be explained in that fashion are δύο, Hom. δύω 'two' vs. δώδεκα 'twelve', δίς 'twice' (Barber 2013: 140), and Aiolic ἴα 'one' (see 4.3.7). ἀνα-βιῶναι 'to revive, to come back to life' is probably a member of the class of intransitive aorists that reflect PIE statives/fientives (see 4.2.2 (iv)) and thus reflects *$g^w ih_3$-éh_1- (Francis 1971: 77–87, Klein 1988: 270); βίᾱ 'force' is at least as likely to reflect *$g^w ih_2$-ah_2- as to be a root noun (cf. the inconclusive discussion of Barber 2013: 133–4), and a laryngeal probably followed the high vowel in βιός 'bow' and similar examples (Barber 2013: 135–7); χιών 'snow' could owe its syllabic ι to the lost zero-grade stem *$\acute{g}^h$im- (Barber 2013: 137); κύων 'dog' could owe its syllabic high vowel to its oblique stem κυν-, and so on.

Examples of SL syllabic alternants of nonvocalic sonorants are also hard to find; two plausible examples are:

[40] How this situation was affected by the surface exceptions to GL that developed as the rule was restricted and fragmented remains to be investigated. It is not clear that they would have made much difference to the intelligibility of learner errors, but if they did, an early reversal of GL would be more likely than a later reversal—in which case it would be difficult to distinguish that scenario from one in which GL had not applied in the dialects in question.

[41] Barber is extremely cautious about drawing conclusions. While such an approach is certainly valuable, especially in sifting the evidence, I believe that we can be somewhat more definite, so long as we remember that every statement about prehistory is in principle probabilistic.

δαπάνη 'expense', orig. collective to *dh$_2$pn̥óm 'sacrificial meal' (cf. ON *tafn* 'sacrifice', Lat. *damnum* 'loss');

πλατάνιστος 'plane tree' (lit. 'the broadest one') ← *πλατανός 'broad' < *pl̥th$_2$n̥ós (cf. OIr. *lethan*, Welsh *llydan*; but Rix's Law cannot be absolutely excluded in this case, see 3.2.2).

But most examples of suffixal -αν-, -αρ-, etc., are of other origin, or of unclear origin; for instance, the present stems in -ανε/ο- must ultimately reflect thematization of infixed present stems ending in *-n̥H- (see 4.2.1 (ii)).

However, there is abundant evidence for the development of *-y- ~ *-i- following a non-initial consonant or cluster. The pattern of Homeric comparative adjectives in *-joh- ~ *-jον- (originally s-stems, see 5.4.2 (ii)) strongly suggests that SL remained a phonological rule well down into the separate prehistory of Greek (see the comprehensive discussion of Barber 2013: 145–86). Though few actual examples can reflect PIE elatives with accented full-grade roots (because most have been remodeled on the basis of the corresponding positive adjectives), a majority of those with light root-syllables ending in consonants exhibit reflexes of the appropriate SL alternant beginning with *j (note that I have silently corrected the Atticizing spellings of our received text, replacing unoriginal long vowels in roots; see e.g. Wackernagel 1916: 13 with references):[42]

μέζων 'greater' *Il.* 15.121, etc.; Myc. nom. pl. *me-zo-e*, neut. *me-zo-a$_2$* < PIE *még-yos- (Av. neut. *maziiō*; remodeled in Lat. neut. *maius*);

κρέσσων 'more powerful' *Il.* 1.80, etc. ←< pre-Gk *krét-yos-, cf. κρατύς 'powerful' < *kr̥tús;

χείρων (i.e. χέ̆ρων) 'inferior' *Il.* 20.434, etc. ←< *χερ-joh- (etymology unknown);

acc. sg. πάσσονα 'stouter, more strongly built' *Od.* 5x ←< *παχ-joh-, cf. παχύς;

βράσσων 'shorter' *Il.* 10.226 ←< *βραχ-joh-, cf. βραχύς;

θάσσον adv. 'more quickly' *Il.* 2.440, etc. ←< *θαχ-joh-, cf. ταχύς;

μάσσον adv. 'longer, farther' *Od.* 8.203 ←< *μακ-joh-, cf. μακρός;

ὑπολίζονες nom. pl. 'much smaller' *Il.* 18.519 ←< *ὀλιγ-joh-, cf. ὀλίγος;

μάλλον adv. 'more, rather' *Il.* 1.563, etc. (very common) ←< *μαλ-joh-, cf. μάλα, sup. μάλιστα.

To this list can be added two examples which happen not to occur in Homer:

τοὔλασσον 'the lesser', Theognis 269 ←< *ἐλαχ-joh-, cf. ἐλάχιστον 'the least' *Hymn to Hermes* 573;

βάσσων 'deeper', Herodian (somewhat doubtful, Seiler 1950: 52) ←< *βαθ-joh-, cf. βάθιστον 'deepest' *Il.* 8.14.

[42] The preform of μείων 'less' is unclear; it might reflect *méw-yos- or *méyw-iyos- (Myc. *me-u-jo* ~ *me-wi-jo*; see Aura Jorro 1999 s.v.). ἀμείνων 'better' seems to be an n-stem that has been attracted into this class of comparatives because of its meaning; see Frisk s.v. with references.

Only three Homeric comparatives with roots of this shape exhibit syllabic -ι- in the suffix:[43]

κακίων 'worse' *Od.* 4x, cf. κακός, sup. κάκιστος (but Myc. nom. pl. *ka-zo-e*);
γλυκίων 'sweeter' *Il.* 1.249, etc., cf. γλυκύς (but nom. pl. neut. γλύσσονα Xenophanes 38.2);
φιλίων 'more welcome' *Od.* 19.351 = 24.268, cf. φίλος (but usual cptv. φίλτερος, sup. φίλτατος).

A further example that might fail to occur in Homer by chance is

βράδιον adv. 'more slowly', Hesiod *Works and Days* 528, cf. βραδύς, sup. nom. pl. βάρδιστοι *Il.* 23.310, 530.[44]

On the other hand, almost all comparatives of this class with heavy root-syllables ending in consonants exhibit syllabic -ι- in the suffix, not only in Homer but in later Greek as well. Homeric examples—mostly nom.-acc. sg. neut., for metrical reasons—include:

καλλίονες nom. pl. 'more handsome' *Od.* 10.396 (and κάλλιον 'better, more appropriate' ten times);
κέρδιον 'better, more fitting' *Il.* 3.41, etc. (more than thirty times);
ἄλγιον 'worse, harder to bear' *Il.* 18.278, etc.;
ῥῑ́γιον 'worse, more frightful' *Il.* 1.325, etc.;
αἴσχιον 'more shameful' *Il.* 21.437.

Posthomeric examples[45] include:

ἥδιον neut. 'more pleasant' Herodotos 2.46.2; ᾅδιον Sappho 62.3;
ὕψιον adv. 'more loftily' Pindar fr. 213.1;
πόρσιον adv. 'further' Pindar *Olympian* I.114.

There are only two exceptions in Homer:

ᾱ̃σσον adv. 'nearer' *Il.* 1.335, etc. (twenty-five times) < *ἄγχ-jον, cf. ἄγχι 'near';
ἥσσων 'inferior' *Il.* 16.722, etc. (four times) ←<*ἡ̄κ-joh-, cf. adv. ἦκα 'a little'.

Though the Ionic derivative ἑσσõσθαι 'be defeated' exhibits a short vowel in the root, that must be an (unexplained) innovation, since all other members of this word-family exhibit η.

[43] Hom. βραχΐων 'arm', though apparently derived from βραχύς, was not necessarily a comparative in origin (Ruijgh 1968: 147–8). However, see now Kostopoulos forthcoming (b), on this form and the Attic comparatives with lengthening.
[44] κοθρασίων in Alkman 87 is too corrupt to be of any use; see Campbell (1988) *ad loc.*
[45] I omit those that occur only with long ῑ in Attic and those that are not attested before the Hellenistic period; for comprehensive discussion, see Seiler (1950).

I have presented this pattern in detail because it is *exactly* the pattern we should expect to find if SL had been a phonological rule applying to this class of forms for some time during the prehistory of Greek but was no longer applicable at the time of our earliest texts.

Somewhat surprisingly, this conclusion is corroborated by the pattern of thematic nominals in *-yo- (Barber 2013: 187–213). An overwhelming majority of old or probably old examples with non-syllabic *-y- exhibit light preceding syllables (pp. 211–13); the following are typical:

PIE *ályos, neut. *ályod 'other' (Lat. *alius*, *aliud*, Lydian neut. *aλad*) > ἄλλος, ἄλλο;
PIE *médʰyos 'middle' (Skt *mádʰyas*, Lat. *medius*) > μέσος;
PIE *kóryos 'detachment' (Goth. *harjis*, Lith. *kãrias*, both 'army'; OIr. *cuire* 'company, host') > *κοιρο- in Hom. κοίρανος 'commander';
PIE *kʷóti 'how many?' (Skt *káti*, Lat. *quot*) → *kʷótyos > πόσος;
PIE *sókʷh₂oy- 'companion' (Skt *sákʰā*) → *sókʷyos (with regular loss of *h₂, see 2.2.4 (i); Lat. *socius* 'ally', OE *seċġ* 'retainer') in denom. *hą-hoκjε-jε/o- 'accompany' > Hom. ἀοσσεῖν 'to help';
PIE *ā́peros 'bank, shore' (OE *ōfer*, Middle High German *uover*), deriv. *ᾰ̄περjος > ᾰ̄πε̄ρος 'mainland' > Att.-Ion. ἤπε̄ρος;
(post-)PIE *pedyós 'foot-, of feet' (cf. Lat. *ped-* 'foot', etc.) > πεζός 'on foot';
(post-)PIE *h₃ókʷyos 'eye-, of eyes' (cf. Toch. B *ek* 'eye', etc.) in Hom. μελάνοσσος 'black-eyed';
(post-)PIE *h₃néryos 'dream-, of dreams' (cf. Hom. ὄναρ 'dream'; coll. *h₃nṓr with suffix *-yo- in Arm. *anowrǰ* 'dream') > ὄνε̄ρος 'dream-god, dream';
PIE *kóm 'with' (Lat. *cum*) in pre-Gk *komyós 'common' > κοινός;
Gk *ξυνjός 'common' (cf. ξύν 'with') > ξῡνός.

By contrast, old nominals with *-yo- following a heavy syllable ending in a consonant are very few; a possible example is λοῦσσον 'fir-tree pith' (Barber 2013: 94 with references). On the other hand, the heavy SL alternant *-io- has spread very widely in Greek, probably encouraged by the fact that there was at least one homonymous suffix that occurred after light roots (see 2.2.4 (ii)); derived adjectives like δαιμόνιος 'supernatural, extraordinary', σκότιος 'dark, clandestine', etc., are common even in Homer. In this class of forms SL had clearly broken down well before the time of our earliest texts.

Among present stems in *-ye/o-, all trace of the heavy SL alternant *-ie/o- has been lost in Greek (Barber 2013: 218–19, 244–7, 293–375). Barber establishes a probable reason for this peculiarity: during the earliest part of the separate prehistory of Greek, the suffix was added almost exclusively to light root-syllables (as in Vedic; pp. 224–44), partly because it was often added to zero-grade forms and partly by sheer accident; almost all the examples that violate SL can have been created after SL had ceased to be a generally applicable phonological rule. However, it seems clear that in at least one instance an inherited suffix *-ié/ó- was replaced by *-yé/ó- (*pace* Barber 2013: 116–18):

PIE *h_2ḱ-$h_2$ows-ié/ó- 'be sharp-eared' (Goth. *hausjan*, OE *hīeran*, both 'to hear') > *akowsié/ó- >→ *ἀκοϝhjε/ο- > ἀκούε̄ν 'to hear' (see 3.6.3 on the loss of *j).

The compound is opaque both in Germanic and in Greek and is therefore probably inherited. So far as I can see, this example shows that the light alternant *-ye/o- was generalized in present stems at some point in the prehistory of Greek.

A more complex case are the feminine nominals in short -α, most of which reflect the PIE type in *-ih_2 ~ *-yáh_2- (see 2.3.1, 2.4.2 (iii)). A disyllabic reflex -ια typically appears after obstruent-plus-sonorant clusters (see 3.2.3) and can reflect the operation of SL, at least by generalization from the oblique stem *-iáh_2- > -ιᾱ- —though the fact that the same outcome appears in πρίασθαι 'to buy' strongly suggests that SL also applied directly to the reflex of *ih_2. In all other cases *y was generalized, possibly because at an early period a large proportion of these feminines were formed to athematic stems with zero-grade suffixes in the oblique cases (thus u-stem *-u-yáh_2-, participial *-n̥t-yáh_2-, etc.).

Finally, one detail of the formation of present stems suggests that the converse of SL might have been (part of) a phonological rule at some point in the prehistory of Greek. Present stems in -αν-ε/ο- probably reflect thematization of *-n̥H-, extracted from nasal-infixed presents of laryngeal-final roots and generalized as a suffix; but it is striking that that suffix occurs exclusively after heavy root-syllables. After light roots ending in a consonant we instead find -νε/ο-; the only unarguable examples are δάκνε̄ν 'to bite (serially), to be biting', τάμνε̄ν 'to cut (several), to be cutting', and κάμνε̄ν 'to be working (hard), to struggle, to be tired', but there are no clear counterexamples. However, I know of no other evidence that points in the same direction.

3.6.2 Word-initial *y

PIE word-initial *y- appears in Greek as ζ-. In Classical Attic and Ionic (though not necessarily in other dialects) zeta spells the consonant cluster /sd/, phonetically [zd]; in our text of Sappho and Alkaios it is spelled σδ. A probable chain of natural sound changes that will give that result is *[j] (i.e. the front unround semivowel, clearly the pronunciation of PIE *y) > *[ɟ] (as in some dialects of Spanish) > *[ʤ] (as in Italian) > *[ʣ] (as in Old Frisian) > [zd] (a metathesis parallel to the one that yielded *žd* in Old Church Slavonic). The following examples are secure:

PIE *yugóm 'yoke' (Skt *yugám*, Lat. *iugum*) > *ʤugón > ζυγόν;
PIE *yéwgos 'yoke (of oxen)' (Lat. pl. *iūgera*, a measure of land originally defined by what a yoke of oxen could plow in a specified time) > *ʤéwgos > ζεῦγος, Myc. dat. pl. *ze-u-ke-si*;
PIE *yewg- 'join' (cf. Skt aor. subj. 3sg. *yójate*) in aor. ζεῦξαι, etc.;
PIE *yéwos 'grain' (Skt *yávas*) in Hom. pl. ζειαί (either with metrical lengthening or a deriv. in *-yā-; see Frisk s.v.);
PIE *yes- 'bubble' (cf. Skt *yásyati* 'it foams') in pres. *yés-e/o- (cf. OHG *jesan* 'to ferment') > *ʤéh-e/o- (or the like) > ζε̄ν 'to boil', Myc. fut. ptc. *ze-so-me-no*;
PIE *yoh$_3$s- 'put on a belt' (cf. Av. *yåŋhaiia-* 'gird') > *ʤōh- in aor. ζῶσαι, ζώνη 'belt', etc.;
PIE *yuHs- 'broth' (Lat. *iūs*) > *ʤūh- in ζῡ́μη 'yeast'.

Evidently the first stage of this development occurred before the Mycenaean period; the last three demonstrate that it also occurred before *h-copying (see 3.5.2 *ad fin.*).

3.6.3 Postconsonantal *y

The development of postconsonantal *y in Greek was even more complex than the development of *s adjacent to sonorants. Exactly what happened was conditioned by the preceding consonant, as follows.

When preceded by a sonorant or *h which was in turn preceded by *w, *y was lost without a trace before any other relevant sound changes occurred. There are three certain examples:

PIE *h$_2$ḱ-h$_2$ows-ié/ó- 'be sharp-eared' (Goth. *hausjan*, OE *hīeran*, both 'to hear') > *akowsié/ó- >→ *ἀκοϝhjέ/ó- > *ἀκοϝhέ/ó- >→ ἀκούε̄ν 'to hear';
PIE *h$_2$árh$_3$wr̥ 'plowing' (OIr. *arbor* 'grain, crop') > *árowr̥ → *ἄροϝϝjα > Hom. ἄρουρα 'plowland, plowed field' (Barber 2013: 296);
pre-Gk *élh$_2$wr̥ 'driving' (r/n-stem, cf. aor. ἐλάσαι 'to drive'): derived pres. *ἐλαϝν-jε/o- > ἐλαύνε̄ν 'to drive (several), to be driving' (Barber 2013: 89, 296).

A fourth possible example is:

pre-Gk *érewr̥ 'search' →*ἔρεϝνjα > ἔρευνα;

it is true this noun does not appear before the 5th century, while the verb ἐρευνᾶν is attested already in Homer (three times), but it does not follow that the noun is a backformation (as Frisk s.v. ἐρευνάω states); accidents of attestation might account for that pattern. Whether *y was lost after other consonant clusters is unclear. A plausible example is

PIE *$h_2$ugsié/ó- 'grow' (?; cf. Av. 3sg. *uxšiieiti*) >→ *αὐξjε/ο- > αὔξεσθαι (*LIV* s.v. **h_2u̯eks*);

however, it is also possible that the prehistory of this stem was quite different, involving a full-grade root (see 3.2.2) and no *y (cf. Barber 2013: 288).

After single consonants and other clusters *y survived and triggered extensive changes, most of which clearly occurred before the Mycenaean period. (For extensive discussion and a possible relative chronology, see Risch 1979, with discussion by the conferees on pp. 278–81.)

The cluster *ly eventually yielded λλ in most dialects. The only phonetically natural path to that outcome is *ly > *[lʲː] > λλ, i.e. mutual assimilation of *[l] and *[j], yielding a long palatalized lateral, followed by depalatalization of the long lateral. Since an alternative outcome is attested (see below), it is clear that only the stage *[lʲː] had been reached in Proto-Greek. Only three of the examples are certainly inherited from PIE:

PIE *ályos, neut. *ályod 'other' (Lat. *alius*, *aliud*, Lydian neut. *aλad*) > ἄλλος, ἄλλο;
PIE *sál-ye/o- 'be jumping' (Lat. *salīre*) > ἅλλεσθαι;
PIE *stél-ye/o- 'make ready' (OCS *posteljetŭ* '(s)he will spread out') > στέλλε̄ν 'to equip, to provide; to send' (*LIV* s.v. **stel*),

though the PIE meaning of the third example is somewhat difficult to recover. Several Homeric presents are archaic denominatives, constructed by deleting the thematic vowel of the noun or adjective and adding *-jε/ο- at some point within the prehistory of Greek. At least two are widely attested and likely to be fairly old:

PIE *póyḱos 'decorated' *vel sim.* (cf. Skt *purupéśas* 'multiform', Goth. *filufaihs* 'manifold') >→ Gk *ποικιλό-ς 'many-colored' (Hom., etc., ποικίλος by Wheeler's Law, see 3.8) → pres. *ποικιλ-jε- 'make many-colored' > ποικίλλε̄ν 'to embroider';
ἄγγελο-ς 'messenger' (loanword, see Frisk s.v.) → pres. *ἀγγελ-jε- 'be a messenger' > ἀγγέλλε̄ν 'to announce, to proclaim'.

Other similar examples are δαιδάλλε̄ν 'to decorate, to embellish' (δαίδαλος 'marvellously made') and ναυτίλλεσθαι 'to sail' (ναυτίλος 'sailor'). The antiquity of any given example is of course a matter of guesswork, because the formation clearly became productive; but the fact that it became productive is indirect evidence for a 'critical mass' of early examples (not all of which need have survived to be attested, of course). A number of non-denominative presents in -λλε/ο- might reflect *-ly- or *-ln-; that problem will be discussed in 5.2.2.

A different outcome is attested for Cyprian: on the Idalion bronze the gen. pl. of 'the other' appears as *to-na-i-lo-ne* *τõν αἴλōν (Masson 217.14).[46] It seems clear that in this dialect *[lʲlʲ], instead of being depalatalized, was dissimilated to [jl], at least when a low vowel preceded. Whether that amounts to a violation of the Obligatory Contour Principle (OCP)[47] is an interesting question, but in any case an identical development is well attested in another class of cases. When preceded by *a or *o (but not by other vowels), the clusters *ny, *ry, and *wy were first assimilated to *[nʲː], *[rʲː], and (presumably) *[ɥː], then dissimilated to [jn], [jr], and [jw]—i.e., ιν, ιρ, and ιϝ—respectively. This development occurred in all the attested dialects, so in principle the entire process could have run its course in Proto-Greek. Examples are fairly numerous; some were inherited from PIE, while many more can be reconstructed on the basis of related Greek words. Inherited examples include:

PIE pres. *gʷm̥-yé/ó- 'step (repeatedly), walk' (Lat. *venīre* 'to come') > *gʷąm-yé/ó- > *γʷα̨νjε/ο- > βαίνε̄ν 'to go';
PIE *h_1n̥$h_3$mn̥-yé/ó- 'name' (verb; Goth. *namnjan*, OE *nemnan*) >→ *ὀνομα̨ν-jε/ο- > ὀνομαίνε̄ν 'to name';
PIE *mn̥yétor '(s)he is mentally active' → post-PIE *mn̥yétoy (Skt *mányate* '(s)he thinks') > *μα̨νjετοι >→ μαίνεται '(s)he is raving';
PIE *ǵʰr̥yé/ó- 'be pleased with' *vel sim.* (Old Lat. *horitur* '(s)he encourages, urges') > *χαρjε/ο- > χαίρε̄ν 'to rejoice, to be glad';
PIE *kóryos 'detachment' (Goth. *harjis*, Lith. *kãrias*, both 'army'; OIr. *cuire* 'company, host') > *κοιρο- in Hom. κοίρανος 'commander';
PIE *$h_2$áwis ~ *$h_2$áwy- 'bird' (Lat. *avis*) > *αἰϝ- in αἰϝετός > αἰετός 'eagle';
PIE *plówyom 'boat' (ON *fley*) > *πλόϝjον > πλοῖον.

Greek innovations on a PIE basis include:

PIE *kóm 'with' (Lat. *cum*) in pre-Gk *kom-yó-s 'common' > *κονjός > κοινός;

[46] Elean αἰλότρια might be an error (Schwyzer 1939: 272); the usual form of 'other' in Elean is the familiar ἄλλος.

[47] On the OCP, see, e.g., Goldsmith (1990: 309–18). The basic idea is that identical adjacent segments (or tones, etc.) are not allowed; in a word such as πολλοί the geminate 'λλ' is actually a single consonant linked to two timing slots. One might therefore expect that geminates would not develop into sequences of different segments, yet it seems clear that *njnj, etc., did develop into *jn, etc., when preceded by *a and *o in the prehistory of Greek. Since the OCP is a matter of the syntagmatic organization of sounds, not of phonetics, it seems possible that some combination of misperception and difficulty articulating a geminate might simply override the OCP in the course of language acquisition; in effect, learners might fail to learn the geminate. Alternatively, the fact that the geminate is partly in the coda of one syllable and partly in the onset of the next might make it possible for the beginning and end of the geminate to diverge. For similar West Germanic cases involving geminate semivowels, see Ringe and Taylor (2014: 53, 65–7).

PIE pres. *u-né-b^h- 'be weaving' (Skt 2sg. *sám unap*) → *ub^h-né-H- (Skt inj. 2sg. *ub^{h}nā́s*, 3sg. with augment *aub^{h}nāt*) → *ub^h-n̥-H-yé- > *ὐφανjε- > ὑφαίνε̄ν;
PIE *h$_2$ánkō 'sharp bend' >→ *ankṓ (OE *anga* 'sting, goad') > ἀγκών 'elbow'; fem. deriv. *ἄνκονjα 'bent arm' in Hom. dat. pl. ἀγκοίνῃσι.

Derivatives of recognizable Greek words and roots are numerous, e.g.:

εὐφραίνε̄ν 'to gladden; to enjoy oneself' < *εὐφραν-jε-, cf. εὔφρων 'cheerful, glad';
pres. φαίνεσθαι 'to appear' < *φαν-jε-, cf. aor. pass. φανῆναι (parallel to χαίρε̄ν, χαρῆναι, see above);
pres. ῥαίνε̄ν 'to sprinkle' < *ῥαν-jε-, cf. aor. pass. ptc. ῥανθείς, both in Pindar;
ἐχθαίρε̄ν 'to hate' < *ἐχθαρjε- with *αρ < *r̥, cf. ἐχθρός 'hated, enemy';
χίμαιρα 'she-goat' < *χίμαρjα, cf. χίμαρος 'he-goat';
μοῖρα 'portion, share; fate' < *hμόρjα, cf. μόρος 'doom', ἕμαρται 'it is fated';
pres. καίε̄ν 'to be burning (something), to burn severally' < *καίϝε̄ν < *καϝ-jε-, cf. Hom., Att. καῦμα 'burning heat'.

When preceded by *e, *i, or *u the clusters *ny and *ry also underwent the assimilation to *[n^j:] and *[r^j:], but subsequently *[n^j:] and *[r^j:] were depalatalized and developed exactly like *Rh- and *hR-clusters in at least most dialects; their development will be treated in 5.2.2, where possible exceptions and the outcome of *ewy will also be discussed.

The clusters *py and *p^{h}y both appear in all dialects as πτ. Such an outcome can only be the result of a sequence of sound changes. The penultimate stage must have been *ptʃ, as in Old Provençal subjunctive 3sg. *sapcha* 'that (s)he may know' < *sapja (cf. Spanish *sepa*) < Lat. *sapiat* 'that (s)he may be wise' (Janko 1977); the palatal semivowel must first have been devoiced by the preceding consonant and must then have developed into a fricative, which then developed into an affricate, ultimately to be deaffricated to τ. One example is root-internal:

PIE *pyah$_2$k- 'beat' (Toch. B *pyāktsi* 'to pound in', Hackstein 1992) > *πtʃᾱκ- > πτᾱκ- in Dor. πτᾱ́σσε̄ν, Ion. πτήσσε̄ν 'to cower'.

There are at least five inherited present stems in *-ye/o-:

PIE *klép-ye/o- 'be stealing' (Toch. B inf. *kälypītsi*) > *κλεπtʃε/ο- > κλέπτε̄ν;
PIE *h$_1$rép-ye/o- 'be snatching' (Lat. *rapere* with remodeled root) > *ἐρεπtʃε/ο- > Hom. ἐρεπτόμενος 'devouring';
PIE *spéḱ-ye/o- 'be looking' (Lat. inf. *cōnspicere*, Skt 3sg. *páśyati* '(s)he sees') >→ *sképye/o- > *σκεπtʃε/ο- > σκέπτεσθαι;

PIE *kh₂p-ié/ó- 'be grabbing' (Lat. *capere* 'to take', OE *hebban* 'to lift') >→ *kapyé/ó- > *καπʧε/ο- > κάπτε̄ν 'to gulp down';
PIE *$g^wh_2b^h$-ié/ó- 'be dipping in water' (ON *kvefja*) >→ *g^wap^hyé/ó- > *γ^wαπʧε/ο- > βάπτε̄ν.

A few others were constructed to roots that might have been inherited, e.g.:

PIE *d^hrub^h- 'break up' (?; cf. Latvian pl. *drubazas* 'splinters'?) > *t^hrup^h- in pres. *t^hrup^h-yé/ó- > *θρυπʧε/ο- > θρύπτε̄ν (cf. aor. passive τρυφῆναι);
pre-Gk *t^hap^h- 'bury' (< *d^hm̥b^h-, cf. Arm. *damban* 'grave'?; so *LIV* s.v. 2.*d^hemb^h*, but only the zero grade of this root is attested anywhere) in pres. *t^hap^h-yé/ó- > *θαπʧε/ο- > θάπτε̄ν (cf. aor. passive ταφῆναι).

There is indirect evidence that the entire sequence of sound changes had run its course by the Mycenaean period. The Linear B syllabary includes a sign for *pte*, its value guaranteed by multiple attestations of *ra-pte*, nom. pl. *ra-pte-re*, etc. = *ῥαπτήρ 'stitcher, tailor', with derived fem. nom. pl. *ra-pi-ti-ra₂* = ῥάπτριαι, the latter actually attested in 1st-millennium Greek (Aura Jorro 1999 s.vv.). That is the only sign in the syllabary that writes a sequence of two stops, but there are several signs that write sequences of consonant plus semivowel. It is reasonable to infer that at the time the syllabary was created the value of the sign was *pye (Palmer apud Janko 1977); if that is true, *py had certainly become *pt* by the Mycenaean period.

The sound-change outcome of *by is undiscoverable. There are two presents in -πτε/ο- to roots ending in β, namely βλάπτε̄ν 'to harm' (cf. noun βλάβη) and καλύπτε̄ν 'to cover' (cf. καλύβη 'hut'), but both could have been backformed from the corresponding sigmatic aorists. I can find no other potential examples.

The development of *$k(^h)$y and *$t(^h)$y clusters has been treated most recently by Kostopoulos forthcoming (a), on which the following discussion partly depends.

The outcome of the clusters *ky and *k^hy differs from dialect to dialect. Most dialects exhibit σσ; Attic, West Ionic, Boiotian, and Cretan exhibit ττ (variously spelled in Cretan inscriptions; Lejeune 1972: 106). The distribution of the outcome ττ over a compact area including Attica and the regions immediately to the north is a striking areal feature cutting across older dialect divisions; it suggests very strongly that the difference between σσ and ττ is the result of recent changes that might have spread from dialect to dialect, and that the Proto-Greek state of development was at most *tts, more likely *tʧ (see further below). That is corroborated by the use of a special symbol **T** for this cluster in early East Ionic inscriptions, typically varying with σσ in all but the earliest (cf. *DGE* 701, 707, 710, 732, 744). In addition to the examples of *ky < *k^wy (for which, see 3.4.3) and a large number of comparatives which must have been formed within Greek (for which, see 3.6.1), there is a present in *-ye/o- made to an inherited root:

PIE *pyah₂k- 'beat' (Toch. B *pyāktsi* 'to pound in', Hackstein 1992) > *πtʃᾰκ- > πτᾱκ- in Dor. πτᾱ́σσεν, Ion. πτήσσεν 'to cower'.

There are also several archaic present stems formed directly to consonant-stem nouns and adjectives with the inherited denominative suffix *-yé/ó-, as well as some other derived presents and some isolated nouns and adjectives:

φυλάσσε̄ν, Att. φυλάττε̄ν 'to guard' < *φυλακ-jε/o-, cf. φύλακ- '(a) guard';
κηρῡ́σσε̄ν, Att. κηρῡ́ττε̄ν 'to announce, to proclaim' < *κηρῡκ-jε/o-, cf. κήρῡκ- 'herald';
Hom. ἑλισσέμεν 'to whirl, to coil', Att. ἑλίττε̄ν 'to roll' < *hελικ-jε/o-, cf. ἕλικ- 'spiral';
πτύσσε̄ν 'to fold' < *πτυχ-jε/o-, cf. Hom. πτύχες 'folds, layers';
ὀρύσσε̄ν, Att. ὀρύττε̄ν 'to dig' < *ὀρυχ-jε/o-, cf. δι-ώρυχ- 'trench, canal' (possibly deverbative, but early enough to preserve the original root-final consonant);
μαλάσσε̄ν, Att. μαλάττε̄ν 'to soften', deriv. of μαλακός 'soft';
ταράσσε̄ν, Att. ταράττε̄ν 'to disturb', deriv. of ταραχή 'uproar';
πίσσα, Att. πίττα 'pitch' < *πίκjα, cf. Lat. *pic-*;
δισσός, Att. διττός 'twofold' < *διχjός, cf. δίχα 'in two, apart'.

In word-initial position geminate consonants did not normally occur in Greek, and that explains why the outcome of these clusters was different word-initially (Kostopoulos, *op. cit.*):

σᾱ́μερον, Ion. σήμερον, Att. τήμερον 'today' < *κj-ᾱ́μερο-, cf. Hitt. *kī* neut. 'this', Lat. *cis* 'on this side', etc., and Hom. ἦμαρ, Att. ἡμέρᾱ, Doric, etc., ἁμέρᾱ 'day';
σᾶτες, Ion. σῆτες, Att. τῆτες, Myc. *za-we-te* 'this year' < *κjᾱ́-ϝετες, formed by lexical analogy with the preceding to PIE endingless loc. *wétes 'in a year';
Hom. σεύεσθαι 'to rush' < PIE *k^wyew-, cf. Skt *cyávate* 'it moves'.

The last example occurs mostly in verse, but a compound derivative πανσυδί 'with all speed' is also attested in Attic prose, and Kostopolous (*op. cit.*) cites an early Cretan equivalent παν]σεϝδί, as well as Boiotian σᾱ́ετες 'this year'. It seems clear that geminate *ttʃ and word-initial *tʃ did not always develop in parallel in a given dialect; Kostopoulos suggests, reasonably, that dialects in which the outcome was σ- experienced an early merger of the reflexes of *k(^{h})y and *t(^{h})y. Mycenaean spells the outcome of the former with the z-signs, to judge from *za-we-te* and nom. pl. *ka-zo-e* 'inferior' < *κάκ-yoh-; cf. κακός 'bad'.

The development of *ty and *t^hy presents the same sort of dichotomy as the development of *hy (see 3.5.1). When there is a morpheme boundary between the consonants and a vowel immediately precedes, we observe the same outcomes as for *ky and *k^hy. Secure examples include:

πάσσēν, Att. πάττēν 'to sprinkle' < (?) PIE *k^wát-ye/o-, cf. Lat. *quatere* 'to shake';[48]

βλίσσēν, Att. βλίττēν 'to harvest honey' < *mlit-yé/ó-, cf. μέλιτ- 'honey'; the zero grade of the base induced by the accented suffix demonstrates that this is an old derivative;

νῆσσα, Att. νῆττα 'duck' < *νά̄τ-jα < *n̥h_2t-, cf. Skt *ātís*, etc.;

Hom. ἐρεσσέμεναι 'to row' < *ἐρετ-jε/o-, cf. ἐρετμόν 'oar';

Hom. λίσσεσθαι 'to beg, to entreat' < *λιτ-jε/o-, cf. aor. λιτέσθαι;

Hom., etc., κρέσσων 'more powerful; better' ←< pre-Gk *krét-yos-, cf. κρατύς 'powerful'; Att. κρε̄́ττων has a lengthened vowel, on which, see now Kostopoulos forthcoming (b);

Arkadian ἔασσα fem. 'being' < *ἐhα̨τ-jα < *$h_1$sn̥tíh_2 (Skt *satī́*) ← PIE *$h_1$sóntih_2;

adj. suffix -(ϝ)εντ- 'having ...', fem. -(ϝ)εσσα, Boiot. -ϝεττα < *-ϝετ-jα ← *-ϝα̨τ-jα < post-PIE *-wn̥t-ih_2, cf. Skt *-vat-ī*;

Hom. ipf. κορύσσετο 'he was putting on his helmet' < *κορυθ-jε/o-, cf. κόρυθ- 'helmet';

πυρέσσēν, Att. πυρέττēν 'to have a fever' < *πυρετ-jε/o-, cf. πυρετός 'burning heat, fever'.

(There are also some more obscure examples; see Lejeune 1972: 103.) The root of the last example has been reanalyzed as πυρεκ- (aor. πυρέξαι, etc.) because the present stem—no doubt the stem most frequently used, since the verb is naturally imperfective—is ambiguous (see 5.4.2).

However, in all dialects *ty and *t^hy appear as single σ after ν or a diphthong; typical are:

πᾶσα fem. 'all' < πάνσα (attested in Arkadian, Thessalian, Argolic, and Cretan) < *πάντjα, cf. masc./neut. παντ-;

pres. ptc. suffix fem. -ōσα < -ονσα (attested in Arkadian, Argolic, and Cretan) < *-οντjα, cf. masc./neut. -οντ-.

The few word-initial examples likewise exhibit a reflex σ- in all dialects:

PIE *$tyeg^w$- 'retreat' *vel sim.* (Skt *tyájati* '(s)he abandons') > σέβεσθαι 'to be ashamed', later 'to reverence, to do homage to';

PIE *d^hyah_2- 'indicate' *vel sim.* (Skt *d^hyā-* 'think') in *t^hyámn̥ 'indication' > σᾶμα > Att.-Ion. σῆμα 'sign, marker'.

Evidently the cluster was not geminate in these positions (Kostopoulos, *op. cit.*).

[48] I prefer this simple and obvious etymology to the speculative connections posited in *LIV* s.v. **(s)ku̯eh₁t*.

Since the outcomes of these clusters clearly merged with those of dental plus *s (see 3.7), it is tempting to suggest that *ty and *tʰy were at first affricated to *(t)ʦ, unlike of *ky and *kʰy (see above). However, the reflex of *ty after *r shows that that cannot be correct:

PIE *wert- 'turn' (3sg. Skt *vártate*, Lat. *vertitur*) → *wért-ye/o- > *wérʧe/o- > *wérʃe/o- > ἔρρε͂ν 'to go away (badly / to a bad place)' (Forssman 1980: 186–98);

pre-Gk *krét-yos- 'more powerful' (see above) → pre-Doric *kárt-yon- > *kárʃon- > κάρρων Alkman 105.

We saw above (in 3.5.1) that the inherited cluster *rs survived intact when the accent immediately preceded. It follows that these words could never have passed through a stage in which they exhibited *rs; their development must have been diverted, so to speak, before it would have reached that point. It follows further that the majority development of the clusters in question was *t(ʰ)y > *(t)ʧ > *(t)ʦ, followed by divergent further development in the dialects. On the other hand, Kostopoulos' suggestion that the development of *t(ʰ)y was at every time 'ahead of' *k(ʰ)y is very likely to be true.

As adumbrated above, there is a further wrinkle. When there is no morpheme boundary between the consonants the outcome is different in Attic-Ionic and Arkadian (and presumably Cypriote and Mycenaean, though the syllabaries do not permit firm inferences on this point). The examples are the following.

PIE *medʰyos 'middle' (Skt *mádʰyas*, Lat. *medius*) > *μέθjος > Att.-Ion., Ark. μέσος but Lesb., Heraklean, Argolic μέσσος, Boiot., Cret. μέττος; cf. Myc. *me-sa-to* 'of middling quality';

PIE *kʷóti 'how many?' (Skt *káti*, Lat. *quot*), *tóti 'that many' (Lat. *tot*), *Hyóti 'as many as', thematized as *κʷότjος, *τότjος, *hότjος > Att.-Ion. πόσος, τόσος, ὅσος, Ark. ὅσος, Myc. *to-so*, but Lesb. ὄσσος, Delphian, etc. ὅσσος, Cret. ὅττος;

PIE *próti 'toward, against' (Skt *práti*), deriv. *prótyō 'forward' > Att.-Ion. πρόσω, to which ὀπίσω 'backward' was formed.

In Homer these words vary between -σ- and -σσ-, whereas words of the preceding class do not.

The examples without an intervening morpheme boundary strongly suggest that σ is the regular sound-change outcome in South Greek, and that the examples with a geminate have been remodeled in some way. Since the geminate examples exhibit ττ in Attic, that remodeling must have occurred at a stage when the reflex of these clusters was still an affricate. How to reconcile that conclusion with the Homeric variation σσ ~ σ remains unclear, but it seems at least possible that the Homeric forms with σσ are Aiolisms. The chronology of developments is also unclear. The most straightforward interpretation of the pattern would recognize the split between *t(^{h})+y and *t(^{h})y with no morpheme boundary as the first change distinguishing the South Greek dialect group from the rest, but the actual course of development need not have been that simple. For instance, it is possible that the split occurred in Proto-Greek, *t(^{h})y yielding *ʦ, for instance, while *t(^{h})+y was remodeled as *ʦy > *tʦ, the latter eventually merging with simple *ʦ in the *non*-South Greek dialects. In the current state of our knowledge it seems impossible to make more detailed suggestions. In any case it is clear that clusters of dental plus *s gave exactly the same outcomes in all dialects (see 3.7); thus Kostopoulos' suggestion that the penultimate stage of development was *ʦ must be correct.

Finally, *dy and *gy eventually appear as ζ, which was clearly /sd/ in Attic-Ionic (and is actually spelled σδ in our text of Sappho and Alkaios); the development must have been approximately *dy, *gy > *dʤ > *dʣ > [zd]. Some dialects might not have progressed beyond the penultimate stage; that the letter zeta was used for /ts/ in Etruscan suggests that it was pronounced [dz] or the like in some dialect(s) of Magna Graecia. In Thessalian, Boiotian, Elean, and Cretan we find δδ, which could reflect assimilation either of [dz] or of [zd]. Several examples are inherited:

PIE nom. sg. *dyḗws or *dyéws 'sky, day' (Skt *dyáus*) > Ζεύς;
(post-)PIE *pedyós 'foot-, of feet' (cf. Lat. *ped-* 'foot', etc.) > πεζός 'on foot';
PIE *méǵ-yos- 'bigger, greater' (Av. neut. *maziiō*; remodeled in Lat. neut. *maius*) > *μέζoh- in Myc. nom. pl. *me-zo-e*, neut. *me-zo-a*$_2$; → μέζων (see 5.4.2; Att. με̄́ζων, see Kostopoulos forthcoming (b));
PIE *néygʷ- ~ *nigʷ- 'wash' (Skt pres. 3sg. mid. *nenikté*), pres. *nigʷ-yé/ó- (OIr. 3sg. *nigid*) > *νιγjε/ο- > νίζε̄ν.

Others are derivatives of inherited roots:

PIE *ǵʰed- 'defecate' (Skt pres. 3sg. *hadati*) in pres. *χεδ-jε/ο- > χέζε̄ν;
PIE *h$_3$od- 'smell' (cf. Lat. noun *odor*) in pres. *ὀδ-jε/ο- > ὄζε̄ν;
PIE *h$_2$tug- 'frightful' (Hitt. *hatugis*) in denom. *ἀτυγ-jε/ο- > Hom. ἀτύζεσθαι 'to be scared witless' (cf. Benveniste 1937);
PIE *stag- 'drip' (cf. σταγών 'drop', Lat. *stagnum* 'pool') in pres. *σταγ-jε/ο- > στάζε̄ν;
PIE *stig- 'pierce' (OE *stician*) in pres. *στιγ-jε/ο- > στίζε̄ν 'to tattoo'.

Still others can be recognized from their relations to other Greek stems or words, e.g.:

pre-Gk pres. *slagʷ-yé/ó- 'seize (severally), be catching' > *hλαγ-jε/o- > Hom. λάζεσθαι, aor. *hλαγʷ-ε/o- > λαβε̄ν;
φράζεσθαι 'to think about, to ponder' < *φραδ-jε/o-, cf. Hom. φράδμων 'wise', etc.;
παίζε̄ν 'to play' < *παϝιδ-jε/o-, cf. Hom. παϊδ- 'child';
ἁρπάζε̄ν 'to snatch' < *hαρπαγ-jε/o-, cf. ἅρπαγ- 'seizure, robbery';
σφάζε̄ν 'to slaughter' < *σφαγ-jε/o-, cf. noun σφαγή.

The class of present tenses created by this sequence of sound changes participated in extensive remodeling. On the one hand, because presents in -ζ- could reflect roots in -δ- or in -γ- they often acquired unetymological sigmatic stems; for instance, the Attic aorist of ἁρπάζε̄ν is ἁρπάσαι instead of expected ἁρπάξαι (attested in Pindar), while in West Greek dialects the aorist of δικάζε̄ν 'judge' is usually δικάξαι (Attic-Ionic δικάσαι). On the other hand, because sigmatic stems in -ξ- might reflect an underlying voiced or voiceless root-final velar, presents in -σσ-/-ττ- have spread widely at the expense of those in -ζ-; for instance, 'to arrange, to marshall (troops)' is everywhere τάσσε̄ν or τάττε̄ν (with whatever infinitive ending is normal in the relevant dialect), even though all the derivatives show that the root is ταγ-.

The sequence of sound changes that eventually yielded /sd/ permits a limited inference about the inflection of one lexeme. The reduplication of Hom. δίζηαι 'you seek', διζήμενος 'seeking' makes sense only if the root was still *δjᾱ-, at least underlyingly; it follows that that present stem must have been in existence before this sequence of sound changes had progressed very far.

3.7 Other clusters of dental stops

Some other clusters of dental stops yielded eventual outcomes similar to those of *t(ʰ)y; for that reason this is a convenient point at which to discuss them.

Of the examples of *tw that have been suggested, only four are beyond serious question. Two are word-initial:

PIE *twé 'you' (acc. sg., accented) > *ʦϝέ > σέ;
PIE *tweys- 'shake' (cf. Skt *atviṣanta* 'they have been inflamed' *RV* VIII.94.7 with zero- grade root) in pres. *twéys-e/o- > *ʦϝέjhε/o- > σείε̄ν.

Whether σ- was the outcome in all dialects is unclear. Both σέ and σείε̄ν occur in literary documents of all dialects; I have not found either in inscriptions. Literary Doric also has 2sg. pronoun forms beginning with τ-, but those could reflect PIE enclitic *te, or even leveling from nom. sg. τύ (the reverse of the leveling in Attic-Ionic). The two word-internal examples do exhibit different outcomes in different dialects:

PIE *kʷetwóres masc. 'four' (Skt *catvā́ras*) >→ *κʷέʦϝVρες > Boiot. πέτταρες, Att. τέτταρες, Ion., Ark. τέσσερες, Lesb. πέσσυρες (but West Greek τέτορες has lost the *w, possibly by leveling from τέταρτος 'fourth', which has lost it in all dialects);

PIE *sēmi- 'half-' (Lat. *sēmi-*) > ἡμι-, derived noun *ἥμιτυς (Att.-Ion. ἥμισυς, also used as an adj.) thematized as *ἥμιτϝο- in Ark., Delphian, etc., noun ἥμισσον, Boiot. εἵμιττον.[49]

In these cases the outcomes are identical with those of *t(ʰ)+y; it therefore seems reasonable to posit a development *tw > *ʦw > Proto-Greek *tʦ, with simplification of the geminate in word-initial position (so Kostopoulos forthcoming (a)).

Most of the examples of *θϝ which have been claimed are doubtful; for instance, it is not at all clear that the root of θανε͂ν 'to die' is cognate with that of Skt *ádʰvanīt* 'it smoked', nor that ὀρθός 'upright' is the same word as Skt *ūrdʰvás* 'lofty'. However, the mediopassive 2pl. ending -σθε must ultimately be connected with Skt *-dʰva* (*yájadʰva* 'you (pl.) sacrifice' *RV* VIII.2.37), and at least in that ending the *w has been lost without a trace. But since the ending has clearly been remodeled, it seems best to postpone discussion of it until 4.2.6.

Finally, clusters of dental stop plus *s exhibit the same outcomes as *t(ʰ)y with no internal morpheme boundary—strikingly, as there was always a morpheme boundary between the dental stop and the *s. In word-final position the outcome is -ς in all dialects (just as *t(ʰ)y yields word-initial σ- in all dialects); non-neuter nom. sg. forms of stems ending in dental stops provide virtually all the examples. After consonants the outcome is likewise -σ- everywhere, e.g.:

dat. pl. *πάντ-σι 'to all' > Ark. πάνσι, Myc. *pa-si*, Att.-Ion., etc. πᾶσι;
dat. pl. *ἑλόντ-σι 'to those who have taken' > Cret. ἐλόνσι, Att.-Ion., etc., ἑλõσι.

After long vocalic nuclei the outcome is likewise -σ-, e.g.:

dat. pl. *πάϝιδ-σι 'to children' > *παῖσι → παισί with analogical shift of accent;
onomastic element *Πειθ-σι- 'persuading' > Πεισι- > Lakonian Πειhι-.

After short vowels there are numerous examples among sigmatic aorists and futures; Attic-Ionic and Arkadian exhibit single -σ- (varying with -σσ- in our text of Homer), Boiotian and Cretan geminate -ττ-, and the remaining dialects -σσ-. The following examples are typical:

[49] PGk η became /eː/ in Boiotian; when the Ionic alphabet was adopted it was spelled ει (Buck 1955: 25).

aor. *δατ-σα- 'divide' (pres. Hom. 3pl. δατέονται, Cret. inf. δατε̄θθαι) in Hom. inf. δάσσασθαι ~ δάσασθαι, Ark. δάσασσθαι (*DGE* 661), but Cret. ἀποδάτταθθαι;
aor. *δικαδ-σα- 'judge; bring a lawsuit' (pres. δικάζε̄ν) in Att.-Ion. inf. δικάσαι, Ark. mid. δικάσασθαι (*DGE* 657, with other examples), but Lesb. 3pl. κατεδίκασσαν, Argolic opt. 3pl. δικάσσαιεν (*DGE* 85);
aor. *λογιδ-σα- 'reckon' (pres. λογίζεσθαι) in inf. Att.-Ion. λογίσασθαι but Boiot. ἀπολογίτταστη.

This pattern tends to corroborate the inference that -σ- was the regular sound-change outcome of *t(^{h})y with no internal morpheme boundary in Attic-Ionic and Arkadian.

3.8 Accent in Proto-Greek

A recent comprehensive account of the development of Ancient Greek accent is Probert (2006a: 83–96), on which this section principally relies.

Contraction of vowels in hiatus (often after the loss of an intervening laryngeal, see 3.2.1) seems to have created the Greek contrast between acute and circumflex intonations, which did not exist in PIE (Jasanoff 2004: 248):[50] when the PIE accent fell on the first vowel the result was a Greek circumflex, contrasting with the preexisting acute. The clearest examples are nominal endings:

PIE gen. pl. *-óHom and thematic *-ó-oHom > -ῶν;
PIE thematic dat. sg. *-ó-ey > -ῶι, and ah_2-stem *-áh_2-ay > -ᾶι (> -ῆι)
PIE gen. sg. *-áh_2-s → (?) *-áh_2-as > -ᾶς (> -ῆς).

Contrast, e.g., PIE *ph_2tḗr 'father' > πατήρ, post-PIE *b^{h}o$h_2$náh_2 'voice' > φωνᾱ́ (> φωνή), etc. This became (at least part of) the basis of a rule assigning circumflex accent to accented genitive and dative endings containing long vowels or diphthongs, e.g. in thematic dat. pl. -οῖς ←< PIE inst. pl. *-ṓys (cf. Jasanoff 2004: 248 fn. 2); thus the α-stem gen. sg. ending is an uncertain example, since it could reflex *-áh_2-s as modified by the new rule.

The 'law of limitation', according to which the accent can fall only on one of the last three syllables of a word (or the last two, if the final syllable is long for accentual purposes), operates in all Ancient Greek dialects, so far as we can tell, and is thus probably a Proto-Greek innovation (Probert 2006a: 84–5 with references); that such a rule spread through a dialect network without being modified or acquiring exceptions does not seem likely. It was certainly in operation before quantitative

[50] However, it is not clear to me that all vowel sequences not originally interrupted by a laryngeal had already been contracted into long vowels in PIE (Jasanoff 2004: 247–8). Identical long vowels clearly had contracted in the thematic subjunctive, but the correspondence between circumflexed thematic dat. sg. Gk -ῶι and Lith. non-acute *-ui* strongly suggests that *-o-ey was still disyllabic in PIE.

metathesis occurred (and therefore before the Homeric poems were composed, Probert 2006a: 84–5 with references; see 6.2 below), and before the late contractions of vowels occurred (see 7.2.3). More significantly, it must have been in place before the loss of word-final stops (see 3.5.3) and before the loss of voiceless dental stops before -ι noticed by Warren Cowgill (see 3.4.6), since it is precisely word-final ι-diphthongs resulting from those changes that are *not* treated as short by the accent law. The assignment of the law of limitation to Proto-Greek is therefore practically certain.

The application of the recessive accent rule to (most) finite forms of Greek verbs, which must reflect the accentlessness of PIE verbs in main clauses (see 2.2.5), also appears to be a Proto-Greek innovation (Probert 2006a: 87 with references).

An innovation which is at least pan-Greek, and might be Proto-Greek, is Wheeler's Law, which retracted final-syllable accent by one syllable if the word had the prosodic shape ¯ ˘x (Probert 2006a: 88); a plausibly inherited example is:

> ἀγκύλος 'bent, crooked' < *h_2(a)nkulós (cf. PGmc *angulaz 'fishhook' > ON *ǫngull*, with Verner's Law voicing showing that the accent was not on the root-syllable).

However, though Wheeler's Law apparently operated in all the dialects (Probert 2006a: pp. 95–6), there are numerous lexical exceptions, and though many might have arisen at a later period (pp. 91–5), it is also possible that Wheeler's Law spread through a dialect continuum word by word (or derivational category by category).[51]

In the paradigms of polysyllabic nominals Greek has mostly fixed the accent on the same syllable in all forms; exceptions are few and are usually (relative) archaisms. In monosyllables, however, except for participles, alternating accent actually became productive, so that genitive and dative forms that do not have the accent on the ending (e.g. πάντων) are the archaisms. Even nouns that became monosyllabic relatively late have largely adopted alternating accent; for instance, in Attic *ὄ̈ατος gen. 'ear's' (cf. Hom. οὔατος) > *ὦτος → ὠτός. The pattern could have arisen indefinitely early in the prehistory of Greek, though obviously the details shifted over time.

3.9 Relative chronology of sound changes

It is clear from the above discussion that the relative chronology of Greek sound changes can be recovered only in part. Figure 3.1 presents a flow chart that shows the relative chronologies of changes that can be inferred with greater or less confidence; because the chart cannot include discussion, it is important to use it with the text, not by itself. The pattern of relative chronologies is quite

[51] See now also Dieu (2021), who argues that various apparent examples of Wheeler's Law reflect other processes. I am grateful to Philomen Probert for the reference.

different from those that can be inferred between sound changes from PIE to Proto-Germanic; in that case it was possible to reconstruct chronologies linking as many as ten sound changes (Ringe 2017: 176), whereas the longest sequences of changes on the following pages include only four. It is also striking that five separate relative chronologies converge on Grassmann's Law.

I have introduced into the chart a horizontal line labeled 'Mycenaean' representing the stage of the language represented in the Linear B tablets, but the line is not continuous, since the syllabary does not reveal whether some sound changes had or had not occurred by the Mycenaean period.

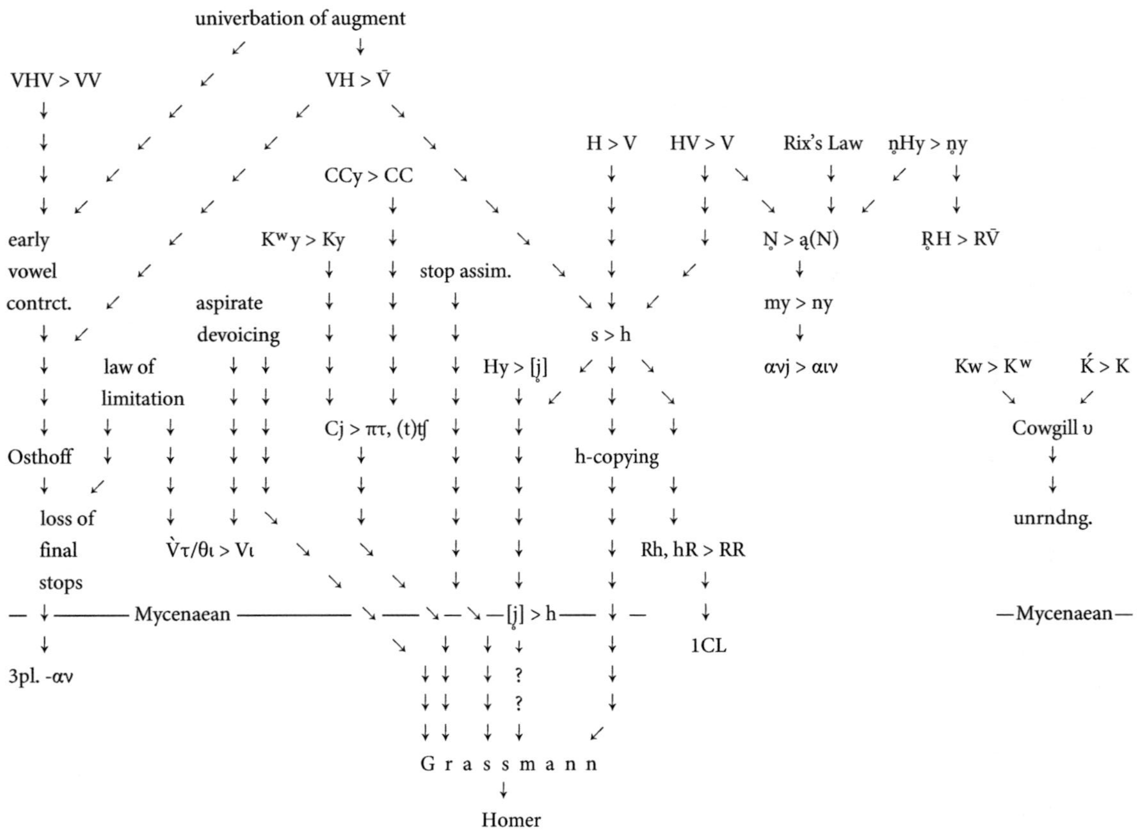

Figure 3.1 Relative chronologies of sound changes

4
The development of Proto-Greek inflectional morphology

4.1 Introduction

Greek underwent no major restructuring of its inflectional morphology in its development from PIE. As in all daughters, the system of nominal inflection was reoriented around stem types defined by their final segment; as in most, it was simplified somewhat. The verb system underwent modest elaboration with little loss of inherited material.

It is even harder than in the case of phonological changes to determine which changes in inflection had occurred by the time the attested dialects began to diverge; there is little evidence of relative chronology, and thus no way to distinguish early changes from later parallel developments or developments that spread from one dialect to another. In practice we are often constrained to ascribe to Proto-Greek those innovations that appear in all the dialects (including Mycenaean, so far as it offers evidence).

4.2 Changes in verb inflection

As I noted in 2.3.3 (v), the final development of the PIE derivational aspect system into an inflectional system marking aspect appears to have occurred in the individual development of Greek. In all attested dialects of Ancient Greek the paradigm of a verb is built on a set of stems, of which the most central, the present and aorist, indicate imperfective and perfective aspect respectively. (That is still true in Modern Greek.) The inherited perfect still expressed stative aspect in Proto-Greek, though by the time the Homeric poems were composed it had begun a long and complex semantic development. In addition, stems expressing future tense had developed, making the system of stems a hybrid aspect-and-tense system.

Reduplication remained a productive process in the Greek perfect; reduplicated presents and aorists had become relic categories by the Classical period. Present stems were normally reduplicated with ι, aorist and perfect stems with ε. Only the first consonant of a cluster was reduplicated. For the most part these reduplication rules were inherited from PIE; notable changes were the replacement of the reduplicating vowel *e by *i in a few present stems and the reduplication of *st-,

The Linguistic Roots of Ancient Greek. Don Ringe, Oxford University Press.
 DOI: 10.1093/9780191989162.003.0004

at least, by *s- (rather than by the whole cluster). In addition, the complex pattern of 'Attic' reduplication, which will be outlined in 4.2.3 (i), developed. All these developments could be of PGk date.

In the following sections I will discuss the Greek stem types one by one, closing with sections on the mood suffixes, the augment, the person-and-number endings, and participles and infinitives.

4.2.1 The development of present stems

4.2.1 (i) Simple and reduplicated athematic presents

Though Greek preserves fewer athematic root-presents than Sanskrit (and many fewer than Hittite), more than twenty survive to be attested in the Homeric poems, and ten are still in use in Classical Attic. Clearly inherited examples include the following; I cite the indicative 3sg. (active, unless the verb is deponent), since that is the form most easily comparable between daughters.

PIE *$h_1$esti '(s)he is' (Hitt. *ēszi*, Skt *asti*, Lat. *est*, Goth. *ist*) > ἐστι;
PIE *b^ha$h_2$ti 'it shines, it illuminates' (Skt *b^hāti*) → '(s)he makes clear' → '(s)he says' (cf. Lat. *fātur*) > φᾱτι > Att.-Ion. φησι;
PIE *$h_1$éyti '(s)he is going/walking' (Skt *éti*, Lat. *it*) > εἶτι (preserved e.g. in Kyrenaian, Buck 115.57) > Att.-Ion. εἶσι;
PIE *h_2wḗ$h_1$ti '(wind) is blowing' (Skt *vā́ti*) > Hom. ἄησι;
PIE *tḱéyti '(s)he settles', pres. 3pl. *tḱiénti (Skt 3sg. *kṣéti*, 3pl. *kṣiyánti*, Av. *šaēiti*, *šiieiṇti*) > Myc. 3pl. *ki-ti-je-si* *κτιjένσι, Hom. ptc. ἐϋκτίμενος 'well settled';
PIE *h_1ḗdsti '(s)he is eating' ~ *$h_1$ed- (Hitt. *ēz'zi*, Skt *átti*) in Hom. inf. ἔδμεναι 'to eat';
PIE *ḱéyor '(s)he is lying down' (Luvian *ziyar*) → *ḱéytoy (Skt *śéte*) >→ κεῖται;
PIE *ḗsor '(s)he is sitting down' (Hitt. *esa*) → *ḗstoy (Skt *ā́ste*) >→ Hom. ἧσται;
PIE *stéwor '(s)he is well known' (cf. Hitt. *istuāri* 'it becomes clear' with shifted accent, Skt *stáve* '(s)he is praised' with innovative *-oy) >→ Hom. στεῦται '(s)he boasts';
PIE *wésto '(s)he was wearing' (cf. Hitt. *wēstat*, Skt *ávasta*) >→ Hom. ἕστο;
PIE *h_2aǵ- 'say' (Arm. thematized *asê*, with *s* < *ḱ < *ǵ before 3sg. *-ti revealing original athematic inflection; derived press. Lat. *ait* '(s)he affirms', Toch. B subj. *ākṣäṃ* '(s)he will proclaim') in augmented ipf. 3sg. *é h_2aǵ-t '(s)he said' > *ἆκτ > Att. quotative ἦ.

φάναι 'to say' and ἰέναι 'to go' have preserved their ablaut alternations; in ἔναι 'to be' and Hom. ἀήμεναι 'to blow' the inherited alternations have been eliminated by regular sound change, since both *ēh_1 and *eh_1 yielded η, while both *$h_1$es- and *h_1s- yielded ἐσ- ~ *hεh- → *ἐh-. The Homeric poems preserve traces of a couple of other examples. A probable athematic subjunctive Hom. ἐρείομεν 'let's ask' *Il.* 1.62 was adduced in 3.2.2. Much more numerous are forms of δέχθαι 'to receive', which might be attested also in Mycenaean (*de-ko-to* = Hom. δέκτο?—but see the discussion of Aura Jorro 1999 s.v.). Most are past indicative or non-finite and so could be aorists, but δέχαται *Il.* 12.147 is clearly a present, and the generalization of -χ- in athematic 3pl. forms neatly explains the unetymological -χ- of Att. present δέχεσθαι (non-Attic δέκεσθαι, cf. Lat. *decēre* 'to be acceptable; so Chantraine 1973: 296–7).[1] An example attested from an outlying dialect is:

> PIE *grés- (*grás-?) ~ *gr̥s- 'eat' vel sim. (cf. Skt 3sg. *grásate* '(s)he swallows', thematized), iptv. 2sg *gr̥sdʰí > Cyprian *ka-ra-si-ti* *γράσθι 'eat!' (Masson 264.1, *LIV* s.v. **gres*).

Greek also has a conspicuous group of middle root-presents of the shape (C)V̆CV̆-. Their prehistories are not entirely clear, because none has a stem-cognate in any other branch of the family; even the roots of ἄγασθαι 'to be astonished' and ἔρασθαι 'to love' cannot be provided with convincing etymologies. At least the following are probably inherited:

> PIE *ḱremh₂- 'be limp' vel sim. (cf. Skt *śramat* 'it will tire', *RV* II.30.7) in pres. κρέμαται 'it is hanging'; conceivably this stem was constructed by lexical analogy with 'lie' and 'sit' (see above), but in that case the innovation must have been very early, since there is also an archaic transitive or causative nasal-infixed present (see 4.2.1 (ii));
> PIE *deyh₂- 'shine' (cf. Skt pf. *dīdā́ya*) in Hom. ipf. δέατ' 'he seemed' *Od.* 6.242 and Ark. subj. δέᾱτοι '(if / however much) it seems', *DGE* 656.10, 18.

On these two stems, see *LIV* s.vv. **ḱremh₂*, **dei̯h₂*; on Hom. δίενται 'they are rushing' *Il.* 23.475 and ὄνοσαι 'you object' *Od.* 17.378, which seem to me to be more problematic, see *LIV* s.vv. **dei̯h₁*, **h₂neh₃*. On the tangle of forms surrounding Hom. ἔρυσθαι 'to draw out; to ward off', see Chantraine (1973: 294–5) and especially Hackstein (2002a: 83, 123–8); on Hom. ῑ̔ετο 'he strove', which might in part be reduplicated, Chantraine (1973: 293–4), Frisk s.v. ἵεμαι, and *LIV* s.v. 1. *u̯ei̯h₁*. How ἐπίστασθαι 'to understand', a transparent compound of στα- 'stand', got attracted into this class remains unclear; the early loss of the reduplicating syllable *hι- posited by Wackernagel (1895: 20–1) (in support of an incorrect etymology of αὐτός!) is unmotivated.

[1] The recognition that Hom. δέκτο, etc., are imperfects eliminates the putative evidence for a root-aorist made to this root, *pace LIV* s.v. **deḱ*. That Arm. *etes* '(s)he saw' is synchronically an aorist proves nothing; after all, so is *eber* '(s)he brought', obviously a cognate of ipf. ἔφερε '(s)he carried'. So far as I can see, there is no unimpeachable evidence for PIE unaffixed presents and aorists made to the same root; see Ringe (2012) for further discussion.

Reduplicated athematic presents are also comparatively well represented in Greek. The reduplicating vowel -ι- has been generalized in this group, replacing *-ε- in two or three common verbs. The following are clearly inherited:

- PIE *h$_1$íh$_1$yeh$_1$ti '(s)he is making' (possibly reflected in Hitt. *iezzi*) > *ἴ̆ϳητι >→ Att. ἵ̆ησι '(s)he is sending', with rough breathing leveled in from aor. ἡκ- ~ ἑ- ←< *h$_1$yeh$_1$-(Peters 1976);
- PIE *d^{h}éd^{h}eh$_1$ti '(s)he is putting' (Skt *dád^{h}āti*) >→ τίθητι > Att.-Ion. τίθησι;
- PIE *dédoh$_3$ti '(s)he is giving' (Skt *dádāti*) >→ δίδωτι > Att.-Ion. δίδωσι;
- PIE *stístah$_2$ti '(s)he is standing up' (thematized in Skt *tíṣṭ^{h}ati*, Lat. *sistit*) > (trans.) ἵστᾱτι > Att.-Ion. ἵστησι;
- PIE *g^{w}íg^{w}ah$_2$ti '(s)he steps (repeatedly), (s)he strides' (Skt *jígāti* '(s)he goes'), zero-grade stem *g^{w}íg^{w}h$_2$- > βιβα- in Hom. ptc. μακρὰ βιβᾱ́ς 'taking long strides';
- PIE *ǵ^{h}íǵ^{h}eh$_1$- (*g^h? meaning? cf. Skt *jáhāti* '(s)he leaves (it)' and *jíhīte* '(s)he moves', and see *LIV* s.vv. **ĝ^{h}eH*, **ĝ^{h}eh$_1$*, and **g^{h}eh$_1$*) in Hom. κιχήμεναι 'to come upon, to overtake, to find'.

Possibly inherited is πιμπλη- ~ πιμπλα- 'fill', but the stem has been remodeled: the root is PIE *pleh$_1$-, whose zero-grade *pl̥h$_1$- would by regular sound change yield πλη-, identical with the full grade, while the nasal in the reduplicating syllable must also an innovation. Hom. iptv. 2sg. ἐμπίπληθι *Il.* 21.311 could be an archaism with the original zero grade of the root. The ablaut of the stem has obviously been remodeled on that of other reduplicated athematic presents, but the source of the intrusive nasal remains a puzzle; for suggestions, see Schwyzer (1939: 689) and *LIV* s.v. **pleh$_1$-*, fn. 7 with references. Also obviously remodeled is ὀνίνησι 'it benefits', a verb whose proposed non-Greek cognates are doubtful; for suggestions see *LIV* s.v. **h$_3$neh$_2$*.

A number of reduplicated athematic presents are clearly innovations. Attic κιχράναι 'to furnish, to lend', Delphian iptv. 3sg. κιχρέτω *DGE* 324.20, etc., do not appear before the 4th century BC and are almost certainly backformations to aor. χρῆσαι (Frisk s.v. κίχρημι). The same process probably underlies Hom. δίδη 'he tied them up (separately)' *Il.* 11.105 in spite of its early appearance (Frisk s.v. 1. δέω, Schwyzer 1939: 688). It is possible that Hom. ἵ̆ληθι 'be propitious!' (twice) was originally a perfect, cognate with Lesb. ἔλλαθι < *he-hla-; see the discussion of Schwyzer (1939: 689) and Frisk s.v. ἱλάσκομαι, both with numerous references. The prehistory of some other examples cannot be recovered for lack of external stem-cognates (or even, in some cases, root-cognates). In the case of Hom. δίζηαι 'you seek' we can at least say that the reduplicated present was formed when the root was still *δjᾱ- (see 3.6.3 *ad fin.*).

4.2.1 (ii) Nasal-affixed presents

As in other daughters of PIE, the class of nasal-infixed presents has been split in Greek, and its fission products have not all survived equally well. Five inherited presents with external cognates to roots ending in *h_2 survive in Homeric Greek, though in every case but one the ablaut of the root has been remodeled:

PIE *mr̥-n-h_2- 'crush' vel sim. (Skt iptv. *mr̥ṇīhí*) > Hom. mid. μάρνασθαι 'to fight';
PIE *pr̥-ná-h_2-ti '(s)he sells' ~ *pr̥-n-h_2- (OIr. *renaid*) > *παρνα- → Hom. περνᾱ́ς 'selling', περνάμεν(α) 'sold';
PIE *dm̥-ná-h_2-ti '(s)he overcomes, (s)he tames' ~ *dm̥-n-h_2- (OIr. *damnaid* '(s)he ties up; (s)he breaks (a horse)') > *δάνησι ~ *δανα- → Hom. δάμνησι '(s)he overcomes', pass. ipf. δάμνατο 'they (neut. pl.) were overcome';
PIE *k(e)d-ná-h_2-ti '(s)he spreads (it) out' ~ *k(e)d-n-h_2- (Toch. B *katnaṃ*) >→ Hom. διασκιδνᾶσιν 'they scatter (it)', κίδναται '(dawn) spreads', ἐσκίδναντο 'they dispersed';
PIE *pl̥-n-h_2- 'approach' (cf. OIr. *ad·ella* '(s)he visits') >→ Hom. πίλναται '(s)he touches the surface', προσεπίλνατο 'it was approaching'.

At least these five examples are Proto-Greek. Several others are highly likely:

PIE *ḱérh$_2$- ~ *ḱr̥h$_2$- 'mix' (cf. Skt ptc. *ā́śīrtas* 'mixed') in pres. *ḱr̥-ná-h_2- 'be mixing' >→ Hom. ipf. κίρνη '(s)he mixed';
PIE *ḱrémh$_2$- ~ *ḱrm̥h$_2$- 'be slack' → 'hang' (caus. *kromh$_2$-éye- in Goth. iptv. 2pl. *hramjiþ* 'crucify', *pace* Frisk s.v. κρεμάννυμι) in pres. *krm̥-n-h_2- >→ κριμνα- in pres. ptc. gen. pl. κριμνάντων 'while weighing (anchor)', Pindar *Pythian* IV.25;
pre-Gk *p(e)th$_2$- 'spread' in *p(e)t-n-h_2- >→ Hom. πιτνᾱ́ς 'stretching forth', πίτναντο 'they were spread out'.

(More problematic is Hesykhios' λίναμαι· τρέπομαι, whose meaning (if correctly transmitted; see Wackernagel 1916: 206 fn. 1) doesn't fit especially well with OIr. *lenaid* '(s)he follows', nor with Skt *lināti* 'it fits', while its form doesn't match Goth. *aflinnan* 'to depart' (see Frisk s.v. λιάζομαι).)

Except for the first one listed, which is *praesens tantum*, the well-attested presents of this group are associated with sigmatic aorists περασα-, δαμασα-, (σ)κεδασα-, πελασα-, κερασα-, κρεμασα-, πετασα-, which are plausibly interpreted as remodelings of the root-aorists that one would expect to be associated with nasal-infixed presents (cf. Strunk 1967: 120–2). That raises the question of how pres. κρέμασθαι 'to hang (intr.)' is related to this complex of stems.

If it is not an innovation (see above), the pair κρεμα-: *κριμνᾱ- could be an extreme archaism, since the nasal-infixed present is effectively the causative of the root-present, as is normal in Hittite and probably in PIE (see 2.3.3 (i)). But in that case the reinterpretation of the unaffixed stems as aorists could be yet another indication that the aspect system was still derivational down into the separate prehistory of Greek. Without further information it does not seem possible to decide this question. The generalization of ι in the root-syllables of most of these presents is clearly an innovation, but its source is uncertain. It might have been introduced from reduplicating syllables by native learner error (Schwyzer 1939: 695 with references).

A completely fossilized nasal-infixed present is:

PIE *du-ná-h₂- ~ *du-n-h₂- 'fit' (root *dewh₂-, cf. Toch. B pres. 3sg. *tswetär* (intrans.), Goth. *taujan* 'to make', orig. causative *'to fit together', Ringe 1996: 31) > passive δύνασθαι 'to be able', orig. *'to be fitted for'.

Only the present survives in Greek; so far as we can tell, that could already have been the Proto-Greek situation. The rest of the paradigm was built to the present at a later date.

On thematized presents which might originally have belonged to this group see further below.

There seem to be only two other nasal presents in which -ν- is unarguably an infix, and one has been thematized:

PIE *gah₂u- 'be glad, rejoice'[2] (*LIV* s.v. **geh₂u̯*) in *gh₂-n̥-u- > Hom. pres. 3sg. γάνυται (Frisk s.v. γάνυμαι);

PIE *kwas- 'kiss' (Hitt. 3sg. *kuaszi*, 3pl. *kuassanzi*) in pres. *ku-né-s- >→ κυνε͂ν (*LIV* s.v. **ku̯as*).

A somewhat problematic case is Hom. κί́νυντο 'they were moving' and its thematized variant κῑνε͂ν. The latter almost certainly reflects *...νεϝ-ε/ο-; the sigmatic aorist κῑνῆσαι, etc., must be later formations, created after the loss of intervocalic *ϝ (Frisk s.v. κῑνέω). The problem is the word's etymology. We might expect it to be part of the large family of reflexes of PIE *kʷyew- 'move', in which case the -ν- would clearly be an infix. The initial κ- is not an insurmountable problem, since labiovelars were delabialized before *y (see 3.4.3) and the resulting *k- could have been leveled through the paradigm. But the long ῑ in all forms of this present is difficult to account for. Positing a different synonymous root *keyH- or the like (*LIV*

[2] Or adj. 'glad'? Cf. Hitt. *tēpu-* 'little, few', *tepnu-* 'make little/few'. The Greek present is not synchronically factitive, but since its inflection is mediopassive it could originally have meant *'be gladdened, get happy'.

s.v. **kei̯h_2* with references) might or might not be the right solution, but there is definitely a problem with this verb.

Most Greek presents with a nasal affix are clearly suffixed; that is not surprising, since in all the most conservative daughters of PIE (including even Hittite) a suffix *-néw- ~ *-nu- has developed. A substantial group of Gk nasal-suffixed presents exhibits a suffix -νῡ- ~ -νυ-, with ablaut remodeled on laryngeal-final roots that had evolved an alternation -V:- ~ -V- (see above). Several such presents might be inherited, if not from PIE then from an intermediate protolanguage, because they have apparent cognates in Indo-Iranian or in other daughters:

(post-)PIE *pstr̥-néw- ~ *pstr̥-nu- 'sneeze' (Lat. *sternuere*) > πτάρνυσθαι (aor. πταρε̃ν);
(post-)PIE *h$_2$r̥-néw- ~ *h$_2$r̥-nu- 'take, receive' (Arm. pres. 3sg. *aṙnow*) > Hom. ptc. ἀρνύμενος;
(post-)PIE *h$_3$r̥-néw- ~ *h$_3$r̥-nu- 'rise, raise' (Skt *r̥ṇóti* 'sets in motion', at least in part, cf. *LIV* s.v. **h$_3$er*) > Hom. ὄρνυται 'it rises', etc.;
(post-)PIE *tn̥-néw- ~ *tn̥-nu- 'stretch' (Skt *tanóti*) > Hom. τάνυται 'it is stretched';
post-PIE *wes-néw- ~ *wes-nu- 'clothe' (Arm. pres. 3sg. *z-genow* 'puts (clothes) on') > Hom. ipf. 3sg. κατα-είνυσαν (ει = ε̄) 'they covered' (*Il.* 23.135); this example could be comparatively old, reflecting a causative that replaced PIE *woséye/o-;
post-PIE *dē̑k-néw- ~ *dē̑k-nu- 'cause to accept' (?; probably with analogical lengthened grade, but cf. Skt *dāśnóti* 'propitiates', *RV* VIII.4.6) > Hom. *δηκνύμενος 'receiving' (mss. δεικνύμενος, but cf. Frisk s.v. δηδέχαται with references).

A special problem are the competing presents κτε̄́νε̄ν and κτε̄νύναι 'kill'. The latter looks like a stem-cognate of Skt *kṣaṇóti* 'destroys', attested in the Brahmanas (cf. Frisk s.v. κτείνω with references, *LIV* s.v. *tken*), with analogically adjusted root-ablaut; yet it appears first in Classical Attic, while the thematic present, which can only reflect *κτεν-jε/o-, is well attested in Homer and everywhere else (including Classical Attic). It is not impossible that the present in -νυ- is an Attic archaism, but absent other evidence it seems prudent to suspend judgment.

A substantial majority of Greek present stems in -νῡ- ~ -νυ- do not have stem-cognates in other IE languages. Frequently encountered examples include (cited as Attic infinitives) κατᾱγνύναι 'to break' (*κατα-ϝαγ-), ῥηγνύναι 'to break', πηγνύναι 'to fix, to fasten', ζευγνύναι 'to yoke', δεικνύναι 'to show', ὀμνύναι 'to swear', ζωννύναι 'to put on a belt', σβεννύναι 'to extinguish', and ἀπ-ολλύναι 'to perish'. The geminate sonorants of the last three show that they were created (or remodeled) well after the Proto-Greek period, since they did not undergo the early changes of sonorant clusters (see 5.2.2).

There are also examples that have been thematized. One is attested both as an athematic and as a thematic stem:

> post-PIE *k^wi-néw- ~ *k^wi-nu- 'pay, repay' (*LIV* s.v. 3. **k^u̯ei̯*) > *τινευ- ~ *τινυ- → Hom. τείνυται, Cret. ἀποτεινύτω (root-ablaut leveled in from aor. τεῖσαι, Schwyzer 1939: 697, *LIV* 339–40 with fn. 5 and references) and *τινϝε/ο- > Hom. τῑ́νε̄ν, Att. etc. τίνε̄ν (see 7.2.2).

Another was mostly thematized directly but is also attested with a thematic consonantal extension:

> post-PIE *$d^h g^{wh}$i-néw- ~ *$d^h g^{wh}$i-nu- 'perish' (*LIV* 131–3) > *χ^wθινευ- ~ *χ^wθινυ- → *φθινϝε/ο- > Hom. φθῑ́νε̄ν, Att. etc. φθίνε̄ν; also extended in Hom. φθινύθε̄ν 'perish' and 'destroy'.

A third has no convincing cognates in other IE languages but appears to be old: Hom. φθᾱ́νει 'it gets ahead of, it outpaces' (twice), Att. etc. φθάνε̄ν 'to anticipate, to get (somewhere) ahead of' < *φθανϝε/ο-. Finally, the most interesting example has been thematized twice, probably originally in different dialects. On the one hand, the full grade of the stem was thematized, and the result is widely attested:

> PIE *seyk- 'arrive, reach (a place)' in (post?-)PIE pres. *sik-néw- ~ *sik-nu- (*LIV* s.v. **sei̯k*) >→ *hικνεϝ-ε/ο- > ἱκνε̄σθαι (twice in the *Odyssey*; Ionic, Attic, etc. aor. ἱκέσθαι).

On the other hand, the usual Homeric present reflects thematization of the zero grade:

> *sik-néw- ~ *sik-nu- >→ *hikn̥w-e/o- > *hικανϝε/ο- > Hom. ἱκᾱ́νε̄ν.

The same form of the suffix recurs in Hom. κιχᾱ́νε̄ν 'to find', but because the stem is also reduplicated that must be a later innovation.

Two nasal-infixed presents to roots in *-y- leveled the full root into the position before the nasal, yielding presents in *-ny- that were then thematized (Warren Cowgill, p.c. ca. 1978; *LIV* s.v. **k̂lei̯* with references):

> PIE *ḱl̥-né-y- ~ *ḱl̥-n-y- 'lean' → *ḱli-né-y- ~ *ḱli-n-y- → *ḱlinye/o- > Hom., etc. κλῑ́νε̄ν;
> PIE *kr̥-né-y- ~ *kr̥-n-y-[3] 'sift, separate' *kri-né-y- ~ *kri-n-y- → *krinye/o- 'distinguish, decide' > Lesb. ptc. κριννόμεναι (Alkaios 130B.17), Pelasgiote Thess. κρεννέμεν, otherwise κρῑ́νε̄ν.

[3] At least if Lat. perf. *crēvisse* owes its vowel to lexical analogy with *lēvisse*; in any case there is no trace of *h_1 in the Greek or Celtic forms (so Barber 2013: 371–2). For a somewhat different reconstruction, see *LIV* s.v. **kreh₁(i̯)*.

A considerable number of Greek thematic presents with suffix -(α)νε/ο- exhibit no certain evidence of any PIE consonant following the *-n-. When the root of the verb is heavy the suffix is consistently -ανε/ο-. Strikingly, most Homeric examples are obvious innovations, attested only once or a few times and restricted to epic Greek; typical are ἐκ ... ληθάνει 'it makes (me) forget' *Od.* 7.220–1 (beside ἐλήθετο 'he forgot', etc.; λήθε̄ν thirty-four times) and ἰσχάνε̄ν 'to hold' four times (beside ἴσχε̄ν fifty-two times, ἔχε̄ν 689 times). But two such Homeric stems are more widely attested:

pre-Greek *$h_2$mert- 'miss (a mark)' (cf. Hom. νημερτής, 3.2.3) in aor. ἁμαρτε̃ν 'to miss, to err' (with zero-grade αρ < *r̥ and apparently /h-/ by lexical analogy), pres. ἁμαρτάνε̄ν (ipf. 3sg. ἡμάρτανε three times in Homer);
Greek ἐχθ- 'hate' (see 3.4.4) in aor. ἀπ-εχθέσθαι 'to incur hatred', pres. ἀπ-εχθάνεσθαι (ἀπεχθάνεαι *Od.* 2.202).

Similar Classical Attic examples—none of which has problem-free external root-cognates—include:

pre-Greek *awisd^h- 'perceive' (?; cf. Skt *āvís* 'visible, evident', Lat. *audīre* 'to hear') in aor. αἰσθέσθαι (cf. ἄϊσθε 'he breathed out (his life)', *Il.* 20.403?), pres. αἰσθάνεσθαι;
aor. βλαστε̃ν 'to sprout', pres. βλαστάνε̄ν;
aor. κατα-δαρθε̃ν 'to fall asleep' (Hom. 3sg. ἔδραθε), pres. κατα-δαρθάνε̄ν;
aor. ὀλισθε̃ν 'to slip' (ὄλισθε(ν) *Il.* twice), pres. ὀλισθάνε̄ν.[4]

It seems clear that this suffix was used productively to form presents to thematic aorists with heavy root-syllables; whether it had already become productive in Proto-Greek is necessarily unclear. In principle -ανε/ο- could reflect a thematization *-n̥H-e/o- of a suffix *-néH- ~ *-n̥H- extracted from the infixed presents of laryngeal-final roots. But -αν- could also reflect just *-n̥-, the Sievers' Law alternant of *-n- that is expected after heavy syllables. The few examples of nasal-suffixed presents to light roots actually suggest as much. Two were made to laryngeal-final roots:

PIE *temh_1- 'cut' (*LIV* s.v.; cf. full grade *témh_1- in τέμενος 'land reserved for a god', zero-grade *tm̥$h_1$tós 'cut' in Hom. ἐΰτμητος 'well-cut'), pres. *tm̥-né-h_1- ~ *tm-n̥-h_1- (cf. Middle Irish *tamnaid*), aor. *témh_1- ~ *tm̥h_1- >→ aor. τεμε̃ν, pres. τάμνε̄ν, with root-vowels leveled in the dialects (ε in Attic, α in our text of Homer and widely elsewhere);

[4] The etymology ὀλισθ- < *$h_3$lisd^h- ← *$h_3$slid^h- (cf. Skt. *ásrid^{h}ānas* 'not going wrong', OE *slīdan* 'to slide', etc.; *LIV* s.v. *$h_3$sleịd^h) is ingenious and attractive—one might almost say inspired—but uncertain, and it does not affect our assessment of the Greek paradigm.

PIE *ḱemh$_2$- 'get tired' (*LIV* s.v.; cf. zero-grade *ḱm̥h$_2$tós 'tired' > *κμᾱτός in Hom. h. ἄκμητος 'tireless'), pres. *ḱm̥-né-h$_1$- ~ *ḱm-n̥-h$_1$- (cf. Vedic Skt 2sg. *śamnīṣe*) >→ aor. καμε̄ν, pres. κάμνε̄ν.

There are just enough stem-cognates to suggest that nasal-infixed presents to these verbs were inherited, but the root-final laryngeal has somehow been lost; alternatively, a 'converse of Sievers' Law' might have operated in the prehistory of Greek, though only in derived environments, since δαπάνη, for instance, was not affected (see 3.6.1). In any case Greek evidently evolved a present stem suffix -νε/ο-. That is clear from the remaining example with a light root:

PIE *denḱ- 'bite' (?; *LIV* s.v., cf. Skt *daṃśayati* '(s)he causes to bite', first attested in the Sūtras) ~ *dn̥ḱ- in aor. δακε̄ν (*Il.* thrice), pres. δάκνε̄ν (Att., Ion.).

The obvious conclusion to be drawn is that there is nothing very old in this whole complex of present stems, especially since none of the examples in -ανε/ο- has stem-cognates in other IE languages.

The same can be said of the presents in -ανε/ο- that also exhibit a nasal-infix in the root. In two of the Homeric examples, and perhaps in one later example, the root-internal nasal is etymologically part of the root:

(post-)PIE *g^{h}end- ~ *g^{h}n̥d- 'grasp' (cf. Lat. *prehendere*; *LIV* s.v. **g^{h}ed*, and see further below): aor. *g^{h}n̥d-é/ó- > χαδε̄ν, desiderative *g^{h}énd-se/o- > fut. 3sg. χείσεται 'will contain, will have room for' *Od.* 18.17 (ει = ε̄); perf. *g^{h}eg^{h}ónd- 'contain' in plup. 3sg. κεχόνδει 'it contained' *Il.* 24.192; on the root-ablaut of pres. χανδάνε̄ν see below;

pre-Gk *leng^h- ~ *ln̥g^h- 'get by lot': aor. *ln̥g^h-é/ó- > λαχε̄ν, perf. *lelóng^h- in 3pl. λελόγχασιν 'they have (by the working of fate)' *Od.* 11.304; pres. λαγχάνε̄ν as for χανδάνε̄ν;

pre-Gk *mend^h- ~ *mn̥d^h- 'learn' (?; see Frisk s.v. μανθάνω for possible cognates): aor. *mn̥d^h-é/ó- > μαθε̄ν (thrice in Homer); pres. μανθάνε̄ν (5th c.) as for χανδάνε̄ν.

It is often suggested that χανδάνε̄ν reflects a PIE nasal-infixed present, but that is not what the distribution of facts argues. Not all the cognates adduced are equally certain, but in most the nasal is synchronically part of the root; *g^{h}ed- appears only in the family of PGmc. *-getaną and in Lat. *praeda* 'plunder, booty' (*praihed-). It is certainly possible that the form of the root with an internal nasal began its career as a nasal-infixed present, but it needs to be remembered that partially similar roots with apparently identical meanings are not rare in IE (e.g. *g^{w}em- and *g^{w}ah$_2$-, both 'step'). Klingenschmitt (1982: 184, fn. 26), suggests that the root-vocalism of pres. χανδάνε̄ν can be explained by reanalysis of a nasal-infixed present: the heavy Lindeman variant *g^{h}n̥éd- was reinterpreted as *g^{h}n̥-né-d-, and the sequence *-n̥n- yielded -αν-. But if that were true the reanalysis must have occurred very early, and it is difficult to see why the future and perfect continue to exhibit the expected inherited ablaut grades of *g^{h}end-; it seems much more likely that the first α of χανδάνε̄ν was simply leveled in from the aorist, the pivotal member of an eventive verb in early Greek.

But though the nasals in the roots of these presents were not originally infixed (at least from a Greek point of view), they were certainly reinterpreted as an infix by native learners. That reanalysis is already underway in the Homeric poems; it will be described in 5.4.2, where other nasal-infixed stems that have been claimed to be inherited (λιμπάνε̄ν, πυνθάνεσθαι) will also be discussed.

Mention should also be made of one more development of nasal-infixed presents, namely the extension of the zero grade with *-ye/o-. An example probably based on an inherited stem is:

> PIE pres. *u-né-b^h- 'be weaving' (Skt 2sg. *sám unap*) → *ub^h-né-H- (Skt inj. 2sg. *ub^{h}nā́s*, 3sg. with augment *aub^{h}nāt*) → *ub^h-n̥-H-yé/ó- > *ὐφανjε/o- > Hom., etc. ὑφαίνε̄ν.

A more involved example is the only Greek present still reduplicated with *e:

> PIE *térh$_1$- ~ *tr̥h$_1$- 'bore' (Hom. τέρετρον 'auger, gimlet', τρητός 'perforated', 3.2.3) in press. *téterh$_1$- ~ *tétr̥h$_1$- and *tr̥-né-h$_1$- ~ *tr-n̥-h$_1$- (?) >→ *te-tr-n̥-h$_1$-yé/ó- > τετραίνε̄ν (directly attested only from the 5th century, but implied by Hom. aor. τέτρηνε).

As the derivation just given suggests, this looks like a conflation of two different present stems. Unfortunately neither has an external stem-cognate; all the other languages that preserve the verb appear to exhibit thematized root-presents (*LIV* s.v. **terh$_1$*).

4.2.1 (iii) Affixed thematic presents

This section deals with affixed thematic presents other than those in *-ye/o-, for which, see 4.2.1 (v).

Though all the thematic nasal suffixes of Greek presents must ultimately have arisen from athematic formations, the same does not seem to be true of reduplicated thematic presents. Three do reflect original athematic stems:

> PIE *tétek̑- ~ *tetk̑- 'fashion, make' (3pl. *tétk̑n̥ti > Vedic Skt *tákṣati*, to which 3sg. *tā́ṣṭi* was backformed) >→ *τιτκε/ο- > τίκτε̄ν 'be giving birth' (aor. τεκε̃ν);

PIE *ǵiǵénh₁- ~ *ǵiǵn̥h₁- 'beget' (cf. Vedic Skt aor. *ájījanat*, Lat. pres. *gignere*) >→ mid. γίγνεσθαι 'be born, become' (aor. γενέσθαι); exactly how the laryngeal was lost remains unclear, but the full grade of the Sanskrit stem argues that the paradigm was originally ablauting, therefore athematic;

PIE *nínes- ~ *nins- 'escape, return safely' (cf. Vedic Skt *níṃsate* '(s)he greets', inj. *niṃsata* 'it returns (to the earth)' (?) *RV* X.74.2) >→ Hom. acc. νῑσόμενον 'returning', νῑ́σοντο 'they usually retreated', etc.

Positing an originally athematic stem for the last example is probably the best explanation for the survival of the -σ-: in an athematic middle stem *ninh- ~ *nins- the latter alternant, which must have occurred in the pivotal 3sg., can have been leveled through the paradigm when the alternation *s ~ *h was no longer automatic, and only then was the stem thematized.[5] But two other stems are thematic in every language in which they are attested, one even in Hittite:

PIE *mímne/o- 'be waiting' (Hitt. *mimmai* '(s)he refuses' ← *'hesitates') > μίμνε̄ν;

PIE *sísde/o- 'be (in the act of) sitting down' (Skt 3sg. *sī́dati*, Av. *niš.hiδaiti*, Lat. *cōnsīdere*) > ἵζεσθαι.

The remaining two examples appear to be innovations confined to Greek:

pre-Gk *sí-sǵʰ-e/o- 'hold' > *hiskʰe/o- > ἴσχε̄ν, beside more common ἔχε̄ν (cognate with Skt *sáhate* '(s)he prevails'); the reduplicated present is directly attested only in Homer (and Homericizing later Greek), but indirectly also in Att. ὑπισχνε̃σθαι 'to promise' with further suffixation;

pre-Gk *pi-pt-e/o- 'be falling' >→ πῑ́πτε̄ν (vs. e.g. Skt *pátati* 'it flies, it falls').

In our text tradition the reduplicating vowel of the latter stem is consistently long (e.g. ipf. πῖπτε(ν), πῖπτον in Homer), which cannot be original; lexical analogy with ῥῑ́πτε̄ν 'throw' is the most likely explanation.

Of the many presents in -σκε/o- that are attested already in Homer, only four have clear stem-cognates elsewhere in the family (cf. Zerdin 2000: 39–41):

PIE *h₁sḱé/ó- 'be habitually' (underlyingly */h₁s-sḱé/ó-/ with reduction of geminate *ss; cf. Palaic iptv. *iska* 'be!', Old Lat. 3sg. *escit* 'will be', Toch. B copula 3pl. *skente*, and see Hackstein 1995: 277–82, *LIV* s.v. 1. **h₁es*, both with references) > Hom. iterative ipf. 3pl. ἔσκε;

PIE *misḱé/ó- 'mix continuously' (underlyingly */miḱ-sḱé/ó-/; cf. Lat. *miscēre*), remodeled as *μιγ-σκέ/ó- > μίσγε̄ν 'to be mixing';

[5] This solution goes back at least to Pokorny (1959) s.v. *nes-*. For alternative explanations, see Frisk s.v. νέομαι, *LIV* s.v. **nes*, and Barber (2013: 259–60), all with references.

PIE *g^{w}m̥-sḱé/ó- 'step repeatedly, walk' (cf. Skt 3sg. *gácc^{h}ati* '(s)he goes') > βάσκε̄ν;

PIE *ǵn̥h$_3$-sḱé/ó- 'recognize on sight' (cf. Lat. *nōscere*, OPers. subj. 3sg. *xšnāsātiy*) > γνώσκε̄ν (attributed to Epirote by a grammarian, Filos 2018: 238) → γιγνώσκε̄ν.

How and why 'mix' was remodeled as μειγ- does not seem to be recoverable; the origin of the reduplication in γιγνώσκε̄ν is likewise obscure. A possible fifth example is:

PIE *h$_2$lu-sḱé/ó- 'keep away, avoid' (?; Toch. B /aləskə/e-/, Hackstein 1995: 215–16, *LIV* s.v. **h$_2$leu̯*) > ptc. ἀλύσκων (twice in *Od.* 22); but see now Peyrot (2013: 584).

A larger number of Homeric examples, plus a couple attested only later, could also be inherited; the absence of stem-cognates might be attributed to the fact that even root-cognates of these verbs are very sparse (and in some cases doubtful). The following exhibit the expected zero grade of the root and no obvious complications:[6]

PIE *d^{h}erh$_3$- 'jump' (cf. Middle Irish ipf. 3sg. *no·daired* '(the bull) kept mounting', *LIV* s.v. **d^{h}erh$_3$* with references) in pre-Gk *d^{h}r̥h$_3$-ské/ó- > Hom. θρώσκε̄ν, aor. θορε̃ν;

PIE *g^{h}an- 'gape' (ON *gana, LIV* s.v. *g^{h}an*) in pre-Gk *g^{h}n̥-ské/ó- > Ion., Att. χάσκε̄ν, aor. χανε̃ν;

PIE *d^{h}enh$_2$- 'run (away)' (?; see *LIV* s.v.) in pre-Gk *d^{h}n̥h$_2$-ské/ó- > θνᾱ́σκε̄ν 'to be dying' > Att.-Ion. θνῄσκε̄ν,[7] aor. θανε̃ν;

PIE *melh$_3$- (?; see *LIV* s.v.) in pre-Gk *ml̥h$_3$-ské/ó- > Hom. προ-, κατα-βλώσκε̄ν 'to come forward/down', aor. Hom., Dor. μολε̃ν;

post-PIE *k^{w}end^{h}- (?; see *LIV* s.v.) in pre-Gk *k^{w}n̥t^{h}-ské/ó- > πάσχε̄ν 'to experience', aor. παθε̃ν.

In addition, there are two examples with both reduplication and the suffix -σκε/ο- that might have developed from inherited presents in *-ské/ó-, like γιγνώσκε̄ν:

PIE *terh$_3$- 'wound' (cf. Vedic Skt nt. *turám* 'wounded', *RV* VIII.79.2) in pre-Gk *tr̥h$_3$-ské/ó- > *τρώσκε̄ν → Ion., Att. τιτρώσκε̄ν, Hom. aor. 3sg. ἔτορε 'it pierced' *Il.* 11.236;

[6] I do not include ἔρχεσθαι 'go, come', since a sound-change *ρσκ > ρχ is unparalleled; it seems much more likely that the verb is cognate with the OIr. imperative *eirgg* 'go!' (see *LIV* s.v. **h$_1$erǵ^{h}*, of which the original meaning is probably not 'besteigen').

[7] Though θνῄισκε̄ν is certainly an innovation, it is not merely a spelling variant, since it appears consistently in 4th-century Attic inscriptions (Threatte 1980: 372, 1996: 505; once θνείσκω with the regular sound-change development of ηι, Threatte 1980: 739).

PIE *mnah₂- (?; see *LIV* s.v. **mneh₂*) in pre-Gk *m̥nh₂-ské/ó- 'remind, remember' > mid. 3sg. μνήσκεται (Anakreon, elegiac fr. 2.4) → μιμνήσκε̄ν, -εσθαι.[8]

But it seems just as likely that the latter example was modeled on γιγνώσκε̄ν, since 'recognize' and 'remember' belong to the same semantic area; and it is clear that this reduplicated formation remained marginally productive in Greek, eventually yielding Hellenistic πιπρᾱ́σκε̄ν as a replacement for Hom. περνα- 'sell', for instance.

4.2.1 (iv) Unaffixed thematic presents

As in most daughters (though not in Anatolian or Tocharian, see 2.3.3), the largest group of inherited thematic presents exhibits e-grade of the root and no affix. Some of these clearly reflect thematization of athematic presents, but even in those cases related languages often exhibit a parallel thematization. The three which appear in Tocharian are represented in Greek as well:

PIE *h_2áǵe/o- 'be driving' (3sg. Toch. B *āśäṃ*, Skt *ájati*; Lat. *agere*, etc.) > ἄγε̄ν;
PIE *b^hére/o- 'be carrying' (3sg. Toch. B *paräṃ*, Skt *b^hárati*; Goth. *baíran*, etc.) > φέρε̄ν;
PIE *g^wíh₃we/o- 'be alive, live' (3sg. Toch. B *śaiṃ*, Skt *jīvati*; Lat. *vīvere*, etc.) → *g^wyóh₃we/o- (with the same analogical full grade as ζωός, see 3.2.3) > Hom., etc. ζώε̄ν.

Many others have stem-cognates in conservative IE languages; typical are:

PIE *b^héyd^{h}e/o- 'trust' (Lat. *fīdere*, Goth. *beidan* 'to wait for') > πείθεσθαι 'to obey';
PIE *dére/o- 'tear' (OCS 3sg. *deretŭ*; Goth. *gataíran* 'to break, to destroy') > δέρε̄ν 'to skin';
PIE *éwse/o- 'burn (trans.)' (Skt 3sg. *óṣati*, Lat. *ūrere*) >→ εὕε̄ν 'to singe' (diphthong reintroduced from aor. εὖσαι);
PIE *géme/o- 'squeeze' vel sim. (Lat. *gemere* 'to sigh') > γέμε̄ν 'to be full';
PIE *h₁réwge/o- 'belch' (Lat. *ē-rūgere*) > ἐρεύγεσθαι 'to disgorge';
PIE *h₂ánǵ^{h}e/o- 'choke' (Lat. *angere*) > ἄγχε̄ν;
PIE *h₂lége/o- 'care about' (Lat. *dī-ligere* 'to love') > Hom. 3sg. ἀλέγει;
PIE *(h₃)méyǵ^{h}e/o- 'urinate' (Skt 3sg. *méhati*, Lat. *meiere*, ON *míga*) > ὀμείχειν, Hesiod *Works and Days* 727;
PIE *léǵe/o- 'collect' (Lat. *legere* 'to collect; to read') > λέγε̄ν 'to say', συλ-λέγε̄ν 'to collect';
PIE *néme/o- 'distribute' (Goth. *niman* 'to take') > νέμε̄ν;
PIE *pérde/o- 'fart' (Skt 3sg. *pardate*) > πέρδεσθαι;
PIE *péte/o- 'fly' (Skt 3sg. *pátati*; Lat. *petere* 'to go for, to seek') > πέτεσθαι;

[8] However, μνᾶσθαι 'to court' seems just as likely to be a denominative to *βνᾱ- < *g^wnah₂- 'woman' (Meister 1921: 88; cf. Modern English *womanize*).

PIE *pléwe/o- 'float' (Skt 3sg. *plávate*; Lat. *pluere* 'to rain') > *πλέϝēν 'to sail' > πλε̃ν;
PIE *sékʷe/o- 'accompany, follow' (Skt 3sg. *sácate*, Lat. *sequī*) > ἕπεσθαι;
PIE *sérpe/o- 'crawl' (Skt 3sg. *sárpati*, Lat. *serpere*) > ἕρπēν;
PIE *snéygʷʰe/o- 'snow' (OHG *snīwan*; OLat. 3sg. *nīvit*?[9]) > νείφēν;
PIE *(s)tége/o- 'cover' (Lat. *tegere*) > στέγēν;
PIE *ténge/o- 'moisten' (Lat. *tingere*) > τέγγēν;
PIE *tréme/o- 'tremble' (Lat. *tremere*) > τρέμēν;
PIE *trése/o- 'fear' (Skt 3sg. *trásati*) > *τρέhēν > τρε̃ν;
PIE *wéǵʰe/o- 'convey' (Skt 3sg. *váhati*, Lat. *vehere*) > Pamphylian iptv. 3sg. ϝεχέτō, Brixhe 3.24? But see the discussion of Brixhe (1976: 183).

Among those that clearly reflect earlier athematic presents are:

PIE *h₃rḗǵ- ~ *h₃réǵ- 'make straight' (Vedic Skt *rā́ṣṭi* 'he rules' *RV* I.104.4) → *h₃réǵe/o- (Lat. *regere* 'to guide, to rule') > ὀρέγēν 'to stretch out';
PIE *h₂mḗlǵ- ~ *h₂mélǵ- 'stroke, milk' (Vedic Skt *sáṃ sā́nu mārjmi* 'I stroke (his) back' *RV* II.35.12; Lith. 3sg. *mélža* '(s)he milks' with lengthened grade thematized) → *h₂mélǵe/o- 'milk' (OE *melcan*) > ἀμέλγēν;
PIE *trép- ~ *tr̥p- 'turn' (Hitt. 3sg. *teripzi* '(s)he plows') → *trépe/o- > τρέπēν;
PIE *sép- ~ *sp- 'take care of' (Gāthā-Av. 3sg. *haptī* '(s)he keeps') → *sépe/o- (Vedic Skt 3sg. *sápati* '(s)he honors') > Hom. ἕπēν;
PIE *dʰéwgʰ- ~ *dʰugʰ- 'produce' (Skt 3sg. *dógdʰi* '(s)he milks', *duhé* 'it gives milk') → *dʰéwgʰe/o- > Hom. τεύχēν 'to fashion, to make';
PIE *léyǵʰ- ~ *liǵʰ- 'lick' (Skt. 3sg. *réḍʰi*) → *léyǵʰe/o- > λείχēν;
PIE *h₁léngʰ- ~ *h₁l̥ngʰ- 'clear oneself by oath' (Hitt. 3sg. *linkzi* '(s)he swears') → *h₁léngʰe/o- > ἐλέγχēν 'to shame, to cross-examine, to refute'.

It is difficult to say whether any of these thematizations had occurred by the Proto-Greek stage, since athematic presents continued to be thematized within the attested history of Greek (see 5.4.2 (i)). Note that the accentuation of the adjective ἑκών 'willing' agrees with that of Skt athematic *uśánt-* 'wanting', suggesting that whatever forms of the stem survived into Proto-Greek were still athematic.[10] One stem, though, probably was thematized well before the separate prehistory of Greek, since its Hittite cognate is inflected according to the hi-conjugation, which in Nuclear IE survived only as the perfect (see 2.3.3 (i)):

[9] Or possibly *nivit*, since the only attestation is in a senarius of Pacuvius: *nĭ̄vit sagittīs; plumbīs, saxīs grandinat.*

[10] The ablaut of the root is more of a problem. Indo-Iranian reflects *wéḱ- ~ *uḱ- (e.g. Skt 3sg. *váṣṭi*, 3pl. *uśánti*), but Hittite clearly reflects Narten ablaut *wḗḱ- ~ *wéḱ- (3sg. *wēkzi*, 3pl. *wekkanzi*). In effect, the surviving Greek participle has the accent of the Sanskrit paradigm but (apparently) the root-ablaut of the Hittite paradigm, and there is more than one way in which that could have come about.

PIE *spónd- ~ *spénd- 'pour a libation' (Hitt. 3sg. *ispanti* ~ *sipandi*) → *spénde/o- > σπένδε̄ν.

Much more startling are those Greek thematic presents that reflect inherited aorist subjunctives. A clear example, noted in *LIV* s.v. **ĝeu̯s*, is:

PIE aor. *ǵéws- ~ *ǵus- 'taste' (Skt *juṣāṇá*- 'enjoying', multiply attested in the Rigveda), subj. *ǵéws-e/o- (Vedic Skt *jóṣat*, *joṣati*, four times in the Rigveda) → Gk pres. *γεύhε/ο- >→ γεύεσθαι;

equally clear is an example whose PIE present was nasal-infixed:

PIE pres. 3sg. *linékʷti, 3pl. *linkʷénti 'leave behind' (Skt *riṇákti*, *riñcánti*; cf. Lat. *linquere*), aor. *léykʷ- ~ *likʷ- (cf. Lat. perf. 3sg. *līquit*, Gk aor. λιπε̄ν (thematized, see 4.2.2)), subj. *léykʷ-e/o- → Gk pres. *λείκʷε/ο- >→ λείπε̄ν.

Both these aorist subjunctives also became presents in Germanic (cf. Goth. *kiusan* 'to test', *leiƕan* 'to lend'), but since Germanic abandoned the inherited contrast of aspects, as well as the contrast between indicative and subjunctive, that is not surprising (Ringe 2017: 182–6). In Greek it is surprising, because those contrasts have remained integral to the verb system (even in Modern Greek). A similar case is Hom., etc. στείχε̄ν 'to go, to march', which matches Goth. *steigan* 'to ascend', both probably reflecting an aorist subjunctive, since a nasal-suffixed present can be reconstructed from Vedic Skt pres. 3sg. *prá stiṅnoti* 'he makes progress' (*Maitrāyaṇī-Saṃhitā* 2.1.12) and OCS *postignǫti* 'to reach, to arrive at' (Ringe 2012: 129). Further examples, typically surviving along with zero-grade thematic aorists, are φεύγε̄ν 'to be trying to escape', τέρπεσθαι 'to enjoy oneself', and Hom. δέρκεσθαι 'to see' and κλέεσθαι 'to be renowned' (Ringe 2012: 127–8). Even Hom. πεύθεσθαι 'to find out', which matches not only Goth. *anabiudan* 'to command' but also Skt 3sg. *bódʰati* '(s)he observes', can reasonably be suspected of reflecting an aorist subjunctive; so can Hom. 3sg. πέλει, πέλεται 'it is' as well as Skt 3sg. *cárati* '(s)he wanders' and Lat. *colere* 'to cultivate', given that an affixed present to *kʷel- 'turn' actually survives in Hom. περι-τελλόμενος 'revolving' (Ringe, *loc. cit.*).[11] Such 'crossovers' between aspect and mood forms would be a bit less surprising if the categories in question were still derivational, rather than inflectional, for some time during the individual prehistory of Greek, and that is probably the conclusion that we should draw. But by the Proto-Greek period the attested inflectional system was fully in place, so far as we can tell; it is noteworthy

[11] Of course the original paradigm has undergone a lexical split, but that need not have happened until after the conditioned developments of labiovelars, after the Mycenaean period. It follows that the present stem πελε/ο- need not be an Aiolism; it could simply have been created to aor. πλε/ο- after *kʷ had become π before consonants.

that there seem to be no mismatches between present and aorist stems among the attested Greek dialects, for example.

Simple thematic presents with zero-grade roots that have stem-cognates in other branches are notoriously hard to find in any daughter of PIE; most reflect thematization of the zero-grade alternant of an athematic present. At least two Greek examples clearly reflect such a development (*LIV* s.vv. **gerbʰ*, **gleu̯bʰ*):

PIE *gérbʰ- ~ *gr̥bʰ- 'cut (into)' (cf. OE *ċeorfan* 'to cut', with full grade thematized) >→ Gk *γρ̥φέ/ó- > γράφε̄ν Hom. 'to scratch, to graze (with a weapon), to engrave', later 'to write';
PIE *gléwbʰ- ~ *glubʰ- 'carve' (cf. OE *clēofan* 'to split', Lat. *glūbere* 'to peel', both with full grade thematized) >→ Gk γλύφε̄ν.

A possible exception to the usual pattern is a present made to PIE *lewH- 'cut (a rope)', which appears in Greek as Hom. 3sg. λύει '(s)he unties, (s)he lets loose', etc. (mostly with ῠ) and in Latin as *(poenās) luere* 'to pay the penalty' (see *LIV* s.v. *leu̯H*). But a nasal-infixed present is also attested in Skt 3sg. *lunā́ti* '(s)he cuts off' (in the Brāhmaṇas), which because of its short *u* must be comparatively old; that raises the suspicion that the thematic present might reflect an inherited thematized aorist. There are a fair number of thematic presents of this type attested already in Homer; how many of them were inherited from Proto-Greek is necessarily uncertain.

4.2.1 (v) Presents in *-ye/o-

The final category of inherited presents exhibits the suffix *-ye/o-, both accented and unaccented; they are very numerous, and in Greek they have ramified into a range of different types with different histories and productivities. As I noted in 3.6.1, the heavy Sievers' Law variant of this suffix has been eliminated completely in Greek.[12]

Some basic PIE verbs constructed presents with full-grade roots and an unaccented suffix (to judge from the few examples in which evidence for the accent survives). Several such presents survived in Greek; clear examples with stem-cognates elsewhere include:

PIE *spéḱ-ye/o- 'look at, watch' (Old Lat. *specere*, 1sg. *speciō*; Skt 3sg. *páśyati* '(s)he sees') >→ *sképye/o- (with metathesis) > σκέπτεσθαι;
PIE *gʷʰédʰ-ye/o- 'ask for' (Goth. *bidjan*, Av. 1sg. *ǰaiδiieimi*) > θέσσεσθαι (Hesychios);
PIE *stél-ye/o- 'make ready' (OCS *posteljetŭ* '(s)he will spread out') > στέλλε̄ν 'to equip, to provide; to send' (*LIV* s.v. **stel*);

[12] For valuable extensive discussion of these stems, especially but not only in light of Sievers' Law, see Barber (2013: 217–375), especially the conclusions of pp. 363–4.

PIE *h_2arh_3- 'plow', pres. *$h_2$árye/o- (Middle Irish 3sg. *airid*) → *$h_2$ár$h_3$ye/o- (by leveling from related forms; cf. Lat. *arāre*) > *ἀροjε/ο- > ἀρõν.

Further likely examples include:

PIE *snéh_1-ye/o- 'twist, spin (thread)' (OIr. 3sg. *con·sní* '(s)he contends for', Lat. *nēre* 'to spin') > *νηjε/ο- > νῆν (but a root-present is also possible; so *LIV* s.v. **sneh₁*);
PIE *knáh_2-ye/o- 'scrape' (Lith. 3sg. *knója* '(s)he peels', OHG *nuoen* 'to plane, to smooth') > *κνᾱjε/ο- 'grate (cheese)' > ipf. 3sg. ἐπὶ ... κνῆ *Il.* 11.639, Att. inf. κνῆν;
PIE *plóh_3-ye/o- 'float' (OE *flōwan* 'to flow') > Ion. πλώε̄ν 'to sail';
PIE *srég-ye/o- 'color, dye' (Vedic Skt *rajyate* '(s)he blushes', *Atharvaveda*) > ῥέζε̄ν (Epicharmos fr. 106, but see the cautions of Barber 2013: 356–7).

Underived presents in accented *-yé/ó- with zero-grade roots may have been more numerous in PIE. Examples that survive in Greek with stem-cognates elsewhere include at least the following:

PIE *wr̥ǵ-yé/ó- 'be working, be making' (Goth. *waúrkjan*, Av. 3sg. *vərəziieiti*) > PGk *ϝρ̥ζε/ο- > Myc. 3sg. *wo-ze* */wórʤei/ vel sim., >→ *ϝέρσδεhεν (with ε leveled in from aor. *ϝέρξαι) > Hom. ἔρδειν (cf. Barber 2013: 355–6);[13]
PIE *nig^w-yé/ó- 'be washing' (OIr. 3sg. *nigid*, Thurneysen 1946: 119) > *νιγjε/ο- > νίζε̄ν;
PIE *kh_2p-ié/ó- 'be grabbing' (Lat. *capere* 'to take', OE *hebban* 'to lift') >→ *καπjε/ο- > κάπτε̄ν 'to gulp down';
PIE *$g^wh_2b^h$-ié/ó- 'be dipping in water' (ON *kvefja*) >→ *$γ^w$αφjε/ο- > βάπτε̄ν;
PIE pres. *g^wm̥-yé/ó- 'step (repeatedly), walk' (Lat. *venīre* 'to come') > *$γ^w$ą̥νjε/ο- > βαίνν 'to go';
PIE *mn̥yétor '(s)he is mentally active' → post-PIE *mn̥yétoy (Skt *mányate* '(s)he thinks') > *μą̥νjετοι >→ μαίνεται '(s)he is raving';
PIE *$h_2$tug-yé/ó- 'be terrified' (Skt *tujyáte* 'flees', *RV* I.84.17; cf. Hitt. *hatugis* 'frightful', Benveniste 1937) > Hom. ptc. ἀτυζόμενος 'scared witless, crazed';
PIE *dh_1-ié/ó- 'be tying' (Vedic Skt *dyati*, *Atharvaveda*) > *δέjεhεν > δε̄ν;
PIE *sr̥h_3-yé/ó- 'rush' vel sim. (Hitt. *sarhieddu* 'let him attack', *LIV* s.v. **serh₃*) > *hρωjε/ο- > Hom. ipf. 3pl. ῥώοντο 'they moved swiftly' *Il.* 18.411, 417.

There are other potential examples, but some can be suspected of reflecting parallel development; most notoriously, though the long ῡ of Att. φῡ́εσθαι 'to grow' suggests that it could reflect *b^huH-ye/o-, like Lat. *fierī* 'to become' and OIr. *biïd* 'it customarily is', it is much more likely to be a post-Homeric innovation based

[13] On the alternative present ῥέζε̄ν, see Barber, *loc. cit.*, with references.

on the inherited root-aorist (see Frisk s.v. φῦομαι, *LIV* s.v. *b^h*u̯eh*$_2$, n. 15).[14] The root-ablaut of some Greek presents in *-ye/o- is uncertain for various reasons. In at least one case the ambiguity is phonological:

PIE *$h_2$áws-ie/o- or *$h_2$us-yé/ó- 'to draw (water)' (probably either would yield Palaic 3pl. *hussīnta* and Lat. *haurīre*, the latter with hypercorrect or analogical *h*-) > Hom. subj. 3sg. αὔῃ '(lest) he have to fetch fire' *Od.* 5.490.

In some cases the reconstruction of the PIE root is uncertain. For instance, I adduced the following examples with full-grade roots in 3.6.3 above:

PIE *sál-ye/o- 'be jumping' (Lat. *salīre*) > ἅλλεσθαι;
PIE *k^wát-ye/o- (?) 'shake' (Lat. *quatere*) > πάσσε̄ν, Att. πάττε̄ν 'to sprinkle';

LIV s.vv. 1. **sel*, **(s)ku̯eh*$_1$*t* suggest alternative reconstructions, less straightforward (especially in the latter case) but not impossible, according to which these presents would have zero-grade roots.

In some cases the comparative facts suggest fairly strongly that a Greek present in *-ye/o- might not be original even if there seem to be stem-cognates in other languages. For instance, it is reasonable to posit

PIE *$\acute{g}^h$r̥yé/ó- (?) 'be pleased (with)' (Old Lat. 3sg. *horitur* '(s)he encourages, urges') > *χαρjε/ο- > χαίρε̄ν 'to rejoice, to be glad',

but there is also evidence for a full-grade present with the same suffix, namely

PIE *$\acute{g}^h$érye/o- (?; Skt 3sg. *háryati* '(s)he accepts gladly', Sabellian *herye- 'wish' in 3sg. subj. Oscan **heriiad**, fut. Umbrian *heriest*).

At least one must be an innovation, and both could be; the difference in ablaut actually suggests a root-present, though it is unclear why its reflexes have been suffixed with *-ye/o- in all the daughters rather than simply thematized. Another such case is

PIE *$h_1$rép-ye/o- (?) 'snatch' > Gk ἐρέπτεσθαι 'bite off, consume' but *h_1r̥p-yé/ó- (?) >→ Lat. *rapere* (see the notes at *LIV* s.v. **rep*, likewise noting the possibility of a root-present).

[14] That Gk τύπτε̄ν 'to beat' < *tup-yé/ó- is cognate with 3sg. Luvian *tūpīti*, Lycian *tubidi* (*LIV* s.v. **(s)teu̯p*) is doubtful; Melchert (1994a: 76, 242), etc., reconstructs the Proto-Anatolian stem as *(s)toubéye/o-, since the lenition of the 3sg. ending is best explained by unaccented vowels both preceding and following (p. 60).

A case of a somewhat different kind is

> PIE *klép-ye/o- 'be stealing' (?; Toch. B inf. *kälypītsi*; Hackstein 1995: 216–17) > κλέπτε̄ν, but
> PIE *klép-e/o- (?) > Old Lat. *clepere*, Goth. *hlifan*.

That Gothic exhibits a simple thematic present proves nothing, since that language has remodeled even some j-presents that survive elsewhere in Germanic (*sitan*, *ligan*, *swaran* in place of *sitjaną 'to sit', *ligjaną 'to lie', *swarjaną 'to swear'), but the Old Latin simple thematic present is less likely to be a secondary development; once again remodeling of a root-present should at least be considered (see also Hackstein 1995: 216–17, Barber 2013: 358). A similar case is

> PIE *wert- 'turn', pres. usually *wért-e/o- (3sg. Skt *vártate*, Lat. *vertitur*; Goth. *waírþan* 'to become'), but *wért-ye/o- > ἔρρε̄ν 'to go away (badly / to a bad place)' (Forssman 1980: 186–98).

These last two cases suggest that Greek might have remodeled some simple thematic presents as presents in *-ye/o- (*LIV* s.vv. **klep*, **u̯ert*; see also Barber 2013: 359–60). Possibly the strongest argument in favor of such a hypothesis is

> PIE *pek^{w}- 'cook, ripen', pres. usually *pék^{w}-e/o- (Lat. *coquere*, 3sg. Skt *pácati*, OCS *pečetŭ*, Lith. *kẽpa*, the last two '(s)he bakes'), but *pék^{w}-ye/o- > πέσσε̄ν, Att. πέττε̄ν.

The latter appears to be cognate with Vedic derived intransitive *pácyate* 'it ripens', but since the Greek verb is transitive (in the active) its stem formation is more likely a Greek innovation (as suggested cautiously by Hackstein 1995: 89).

Greek definitely did remodel some athematic root-presents by adding the suffix *-ye/o-. Clear examples include:

> PIE *g^{wh}én- ~ *g^{wh}n̥- 'hit, kill' (3sg. Hitt. *kuēnzi*, Skt *hánti*) >→ *χ^{w}εν-jε/o- > Hom. θεινέμεναι 'to smite' (ει = ε̄);[15]
> PIE *wémh$_1$- ~ *wm̥h$_1$- 'vomit' (Skt 3sg. *vámiti*) >→ *ϝεμε-jε/o- > ἐμε̄ν;
> PIE *séwH- ~ *suH- 'rain' (Toch. B 3sg. *suwaṃ*) >→ *hῡ-jε/o- > ὕ̄ε̄ν (*H = *h$_2$ if Hitt. hi-conjugation *suhha-* 'pour out' is related).

The productive function of accented *-yé/ó- in PIE was the formation of derived presents from nouns and adjectives. Precisely because of its productivity, most

[15] A sparsely attested thematic stem θενε/ο- seems to have been construed as an aorist by Greek poets (e.g. θενών 'smiting', Pindar *Olympian* 7.28). That could reflect another 'aspect crossover' like pres. λείπε̄ν, and if that is what happened the present could have been formed to the aorist by suffixation; but we do not really have enough evidence to say for certain what happened.

examples attested in the daughters are innovations, but at least two Greek examples were almost certainly inherited:

PIE *h_1n̥$h_3$mn̥-yé/ó- 'name' (Goth. *namnjan*, OE *nemnan*) >→ *ὀνομα̥ν-jε/ο- > ὀνομαίνε̄ν 'to name';
PIE *h_2ḱ-$h_2$ows-ié/ó- 'be sharp-eared' (Goth. *hausjan*, OE *hīeran*, both 'to hear') > *akowsié/ó- >→ *ἀκοϝhjε/ο- > ἀκούε̄ν 'to hear'.

The former has plausible external cognates and was evidently derived before -τ- was introduced into the paradigm of ὄνομα; the latter is semantically opaque and therefore synchronically underived both in Greek and in Germanic. Also likely to have been inherited is

Att. βλίττε̄ν 'to harvest honey' < *mlit-yé/ó-, formed to the zero grade of μέλι, μέλιτ- 'honey' < PIE *mélit- (cf. Hitt. *milit*, Luvian *mallit*, Goth. (thematized) *miliþ*);

the ablaut of the verb's base is an unparalleled archaism. Other apparent stem-cognates are more likely to be parallel innovations. For example, the participles Vedic Skt *sumanasyámānas* (five times in the Rigveda) and pl. εὐμενέοντες (Pindar *Pythian* IV.127), though both meaning 'well disposed, wishing ... well' and potentially reflecting an inherited *$h_1$su-menes-yé/ó-, are almost certainly parallel formations, as is suggested both by the morphology (middle in Sanskrit, active in Greek) and the syntax (intransitive in Sanskrit, transitive in Greek); also likely to be parallel formations are Vedic Skt ptc. du. *vasnayántā* 'bargaining' (*RV* VI.47.21) and ὠνε̄σθαι 'to bargain for, to buy' (subj. 2sg. ὠνῆι Hesiod *Works and Days* 341) in spite of the fact that their earliest attestations are more or less synonymous.

Some other denominatives must be at least comparatively early formations. Two others in -αινε/ο- were made to inherited neuter nouns in *-n̥- before the spread of -τ- through that class (cf. Barber 2013: 295):

Hom. (*)πε̄ραίνε̄ν 'to fasten (a rope); to finish',[16] Att. περαίνε̄ν 'to complete, to finish' < *περϝν̥-jε/ο- ← *πέρϝαρ, *πέρϝν̥- (Hom. πε̄ραρ 'cord', pl. πε̄ρατα also 'ends, limits') ←< PIE *pérwr̥, *pr̥wén- 'end of a rope' >→ Vedic Skt *párus*[17] (*RV* X.100.5), *párvan-* 'node, joint';
Hom., Att.-Ion. σημαίνε̄ν 'to give a sign, to indicate' ← σῆμα, non-Att.-Ion. σᾶμα 'sign' < PIE *d^hyá$h_2$mn̥ > Skt *d^hyā́ma* 'thought' (?, Brugmann apud Frisk s.v. σῆμα; the meaning of the protoform is no longer recoverable with certainty).

[16] Actually attested are aor. ptc. du. πειρήναντε 'having fastened' *Od.* 22.175, 192 and perf. pass. 3sg. πεπείρανται '(these things) are past and gone' *Od.* 12.37, but since those stems are later formations based on the present, the inference of a present in -αίνε̄ν is not doubtful.

[17] *párur was reinterpreted as /párus-/ because /r/ and /s/ have the same phonetic realizations in many sandhi environments, whence *páruṣ-* half a dozen times in the Rigveda.

Especially striking is μιαίνε̄ν 'to stain, to bloody, to defile', derivationally related to adj. μιαρός 'stained, bloodied, defiled'. The alternation between -αρ- and -αν- is reminiscent of PIE r/n-stems like *pérwr̥, yet no related noun is attested and there are no convincing external cognates. Speculation about the origin of this derivational pair seems unprofitable, but it is probably old. Similar is Hom. κῡδαίνε̄ν 'to glorify', cf. κῡδρός 'glorious', κῦδος 'glory', κῡδι- 'glorifying', but in this case we have a whole set of derivatives obviously belonging to the inherited Caland system, regardless of the root's exact etymology (see Frisk s.v. κῦδος).

In light of examples like the last two, Schwyzer (1939: 725) suggests that denominative presents in which the thematic vowel *-o- seems to have been deleted before the addition of *-yé/ó- (see below) actually reflect a more complex development: both denominative presents and thematic adjectives were formed to athematic nouns, typically in *-l-, *-r-, or *-n-; then the nouns were lost, so that the presents appeared to have been formed directly to the thematic adjectives; finally that pattern was generalized to other thematic adjectives. What is awkward about this scenario is that only the innovative examples survive; not a single word-family that actually illustrates the whole development can be cited. It seems reasonable to propose an alternative. In Vedic, denominative presents to thematic nominals normally end in *-a-yá-*, just as the corresponding Greek class normally end in -ε-ε/ο-; but there are a few in which the nominal thematic vowel is dropped (see e.g. Macdonell 1910: 399–400). Since the thematic vowel is normally dropped before the adjective suffix *-yo- ~ *-io- (cf. e.g. ἵππος: ἵππιος), it seems possible that it was originally dropped also before the denominative suffix (so Barber 2013: 297). Probably none of the attested examples is inherited (there seem to be no Greek–Sanskrit cognate pairs), but this group of denominatives is likely to be older, on the average, than the much larger class in which the thematic vowel of the nominal is not dropped. Stems attested in Homer include, e.g.:

Hom. ἐχθαίρε̄ν 'to hate' < *ἐχθρ̥-jε/ο- ← ἐχθρός 'hated';
καθαίρε̄ν 'to cleanse' < *καθαρ-jε/ο- ← καθαρός 'clean';
ῑ̔μέ̄ρε̄ν 'to desire' < *ῑ̔μερ-jε/ο- ← ῑ̔́μερος 'desire' (Barber 2013: 297 n. 3, 369 with references);
ποικίλλε̄ν 'to make variegated, to embroider' (ποίκιλλε 'he depicted', *Il.* 18.590) < *ποικιλ-jε/ο- ← ποικίλος 'many-colored';
ἀγγέλλε̄ν 'to deliver a message, to announce' ← ἄγγελος 'messenger';
φαρμάσσε̄ν, Att. φαρμάττε̄ν 'to cure' (φαρμάσσων 'tempering (metal)' *Od.* 9.393) < *φαρμακ-jε/ο- ← φάρμακον 'drug, cure';
Hom. χαλέπτει 'is angry with' *Od.* 4.423 < *χαλεπ-jε/ο- ← χαλεπός 'difficult, hard to bear, hard to deal with'.

Since ἄγγελος is clearly a loanword, this way of forming denominatives from thematic nominals must have been a productive option well down into the separate prehistory of Greek.

Denominatives formed from consonant-stem nominals are numerous. Those formed from n-stems and r-stems typically exhibit zero-grade *-αν- < *-n̥- and *-αρ- < *-r̥- before the denominative suffix (Barber 2013: 295), which is probably an archaism, but otherwise the bases do not ablaut. Stems attested early include, e.g.:

ποιμαίνε̄ν 'to pasture, to tend (sheep)' < *ποιμν̥-jε/ο- ← ποιμήν 'shepherd';
εὐφραίνε̄ν 'to gladden' ← ἐΰφρων 'cheerful';
(*)τεκταίνεσθαι 'to make (of wood)'[18] ← τέκτων 'carpenter, joiner';
τεκμαίρεσθαι 'to indicate, to foretell, to decree' < *τεκμρ̥-jε/ο- ← τέκμωρ 'sign, goal, solution (of a problem)';
Hom. ipf. 3sg. μελαίνετο 'it became black'< *μελαν-jε/ο- ← μέλᾱς, μέλαν- 'black';
Hom. κορύσσε̄ν 'to put a helmet on (someone), to equip' < *κορυθ-jε/ο- ← κόρυς, κόρυθ- 'helmet';
φυλάσσε̄ν, Att. φυλάττε̄ν 'to guard' < *φυλακ-jε/ο- ← φύλαξ, φύλακ- 'guard';
κηρῡ́σσε̄ν, Att. κηρῡ́ττε̄ν 'to proclaim' ← κῆρυξ, κήρῡκ- 'herald';
Hom. ἀνασσέμεν 'to be lord, to rule' < *ἀνακ(τ)-jε/ο- ← ἄναξ, ἄνακτ- 'lord';
Hom. ἱμάσσε̄ν 'to whip' < *ἱματ-jε/ο-, apparently with zero grade of ἱμᾱ́ς, ἱμάντ- 'thong' (Barber 2013: 296 with n. 2);
Hom. (*)πεμπάζεσθαι 'to count (on one's fingers)'[19] < *πεμπαδ-jε/ο- ← πεμπάς, πεμπάδ- 'group of five';
ἐρίζε̄ν 'to quarrel' < *ἐριδ-jε/ο- ← ἔρις, ἔριδ- 'strife';
ἁρπάζε̄ν 'to snatch, to rob' < *ἁρπαγ-jε/ο- ← ἅρπαξ, ἅρπαγ- 'unlawful taking', Hesiod *Works and Days* 356.

Denominatives made to s-stems introduce a further complication. Beside the forms in -ε-ε/ο- that are normal throughout Greek, Homer has competing forms in -ει-ε/ο-. For instance, we find ipf. 3pl. ἐτέλειον 'they fulfilled, they completed' (*Il.* twice) ~ τέλεον 'they completed' (*Il.* twice) < *τελεh-jε/ο- ← τέλος, τέλε- < *τέλεh- 'end'. This looks like a further instance of the phenomenon observed in gen. sg. -οιο ~ -ō < *-οο (see 3.5.1), but it cannot be: there was a clear morpheme boundary before the *-j-, yet the majority outcome looks like the outcome of *-hj- with no morpheme boundary. It is much more likely that alternants like τελε-ε/ο-, with no ι, were backformed to aorists like τελέσσαι, on which, see 4.2.2 (iii) below. If γελᾶν 'to laugh' ultimately reflects *γελαh-jε/ο- (as seems possible, considering that most of its derivatives exhibit -σ-), it must have undergone a similar development; but in the absence of stem-cognates its prehistory is necessarily uncertain. A more certain case with yet another vowel is ἱδρῶν 'to sweat' (ptc.

[18] Securely inferred from aor. 3sg. τεκτήνατο *Il.* 5.62, etc.
[19] Securely inferred from aor. subj. 3sg. πεμπάσσεται '(when) he has counted'; *Od.* 4.412.

ἱδρώων already in Homer), plausibly derived from an s-stem ἱδρώς (Frisk s.v.; see especially Chantraine 1973: 54).[20]

In the absence of stem-cognates elsewhere, we cannot be certain that any specific denominative present made to a consonant stem was already in existence in Proto-Greek, though all the types attested in Homer very likely reflect Proto-Greek formations.

A stem which might or might not be denominative is

Hom. ἐρεσσέμεναι 'to row' < *ἐρετ-jε/ο-, cf. ἐρετμόν 'oar';

the related noun suggests a verb root *ἐρετ-, but potential cognates exhibit no *-t- (cf. *LIV* s.v. 2. *$h_1$reh$_1$*), nor does ἐρέτης 'rower' with suffix *-τᾱ-. If the suffix of this noun were simply *-τ- at an earlier stage of the language, the verb could be an unremarkable denominative; that would obviate the objection of Barber (2013: 248 n. 63) that a denominative deleting *-ᾱ- is without parallel. In that case this would be another very early denominative.

Denominative presents made to nominals ending in vowels in which the vowel is not deleted are very common in Greek. One large class is in *-ε-jε/ο- derived from thematic nominals; Homeric examples include:

φιλέε̄ν 'to love, to treat kindly' < *φιλε-jε/ο- ← φίλος 'one's own, dear, beloved';
νοε̄ν 'to perceive, to think' ← νόος 'mind';
μῡθε̄σθαι 'to speak, to tell' ← μῦθος 'talk, speech';
αἰνε̄ν 'to tell, to praise' ← αἶνος 'story, praise';
ἀρῑθμε̄ν 'to count' ← ἀρῑθμός 'number';
χωρε̄ν 'to give ground, to make way' ← χῶρος 'ground, place';
ipf. 3pl. διεμέτρεον 'they measured out' *Il.* 3.315 ← μέτρον 'measure';
ipf. 3pl. ὤπλεον 'they got (the wagon) ready' *Od.* 6.73 ← ὅπλα 'gear, harness';
αἰτε̄ν 'to ask (for)' ← *αἰτο- 'portion, share' ← αἴνυσθαι 'to take' (Frisk s.v. αἰνέω).

In the absence of external cognates no single example can be reconstructed securely for Proto-Greek, but the type is certainly inherited, since *-ε-jε/ο- corresponds perfectly to Vedic Skt *-a-yá/á̄-* < PIE *-e-yé/ó- (note the absence of lengthening by Brugmann's Law before the *y, showing that the PIE vowel was not *o).

Another large class is in *-α-jε/ο-. These must originally have been denominatives of noun stems in long *-ᾱ-, but for the most part the *α of the verb stems is short, apparently by analogy with the class in *-ε-jε/ο- (whereas in the aorist

[20] Att. ῥῑγῶν 'to shiver' was almost certainly modeled on ἱδρῶν (Frisk s.v. ῥῖγος). Whether any of the Homeric present-stem forms in γελω-ε/ο- are denominative from γέλως is difficult to say; see Chantraine (1973: 365–6) for discussion.

the analogy worked in the opposite direction—see 4.2.2 (iii) below). That shortening had not yet occurred in Proto-Greek, since forms with preserved ᾱ are attested or inferrable for several dialects (Meister 1921: 90). Homeric examples include:

> τῑμᾶν 'to honor' < *τῑμα-jε/ο- ← τῑμᾱ́ (> Att.-Ion. τῑμή) 'honor';
> βοᾶν 'to shout' ← βοᾱ́ (βοή) 'shout';
> βιᾶσθαι 'to overpower' ← βίᾱ (Ion. βίη) 'strength, force';
> iptv. 2sg. αὔδᾱ 'speak!' ← αὐδᾱ́ (αὐδή) 'voice'.

This formation too must be inherited, since it reappears in Vedic (cf. Macdonell 1910: 400), in Germanic class II weak verbs, and in the Latin first conjugation, though in all those languages the *ā is not shortened. At least one derived verb in -ᾶν has a different origin, and it is the only one which has clear external cognates (Watkins apud Tucker 1981: 20):

> PIE *néwo- 'new' (cf. Hitt. *nēwas*, Lat. *novos*; Gk νέος 'young') → *néwa-h_2- 'make new, renew' (Hitt. 3sg. *newahhi*; Lat. *novāre* 'to renew; to plow fallow ground) >→ νεᾶν 'to plow fallow ground'.

The derived meaning shared with the Latin word shows that this verb is inherited. Though it looks exactly like a denominative in *-α-jε/ο-, it does not fit the usual pattern of derivation at all: it is a factitive derived from a thematic adjective, exactly like the Hittite hi-conjugation verb. How it acquired its attested shape in Greek does not seem to be recoverable in any detail, but in some form or other it must have been present in Proto-Greek.

The origins of the third group of 'contract presents', in *-ο-jε/ο-, are more complex and in part disputed. The most important study of these stems is Tucker (1981), whose discussion of this class of presents and their associated stems can be summarized as follows. There are two derivational types in Homer. One is derived from nouns and is instrumental in meaning, while the other is derived from adjectives and is factitive (Tucker 1981: 16 with references). To the former the attested presents derived from o-stems are χολῶσθαι 'be angry' (twice in *Il.* 8; χόλος 'anger'), ῥυπόω 'I am dirty' (twice in the *Odyssey*; pl. ῥύπα 'dirt'), θεειοῦται *Od.* 23.50 'he fumigates' (θέειον 'sulfur'), iptv. κάκου *Od.* 4.754 'afflict' (nt. κακόν 'evil'), and from nouns of other types γο̄νοῦσθαι 'clasp the knees of, implore' (γοῦνα 'knees'), κορυφοῦται *Il.* 4.426 'it is crested' (κορυφή 'crest'), and παχνοῦται *Il.* 17.112 'is chilled' (πάχνη 'hoarfrost'). Mediopassive perfects are surprisingly common in this group of verbs in Homer and appear to be attested even in Mycenaean. Since there is no comparable formation in other IE languages, Tucker suggests plausibly that the perfects are actually the oldest members of these paradigms and are Greek innovations on which the rest of the paradigm was subsequently built (Tucker 1981: 16–17). We will return to them in 4.2.3 (ii) below.

By contrast, the factitives never have perfects in Homer, and there are even fewer present stems attested, namely σαῶν 'to save' (*σάος 'safe'), γυμνοῦσθαι *Od.* 6.222 'to strip' (γυμνός 'naked), and probably δηϊόων 'cutting down, slaying' (δήϊος 'hostile' or the like; Tucker 1981: 31 fn. 7). Tucker therefore accepts the widespread view that these too are Greek innovations (pp. 15, 30 fn. 4) and suggests a fairly complex scenario by which they might have developed from the inherited type of νεᾶν (pp. 19–22). However, Dishington has made a persuasive case that the Gothic factitives of the third weak class are cognate with the Greek factitives in *-o-jε/o- (Dishington 1976; see Ringe 2017: 204–5 on the phonology), and Melchert (1997a: 136–7) suggests that a class of Anatolian denominatives might also be cognate.[21] It therefore seems likely that Greek inherited a class of factitive presents in *-o-yé/ó- as well. If that is true, we need to account for the rarity of such presents in Homer; but that is not necessarily a challenge. Even counting their sigmatic stems in -ωσ- and their perfects, this is by far the smallest of the 'contract' classes in Homer; moreover, the fact that a large proportion of the epics is third-person narrative militates against the appearance of present stems, even though Homer does not hesitate to use imperfects instead of aorists when it is metrically convenient. Thus the small number of factitive stems in *-o-jε/o- is plausibly a statistical accident.

Two Attic-Ionic denominatives consistently exhibit a long *ᾱ before the original suffix; in Attic they appear as πεινῆν 'to be hungry' and διψῆν 'to be thirsty'. Both exhibit a long vowel in Homer as well (πεινάων *Il.* thrice, πεινήμεναι *Od.* 20.137; διψάων *Od.* 11.584). It seems possible that these two stems, which must have been learned early and form an obvious semantic pair, simply failed to undergo the analogical shortening that affected most α-contract presents. There are several more such stems in Homer, but as the syllable before their unexpected long vowel is always heavy, we have to reckon with the possibility that these forms have been adjusted to fit the meter (cf. Risch 1974: 322); another possibility is that they are Aiolisms, as suggested by the obviously non-Ionic participles in -ᾱ́ων (Meister 1921: 89).

Denominatives from most other types of vowel stems, such as Hom. μηνίε̄ν 'be angry, rage' (μῆνις 'anger') and κορθύεται *Il.* 9.7 '(the wave) rolls itself up' (κόρθυς 'sheaf' *vel sim.*) are uncommon and unimportant, with one exception: presents in -εύε̄ν, at first derived from nouns in -εύς. (See 4.3.3 *ad fin.* for discussion of this suffix.) The phonology of the denominative presents requires some

[21] However, Vedic presents in *-ā-yá/á-* derived from o-stems, which could reflect *-o-yé/ó- with lengthening of *o by Brugmann's Law, do not seem to be connected with these formations; note especially that most examples are clearly not factitives derived from adjectives, a large number actually being statives (Macdonell 1910: 399).

discussion. The noun suffix was originally *-ηϝ-, as is demonstrated by Homeric βασιλή-, the stem before vocalic endings without exception; the short diphthong of the nom. sg. and the dat. pl. reflects the working of Osthoff's Law, operating either as a regular sound change (see 3.5.3) or as a phonological rule before it was lost. The derived present stem must therefore originally have ended in *-ηϝ-jε/o-, which by OL yielded *-εϝ-jε/o-. The outcome of this sequence by regular sound change seems to have been -εjjε/o- (see 5.2.2), and that is what we find in Elean, a West Greek dialect; for instance, *DGE* 424, a 4th-century inscription, attests (l. 1) φυγαδείην = φυγαδεύε̄ν 'to exile, to banish' and (l. 5, with lowering of ε to α after ρ) κατιαραίων = καθιερεύων, usually 'dedicating' but in Elean apparently 'informing' or 'bringing a charge' (see Buck 1955: 125, 262–3). In other dialects (so far as we have evidence) -ευ- has been leveled into the present stem from the aorist. Homeric examples clearly derived from nouns in -εύς include:

βασιλεύε̄ν 'be king, rule' ← βασιλεύς 'king';
ἱερεύε̄ν 'sacrifice' ← ἱερεύς 'priest';
χάλκευον *Il.* 18.400 'I forged' ← χαλκεύς 'smith'.

But already in Homer's time presents in -εύε̄ν had been derived from nouns of other stem classes, e.g. ἀγορεύε̄ν 'make a speech' ← ἀγορή 'assembly'. Though the phonology of the Elean examples at least suggests that the first presents in *-ηϝ-jε/o- might date back to Proto-Greek, it is impossible to say how early any of the various extensions of the formation occurred, given that most or all Greek dialects remained in contact and could have borrowed innovations from one another.

Greek has created a considerable number of further denominative present suffixes by resegmentation, of which the most important are -ιζε/o-, -αζε/o-, -αινε/o-, and -ῡνε/o-, all with reflexes of *-ye/o-. So far as I can see, none of them can be projected back into Proto-Greek with any confidence.

There are also deverbative presents in *-Vye/o-, at least one class of which was inherited. In Indo-Iranian and Germanic a type of present with an o-grade root and suffix *-éye/o- is well represented, and relics occur in other IE languages, including Greek. Some are causative in meaning, while others appear to be iterative. About half a dozen Greek examples have certain or probable stem-cognates in other IE languages:

PIE *doḱéye/o- 'cause to accept, make acceptable' (Lat. *docēre* 'to teach') > δοκε̄ν 'to seem good' (root *deḱ-, cf. Ion. δέκεσθαι);
PIE *spoḱéye/o- 'keep looking, look intently' (Skt mp. iptv. 2sg. *spāśáyasva* 'spy out, detect' *RV* I.176.3) >→ σκοπε̄ν 'to look at, to examine' (root *speḱ-, cf. σκέπτεσθαι, Skt 3sg. *páśyati* '(s)he sees');
PIE *woǵʰéye/o- 'cause to convey' (Skt 3sg. *vāháyati*) > Hom. ὀχέεσθαι 'to drive (horses)' *Il.* 10.403, 17.77;

PIE *krotéye/o- 'keep shaking, rattle' (OCS *krotiti* 'to break (a horse)') > Hom. ptc. κροτέοντες *Il.* 15.453 (root *kret-, cf. OHG *redan* 'to sift');
PIE *kowh₁éye/o- 'pay close attention' (Lat. *cavēre*[22] 'take care, beware') > 2sg. κοεῖς 'you notice' Anakreon 360.2 (*LIV* s.v. **(s)keu̯h₁*);
PIE *worséye/o- 'make it rain' (Skt 3sg. *varṣáyati*) > ὀρε̃ν 'to urinate' (*LIV* s.v. **h₂u̯ers*);
PIE *srobʰéye/o- 'keep slurping/drinking' (Lat. *sorbēre* with analogical zero grade of the root, see *LIV* s.v. **srebʰ*) > ῥοφε̃ν.

It can be seen that these stems are more or less isolated derivationally in attested Greek, and that some have undergone shifts in meaning; they are relics, not the results of a derivational process that is still productive. It follows that even examples without external stem-cognates must be relatively old, though of course we cannot assert that any individual example already existed in Proto-Greek. Other such stems made to clearly inherited roots include the following. Two were originally causatives:

φοβε̃ν 'to frighten' ← Hom. 'to put to flight' ← φέβεσθαι 'to flee', root *bʰegʷ- 'run away' (cf. Lith. 3sg. *bėga* '(s)he runs');
σοβε̃ν 'to scare away (birds)' ← Hom. 2pl. σέβεσθε 'you feel shame' *Il.* 4.242 ← *'yield, give way', root *tyegʷ- (cf. Skt *tyajati* '(s)he abandons').

Most, however, including less certain examples not adduced here, were iteratives:

φορε̃ν 'to carry customarily, to wear' ← φέρε̄ν 'to carry', root *bʰer- (see 4.2.1 (iv); the apparent stem-cognate Av. *bāraiia-* is causative rather than iterative);
τρομε̃ν 'to tremble' ← τρέμε̄ν, root *trem- (see 4.2.1 (iv));
Hom. τροπε̃ν 'to turn' ← τρέπε̄ν, root *trep- (see 4.2.1 (iv));
Hom. ὀχέων 'enduring', ὀχέεσκον 'I used to endure' *Od.* 11.619[23] ← ἔχε̄ν 'to hold', root *segʰ- (see 4.2.1 (iv));
Hom. ὑποκλοπέοιτο '(whether anyone) was lurking' *Od.* 22.382 ← κλέπτε̄ν 'to steal, to do in secret', root *klep- (see above);
ποθε̃ν 'to long for' ← *'to keep asking for' < *gʷʰodʰéye/o-, root *gʷʰedʰ- (see the beginning of this section).

[22] With *av* < pretonic *ow at a very early date, cf. Vine (2006).

[23] Considering that this stem is iterative, it seems reasonable to translate *Od.* 1.296–7

οὐδέ τί σε χρὴ
νηπιάας ὀχέειν, ἐπεὶ οὐκέτι τηλίκος ἐσσί.

as 'and you don't need to keep hanging on to childish ways, since you're not that age any more' (cf. W. H. D. Rouse's translation 'you ought not to play about in the nursery any longer').

One is attested in both functions:

epic ptc. πυρ-πολέοντας 'tending the fires' *Od.* 10.30, inf. πολεῖν 'to plow' Hesiod *Works and Days* 462 < *kʷoléye/o-, causative of *kʷel- 'turn';
Att. poet. πολε̃ν 'to go all over (a place)' < *kʷoléye/o-, iterative of *kʷel-.

Several other, roughly similar formations are also attested in Greek. A formation with long *ō in the root and a suffix *-ie/o- might be of PIE date; a possible example is Lat. *sōpīre* 'to put to sleep' (though see Weiss 2016 for counterarguments). But examples are few and scattered: *LIV* lists only twenty-five for the whole family, of which thirteen are marked as uncertain to one degree or another, and most are securely attested in only one subgroup. In Greek the few clear examples have adopted the suffix *-éye/o- of the short-vowel type:

Hom. πωλε̃σθαι 'to go around, to go frequently', iterative of *kʷel- 'turn';
ὠθε̃ν 'to push', iterative of *wedʰh_1- (cf. Skt aor. *ávadʰīt* '(s)he has killed');
πωλε̃ν 'to sell' must also belong here (so Frisk s.v. πωλέω), though no good root-cognate can be cited.

There are a handful of examples in *-αϳε/o-, and their origin is still more uncertain. The presents ποτᾶσθαι and πωτᾶσθαι, both 'to fly around' and both attested in Homer, offer support for the hypothesis that their root ended in the second laryngeal in PIE, since they can be regular reflexes of *poth$_2$áye/o- (with underlying /é/) and *pṓth$_2$ie/o- (so *LIV* s.v. **peth$_2$*); but ποτε̃σθαι, with no reflex of a laryngeal, is Homeric too. Moreover, plausible evidence for the laryngeal is confined to Greek (Hackstein 2002a: 140); for instance, note that the Skt root is *pat-*, not the '*patʰ-*' that would be expected if it had been laryngeal-final. There are also examples of deverbatives with e-grade roots; the full range of types is laid out in Schwyzer (1939: 717–20). The antiquity of these formations is unclear to me.

4.2.2 The development of aorist stems

4.2.2 (i) Root-aorists

Ancient Greek had fewer types of aorist stems; most have at least occasional stem-cognates in other IE languages, though all have undergone important developments within the separate prehistory of Greek.

Root-aorists are already an unproductive relic type in Homer, but the epics attest more stems than later Greek documents do. Many have unproblematic stem-cognates in other IE languages and were clearly inherited:

PIE *g^{w}áh$_2$- ~ *g^{w}h$_2$- 'step' (Skt 3sg. *ágāt*) > Dor. 3sg. ἔβᾱ, Hom. 3sg. ἔβη, βῆ, 2du. βάτην, 3pl. ἔβαν, βάν < *g^{w}h$_2$ánd (PIE 3pl. *-énd with laryngeal coloring);

PIE *stáh$_2$- ~ *sth$_2$- 'stand up' (Skt 3sg. *ást^{h}āt*) > Dor. 3sg. ἔστᾱ, Hom. 3sg. ἔστη, στῆ, 3pl. ἔσταν, στάν;

PIE *b^{h}úH- 'become' (Skt 3sg. *áb^{h}ūt*) > 3sg. ἔφῡ;

PIE *dráh$_2$- ~ *dr̥h$_2$- 'run' (Skt iptv. 3sg. *drā́tu*) > Att. 3sg. ἀπ-έδρᾱ '(s)he ran away', cf. Hom. ptc. ἀποδρᾱ́ς;

PIE *ǵnóh$_3$- ~ *ǵn̥h$_3$- 'recognize' (Lat. pf. 3sg. *nōvit* '(s)he knows (someone)') > 3sg. ἔγνω;

PIE *d^{h}g^{wh}éy- ~ *d^{h}g^{wh}i- 'perish' (Skt iptv. 2sg. *kṣid^{h}í* 'destroy!' *Samaveda* 1.336; see *LIV* s.v. **d^{h}g^{uh}ei̯*) > Hom. mp. 3sg. ἔφθιτο;

PIE *ḱléw- ~ *ḱlu- 'hear' (Skt iptv. 2sg. *śrud^{h}í*) > Hom. iptv. 2sg. *κλύθι (always line-initial, hence written κλῦθι);

PIE *léwH- ~ *luH- 'untie, release' (Lat. pf. 3sg. *luit* '(s)he atoned for') → *lu- by resegmentation in Hom. mp. 3sg. λύτο 'gave way, broke up' (λῦτο *Il.* 24.1 by the same process as κλῦθι, see above);

PIE *k^{w}réyh$_2$- ~ *k^{w}rih$_2$- 'buy' (Toch. B pret. 1pl. *käryāmtte* 'we bought') > Hom. 3sg. πρίατο;

PIE *pléh$_1$- ~ *pl̥h$_1$- 'fill' (Lat. pf. 3sg. *implēvit*) > Hom. mp. 3sg. πλῆτο 'it was filled'.

Note that in the last stem Hom. πλη- can reflect zero-grade *pl̥h$_1$- (and probably does, since the stem is mediopassive); in fact regular sound change made the full grade and zero grade of the root identical, and the same is true of γνω- and δρᾱ-. That might have contributed to the leveling which has affected βᾱ- and στᾱ-, in which most dual and plural forms exhibit a full-grade root instead of the expected zero grade even in Homer; the fact that φῡ- had never exhibited ablaut might also have been a contributing factor. In one root an inherited zero grade has been generalized:

PIE *télh$_2$- ~ *tl̥h$_2$- 'lift' (Old Lat. subj. 3sg. *attulat*) > *τελα- (cf. Hom. τελαμών 'shield-strap') ~ τλᾱ-, the latter in 1sg. ἔτλᾱν 'I have endured', Pindar *Isthmian* VII.37, and in Hom. 3sg. ἔτλη, τλῆ, etc., to which 3pl. ἔτλαν (*Il.* 21.608) was formed by rule.

Homer also preserves a number of inherited consonant-final root-aorists:[24]

*h$_3$ór- ~ *h$_3$r̥- 'rise' (Skt 3sg. *prá ārta* 'it came forth' *RV* IV.1.12, Av. iptv. 2sg. *uz-ārəšuua* 'arise!') > Hom. 3sg. ὦρτο 'it arose' (augmented);

[24] But ἐλέγμην 'I was counted' *Od.* 9.335, λέκτο 'he counted' *Od.* 4.451 could be archaic s-aorists with *-s- lost by sound change between consonants (Harðarson 1993: 205); so far as I can see, the same could be true of κατέπηκτο 'it stuck (in the ground)' *Il.* 11.378. On δέκτο, see fn. 1 above.

*ár- ~ *r̥- 'fit' (Skt 3pl. *sám aranta* 'they met' *RV* VII.25.1, thematized; cf. Hitt. *natta āra* 'it isn't right/fitting') > Hom. ptc. ἄρμενος 'fitting';
*sál- ~ *sl̥- 'leap' (Skt 3sg. *ásarat* 'it flowed', thematized (?)) > *hαλ- > Hom. 3sg. ἆλτο (Aiolic?; see Chantraine 1973: 482), ptc. ἐπι-άλμενος.

Two such stems require some discussion. For PIE *legʰ- 'lie down' *LIV* reconstructs a simple thematic present, but the root was eventive (the corresponding stative was *ḱey-) and should therefore have had an unaffixed aorist. It should follow that Hom. aor. 3sg. λέκτο '(s)he lay down' is inherited, even though the only stem-cognate is OCS 3sg. *-leže* (thematized); Hesykhios' λέχεται· κοιμᾶται must be an innovation, not necessarily an early one. For Hom. aor. 3sg. μίκτο 'he mingled' (intrans.) there are no external stem-cognates, but the fact that a present in *-ḱé/ó- is reconstructable for PIE and actually survives in Greek (see 4.2.1 (iii)) suggests that this affixless aorist is also inherited. An athematic form attested only in Attic and Cyprian[25] that must nevertheless be old is iptv. 3sg. πῖθι 'have a drink!'; otherwise the aorist has been thematized as πιε̄ν.

A couple of Homeric root-aorists are more questionable. Since the Homeric present σεύεσθαι 'to rush, to hurry' has no stem-cognates, we might expect the aorist ἔσσυτο to be the inherited member of the paradigm. But I have argued elsewhere that it is only the sparsely attested root-present σεῦται 'is hurrying' (Sophokles *Trakhiniai* 645) that has an indisputable stem-cognate in Vedic pres. ptc. *cyávānas* 'moving, in motion' (Ringe 2012: 128 with references), and if that is true, the root-aorist must be a Greek innovation. (See further below on the process by which innovative affixless aorists may have been created.) In the case of Homeric aor. χύτο 'it gushed, it flowed' and pres. χέε̄ν < *χέϝε/ο- 'to pour' no stem-cognates can be cited; the reduplicated Skt present 3sg. *juhóti* '(s)he sacrifices' suggests that the Greek aorist is original and the Greek present was originally an aorist subjunctive, like λείπε̄ν (see 4.2.1 (iv) above),[26] but other scenarios are possible.

Three common root-aorists have undergone a surprising development in Greek: they exhibit a suffix -κ- in the indicative active singular, but not (originally) in other forms. Thus for 'put' we find in Homer act. ind. 3sg. ἔθηκε but 3pl. ἔθεσαν, subj. 3sg. θήῃ, opt. 3sg. θείη, iptv. 2sg. θές, inf. θεῖναι ~ θέμεναι, ptc. -θείς, and mediopassive ind. 3sg. ἔθετο, etc.; so also δωκ- ~ δο- 'give' and ἡκ- ~ ἑ- 'send, throw'. Nor are the forms with *-k- confined to Greek; ἔθηκε is plausibly related to Lat. pf. 3sg. *fēcit* '(s)he made' and late Phrygian αδδακετ 'does (something bad) to', while ἡκ- recalls Lat. pf. 3sg. *iēcit* '(s)he threw'. But in other IE languages the *-k- is part of the root, so far as we can tell from Lat. *facere* 'to make', *iacere* 'to throw', Venetic *vhagsto* '(s)he made'. Moreover, most IE languages exhibit only forms without *-k-; typical are Skt 3sg. *ádʰāt* '(s)he put', *ádāt* '(s)he gave' and (for *h₁yeh₁-)

[25] Masson 207b, 346, 347.
[26] Or possibly constructed to the Greek s-aorist (*LIV* s.v. **ĝʰeu̯*).

Lycian *adi* = Toch. A *yaṣ* '(s)he makes'. Finally, an extended root such as *$d^h eh_1 k$- must be a post-PIE innovation, since it violates the constraint against having a breathy-voiced stop and a voiceless stop in the same root (see 2.2.1). What are we to make of this configuration of facts?

The extended root most widely attested is *$d^h eh_1 k$-. That it appears both in Greek and in Phrygian is no surprise, given the similarities between those languages, but its appearance also in Italic can only mean that it was created in the common ancestor of the non-Anatolian, non-Tocharian daughters.[27] Apparently Greek inherited both a root θη- ~ θε- and a root θηκ- ~ *θεκ- in the meaning 'put'; it may or may not have inherited a reflex of *$h_1 yeh_1 k$-, since both Gk ἡκ- and Lat. *iēc-* could have been constructed to match the reflexes of *$d^h eh_1 k$- by lexical analogy. Moreover, competition between θη- and θηκ- might actually be attested: though most dialects exhibit active indic. 3sg. ἔθηκε, ἀνέθηκε, etc., an alternative form ἀνέθε̄ is clearly attested in early Boiotian inscriptions (Dubois 1986a). Sara Kimball has demonstrated how the two paradigms could have been conflated, starting from expected sound-change outcomes:

1sg.	*$éd^h ēm$	>	*ἔθην	ἔθηκα	<	*$éd^h eh_1 k\r{m}$
2sg.	*$éd^h eh_1 s$	>	*ἔθης	*ἔθηξ	<	*$éd^h eh_1 ks$
3sg.	*$éd^h eh_1 t$	>	ἔθη	ἔθη	<	*$éd^h eh_1 kt$

(cf. Kimball 1991: 142, 150)

Though the details of the process are not recoverable, the fact that the pivotal active indic. 3sgs. both should have become ἔθη by regular sound change, and the survival both of that form and of 1sg. ἔθηκα, make a confusion of the two paradigms by native learners highly plausible. The resulting pattern may have been extended to ἡκ- ~ ἑ- and was certainly extended to δωκ- ~ δο-. The survival of ἔθη (spelled -εθε̄) in Boiotian, a dialect notable for its archaisms in verb inflection, shows that this process had not occurred or at least was not complete in Proto-Greek, though it was apparently complete in Mycenaean, to judge from *te-ke*, *do-ke*, and their compounds.

4.2.2 (ii) Thematic aorists

How early the thematic aorist developed is still an open question, but at least it can be said that one example is widely attested in the IE family:

> Toch. B *lac* '(s)he went out' = OIr. *luid* '(s)he went' = Gk ἤλυθε '(s)he came' < *$h_1 lud^h éd$, augmented *é $h_1 lud^h ed$ '(s)he arrived' (vel sim.).

[27] The element *-k-, whatever its function might originally have been, could actually be somewhat older, since it appears in the Tocharian non-present stem *(s)taka- 'be', evidently an extension of PIE 'stand' (cf. Toch. A subj. 1sg. *tām* 'I will be' vs. iptv. 2sg. *päṣtāk* 'be!' and TB subj. /táka-/, pret. /taká-/). For further discussion, see Hackstein (2002a: 136 with fn. 1).

Even this example might have been a root-aorist in PIE (see *LIV* s.v. *$^*h_1leu̯d^h$*, where the problem of determining which forms are cognate is discussed and the possibility of multiple roots is raised in the notes). All other thematic aorists show clear signs of secondary thematization (see especially the discussion of Cardona 1960); even the equation Gk ἔϝιδε '(s)he caught sight of' = Skt *ávidat* '(s)he found' is undercut by Lat. *vīdit* '(s)he saw', whose full grade forces the reconstruction of an ablauting athematic paradigm *wéyd- ~ *wid- 'catch sight of'. A few aorists were clearly thematized after the Proto-Greek period, since both athematic and thematic forms occur in Homer (indic. always ἔκλυε, etc., but iptv. always κλῦθι, κλῦτε; ἔφθιεν 'he ate (his heart) out', *Il.* 18.446, but mp. usually ἔφθιτο; ἔκτανε 'slew', etc., beside ἔκτα, etc., the latter backformed to mp. κτάσθαι; usually ὦρτο, etc., but ὤρετο *Il.* thrice, and only subj. ὄρηται (*Od.* thrice), opt. ὄροιτο (*Od.* 14.522).)[28] Thematic πιεῖν 'to take a drink' must also be a post-PGk innovation, given the survival of iptv. 2sg. πῖθι (see 4.2.2 (i)).

A number of Greek thematic aorists have stem-cognates elsewhere, either athematic or thematic, showing that they are inherited. So far as can be determined, most had already been thematized in Proto-Greek. In addition to the stems adduced above, note the following:

PIE *léyk^w- ~ *lik^w- 'leave behind' (Lat. pf. 3sg. *līquit*) → *lik^wé/ó- (Arm. 3sg. *$elik^h$*) > λιπεῖν;

PIE *b^héwg- ~ *b^hug- 'run away' (Lat. pf. 3sg. *fūgit*) → *b^hugé/ó- > φυγεῖν;

PIE *g^hrawH- ~ *g^hruH- (?; see *LIV* s.v. *$^*g^hreh_1u̯$*) 'run into' (Lat. pf. 3sg. *ingruit* '(s)he rushed into') → *g^hrawé/ó- > Hom. 3sg. ἔχραε '(s)he attacked; (s)he was eager to';

PIE *b^héwd^h- ~ *b^hud^h- 'become alert' (Skt. inj. 3pl. *bud^hánta* 'they wake up') → *b^hud^{h}é/ó- > πυθέσθαι 'to learn about';

PIE *Hné(n)ḱ- ~ *Hn̥ḱ- 'bring'[29] (Skt 3sg. *ā́naṭ* '(s)he has reached') >→ ἐνεγκεῖν;

PIE *dérḱ- ~ *dr̥ḱ- 'look at' (Skt 3pl. *ádr̥śran*) → *dr̥ḱé/ó- > Hom. δρακεῖν 'to look (at)';

PIE *térp- ~ *tr̥p- 'have enough of' (Skt neut. ptc. as adv. *tr̥pát* 'to satiety') → *tr̥pé/ó- > Hom. subj. ταρπώμεθα[30] 'we are refreshed';

[28] It is difficult to say how many of these stems are artificial poetic creations. At least ὤρετο, always in ὅτε δ' ὤρετο immediately before the bucolic diaeresis, looks suspiciously like a form created by formulaic modification (see Chantraine 1973: 392 and the discussion of Roth 1990: 62–3); the subjunctive and optative forms might actually have been part of the athematic paradigm.

[29] The Greek stem suggests initial *h_1, whereas OIr. pf. *tánaic* '(s)he arrived, (s)he came' suggests *h_2 (or, in principle, *h_3). Possibly we need to recognize two roots (so *LIV* s.vv. *$^*h_1neḱ$*, *$^*h_2neḱ$*), but that seems less economical than positing an assimilation of vowels in adjacent syllables—most likely in Greek. I accept the traditional view that the internal nasal in the Greek form is a purely phonetic development, not a relic of reduplication, because it appears in a large number of forms in multiple daughters (e.g. pf. 3sg. *He-Hnónḱ-e > Skt *ānáṃśa*, OIr. *t-ánaic*, the latter with /gʲ/ < *gg < *nk).

[30] For expected *τραπ- by leveling on pres. τέρπεσθαι.

PIE *pérh₃- ~ *pr̥h₃- 'grant' (Skt iptv. 2sg. *pūrdʰí* 'give!') >→ Hom. 3sg. πόρε;
PIE *h₂ár- ~ *h₂r̥- 'get a share of' (Arm. 3sg. *aṙ* '(s)he took') → ἀρέ/ό- in Hom. 3pl. ἄροντο 'they have won (prizes)';
PIE *kʷél- ~ *kʷl̥- 'turn (once)' (Arm. 3sg. *ełew* '(s)he became') → πλέ/ό- in Hom. 3sg. ἔπλετο 'it has become'.

A larger number of thematic aorists are shown to be comparatively old by the fact that their presents are affixed, or there is no present (or a suppletive present); if the root is inherited, it is very likely that the unaffixed aorist was too. In addition to πταρε͂ν 'to sneeze' (pres. πτάρνυσθαι), ἱκέσθαι 'to arrive' (pres. ἱκνε͂σθαι, Hom. ἱκα̃́νε͂ν), τεμε͂ν 'to cut' (pres. τάμνε͂ν), καμε͂ν 'to get tired' (pres. κάμνε͂ν), δακε͂ν 'to bite' (pres. δάκνε͂ν), and χαδε͂ν 'to grasp' (pres. χανδάνε͂ν), which were adduced in 4.2.1 (ii), and τεκε͂ν 'to give birth' (pres. τίκτε͂ν), γενέσθαι 'to be born, to become' (pres. γίγνεσθαι), χανε͂ν 'to gape' (pres. χάσκε͂ν), θορε͂ν 'to leap' (pres. θρώσκε͂ν), θανε͂ν 'to die' (pres. θνήσκε͂ν), and Hom. τορε͂ν 'to pierce' (pres. Att. τιτρώσκε͂ν 'to wound'), which were adduced in 4.2.1 (iii), the following cases seem especially clear:

PIE *h₁ger- 'wake up', stative pf. *h₁geh₁góre (Skt. *jāgā́ra*) in aor. ἐγρέσθαι, pf. ἐγρηγορέναι;
PIE *bʰag- 'share' (Skt pres. 3sg. *bʰájati* '(s)he distributes') in aor. φαγε͂ν 'to eat';
PIE *drem- 'run' (Khotanese 3sg. *dremäte* '(s)he drives away', see *LIV* s.v.) in aor. δραμε͂ν;
PIE *h₂algʷʰ- 'earn' (Skt pres. 3sg. *árhati* '(s)he deserves') in aor. 1sg. ἦλφον 'I earned' *Il.* 21.79, pres. ἀλφάνε͂ν in Attic drama.

Even if external cognates for the root are sparse or doubtful, widely attested thematic aorists with affixed presents (or no present) are reasonably likely to go back to Proto-Greek. In addition to ἁμαρτε͂ν 'to miss (a mark), to make a mistake' (pres. ἁμαρτάνε͂ν), αἰσθέσθαι 'to perceive' (pres. αἰσθάνεσθαι), βλαστε͂ν 'to sprout' (pres. βλαστάνε͂ν), κατα-δαρθε͂ν 'to fall asleep' (Hom. 3sg. ἔδραθε; pres. κατα-δαρθάνε͂ν), ὀλισθε͂ν 'to slip' (pres. ὀλισθάνε͂ν), χαδε͂ν 'to grasp' (pres. χανδάνε͂ν), λαχε͂ν 'to get by lot' (pres. λαγχάνε͂ν), and μαθε͂ν 'to learn' (pres. μανθάνε͂ν), adduced in 4.2.1 (ii), and μολε͂ν 'to come, to go' (pres. βλώσκε͂ν) and παθε͂ν 'to experience' (pres. πάσχε͂ν), adduced in 4.2.1 (iii), one might mention:

Hom. 3sg. κίε '(s)he went (away)', pres. κῑ́νυντο 'they were moving', thematized κῑνε͂ν (see 4.2.1 (ii));
ἀπ-ολέσθαι 'to perish', pres. ἀπ-όλλυσθαι (cf. Lat. *ab-olēre* 'to wipe out'?);
βαλε͂ν 'to hit (with a missile), to throw', pres. βάλλε͂ν (cf. OIr. 3sg. *at·baill* '(s)he dies'?);

λαβε̃ν 'to take hold of', East Argolic ptc. λhαβόν *DGE* 116, pres. Hom. λάζεσθαι, root *hλαγ^w-;

ἀγρέσθαι 'to assemble (intr.)' (but Hom. 3pl. ἀγέροντο, suggesting an original ablauting root-present, *LIV* s.v. *h_2*ger*), pres. ἀγε̄́ρε̃ν;

Hom. λιτέσθαι 'to beg, to beseech', pres. λίσσεσθαι;

φάε (*φάϝε) '(dawn) appeared' *Od.* 14.502, Hom. pres. πιφαυσκέμεν 'to light (a fire), to show';

ἑλε̃ν 'to take' (cf. Goth. *saljan* 'to sacrifice', OE *sellan* 'to give'?).

However, this line of argument cannot be pushed too far; for instance, ἀπ-εχθέσθαι 'to incur hatred' (pres. ἀπ-εχθάνεσθαι) was obviously made to a 'root' extracted from ἐχθρός 'hostile', a process which cannot be dated with any confidence.

Quite different from all the above are paradigms with zero-grade thematic aorists and full-grade presents, of which only the presents have secure stem-cognates in other IE languages. I have argued elswhere that those aorists are specifically Greek creations (Ringe 2012: 125–31). A few of the corresponding presents were originally athematic, and it's conceivable that their aorists arose from the ablauting present by paradigm split, though the details of such a process are beyond recovery. But I suspect that most of these aorists were formed on the model of pairs like λείπε̃ν: λιπε̃ν, in which the present was originally an aorist subjunctive (see 4.2.1 (iv)). At least the following are almost certainly Greek innovations, one way or another:

Hom. ἐπι-σπε̃ν 'to meet (death or fate)', μετα-σπών 'following': pres. ἕπει '(evil) besets' *Od.* 12.209, ἔφ-επε 'he was driving', ἀμφί-επον 'they took care of', etc. ←< PIE *sép- ~ *sp- 'take care of', cf. Gāthā-Av. 3sg. *haptī*;

Hom. 3sg. τύχε 'he/it happened to hit', later τυχε̃ν 'to hit (a mark); to happen to': pres. Hom. τεύχε̃ν 'to fashion, to make (as a craftsman)' ←< PIE *d^{h}éwg^h- ~ *d^{h}ug^h- 'produce', cf. Skt 3sg. *dógd^{h}i* '(s)he milks', mp. *duhé* 'it produces milk'; the Greek forms exhibit paradigm split;

Hom. 3sg. ἔτραπε '(s)he turned (it)', ἐτράπετο '(s)he turned' (intrans.): pres. τρέπε̃ν ←< PIE *trép- ~ *tr̥p-, cf. Hitt. 3sg. *teripzi* '(s)he plows';

σπέσθαι 'to follow': pres. ἕπεσθαι < PIE mp. *sék^w-e/o-, cf. Skt. 3sg *sácate*, Lat. *sequī*;

σχε̃ν 'to take hold of, to get': pres. ἔχε̃ν 'to hold, to have' < *hεχε/o- < PIE *séǵ^h-e/o-, cf. Skt 3sg. *sáhate* '(s)he prevails';

ἐπι-πτέσθαι 'to fly at' *Il.* 4.126 (and other cpds.): pres. πέτεσθαι < PIE *pét-e/o-, cf. Skt 3sg. *pátati*, Lat. *petere* 'to go for, to seek';

Hom. πιθέσθαι 'to obey': pres. πείθε̃ν 'to persuade' < PIE *b^{h}éyd^h-e/o- 'trust', cf. Lat. *fīdere*, Goth. *beidan* 'to wait for';

Hom. 3sg. ἤρυγεν 'he bellowed' *Il.* 20.403, 404: pres. ἐρεύγεσθαι 'to belch, to bellow' < PIE *$h_1$réwg-e/o- 'belch', cf. Lat. *ē-rūgere*;

ἀπο-παρδε̃ν 'to fart': pres. πέρδεσθαι < PIE mp. *pérd-e/o-, cf. Skt 3sg. *pardate*.

A couple of further examples, less certain because of the sparsity of cognates, are listed in Ringe (2012: 126–7).

A final category of simple thematic aorists are onomatopoeic, often occurring in paradigms that contain a stative perfect but no present (or an obviously derived present). In such cases the aorist is almost certainly the oldest member of the paradigm, but just how old any individual example might be is indeterminable. Homeric examples include λάκε 'it crashed, (the bones) crunched' *Il.* thrice beside pf. ptc. λεληκώς 'shrieking' *Il.* 22.141; ptc. μακών 'groaning, with a groan' beside pf. ptc. μεμηκώς 'screaming' *Il.* 10.362; μύκε '(the shield) made a hollow sound' *Il.* 20.260, μύκον '(the gates) groaned' thrice beside pf. ἀμφι-μέμῡκεν 'it echoes' *Od.* 10.227, plup. μεμῡ́κει '(the meat) was mooing' *Od.* 12.395 and pres. ptc. μῡκώμεναι 'mooing' *Od.* 10.413; ἀν-έκραγον 'I have blurted it out' *Od.* 14.467.

Reduplicated thematic aorists are a small but conspicuous group in the Homeric poems; a couple also occur in later Greek. They seem to have had diverse origins.

One example demonstrably dates back to the last common ancestor of Greek and Indo-Iranian:

> PIE *wek^w- 'speak, say', aor. *wé-wk-e/o-,[31] augmented 3sg. *é wewked (Skt *ávocat*) → *é wewk^{w}ed (with the labiovelar leveled in from other forms) > *ἔ̆ϝευκ^{w}ε > *ἔ̆ϝεικ^{w}ε (by dissimilation) > Hom. ἔειπε.

Also probably inherited is Hom. ἤραρε '(s)he fit (it)', ptc. ἀραρών, etc. (ten times in Homer), which matches the Armenian thematic aorist 3sg. *arar* '(s)he made' (Bendahman 1993: 83). The stem is normally transitive (see the discussion of Bendahman 1993: 80–2 on exceptions) and thus contrasts with the fossilized participle ἄρμενος 'fitted' (thrice).

Three further Homeric examples of similar shape are relatively old, perhaps Proto-Greek, though at least one must have been a specifically Greek creation. The PIE root-present 3sg. *g^{wh}énti '(s)he hits, (s)he kills' is well attested in Hitt. *kuēnzi*, Skt *hánti*, and Av. *jaiṇti*; it survives in Homeric Greek remodeled as *g^{wh}én-ye/o- > θε̄νέμεναι 'to smite' (see 4.2.1 (v)). Strikingly, most of the languages in which it is attested, directly or indirectly, exhibit no stem that could reflect an inherited aorist (see *LIV* s.v. *$g^{u̯h}$*en*); the Skt aorist is suppletive *ávad^{h}īt*. Hom. Gk aor. πεφνέμεν < *χ^{w}e-χ^{w}ν-ε/ο- is therefore almost certainly a Greek creation, though its paradigmatic relationship to θε̄νέμεναι shows that it arose before the split of labiovelars into labials and dentals and could therefore be Proto-Greek.[32] A similar but more obscure case is ἔτετμε '(s)he encountered, (s)he overtook' eight times beside pres. 3sg. τέμει 'it [the plow] reaches (the boundary-furrow)' *Il.* 13.707 (Chantraine 1973: 309); since external cognates are uncertain we cannot say with

[31] With automatic unrounding of *k^w next to *w.

[32] The analysis of Av. *-jaγnat* is too uncertain for it to be accepted as a cognate stem; see *LIV*, *loc. cit.*, for discussion.

any certainty how old these stems are, but the fact that the paradigm is sparsely attested even in Homer suggests that it too might be of Proto-Greek date. The final example is more puzzling. Hom. aor. ἐκέκλετο '(s)he called' has long been considered part of the same paradigm as pres. κέλεσθαι 'to tell (someone to do something)', though the aorist mostly governs the dative while the present governs the accusative (see the discussion of Bendahman 1993: 110–12, 114). Of course a single paradigm might have been split lexically some time before the composition of the epics, or modification of inherited formulas containing an obsolete verb might eventually have led to the observed pattern. Deriving the aorist stem from a root *$kleh_1$- 'call' (Bendahman 1993: 112–14, *LIV* s.v.) raises further problems, since the disappearance of the laryngeal is difficult to motivate. In any case outside cognates are problematic (see *LIV* s.v. **kel*), but the shape and distribution of this aorist suggest that it is an archaism within Greek (so Bendahman, *loc. cit.*).

Another reduplicated aorist, common to all the Greek dialects (so far as our evidence goes), was almost certainly created by lexical analogy. Though the aorist ἐνεγκε͂ν 'to bring' is not etymologically reduplicated, it looks as though it were; it must be the model for ἀγαγε͂ν 'to lead' (so Bendahman 1993: 55–6 with references). Though creation of a new stem by lexical analogy is always a surprise, there are several reasons to accept this scenario (Bendahman, *loc. cit.*):

1) no other IE language has an inherited aorist for this verb, only the thematic present (Gk ἄγε͂ν) being shared (*LIV* s.v. 1. *$h_2e\hat{g}$);
2) the idiom ἄγε͂ν καὶ φέρε͂ν 'to plunder' (lit. 'to drive (off) and carry (away)') shows that the two verbs were semantically linked;
3) in the Hellenistic period the perfect ἐνηνοχέναι 'to have carried/brought' was evidently the model for *ἀγηγοχέναι > ἀγηοχέναι (by dissimilatory loss) 'to have led'.

The largest group of reduplicated thematic aorists are constructed to light roots of the shape CVC-; they are practically confined to epic language. This group has been compared repeatedly to the Sanskrit reduplicated aorist, which is causative in function (Whitney 1889: 308–9), and to the Tocharian causative aorist, which is reduplicated in Toch. A and exhibits evidence of once having been so in Toch. B (see e.g. Kim 2003, Malzahn 2010: 170–89, both with references). But these Greek aorists have no certain stem-cognates in other IE languages—none at all[33]—and while there are more than a dozen such stems, no more than three are clearly causatives. For our purposes the following observations seem appropriate.

Since reduplicated causative aorists and preterites do occur in other IE languages, it seems reasonable to adopt the working hypothesis that Greek inherited such a formation, though it is possible that none of the inherited examples survive

[33] That τεταγών 'having seized' (*Il.* 1.591, 15.23) is cognate with Lat. *tetigisse* 'to have touched' is very uncertain, as *LIV* admits s.v. **teh_2g* fn. 3.

to be attested. If we ask which attested stems might conceivably be such survivals, by far the best candidate is Hom. δέδαε '(s)he taught' (see the discussion of Bendahman 1993: 69–71). It is unarguably the causative that corresponds to Hom. δαήμεναι 'to learn' and is clearly an archaism, since even in Homer it is beginning to be replaced by δίδαξε, the innovative sigmatic aorist that took over its function in later Greek; moreover, its root was inherited (see *LIV* s.v. **dens*). If any PGk reduplicated causative aorist survives, this is it. Also clearly causative is subj. 3pl. λελάχωσι *Il.* thrice, 2pl. λελάχητε *Il.* 23.76 'give someone a share of (fire by cremation)', since the usual aorist λαχε͂ν means 'get a share of' and there is no difference of voice between the forms (Bendahman 1993: 61–2); but in this case even the root has no cognates outside Greek.

A more complex case is ἐκλέλαθον 'they made him forget completely' *Il.* 2.600, λελάθηι 'he may make him forget' *Il.* 15.60. The corresponding mediopassive λελαθέσθαι, of which forms occur seven times in the poems, could mean 'make oneself forget' (so Bendahman 1993: 63–4), but could as well mean simply 'forget', so that the causative function might appear to be expressed by the active voice. But while mediopassive forms of other stems of this verb do also mean 'forget', the active forms normally mean 'escape the notice of'; the only other causative forms are the gnomic aorist ἐπέλησεν 'it makes one forget' *Od.* 20.85, a sigmatic aorist that is unique for this verb, and ἐκ δέ με πάντων | ληθάνει ὅσσ' ἔπαθον 'and makes me forget all that I have suffered' *Od.* 7.220–1, a unique present stem that combines the full-grade root of λήθε͂ν and the nasal-suffix of λανθάνε͂ν. Both these stems are certainly late innovations, and the two active forms of λελαθε/ο- could be too. On the other hand, the reduplicated aorist could have been created as a causative, and its mediopassive forms would then automatically mean either 'make oneself forget' or just 'forget'. Once again a decision seems unattainable because the verb has no clear cognates in other IE languages.

Other potential causatives seem to me less certain. For instance, the phrase ἀμπεπαλὼν προΐει means 'he Xed and threw' (*Il.* eight times, *Od.* 24.522) or iptv. 'X and throw!' (*Od.* 24.519), and the object is always a spear (usually δολιχόσκιον ἔγχος, but δόρυ *Il.* 20.438), so ἀμπεπαλών must be whatever you do with a spear just before you throw it. It could mean 'having lifted', and in that case it could be a causative to ἀνέπαλτο 'he sprang up' (*Il.* thrice); but the difference in voice could account for that, so reduplication does not necessarily mark causative function in this participle.

The case of λελαθε/ο- (see above) suggests how non-causative reduplicated aorists might have been created even if the original function of the formation was causative. Greek is notorious for pressing the voice opposition into service to express causativity or transitivity. For instance, both Skt *tíṣṭʰati* and Lat. *sistere* are intransitive, though active, but in Greek the active ἱστάναι is transitive (or causative) 'to stand (something) up'; Lat. *fīdere* means 'to trust' and Goth. *beidan* 'to wait for', but in Greek it is mediopassive πείθεσθαι that means 'to trust, to obey', active πείθε̄ν having acquired the causative meaning 'to persuade'. Under the circumstances it is not surprising that while the aorist of πείθεσθαι is usually πιθέσθαι, that of πείθε̄ν is usually πεπιθε̃ν[34]—and in the absence of aorist stem-cognates in other IE languages, there is more than one way in which that situation could have come about. This is another reason why we should be reluctant to claim that any of these stems existed in Proto-Greek.

One reduplicated aorist, however, might preserve a trace of its prehistory. It seems clear that τετυκεῖν 'to prepare (a meal for others)' *Od.* 15.77, 94, τετυκέσθαι 'to prepare (one's own meal)'[35] belong with τεύχε̄ν 'to make, to fashion', but the consistent root-final -κ- is anomalous. The obvious source would be assimilation to a following *s or *t, but that could have occurred only if the stem had originally been athematic.[36] Unfortunately that inference leads no further.

Reduplicated aorists of other types (e.g. Hom. ἄλαλκε '(s)he warded off', ἐνένῑπε and ἠνί̄πατε '(s)he rebuked', etc.) seem to be Greek innovations of uncertain date; some might be artificial creations of the oral epic tradition (cf. Roth 1990: 63, Bendahman 1993: 100–8).

4.2.2 (iii) Sigmatic aorists

This is the fully productive active and middle aorist in Greek. For that reason the Proto-Greek status of any given example can be established with certainty only by outside stem-cognates or archaic features of inflection; other sigmatic aorists can be later creations. On the other hand, the formation and/or the paradigmatic relationships of numerous examples argue that they are relatively old and could be Proto-Greek.

Until late in the 20th century it was believed that the PIE s-aorist was a relatively late development, both because few examples were well attested in more than two daughters and because its ablaut made no sense in terms of PIE patterns then known. Since then the Tocharian languages have added substantially to the number of reconstructable s-aorist stems (see *LIV passim*) and it has become clear that the acrostatic ablaut of the formation is not in fact anomalous (Strunk 1985). Greek examples can be sorted as follows in terms of how likely to be inherited they are.

We are now able to cite four Greek sigmatic aorists with stem-cognates in two other branches of the family:

PIE *dḗyḱs- ~ *déyḱs-[37] 'point at' (Gāthā-Av. injunctive 2sg. *dāiš* 'show', Lat. pf. *dīxisse* 'to have said') >→ δεῖξαι 'to show';

[34] Though sigmatic πεῖσαι has begun to compete with it.

[35] Bendahman (1993: 76) also notes this distinction.

[36] For alternatives, all of which strike me as less likely, see Bendahman (1993: 76–7).

[37] I question the judgment of *LIV* s.v. **dei̯ḱ* that these are parallel innovations; in my opinion Skt *ádiṣṭa* is more likely to be an innovative s-aorist form (cf. 1sg. *ádikṣi*), and Skt pres. *diśá-*, Lat. *dīcere* 'to

PIE *wḗǵ^{h}s- ~ *wéǵ^{h}s- 'bring in a vehicle' (Skt 3sg. *ávāṭ*, Lat. *vēxisse*) >→ Cyprian 3sg. *e-we-xe* *ἔϝεξε '(s)he brought/dedicated' (Masson 245.2);
PIE *h_3rḗǵs- ~ *$h_3$réǵs- 'put in a straight line' (Lat. pf. *rēxisse*, Toch. B 3sg. *reksa* '(s)he covered') >→ ὀρέξαι 'to reach';
PIE *plḗws- ~ *pléws- 'float (from/to)' (Skt mp. 3sg. *aploṣṭa* 'it floated off', Toch. B 3sg. *plyewsa* 'it hovered') >→ πλεῦσαι 'to sail'.[38]

It is striking that the presents of all four of these verbs were unaffixed in PIE (a root-present in the first instance, simple thematic presents in the others); if the hypothesis that only one stem of a verb could be unaffixed in PIE is even approximately correct, an s-aorist is what we would expect for all four. Note that Greek has generalized the (short) e-grade; that is an exceptionless development in the sigmatic aorist (Schwyzer 1939: 751).[39]

Two other Greek sigmatic aorists have possible external stem-cognates in Anatolian, the outlying branch of the family, and are therefore also good candidates for inheritance:

PIE *ḱḗrs- ~ *ḱérs- 'cut (off)' (Hitt. pres. 3sg. *karszi*) >→ Hom. κέρσαι;
PIE *h_2ḗrh_3s- ~ *$h_2$árh_3s- 'break ground' (Hitt. pres. 3sg. *harszi*) >→ ἀρόσαι 'to plow'.

A larger number of possible stem-cognates are found in Latin:

PIE *klḗps- ~ *kléps- 'steal' (Old Lat. 3sg. *clepsit*) >→ κλέψαι;
PIE *spḗḱs- ~ *spéḱs- 'look' (Old Lat. pf. 3sg. *spexit*) >→ σκέψασθαι;
PIE *tḗngs- ~ *téngs- 'moisten, get (something) wet' (Lat. pf. *tīnxisse*) >→ τέγξαι;
PIE *pḗk^{w}s- ~ *pék^{w}s- 'cook' (Lat. pf. *coxisse*) >→ πέψαι;
PIE *ḗws- ~ *éws- (underlyingly /ews-s-/) 'to burn' (Lat. pf. *ussisse*) >→ εὗσαι 'to singe';
PIE *h_2ḗws- ~ *$h_2$áws- (underlyingly /-s-s-/) 'to fetch' (Lat. pf. *hausisse* 'to have drawn (water)') >→ ἐν-αῦσαι 'to kindle, to light (a fire)';
PIE *h_2ḗnǵ^{h}s- ~ *$h_2$ánǵ^{h}s- 'to squeeze, to choke' (Lat. pf. *ānxisse*, acc. to Priscian) >→ ἄγξαι;
PIE *lḗyǵ^{h}s- ~ *léyǵ^{h}s- 'lick (once)' (Lat. pf. *līnxisse* (Priscian) with *-n-* leveled in from pres. *lingere*) >→ λεῖξαι;
PIE *k^{w}ā́ts- ~ *k^{w}áts- 'shake' (see 3.6.3 with fn. 49; Lat. pf. *quassisse*) >→ πάσαι 'to sprinkle'.

say', Goth. *gateihan* 'to announce, to report' all reflect direct thematization of an ablauting root-present *déyḱ- ~ *diḱ-, which should belong to the same paradigm as an s-aorist.

[38] With -σ- reintroduced in place of *-h- at some point before the loss of intervocalic *ϝ in the thematic present.

[39] A fifth example, potentially reconstructable from Hom. mp. ἕσ(σ)ασθαι 'put on a garment', Arm. 3sg. *zgec^{h}aw*, and Toch. B 3sg. *wässāte*, is uncertain: in Greek and Armenian it is the aorist of the (originally causative) present in *-néw- ~ *-nu- and as such is likely to be an innovation (*LIV* s.v. 1. *u̯es, fn. 6).

Of course any individual pair of stems could reflect parallel development, since the sigmatic aorist has been highly productive in Greek and can have been so in the prehistory of Latin. But modern cladistic studies of the family show that Greek and Italic are not closely related, and that increases the probability that at least some of these apparent stem-cognations are real. Note also the implication of present tenses such as εὕε̄ν < *éws-e/o-, with roots ending in *ws. Such presents should have undergone the 1CL; their attested shapes can only have been remodeled on their s-aorists. But it follows that s-aorists to at least a few such verbs were in existence before the 1CL occurred; and it also follows that they either had not acquired the stem vowel -α/ε-, so that *their* *ws were not intervocalic in most forms, or else that they had restored the suffixal *-s- (*éws-s-V-, etc.). By contrast, s-aorists certainly attested only in Greek and Indo-Iranian are few, and only one is represented in the Rigveda:

> PIE *wḗyh₁s- ~ *wéyh₁s- 'hurry' (Skt subj. 3sg. *véṣat RV* I.180.6) >→ Hom. 3sg. εἴσατο 'he rushed, it sped'.

(See further *LIV* s.vv. 2. **hu̯es*, **sreu̯*, **tres*.)

That Vedic Sanskrit is attested so early, yet shares few s-aorists with other daughters, is one factor that led earlier scholars to conclude that most s-aorists were post-PIE developments; but given that Greek and Indo-Iranian are obviously closely related, and that Greek shares more s-aorists with more distant relatives, we should consider the possibility that the s-aorist underwent a sharp decline in the prehistory of Indo-Iranian, followed by a resurgence.

Sigmatic aorists made to vowel-final roots normally exhibit -σ-, which must have been leveled in from the aorists of consonant-final roots at some time after the PGk sound change *s > *h (see 3.5.1). Two aorists which did not restore -σ- must be of PGk date, even though neither has clear stem-cognates elsewhere (*LIV* s.vv. **ǵʰeu̯*, **keh₂u̯*):

> pre-Gk *ǵʰew-s- 'pour' > *χεϝ-h- > *χε̄ϝ- (by the 1CL, see 5.2.2) > χε- (by loss of intervocalic *ϝ and prevocalic shortening, see 6.2) > Hom. 3sg. χέε, etc.;
> pre-Gk *kaw-s- 'set on fire, burn' > *καϝ-h- > *κᾱϝ- > Att.-Ion. κη- > Hom. 3sg. ἔκηε, etc.

However, most Greek sigmatic aorists do appear to be innovations. Those made to denominative presents are necessarily Greek innovations, since derived presents had no aorists in Nuclear IE (so far as we can tell). Evidently such an aorist as φυλάξαι 'to guard' was constructed to pres. φυλάσσε̄ν on the model of such underived examples as aor. κλέψαι 'to steal', pres. κλέπτε̄ν—and that could have happened at any time.

Part of the development of the s-aorist can perhaps be reconstructed by examining the aorists of denominative verbs derived from stems in vowels. The creation of aorists to such stems seems to have occurred in at least two stages. A tiny handful of derived presents in *-ϳε/o- delete the entire present suffix before adding the sigmatic suffix:

δόξαι 'to win approval, to be resolved (by a legislature)' ← δοκε͂ν 'to seem good';
ὦσαι 'to shove' ← ὠθε͂ν 'to push (continuously or repeatedly)';
Hom. φῐ́λασθαι 'conceive affection for, show kindness to' *Il.* four times ← φιλε͂ν 'to be friendly to, to love' (see 5.2.2 on the phonology).

The fact that one of these archaic stems was constructed to a transparent denominative shows that this cannot be an innovation resulting from the opacity of the presents' derivation; it must be the way in which sigmatic aorists were originally constructed to presents in *-ϳε/o-. The later procedure, still completely productive in Greek, is to retain the vowel before the *ϳ (which may or may not have been lost intervocalically by then); and just as *-ᾱ(ϳ)ε/o- became -ᾰ(ϳ)ε/o- by analogy with -ε(ϳ)ε/o- and -o(ϳ)ε/o-, so *-εσα- was lengthened to -ησα- and *-οσα- to -ωσα- on the model of -ᾱσα-, at least in the well-attested dialects of Ancient Greek. Already in Homer we find the innovative φιλῆσαι a dozen times, of which a substantial majority are in the Iliad.

The lengthening seems to be characteristic only of denominative verbs; sigmatic aorists to primary verbs, such as γελάσαι 'to burst out laughing' and καλέσαι 'to call', have mostly been unaffected. Aorists to presents in *-εh-ϳε/o-, such as τελέσσαι 'to finish', South Greek τελέσαι (Hom. pres. τελείε͂ν) also often remain unaffected. Whether there is any connection between those two phenomena is not immediately obvious.

Is there evidence that bears on the date of any of these developments? We know that the sigmatic aorist suffix participated in the change of *s to *h between sonorants, and that the outcome *h is normal even in a class of aorists that must be Greek innovations:

τέκτων 'carpenter, joiner' → *τεκταν-ϳε/o- > τεκταίνεσθαι 'to make (of wood)', to which was created aor. *τεκταν-hα- > Hom. 3sg. τεκτήνατο *Il.* 5.62.

Of course it doesn't follow that particular sigmatic aorists were created to presents of this type *before* the change of *s to *h, because there must have been a period when the alternation between *s and *h was completely automatic and would thus affect all new formations. But analogical *-s-* has already replaced intervocalic *-h- in sigmatic aorists attested in Mycenaean; clear examples are *e-ra-se* *ἔλασε and *e-re-u-te-ro-se* *ἐλευθέρωσε (Aura Jorro 1999 s.vv., Bartoněk 2002: 326), and there are no clear counterexamples. It is reasonable to conclude, with caution, that the sigmatic aorist began to spread very early in the history of Greek, perhaps in the Proto-Greek period.

The inflection of the sigmatic aorist, especially the spread of 'alphathematic' -α-, will be discussed in 5.4.2 (i).

4.2.2 (iv) Aorists in -ή-

For the most part these are clearly passive in Classical Greek, but in Homer the situation is more complicated. Many are simply intransitive (e.g. δαήμεναι 'to learn'), and a few that cannot be called passive survive in later Greek (e.g. ῥυῆναι 'to (begin to) flow', cf. 3sg. ῥύη *Od.* 3.455; χαρῆναι 'to rejoice'); some function as passives in Homer because of the telic nature of their roots (e.g. ἔβλαβεν *Il.* 23.461, βλάβεν 545 'they got hurt'). Evidently this was originally an intransitive formation, and (as has long been recognized) its only possible source is the class of PIE derived statives/fientives in *-éh$_1$-. That these are aorists in Greek supports the arguments of Harðarson (1998) that the PIE formation was fientive (and therefore perfective); the fact that the cognate formations in Hittite, Tocharian, and Latin are presents can reflect innovations in those branches.

None of the possible stem-cognations in other branches of the family strikes me as certain, but three seem to be plausible:

PIE *tr̥séh$_1$- 'be dry' (Lat. ptc. *torrēns* 'parched, hot') >→ Hom. τερσήμεναι 'to dry out' *Od.* 6.98, τερσῆναι 'to be staunched' *Il.* 16.519 (with e-grade and -ρσ- leveled in from the present);
PIE *mnéh$_1$- ~ *mn̥éh$_1$- 'be mentally active' vel sim. (Lith. *minéti* 'to mention, to commemorate', OCS *mĭněti* 'to believe') >→ Att., Hdt. μανῆναι 'to go crazy';
PIE *tupéh$_1$- 'be stricken' (?; Lat. *stupēre* 'to be stunned') >→ Hom. ἐτύπη 'he had been struck (with)' *Il.* 24.421, ptc. τυπείς 'struck'.

However, two further examples, though they have no external stem-cognates, were certainly already in existence in Proto-Greek:

(post-)PIE *g^{w}ih$_3$óh$_1$- /*g^{w}ih$_3$-éh$_1$-/ 'be/become alive' > Hom. βιῶναι 'to escape alive';
(post-)PIE *wl̥h$_3$óh$_1$- /*wl̥h$_3$-éh$_1$-/ 'be stricken' (?; cf. Hitt. 3sg. *walhzi* '(s)he strikes', *LIV* s.v. **u̯elh$_3$-*) > Hom. ἁλώμεναι ~ ἁλῶναι 'to be taken captive'.

These cannot be root-aorists; they can only be aorists in *-éh$_1$- (Francis 1971: 65–87, Harðarson 1993: 208–10, *LIV* s.v. **g^{u}ieh$_3$* fn. 11). Whether or not they were inherited from PIE, they must have been in existence while the third laryngeal still existed to round the following *e, and that was well before the Proto-Greek period.

The competing (and productive) formation in -θή- is certainly a Greek innovation, as is revealed by the fact that the suffix is often added to full-grade roots even when a zero grade would be unproblematic, e.g. μειχθῆναι vs. μιγῆναι 'to get mixed', etc. (Risch 1974: 250–4). The only possible source for this suffix is resegmentation, the aorist in -ή- to a root extended with -θ- having been reanalyzed as an aorist in -θή- to the corresponding unextended root (Chantraine 1925: 105–6, Risch 1974: 253–4). What the original pair of roots was is of course no longer recoverable—they need not both have survived to be attested. Whether the reanalysis had occurred already in Proto-Greek is also undiscoverable, though the ubiquity of -θή- in Greek dialects suggests that it could have.

4.2.3 Perfect stems

The Nuclear IE perfect underwent a great deal of development and elaboration in the prehistory and history of Ancient Greek. In addition to the active perfect, also attested (directly or indirectly) in Tocharian, Italic, Celtic, Germanic, and Indo-Iranian, Greek has developed a mediopassive perfect which seems to have little to do with the similar Indo-Iranian formation (and nothing at all to do with Old Irish deponent preterites). I will treat them in that order.

4.2.3 (i) Active perfects

I have argued elsewhere (Ringe 2022) that the Nuclear IE perfect was a purely stative formation, any 'resultative' nuances being attributable to the lexical meanings of roots from which it was formed (see also Cowgill 1974a: 563 and Kümmel 2020). Several ancient IE languages exhibit relics pointing in that direction, but the most important evidence is that of Homeric Greek.

Nearly all active perfects in Homer are clearly stative or can easily be interpreted as such (Wackernagel 1904, Chantraine 1927: 8–16). However, only a minority can be shown to be inherited. It is necessary to consider examples made from consonant-final roots and those made from vowel-final (originally, laryngeal-final) roots separately because of the formal divergences between them that occurred within the prehistory of Greek. The lone unreduplicated perfect that can be reconstructed for Nuclear IE survives in Greek, with its ablaut alternations largely intact in Homer:

NIE 1sg. *wóydh$_2$a 'I know' (Skt *véda*, Goth. *wait*, OCS *vědě*) > οἶδα;
NIE 2sg. *wóydsth$_2$a 'you (sg.) know' (Skt *véth^{h}a*) > οἶσθα (see 3.2.1 on the aspirate);
NIE 3sg. *wóyde '(s)he knows' (Skt *véda*, Goth. *wait*) > οἶδε;
NIE 1pl. *widmé 'we know' (Skt *vidmá*) >→ ἴδμεν;
NIE subj. 3sg. *wéydeti '(s)he will know' (Skt *védati*) >→ *εἴδει, transmitted as εἰδῇ (see below);
NIE iptv. 2sg. *widsd^{h}í 'know!' (Skt *vidd^{h}í*) > ἴσθι;
NIE ptc. masc. nom. sg. *wéydwōs 'knowing' (Skt *vidvā́n*, remodeled) >→ εἰδώς;
NIE ptc. fem. nom. sg. *widwésih$_2$ 'knowing' → *widúsih$_2$ (Skt *vidúṣī*) > ἰδυῖα.

This much of the paradigm, at least, must have been present in Proto-Greek. Note that the reconstruction *εἴδει is not doubtful. The Homeric paradigm of this subjunctive makes no sense as transmitted:

εἰδῶ	εἴδομεν
εἰδῇς	εἴδετε
εἰδῇ	εἰδῶσι

Since the 1pl. and 2pl. consistently have a short subjunctive vowel, we expect the other forms to have been εἴδω, εἴδεις, εἴδει, εἴδουσι. The forms actually transmitted, which are identical with the Classical Attic forms, can have been substituted for them in the transmission of the text without disrupting the meter; in the case of the 1pl. and 2pl. that was not possible, which is why the older, genuinely Homeric forms survive.

Two other inherited consonant-final perfects that still exhibit traces of their original ablaut in Homer are:

NIE 3sg. *memóne '(s)he has in mind' (Lat. *meminit*, Goth. *ga-man* '(s)he remembers'; cf. Goth. 1sg. *man* 'I think so') > μέμονε '(s)he intends, (s)he is eager'; 1pl. *memn̥mé >→ μέμαμεν, ptc. *memn̥wṓs >→ μεμαώς;
(post-)NIE 3sg. *ǵeǵónh₁e '(s)he is born' > γέγονε (but Skt transitive *jajā́na* either has undergone a shift in function or is an innovation); ptc. fem. *ǵeǵn̥h₁wésih₂ >→ ἐκγεγαυῖα 'born of' *Il.* 3.418.

The latter stem lost its laryngeal by reanalysis early in the prehistory of Greek (so that the Homeric participle exhibits -α- < *-n̥-, not *-n̥h₁-); that could have been a PGk development, though it did not affect derived nominals like γένεσις and (κασί)γνητος. In both paradigms the zero-grade stems μεμα-, γεγα- have been generalized to forms with vowel-initial endings, e.g. 3pl. μεμάᾱσι, γεγάᾱσι; that is likely to have occurred not long before the composition of the Homeric poems, since such forms consistently remain uncontracted (in contrast to consistent ἑστᾶσι, in which the stem ἑστα- ended in a vowel reflecting a PIE laryngeal). Though it is not clear that Skt *jajā́na* is a genuine cognate of γέγονε, both the ablaut and the intransitive meaning of the latter argue that it existed in Proto-Greek and was probably inherited from NIE. The same can be said of five other stems that have no clear stem-cognates but do exhibit traces of NIE ablaut:

(post-)NIE 1sg. *dedwóyh₂a 'I'm afraid' > PGk *δέδϝοjα > *δέδϝοα > Hom. δείδω (i.e. δέ͞δω, by the 3CL; see 7.2.2); 1pl. *dedwimé >→ δείδιμεν;
(post-)NIE *wewóyke '(s)he resembles' > Hom. ἔοικε '(s)he resembles; it is fitting'; 2du. ἔϊκτον *Od.* 4.27, plup. 3du. ἐΐκτην four times;
(post-)NIE *bʰebʰóydʰe '(s)he trusts' > Hom. πέποιθε; plup. 1pl. ἐπέπιθμεν *Il.* thrice;

(post-)NIE *h_1e$h_1$lówd^h- ~ *h_1e$h_1$lud^h- 'be here, have arrived' >→ Hom. 1sg. εἰλήλουθα and ἀπ-, ἐπ-ελήλυθα (*Od.* three times);
post-NIE 1sg. *k^{w}ek^{w}ónd^hh_2a 'I am one who has suffered' (see *LIV* s.v. **k^{u}end^h*) > Hom. πέπονθα *Od.* 17.284; 2pl. *k^{w}ek^{w}n̥d^{h}sté > πέπασθε *Od.* three times (see 3.4.4 on the phonology), cf. also fem. ptc. dat. sg. πεπαθυίῃ *Od.* 17.555.

While we cannot be completely certain that any one of these stems was present in Proto-Greek, and while the distribution of ablaut grades has been disrupted in every one of them except the last (which is attested only half a dozen times), collectively they show that the alternation between o-grade and zero-grade forms that was inherited from NIE continued to exist in PGk perfects made to roots with internal ε. In many other examples the o-grade has been generalized; only those with potential outside cognates seem worth mentioning:

NIE *$h_1$ge$h_1$góre '(s)he is awake' (Skt *jāgā́ra*) ~ *$h_1$ge$h_1$gr̥- (e.g. in Skt ptc. *jāgr̥vā́n*) > PGk *ἐγήγορε ~ *ἐγηγρ̥- >→ ἐγρήγορε, ptc. ἐγρηγορώς, etc. (influenced by aor. ἐγρέσθαι 'to wake up (intr.)');
(post-)NIE *dedórḱe '(s)he looks' (Skt *dadárśa* is resultative '(s)he has seen' but can have undergone a semantic shift; see Kümmel 2000: 231–3) ~ *dedr̥ḱ- >→ Hom. δέδορκεν 'he glares' *Il.* 22.95, ptc. δεδορκώς *Od.* 19.446;
(post-)NIE *wewórǵe '(s)he is a worker' (?; cf. Av. *vauuarəza* '(s)he has done'?) ~ *wewr̥ǵ- >→ Hom. ἐσθλὰ ἔοργε 'he has done good deeds' *Il.* 2.272, ptc. ὅ τε πολλὰ ἐοργώς 'and the one who has done much' *Il.* 11.320 (both emphasizing the state of the subject, Wackernagel 1904: 4).

The first of these three examples is important because it is the most plausible model for 'Attic' reduplication (cf. Rix 1976a: 73, 204) on the hypothesis that clusters of laryngeal plus stop, being obstruent clusters, were reduplicated in their entirety (Warren Cowgill, p.c. ca. 1978; *LIV* s.v. **$h_1$ger*). Perfect reduplication *VCV̄C*- to roots beginning *VC*- must have spread from this example (and perhaps one or two others that did not survive) after the vocalization of laryngeals but before 'be awake' was remodeled. Whether this was already happening in Proto-Greek is unclear; the only possible evidence is the dialect distribution of Attic reduplication.[40] In the Attic-Ionic dialects it is well attested. There seem to be no Arkadian examples, but Cyprian attests *o-mo-mo-ko-ne* *ὀμώμοκον 'they had sworn' Masson 8.6 and *i-na-la-li-si-me-na* 'inscribed' Masson 217.26, which shows that the formation was common to South Greek. The few forms in Alkaios' verse are identical with Homeric forms (Hamm 1958: 161) and could simply be epicisms; of the Lesbian epigraphical examples, 4th-century κατεληλύθοντος *DGE* 620.9 is probably genuine, but the few other examples are late and can reflect Attic koine influence (cf. Hodot 1990: 207–8). West Greek forms that are early enough that koine influence can (probably) be discounted include Heraklean

[40] I omit doubtful examples from this discussion.

ἀπολώλη 'had been lost' *DGE* 62.39, Cretan inf. ἀμπεληλεῦθεν *Inscriptiones creticae* IV.42.B.4, and Kyrenaian κατεληλευθυῖα Buck 115.102. Such a distribution suggests that Attic reduplication might have been a Proto-Greek innovation. However, 3rd-century Boiotian διεσσείλθεικε *DGE* 485.2, ἀπειλθείοντες *IG* VII.1748.3, 1749.2 argue caution, considering that the inflection of the perfect is relatively conservative in Boiotian (see below).

As is well known, active perfects made to verbs with internal PGk *ᾱ do not exhibit o-grade roots; their ablaut is ᾱ ~ α (Att.-Ion. η ~ α), to the extent that they exhibit ablaut at all. Typical examples are:

τέθᾱλεν 'it blooms' Sappho 2.9, 'he prospers' Bakkhylides 10.40, ptc. φύλλοισι τεθηλώς 'leafed out' *Od.* 12.103, fem. τεθαλυῖα Homer six times;
λέλᾱκα 'I screech' Alkman 1.86, ptc. λεληκώς 'shrieking' *Il.* 22.141, fem. λελακυῖα *Od.* 12.85;
πεπᾱ́γαισιν 'they are frozen' Alkaios 338.2, παρὰ δ' ἔγχεα μακρὰ πέπηγεν 'and (their) long spears are stuck (in the ground) beside (them)' *Il.* 3.135.

A fuller list of examples is given at Kimball (1988: 242–3). As Kimball also observes, there is indirect evidence that this was not the PGk situation. Hesykhios records a mediopassive perfect τέθωκται· τεθύ̄μωται 'is enraged', τεθωγμένοι· μεμεθυσμένοι 'drunk' and an aorist θῶξαι· μεθύσαι 'to intoxicate', clearly related to θήγε̄ν Hom. 'to sharpen', later 'to provoke', aor. ptc. θᾱ́ξαις 'whetting' Pindar *Olympian* X.20; the o-grade of these forms makes no sense unless they were formed to a lost active perfect *τέθωγε 'it is sharp'. The prehistories of the two perfects of this type that might conceivably have outside cognates must therefore be reconstructed as follows:

(post-)NIE *pepóh$_2$ǵ- ~ *peph$_2$ǵ- 'be fixed' (cf. Lat. trans. pf. *pepigisse* with resultative meaning?) > PGk *πεπωγ- ~ *πεπαγ- → πεπᾱγ- > πεπηγ-;
(post-)NIE *wewóh$_2$g- ~ *wewh$_2$g- 'be broken' (cf. Toch. B pret. ptc. *wawākau* 'split'?) > PGk *ϝεϝωγ- ~ *ϝεϝαγ- → *ϝεϝᾱγ- > Att. ἐᾱγέναι.

Roots with PGk internal η normally preserve the o-grade, though none has stem-cognates elsewhere:

PIE *wreh$_1$ǵ- 'break' (see *LIV* s.v. **u̯reh$_1$ĝ-*), pf. *wewróh$_1$ǵe 'it is broken' remodeled in Att. ἔρρωγε;
(post-)NIE *sweh$_1$-d^h- 'become accustomed' (cf. Lat. pres. *suēscere*), pf. *seswóh$_1$d^{h}e '(s)he is accustomed' > Hom. ἔ̆ωθε.

That must have been the Proto-Greek situation as well.

Vowel-final active perfects have acquired an extension -κ- in the indicative singular and the subjunctive (i.e. in all forms which usually have a full-grade root). At least two directly reflect NIE perfects, namely *b^{h}e-b^{h}úH- 'be (by nature or growth)' (cf. Skt 3sg. *babʰū́va*[41] 'it is (by nature)' *RV* VII.103.7; cf. Kümmel 2000: 344) and *ste-stóh₂- ~ *ste-sth₂- 'be in a standing position' (cf. Skt 3sg. *tastʰau* 'she stands erect' *RV* III.55.14). The Greek innovations in the inflection of these stems can be illustrated by their Homeric paradigms:

indic. 3pl. πεφύᾱσι(ν) four times (πεφῡ́κασι *Od.* 7.114), subj. 3sg. πεφῡ́κῃι *Il.* 4.483, ptc. πεφυυῖα, etc. four times, plup. 3sg. πεφῡ́κει five times;
indic. 2sg. ἕστηκας *Il.* 5.485, 3sg. ἕστηκε(ν) ten times, 2du. ἕστατον *Il.* 23.284, 1pl. διέσταμεν *Il.* 21.436, 2pl. ἀφέστατε *Il.* 4.340, 3pl. ἑστᾶσι(ν) nine times (ἑστήκᾱσιν *Il.* 4.434), subj. 3sg. ἑστήκῃι twice, opt. 3sg. ἀφεσταίη twice *Od.*, iptv. 2sg. ἕσταθ' *Od.* 22.489, 2du. ἕστατον *Il.* 23.443, 2pl. ἕστατε *Il.* 20.354, inf. ἑστάμεν(αι) seventeen times, ptc. ἑσταότος, etc. thirty-eight times, plup. 3sg. ἑστήκει(ν) twenty-one times, 1pl. ἕσταμεν *Od.* 11.466, 3pl. ἕστασαν thirty-two times.

The former stem was anomalous in NIE in that it did not ablaut because the root did not ablaut; in the latter the inherited full-grade *oh₂ > *ω was replaced by *ᾱ > η, as expected (see above), and in this case there is no indication that that could not have occurred at the PGk stage. But in both stems, and in all other Greek perfect stems ending in vowels, -κ- was inserted between the stem and the endings in the singular of the indicative (both perfect and pluperfect) and in the subjunctive. The Boiotian dialect, which preserves a range of archaisms, also normally exhibits -κ- in the indicative singular of vowel-final perfect stems but not in other forms (Ringe 1984: 175–86; see also 7.3.3 below); unfortunately the only Boiotian perfect subjunctive is periphrastic δεδωῶσα ἴῃ (*DGE* 462.A.30).

As Kimball (1991: 148) points out, sg. -κα, -κας, -κε of aor. ἔθηκα, etc., could have been parsed by native learners as endings appropriate for vowel-final stems; in that case their spread to the perfect would have been a natural development (pp. 151–2), especially since 1sg. -α, 3sg. -ε were normal perfect endings. But a later generation of native learners apparently re-parsed the perfect forms as πέφῡκ-ε, etc., reinterpreting -κ- as part of the full-grade alternant of the stem; the result was that it spread to the only other full-grade forms in the paradigm, namely the subjunctive.

How much of this development had already occurred in PGk? Even the introduction of the endings -κα, -κας, -κε could have occurred at that stage only if the active indicative singular of ἔθηκα were already in place, and as we have seen, a relic of a κ-less paradigm appears to be actually attested (4.2.2 (i)). Under the circumstances we cannot be certain what the PGk situation was. In any case

[41] Note that this perfect is revealed to be an archaism by a double anomaly: a regular perfect to this root could only be '*bubʰā́va*', with different vowels both in the root and in the reduplicating syllable.

the spread of -κ- in these perfect paradigms was an ongoing process (except in Boiotian); for instance, in Homer it has begun to spread into the 3pl. (note the two examples above), there are occasional examples of participles with -κ-, and δείδω 'I'm afraid' (see the beginning of this section) has largely been replaced by δείδοικα. These are clearly later phenomena and will be addressed in 7.3.3.

The ablaut pattern of perfects built to roots of the shape *CeRH- has undergone substantial evolution in Greek. For instance, the NIE perfect of *telh$_2$- 'lift' can only have been *tetólh$_2$- ~ *tetl̥h$_2$-, surviving in Old Lat. *tetulit* (*LIV* s.v. **telh$_2$*). In Greek we would expect to find *τετολ(α)- ~ *τετλᾱ- > τετλη-. The former type is never found (except for *ǵegónh$_1$e > γέγονε, on which see above). The latter appears consistently in Homeric participles: τετληότι nine times, τετληότες *Il.* 5.873, τετληυῖα *Od.* 20.23. Otherwise it has been replaced by a 'hyper-zero-grade' τετλα-, apparently formed to τετλη- as if the latter were full-grade. It seems possible that indicative sg. τετληκ- was constructed to τετλη- in the manner outlined above, and then τετλα- was constructed to τετληκ- on the model of 'stand', but I can think of no way to demonstrate that. The facts regarding Hom. κέκμηκε 'is exhausted' and τέθνηκε 'is dead' are precisely parallel. None of these developments can be projected back into PGk with any confidence.

Since I do not think that the comparative evidence justifies the reconstruction of a pluperfect for PIE, I believe that the Greek active pluperfect is an innovation; its inflection must be innovative in any case, since no related language exhibits any similar paradigm. We are very poorly informed about the inflection of the pluperfect outside of Attic-Ionic, since most of the epigraphical examples can (and in many cases clearly do) reflect Attic influence. Three examples are early enough to be taken seriously:

Heraklean ἀπολώλη 'had been lost' *DGE* 62.39;
Delphian ἐφεστάκεον 'they were in charge' *Fouilles de Delphes* V.20.39 (*DGE* 326, notes);
Cyprian *o-mo-mo-ko-ne* *ὀμώμοκον 'they had sworn' Masson 8.6.

(Cyprian *a-no-ko-ne* *ἄνωγον 'they ordered' Masson 217.2 is also etymologically a pluperfect but might have been reinterpreted as an imperfect, as in Homer, so that its ending has more than one potential source.) The first two examples demonstrate that in at least some West Greek dialects the 3sg. originally ended in *-εε, as in Attic-Ionic: Heraklean -η is the sound-change outcome of that ending (see 7.2.3), while Delphian 3pl. -εον was obviously constructed to it. But Cyprian -ον strongly suggests that the PGk pluperfect 3sg. ending was just *-ε, identical with the perfect 3sg. ending. All hypotheses regarding the inflection of the active pluperfect are necessarily speculative, but Berg (1977) still seems the most plausible to me. For very different scenarios, see Jasanoff and Katz (2017) with references.

4.2.3 (ii) Mediopassive perfects

A large number of mediopassive perfects are attested already in Homer; many are passives, some with a resultative meaning. This is not surprising, considering that such stems are already well attested in Mycenaean, especially passive participles, some constructed to basic verbs (*de-de-me-no* 'bound', *ke-ka-u-me-no* 'burnt', etc.) but others obviously denominative (*a-ra-ro-mo-te-me-no* 'assembled', *qe-qi-no-me-no* 'turned on a lathe' (?) with 3sg. *qe-qi-no-to*, etc.; see Bartoněk 2002: 328, 332). However, not all mediopassive perfects can be equally old.

It is clear that mediopassive perfects with e-grade roots (λέλειπται 'is left, remains', etc.) cannot be inherited, since according to the inherited ablaut system for perfects a mediopassive perfect ought to have a zero-grade root (Chantraine 1973: 432, Risch 1974: 342, etc.). Mediopassive perfects of derived verbs also cannot be inherited, since there is no good evidence that derived verbs constructed perfects at all in NIE. Whether either of these types could have developed already in PGk is difficult to say.

But most mediopassive perfects with zero-grade roots do not seem to have been inherited either. There is only one with a highly plausible stem-cognate in another IE language (*LIV* s.v. **k̂lei̯*):

> ?Central IE mp. *k̂e-k̂li- 'lean, rest' (cf. Skt *śiśriye* '(Agni) is set (in the wood)' *RV* X.91.2, opt. *śiśrīta* 'would remain fixed' *RV* I.149.2) > κεκλι- in ἐγκέκλιται '(the burden) rests' *Il.* 6.78, ἐκέκλιτο '(the spear) was right up against (a cloud)' *Il.* 5.356, etc.

Since Greek and Indo-Iranian clearly started out in the same area of the Central IE dialect continuum, it is possible that this example is a common inheritance. Also worth considering as a possible cognate pair is:

> ?Central IE mp. *ste-str̥h₃- 'be scattered, be strewn' (Skt *tistiré* '(the barhiṣ) is strewn' *RV* III.41.2) >→ ἔστρωτο '(an oxhide) was spread out' *Il.* 10.155.

Other potential examples, however, are more problematic. Though Skt *cucyuvé* (*RV* VIII.45.25) looks like a potential cognate of Hom. Gk ἔσσυται '(my θῡμός) is eager' *Od.* 10.484, the equation is almost certainly a mirage: the (rare) Skt stem is transitive, meaning something like 'has set in motion', while the Homeric stem is an intransitive stative. Homeric κέχυται, etc. is consistently passive—'it is poured', 'they are scattered', etc.—while its apparent Skt cognate *juhvé* is middle in at least two of its three occurrences (Grassmann 1996 s.v. *hu*, *LIV* s.v. *ĝʰeu̯*). Since the formation is productive both in Greek and in Indo-Iranian, most apparently shared examples can easily have been parallel innovations.

However, it is likely that PGk already possessed a nucleus of mediopassive perfect stems with zero-grade roots. Especially persuasive are examples like πέφαται 'he lies slain' and ἕμαρται 'it is fated', whose shapes are opaque in Homeric Greek but would have been much more transparent in PGk. On the other hand, the coexistence of an active intransitive and a mediopassive perfect strongly suggests that the latter is an innovation; Mycenaean *te-tu-ko-wo-a₂*, Hom. τετευχώς *Od.* 12.423 vs. Hom. τετυγμένος, all meaning 'fashioned, made', are the obvious example.

4.2.4 Future stems

It is now generally agreed that Greek future stems, like those of Indo-Iranian, Balto-Slavic, and Celtic, are the reflexes of NIE desideratives. At least a handful of desideratives survive as present stems in the daughters; the most obvious example is Lat. *vīsere* 'to visit, to go to see, to behold' < *wéyd-se/o- 'want to see', and a present stem which Greek shares with Sanskrit must also originally have been desiderative (*LIV* s.vv. **$h_2$elk*, **$h_2$leks*):

> NIE *$h_2$lek- 'ward off' (cf. Hom. aor. ἄλαλκε) → *$h_2$lék-se/o- 'want to ward off' → 'ward off, defend' (Skt 3sg. *rákṣati*) > Hom. ἀλεξέμεναι.

Two slightly different desiderative suffixes survive as Greek future suffixes, a default *-se/o- and an extended *-$h_1$se/o-; the latter > *-εhε/o- > 'liquid future' -εε/o-, as in μενε͂ν 'to be going to stay' < *μενεhε/o-. It seems likely that a genuine future stem already existed in PGk, if only because there are no relic futures with an overtly desiderative meaning. On the other hand, the curious fact that active verbs often have middle futures could conceivably be an indirect reflex of their originally desiderative function.

While both these future suffixes must have been present in PGk, it is difficult to find unproblematic stem-cognates in related languages. That is not surprising, given that the desiderative was a peripheral category of the NIE verb that was widely lost in the daughters. A good many Greek futures resemble Indo-Iranian or Old Irish subjunctives (*LIV passim*), but that can be an accident, since all the relevant formations were marked by suffixes beginning with *-s- which need not have been etymologically identical. At least one cognate pair seems solid (*LIV* s.v. 2.**deh₁*):

> NIE *déh₁-se/o- or *dáh₂-se/o- 'want to meet' (Skt 3sg. *ábhi dāsati* '(s)he is hostile') > fut. *δᾱhε/o- or *δηhε/o- > Hom. δήεις 'you will find'.

The other proposed cognations that seem at least possible are the following:

> ?PIE *démh₂-s- 'want to tame' (Hitt. *damass-* 'press, oppress'?; but see Melchert 1994a: 70–1 on the phonological problems) >→ NIE *démh₂-se/o- >→ fut. *δαμαhε/o-(remodeled on pres. δαμνη/α- and aor. δαμασ(σ)α-, *LIV* s.v. 2. **demh₂*) in 3sg. δαμᾶι 'is going to overwhelm' *Il.* 1.61;

?NIE *démh$_2$-se/o- 'want to build' (Proto-Tocharian trans. pres. *tsəm-ṣə/së-, with the laryngeal reflex *-a- deleted, as typically in Tocharian derived transitives, in Toch. B 2sg. *tsamṣt* 'you cause to grow', TA 3sg. *tsmäṣ*) > *δεμαhε/ο- →[42] fut. *δεμεhε/ο- > Myc. ptc. masc. pl. *de-me-o-te* *δεμέhοντες '(men) going to build', Att. δεμε̄ν;

?NIE *kél-se/o- 'want to drive' (?Toch. 'bear, endure': Toch. B pres. 3sg. *kälṣäṃ*, 3pl. *kälseṃ*, Toch. A ptc. *kläsmāṃ*; on the possible semantic development see *LIV* s.v. **kel*) > κέλσε̄ν '(that it) was going to land (i.e. was going to find refuge)' Aischylos *Hiketides* 331.

Perhaps a better guide to the PGk situation are the attested Greek futures that are anomalous in one way or another. Two are isolated in suppletive paradigms:

PIE *h$_3$okʷ- 'see' (fossilized reduplicated desiderative *h$_3$í-h$_3$kʷ-se/o- in Skt 3sg. *ī́kṣate* '(s)he sees', *LIV* s.v. **h$_3$ekʷ*), desid. *h$_3$ókʷ-se/o- > fut. ὄψεσθαι;

pre-Gk *oys-se/o- 'want to carry/bring' (cf. οἰστός 'bearable', Frisk s.v. οἴσω) > fut. οἴσε̄ν.

A few (in addition to δήεις) have failed to reintroduce -σ- between vowels as expected:

pre-Gk *píh$_3$-se/o- 'want to drink' > fut. πί̄εσθαι;[43]

pre-Gk *ǵʰéw-se/o- 'want to pour' > *χεϝ-hε/ο- > *χε̄ϝε/ο- > χεε/ο- > Att. fut. χε̄ν;

pre-Gk *élh$_2$-se/o- 'want to drive' > ἐλα-hε/ο- > Hom. *ἐλάε̄ν (transmitted as ἐλάαν, *Od.* 5.290).

Finally, there are a few with an etymologically justified e-grade root which is not well supported by the rest of their paradigms:

pre-Gk *gʰénd-se/o- 'want to grasp' > fut. χέ̄σεσθαι (pres. χανδάνε̄ν, aor. χαδε̄ν, Hom. plup. 3sg. κεχόνδει);

pre-Gk *kʷéndʰ-se/o- 'want to experience' > fut. πέ̄σεσθαι (pres. πάσχε̄ν, aor. παθε̄ν, Hom. pf. 1sg. πέπονθα);

pre-Gk *h$_1$léwdʰ-se/o- 'want to arrive' > fut. ἐλεύσεσθαι 'to be going to come' (Hom. aor. 3sg. ἤλυθε, pf. 1sg. εἰλήλουθα ~ ἀπελήλυθα).

[42] Exactly how this replacement occurred remains unclear. It is possible that an anomalous future was simply remodeled to conform to the majority type; but *demh$_2$- 'build', like *ǵenh$_1$- 'be born', has lost its laryngeal completely in Greek verb forms except in the preconsonantal zero-grade stem (δμᾱ- > δμη-, γνη-), and if that occurred very early the fut. *δεμεhε/ο- could have been formed within the separate prehistory of Greek.

[43] This must be the model for unexpected fut. ἔδεσθαι 'be going to eat' (Warren Cowgill, p.c. ca. 1976).

4.2.5 Mood suffixes and the augment

Greek inherited from Core IE a subjunctive suffix that was *-e/o- for athematic stems and *-ē/ō- (i.e. thematic *-e/o- plus subjunctive *-e/o-) for thematic stems. Though the latter, as -η/ω-, has spread to all stems in literary Greek of the Classical period, there are numerous indications in Homer that PGk athematic stems still had short-voweled subjunctives in -ε/ο-:

Hom. εἴδομεν '(so that) we may know', εἴδετε '(so that) ye may know' (see 4.2.3 (i));
ἐρύσσομεν ... ἀγείρομεν ... θείομεν ... βήσομεν 'let's launch (a ship) ... let's assemble (a crew) ... let's put (a hecatomb in it) ... let's embark (Chryseis)' *Il.* 1.141–4, all sigmatic aorist subjunctives (and see Chantraine 1973: 454–5, 458–9 for much longer lists of examples);
Hom. ἴομεν 'let's go'.

Sigmatic aorist subjunctives in -ε/ο- survived longest in the dialects of the Asia Minor seaboard and the islands offshore, as well as in the southern Doric islands (Buck 1955: 119–20), e.g.:

χαλάσσομεν δὲ τὰς θυμοβόρω λύας 'and let's let go of heart-consuming strife', Alkaios 70.10;
ἢν δὲ μὴ πρήξοισιν 'if they do not exact the penalty', *DGE* 688A.16–17, Ionic (Chios), 5th century BC;
ὃς ἂν τὰ(ς) στήλας ... ἢ κατάξει ἢ φοινικήια ἐκκόψει ἢ ἀφανέας ποιήσει 'whoever either breaks the stelae or chisels out the letters or makes them illegible', *DGE* 710B.35–9, Ionic (Teos), 5th century BC;
αἰ μέγ κα ὑποκύψει 'if it submits', *DGE* 251A.20, Koan, 4th century BC;
αἰ δέ κα δόξει 'if it is agreed', *DGE* 244.13, Astypalaian;
νικῆν δ' ὀτερά κ' οἱ πλίες ὀμόσοντι 'whichever side the majority swears (in favor of) shall win (the suit)', Buck 118.11–12, Cretan (Gortyn), 3rd century BC;
αἴ κα τῶι θεῶι τὰν τιμὰν ἐρεῖσες 'if you have deposited the price for the god', Buck 115.8–9, Kyrenaian, early 4th century BC.

In this respect they preserved the PGk situation.

The optative had undergone somewhat less change by the classical period. The inherited thematic optative suffix -οι- underwent no change at all. Athematic *-yéh$_1$- ~ *-ih$_1$- should have given *-η- ~ *-ι- after vowels; after consonants the *-y- of the full-grade alternant should have caused the sound changes characteristic of y-clusters (see 3.6.3). What we actually find in athematic vowel stems is -Vιη- ~ -Vι-, in which the -ι- of the full-grade alternant cannot reflect intervocalic *y. The most plausible explanation is that these athematic optatives have been remodeled on the present optative of 'be', in which such an outcome was phonologically regular (see 3.5.1):

PIE opt. 3sg. *$h_1$siéh$_1$t 'let him be' (Skt *syā́t;* cf. Old Lat. *siet*) >→ *esyēd > *ἐhjη > εἴη.

There would have been no motivation for this remodeling until intervocalic *y was variably lost; thus the remodeling probably occurred well after PGk, roughly in the Mycenaean period.

After consonants the inherited athematic suffix persists only in the Cretan sigmatic aorist, e.g.:

αἰ δὲ κοσμησίε̄, ὄπε̄ δικακσίε̄,[44] αὐτὸν ὀπῆλεν διπλεῖ 'if he should become kosmos (again), however he may judge, he himself is to owe double the amount'; Buck 116.2, Dreros, 6th (7th?) century BC.

However, that is enough to demonstrate that PGk sigmatic aorist optatives were constructed with the inherited athematic optative suffix (and note that in these examples Siever's Law has applied, as expected etymologically). The sigmatic optative aorists in -αι- and -ειε must therefore be post-PGk innovations.

As I noted in 2.3.2, the augment *é, which behaves like a separate word in terms of accent, is attested only in the eastern end of the Core IE area: Greek, Phrygian, Armenian, and Indo-Iranian. Its distribution in attested Greek is odd: in Mycenaean it is mostly absent; in Homer it is optional in past-tense narrative, but usually occurs in the gnomic aorist, which does *not* refer to the past; in later Greek it is normally present in all 'secondary' indicative tenses in all functions.

The gnomic aorist is the key to understanding the augment's development. As Delfs (2006) demonstrated, the appearance of the augment in past tenses and in the gnomic aorist, which have nothing in common semantically, is best explained by the hypothesis that it originally indicated hearsay, i.e. statements for which the speaker did not vouch personally; Delfs adduces a similar particle in Wintu, an aboriginal language of California, which likewise developed into a past tense marker. The fact that Greek attests both divergent functions of the augment suggests that it might still have been an evidential marker in Proto-Greek.

On the other hand, the shape of the augment in Greek suggests that it had already become a prefix in Proto-Greek. Before most consonants, including those that were lost within the separate prehistory of Greek, it underwent no change;

[44] Buck's δικασσίε̄ is a misprint; see the original publication, Van Effenterre and Demargne (1937: 334).

but before laryngeals it underwent the usual contractions and compensatory lengthenings, e.g.:

PIE *$h_1$ludʰéd '(s)he arrived' (Toch. B *lac* '(s)he went out', OIr. *luid* '(s)he went'), with augment *é $h_1$ludʰed > Hom. ἤλυθε '(s)he came';
PIE *é $h_1$est 'it is said that (s)he was' (Skt *ā́s* '(s)he was') > Dor. ἦς '(s)he was';
PIE *é h_2aǵed 'it is said that (s)he was leading/driving' (Skt *ā́jat* '(s)he drove') > ᾶγε '(s)he was leading' > Att.-Ion. ἦγε;
PIE *é $h_3$reǵsn̥d 'it is said that they reached' >→ ὤρεξαν.

Strictly speaking it is not completely clear that laryngeals were still in place when these developments occurred—conceivably the immediate predecessor of a form like ἤλυθε was *é eludʰed or the like—but it is clear that these contractions, which yielded lower mid long vowels in all the dialects, occurred long before most other vowel contractions in Greek, which yielded higher mid long vowels in many dialects. It seems reasonable to infer that, whatever its function was in Proto-Greek, the augment had become part of the inflectional morphology and was no longer an independent sentence particle.

4.2.6 Personal endings

Greek has lost one person-and-number ending altogether: there are no longer any inherited 1du. verb forms, and the 1du. pronouns are (as expected) used with 1pl. verbs; so far as we can tell, that was already the Proto-Greek situation. The unique Homeric 1du. form περιδώμεθον 'let's wager' *Il.* 23.485 is obviously an innovation, with an ending constructed from 1pl. -μεθα and 2du. -σθον (Chantraine 1973: 478); whether it ever existed outside of epic diction is undiscoverable.

In Classical Greek the primary endings are arguably the default set; otherwise it is difficult to see why 1sg. -μι would have spread to the optative. However, it is clear that the secondary endings were the default set in PIE, and they probably remained so in Proto-Greek. I therefore begin with the secondary endings of the active.

4.2.6 (i) Active secondary endings

The PIE endings and their expected PGk outcomes were the following:

sg.	1	*-m ~ *-m̥	>	-ν ~ -α	du.	1	*-wé	>	*-ϝε
	2	*-s	>	-ς		2	*-tóm	>	-τον
	3	*-t ~ *-d	>	0		3	*-tā́m	>	-τᾱν (> -την)

pl.	1	*-mé	>	*-με
	2	*-té	>	-τε
	3	*-énd ~ *-nd ~ *-n̥d	>	-εν ~ -ν ~ *-α

What is surprising is how many of the expected outcomes are actually attested in Greek; evidently there has been no wholesale overhaul of the system. The 1du. ending, like all 1du. endings, has been lost, with the result that 1du. subjects default to 1pl. concord; when that happened is unrecoverable. The 1pl. ending has acquired a final nasal and become -μεν, probably in PGk, since that is the ending in all Greek dialects which preserve the 2ary ending; whether that has anything to do (historically speaking) with Hitt. 2ary 1pl. *-wen*, 2pl. *-tten* is difficult to say. The expected syllabic reflex of the zero-grade alternant of the 3pl. ending was eventually remodeled to -αν (see 5.4.2 (i)), no doubt on the basis of the full-grade alternant. That would have been most clearly motivated when word-final stops were lost, probably well after the PGk period. Naturally the full-grade alternant *-énd was 'colored' by an adjacent laryngeal; thus such a form as Hom. 3pl. βάν 'they went' can be, and probably is, a direct reflex of PIE $*g^wh_2ánd$ 'they stepped' (underlyingly $*/g^wh_2$-énd/). In thematic stems the *e of *-énd was elided, yielding 3pl. *-o-nd > PGk -ον.

4.2.6 (ii) Active primary endings

The PIE endings and their expected PGk outcomes were the following:

sg.	1	*-mi	>	-μι	du.	1	*-wós	>	*-ϝος
	2	*-si	>	*-σι ~ *-hι		2	*-tés	>	*-τες
	3	*-ti	>	-τι (> -σι)		3	*-tés	>	*-τες

pl.	1	*-mós	>	*-μος
	2	*-té	>	-τε
	3	*-énti ~ *-nti ~ *-n̥ti	>	-εντι ~ -ντι ~ -ατι

Once again many of the expected endings survive in attested Greek. Expected *-μος has been replaced by -μες, no doubt with the vowel leveled in from the secondary ending. 2du. *-tés (Skt $-t^h\acute{a}s$) has been replaced by 2ary -τον—and the result has been that the latter also acquired 1ary 3du. function, giving indirect testimony that the original 3du. primary ending was also *-tés (Skt *-tás*). These modest changes are common to all the dialects whose forms are attested and are probably PGk. The 3pl. endings survive, except for the leveling of -ν- into -ατι (see 5.4.2 (i)); elision of *e in thematic stems yielded 3pl. *-o-nti > -οντι. The only ending which does not survive unaltered anywhere is 2sg. *-σι ~ *-hι. The loss of *h, roughly in the Mycenaean period, reduced the postvocalic alternant to *-ι, which was usually extended with 2ary -ς to mark the form better as a 2sg. The failure of 2sg. *-σι to be attested must be laid to the fact that consonant-final athematic stems are already rare even in Homer.

The anomalous NIE thematic 1sg. *-o-h_2 survives in Greek as -ω. Thematic 3sg. primary ending -ει is best explained as a regular sound-change reflex of *-eti (see 3.4.6 with references). The loss of *t was early, as this ending is attested (by implication) already in Mycenaean, in the sequence *e-ke-qe e-u-ke-to-qe e-ke-e* *hέχει κ^{w}ε εὔχετοί κ^{w}ε hέχεhεν 'she both is in possession of and solemnly affirms that she is in possession of' (Aura Jorro 1999 s.v. *e-ke*).

4.2.6 (iii) Mediopassive secondary endings

The Core IE endings and their expected PGk outcomes were the following:

sg.	1	*-h_2a	>	*-α	du.	1	*-wé$d^h h_2$	>	*-ϝεθα
	2	*-th_2a	>	*-τα (*-θα?)		2	???		
	3	*-to	>	-το		3	???		
pl.	1	*-mé$d^h h_2$	>	-μεθα					
	2	*- $d^h h_2$ué	>	???					
	3	*-nto ~ *-n̥to	>	-ντο ~ -ατο					

There has been much more innovation in this set of endings. The 2sg. ending has been replaced by -σο > (*-ho after vowels) everywhere, thus probably in PGk; the 1sg. ending was apparently first replaced by *-μα, with -μ- leveled in from the active. But in all the dialects for which we have evidence we find -μᾱν (> -μην), with a syllable coda of unclear origin. What should have happened to the 2pl. ending by regular sound change is unclear; it looks as if the outcome was at first *-θϝε, the laryngeal having somehow been lost, with further regular development to *-θε and then remodeling to -σθε (on which, see below). In any case the dual endings, 2du. -σθον and 3du. -σθᾱν (> -σθην), were obviously constructed to -σθε on the model of the active endings (-τον and -τᾱν, cf. 2pl. -τε). How many of these developments had occurred by the PGk period is difficult to say, but they appear to be shared by all the dialects.

4.2.6 (iv) Mediopassive primary endings

The Core IE endings and their expected PGk outcomes were the following:

sg.	1	*-$h_2$ay	>	*-αι	du.	1	*-wós$d^h h_2$	>	*-ϝοσθα
	2	*-t$h_2$ay	>	*-ται (*-θαι?)		2	???		
	3	*-toy	>	-τοι		3	???		
pl.	1	*-mós$d^h h_2$	>	*-μοσθα					
	2	*- $d^h h_2$ué	>	???					
	3	*-ntoy ~ *-n̥toy	>	-ντοι ~ -ατοι					

Just as in the secondary endings, *-αι has been recharacterized as -μαι with active -μ-; just as in the active, *-μοσθα has been remodeled to -μεσθα, well attested in Homer. Once again the 2sg. ending has been replaced by *-σοι (> -οι) and 2du.,

3du. -σθον have been remodeled on -σθε. But two details of these endings require more discussion, namely the syllable coda -οι vs. -αι and the -σ- of -σθε.

More than thirty years ago the late Jordan Greenwald proposed (p.c.) a highly plausible explanation of the -σ- of the 2pl. ending. We need to start with the inherited 1pl. and 2pl. endings, assuming that the mp. 2pl. ending was *-θε:

	active		mediopassive	
	1ary	2ary	1ary	2ary
1pl.	-μες	-με(ν)	-μεσθα	-μεθα
2pl.	-τε	-τε	*-θε	*-θε

Since there was a clear difference between the 1ary and 2ary mediopassive 1pl. endings, marked by -σ- in the former, it would have been natural for native learners to extend the difference to the mediopassive 2pl. endings:

	active		mediopassive	
	1ary	2ary	1ary	2ary
1pl.	-μες	-με(ν)	-μεσθα	-μεθα
2pl.	-τε	-τε	-σθε	*-θε

However, since there had never been any difference between the 1ary and 2ary *active* 2pl. endings, a later generation of native learners could have restored that situation in the corresponding mediopassive endings by extending -σθε to secondary function as well, yielding the immediately reconstructable set of endings. When this happened is impossible to say, but at least two statements can be made. One is that the distinction between 1ary -μεσθα and 2ary -μεθα must have been lost relatively late in the prehistory of Homeric Greek, since the poems preserve both endings (though not their functions, using them interchangeably for metrical purposes); thus the creation of -σθε need not have been very early, and its spread to secondary function must of course have been later. The other is that the remaining mediopassive endings beginning with -σθ- must have been modeled on -σθε. Thus unless the creation of 1ary -σθε, at least, occurred before the PGk period it is very unlikely that the entire set of attested mediopassive endings was already present in Proto-Greek.

The identity of the diphthong in the coda of the singular and 3pl. endings is a more difficult problem. Most of the attested dialects exhibit -μαι, -(σ)αι, -ται, -νται ~ -αται (or their reflexes, e.g. Boiotian 3sg. -τη, 3pl. -αθη), but Arkadian instead has 3sg. -τοι, 3pl. -ντοι, and a 2sg. κεῖοι 'you lie' is attested on two nearly identical curse tablets (Otto Hoffmann 1900: 101–3); Mycenaean concurs with 3sg. *-to* (see 4.2.6 (ii) for an example). Nearly all the older literature observes that these endings could have been constructed to 2ary -(σ)ο, -το, -ντο and can therefore be innovations. So far as I can see, that is still a possibility. However, it now seems clear that the PIE third-person endings were *-tor, *-ntor (see 2.3.3 (iii)), and the most economical explanation for the Mycenaean and Arkadian (and probably Cyprian) endings is a straightforward replacement of *-r with *-y, yielding -τοι, -ντοι. In that case the -αι of the other dialects can only have been leveled in from 1sg. -μαι, necessarily spreading through a dialect continuum, since the dialects with -αι in all four endings do not constitute a clade. A more definitive solution will depend on the discovery of further evidence.

4.2.6 (v) Imperative endings

The PIE active imperative 2sg. was endingless, though it was sometimes extended with an emphatic particle *-d^hí which was reinterpreted as a 2sg. ending in some daughters, including Greek (cf. Hitt. *īt* = Skt *ihí* = ἴθι, all < PIE *h_1id^hí, whereas Lat. *ī* reflects older endingless *$h_1$éy). The other second-person imperative endings seem to have been identical with the 2ary endings, and that has continued to be the case in Greek.

The 3sg. imperative, however, was replaced in Greek by the displaced imperative in *-tṓd, which in Greek is always 3sg. and does not indicate temporal displacement. Other third-person imperative endings were constructed from that inherited ending. It appears that *-tōd was reanalyzed as */-t-ō-t/, doubly marked as 3sg., and a 3pl. */-nt-ō-nt/, likewise with double marking, was constructed to match it (Ringe 1997). That had already occurred when Osthoff's Law operated in Greek (see. 3.5.3), because the outcome was -ντον in Lesbian, in Rhodian inscriptions from Phaselis, and in Pamphylian (where it became -δυ by regular sound change, Brixhe 1976: 21, 74). The loss of word-final stops must have been later still.

3pl. -ντον is shown to be an archaism by its persistence in dialects on the edge of the Greek *Sprachraum* that do not otherwise share innovations. Elsewhere this ending was remodeled or replaced, necessarily after the PGk period, since the dialects do not agree. The prehistory of third-person imperative endings will be taken up again in 7.3.1.

4.2.6 (vi) Perfect active endings

The NIE endings of the singular indicative survive in Greek:

1sg.	*-h_2a	>	-α
2sg.	*-th_2a	>	-θα (see 3.2.1)
3sg.	*-e	>	-ε

2sg. -θα was mostly replaced by -ας on the model of the sigmatic aorist (in which the 1sg. ending was also -α, though < *-m̥, and the 3sg. ending had become -ε), but that must have happened long after the PGk period. Otherwise the Greek perfect has adopted the endings of the athematic present. However, at some point the zero-grade 3pl. ending *-n̥ti was generalized in the perfect; its reflex -ατι survives in the northern West Greek dialects, and *-ą̥ti must have been the PGk ending (unless *-ēr or *-r̥s survived, for which there is no evidence at all).

4.2.7 Participles and infinitives

Like all the branches of Nuclear IE,[45] but unlike Anatolian, Greek has interpreted *-ónt- ~ *-nt- as an active participle suffix and *-mh$_1$nó- as a mediopassive participle suffix; the NIE perfect participial suffix *-wós- ~ *-us- also survives, e.g. in Mycenaean *te-tu-ko-wo-a$_2$* *τετυχϝóhα nt. pl. 'fashioned, made'.

Infinitives are another matter. All the Greek active infinitives seem to have originated as caseforms of NIE deverbal nouns, and some endings have plausible Sanskrit cognates. The distribution of the suffixes -μεναι, -μεν, *-hεναι, and *-hεν will need to be discussed in some detail in 5.3.2, and only in the light of that discussion can we suggest what the PGk situation was; but it seems clear that Vedic Skt *-máne* and *-ṣáni* are roughly cognate with the Greek suffixes. Sigmatic aorist -σαι is harder to assess because it is unclear whether its α spread from the indicative; mediopassive -σθαι, whatever its antecedents might have been, has obviously been remodeled to fit the mediopassive personal endings with -σθ-.

In spite of their nominal origin, all Greek infinitive endings are appended to aspect-and-tense stems; it is reasonable to project that innovation into Proto-Greek and impossible to say how it occurred in detail.

4.2.8 The accent of Greek verb forms

As is well known, the accent of verbs in the Attic and Ionic dialects—those which are well enough attested to give us some confidence in the tradition—can be described as follows.

1) all forms of the present indicative of ἔναι 'be' and φάναι 'say', except the 2sg., are enclitic;
2) otherwise finite forms normally have recessive accent *before the operation of vowel contraction*, except that
   a) the accent cannot recede beyond the augment; but
3) there are a handful of imperatives that do not have recessive accent, and
4) the accent of the non-finite forms (participles and infinitives) is not uniform and must be learned.

It is interesting to confront these general rules with the rules governing the accent of verbs in Vedic Sanskrit, which probably reflect the NIE or Core IE system (and certainly the system immediately ancestral to both Greek and Indo-Iranian). In subordinate clauses in Vedic the finite verb is accented, and if it occurs with a preverb the two are univerbated; in main clauses there is no univerbation, and the

[45] On Tocharian, see now Fellner (2021).

finite verb is *unaccented*. Obviously the Greek rule (1) is a relic of such a system: for some forms of ἔναι and φάναι the main-clause accentuation has been generalized. But the Greek rule (2) is also a relic of the same system, at one remove: main-clause accentlessness was generalized, and recessive accent was assigned to the accentless forms. That makes exception (2a) informative: at the time when accentless finite forms were generalized, the augment was still an independent particle, and it was accented.

Most athematic stems must have been inherited with alternating accent, and the accent of pf. inf. -έναι and ptc. -ώς, fem. -υῖα must be a relic of that situation. Sigmatic aorists, however, should have been accented on the root throughout, and in attested Greek their infinitives and participles still are (subject to general restrictions on where the accent can fall); the infinitives and participles of thematic presents and of futures exhibit the same pattern. However, thematic aorists and aorists in -ή- were clearly accented on the stem vowel (cf. λιπε͂ν, λιπέσθαι, λιπών, λιποῦ, μιγῆναι, μιγές, as well as imperatives λαβέ, etc.; Smyth 1956: 143).

4.3 Changes in nominal inflection

The inflection of nominals underwent more change in Greek than the inflection of verbs. The PIE accent-and-ablaut system survived only in relics, and there was a modest reorganization of stems on the basis of stem-final segment. The case system was also simplified somewhat.

4.3.1 Cases

Like all the daughters of Nuclear IE, Greek has lost the allative case, though at least one and possibly several adverbs with originally allative endings survive. The clearest example is

PIE allative *$\acute{g}^h$m̥áh$_2$ 'to the ground' + deictic *-í > Hom. adv. χαμαί.

The other plausible examples are prepositions/preverbs; the one with the most solid etymology is

PIE *kát(a)h$_2$ 'down' (cf. Hitt. *katta*) > κατά.[46]

Greek has also lost the ablative case; in 1st-millennium Greek the only clear relics of the ablative are a scattered handful of West Greek adverbs like

[46] The oxytonesis of this and other prepositions is likely to be a grammarians' fiction, reflecting underlying accentlessness. Note that when postposed this lexeme surfaces as κάτα (and so also other similarly accented prepositions).

Delphian ϝοίκω 'from home' *DGE* 323.C.23, -ω < *-ōd < *-oad ← NIE *-e-ad.

However, the Mycenaean data introduce an interesting complication. It seems reasonably clear that the unambiguous inst. pl. *-pi* *-φι functions as an ablative with some names of places (Hajnal 1995: 154–85), and it follows that in the Mycenaean dialect there was at least a partial syntactic merger of the inherited instrumental and ablative. That seems likeliest to have been prompted by the accidental synonymy of o-stem abl. sg. *-ō < *-ōd < *-oad (see above) and inst. sg. *-ō < *-oh$_1$, and in fact the Mycenaean o-stem ending *-o* can in some environments be plausibly interpreted as such a syncretic ending (cf. Hajnal 1995: 247–72). The fact that in 1st-millennium Greek dialects the ablative has obviously undergone syntactic merger with the genitive strongly suggests that the ablative-instrumental merger of Mycenaean was not shared with other contemporary dialects—and it follows that the ablative was still a living case in Proto-Greek.

Evidence for the locative case in Greek is differently distributed but leads to the same conclusion. No attested dialect of Greek distinguishes the dative and locative functionally, but the distinctive consonant-stem singular endings *-ey and *-i are both well attested. While the former survives in the 1st millennium only in compounds like Cyprian *ti-we-i-pi-lo* (Masson 327.8) = Hom. Διείφιλος 'friend-to-Zeus',[47] both endings are still in productive use in Mycenaean: the dat. sg. of s-stems often ends in *-e-i* *-εh-ι, but that of other consonant stems usually ends in *-e* *-ει (cf. Bartoněk 2002: 225–72). However, the distribution is not perfect, and it seems likely that *-ει was being replaced by -ι (Thompson 1997: 327–9). Since the competition between the two endings has not been resolved in Mycenaean, it seems unlikely that the two had become isofunctional already in Proto-Greek.

That the instrumental was a living case in Mycenaean has long been recognized (see the discussions of Hajnal 1995 and Bartoněk 2002 with references). It thus appears that Proto-Greek, like Sanskrit, still preserved a system of eight nominal cases.

4.3.2 Accent and ablaut

The elaborate PIE system of nominal ablaut has largely been lost in Greek, and many accent alternations have been leveled. It seems clearest to structure the discussion around a number of examples.

Ablaut between *ĕ and *ŏ has been eliminated from Greek noun paradigms, except for the innovative acrostatic neuter s-stems; for instance, Hom. γένος

[47] The manuscripts actually read Διίφιλος (as Wolfgang de Melo reminds me), and in principle the apparent long ι could have been lengthened metrically as the third of five successive light syllables; but the Cyprian name and a handful of others, such as Attic Διειτρέφης, show that it actually reflects the late graphic confusion of ει and long ι because the two merged in the 3rd century BC.

'lineage', gen. γένεος preserves the ablaut of PIE *ǵénh$_1$os, gen. *ǵénh$_1$es-os unchanged, and such nouns remain common in Ancient Greek.

Only the kinship terms and some other nouns in -ήρ preserve all three ablaut grades: the lengthened grade (in the nom. sg.), the full grade, and the zero grade. The paradigm of πατήρ 'father' (Skt *pitā́*, Lat. *pater*, etc.) is maximally conservative in that regard:

	Attic Greek			PIE	
	sg.	pl.		sg.	pl.
nom.	πατήρ	πατέρ-ες		*ph$_2$tḗr	*ph$_2$tér-es
acc.	πατέρ-α	πατέρ-ας		*ph$_2$tér-m̥	*ph$_2$tér-n̥s
gen.	πατρ-ός	πατρ-ῶν		*ph$_2$tr̥-és	*ph$_2$tr̥-óHom
dat.	πατρ-ί	πατρά-σι	(loc.)	*ph$_2$tér(-i)	*ph$_2$tr̥-sú
voc.	πάτερ			*ph$_2$tér	

It can be seen that even the 5th-century Attic forms are largely the reflexes of the PIE forms by regular sound change and minor phonological and morphological adjustments (desyllabification of *r̥ at some point after *h$_2$ between consonants had become α, generalization of gen. sg. *-os, loc. pl. *-su → -σι under the influence of sg. -ι, etc.). The retracted accent of πατράσι might be the result of Wheeler's Law (Probert 2006a: 91), though it could also reflect an innovative rule fixing the accent on the second syllable of the paradigm ('columnar accent'—the only plausible explanation for Skt *pitŕ̥ṣu*). The paradigms of μήτηρ[48] 'mother' (Skt *mātā́*, Lat. *māter*, etc.), θυγάτηρ[49] 'daughter' (Skt *duhitā́*), and γαστήρ 'belly' are similar, the last apparently for purely formal reasons. Homer preserves a similar paradigm of ἀνήρ 'man, male human being' (Skt *nā́*, PIE *h$_2$nḗr): sg. acc. ἀνέρα (with metrical lengthening of ἀ-), gen. ἀνδρός, etc., but also forms leveled in both directions (sg. acc. ἄνδρα, gen. ἀνέρος, etc.).

By the Classical period most polysyllabic n- and r-stems had eliminated either the full grade of the stem (thus sg. acc. ἄνδρα, gen. ἀνδρός, etc.) or the zero grade; note the following inherited examples:

PIE *ḱwṓ ~ *ḱuṓ 'dog', acc. *ḱwón-m̥, gen. *ḱun-és (Toch. B *ku*, obl. *kweṃ*; Skt *śvā́, śvā́n-am, śún-as*) >→ κύων, κύνα, κυνός;

PIE *poh$_2$imḗ(n) 'shepherd', acc. *poh$_2$imén-m̥, gen. *poh$_2$imn-és (Lith. *piemuõ*) >→ ποιμήν, ποιμένα, ποιμένος;

PIE *h$_2$áḱmō 'stone', acc. *h$_2$áḱmon-m̥, gen. *h$_2$ḱ(m)n-és (Skt *áśmā, áśmān-am, áśman-as ~ áśn-as*) >→ ἄκμων 'anvil', ἄκμονα, ἄκμονος.

[48] Accent shifted to agree with voc. sg. μῆτερ for obvious reasons.
[49] Accent shifted to agree with 'mother'.

Among the latter group the dat. pl. (reflecting the PIE loc. pl.) occasionally preserves an archaic zero grade; for instance, though most forms of ἀστήρ 'star' (Hitt. *hasterz*, PIE *$h_2$stḗr) are made to a stem ἀστέρ-, the dat. pl. is ἀστράσι. Quite a few of these nouns have leveled the lengthened grade of the nom. sg. through the entire paradigm. An inherited example is

> *$h_2$ánkō 'bend' → *$h_2$ankṓ (cf. OE *anga*, OHG *ango* 'goad' with Verner's Law voicing) >→ ἀγκών 'elbow', sg. acc. ἀγκῶνα, gen. ἀγκῶνος.

Most striking are the agent nouns in -τήρ. More than forty-five are attested in Homer (Risch 1974: 30–1), and in every single one the lengthened-grade η has been leveled through the paradigm.[50] In all these leveled paradigms the accent has been fixed on the same syllable in all forms (subject to the law of limitation). Since it is clear that leveling proceeded on a lexical basis, we cannot know how far it had gone in the paradigm of any given noun in Proto-Greek (except that it cannot have gone farther than in our attested examples). But an instance of lexical split argues caution:

> PIE *léymō 'lake', acc. *léymon-m̥, gen. *limn-és, loc. *limén(-i) (cf. Toch. B *lyam*, A *lyäm* < leveled *limn̥) >→ λειμών, λειμῶν- 'water meadow' and λιμήν, λιμέν- 'harbor'; double zero grade reflected in deriv. (orig. collective) λίμνη 'pool'.

It seems clear that the full range of ablaut grades of this noun survived down into the separate prehistory of Greek, and the same could be true of almost any ablauting noun of this group.

By contrast, neuter n-stems in *-mn̥ ~ *-mén- have all acquired recessive accent in Greek (like other polysyllabic neuters—see below). The stem consistently ends in -ματ-; the source of the -τ- is unknown (see e.g. Buck and Petersen 1949: 221 for some half-hearted suggestions). The few etymologically underived examples, such as ὄνομα and στόμα, have been assimilated to the derived type, the former, at least, with remodeling of its ablaut.

PIE i-stems and u-stems have developed somewhat differently in Greek. The nom. and acc. sg. forms are uniformly -ις, -ιν and -υς, -υν, suggesting that proterokinetic inflection has been generalized. But in the gen. and dat. sg. the most conservative attested forms seem to be Hom. πόληος, πόληϊ. The latter is clearly PIE loc. sg. *-ēy (< **-ey-i by Stang's Law) plus *-i (again), and it seems clear that the gen. sg. has been remodeled on that basis. The u-stem singulars are more straightforward, with reflexes of gen. *-éw-os, loc. sg. *-éw-i. The plural endings of

[50] Of course it is true that many are attested only once or a few times (though only θηητήρ 'critic, connoisseur' *Od.* 21.397 is attested only in the nom. sg.). But κρητήρ 'mixing bowl' appears forty times in the poems and μνηστῆρες more than 200 times in the *Odyssey*, always with η in the second syllable.

both stem types agree closely with their Vedic cognates—except that the dat. pl. has been remodeled to -εσι, an outcome that probably was not present in Proto-Greek.

Among monosyllabic consonant stems PIE *dyḗws or *dyéws 'sky, day; Sky-god' (Skt *dyáus*) retains its original ablaut to some extent:

	Greek	PIE
nom.	Ζεύς	*dyḗw-s or *dyéws
acc.	Δί-α, Dor. Ζῆν-α	*dyḗ-m
gen.	Δι-ός, Dor. Ζην-ός	*diw-és
dat.	Δι-ί, Dor. Ζην-ί	*diw-éy, loc. *dyéw(-i)
voc.	Ζεῦ	*dyéw

The Attic-Ionic dialects, at least, have leveled the zero grade of the root into the accusative, but in at least some Doric dialects the original accusative survived, was extended with the productive consonant-stem ending -α, and was then the basis for a new gen. and dat. It follows that the inherited accusative still existed, probably unchanged except by sound change, in Proto-Greek. Most other monosyllabic nouns leveled a single ablaut grade through the paradigm, sometimes with an additional lengthened grade for the nom. sg. and/or a relic dat. pl. with zero grade. The following are typical:

PIE *pṓd-s 'foot', acc. *pód-m̥, gen. *ped-és (Skt *pā́t, pā́d-am, pad-ás*; Lat. *pēs, ped-em, ped-is*) >→ πṓς,[51] πόδα, ποδός;

PIE *$h_1$dónt-s 'tooth', acc. *$h_1$dónt-m̥, gen. *$h_1$dn̥t-és (Skt *dán, dánt-am, dat-ás*; Lat. *dēns, dent-em, dent-is*) >→ ὀδṓς, ὀδόντα, ὀδόντος;

PIE *nók^{w}t-s 'night', acc. *nók^{w}t-m̥, gen. *nék^{w}t-s (Lat. *nox, noct-*; Hitt. *nekuz mēhur* 'evening time') >→ νύξ, νύκτα, νυκτός;

PIE *wṓk^w-s 'voice' (Lat. *vōx*), acc. *wók^w-m̥ (Toch. B *wek*), gen. *wek^w-és (?; Av. *vacō*) >→ Hom. acc. ὄπα, gen. ὀπός;

PIE *ǵ^{h}wḗr, acc. *ǵ^{h}wér-m̥ (?) 'wild animal' (Lith. *žvėrìs*; cf. Lat. *ferus* 'wild') > *χ^{w}ήρ >→ θήρ, acc. θῆρα;

PIE *b^{h}ṓr 'one who carries', acc. *b^{h}ór-m̥ (?) >→ φώρ 'thief', acc. φῶρα;

φρήν 'midriff, mind' (etymology?), acc. φρένα, gen. φρενός, pl. dat. φρεσί, Dor. φρασί (with α < *ą < *n̥).

As usual, we cannot tell exactly what the paradigm of each of these nouns was in Proto-Greek. There are also isolated forms, especially in Homeric formulas, e.g.:

[51] Hesykhios attests a Doric πῶς, but the context suggests that the transmission is faulty (Piwowarczyk 2015: 275). It is clear that a nom. sg. *pṓds existed, since otherwise there is no plausible source for PGmc. *fōt-; moreover, if Greek had inherited a nom. sg. *πώς (parallel to κλώψ 'thief') it is easier to understand why the Att.-Ion. nom. sg. is πṓς rather than *πός: the vowel was simply raised to bring it into conformity with πόδα, πόδες, etc. But direct evidence for *πώς apparently does not exist.

κατὰ ὦλκα 'down the furrow' *Il.* 13.707, εἰ ὦλκα διηνεκέα προταμοίμην 'whether I could cut a straight furrow' *Od.* 18.375 (note that in both cases *ἄολκα can be restored, Schindler 1972b: 77) < PIE *$h_2$wólkm̥, root *$h_2$welk- 'pull';

ἀλκὶ πεποιθώς 'relying on his defensive capability' six times at line-end < *h_2l̥k-, root *$h_2$lek- 'protect';

εἰς ὦπα 'in(to) the face' six times ←< PIE collective *h_3ṓk^w 'eyes, face'.

Such forms suggest that the ablaut of surviving PIE root-nouns was better preserved in Proto-Greek. There are also, of course, root-nouns that do not exhibit ablaut in any daughter and probably did not in PIE; obvious examples are ἅλς 'salt' and μῦς 'mouse'.

The accent patterns of consonant stems have been redistributed in Greek. Nouns which remained or became polysyllabic in Greek usually acquired fixed accent on one particular syllable; thus PIE monosyllabic *$h_1$dónt-s, *$h_1$dn̥t-és appears in Greek as ὀδός, ὀδόντος (see above). Conversely, nouns which remained or became monosyllabic in Greek usually exhibit alternating accent, with the accent on the gen. and dat. endings but on the stem in the other cases; thus *nók^wt-s, *nék^wt-s appears in Greek as νύξ, νυκτός (see above). Two m-stems whose inflection had been parallel in PIE diverged in Greek because one became monosyllabic and the other did not:

PIE *d^hé$ǵ^h$ōm (< **-om-s) 'earth', acc. *d^hé$ǵ^h$ōm (< **-om-m̥), gen. *$ǵ^h$m̥-és (< **$d^h$$ǵ^h$-), loc. *$d^h$$ǵ^h$ém(-i) (cf. Hitt. nom.-acc. *tēkan*, Ved. Skt acc. *kṣā́m*, gen. *jmás*, loc. *kṣámi*) >→ Hom. χθών, χθόν-α, χθον-ός, dat. χθον-ί;

PIE *$ǵ^h$éyōm 'winter', acc. *$ǵ^h$éyōm, gen. *$ǵ^h$im-és, loc. *$ǵ^h$iém(-i) (cf. Lat. *hiems*) >→ χιών 'snow', χιόν-α, χιόν-ος, χιόν-ι.

Other nouns that have become monosyllabic and acquired alternating accent include:

PIE *mḗh_1n̥s 'moon, month', acc. *mḗh_1n̥s-m̥, gen. *méh_1n̥s-os (Skt *mā́s*, Lat. *mēnsis*) >→ Hom. μείς (i.e. μέ̄ς, *Il.* 19.117), μῆν-α, μην-ός;

PIE *$ǵ^h$ésōr 'hand' (cf. Hitt. *kissar*): obl. stem *$ǵ^h$esr- > *χεhρ- > χέ̄ρ, acc. χε̄ρ-α, gen. χε̄ρ-ός;

PIE coll. *páh$_2$wōr 'fire', gen. *ph$_2$un-és (cf. Hitt. *pahhur*, *pahhuenas*) >→ *ph$_2$uṓr, *ph$_2$ur-és (cf. Toch. B *puwar*) >→ πῦρ, πυρ-ός.

With the last contrast ὕδωρ 'water' ←< *udṓr (Skt *udā́ RV* twice) ← coll. *wédōr (cf. Hitt. *witār*), which remained polysyllabic and acquired the recessive accent typical of polysyllabic neuter consonant stems (gen. ὕδατος). As this last example illustrates, polysyllabic neuter consonant stems acquired recessive accent, apparently by generalization from the very common acrostatic s-stems (such as γένος) and the direct cases of proterokinetic nouns (e.g. neuter *men-stems and u-stems). Occasional deviations from these rules show that they developed gradually, at least partly after the Proto-Greek period.

4.3.3 Stem types: Nouns

Except that PIE m-stems have become n-stems in Greek (by leveling from endingless forms in which word-final *-m > -ν; see 3.3), Greek has preserved most PIE stem types and created a couple more. I will illustrate them with examples that have exact cognates in other IE languages, to the extent that that is possible.

The number of masculine o-stems matched by clear cognates elsewhere is considerable; note the following:

(post-)PIE *ag^{w}nós 'lamb' (Lat. *agnus*) > ἀμνός;
PIE *áwlos 'tube' (Lat. *alvos* 'belly', Lith. *aũlas* 'leg of a boot') > αὐλός 'double shawm';[52]
PIE *áyd^{h}os 'burning' (Skt *éd^{h}as* 'firewood', OE *ād* 'pyre') > αἶθος;
(post-)PIE *b^{h}āǵós 'tree sp.' (Lat. *fāgus* 'beech') > φηγός 'Vallonea oak';
PIE *dólos 'bait, trick, deceit' (Lat. *dolus*) > δόλος;
PIE *d^{h}óh$_1$mos 'thing put' (Goth. *doms* 'reputation', OE *dōm* 'judgment') > θωμός 'heap';
PIE *d^{h}uh$_2$mós 'smoke' (Skt *d^{h}ūmás*, Lat. *fūmus*) > θῡμός 'emotion, spirit (etc.)';
PIE *éḱwos 'horse' (Skt *áśvas*, Lat. *equos*) >→ ἵππος (see 3.4.3);
PIE *ǵómb^{h}os 'row of teeth' (Skt pl. *jámb^{h}āsas*, OE *camb* 'comb') > γόμφος 'peg';
PIE *g^{h}órtos 'enclosure' (Lat. *hortus* 'garden') > Hom. χόρτος;
PIE *h$_2$áǵros 'pasture' → 'field' (Skt *ájras*, Lat. *ager*, Goth. *akrs*) > ἀγρός;
PIE *h$_2$ónkos '(a) bend' (Lat. *uncus* 'hook') > ὄγκος 'barb';
PIE *h$_2$ŕ̥tḱos 'bear' (Hitt. *hartaggas*, Skt *ŕ̥kṣas*, Av. *aršō*, Lat. *ursus*) > ἄρκτος;
PIE *h$_3$ósdos 'branch' (Goth. *asts*) > ὄζος;
PIE *kápros 'male animal' (Lat. *caper*, ON *hafr*, both 'goat') > κάπρος 'boar';
PIE *k^{w}ék^{w}los 'wheel' (OE *hwēol*) > κύκλος;
PIE *k^{w}ólos 'axis' (Toch. B *kele* 'navel') > πόλος;
PIE *neg^{wh}rós 'kidney' (extended in Lat. dial. pl. *nefrōnēs*, etc.) > νεφρός;
PIE *órsos 'arse' (Hitt. *ārras*, OE *ears*) > Att. ὄρρος;
PIE *ṓmsos 'shoulder' (Toch. B *āntse*) > ὦμος;

[52] Occasional shifts of accent in this and other isolated words must be the result of lexical analogies; I will pass over them in silence if I have no specific suggestion to make.

PIE *stah$_2$urós 'stake, pale' (ON *staurr*) > σταυρός;

PIE *swéḱuros 'father-in-law' (Skt *śváśuras*, Lat. *socer*) >→ ἑκυρός (accent by lexical analogy with fem. ἑκυρᾱ́, the latter ←< *sweḱrúh$_2$ by lexical analogy with the masc.);

PIE *táwros 'bull' (Lat. *taurus*) > ταῦρος;

PIE *tórmos 'borehole' (OE *þearm* 'intestines') > τόρμος 'socket';

PIE *udrós 'water-dwelling animal' (Skt *udrás*; ON *otr* 'otter') > ὕδρος 'water snake';

PIE *wésperos 'evening' (Lat. *vesper*) > ἕσπερος (on the rough breathing, see 3.5.5 and 6.2);

PIE *wl̥k^{w}os 'wolf' (Skt *vŕ̥kas*, Lith. *vil̃kas*, Goth. *wulfs*) → *lúk^{w}os > λύκος.

A few masculine o-stems appear to be substantivized inherited adjectives:

PIE *alb^{h}ós 'white' (Lat. *albus*, Hitt. *alpās* 'cloud') > ἀλφός 'white skin disease';

PIE *ā́peros 'bank, shore' (OE *ōfer*, Middle High German *uover*) → adj. (?) *ā́peryos > ᾱ̆πε̄ρος 'mainland' > Att.-Ion. ἤπε̄ρος;

PIE *neptiós 'of grandsons/nephews' (Av. *naptiiō* 'descendant', late Church Slavonic *netĭjĭ* 'nephew') >→ ἀνεψιός 'cousin'.

A few others are agent or result nouns of an originally productive type that have acquired specialized meanings:

PIE *d^{h}óyǵ^{h}os 'shaped clay' (Goth. *daigs* 'dough'; cf. Skt *dehī́* 'rampart') > τοῖχος 'wall';

PIE *sólkos 'thing pulled' (Lat. *sulcus* 'furrow') >→ ὁλκός 'furrow' (by lexical confusion with *solkós 'thing to haul with', which also survives as ὁλκός in Greek);

PIE *d^{h}rog^{h}ós 'runner' (OIr. *droch* 'wheel') > τροχός 'wheel'.

There is at least one inherited feminine o-stem and another whose original gender is doubtful:

PIE *snusós fem. 'daughter-in-law' (Arm. *now*, gen. *nowoy*; shifted into the ā-stems in Skt *snuṣā́*, etc.) > νυός;

PIE *sámh$_2$d^{h}os 'sand' (PGmc masc. *samdaz > ON *sandr*, Middle High German *sam(b)t*, etc.) > fem. ἄμαθος.

One clearly inherited example might have been either masculine or neuter:

PIE *misd^{h}ó- 'reward' (Skt *mīḍ^{h}ám* 'contest (for a prize)') > μισθός 'pay, wages'.

There are few shared neuter o-stems, e.g.:

PIE *gérsom 'brushwood' (ON *kjarr* 'underbrush') > Att. γέρρον 'wickerwork';
PIE *$h_2$árh$_3$trom 'plow' (OIr. *arathar*) > ἄροτρον;
PIE *ksuróm 'razor' (Skt *kṣurám*) > ξυρόν;
PIE *méh$_1$lom or *mḗlom 'animal' (OIr. *míl*) > Hom. μῆλον 'sheep, goat';
PIE *pédom 'footing' (Hitt. *pēdan* 'place') > πέδον 'ground';
PIE *plówyom 'boat' (ON *fley*) > πλοῖον;
PIE *wérǵom 'work' (OE *weorc*) > ϝέργον (attested in Arkadian) > ἔργον;
PIE *yugóm 'yoke' (Hitt. *iukan*, Skt *yugám*, Lat. *iugum*) > ζυγόν.

One is difficult to reconstruct exactly:

PIE *(h_2)ōwióm 'egg' (?, cf. Lat. *ōvom*) > ᾠιόν.

One is possible but not certain:

PIE *peróm 'feather' (?; OCS *pero*; cf. also Toch. B pl. *parwa*) >→ πτερόν (by lexical analogy with aor. πτέσθαι?; but see Frisk s.v. with references).

Another is a substantivized adjective, possibly but not necessarily reflecting shared history:

PIE coll. *énterah$_2$ 'things on the inside, guts' → neut. pl. (PGmc. *inþarō > ON *iðr*) > ἔντερα.

Finally, two appear to be loanwords from an unknown source (or sources):

post-PIE *mā́lom 'apple' (Lat. *mālum*) > μᾶλον > Att.-Ion. μῆλον;
post-PIE *pŕ̥som 'leek' (Lat. *porrum*) > πράσον.

Since Greek and Italic shared no early prehistory after reaching the Mediterranean (so far as we can tell), these words must have been borrowed either early or from a non-IE language family widely represented in the Mediterranean basin.

As is usual in IE languages, fairly few feminines in *-ah$_2$- have exact cognates elsewhere, but at least the following can be cited:

PIE *bʰáh$_2$mah$_2$ 'illumination' (cf. Skt *bʰāti* 'it illuminates') → 'clarification' → 'reputation' (Lat. *fāma*) > φήμη;
PIE *bʰugáh$_2$ 'flight, running away' (Lat. *fuga*) > φυγή;
PIE *Hyéh$_1$gʷah$_2$ 'strength' vel sim. (Lith. *jėgà*) > ἥβᾱ 'youth' > Att.-Ion. ἥβη;
PIE *h$_1$roHwáh$_2$ 'rest' (OE *rōw*) > Hom. ἐρωή 'lull, pause (in battle)';
PIE *h$_2$ánkulah$_2$ 'loop (in a cord)' (PGmc. *anhulō > ON *ál* 'strap') > ἀγκύλη;
PIE *(h$_3$)migʰláh$_2$ 'cloud' (Lith. *miglà*, OCS *mĭgla*) > ὀμίχλη 'mist';

PIE *krásnah$_2$ 'moving water' vel sim. (ON *hrǫnn* 'wave') > κρᾱ́νᾱ, Att. κρήνη 'spring';
PIE *k^{w}oynáh$_2$ 'recompense' (Av. *kaēnā* 'punishment', OCS *cěna* 'price') > ποινή 'weregild, penalty';
PIE *nébʰelah$_2$ 'cloud' (Lat. *nebula* 'fog') > νεφέλᾱ > Att.-Ion. νεφέλη;
PIE *pl̥h$_2$mah$_2$ 'flat hand' (Lat. *palma*, OIr. *lám* 'hand', OE poet. *folm* 'hand') > Hom. παλάμη;
PIE *póywah$_2$ 'meadow' (cf. Lith. *píeva*) > PGk *ποίϝᾱ 'grass' > Ion. ποίη, Att. *ποίᾱ > πόᾱ.

Two are clearly collectives to o-stem nouns attested in other IE languages:

PIE *dh$_2$pn̥óm 'sacrificial meal' (ON *tafn* 'sacrifice', Lat. *damnum* 'loss'), coll. in *-ah$_2$- > δαπάνη 'expense';
PIE *sóngʷʰos 'chanting' vel sim. (Goth. *saggws* 'song'), coll. *songʷʰáh$_2$ > *honkʷʰᾱ́ > ὀμφή 'oracular voice'.

One originally proterokinetic h$_2$-stem became an ordinary ᾱ-stem in Greek:

PIE *ḱáh$_2$ih$_2$ ~ *ḱh$_2$iáh$_2$- 'shadow' (Skt *cʰāyā́*, Toch. B *skiyo*; see Ringe 1996: 18 with references) > σκιᾱ́.

Another underwent further developments. PIE *g^{w}énh$_2$- ~ *g^{w}náh$_2$- 'woman' (OIr. *ben*, gen. sg. *mná*) was apparently regularized as *g^{w}enáh$_2$ (OCS *žena*), and that appears to be the source of γυνᾱ́ > Att.-Ion. γυνή (see 3.4.3). The rest of the paradigm, however, is built to an extended stem γυναικ- which exhibits alternating accent. Schwyzer (1939: 582–3) suggests that the voc. sg. γύναι, which could reflect an earlier *γύναικ (see 3.5.3), might instead be an inherited voc. sg. in *-ay, cognate with the Skt ā-stem voc. sg. -*e*—presumably the late PIE voc. sg. *-a created by loss of the laryngeal in utterance-final position (see 2.2.4 *ad fin.*) plus the *hic-et-nunc* particle *-i; but that still does not explain the -κ-. In any case the survival of Boiotian βανᾱ́ (Corinna 664a.2), the first syllable of which must reflect *n̥, shows that the history of this word was more complex than can be reconstructed from the surviving evidence.

Greek also exhibits an unusually large number of masculine ᾱ-stems, originally identical in inflection to the feminines, but over time acquiring a nom. sg. in -ᾱς (> Att.-Ion. -ης) and a gen. sg. in -ᾱο (> Att.-Ion. -εω; see 6.2). A large proportion are fairly recent creations using an innovative agentive suffix -τᾱς (> -της), but there is also a compound type that appears to be older. Buck and Petersen (1949: 2–3) suggest that they began as exocentric compounds of fem. ᾱ-stems, so that Hom. κλυτοτέχνης, for instance, is literally 'whose τέχνη is κλυτή'; since some could be associated with verbs as well (e.g. -νῑ́κης with νῑκᾶν), they were reinterpreted as agentives. But it is striking that Latin also has ā-stem masc. agentives, and they are deverbal, at least synchronically (*advena* 'newcomer', *agricola* 'field-cultivator, farmer', etc.); moreover, there is some evidence for *-ah$_2$- as an individualizing suffix in Anatolian (Melchert 2014b: 260–3). It seems likely that the last word has not been said about the origin of these masculines. In any case their formation was (at least somewhat) productive in the various daughters of the family, with the result that examples shared between subgroups do not seem to be discoverable.

Greek preserves a single inherited feminine noun in *-ih$_2$- ~ *-yáh$_2$-:

PIE *pótnih$_2$ 'lady, mistress' (Skt *pátnī*) > Hom. πότνια.

Of course it is true that Greek and Indo-Iranian probably began their development as adjacent or nearly adjacent dialects at the eastern end of the Central IE continuum, so this particular example might not be all that ancient. But the suffix reappears in Celtic; for instance, Skt *rā́jñī* 'queen' is cognate with OIr. *rígain* (< *rīganī < *h$_3$rḗǵn̥ih$_2$). The pattern of facts thus suggests that this example is at least as old as Core IE. At least one other inherited noun has been extended with this feminine suffix:

*ánh$_2$t- ~ *n̥h$_2$t- 'duck' (Lat. *anas*, Skt *ātís*) >→ *nā́t-ya > Att. νῆττα.

Derived stems in *-uh$_2$- do not seem to survive (note that PIE *sweḱrúh$_2$, the most securely reconstructable example, has been remodeled as ἑκυρᾱ́), unless an example is:

PIE *gʰéluh$_2$(s) 'tortoise' (OCS *žely*) > χέλῡς.

PIE i-stems are mostly relics in Greek, with the exception of the action/result nouns in -σι- < *-ti-. At least the following have cognates in other IE languages:

PIE *h$_2$ówis ~ *h$_2$áwi- 'sheep' (Kimball 1987: 189; Lycian acc. sg. *xawã*, Toch. B *ā$_u$* 'ewe' (Kim 2000b), Skt *ávis*, Lat. *ovis*) > Hom. ὄϊς;
PIE *h$_3$órǵʰis ~ *h$_3$r̥ǵʰéy- 'scrotum, testicle' (Av. *ərəziš* 'scrotum') > ὄρχις 'testicle';
PIE *h$_3$ḗgʷʰis ~ *h$_3$ógʷʰi- 'snake' (Arm *iž*, Skt *áhis*) > ὄφις;
PIE *pótis 'lord, husband' (Skt *pátis*) > πόσις;
PIE *méh$_1$tis 'measure' (OE *mǣþ*) > Hom. μῆτις 'plan';
PIE *gʷémti- ~ *gʷm̥téy- 'step' (cf. Lat. *con-ventiō*, Goth. *ga-qumþs* 'assembly') >→ βάσις, Hom. ἔκβασις 'exit' *Od.* 5.410;
PIE *ǵénh$_1$ti- ~ *ǵn̥h$_1$téy- 'begetting, birth' (Lat. *gēns*, *genti-* 'clan' and *nātiō* 'people, nation') > γένεσις;
PIE *dʰéh$_1$ti- ~ *dʰh$_1$téy- '(act of) putting' (PGmc *dēdiz 'deed' > Goth. *-deþs*, OE *dǣd*) >→ θέσις;
PIE *stáh$_2$ti- ~ *sth$_2$téy- 'standing, place to stand' → *sth$_2$tís (Skt *sthitís*, OE *stede*, Lat. *statiō*) > στάσις;

PIE *b^háh$_2$ti- ~ *b^hh$_2$téy- 'speech' (Arm. *bay* 'word') >→ φάτις 'saying; oracle'.

(There is inevitably some uncertainty about whether a given noun in *-ti- is inherited, since the formation was productive.) Greek also has a class of nouns in *-oy-, exemplified by πειθώ 'persuasion', which appear to have been originally amphikinetic nouns with a nom. sg. in *-ō; there are no full cognates elsewhere, but the suffix and inflection of Skt *sák^{h}ā* 'companion', acc. *sák^{h}āyam* are clearly cognate.

PIE action/result nouns in *-tu- do not survive as a class in Greek. Surviving u-stem nouns are relics, of which a substantial number are neuter; the following inherited examples seem secure:

PIE *b^hāǵ^{h}us 'arm' (*-ah$_2$-?; Skt *bāhús*) > πᾶχυς 'forearm' > Att.-Ion. πῆχυς;
PIE *ǵénus ~ *ǵénu- 'jaw' (Toch. A du. *śanweṃ*, OIr. *giun* 'mouth') > γένυς;
PIE *suh$_3$yús ~ *suh$_3$iw- 'offspring' (Toch. B *soy* 'son'; see Ringe 1996: 61–3) >→ Hom. υἱύς 'son';
PIE *ǵónu ~ *ǵénu- 'knee' (Skt *jā́nu*, Lat. *genū*) > γόνυ;
PIE *dóru 'tree' (Hitt. *tāru*, Skt *dā́ru*) > δόρυ 'spear-shaft';
PIE *dáḱru 'tear (i.e. eye-water)' (Old Lat. *dacruma*, Skt *áśru* with unexplained loss of *d-) > Hom. δάκρυ;
PIE *wā́stu ~ *wástu- 'settlement' (Skt *vā́stu*, Toch. A *waṣt*, B *ost*) > *ϝάστυ 'citadel' (Myc. *wa-tu*) > ἄστυ.

One is a substantivized adjective:

PIE *méd^{h}us 'sweet' (Skt *mád^{h}us*), neut. *méd^{h}u → 'honey' (Toch. B *mit*) → 'mead' (OE *medu*) > Hom. μέθυ 'wine'.

One inherited u-stem has become a monosyllable:

PIE *náh$_2$us 'boat', gen. *n̥h$_2$wés (Skt *náus*, *nāvás*, Lat. *nāvis*) > ναῦς, νᾱός > Att.-Ion. νηός > νεώς.

One inherited u-stem with a good external cognate seems to have been a loanword from an unknown language, judging both from its double full grade and from the mismatch in the accentuation of the cognates:

post-PIE *peleḱus 'ax' (Skt *paraśús*) > πέλεκυς.

Finally, the derived nouns πάτρως 'father's brother', μήτρως 'mother's brother' appear to be inherited stems in *-ωϝ- (cf. Lat. *patruos*), though not much more can be said about them.

The number of neuter s-stems with cognates in other IE branches is substantial. Two do not exhibit the late PIE acrostatic ablaut pattern (for discussion, see Nussbaum 1986: 139–57):

PIE *kréwh_2s 'raw meat' (Skt *kravís*) > κρέας 'meat';
post-PIE *ḱérh_2s 'horn' > κέρας.

The remainder are of the familiar type well attested in all the most conservative branches:

PIE *ǵén$h_1$os, gen. *ǵén$h_1$esos 'lineage' (Skt *jánas*, *jánasas*, Lat. *genus*, *generis*) > γένος, γένεος > Att. γένος, γένōς;
PIE *g^{wh}éros 'heat' (Skt *háras*) > Att.-Ion. θέρος 'summer, harvest';
PIE *$h_1$rég^{w}os 'darkness' (Goth. *riqis*; Skt *rájas* 'empty space', Arm. *erek* 'evening') > ἔρεβος 'passage to the underworld';
PIE *$h_2$ág^{h}os 'emotional distress' (Goth. *agis* 'fear') > Hom. ἄχος;
PIE *$h_2$ánd^{h}os 'plant' (Skt *ánd^{h}as* 'herb') > ἄνθος 'flower';
PIE *$h_2$ánkos '(a) bend' (Skt *áṅkas* '(a) curve') > ἄγκος 'glen';
PIE *$h_2$pélos 'wound' (noun; Toch. B *pīle*, A *päl*) > ἄπελος 'open wound';
PIE *ḱléwos 'fame' (Skt *śrávas*) > κλέος;
PIE *néb^{h}os 'cloud' (Skt *náb^{h}as*; Hitt. *nēpis*, OCS *nebo*, both 'sky') > νέφος;
PIE *pésos 'penis' (Skt *pásas*) > πέος;
PIE *sédos 'seat' (Skt *sádas*, ON *setr*) > ἕδος;
PIE *sélos 'standing water' vel sim. (Skt *sáras* 'pool') > ἕλος 'floodplain';
PIE *skélos 'crookedness' (Lat. *scelus* 'crime') > σκέλος 'leg';
PIE *srī́gos 'cold(ness)' (Lat. *frīgus*) > ῥῖγος;
PIE *wék^{w}os 'word' (Skt *vácas*) > Hom. ἔπος;
PIE *wétos 'year' (Lat. *vetus* 'old' (!)) > ἔτος;
PIE *yéwgos 'yoke (of oxen)' (Lat. pl. *iūgera*, a measure of land originally defined by what a yoke of oxen could plow in a specified time) > ζεῦγος.

One original neuter s-stem has developed a unique inflection:

PIE *$h_2$áwsos 'ear' (OCS *uxo*) >→ *ówhos (by lexical analogy with *ok^w- 'eye') > South Greek *ὄϝος (cf. Myc. *o-wo-we* *οἰϝ-ωϝής 'with a single ear (i.e. handle)'; Aura Jorro 1999 s.v.) >→ Att.-Ion., Hom. οὖς, gen. οὔατος (i.e. ō̃ς, ὄ̆ατος) >→ Att. ō̃ς, ὠτός (with productive alternating accent in a new monosyllable).

Inherited non-neuter s-stem nouns are rare, but at least three can be cited:

PIE *kónis ~ *kénis- 'dust' (Lat. masc. *cinis* 'ashes') > fem. κόνις;
PIE fem. *$h_2$áwsōs 'dawn' → *$h_2$usṓs (Skt *uṣā́s*) > *hawhṓs > *hāϝώς (preserved in Doric) > Att.-Ion. *hηώς > Hom. ἠώς, >→ Att. ἕως.

One has lost its *-s- completely in Classical Attic:

PIE *méh$_1$n̥s 'moon, month' (Skt *mā́s*, Lat. *mēnsis*) > Hom. μείς 'month' (i.e. μέ̄ς), μην- → Att. μήν.

In addition, though αἰδώς, *αἰδόh- 'respect, self-respect' has no exact cognates elsewhere, its non-neuter s-stem suffix, unique in Greek, appears to be cognate with the suffix of Lat. *honōs*, etc.; that class of nouns probably ultimately reflects amphikinetic collectives.

The n-stems are more evenly distributed between non-neuters and neuters. Of the former at least the following examples are inherited:

PIE *ḱwṓ ~ *ḱuṓ 'dog', gen. *ḱun-és (Skt *śvā́, śún-as*) >→ κύων, κυνός;
PIE *poh$_2$imḗ(n) 'shepherd' (Lith. *piemuõ*) > ποιμήν;
PIE *wr̥ḗ(n) 'lamb' (Arm. *gaṙn*, gen. *gaṙin*) > ϝαρήν (preserved in Cretan) > ἀρήν;
PIE *h$_2$r̥sḗ(n) 'male' (Av. *aršā*) > ἄρσην > Att. ἄρρην;
PIE *h$_2$áḱmō 'stone' (Skt *áśmā*, Lith. *akmuõ*) > ἄκμων 'anvil';
PIE *h$_2$ánkō 'bend' → *h$_2$ankṓ (OE *anga* 'goad') > ἀγκών 'elbow';
PIE *léymō 'lake', loc. *limén(-i) (cf. Toch. B *lyam*, A *lyäm* < leveled *limn̥) >→ λειμών, 'water meadow' and λιμήν 'harbor';
post-PIE *ǵ^{h}éymō 'winter' (deriv. of *ǵ^{h}éyōm 'winter', see below; cf. Skt *hemantás*) > χειμών;
post-PIE *ḱíHō 'column' (Arm. *siwn*) > κίων.

One seems to have been a collective originally:

PIE *térmō 'boundary, boundaries' (Lat. masc. *termō* 'finish line') > masc. τέρμων.

Here, from a Greek point of view, belong the two PIE m-stem nouns:

PIE *d^{h}éǵ^{h}ōm, 'earth', loc. *d^{h}ǵ^{h}ém(-i) (Hitt. nom.-acc. *tēkan*, Skt loc. *kṣámi*) >→ Hom. χθών;
PIE *ǵ^{h}éyōm 'winter', *ǵ^{h}iém(-i) (cf. Lat. *hiems*) >→ χιών.

Two archaic nouns in *-men- survive in Greek:

PIE *h$_1$néh$_3$mn̥ ~ *h$_1$nóh$_3$mn- 'name' (Toch. B *ñem*, Skt *nā́ma*, Lat. *nōmen*) >→ *ἔνομα (cf. Lakonian Ἐνυμα-κρατίδᾱς) > Att.-Ion. ὄνομα;
PIE *stóh$_3$mn- 'orifice' (Hitt. *istaman-* 'ear'; see Melchert 1994a: 73–4) >→ στόμα 'mouth'.

Most of the remaining inherited neuters exhibit the proterokinetic suffix *-men-:

PIE *d^{h}yá$h_2$mn̥ 'thought' (?; Skt *d*^{h}*yā́ma* 'meditation') > σᾶμα 'memorial; sign' > Att.-Ion. σῆμα;
PIE *néwmn̥ 'nod' (Lat. *nūmen* 'presence of a divinity') > νεῦμα;
PIE *sné$h_1$mn̥ 'thread' (Lat. *nēmen*, attested once in an inscription as abl. sg. *nēmine*) > νῆμα;
PIE *térmn̥ 'boundary' (Lat. *termen*) > τέρμα;
PIE *wésmn̥ 'garment' (Skt *vásma*) > *ϝέhμα̨ > ἕμα.

One which did not has undergone a unique development:

PIE *péḱtn̥, gen. *pḱtén-s 'comb' (Lat. *pecten*) >→ masc. κτεν-, nom. sg. κτε̄́ς.

PIE r-stems seem to have been non-neuter. Though they are relics in Greek (except for the agent nouns in *-ter-), the inherited examples are part of the most basic vocabulary:

PIE *ph_2tḗr 'father' (Skt *pitā́*, Lat. *pater*) > πατήρ;
PIE *mah_2tḗr 'mother' (Skt *mātā́*, Lat. *māter*) > μᾱ́τηρ > Att.-Ion. μήτηρ (accent of the nom. sg. leveled on voc. sg. μῆτερ; otherwise μητέρ- ~ μητρ-);
PIE *b^{h}ráh_2tēr 'brother' (Skt *b*^{h}*rā́tā*, Lat. *frāter*) > φρᾱ́τηρ 'member of a brotherhood';
PIE *d^{h}ugh_2tḗr 'daughter' (Skt *duhitā́*, Goth. *daúhtar*) > θυγάτηρ (accent as for 'mother');
PIE *dayh_2wḗr 'brother-in-law' (Skt *devā́*, late Lat. *lēvir*) > δᾱήρ;
PIE *h_2nḗr 'man' (Skt *nā́*) > ἀνήρ;
PIE *$h_2$stḗr 'star' (Hitt. *hasterz*) > ἀστήρ;
PIE *Hyn̥h_2tḗr 'husband's brother's wife', voc. *Hyén$h_2$ter (Skt *yātár-*) >→ Hom. pl. εἰνατέρες (ει = ε̄ by metrical lengthening);
PIE nom. pl. *swésores 'sisters' (Skt *svásāras*) > ἔορες '(female) relatives' (Hesykhios, apparently quoting from a psilotic text);
PIE *ǵénh_1tōr 'begetter, parent' (Lat. *genitor*) > γενέτωρ.

In addition, there are a couple of root-nouns in *-r-:

PIE *ǵ^{h}wḗr 'wild animal' (Lith. *žvėrìs*) > θήρ;
PIE *b^{h}ṓr 'one who carries' → 'thief' (Lat. *fūr*) > φώρ.

There is also an r-stem that has become a monosyllable by generalization of its oblique stem:

PIE *ǵ^{h}ésōr 'hand' (cf. Hitt. *kissar*), obl. stem *ǵ^{h}esr- > *χεhρ- > χε̄́ρ, gen. χε̄ρ-ός.

In place of neuter r-stem nouns PIE seems to have had r/n-stems, with *r in the direct cases and *n in the oblique cases. Some have become r-stems in Greek:

PIE coll. *páh$_2$wōr 'fire', gen. *ph$_2$un-és (cf. Hitt. *pahhur*, *pahhuenas*) >→ *ph$_2$uṓr, *ph$_2$ur-és (cf. Toch. B *puwar*) > → πῦρ, πυρ-ός;
PIE *d^{h}énr̥ 'palm (of the hand)' (OHG *tenar*) > θέναρ, gen. θέναρ-ος;
PIE *wésr̥ 'spring(time)' (Av. loc. *vaŋri*) > Hom. ἔαρ, gen. ἔαρ-ος.

Others have remained r/n-stems in Greek, but their oblique stems have been extended, with *-n̥-t- > -ατ-, exactly as in the oblique stems of nouns in *-men-. The source of the *-t- remains obscure. At least the following are clearly inherited:

PIE *wódr̥ 'water' (Hitt. *wātar*), coll. *wédōr, gen. *udn-és (cf. Hitt. *witār*) >→ *udṓr (Vedic Skt *udā́*) > ὕδωρ, ὕδατ-ος;
PIE *Hyḗk^{w}r̥ ~ *Hyék^{w}n- 'liver' (Skt *yákr̥t*, Lat. *iecur* with full grade generalized) > ἧπαρ, gen. ἥπατ-ος;
PIE *ówd^{h}r̥, 'udder', gen. *uHd^{h}én-s (Skt *ū́d^{h}ar*, gen. *ū́d^{h}n-as*) > οὖθαρ, οὔθατ-ος;
PIE *sókr̥ 'shit' (Hitt. *sakkar*; Wodtko et a. 2008 s.v.), coll. *skṓr > σκῶρ, gen. σκατ-ός;
PIE *pérwr̥ 'knot' (Vedic *párur → *párus* and *párvan-*, both 'joint') > *πέρϝαρ > Hom. πεῖραρ 'end; rope';
post-PIE *ā́mr̥ 'day' (Arm. *awr* < coll. *ā́mōr) > ἆμαρ (cf. pl. ἄματα πάντα *DGE* 661.22 (Arkadian), Buck 59.A.12 (Lokrian)) > Hom. ἦμαρ.

One is attested only in the nom.-acc. sg.:

(post-)PIE *h$_3$ónr̥ 'dream' (Arm. *anowrǰ*, deriv. of a coll. in *-ōr) > ὄναρ.[53]

A considerable number of other inherited consonant stems survive in Greek, mostly without ablaut alternations; the following list is not exhaustive:

PIE du. *h$_3$ók^{w}ih$_1$ 'eyes' (OCS *oči*) > (→) Hom. ὄσσε (see 3.2.3 on the phonology), and coll. *h$_3$ṓk^w >→ Hom. acc. ὦπα 'face';
PIE acc. *wók^{w}m̥ 'voice' (Toch. B *wek*) > Hom. acc. ὄπα;
(post-)PIE acc. *snígʷʰm̥ 'snow' (Lat. *nivem*) > Hom. acc. νίφα;
PIE *pṓd-s 'foot', *pód- ~ *ped- (Skt *pā́t*, *pā́d-am*, *pad-ás*; Lat. *pēs*, *ped-em*, *ped-is*) >→ πός, ποδ-;

[53] The *h$_2$- reconstructed in Wodtko et al. (2008: 303–6) seems uncertain to me. If we discount the forms cited from Hesykhios, it rests only on εὐήνορα οἶνον *Od.* 4.622 if the latter means 'wine which gives good dreams' (see the discussion and references, *loc. cit.*). But at *Od.* 13.19 we find εὐήνορα χαλκόν, in which the adjective obviously must mean something else, and later poets such as Pindar clearly took it to mean 'good-man, brave, glorious'.

PIE *$h_1$dónt-s 'tooth', *$h_1$dónt- ~ *$h_1$dn̥t- (Skt *dán, dánt-am, dat-ás*; Lat. *dēns, dent-em, dent-is*) >→ ὀδός, ὀδόντ-;
PIE *nók^{w}t-s 'night' (Lat. *nox, noct-*) >→ νύξ, νυκτ-;
PIE *$h_3$nog^h- 'nail, claw' (OE *nægl*), extended *$h_3$nog^h-w- (cf. Toch. B pl. *mekwa*, Lat. *unguis*) > *onog^{wh}- > ὄνυχ-;
PIE *dyḗws or *dyéws 'sky, day', *diw- (Skt *dyáus, div-*) > Ζεύς, Δι(ϝ)-;
PIE *g^{w}ṓw-s, *g^{w}ów- 'bovine, head of cattle' (Skt *gáus*, pl. *gā́vas*) > βοῦς, βο(ϝ)-;
PIE *ḱḗr, *ḱr̥d- 'heart' (Hitt. *kēr*, Lat. *cord-*) > Hom. κῆρ (otherwise *ḱr̥d- extended as Hom. κραδίη, Att. καρδίᾱ);
PIE *ǵ^{h}áns 'goose' > *χάνς, *χανh- >→ χᾱ́ν > Att.-Ion. χήν;
PIE *sál-s 'salt' (Lat. *sal*) > ἅλς;
PIE *wih$_1$- 'sinew, strength' (Lat. *vīs*) > Hom. ῑ̆ς, inst. pl. ἶφι;
PIE *h_3b^{h}rúH-s 'eyebrow' (Skt *b^{h}rū́s*) > ὀφρῦς;
PIE *d^{h}ǵ^{h}úH-s 'fish' (Lith. *žuvìs*, gen. pl. *žuvų̃*) > ἰχθῦς (ἰ- unexplained);
PIE *súH-s or *sū́-s 'pig' (Lat. *sūs*, ON *sýr* 'sow') > ὗς and σῦς;
PIE *múHs or *mū́s 'mouse' (Skt *mū́s*, Lat., OE *mūs*, ON *mús*) > μῦς;
PIE *mélid, *mlit- 'honey' (Hitt. *milit*, Luv. *mallit*) >→ μέλι, μέλιτ-.

Finally, there is the odd case of two Greek nouns with stems in -κτ-. One is clearly a loanword from some substrate language:

PGk *ϝάνακτς, gen. ϝάνακτος 'king, lord' (Myc. *wa-na-ka*; Boiot. ϝάναχς, dat. ϝάνακτι, Buck 37) > Hom. ἄναξ, ἄνάκτος.

It is not surprising that this noun has no cognates elsewhere. But the other one apparently does:

PGk *γάλακτ, gen. γάλακτος 'milk' (Lat. *lac, lactis*) > γάλα, γάλακτος.

It seems unlikely that this is a true cognate pair, because its shape is unparalleled, it appears in no other IE language, and the Greek syllable γα- is unaccounted for. But if it is a loanword it exhibits the same startling distribution as πράσον and μᾶλον (see above).

A major innovation among Greek stem types are the nouns in -ήϝ- (nom. sg. -εύς). Since this Greek suffix almost certainly entered the language as a component of loanwords (John Bennett apud Meissner 2016: 27–8), it is necessarily uncertain whether any of the nouns existed in Proto-Greek, but a strong case that some existed at some early stage of the language can be made. Nouns in -εύς are already well attested in Mycenaean, most often as names of trades or professions (Bartoněk 2002: 279–83), e.g. *ka-ke-u* χαλκεύς 'smith', *ke-ra-me-u* κεραμεύς 'potter', *i-je-re-u* ἱερεύς 'priest', but also including pl. *a-pi-po-re-we* (*)ἀμφιφορῆϝες 'two-handled jars' and the culturally important loanword *qa-si-re-u* *γ^{w}ασιλεύς, the title of a subordinate ruler. So far as our evidence goes, all Ancient Greek dialects exhibit this formation, and a reasonable number of examples can be reconstructed for Proto-Greek with due caution (including all those just adduced). Note also that (1) nom. sg. -εύς, dat. pl. -εῦσι consistently exhibit the effects of Osthoff's Law (see 3.5.3), and (2) the sound-change outcome of original *-ηϝ-jέ/ό- in derived present stems is preserved in Elean as -ειε/ο-, but in the other dialects has been leveled to -ευε/ο- (see 4.2.1 (v)). The latter pattern of facts shows that this suffix was part of the language at the time when *-wj- > *-jj-, but that the present stems in question were created early enough to have undergone leveling in most dialects by the time they are attested.

4.3.4 Stem types: Adjectives

Greek adjectives with good cognates elsewhere in the IE family are overwhelmingly either o-stems with ah_2-stem feminines or u-stems with feminines in *-ih_2- ~ *-$yáh_2$-. The suffix of the u-stems is usually just *-u-, but there is a fairly large number of thematic suffixes, which I will discuss first. Inherited adjectives in which the suffix is just *-o- are few:

PIE *néwos 'new' (Hitt. *nēwas*, Skt *návas*, Lat. *novos*) > νέος 'young';
PIE *sénos 'old' (Skt *sánas*, Lith. *sẽnas*) > Att. ἕνη καὶ νέᾱ 'last day of a month' (*'old and new (moon)');
PIE *dl̥h_1gʰós 'long' (Skt *dīrgʰás*, Av. *darəγō*, OCS *dlŭgŭ*) >(?) Hom. δολιχός (see 3.2.3);
PIE *somHós 'same' (Skt *samás*) > ὁμός;
PIE *n̥udros 'waterless' (Skt *anudrás*) > ἄνυδρος;
post-PIE *awtós 'same, self' (Old Phrygian *wen autun* 'himself, ἑᾱυτόν') > αὐτός.

Other thematic suffixes are well represented. The Caland suffix *-ró- is naturally common:

PIE *$h_1$rudʰrós 'red' (Toch. B *ratre*, Lat. *ruber*) > ἐρυθρός;
PIE *$h_1$ln̥gʷʰrós 'light(weight)' (OHG *lungar* 'vigorous') > ἐλαφρός 'light';
PIE *h_2r̥ǵrós 'white' (Skt *r̥jrás* 'shining; swift') > *ἀργρός > ἀργός 'bright';
PIE *lugrós 'lamentable' (Toch. B *lakle* 'pain, suffering') > λυγρός;
PIE *piḱrós 'pointed; punctured' (OCS *pĭstrŭ* 'embroidered, multicolored') > πικρός 'bitter, keen';
(post-)PIE *maḱrós[54] 'thin, lean' (Lat. *macer*, OE *mæġer*) > μακρός 'long'.

[54] The related s-stem noun μᾶκος > μῆκος 'length' and the Homeric superlative μήκιστος 'tallest' seem to show that the root was ablauting and contained a laryngeal, thus *mah_2ḱ-; but as Frisk observes s.v. μακρός, all other related words exhibit a short vowel. I suggest that the oldest recoverable preform

One example is more complex:

(post-)PIE *$h_1$léwd^{h}eros 'free' (Lat. *līber*, Venetic dat. pl. *louderobos* 'for (his) children') > ἐλεύθερος.

Though innovations are not usually shared by Greek and Italic, the double full grade of this example suggests that it is not very ancient.

Verbal adjectives in *-tó- with external cognates are very numerous in Greek:

PIE *mr̥tós 'mortal' (Skt *mr̥tás* 'dead') > Hom. (Aiolic) βροτός;
PIE *d^h$h_1$tós 'placed' (Skt *hitás*) > θετός 'adopted (child)';
PIE *st$h_3$tós 'standing, stationary' (Skt *st^{h}itás* 'having stood up') > στατός 'standing, stalled (horse)';
PIE *tn̥tós 'stretched, stretchable' (Lat. *tentus* 'stretched') > τατός 'stretchable';
PIE *tl̥$h_2$tós 'lifted, liftable' (Lat. *lātus* 'carried, brought') > τλᾱτός > Att.-Ion. τλητός 'bearable, endurable';
PIE *str̥$h_3$tós 'spread out, strewn' (Lat. *strātus*) > στρωτός;
PIE *b^{h}id^{h}stós 'trustworthy' (Lat. *fīsus* 'having trusted') > *φιστός → πιστός;
PIE *wr̥$h_1$tós 'said, sayable' (Goth. neut. *waúrd* 'word') > *ϝρητός > Hom. ῥητός 'stated, specified';
PIE *d$h_3$tós 'given' (Lat. *datus*) > θεό-δοτος 'god-given';
PIE *d^{h}ug^{h}tós 'produced' (Skt *dugd^{h}ás* 'milked') > *θυκτός → *τυκτός 'fashioned' in Hom. εὔτυκτος 'well-made';
PIE *g^{wh}n̥tós 'struck, killed' (Skt *hatás*) > Hom. ἀρηΐ-φατος 'killed in battle';
PIE *ǵn̥$h_1$tós 'born' (Skt *jātás*, Lat. *nātus*) > Hom. κασί-γνητος 'brother', lit. 'co-gnātus';
PIE *h_3r̥tós 'risen, up' (Lat. *ortus*) > κονι-ορτός 'dust-cloud';
PIE *ḱr̥$h_2$tós 'mixed' (Skt *ā́-śīrtas* 'mixed', *RV* VIII.2.9) > *κρᾱτός in Hom. ἄκρητος, Att. ἄκρᾱτος 'unmixed';
PIE *nig^{w}tós 'washed' (Skt *niktás*) > *νιπτός in ἄνιπτος 'unwashed';
PIE *b^{h}ud^{h}stós 'observable' vel sim. (Skt *budd^{h}ás* 'awake') >→ *πυστός in Hom. ἄπυστος 'unheard-of';
PIE *n̥d^{h}g^{wh}itom (ḱléwos) 'imperishable (fame)' (Skt *ákṣitaṃ (śrávas)*) > Hom. (κλέος) ἄφθιτον;
PIE *éwg^{h}tos 'solemnly spoken' (late Av. *aoxtō*) >→ Hom. neut. pl. εὐκτά 'what is desired'; *Il.* 14.98.

By contrast, those in *-nó- and *-wó- with probable outside cognates are relics:

PIE *Hiǵnós 'holy' (cf. Goth. *swikns* 'pure') → *Hyaǵnós (full grade reintroduced from the related verb; Skt *yajñás* 'worship') > ἁγνός 'holy, pure';

is *maḱ-, and that the Greek forms with a long vowel were created on the model of other post-laryngeal vowel length alternations.

PIE *neg^{w}nós 'naked' (Skt *nagnás*; with dissimilation Av. *maγnō*) >→ *mog^{w}nós (as in Avestan) >→ γυμνός (with metathesis);
PIE *g^{w}ih$_3$wós 'alive' (Skt *jīvás*, Lat. *vīvos*) → *g^{w}yoh$_3$wós (full grade reintroduced from the related verb) > ζωός;
PIE *skaywós and *laywós 'left(-hand)' (Lat. *scaevos* and *laevos*) > Hom. σκαιός, poet. λαιός.

Examples with various other thematic suffixes and full outside cognates are likewise isolated:

PIE *ályos 'other' (Lydian *aλa-*, Lat. *alius*) > ἄλλος;
PIE *méd^{h}yos 'middle' (Skt *mád^{h}yas*, Lat. *medius*) > μέσος;
PIE *h$_2$ágrios 'of meadows/fields' (Skt *ajryás*) > Gk ἄγριος 'wild';
PIE *h$_2$(a)ntíos 'opposite' (Goth. *andeis* 'end') > ἀντίος;
PIE *óywos 'single' (Av. *aēuuō* 'one') > οἶος 'lone';
PIE *sólwos 'whole' (Skt *sárvas*) > ὅλος;
PIE *g^{wh}r̥mós 'warm' → *g^{wh}ermós (full grade reintroduced from the related verb, cf. Arm. *ǰerm*) > θερμός;
PIE *h$_2$(a)nkulós 'bent, crooked' (ON *ǫngull* 'fishhook') > ἀγκύλος.

Note also:

PIE *dek̑si- 'right(-hand)' (cf. Skt *dákṣiṇas*, Av. *dašinō*) in *dek̑siwós (Weiss 1996: 212) > δεξιός, possibly with *-wó- by lexical analogy with 'left' (see above).

Somewhat surprisingly, two contrastive adjectives in *-tero- have exact cognates elsewhere:

PIE *údsteros 'farther up/out' (Skt *úttaras*) > ὕστερος 'later';
PIE *dek̑siterós 'right (explicitly opposed to left)' (Lat. *dexter*) > δεξιτερός.

(See also neut. pl. ἔντερα in 4.3.3.) So does a pronominal adjective with the same suffix:

PIE *k^{w}óteros 'which (of two)?' (Skt *katarás*, Goth. *ƕaþar*) > πότερος.

All these types of thematic adjectives must have been present in Proto-Greek; others could have been as well.

Cognates of inherited u-stem adjectives are especially to be found in Indo-Iranian and Gothic; some also have Latin cognates, typically in *-vi-*. Comparison of the cognates' ablaut grades strongly suggests that most of these adjectives were proterokinetic in PIE (ablaut schema *´-u- ~ *-éw-) with feminines, likewise proterokinetic, in *-éw-ih$_2$- ~ *-w-iáh$_2$-; different daughters have leveled differently. The following can be cited:

PIE *b^{h}énǵ^{h}u- ~ *b^{h}n̥ǵ^{h}éw- 'thick' → *b^{h}n̥ǵ^{h}ú- (Skt *bahús* 'much') > παχύς;
PIE *dénsu- ~ *dn̥séw- 'dense' (Lat. *dēnsus*) >→ δασύς 'shaggy, rough';
PIE *d^{h}érsu- ~ *d^{h}r̥séw- 'daring, brave' (cf. noun θέρσος) → *d^{h}r̥sú- (Skt *d^{h}r̥ṣús*) > θρασύς;
PIE *g^{w}ráh$_2$u- ~ *g^{w}r̥h$_2$éw- 'heavy' (Lat. *gravis*) → *g^{w}r̥h$_2$ú- (Skt *gurús*, Goth. *kaúrus*) > βαρύς;
PIE *h$_1$ésu- ~ *h$_1$séw- 'good' (Hitt. *assus*; see Melchert 1994a: 63) >→ Hom. ἐΰς;
PIE *h$_1$léng^{h}u- ~ *h$_1$ln̥g^{wh}éw- 'light(weight)' (cf. Av. superlative *rənjištō* 'swiftest') → *h$_1$ln̥g^{h}ú- (Skt *rag^{h}ús* 'swift') > ἐλαχύς 'little';
PIE *h$_1$wéru- ~ *h$_1$uréw- 'broad' (cf. Skt comparative *várīyas-*) → *h$_1$urú- (Skt *urús*) > εὐρύς;
PIE *krétu- ~ *kr̥téw- 'strong' (substantivized in Skt *krátus* 'power') >→ κρατύς;
PIE *mréǵ^{h}u- ~ *mr̥ǵ^{h}éw- 'short' (Lat. *brevis*) → *mr̥ǵ^{h}ú- (Av. *mərəzu-*) > βραχύς;
PIE *pláth$_2$u- ~ *pl̥th$_2$áw- 'broad' (Lith. *platùs*) → *pl̥th$_2$ú- (Skt *pr̥t^{h}ús*) > πλατύς;
PIE *swáh$_2$du- ~ *suh$_2$déw- 'sweet' (Lat. *suāvis*) >→ *swādú- (Skt *svādús*) > ἡδύς;
PIE *ténh$_2$u- ~ *tn̥h$_2$áw- 'stretched, extended' (Lat. *tenuis* 'thin') → *tn̥h$_2$ú- (Skt *tanús*) > Hom. τανύ-φυλλος 'with long/slender leaves';
(post-)PIE *ṓḱu- ~ *ōḱéw-[55] 'swift' (cf. Lat. comparative *ōcior*) → *ōḱú- (Skt *āśús*) > ὠκύς;
post-PIE *g^{w}r̥dú- 'slow' (Lith. *gurdùs*) > βραδύς.

One inherited u-stem has undergone unexpected developments:

PIE *pélh$_1$u- ~ *pl̥h$_1$éw- 'much' (Goth. noun *filu*) → *pl̥h$_1$ú- (Skt *purús*) >→ πολύς, πολλό- (< *πολυ-λό-?).

The o in the root of this adjective poses the same problem as that in δολιχός (see above).

Other inherited adjectives are isolated. Three have exact cognates in other IE languages:

PIE *méǵh$_2$- 'big' (Skt neut. *máhi*) > μέγας;
PIE *píHwō, fem. *píHwerih$_2$ 'fat' (Skt. *pī́vā*, fem. *pī́varī*) > πῑ́ων, fem. πῑ́ερα;
(post-)PIE masc. nom. pl. *pā́ntes 'all' (Toch. B *poñc*) > πάντες.

[55] The unexpected *ō of this word undoubtedly conceals something more complex, but I see no point in speculating about it.

The extended stem μεγάλο- is obviously parallel to πολλό-; presumably the same process, whatever it was, gave rise to both.

The PIE participles in *-nt- are fully productive in Greek, and their formation and inflection are unsurprising, with one exception: the thematic nom. sg. masc. ends in -ων, which cannot be a reflex of *-o-nt-s. That appears to be an innovation, though how it occurred is unclear (see the discussion of Schwyzer 1939: 566–7). If it was created on the analogy of voc. sg. -ον and neuter nom.-acc. sg. -ον—the simplest explanation—then it must postdate the loss of word-final stops (see 3.5.3).

Comparatives and superlatives can be ascribed to PGk with some confidence, since they closely parallel the Sanskrit formations. The older comparative in *-joh- ~ *-ioh- and superlative in *-isto- had undergone no morphological changes; the -ν- of Homeric and later comparative forms is not yet present in Mycenaean and so must not have been in Proto-Greek. The later and more productive suffixes -τερο- and -τατο- (the latter for expected *-ταμο-, cf. Skt *-tama-*; possibly remodeled on -ιστο-?) can also have been in place in Proto-Greek.

4.3.5 Noun and adjective endings

The number-and-case endings of Greek athematic nouns preserve the PIE system well, with some simplifications, as a confrontation of the two systems demonstrates:

	(post-)PIE	*Greek*
singular		
vocative	-0	-0
nominative	*-s ~ -0, *neuter* -0	-ς ~ -0, *neuter* -0
accusative	*-m ~ *-m̥, *neuter* -0	-ν ~ -α, *neuter* -0
genitive	*-és ~ *-s → *-os	-ος
dative	*-éy	(*Myc.* -e; Διεί-φιλος)
locative	-0´ → *-í	-ι (*dative*)
instrumental	*-éh_1	(*Myc.* -e?)
plural		
nom.-voc.	*-es	-ες
accusative	*-ns ~ *-n̥s	-νς (*W.Argolic, Cretan, etc.*) ~ -ας
genitive	*-óHom	-ων
dative	*-ós → *-mós	
locative	*-sú	-σι (*dative, vowel from the sg.*)
instrumental	*-ís → *-b^hís	(*Myc.* -pi, *Hom.* -φι, *remodeled on* -σι)
dual		
nom.-acc.-voc.	*-h_1e, *neuter* *-ih_1	-ε

As usual, the oblique dual endings are not reconstructable (even for Proto-Greek). The only significant changes (aside from obvious levelings) are the syntactic merger of dative and locative, and later of the instrumental as well.

The prehistory of the Greek thematic endings is almost as straightforward:

	(post-)PIE	*Greek*
singular		
vocative	*-e, *neuter* *-om	-ε, *neuter* -ον
nominative	*-os, *neuter* *-om	-ος, *neuter* -ον
accusative	*-om	-ον
genitive	*-osyo	*Hom.* -οιο, *Thessalian* -οι, *otherwise* -ō
dative	*-oey	-ωι
locative	*-ey → *-oy	*Arkadian, etc. dat.* -οι?
instrumental	*-oh$_1$	(*Myc.* -o)
plural		
nom.-voc.	*-oes	-οι
accusative	*-ons	-ονς (W. *Argolic, Cretan,* etc.)
genitive	*-ōHom	-ων
dative	*-ōs (?) → *-oymos	
locative	*-oysu	*Myc. dat.* -o-i = *-οιhι (→ -οισι)
instrumental	*-ōys	*Myc.* -o = *dat.* -οις
dual		
nom.-acc.-voc.	*-oh$_1$, *neuter* *-oy(h$_1$)	-ω

It is unclear whether the dat. sg. in -οι attested in various dialects is the inherited loc. sg. or the result of regular sound change (since there are virtually no other examples of inherited -ωι). By far the most significant innovation among these endings was the replacement of the inherited nom.-voc. pl. with pronominal -οι.

As is usual in the daughters, collectives in *-h$_2$ and thematic *-ah$_2$ have become neuter nom.-acc.-voc. plurals in Greek. Both the athematic and the thematic formations end in (short) -α; presumably the athematic sound-change outcome has been generalized. However, it is not clear when the reanalysis of these forms as plurals occurred; Greek is (notoriously) one of the archaic IE languages in which neut. pl. subjects trigger singular concord on the verb, suggesting that they might have been grammatically singular far down into the prehistory of Greek.

The prehistory of the ᾱ-stem endings is more complex, because (as in various other daughters) they have been influenced by the thematic endings, undoubtedly because of their association in adjective inflection. In this case a different confrontation is instructive (I give the maximally conservative non-Att.-Ion. forms of ᾱ-stems):

	Greek o-stem	Greek ᾱ-stem	PIE ah$_2$-stem
singular			
vocative	-ε	-α	*-a
nominative	-ος	-ᾱ	*-ah$_2$
accusative	-ον	-ᾱν	*-ām
genitive	-οιο ~ -ō	-ᾱς → *masc.* *-ᾱCo	*-ah$_2$s
dative	-ωι	-ᾱι	*-ah$_2$ay
locative	*Ark., etc., dat.* -οι	*Ark., etc., dat.* -αι?	*-ah$_2$i
instrumental	(*Myc.* -o)	(*Myc.* -a)	*-ah$_2$h$_1$
plural			
nom.-voc.	-οι	-αι	*-ah$_2$as
accusative	-ονς (*W. Argolic, etc.*)	-ανς (*W. Argolic, etc.*)	*-ās
genitive	-ων	*-ᾱ́hων	*-ah$_2$oHom
dat.-loc.	*Myc. dat.* -o-i = *-οιhι → -οισι	*Myc. dat.* -a-i = *-ᾱhι (→ *-ᾱσι)	*-ah$_2$su (*loc.*)
instrumental	*Myc.* -o = *dat.* -οις	*Myc.* -a-pi = *-ᾱφι; (→ -αις)	*-ah$_2$b^{h}is
dual			
nom.-acc.-voc.	-ω	*Myc.* -o, -a-e > -ᾱ	???

The endings of the singular are inherited, but many plural endings have been remodeled. Nom. pl. -αι and acc. pl. -ανς (> -ᾱς) are modeled on the o-stem endings, and since they occur in all the dialects (so far as we know), they can be Proto-Greek innovations. The gen. pl. is more interesting. The PIE ending should have contracted to -ων, becoming identical with the corresponding ending in all the other stem classes; instead it has been replaced by the pronominal ending *-ah$_2$soHom > *-ᾱ́hων (> -ᾱ́ων > Att.-Ion. -ήων > -έων > -ῶν; all stages after the loss of *h are actually attested). That too can be a Proto-Greek innovation. The inst. pl. is still attested in Mycenaean, and a reflex of the inherited dat.-loc. pl. ending appears in the fossilized form Ἀθήνησι, so those two endings must still have been part of the PGk system, though in later Greek they were replaced by -αισι and -αις, again on the model of the o-stems. The Myc. dual *-o* is presumably o-stem -ω (*pace* Szemerényi 1966a: 217–22, whose suggestion does not fit etymologically or structurally); the more transparent *-a-e* seems to be the source of Att.-Ion. -ᾱ. Most striking is the innovative masc. gen. sg., appearing in Mycenaean as *-a-o*, which presumably reflects *-ᾱho, *-ᾱjo, or conceivably *-ᾱhjo. The new ending was evidently created on the model of the o-stem ending, and since the latter could have been analyzed as nom. sg. *-os + *-jo (see 3.6.3), a preform *-ᾱjo is plausible. However, native learners do not necessarily work with analogical proportions, and we do not know what would have happened to *hj, with or without a morpheme boundary, after long vowels because this would be the only example. The innovative ending can be ascribed (with due caution) to Proto-Greek, since the few masc. gen. sg. forms in -ᾱς can be shown to be innovations (Morpurgo 1961). By contrast, masc. nom. sg. -ᾱς is clearly post-Proto-Greek, since forms in -ᾱ survive in outlying dialects (Morpurgo 1961: 105–6).

Finally, something should be said about the Greek dual gen.-dat. ending. The most conservative forms are Arkadian: o-stem -οιυν, ᾱ-stem -αιυν (*DGE* 664). They have no exact cognates in any other IE language. In Homer they appear as -οιϊν, -αιϊν, apparently with assimilation of the υ; in later Attic-Ionic they have contracted to -οιν, -αιν, and the former has spread to consonant stems. What the situation was in Proto-Greek is unrecoverable.

4.3.6 Pronouns

The differences between noun and adjective inflection on the one hand and 'pronominal' inflection on the other have largely been leveled out in Greek, though there are indications that the leveling had not become quite as complete in Proto-Greek. The inflection of the determiner 'that' will illustrate; forms which have undergone morphological replacement are parenthesized:

	Proto-Core IE			*Greek*		
	masc.	*neut.*	*fem.*	*masc.*	*neut.*	*fem.*
singular						
nom.	só	tód	sáh_2	ὁ	τό	ᾱ̔
acc.	tóm	tód	tā́m	τόν	τό	τᾱ́ν
dat.	tósmey		tósya$h_2$ay	(τῶι)		(τᾶι)
gen.	tósyo		tósyah_2s	τοῖο / τõ		(τᾶς)
dual						
nom.-acc.	tóh_1	tóy(h_1)	???	τώ	(τώ)	(τώ)
plural						
nom.	tóy	táh_2	tá$h_2$as	τοί	τά	(ταί)
acc.	tóns	táh_2	tā́s	τόνς	τά	(τάνς)
inst.	tō̃ys		tá$h_2b^h$is	τοῖς		(ταῖς)
gen.	tóysoHom		tá$h_2$soHom	(τῶν)		τᾱ́ων
loc.	tóysu		tá$h_2$su	τοῖσι		(ταῖσι)

The masc.-neut. forms with *-sm-, the fem. forms with *-sy-, and the masc.-neut. gen. pl. have all been replaced; so have all the fem. pl. forms except the gen. pl. Conversely, the masc.-neut. gen. sg. ending and the fem. gen. pl. ending have spread to all other o- and ᾱ-stem nominals. However, there is indirect evidence that *-sm- had not yet disappeared in Proto-Greek, for which we must examine the interrogative/indefinite pronoun:

	Proto-Core IE			*Greek*	
	masc.	*neut.*	*fem.*	*masc.-fem.*	*neut.*
singular					
nom.	kʷéy	kʷíd	kʷíh₂	τίς	τί
acc.	kʷím	kʷíd	kʷíh₂m̥	τίνα	τί
dat.	kʷésmey		kʷésyah₂ay	τέωι	
gen.	kʷésyo		kʷésyah₂s	τέο	
loc.	kʷésmi		kʷésyah₂(i)	(*Cret. dat.* ὅτῑμι—see below)	
plural					
nom.	kʷéyes	kʷíh₂	kʷíh₂es (?)	τίνες	τίνα
acc.	kʷíns	kʷíh₂	kʷíh₂n̥s (?)	τίνας	τίνα / σσα
gen.	kʷéysoHom		kʷíh₂soHom	τέων / τίνων	
loc.	kʷéysu		kʷíh₂su	τέοισι / τίσι	

The feminine forms have been lost completely, as in Latin and Germanic. I have given the Homeric forms of the gen. and dat. sg., which are clearly older than Classical τίνος, τίνι. Though a longer gen. sg. *τεῖο is not actually attested, it might have existed, since it is a plausible model for ἐμεῖο 'of me', etc. (see below). The dat. sg. and oblique plural forms have been built to the inherited gen. sg. Otherwise the acc. sg. *kʷím > *τίν, recharacterized as τίνα, has been made the basis of most of the paradigm. Two remarkable archaisms have resisted the spread of the stem τιν-. One is neut. pl. *kʷíh₂ > *kjá, preserved in the second part of the Attic indefinite relative ἅττα and in *Od.* 19.218:

εἰπέ μοι ὁπποῖά σσα περὶ χροῒ εἵματα ἕστο
'tell me what sort of garments he was wearing around his body'.

The other is the Cretan indefinite relative dat. sg. ὅτῑμι, of which the second part can only be *kʷísmi ← *kʷésmi, demonstrating that *-sm- was still present in pronominal inflection in Proto-Greek.

The only pervasive relic of pronominal inflection in Greek is neuter nom.-acc. sg. -o < *-od. It is inherited in τό and at least also in ἄλλο (cf. Lat. *aliud*), and has spread to αὐτό, ἐκε͂νο, etc.

The personal pronouns have also undergone extensive remodeling in Greek; a number of inherited forms have been lost, and the duals and plurals have been provided with full case inflection. So far as I can tell, the developments were the following.

1st person

sg.	*nom.*	éǵh$_2$	>→	ἐγώ
	acc.	emé ~ me	>	ἐμέ ~ με
	gen.	méme ~ moy	→	ἐμεῖο ~ μεο, adj. *memós >→ ἐμός
	dat.	méǵ^{h}ye ~ moy	>→	ἐμοί ~ μοι
du.	*nom.*	wé		
	oblique	n̥h$_3$mé ~ noh$_3$	>→	acc. *νωϝέ > νώ, >→ νῶε (Katz 1998: 206–10)
pl.	*nom.*	wéy		
	oblique	n̥smé ~ nos	>	acc. *hąhμέ > Lesb. ἄμμε, Dor. ἁ̄μέ

As in Latin, the nom. sg. has been extended with the thematic 1sg. primary ending of the verb. The acc. sg. survives without change, and the remaining sg. forms have been remodeled to match it: the accented dat. sg. by backformation to the enclitic form, the gen. sg. by addition of the ending of the interrogative pronoun or the default determiner. A possessive adjective has also been formed to the inherited gen. sg. and has then undergone dissimilatory loss of one of its *m's (Cowgill 1965: 170, who also suggests *memós >→ Lat. *meus* by loss of the other *m). Of the dual and plural only the accented oblique forms survive, reinterpreted as specifically accusative; the nominatives and the enclitic oblique forms have been lost. The stressed elements *-mé and *-wé have been redistributed, with the former for plurals and the latter for duals (Katz 1998: 195–7). In the dual the accusative form also acquired nominative function (conforming to the syncretism of all other nominals); in the plural new nominative forms have been created in Greek, and both in the dual and in the plural new gen. and dat. forms have been created. How much of that had already happened in Proto-Greek is not recoverable, but if there was a new nom. pl. already in PGk, it was probably the preform of Lesb. ἄμμες and Dor. ἁ̄μές, with only *-s added.

2nd person

sg.	*nom.*	túh$_2$	>	τύ → σύ (with loss of the laryngeal utterance-finally)
	acc.	twé ~ te	>→	σέ ~ *τε → σε
	gen.	téwe ~ toy	→	σεῖο ~ σεο, adj. *tewós > Hom. τεός (Lat. *tuos*)
	dat.	téb^{h}ye ~ toy	>→	σοί ~ τοι → σοι
du.	*nom.*	yú		
	oblique	uh$_3$wé ~ woh$_3$		
pl.	*nom.*	yū́ (< **yúy ?)		
	oblique	uswé ~ wos	>→	acc. *huhmé > Lesb. ὔμμε, Dor. ὑ̄μέ

The developments have largely been parallel to those of the first-person pronoun, with two major differences. In the singular *tw- > σ-, and the resulting alternation between τ and σ was adjusted (and eventually eliminated) in a variety of ways, partly differently in the different dialects. In the dual, we find nom. acc. σφώ, which cannot possibly reflect the PIE form. Its origin remains debatable; for discussion, see Katz (1998: 234–53) with references.

The pronoun (acc.) ἕ, etc., reflecting PIE *swé, can be reflexive in Homer but need not be; it is at least possible that that is an archaism. Its forms are parallel to those of the second person and probably were so in PGk. The corresponding plural beginning with σφ- can only have been built to a inst. pl. (*)σφι which survives in Homer as dat. pl. σφιν (Katz 1998: 228–33); only that form is likely to have existed already in PGk. The initial nasals of non-neuter accusative μιν and νιν have not been given a satisfactory explanation.

4.3.7 Numerals

Greek is one of the languages which preserves PIE *sem- 'one', but the only form that has not been remodeled is neut. nom.-acc. *sém > ἕν; masc. nom. *sḗm has been replaced by more transparent *sém-s > ἕνς. The e-grade has been leveled through the masc. and neut. paradigm. Mycenaean dat. sg. *e-me* *ἐμεί shows that this numeral remained an m-stem far down into the history of Greek; leveling of ν into intervocalic position (ἕνα, ἑνός, ἑνί) is a post-Mycenaean innovation. The fem. direct forms *sémih$_2$, *sémih$_2$m̥ seem to have been remodeled to *smíh$_2$, *smíh$_2$m̥ (> μία, μίαν) early, but both the direct stem *hμία- and an oblique stem *siáh$_2$-[56] > *hιᾶ- must still have been present in Proto-Greek, because the latter is the only plausible source for Lesbian and Homeric ἴα; evidently the dialects leveled *hμ- and *h- in opposite directions.

Greek preserves two nom.-acc. forms of 'two': Hom. δύω reflects PIE masc. *dwóh$_1$, while δύο is apparently endingless. Of course the uninflected form might have lost its laryngeal utterance-finally, but if that is what happened it happened before the daughters began to diverge, because forms in *-o are also attested in other IE languages; see Cowgill (1985b) for discussion. In Homer this numeral appears to be uninflected (Chantraine 1973: 260), but in later Greek it has a transparent gen.-dat. δυοῖν, with alternating accent apparently on the model of 'one'; the same peculiarity has spread to ἄμφω, ἀμφοῖν 'both' (post-PIE *h$_2$n̥tb^{h}óh$_1$; Jasanoff 1976). Neither word has distinctive feminine forms, and that might be an archaism.

'Three' and 'four' also have no distinctive feminine forms, but it is clear that the inherited feminine stems in *-sr- have been lost (they survive in Indo-Iranian and Celtic). Greek forms of 'three' are the regular sound-change reflexes of the PIE forms (with -σί replacing *-sú, as always), except that the dialects exhibit a strong tendency to syncretize the nom. and acc.; but since reflexes both of nom. *tréyes and of acc. *tríns occur (the latter in, e.g., Heraklean nom. τρῖς *DGE* 62.23

[56] With the syllabic alternant of *y by Lindeman's Law; so also in 'two' below.

and Cretan acc. τρίινς *DGE* 179.V.54), both forms must still have been present in Proto-Greek. 'Four' exhibits the productive Greek consonant-stem endings and its ablaut has been leveled, but the outcome is not the same in all dialects. The widespread stem τεσσαρ- (Attic τετταρ-) looks like the sound-change reflex of NIE *kʷetwr̥-; Doric τετορ- ought to reflect *kʷetwór-, but the *w has somehow been lost. Possibly the key to that puzzle is the dat. pl. τέτρασιν attested twice in Pindar: apparently postconsonantal *w was lost before *r̥ and the -τ- was leveled through the paradigm. But in that case the stem τεσσαρ- has also undergone leveling: the *w has been leveled back into its preform after being lost by regular sound change. Evidently this numeral still preserved its ablaut alternation in Proto-Greek.

Higher numerals are for the most part sound-change reflexes of the NIE forms. The discussion of Szemerényi (1960) is still valuable.

5
The initial diversification of Greek dialects

5.1 Introduction

Since linguistic descent is defined by unbroken sequences of native language acquisition, and since divergent descent from a common parent defines a family of languages or dialects, an important endeavor in historical linguistics is the attempt to recover the branching structure of a language's diversification into daughters. In a strict cladistic tree speechforms are grouped together only if they can be shown to share a critical mass of innovations *which are not easily repeatable* and *which other related speechforms do not share*, so as to demonstrate significant exclusively shared history. The requirements that there be a significant number of innovations, that they be not easily repeatable, and that they be exclusively shared are intended, in the first instance, to exclude parallel development by chance, though the motivation for the requirement of exclusivity is also a desire to find a 'clean' tree (if there is one) rather than a dialect network.

Though such a model of diversification is clear in principle—and should always be tested on a dataset first because it is easily falsifiable—it often does not match linguistic reality. If languages or dialects remain in contact as they diversify, they can and usually do continue to share innovations after they have become distinct; Ross (1997, 1998) is perhaps the best exploration of that phenomenon. Since the dialects of Ancient Greek were obviously in contact for many centuries, this is a major problem in assessing how the Greek dialects diversified.

Risch (1955) pointed out that attention both to cladistics and to the relative chronology of changes could help clarify the diversification of the Greek dialects. For instance, it is easy to show that the 'second compensatory lengthening' (2CL) occurred in the Attic-Ionic dialects after they had begun to diverge from all the others (Risch 1955: 64); it follows that the 2CL must have spread through an already diversified dialect continuum. Unfortunately the relative chronology of changes is often not recoverable, so that we cannot always determine which changes occurred before any diversification and which spread through already diversified dialects—and making 'simplifying' assumptions about contingent events, which could easily have happened one way or another, is not good scientific practice. It should be noted that the ability to reconstruct a potential parent dialect for a dialect group is not automatically proof that the group constitutes a clade, both for the reasons just discussed and because nearly identical parent dialects could have been (and probably were) members of a dialect continuum, not cleanly separate ancestors

The Linguistic Roots of Ancient Greek. Don Ringe, Oxford University Press.
 DOI: 10.1093/9780191989162.003.0005

of clades; for valuable discussion of this and related issues, see Morpurgo Davies (1992) and Rau (2018, 2022). We need to consider whether we are willing to accept subgroups that might have coalesced after an initial period of modest divergence. I will return to this question in considering an Aiolic subgroup in 5.2 and a South Greek subgroup in 5.3.

Though my judgments of particular pieces of evidence are (perhaps inevitably) different from those of other scholars, so that we do not always agree in detail, the general picture that is sketched below—modest initial divergence followed by the extensive spread of innovations through a dialect continuum—is comparable to the conclusions of colleagues cited above, as well as those of Meier-Brügger (2005) and Hajnal (2007); cf. also García-Ramón (2018: 99). For an exploration of this problem using computational cladistic methods, see Skelton (2015).

It seems to me that two identifiable groups of dialects require only a summary discussion.

I doubt that West Greek, or any of its potential subgroups, shares a critical mass of distinctive innovations that would justify recognizing it as a coherent clade exclusively sharing history. Of the common West Greek characteristics listed in Thumb and Kieckers (1932: 70–4), Buck (1955: 154–5), and Thompson (2008: 761–3), a good many are actually archaisms (often shared with non-West Greek dialects); some, such as the paradigms πόλις, gen. πόλιος, etc. (replacing inherited πόληος, etc.), and -εύς, gen. -έος, etc. (replacing inherited -ῆος, etc.), the spread of σ-aorist -ξαι at the expense of -σσαι, the spread of the future in -σέε̄ν (see Ruijgh 2007: 422–3 with references), and the active endings of the future passive (Buck 1955: 117) are the results of natural and repeatable changes (again typically shared with other dialects, at least to some extent); and the contractions of vowels in hiatus are known to have occurred at a late prehistoric stage, when the dialects must already have been differentiated. The best support for a West Greek group comes from lexical peculiarities such as πρᾶτος 'first' and τέτορες 'four', of which the latter shows an unexpected loss of *w after *t; but since lexemes are the most easily borrowable components of a language, such support is always relatively weak. Other traits of West Greek will be adduced in the appropriate places below.

Support for an Arkado-Cyprian clade is no better, in spite of the statements of Buck (1955: 144), Thumb and Scherer (1959: 110), Colvin (2014: 99–100), and other scholars. Many features of Arkadian and Cyprian are shared with Attic-Ionic and are characteristic of South Greek (see 5.3). Κάς 'and' and πός 'toward, at' represent not positive innovations but *loss* of the alternatives καί and πρός, which were also present in Proto-Greek and South Greek respectively; and since loss is by far the most easily repeatable type of change, it cannot count for much in subgrouping. The raising of *ε before nasals and of *o word-finally are trivial phonetic changes that are easily repeatable. We are left with ὄνυ 'this', nom. sg. ἱερής (for ἱερεύς), and the fact that prepositions meaning 'from' govern the dative rather than the genitive (Janko 2018: 113)—not extensive support for a dialect group.

Two other dialect groups require much more discussion, namely Aiolic, which includes Lesbian, Thessalian, and Boiotian (plus the Aiolic component of the Homeric oral poetic tradition), and South Greek, which includes at least Mycenaean, Arkadian, Cyprian, and Attic-Ionic. I will discuss those two dialect groups in turn.

5.2 Aiolic

5.2.1 Evidence for an Aiolic group

Two recent treatments of the Aiolic dialect group come to diametrically opposite conclusions, as follows.

Parker (2008) raises the question of whether Aiolic is a viable subgroup at all. He identifies seven characteristics that could provide solid support for an Aiolic clade (Parker 2008: 444–6):

> among regular sound changes, *r̥ > ρο ~ ορ; labiovelars > labials even before e- vowels; *VRh, *VhR, *VRj > *VRR*;
> in inflectional morphology, dat. pl. -εσσι; pf. ptc. -οντ-; fem. ἴα 'one';
> in derivational morphology, patronymic adjectives in -ιος.

As Parker notes, many of these characteristics provide only weak support for an Aiolic clade, as follows.

The patronymics in -ιος are probably an archaism (cf. Debrunner 1917: 142, Buck 1955: 134). Parker argues that the 'double sonorant' outcome of h-clusters (which is not shared by Boiotian) is likewise an archaism; I will discuss that issue at length in 5.2.2 below. In addition, he maintains that the labial outcomes of labiovelars before e-vowels could also reflect failure to undergo a sound change. The development of labiovelars will be treated in greater detail in 5.4.1, but the pattern of reflexes shows that, except for *k^w before high front vowels, labials were the default outcome, appearing in all dialects except before mid front vowels (with rare exceptions). The most economical scenario that can account for the messy pattern of facts seems to be:

1) before front vowels, labiovelars developed allomorphs (probably palatalized) that would eventually develop into dentals, but
   1a) as the new allomorphs spread through the dialect continuum they failed to spread completely to the Aiolic dialects and to Cyprian;
2) then all unaffected labiovelars became labials, the change spreading across the Greek *Sprachraum*.

It should follow that the Aiolic dialects share an archaism, not an innovation, in this detail too (Parker 2008: 445–6). The reflex of *r̥ with ο, as opposed to α, is obviously not an archaism, but it is not restricted to the Aiolic dialects (Buck 1955: 20, Morpurgo Davies 1968, Parker 2008: 446–7), and such a simple sound change is clearly repeatable.

The remaining characteristics are more interesting. Fem. ἴα 'one', as opposed to μία, reflects leveling in an inherited paradigm (Parker 2008: 448–50; see 4.3.7), and while leveling is of course a repeatable change, it is striking that only the Aiolic dialects have leveled in this direction. Remodeling of the active perfect participles in these dialects with present/aorist thematic -οντ-, replacing -ότ- ~ -υίᾱ-, might actually be expected on general grounds; but why didn't the other dialects participate in this obvious leveling? And while dat. pl. -εσσι is not restricted to the Aiolic dialects, most of the dialects that exhibit such an ending form a coherent area, extending from Lesbian through Thessalian and Boiotian into northern West Greek, suggesting that there is some historical connection between them. While Parker is right to maintain that these innovations are not sufficient to establish an Aiolic clade in the strictest sense, it is hard to believe that they do not reveal shared history of some sort.

Parker used established diagnostics for subgrouping in his study; Scarborough, by contrast, employs a new and promising probabilistic method (Scarborough 2016: 185–209). He estimates the probability of each innovation occurring (pp. 188–95) based on its actual incidence in the nineteen Greek dialects exemplified in Buck (1955) (Scarborough 2016: 194–7), then multiplies the probabilities of those innovations shared by all the Aiolic dialects; the result is a statistical demonstration that the isogloss bundle that distinguishes Aiolic is unlikely to be due to chance (pp. 198–9). Since estimates of the probability of each innovation occurring independently are (other things being equal) a better alternative to simply rejecting innovations as evidence if they seem too easily repeatable,[1] it seems clear that Scarborough has demonstrated probable shared history of some sort between the Lesbian, Thessalian, and Boiotian dialects.

I suggest that both Parker and Scarborough are correct, depending on how the question is framed. It does not seem possible to establish an Aiolic clade in the strict sense, especially since we cannot demonstrate that the shared innovations occurred earlier than those that are not shared by all three dialects. However, the Aiolic dialects did share some innovations, not by accident but as historically single events.

[1] The only potential problem is that all the Greek dialects were in contact for centuries, so that an estimate of *independent* 'innovability' based on the incidence of an innovation among the dialects might be inaccurate by an unknown margin. Scarborough is aware of this (p. 191), but (a) it isn't clear how to get a better estimate, and (b) since all probabilities fall between 0 (impossible) and 1 (certain), the product of all the estimates is unlikely to be off by as much as an order of magnitude.

The basic problem is the one mentioned at the beginning of Chapter 3: given that the dialects had all been in contact for a long time, we are often unable to distinguish between changes that occurred in a unitary parent dialect, before divergence, and those that spread later through an already differentiated dialect continuum. This problem is not peculiar to any one approach; it bedevils every attempt to classify the Greek dialects by any method. Demanding exclusively shared innovations is intended, in part, to obviate this problem; but it seems clear that such a strategy is not very effective in the context of a dialect continuum.

In the remainder of this book I will treat the Aiolic dialects as a historically definable *group*, with the explicit understanding that they might not be a *clade*, strictly speaking.

5.2.2 The first compensatory lengthening

The outcome of *VRh, *VhR, and *VRj-clusters, except for *VRj after *a and *o and for *Vlj (see 3.6.3), is a geminate sonorant (*VRR*) in Lesbian and Thessalian, but not in Boiotian; in Boiotian, as in all the other dialects, these clusters are reduced to single sonorants and the preceding vowel is lengthened by the 'first compensatory lengthening' (1CL; see Bechtel 1921: 240–1). The following examples are typical (Buck 1955: 65–7, Lejeune 1972: 121–3, 125–6, 128–9):[2]

- PIE *$h_1$esmi 'I am' (Skt *asmi*) > *esmi > *ἐhμι > Hom., Att., Boiot., etc., ἔ̄μι but Lesb. ἐμμι;
- PIE *wésmn̥ 'garment' (Skt *vásma*) > *ϝέhμα̨ > Hom., Att. ἔ̄μα but Lesb. pl. ἔ̆μματα (Sappho 62.12);
- PIE *n̥smé 'us' (Skt *asmā́n*) > *α̨hμέ > Dor. ἅ̄μέ but Lesb. ἄμμε, Thess. ἀμμέ;
- PIE *krásnah$_2$ 'moving water' vel sim. (ON *hrǫnn* 'wave') > *κράhνᾱ > Dor., Ark. κρᾱ́νᾱ 'spring', Att. κρήνη, but Lesb. acc. κράννᾱν (Alkaios 150.5);
- PIE *$h_1$rég^{w}es- 'darkness' (Goth. *riqis*) in pre-Gk *ἐρεγ^{w}εh-νό- 'dark' > Hom. (Aiolic) (νὺξ) ἐρεβεννή;
- pre-Gk *φαϝεh-νό- 'shining' > Hom. φαε̄νός but Lesb. neut. φάεννον (Sappho 34.2);
- pre-Gk *σελάhνᾱ 'moon' (cf. σέλας 'torch') > Dor. σελᾱ́νᾱ, Att.-Ion. σελήνη but Lesb. σελάννᾱ;
- (post-)PIE *ǵ^{h}éslom 'thousand' (Skt *sa-hásram*), deriv. *ǵ^{h}éslio- > *χέhλιο- > Ion. gen. pl. χειλίων (ει = ε̄) *DGE* 688.D.12, Lakonian acc. pl. τρισχε̄λίōς *DGE* 13.20, acc. pl. fem. Boiot. χειλίᾱς *DGE* 467.15 but Thess. χέλλιας *DGE* 614.29;

[2] A problem is Att. αὗος, Ion. αὖος 'dry, dried out'. It is hard to believe that it is not cognate with Lith. *saũsas* and OE *sēar*, reflecting *sáwsos or the like; but *aws ought to have become *awh and then *ᾱϝ, etc., unless it had been subject to analogical remodeling. For discussion, see Berg and Lindeman (1992 with references).

PIE *$ǵ^h$ésr- 'hand' (Hitt. *kissar*, Toch. B *ṣar*, Arm *jeṙn*) > *χεhρ- > Att., etc. χέ̄ρ but Lesb. nom. pl. χέρρες;
pre-Gk *ναhϝός 'temple' (cf. Hom. ναίε̄ν 'to dwell') > Dor. νᾱϝός, Hom. νηός, Att. νεώς but Lesb. ναῦος (= νάϝϝος);
pre-Gk aor. *κριν-h- 'judge' > Att., etc. 3sg. ἔκρῑνε but Lesb. ἐπέκριννε 'decided' (*DGE* 621.28);
pre-Gk aor. *μεν-h- 'stay' > Att., etc. 3sg. ἔμε̄νε but Thess. ptc. gen. pl. συμμεννάντουν 'so long as they remain' (*DGE* 590.15);
PIE *$méh_1n̥s$- 'moon' (Skt *mā́s*, Lat. *mēnsis* 'month') > *μηνh- 'month', gen. sg.*μηνhός > Att., etc. μηνός but Lesb. μῆννος, Thess. μειννός;
pre-Gk aor. *ἀϝερ-h- 'lift' > Hom. inf. ἀε̄ραι but Lesb. ptc. fem. συναέρραισα (Sappho 81.5);
pre-Gk aor. *στελ-h- 'send' > Att., etc. 3sg. ἔστε̄λε but Lesb. 3pl. ἀπέστελλαν (*DGE* 623.22), Thess. ptc. gen. sg. ἀπυστέλλαντος;
PIE *$h_2$áwsōs 'dawn' → *$h_2$usṓs (Skt *uṣā́s*) > *ἀϝhώς > Dor. ἀ̔ϝώς, Hom. ἠώς, Att. ἕως but Lesb. αὔως (= ἄϝϝως);
pre-Gk pres. *κριν-jε/ο- 'judge' > Att., etc., κρί̄νε̄ν but Lesb. passive ptc. κριννόμεναι (Alkaios 130B.17), Thess. inf. κρεννέμεν (*DGE* 590.14);
pre-Gk pres. *ἀϝερ-jε/ο- 'lift' > Hom. ptc. ἀε̄ρων but Lesb. iptv. 2sg. κὰδ δ' ἄερρε 'take down' (Alkaios 346.2);
pre-Gk pres. *hῑμερ-jε/ο- 'long for, desire' > Hom. inf. ἱ̄με̄ρε̄ν but Lesb. inf. ἰμέρρην (Alkaios 73.5).

Similar Lesbian forms are quoted by the grammarians (see Buck, *loc. cit.*, and Lejeune, *locc. citt.*). The question is how the PGk consonant clusters developed into the forms with geminate sonorants on the one hand and the forms with the 1CL on the other.

The standard suggestion is that these consonant clusters developed independently in Lesbian and Thessalian on the one hand and in the remaining dialects on the other; that is:

> *VRh, *VhR, *VRj (1) > *VRR* in Lesbian and Thessalian by assimilation, but (2) > $\bar{V}R$ in other dialects by the 1CL.

For *VhR sequences, in which the lost consonant was originally adjacent to the vowel that was eventually lengthened, that is obviously plausible. For the other sequences, in which the lost consonant was not adjacent to the vowel, this scenario is at least possible; as I will show in 7.2.2, in the 'third compensatory lengthening' we are forced to posit a direct change *VCw > $\bar{V}C$ with no intermediate stages, and the 1CL could perhaps have been a similar change. This scenario posits two potential clades of dialects, each of which shares a distinctive sound change.

But Cowgill (1969) pointed out that this is not the only possibility. His proposed scenario can be schematized as follows:

1) *VRj > *VR^jR^j, while *VhR and *VRh > *VRR*;
2) palatalized geminate sonorants are depalatalized,[3] leading to the situation in Lesbian and Thessalian;
3) finally, *VRR > $\bar{V}R$ in all dialects *except* Lesbian and Thessalian.

Of course this will work only if there are no counterexamples to change (3), but in fact there are not: except for the reflex of *l^jl^j, which remained geminate in most dialects (see 3.6.3), all attested geminates in dialects other than Lesbian and Thessalian are of later origin (see below). If Cowgill's scenario is correct, Lesbian and Thessalian do not form a clade; they simply failed to share a change shared by all the other dialects (Parker 2008: 450–5).

Either of the scenarios just presented could be correct; while Cowgill's is slightly more complex in terms of the number of changes involved, it is also slightly more likely in phonetic terms, so that Occam's Razor cannot really be invoked. We should look for further evidence that might favor one alternative or the other.

In fact we have already seen evidence favoring Cowgill's alternative in 3.6.3. It is beyond dispute that *lj became geminate *l^jl^j, which was subsequently depalatalized; the only difference is that the resulting λλ did not undergo the 1CL. We have also seen that the change from *ny, *ry, *wy to ιν, ιρ, ιϝ when α or ο preceded is most plausibly modeled not as a brute-force metathesis but with an intermediate stage of palatalized geminates. But if *Ry-clusters developed into palatalized geminates in those cases, it is most economical to suppose that they did so in all other cases too; that is the simplest and most likely sound change that we can posit. It then follows that the persistence of gemination in Lesbian and Thessalian is conservative, not evolved—and that the 1CL operated on geminate *n^jn^j and *r^jr^j after high and front vowels (though not on *w^jw^j—see further below). Once we have arrived at that conclusion, generalizing to include the rest of Cowgill's scenario—i.e. *VRh, *VhR > *VRR* > $\bar{V}R$—seems to be the simplest and most plausible hypothesis that we can construct. I therefore concur with Scarborough (2016: 114–15), who judges gemination followed by lengthening to be the most likely hypothesis (on partly different grounds).

I also suggest that the geminate sonorant stage of development had been reached in PGk, but depalatalization had not occurred, since *lj did not undergo the 1CL anywhere.

There are a handful of Attic and Ionic examples in which the outcomes of these clusters are spelled -ειρ- and -ειν- at unexpectedly early dates; for the forms and discussion, see Kostopoulos (2023: 127–36). Kostopoulos argues (pp. 136–8) that

[3] Except in the cases noted in 3.6.3; see further below.

these forms might actually contain the diphthong ει; if that is true, there might have been a few localities in the (very large) Attic-Ionic dialect area in which *ery and *eny developed differently, and the entire development of these sequences might have been later than is usually supposed.

This is the most convenient place to address the development of *ewj. There is at least a bit of evidence that *wj > *jw after *a and *o (see 3.6.3); what happened after *i, e.g. in Hom. δῖος 'godlike' < *diwyós (cf. Myc. *di-u-jo* ~ *di-wi-jo*) is difficult to determine, since more than one line of development could have yielded ῑ, and whether *ūj was treated as *uwy is also difficult to determine.[4] We have more potential evidence for what happened to *ewy, but the inconclusive discussion of Lejeune (1972: 171–3) gives a good idea of the problems involved. For instance, it seems clear from Myc. *me-u-jo* ~ *me-wi-jo* 'less' and *di-u-jo* ~ *di-wi-jo* that *wj remained unaltered in the Mycenaean period; but then why is 'priestess' always spelled *i-je-re-ja*? The obvious conclusion is that the latter was not derived from a noun in -ήϝ- (so Lejeune 1972: 172 *ad fin.*), but if so, we might have fewer 1st-millennium examples of *-ewj- than we had supposed. Two formations at least seem certain, namely present stems derived from nouns in -ήϝ- and feminines of adjectives in -ύ- ~ -έϝ-. The former end in -ευ-ε/ο- in almost all 1st-millennium dialects, but in -ει-ε/ο- in Elean (see 4.2.1 (v) for examples); since -ευ-ε/ο- is attributable to leveling from aorist -ευ-σα-, the Elean examples are good evidence that the outcome of *-ewj- was in fact -ει-, i.e. /-ejj-/. The feminines of υ-stem adjectives present a more complex picture. In Attic they uniformly end in -ει-α before the 4th century BC (Threatte 1996: 303–4), by which point /ei/ had merged with /e:/ and become subject to shortening; that corroborates the inference from Elean present stems. In Homer about 85% also end in -ει-α, and most of the examples of -ε-α are scattered enough that formulaic modification and metrical exigencies seem likely to explain them. But the formula ὠκέα Ἶρις occurs some twenty times, always in the Iliad, and is clearly an integral part of the poetic tradition. The fact that these feminines appear uniformly with -ε-α in our text of Herodotos might suggest that they are not artificial, and that the suffix in at least some Ionic dialects was actually /-ẽ:a/, with early shortening to /-éa/ (see 6.2), rather than /-éjja/. However, even the old collection of data in Smyth (1894: 197–9) argues caution: it turns out that the Ionic lyric poets avoid -ε-α, and the pattern of attestation is consistent with relatively late development of an earlier diphthongal form. In the poetry of Sappho and Alkaios the feminines of five different u-stem adjectives occur, and every one ends in -ηα—neither '-ευα', as might be expected in an Aiolic dialect,

[4] The obvious example is φῦεν. A 3sg. φυίει is sometimes supplied in Alkaios 10B.5 on the basis of a scholion to Sophokles *Oidipous Tyrannos* 153, but the reading of the scholion is apparently not secure. (I am grateful to Matthew Scarborough for helpful discussion of this point.) The paradigm of ὑιύς 'son', even if we were sure of the original shape of the stem, must have been so vulnerable to leveling that it is not useful for historical phonology.

nor -εια. The most likely hypothesis is that ει > η before vowels, or at least non-high back vowels, in the dialect of the Lesbian poets (though not necessarily in all subdialects of Lesbian; see the comprehensive discussion of Forssman 1975). I infer, with caution, that *εϝj > /ejj/ in all Ancient Greek dialects (so far as we have evidence), though clearly after the Mycenaean period, with divergent development subsequently.

This is also the most convenient place to call attention to some further examples of Lesbian and Thessalian *VRR* corresponding to the $\bar{V}R$ of other dialects that might reflect pre-PGk consonant clusters of other kinds. One is a common noun with an obscure suffix:

PGk *στάλλᾱ 'standing stone' > Lesb., Thess. στάλλᾱ, otherwise στᾱ́λᾱ (> Att.-Ion. στήλη).

The preform was probably *στάλνᾱ (Schwyzer 1939: 283–4, Frisk s.v. στήλη); a suffix *-σᾱ is not completely impossible, but *-νᾱ is much commoner (see the relevant sections of Buck and Petersen 1949). There are a number of similar nouns, many with questionable etymologies. There is also a present stem:

PGk *ὀφέλνεhεν 'to owe' > Hom. (Aiolic) ὀφέλλēν, Att.-Ion. ὀφḗλēν, Dor. ὀφḗλēν (Frisk s.v. ὀφείλω with references).

Whatever the etymology of this root, it is most likely to have had a present in -νε/ο-like τάμνēν, etc. (see 4.2.1 (ii)). Finally, there is an extraordinarily complex family of words well attested in most Greek dialects. One member is an inherited noun:

PGk *γʷολνᾱ́ (*γʷολhᾱ́?) 'decision, consultation (etc.)' > Lesb. βόλλᾱ, Boiot., Ark., etc. βωλᾱ́, Att.-Ion. βōλή.

This seems to have been derived from a simple thematic present with attestations scattered across the South Greek dialect group:

Hom. βόλεται 'wishes, prefers' *Il.* 11.319, ἐβόλοντο *Od.* 1.234, βόλεσθε 16.387 (beside forms of βṓλεσθαι more than thirty times in the two poems together), West Ionic subj. βόληται *DGE* 808.32, 811.31 (both 4th century, ο necessarily short), Arkadian subj. βόλητοι *DGE* 657.46, etc. (the 1CL yields ω in Arkadian, cf. βωλᾱ́ immediately above and see 7.2.4).

But the o-grade root is unexpected in the verb, and the formation of the noun is also surprising; one might expect the noun to have been '*γʷολᾱ́', a garden-variety oxytone fem., derived from a root *γʷελ-. In fact e-grade forms of the verb stem are well attested:

subj. 3sg. Thess. βέλλειτει *DGE* 590.20, Boiot. βείλειτη *DGE* 485.2, Delphian and Lokrian δείληται (ει = ε̄) *DGE* 335.10, 366.A.12, Coan δήληται *DGE* 254.17, 3pl., Heraklean δήλωνται *DGE* 62.146, etc.

So far as we can tell, the e-grade present stem is attested in Thessalian, Boiotian, and all of West Greek, i.e. *except* in South Greek, Lesbian, and Pamphylian. It must reflect a preform *γ^weλ-νε/ο- or *γ^weλ-hε/ο-. If it is the original present, an e-grade desiderative in *-hε/ο- is actually likely, given the meaning of the verb (Chantraine 1973: 311). In that case we might consider positing a PGk present *γ^weλ-hε/ο- and derived noun *γ^wολᾱ́, with the opaque suffix of the present spreading into the noun by lexical analogy, at first outside of South Greek, while conversely the South Greek present was remodeled as *γ^wολ-ε/ο-, with further lexical analogies to follow. It does not seem possible to move beyond these speculations, which of course must remain uncertain; for further discussion see Ringe (2018: 280–2) with further references.

Examples of geminate νν outside of Lesbian and Thessalian are all obviously later creations. The most obvious is Πελοπόννησος < Πέλοπος νῆσος, but it is almost as clear that presents such as Att. κρεμαννύναι 'to be hanging (something) up' can have been remodeled on the corresponding aorists κρεμάσαι, etc., with a fairly recent *-σν- that also became -νν- by a still more recent regular sound change. Examples of λλ that cannot reflect *lj are more of a problem. One is clearly a late secondary development:

ἀπολλύναι 'to destroy' < *ἀπ-ολ-νυ-,

which suggests that examples such as βάλλε̄ν 'to throw', ἀνατέλλε̄ν 'to rise' (of heavenly bodies), and Hom. περιτελλόμενος 'revolving' also exhibit λλ < *λν—especially since *telh_2- 'lift' is known to have had a nasal-infixed present and both *k^wel- 'turn' and *g^welh_1- 'throw' might be expected to (see the relevant entries in *LIV*). But that can only mean that the nasal affix was restored after the 1CL had run its course (Harðarson 1993: 161 fn. 69). More than that cannot be said unless and until further information is forthcoming.

5.3 South Greek

In the middle of the 20th century it became clear that Mycenaean, Arkadian, Cyprian, and Attic-Ionic share several innovations that might lead an observer to recognize them as a dialect group, sometimes called 'South Greek' (Risch 1955: 65–7, 70, Cowgill 1966: 93). Ringe (2018) briefly discusses what seem to me to be the crucial pieces of evidence; in what follows I will expand somewhat on that presentation.

5.3.1 Phonological evidence for South Greek

The most obvious phonological innovation of the South Greek dialects is the replacement of the sequence τι with σι in a wide range of forms. By itself that would not necessarily be strong evidence for a clade, even though it must reflect more than one sound change, because a sequence of changes *ti > ... > *si* is widely attested in other languages across the globe (cf. Ringe and Eska 2013: 257–8). However, the conditioning of this change was partly morphological in Greek; and since sound change is normally conditioned only by phonological factors, the shared quirky pattern of this change is good evidence for a South Greek group, potentially a clade. The best recent discussion is Thompson (2008: 753–8), on which this discussion partly depends; Méndez Dosuna (1985) is also highly relevant.

The change affected athematic 3sg. *-τι except after -σ- (we find ἐστι in all dialects):

PGk *φᾱτι '(s)he says' (Dor. φᾱτι Alkman 6 fr. 4.4, Bakkhylides 27.36; cf. Skt *bʰāti* 'it shines') > Myc. *pa-si* *φᾱσι > Att.-Ion. φησι;
PGk *εἶτι '(s)he is going' (Kyrenaian εἶτι '(nor) shall he go' Buck 115.57; cf. Skt *éti*) > Att.-Ion. εἶσι, Myc. *a-pe-i-si* 'is going away';
PGk *δίδωτι '(s)he is giving' (Dor. δίδωτι Simonides 555.1, Boiot. δίδōτι *DGE* 441; cf. Skt *dádāti*) > Att.-Ion. δίδωσι;
PGk *τίθητι '(s)he is putting' (Delphian τίθητι *DGE* 332.5–6, Boiot. ἀντίθειτι (ει = ē) *DGE* 509.6; cf. Skt *dádʰāti*) > Att.-Ion. τίθησι.

It also affected 3pl. *-ντι and *-ą̄τι:

PGk *ἄγοντι 'they lead' (Koan ἄγοντι *DGE* 108.23; cf. Skt *ájanti* 'they drive') > *ἄγονσι > Att.-Ion. ἄγōσι;
PGk *hέχοντι 'they have' (Heraklean ἔχοντι *DGE* 62.99) > Myc. *e-ko-si* *hέχονσι > Att.-Ion. ἔχōσι;
PGk pf. 3pl. *-ą̄τι (e.g. in Phokian ἱερῑτεύκατι 'they have held a priesthood' *DGE* 353.40–1) > Ark. -ασι (e.g. in ἐσλελοίπασι 'they have missed' *DGE* 657.22).

Though it is more difficult to find entire forms that are exactly cognate, the active primary 3pl. ending is of course frequently attested; cf. on the one hand, Dor. ἵσταντι 'they stand (it)' Pindar *Dithyramb* 2.8, Boiot. ἀντίθεντι 'they dedicate' (i.e. manumit) *DGE* 517.3, Corinthian δίδοντι 'they (customarily) give' *DGE* 128.13, Megarian νῑκõντι 'they (habitually) conquer' *DGE* 166.1, Theran θῡσέοντι 'they shall sacrifice' *DGE* 220.2, etc., and on the other hand Ark. εἰκ ἂν κελεύωνσι 'if they so order' *DGE* 656.15, καθέρπονσι 'they are returning' *DGE* 657.54, Cyprian *e-ke-so-si* *ἕξο(ν)σι 'they shall have' Masson 217.31, Myc. *di-do-si* *δίδονσι 'they give', *do-so-si* *δώσονσι 'they shall give', *ki-ti-je-si* *κτιjένσι 'they inhabit' (cf. Skt *kṣiyánti*), etc., as well as every Attic-Ionic active primary 3pl. form.

But note that this change also occurred in Lesbian: we find 3sg. τίθησιν Alkaios 58.23, 3pl. πίμπλεισιν Alkaios 72.3, ἐπιρρόμβεισι Sappho 31.11–12, φαῖσι Alkaios 343, pf. 3pl. τεθᾱ́λαισι Sappho 96.23–3, πεπᾱ́γαισιν Alkaios 338.2. Nor are these literary Ionicisms or Homericisms, or errors of transmission; in the inscriptions we find 3sg. φᾶσι *DGE* 618.3, 3pl. προτίθεισι *DGE* 622.13, subj. γράφωισι *DGE* 619.3, fut. ἐμμενέοισι *DGE* 620.29, etc., forms with τ being completely unknown. In other words, by this criterion Lesbian is a South Greek dialect.

There seem to be no Pamphylian examples of 3sg. *-τι, but at least the subjunctive 3pl. form ἐξάγōδι < *-ωντι (Brixhe 3.16) shows that that dialect did not participate in the South Greek change.

Word-final -τι has become -σι in two other South Greek forms:

PGk *ϝῑ́κᾳτι 'twenty' (ϝῑ́κατι in e.g. Lakonian, *DGE* 13.B.6, Heraklean, *DGE* 62.37, and Boiotian, *DGE* 524.1; Thessalian ῐ̈κατι *DGE* 617[g]; cf. also Pamphylian φῑ́κατι Brixhe 17.5, 18.5); but >→ εἴκοσι in Attic-Ionic, Arkadian (*DGE* 654.1), and Lesbian (*DGE* 620.21);

PGk *πέρυτι 'last year' (cf. Skt *parút*) > Att. πέρυσι; cf. Att. adj. περυσινός = Myc. *pe-ru-si-nu-wo*.

Once again Lesbian agrees with South Greek. 'Twenty' is especially striking because of the irregularities in the innovative form. The ο is probably due to lexical analogy with the higher decads in -κοντα (so e.g. Thompson 2008: 759), and that might be a repeatable change, given how often numerals influence each other in IE languages, but the replacement of *ϝῑ́- by εἴ- remains without a convincing explanation (cf. Thompson 2008: 759–60) and could only have happened once.

Other word-final -τι remain unaffected: ἔτι 'still, yet' (cf. Lat. *et* 'and'), ἀντί 'opposite, instead of' (cf. Lat. *ante* 'before'), and ἄρτι 'right now' (cf. Arm. *ard*) exhibit no forms with σ in any dialect.

Some word-internal sequences -τι- have also become -σι- in the South Greek dialects; the best attested is

*-κᾴτιοι '-hundred' > West Greek -κάτιοι, e.g. in Heraklean fem. διᾱκάτιαι '200' *DGE* 62.18–19, ϝεξακάτιαι '600' l. 19, etc., Delphian dat. τετρακατίαις '400' *DGE* 324.2–3, Boiot. acc. ὀκτακατίᾱς '800' *DGE* 523.17, Thess. masc. ἑξεικάττιοι '600' *SEG* 2.264.4;
but > Ark. -κάσιοι, e.g. in masc. acc. τριᾱκάσιος '300' *DGE* 654.20–1 and >→ -κόσιοι, e.g. in fem. acc. Lesb. τριᾱκοσίαις '300' *DGE* 622.36, Att.-Ion τριᾱκοσίᾱς, etc., with ο as in εἴκοσι.

In this case too Lesbian aligns with South Greek, specifically with Attic-Ionic. Other scattered examples of the same phenomenon include:

Thess. κατίγνειτος 'brother' *DGE* 617[g] = Hom. κασίγνητος, Lesb. gen. pl. κασιγνήτων *DGE* 632.D.19, Cyprian acc. pl. *ka-si-ke-ne-to-se* Masson 217.3;
Lakonian πλούτιος 'rich' (*Etymologicon Magnum*) = Att.-Ion. πλούσιος, deriv. of πλοῦτος 'wealth';
Delphian fem. ἐνιαυτίᾱ 'yearly' *DGE* 325.44, Koan neut. pl. ἐνιαύτια *DGE* 251.37 = Att.-Ion. ἐνιαύσιος, deriv. of ἐνιαυτός 'year';
Boiot. πλᾱτίος 'adjoining' (Holleaux 1897: 26–49), adv. literary Doric πλᾱτίον 'near' Theokritos 5.28 = Lesbian πλᾱ́σιον Sappho 17.1, 31.3, Hom. πλησίος, Att.-Ion. adv. πλησίον;
West Argolic ῥῡ́τιον 'penalty' *DGE* 83.B.21, East Argolic ἐρρῡτιασμένος 'plundered' *DGE* 104 *passim* = Ion. ῥῡ́σιον 'plunder, pledge, penalty' (Homer and Attic poets), ῥῡσιάζε̄ν 'to seize as a pledge' (Euripides);
Rhodian, Thess. ἐνᾱράτιον *DGE* 614.10 (and see the notes to *DGE* 180) = Att.-Ion. ἐνηρόσιον 'rent for plow-land'.

Those are the secure examples that I am aware of, aside from names and their derivatives, e.g. West Gk Ἀρταμίτιος = Att.-Ion. Ἀρτεμίσιος (see the discussion of Buck 1955: 57–8) and the Mycenaean names collected at Thompson (2008: 754–5). Several South Greek forms show that the non-final sequence -θι- also became -σι-, at least under some circumstances:

Myc. du. *e-pi-ko-ru-si-jo* *ἐπικορυσίω, pl. *o-pi-ko-ru-si-ja* *ὀπικορύσια 'for attachment to helmets', cf. Hom. κόρυς, κόρυθ- 'helmet';
Att. Προβαλῑ́σιος 'of Προβάλινθος' (a deme in the plain of Marathon, see e.g. Talbert et al. 2000: map 59);
Myc. nom. pl. *ko-ri-si-jo* *Κορίνσιjοι 'of Corinth';
Myc. *za-ku-si-jo* *Ζακύνσιος 'of Zakynthos'.

In later Greek the last two have of course been replaced by Κορίνθιος, Ζακύνθιος, re-derived from Κόρινθος, Ζάκυνθος—and that illustrates neatly the difficulty of determining the original scope of this sound change. Especially puzzling is the fact that nouns derived with the PIE suffix *-ti- usually appear with -σι- in all dialects except when -σ- precedes (thus βάσις, στάσις, γένεσις, etc.; but πίστις, etc.), so far as we can tell, with a few lexical exceptions (such as poetic φάτις, cited above, and μῆτις, cited in 4.3.3), and derivatives in -σίᾱ are likewise not restricted to South Greek; Méndez Dosuna (1985: 118–22) shows that they are so pervasive that dialect borrowing is not a realistic hypothesis. Some version of the hypothesis suggested by Thompson (2008: 757), that assibilation was a sound change arrested at the variable stage as it worked its way through the dialect continuum, must be correct. However, when there is a dialect difference, Lesbian groups with South Greek, so far as our evidence goes.

But Lesbian does not participate in the other clear phonological innovation of the South Greek group. We saw (in 3.6.3) that when there was no morpheme boundary between *t or *t^h and *y the consonant cluster developed aberrantly in Attic-Ionic and Arkadian (and presumably Cypriote and Mycenaean). Examples are few but consistent:

PIE *méd^{h}yos 'middle' (Skt *mád^{h}yas*, Lat. *medius*) > *μέθjος > Att.-Ion., Ark. μέσος but Lesb., Heraklean, Argolic μέσσος, Boiot., Cret. μέττος; cf. Myc. *me-sa-to* 'of middling quality';

PIE *k^{w}óti 'how many?' (Skt *káti*, Lat. *quot*), *tóti 'that many' (Lat. *tot*), *Hyóti 'as many as', thematized as *κ^{w}ότjος, *τότjος, *hότjος > Att.-Ion. πόσος, τόσος, ὅσος, Ark. ὅσος, Myc. *to-so*, but Lesb. ὄσσος, Delphian, etc. ὅσσος, Cret. ὅττος;

PIE *próti 'toward, against' (Skt *práti*), deriv. *prótyō 'forward' > Ion. πρόσω (Att. *πόρσω > πόρρω), to which ὀπίσω 'backward' was formed, but Dor. ὀπίσσω Bakkhylides 13.53, Pindar *Nemean* IX.32, Lesb. ὐπίσσω Sappho 19.10.

In Homer these words vary between -σ- and -σσ-, whereas words containing *t(^{h})+y (with a morpheme boundary) do not. As I noted in 3.6.3, it is difficult to figure out what happened in detail. But the fact that Lesbian consistently exhibits σσ in these words shows that, by this criterion, Lesbian is *not* part of the South Greek group. The same pattern of outcomes holds for dental-plus-σ sequences (see 3.7 *ad fin.*).

Finally, a few other monosyllables exhibit the same development as Ark., Cyprian κάς < *κάτj before vowel-initial words:

*πότj, *πρότj > Ark., Cyprian πός, Att.-Ion.,[5] Lesb. πρός (but Thess., Boiot. ποτί, West Greek mostly ποτί ~ ποί, occasionally προτί and its further developments);

aor. iptv. 2sg. *θέθj 'put!', *δόθj 'give' > Att.-Ion. θές, δός; from other dialects I can find only σύνες Pindar *Hyporchemata* 105.1, which can be a Homeric form.

In this case Lesbian does group with South Greek, so far as our meager evidence permits us to judge.

[5] However, the fact that in Homer πρό typically 'makes position' when immediately following a short vowel, while πρός typically does not, strongly suggests that in an earlier stage of the tradition the latter was πός, part of the 'Achaian' stratum of the epic dialect. See Wathelet (1966: 151–4) for discussion.

5.3.2 Morphological evidence for South Greek

The most important morphological piece of evidence for South Greek, but also the most difficult to judge, is the distribution of active infinitive endings. The facts are as follows.

In Attic-Ionic, Arkadian, Cyprian, and Mycenaean the thematic active infinitive originally ended in *-ε-hεν, while the athematic active infinitive ended in -έναι, which in at least some cases might reflect earlier *-hέναι. Examples are numerous:

Myc. *e-ke-e* *hέχεhεν 'to have', *wo-ze-e* *ϝόρζεhεν 'to make', etc. (Bartoněk 2002: 328); no unproblematic athematic examples;
Cyprian *e-ke-ne* *ἔχεν or *ἔχε̄ν, Masson 217.10, etc.; *to-we-na-i* *δοϝέναι 'to give' ll. 5, 15, *to-e-na-i* *δοέναι Masson 306.6–7;
Ark. ἰμφαῖνεν 'to bring to light, to inform' *DGE* 656.24, φέρην 'to bear' *DGE* 665.A.17, aor. λαχῆν 'to get by lot' l. 3; ἦναι (< *ἐhέναι) 'to be' *DGE* 656.10, *DGE* 657.9, etc.; aor. ἀνθῆναι 'to set (it) up' *DGE* 658.9, δῶναι'to give' *DGE* 666.2;
Att.-Ion. ἄγε̄ν, φέρε̄ν, etc., aor. λαχε̄͂ν, etc.; ε̄͂ναι, ἰέναι, aor. θε̄͂ναι, δο̄͂ναι, pf. εἰδέναι, etc.[6]

The remodeling of *-εhεν to -εν in part of the Arkadian *Sprachraum* is an innovation, occurring also in West Greek dialects (see below), though it is unclear how it happened. We are on surer ground with the innovative Attic-Ionic ending -ναι, e.g. in τιθέναι, διδόναι, etc. (pf. τεθνάναι already in Mimnermos 2.10): the ending of aorists such as στῆναι 'to stand (something) up', contracted from *στηέναι, was resegmented and the resulting -ναι affixed to pres. ἱστάναι, etc.

The West Greek situation is equally clear: thematic active infinitives originally ended in *-ε-hεν, while their athematic counterparts ended in -μεν, though the evidence has been complicated by later innovations. Most of the more northwesterly dialects preserve the original situation:

Lakonian ἔχην *DGE* 48.29 vs. ἦμεν *DGE* 44.16, ἀνιστάμεν *DGE* 54.6;
Elean πάσχην *DGE* 424.13 vs. ἦμεν *DGE* 425.21, δόμεν ibid.l. 28;
Phokian ἀπέχειν *DGE* 355.II.27 vs. εἶμεν, I.48, παρίμεν *DGE* 350.6;
Lokrian φάρειν 'φέρε̄ν, to be subject to (a tax)' *DGE* 362.5 vs. ἐξεῖμεν l. 3, μὴ 'ποστᾶμεν 'not to secede' ibid.l. 11;
Megarian παρέχειν *DGE* 154.8 vs. εἶμεν *DGE* 153.14, τῑμᾱθῆμεν *DGE* 154.9;
Corinthian ἔχειν *DGE* 138.18, λαβεῖν *DGE* 147.3 vs. εἶμεν *DGE* 131.12, δόμεν *DGE* 128.12, ἀναγραφῆμεν *DGE* 147.7.

[6] On later Ionic innovations, especially in West Ionic, see Buck (1955: 123, 125).

However, some dialects have shortened thematic -ην or -ε̄ν to -εν, possibly on the model of athematic -μεν:

Delphian ἄγεν *DGE* 325.21, cf. εἶμεν l. 22, διδόμεν *DGE* 322.2;
Heraklean ἔχεν *DGE* 62.116, cf. ἦμεν *loc. cit.*, πεφυτευκῆμεν l. 142;
East Argolic φέρεν *IG* IV.823.60, cf. ἀποδόμεν *DGE* 104.11–12;
Astypalaian ἐσέρπεν *DGE* 242.1, cf. ἀναθέμεν *DGE* 244.21.

The shortening is certainly an innovation, because in a few dialects it even affects *-ε-εhεν:

West Argolic fut. ἐμμενέν *DGE* 85.7, cf. ἦμεν *DGE* 85.11, ἐγδόμεν *DGE* 90.18;
Theran λαμβάνεν *DGE* 227.B.116, τελέν l. 38, cf. θέμεν ll. 14, 20;
Kyrenaian θῦεν Buck 115.5, τεκέν l. 100, σῑγέν l. 136, cf. ἐξίμεν l. 135.

If remodeling on the basis of -μεν is the correct explanation for this peculiarity, its presence in the Arkadian subdialects of Tegea and Mantineia (see above) must be due to the influence of neighboring West Argolic. In Rhodian the opposite leveling has occurred, yielding athematic -μειν:

Rhodian παρέχειν *DGE* 281.13; athematic ἐξήμειν l. 4, ἐκθέμειν l. 3.

The same leveling occurred in some subdialects of Cretan, yielding -μην, yet shortened thematic -εν is also attested in Cretan. Without an investigation of all the material in greater depth it will not be possible to figure out exactly what happened.

As has long been recognized, Thessalian was not a uniform dialect. In Thessaliotis, the western plain, we apparently find the same system as in West Greek (though see the footnotes to the following forms):

thematic ἐξξανακάδ(δ)ε̄ν *DGE* 557.8–9,[7] φεύγε̄ν *DGE* 561.2,[8] ἔχειν *DGE* 567.4; I can find no athematic examples, but Phthiotis (to the south) yields εἶμεν *DGE* 556.5—which unfortunately could be a Doric koine form.

But in Pelasgiotis, the eastern plain, -μεν has spread to the thematic stems, yielding -έ-μεν:[9]

thematic κρεννέμεν *DGE* 590.14, πρᾱσσέμεν l. 17, etc.; athematic ἔμμεν l. 20, ἐσδόμεν ll. 20–1, etc.

[7] But Colvin (2007: 93) notes that there are clear non-Thessalian forms in this inscription; in particular, χρέ̄μασιν in place of expected χρε̄μάτεσσι can only be Attic or Ionic.
[8] But (as Matthew Scarborough reminds me) this is a verse epigram which might contain epic forms.
[9] The appearance of this ending in Homer, like the presence of προτί and some other details, suggests that the 'Aiolic' element in Homer might be specifically Thessalian.

Boiotian exhibits the same innovation, e.g.:

> thematic ὑπαρχέμεν *DGE* 450.13; athematic εἶμεν *DGE* 523.11, ἀποδόμεν l. 12, etc.

Since all other dialects have thematic active infinitives reflecting *-ε-hεν, directly or indirectly, this is obviously an innovation, probably a historically shared innovation (one way or another).

The infinitives of Lesbian present a unique pattern. The thematic infinitive ends in -ην < *-ε-hεν, e.g. in κόπτην 'to coin (money)' *DGE* 619.19, πάθην 'to suffer (punishment)' l. 17. Athematic -μεναι is found on monosyllabic stems:

> ἔμμεναι 'to be' (frequent), κατθέμεναι *DGE* 619.17, ἀπυδόμεναι 621.45, ἐπιδόμεναι 623.42, δόμεναι 631.12, etc.

Otherwise the thematic ending has spread to athematic stems too, typically appearing as vowel length plus -ν:

> ἐπιμελήθην *DGE* 623.46, δίδων 630.15, προνοήθην 631.7, ὄμνῡν 632.C. 10–11, etc.

Occasionally one finds the same ending on monosyllabic stems, e.g. in πρόστᾱν *DGE* 623.43. It seems clear that -μεναι was originally the active infinitive ending for all athematic stems, considering its distribution in the Homeric poems (e.g. ἔδμεναι *Il.* 4.345 etc., ζευγνύμεναι 3.260, δαήμεναι 6.150 etc.; see Bechtel 1921: 98, Chantraine 1973: 485–8).

There is one further surprise. Though Pamphylian did not participate in the South Greek change of *-τι to -σι, as we have seen (5.3.1), it does have South Greek infinitives, to judge from athematic ἀφιιέναι Brixhe 3.6 (so Brixhe 1976: 123–4).

From this welter of facts one clear conclusion emerges: PGk thematic infinitives ended in *-ε-hεν; on that all the dialects agree except Pelasgiote Thessalian and Boiotian, and an obvious analogical source for their -έμεν is their athematic -μεν. We need to account for the origin of the athematic endings -μεν, -μεναι, and -έναι. If we are willing to posit two athematic active infinitive endings for Proto-Greek, distributed according to some principle no longer recoverable, several solutions are possible; in particular, Lesbian (and Homeric) -μεναι could be a kind of compromise form between the others, no doubt motivated by dialect contact. But that is not the most parsimonious solution available; consequently it is neither the most probable nor the best solution available, absent further evidence. The best solution, other things being equal, is to account for -μ- and -αι by positing a single preform, which can only be -μεναι.

If that is true, -μεναι is a further Lesbian archaism. Thessalian, Boiotian, and West Greek have remodeled *-μεναι to -μεν under the influence of the thematic ending; that is especially plausible because West Ionic independently remodeled -ναι to -ν much later (Buck 1955: 123). South Greek, on the other hand, remodeled *-μεναι to -(*h)έναι, also under the influence of the thematic ending. A further reason to believe this scenario is that -μεναι and *-hεν are the only two Greek infinitive endings that might have approximate cognates in Vedic. Lesbian/Homeric -μεναι appears to be cognate with Vedic *-máne* (Bechtel 1921: 98, cf. Macdonell 1910: 410), and in fact Hom. ἴδμεναι 'to know' is more or less identical with Vedic *vidmáne*; the endings might not be exactly cognate—the Vedic forms are synchronically datives, while the Greek ending looks like a fossilized allative—but the stem formation is. Greek *-hεν, on the other hand, is patently cognate with Vedic locative infinitive *-ṣáṇi* (Macdonell 1910: 412), the only difference being the presence or absence of the *hic-et-nunc* particle *-i.

A further consequence of this argument is that, to judge from infinitive endings, Pamphylian is a marginal member of South Greek—just as Lesbian is on phonological grounds (see 5.3.1).

Other morphological evidence for South Greek is indecisive. The active 1pl. ending is -μεν in Attic-Ionic and Lesbian (to judge from the Lesbian poets) and -μες in West Greek, but examples from other dialects are rare. One Arkadian form ἐδικάσαμε[(*IG* V-2.262.18, *DGE* 661.18) is too badly damaged for certainty (see Buck 1925: 137, Ringe 2016: 280 with references), though Dubois (1986c: 104) reads ἐδικάσαμεν. The other is unambiguously ὠμόσαμες (Te Riele 1967: 212 l. 16). Dubois (1986b: 177–8) suggests that both could be native, since Proto-Greek must have had both endings and different subdialects of Arkadian might have generalized differently; but it is also true that one or the other, or even both, could reflect Attic koine and/or Doric koine influence. All Boiotian and Thessalian forms are late (Scarborough 2016: 104–5) and can be suspected of Attic koine influence to varying degrees, though it is at least worth noting that all end in -μεν, not in -μες.

South Greek does have a distinctive form of the conjunction 'when', namely Att.-Ion., Ark. ὅτε, Cyprian, Myc. *o-te*, vs. Lesbian ὄτα, Boiot., West Greek ὅκα; but since in Attic-Ionic we also find ἔπειτα 'thereupon', with the same suffix as in Lesbian, it seems clear that the dialects have made different choices from among inherited alternatives, and it is difficult to judge the cladistic relevance of that fact. The pattern of variants of the conjunction 'if' is even harder to judge. Outside of South Greek the form is universally αἰ (> Boiot. ἠ by regular sound change), but South Greek exhibits two forms. In Arkadian we find only εἰ, in Cyprian only ἠ; Attic-Ionic exhibits εἰ when the conjunction is not contracted with the conditional particle, but when that contraction does occur we find *ἠάν > Att. ἐάν, Ion. ἤν. In this case too we cannot say for sure which dialects have innovated. In the case of the irrealis particle all the dialects have innovated by losing inherited alternatives. The particle seems originally to have been *kém ~ *k̥m (Vedic Skt *kám*), with sound-change outcomes κεν ~ κα ~ *καν in Proto-Greek (Forbes 1958c); the last was 'recut' to give ἄν in Attic-Ionic and Arkadian, though Ark. εἰκ ἄν shows that the particle originally had an initial κ-. In West Greek and Boiotian we find κα; in the other dialects, including Cyprian, κε(ν).[10]

There is also the distribution of forms of the definite article. In NIE the nom. sg. masc. and fem. were *só and *sáh_2 respectively, while all other forms began with *t-; in particular, the nom. pl. masc. and fem. were *tóy and *tá$h_2$as respectively (cf. Skt *sá, sā́, té, tā́s*, and Goth. *sa, so, þai, þos*). West Greek (except Cretan), Boiotian, and Thessaliote Thessalian preserve the original distribution of initial consonants, so that the forms are typically ὁ, ἁ, τοί (> Boiot. τῡ́), ταί (> Boiot. τή). But in the whole South Greek group, as well as in Lesbian, Pelasgiote Thessalian, and Cretan Doric, the initial of the masc. and fem. nom. sg. forms has spread to the corresponding plurals, giving οἱ and αἱ (or, in psilotic dialects, οἰ and αἰ). This could be a South Greek characteristic which has spread more widely than usual beyond that dialect group, i.e. not only to Lesbian but also to eastern Thessalian; but the fact that the same peculiarity occurs in Cretan argues caution. There it could be taken as a South Greek substrate phenomenon, and the fact that we also find Ἄρτεμις instead of the usual West Greek Ἄρταμις in Cretan might lend credence to that interpretation (cf. Buck 1955: 8, 169). But independent parallel innovation is difficult to exclude, and that fact casts doubt on the usefulness of this innovation as a marker of South Greek.

Finally, there is the vexed problem of ἱερός 'holy, sacred'. The familiar form of the word is confined to Mycenaean, Arkadian, Cyprian, and Attic-Ionic, i.e. to South Greek in the strictest sense; we find ἱαρός in West Greek, Boiotian, and Pamphylian, while the Lesbian form is ἶρος (Buck 1955: 24). The distribution of forms suggests fairly strongly that South Greek and Lesbian have each innovated, though of course we cannot be sure, especially given the uncertain etymology of the word (see Frisk s.v.).[11]

5.3.3 An assessment of South Greek

From the above discussion it seems clear that South Greek, like Aiolic, cannot be shown to be a strict clade; on the contrary, the fact that Lesbian shares only one of the South Greek innovations while Pamphylian shares only another

[10] For an alternative (and very different) reconstruction of the prehistory of this particle, see Colvin (2016).

[11] The proposed connection with Skt *iṣirás* 'rushing, active' rests on an interpretation of Indo-European polytheism that might best be described as Wagnerian. The pattern of derivatives in -εύς in Mycenaean, which of course include *i-je-re-u* = ἱερεύς, suggests that the adjective was a loanword in Greek (see Meissner 2016: 27–8).

(so far as we can tell) strongly suggests that the innovations spread across dialect boundaries. However, again like the Aiolic dialects, the South Greek dialects clearly share linguistic history in some sense.

5.4 Other widely shared early innovations

Ancient Greek dialects share numerous innovations in distributions that do not coincide with the limits of dialect groups outlined above. Many of them were comparatively recent (from the perspective of the 8th century BC), but others appear to have occurred, or could have occurred, several centuries earlier. Though it is difficult to date any particular innovation, it is convenient to sort them roughly into an earlier and a later group. The (potentially) earlier group will be dealt with here.

5.4.1 Early phonological innovations

5.4.1 (i) Labiovelars

The most obvious of the early 'messy' innovations is the treatment of labiovelars. In Mycenaean they were still written with a separate set of syllabic signs,[12] but all the 1st-millennium dialects had eliminated them, in two different patterns, broadly speaking.

The outcome of labiovelars before back vowels and before consonants was the same in all the 1st-millennium dialects: they became bilabials. That is a natural change that can have occurred in a single step. The numerous examples include:

PIE *k^{w}óteros 'which (of two)?' (Skt *katarás*, Goth. *ƕaþar*) > πότερος;
PIE *k^{w}óti 'how many?' (Skt *káti*, Lat. *quot*) → *κ^{w}ότjος > Att.-Ion. πόσος;
PIE *k^{w}át-ye/o- pres. 'shake' (Lat. *quatere*) > πάσσε̄ν, Att. πάττε̄ν 'to sprinkle';
PIE *k^{w}rih$_2$tó '(s)he bought' (cf. Toch. B *käryāmtte* 'we bought') > Myc. *qi-ri-ja-to*, ἐπρίατο;
PIE *Hyḗk^{w}r̥ ~ *Hyék^{w}n- 'liver' (Skt *yákr̥t*, Lat. *iecur* with full grade generalized) >→ἦπαρ ~ ἥπατ-;
PIE acc. *wók^{w}m̥ 'voice' (Toch. B *wek*) > Hom. acc. ὄπα;
PIE *h$_3$ok^{w}- 'eye' (Toch. B *ek*, OCS *oko*) > ὀπ- in ὀφθαλμός, dat. pl. Hom. ὄμμασι, Lesb. ὀππάτεσσι;
PIE coll. *h$_3$ṓk^{w} 'eyes, face' >→ Hom. acc. ὦπα 'face';

[12] Excepting, of course, those that had already been unrounded next to *u or before *y (see 3.4.3). Labiovelars were often reintroduced next to *u by leveling; see Lejeune (1972: 43–53) for numerous examples and for comprehensive discussion of the development of labiovelars.

PIE aor. *pḗk^{w}s- ~ *pék^{w}-s- 'cook' (Lat. pf. *coxisse*) >→ πέψαι;[13]
PGk *ἄνθρωκ^{w}ος 'human being' (Myc. *a-to-ro-qo*) > ἄνθρωπος;
PIE *g^{w}ṓws, *g^{w}ów- 'bovine' (Skt *gáus, gáv-*) > Myc. *qo-o, qo-u-*, βοῦς, βου- ~ βο(ϝ)-;
PIE pres. *g^{w}m̥-yé/ó- and *g^{w}m̥-sḱé/ó- 'step (repeatedly), walk' (Lat. *venīre* 'to come', Skt *gácc^{h}ati* '(s)he goes') > βαίνε̄ν 'to go', Hom. also βάσκε̄ν;
PIE *é g^{w}ah$_{2}$t 'it is said that (s)he stepped' (Skt *ágāt* '(s)he has gone') > ἔβᾱ '(s)he went'> Att.-Ion. ἔβη;
PIE *g^{w}h$_{2}$b^{h}-ié/ó- 'be dipping in water' (ON *kvefja*) > βάπτε̄ν;
PIE *g^{w}ráh$_{2}$u- ~ *g^{w}r̥h$_{2}$áw- 'heavy' (Lat. *gravis*) → *g^{w}r̥h$_{2}$ús (Skt *gurús*, Goth. *kaúrus*) > βαρύς;
PIE *g^{w}l̥h$_{1}$tós 'thrown, throwable' (cf. Skt *udgūrṇas* 'raised, brandished' with alternative suffix *-nó-) > *βλητός in Hom. ἀπόβλητος 'disposable, worthless';
PIE *g^{w}r̥h$_{3}$tós 'swallowed, swallowable' (cf. Skt *gīrṇás* with alternative suffix *-nó-) > βρωτός 'edible';
PIE *Hyéh$_{1}$g^{w}ah$_{2}$ 'strength' vel sim. (Lith. *jėga*) > ἥβᾱ 'youth' > Att.-Ion. ἥβη;
PIE *néyg^{w}- ~ *nig^{w}- 'wash' (Skt pres. 3sg. mid. *nenikté*), pre-Gk aor. *νιγ^{w}-σ- > νίψαι, cf. also Hom acc. χερνίβα 'basin' ('hand-washer') and probably Myc. pl. *ke-ni-qa*;
(post-)PIE *ag^{w}nós 'lamb' (Lat. *agnus*) > ἀμνός;
post-PIE *g^{w}r̥dú- 'slow' (Lith. *gurdùs*) > βραδύς;
PGk *γ^{w}ασιλήύς (title of a subordinate ruler, Myc. *qa-si-re-u*) > βασιλεύς;
PGk *φοργ^{w}ᾱ́ 'pasturage' (Myc. *po-qa*) > φορβᾱ́ > Att.-Ion. φορβή;
PIE *snig^{wh}- 'snow' (Lat. *nix, niv-*) > Hom. acc. νίφα;
PIE *sóng^{wh}os 'chanting' vel sim. (Goth. *saggws* 'song'), coll. *song^{wh}áh$_{2}$ > *hονχ^{w}ᾱ́ > ὀμφή 'oracular voice';
PIE *neg^{wh}rós 'kidney' (cf. Lat. dial. pl. *nefrōnēs*, OHG *nioro*) > νεφρός;
PIE *h$_{1}$ln̥g^{wh}rós 'light(weight)' (OHG *lungar* 'vigorous') > ἐλαφρός 'light';
PIE *d^{h}eg^{wh}- 'burn' (Skt 3sg. *dáhati*) > τεφ- in τέφρᾱ 'ashes';
PIE *n̥d^{h}g^{wh}itom (ḱléwos) 'imperishable (fame)' (Skt *ákṣitaṃ* (*śrávas*)) > Hom. (κλέος) ἄφθιτον.

(Examples that gave rise to alternations between labials and dentals will be adduced below, as will examples that might have been expected to give rise to alternations but did not.) It can be seen from the above examples that this sound change postdated not only the Mycenaean period but also many of the early sound changes discussed in Chapter 3; on the other hand, it predated the Attic-Ionic fronting of

[13] Cf. Myc. *a-to-po-qo* *ἀρτοπόκwος 'baker'. The κ of Att. ἀρτοκόπος is surprising; if it is not simply the result of dissimilation (from *-πόπος), the only available explanation seems to be that the second part of the compound was remodeled on pres. *πεκ-jε/o- (see 3.4.3) and that metathesis then occurred. Dissimilation seems more likely.

*ᾱ (cf. ἔβη, ἥβη, φορβή, ὀμφή). The only clear counterexamples are the East Ionic derivatives of interrogative *kʷo- that exhibit κ instead of the expected π: κόθεν, κοῖος, κόσος, κότε, κότερος, κοῦ, κῶς, and the corresponding indefinite forms, as well as κω, all well attested in Herodotos and other authors and at least once in an inscription (see Bechtel 1924: 87–9 for discussion in depth). So far as I can see, the only possible explanation is that the labiovelar was delabialized in οὔκω and οὔκως and κ then spread by lexical analogy, first to the corresponding positives, then to the other derivatives of this stem.

The dialects exhibit divergent outcomes before mid front vowels: most exhibit dentals, but labials appear in Lesbian, Thessalian, Boiotian, and Cyprian (!). The change from labiovelars to dentals could not have occurred in a single step; a plausible sequence of changes for the voiceless stop might be *kʷ > *[cᶣ] (palatalization) > *[tɕ] (affrication and unrounding) > [ts] > τ. In those dialects with dental outcomes there are often related words with labial outcomes before other sounds. The following are typical:

PIE masc. *kʷetwóres 'four' (Skt *catvā́ras*, Toch. B *śtwer*) >→ Lesb. πέσσυρες, Boiot. πέτταρες, Thess. combining form πετρο- vs. Att. τέτταρες, Ion., Ark. τέσσερες, West Greek τέτορες, combining form τετρα- (cf. Myc. *qe-to-ro-*);

PIE *pénkʷe 'five' (Skt *páñca*) > Lesb. πέμπε in πεμπεβόηα 'made of five oxhides' Sappho 110.2 vs. Att.-Ion., Ark., WGk πέντε 'five' —but πέμπτος 'fifth';

PIE *kʷey- 'pay' in Thess. ἀππεισάτου 'let him pay' *DGE* 614.28, Boiot. ποταποπῑσάτω 'let her pay in addition' *DGE* 523.163, Cypr. *pe-i-se-i* 'he shall pay' Masson 217.12, 25[14] vs. Ark. ἀπυτεισάτω *DGE* 656.35, Att.-Ion., WGk τεῖσαι —but PIE *kʷoynáh₂ 'recompense' (Av. *kaēnā* 'punishment', OCS *cěna* 'price') > Att.-Ion. ποινή 'weregild, penalty';

PIE *kʷel- 'turn' in Lesb. πέλεται 'is' Sappho 50.1 (also Homer) vs. Hom. περιτελλομένου 'revolving' *Od.* 11.295 —but PIE *kʷólos 'axis' (Toch. B *kele* 'navel') > πόλος;

PIE *kʷels- 'make a groove' (Hitt. *gulszi* '(s)he engraves') in Hom. τέλσον (ἀρούρης) 'boundary (of the field)';

PGk *κʷηλ- 'far' in Lesb. πήλοι Sappho 1.6 vs. Hom. τῆλε;

PIE *gʷelbʰ- 'womb' (Skt *gárbʰas*) > Att.-Ion. δελφῦς and (probably) West Greek, Att.-Ion. Δελφοί vs. Boiot. Βελφοί, Thessaliote Βελφαίō *DGE* 557.10;

PIE *n̥gʷḗn 'gland' (Lat. *inguen* 'groin') > Ion. ἀδήν;

PIE *gʷʰen- 'hit, kill' in Hom. pres. θε̄νέμεναι 'to slay' —but reduplicated aor. πεφνέμεν and pf. 3sg. πέφαται 'he lies slain';

[14] This is the only example of the labial outcome before an e-vowel in Cyprian, but there are no counterexamples, and lexical analogy with (e.g.) ποινά̄ doesn't strike me as likely, considering how different the verb and its derived nominals had become.

PIE pres. *g^{wh}éd^h-ye/o- 'to beg' (OPers. *jadiyāmiy* 'I pray') > θέσσεσθαι (Hesych.) —but derived noun πόθος 'desire';
PIE *g^{wh}éros 'heat' (Skt *háras*, Arm. *ǰer*) > Att.-Ion. θέρος 'summer, harvest'.

To these examples can be added the lexical family of βόλεσθαι 'to want' (see 5.2.2) and a word of obscure origin:

WGk, Ark. ὀδελός 'spit; obol' *DGE* 179.II.14, 654.19, etc., vs. Thess. ὀβελλός *DGE* 614.20, Hom. pl. ὀβελοί —but Att. ὀβολός.

To this usual pattern of development there is one exception: PIE *k^we 'and' > τε in all dialects (possibly except Cyprian, in which the word is unattested, Lejeune 1972: 49). Parker (2013: 220), Scarborough (2016: 71–3), and (for the Thessalian examples) García Ramón (2020: 306, 314–15) note that all the epigraphical examples in Aiolic dialects are late enough that Attic koine influence cannot be excluded, with the exception of an early Boiotian inscription in verse in which τε could be an epicism; and further that the repeated appearance of τε in the poetry of Sappho and Alkaios could likewise be a Homeric borrowing. That seems to me to be the most probable solution.

In simple thematic presents and aorists made to roots ending in a labiovelar, and in neuter s-stems made to such roots, we might expect to find an alternation between labials and dentals in those dialects in which labiovelars became dentals before e-vowels, yet we never do; the labial outcomes have been leveled through every relevant paradigm. The following are typical:

PIE *wék^wos, *wék^wes- 'word, speech' (Skt *vácas*) >→ ἔπος, ἔπε-;
PIE reduplicated aor. *we-wk-e/o- 'say' (Skt *voca-*) → *wewk^we/o- (labiovelar restored from other stems) > PGk *ϝει$κ^w$ε/ο- (dissimilation of *wew- to *wey-) >→ εἰπε̃ν;
PIE pres. *sék^wetor '(s)he accompanies', *sék^wontor 'they accompany' (Skt *sácate, sácante* with remodeled endings; see 2.3.3 (iii)) >→ ἕπεται, ἕπονται (also with remodeled endings, see further 4.2.6 (iv));
PIE aor. subj. *léyk^we/o- 'leave' (see 4.2.1 (iv)) >→ pres. λείπε̄ν;
PIE *$h_1$rég^wos, *$h_1$rég^wes- 'darkness' (Skt *rájas* 'empty space', Goth. *riqis*) > ἔρεβος, ἐρέβε- 'passage to the underworld';
PIE pres. *tyég^we/o- 'retreat' (Skt *tyája-* 'abandon') >→σέβεσθαι 'to be ashamed';
pre-Gk aor. *slag^wé/ó- 'grab' (cf. Hom. pres. λάζεσθαι with ζ < *gy < *g^wy, see 3.4.3) >→ λαβε̃ν;
(post-)PIE pres. *snéyg^{wh}e/o- 'be snowing' (OHG *snīwan*) >→ νείφε̄ν;
PIE *$h_2$alg^{wh}- 'earn' (cf. Skt pres. 3sg. *árhati* '(s)he deserves') in Hom. aor. ἀλφε̃ν.

Before *i and *ī there is yet another pattern of outcomes. In all dialects $*k^w$ was palatalized in that position, and in most it appears as τ:

PIE $*k^w$íd 'what?', $*k^w$id 'something' (Lat. *quid*, *ali-quid*, Skt focus particle *cit*, etc.; cf. Myc. *jo-qi* 'ὅττι, whatever') > τί, τι;
post-PIE $*k^w$i-néw- ~ $*k^w$i-nu- 'pay, repay' (see 4.2.1 (ii)) > *τινευ- ~ *τινυ-, thematized as *τινϝε/ο- > Hom. τῑ́νειν, Att. etc., τίνε̄ν (see 7.2.2);
PGk $*κ^w$ῑμᾱ́ 'respect, honor' (if related to Skt *ní cikāya* '(s)he perceives', see *LIV* s.v. 1. **ku̯ei̯*) > τῑμᾱ́ > Att.-Ion. τῑμή.

However, the aspirated labiovelar appears as φ in the only certain example:

PIE $*h_3$ḗ$g^{wh}$is ~ $*h_3$óg^{wh}i- 'snake' (Arm. *iž*, Skt *áhis*) > ὄφις.

The situation of the voiced labiovelar before front high vowels is less clear. The usual outcome is β:

PIE $*g^w$i(H)- 'bowstring' (Skt *jyā́*, disyllabic at *RV* VI.75.3) > Hom. βιός 'bow';
PIE $*g^w$ih_2áh_2- 'force' (Skt *jyā́*) > βίᾱ > Ion. βίη;
(post-)PIE $*g^w$ih_3óh_1- /$*g^w$ih_3-éh_1-/ 'be/become alive' (cf. $*g^w$i$h_3$wós 'alive' > Skt *jīvás*, Lat. *vīvos*) > Hom. βιῶναι 'to escape alive'.

However, there are also two possible examples of an outcome δ. One is found in the Heraklean tables:

ταῦτα δὲ πάντα πεφυτευμένα παρhεξόντι καὶ ἐνδεδιωκότα, ὅσσα ἐν τᾶι συνθήκᾱι γεγράψαται *they shall present (for inspection) all the aforesaid (fully) planted and* the plants settled in (?), however many shall have been written in the agreement.
DGE 62.120–1

It is highly likely that the perfect participle ἐνδεδιωκότα is part of the paradigm of the Heraklean verb that corresponds to Hom. βιῶναι (see above), and in that case we have an alternative outcome for the voiced labiovelar before ι. The same is at least suggested by a comparison of some Mycenaean forms with forms current in later Greek:

Myc. *qe-qi-no-me-no*, *qe-qi-no-to* (mediopassive perfect participle and 3sg. (?) describing the decoration of furniture; see Aura Jorro 1999 s.vv.), cf. Att.-Ion. δῑ́νη 'whirlpool', etc.?

If the Mycenaean forms mean '(has been) turned (on a lathe)' or the like, this South Greek word family would be another example of $*g^w$ > δ before a high front vowel.

What are we to make of this complex pattern of outcomes? The following solution, following Parker (2013: 222–4), seems to me optimal.

It seems clear that the development of labiovelars to bilabials was the default outcome even where it was not the only outcome; the most economical hypothesis is that that change occurred last, affecting all labiovelars that had not already been changed into something else (Lejeune 1972: 47, 52, Parker 2008: 446, 2013: 223). Since the earlier changes were not the same in all dialects, the change to bilabials must have spread through a dialect continuum, to the extent that it was not an independent change (see below). But even the palatalization of *k^w (eventually resulting in τ) before high front vowels, which affected all dialects, must have spread from dialect to dialect because it is demonstrably post-Mycenaean (Parker 2013: 222). The simplest chronology that can be constructed is:

1) palatalization of *k^w before high front vowels, plausibly the leading edge of the following change;
2) palatalization of all labiovelars before mid front vowels, not spreading to Boiotian, Thessalian, Lesbian, and Cyprian because of their relative isolation; with respect to this change note that
   a) it probably occurred after the substantial Greek settlement of Cyprus upon the collapse of Mycenaean civilization, and
   b) both Lesbian and Boiotian are notable for other archaisms;
3) labiovelars > bilabials, possibly partly independently in some dialects, since such a change is common enough in other languages.

There is documentary evidence that the change of labiovelars to dentals occurred in more than one stage, since intermediate stages are attested in Arkadian and Cyprian. Arkadian spellings suggest an affricate: ὄζις 'ὅστις, whoever' Buck 16.4, ὀиέοι 'ὅτῳ, in the case of anyone who' *DGE* 661.14, εἴ иις 'if anyone' l. 25, etc.; Cyprian writes *si-se* for τις, e.g. at Masson 217.10, but since the syllabary does not distinguish all the consonant phonemes it is difficult to say what that means phonetically. There is no reason to believe that Arkadian and Cyprian did not participate in the palatalization of *k^w before high front vowels at the same time as the other dialects (roughly speaking); the subsequent changes to the palatalized labiovelar simply proceeded more slowly than in the other dialects.

To the change *k^w > τ there is a surprising exception, a velar outcome κ in Thessalian κις 'anyone', e.g. in *DGE* 614.26. As with the Ionic κ's, there is a simple explanation: the velar outcome has been generalized from οὔκις 'no one' (pace Dunnett 1970; see 3.4.3).

5.4.1 (ii) Syllabic liquids

The only other 'scattered' phonological innovation that seems to have been early is the resolution of the syllabic liquids *r̥ and *l̥; because of the distribution of inherited phonemes, nearly all the examples involve *r̥. The comprehensive discussion of van Beek (2022) is essential for serious students of Greek; as usual, I will offer a summary of relevant points, sometimes preferring alternative solutions.

Since the dialect reflexes diverge, it is clear that *r̥ and *l̥ still existed as contrastive sounds in some form or other in Proto-Greek. How long they survived is a vexed question. The discussion of van Beek (2022) is very useful, but one of the hypotheses on which it is based is probably untenable, namely that *r̥ survived longer in the epic dialect than in spoken Ionic and underwent a separate regular development to ρα at a later date in epic Greek (van Beek 2022: 237–88). Since the pronunciation of a native language is acquired in the first few years of life, and since it is impossible to believe that small children learned the epic dialect natively, we must imagine some generations of oral poets in training learning to pronounce consistently a phoneme that was foreign to them. Van Beek's suggested scenario for that process (pp. 259–62) is not convincing. But if we cannot posit a separate chronology for epic Greek, we will not be able to do without the traditional assumption of metathesis in at least a few words (which van Beek wishes to exclude).

I begin with a consideration of word-initial and word-final *r̥. It is true that the former should have existed in full words only as the zero grade of word-initial *Vr-, and the only possible example is Hom. ἄρμενος 'fitted': the root cannot have begun with the second laryngeal, to judge from Hitt. *natta āra* 'it's not right', and if it had begun with the first laryngeal the zero grade would have given ἐρ- by Rix's Law (see 3.2.2). Unfortunately we cannot be sure that ἄρμενος does not exhibit a full-grade root. It is possible that Hom. ἄρ ~ ῥα reflects an enclitic particle *r̥ (cf. Lith. *ir̃* 'and') in which initial *r was permissible in PIE because the clitic was not a phonological word; either the double form of this particle is a *prima facie* case of metathesis or, especially considering its enclitic nature, the double outcome of *r̥ might reflect regular sound changes dependent on the prosody of the preceding word, along the lines of Hoenigswald (1953: 289–90). However that may be, nearly all examples of ἀρ- do result from Rix's Law (van Beek 2022: 16–17) and are of no further relevance here.

Word-final *r̥ nearly always appears as -αρ, and for that reason and others van Beek suggests, following much earlier work, that that outcome is the result of a regular sound change at least in South Greek (van Beek 2022: 18, 416). However, nearly all examples of *-r̥ > -αρ are neuter r/n-stem nouns with oblique stems in -ατ- < *-n̥t- (or, in a few cases, leveled -αρ- < word-internal *-r̥-), which could be the source of their α, as van Beek observes (pp. 417–18). Typical examples include:

PIE *Hyḗk^{w}r̥ 'liver' (see 3.2.1) > ἧπαρ;
PIE *pérwr̥ 'end of a rope' (Skt *párus*, *RV* X.100.5, and see 4.3.3) > *πέρϝαρ > Hom. πε͂ραρ 'cord';
PIE *d^{h}énr̥ 'palm (of the hand)' (OHG *tenar*) > θέναρ;
PIE *wésr̥ 'spring(time)' (cf. Av. loc. *vaŋri*) > Hom. ἔαρ;
PIE *ówd^{h}r̥, 'udder' (cf. Skt *ū́d^{h}ar*, Lat. *ūber*) > οὖθαρ;
post-PIE *ā́mr̥ 'day' (Arm. *awr* < coll. *ā́mōr) > ἄμαρ (cf. pl. ἅματα πάντα *DGE* 661.22 (Arkadian), Buck 59.A.12 (Lokrian)) > Hom. ἦμαρ.

That makes the pattern of attestation of Hom. ἦτορ 'heart' more than a little interesting. The word is clearly a neuter consonant stem, but it is attested only in the nom. and acc. sg.—in other words, the potential source of α by leveling has been lost in the epic tradition, and -ορ could be a regular sound-change outcome of final *-r̥. Homeric and Cyprian αὐτάρ 'but' is not a clinching counterexample, since it is a compound whose second component can reflect development of initial *r̥ in an enclitic (see above). It seems we must conclude that while the sound-change outcome of word-final *-r̥ is -Vρ, the identity of the vowel can have been different in different dialects, and that Homeric ἦτορ can be attributed to the Akhaian or Aiolic component of the oral tradition (Aiolic if αὐτάρ is a counterexample after all; see van Beek 2022: 419).

The Mycenaean evidence is sparse and difficult to interpret. Two examples appear to show an outcome ορ:

PIE *wr̥ǵyéti (Av. *vərəziieiti*) > *wo-ze* *ϝόρζει '(s)he is working (the land)'; inf. *wo-ze-e*, ptc. *wo-zo*, pl. *wo-zo-te*, mp. *wo-zo-me-no*;
PGk *(κ^{w})τρ̥πεδjα 'four-footer' > *to-pe-za* *τόρπεζα 'table' (cf. Att.-Ion. τράπεζα).

Two others seem to show ρο:

PGk *κ^{w}ετρ̥- 'four-' in inst. pl. *qe-to-ro-po-pi* *κ^{w}ετρόποδφι (cf. Hdt. pl. τετράποδα);
place name *ma-to-ro-pu-ro*, apparently *Μᾱτρόπυλος, of which the first part is likely to be 'mother'; the variant *ma-to-pu-ro* can be an error.

The 1st-millennium combining form of 'mother' shows that a linking vowel -o- is not completely out of the question, though at an early date that seems less likely. The final example is damaged:

PIE loc. pl. *d^hugh$_2$tr̥sú (cf. Skt *duhitū́ṣu*) >→ dat. pl. *tu-ka-ṭạ-ṣị* θυγατάρσι 'to the daughters'?

That is the usual reading of this form (Sacconi 1974: 32), but some specialists (e.g. Lejeune 1972: 127, 197) read *tu-ka-to-si*. The signs *ta* and *to* are not extremely similar, but both are rectilinear and vertical, and the tablet is damaged enough to raise doubts; in addition, a single example could be an error.

It seems clear that the normal outcome of *r̥ in Lesbian, Thessalian, and Boiotian is ρο (van Beek 2022: 117–29). Clear examples include:

PIE *mr̥tós 'mortal' (Skt *mr̥tás* 'dead') > Hom. (Aiol.) βροτός;
PIE *mr̥ǵ^{h}éw- 'short' in Lesb. βρόχε(α) 'briefly' Sappho 31.7, Thess. Μροχō̃ 'Shorty' *SEG* 24.406 (Att.-Ion. βραχύς);
(post-)PIE aor. *tr̥pé- 'turn' > Lesb. τρόπην 'to turn' Alkaios 70.9 (Att.-Ion. τραπε͂ν);
PGk aor. *ἀμρ̥τέ- 'miss a mark' in Lesb. ἄμβροτε 'he made mistakes' Sappho 5.5, inf. ἀμβ[ρό]την 'to break the law' *DGE* 619.15–16 (Att.-Ion. ἁμαρτε͂ν);
PGk *στρ̥τός 'camp' in Lesb. acc. στρότον 'army' Sappho 16.1, στρότᾱγοι 'generals' *DGE* 620.7, Boiot. ἐσστροτεύαθη 'they have campaigned' *DGE* 521.6 (Att.-Ion. στρατός, etc.).

The clearest example of ορ is ἐμμόρμενον 'fated' at Alkaios 39.7 (Att. εἱμαρμένον); it can owe the shape of its root (and might even owe its vowel) to analogy with active ἔμμορε (four times in Homer). Examples with α-vocalism can reflect dialect borrowing.

For Cyprian there is very little evidence that can't be questioned. *ka-te-wo-ro-ko-ne* *κατήϝοργον 'they besieged' Masson 217.1 is almost certainly a thematic aorist with zero-grade *r̥ in the root; on *a-u-ta-ra-* *αὐτάρ 'but, however' Masson 235.2, shared only with epic, see above.

Much of the apparent Arkadian evidence can likewise be impugned (see Morpurgo Davies 1968). Possibly the best evidence is fem. gen. τετόρτᾱυ 'of the fourth' *DGE* 656^g.104 (Att.-Ion. τετάρτης) and dat. πανᾱγόρσῑ 'festival' *DGE* 654.26, gen. τριπανᾱγόρσιος l. 8, in which a zero grade of ἀγερ- 'gather' is expected. Once again, examples with α-vocalism can reflect dialect borrowing. Note that Arkadian acc. pl. δαρχμάς (*DGE* 654.8) can reflect metathesis of ρ and a short vowel; the root is normally δραχ-, which can reflect either *dr̥ǵ^h- or *dr̥n̥g^h- (*LIV* s.v. **dreg^h*).

In Attic-Ionic and the West Greek dialects the outcomes are αρ ~ ρα and αλ ~ λα. We find αρ and αλ before vowels, typically when a laryngeal has been lost, and before *y:

PIE *wr̥ḗ(n) 'lamb' (Arm. *gaṙn*, gen. *gaṙin*) >→ ϝαρήν (preserved in Cretan) > ἀρήν;
PIE *g^{w}ráh$_2$u- ~ *g^{w}r̥h$_2$áw- 'heavy' >→ *g^{w}r̥h$_2$ús (Skt *gurús*) > Gk βαρύς;
PIE *ǵ^{h}r̥yé/ó- 'be pleased with' vel sim. (Old Lat. *horitur* '(s)he encourages, urges') >*χαρjε/ο- > χαίρε͂ν 'to rejoice, to be glad';
pre-PGk *iswo-k^{h}esr̥-ya 'arrow-handed (fem.)' > *ἰhϝο-χεhαρ-jα > Hom. (Ἄρτεμις) ἰοχέαιρα (Heubeck 1956);
pre-Gk aor. *γ^{w}λ̥h$_1$-έ/ό- 'throw' (cf. Skt ptc. *udgūrṇas* 'lifted, raised') > βαλε͂ν.

We find preconsonantal ρα and λα in the roots of u-stem adjectives, apparently regardless of where the full-grade vowel was:

PIE *mréǵ^{h}u- ~ *mr̥ǵ^{h}éw- 'short' (Lat. *brevis*) → *mr̥ǵ^{h}ús (Av. *mərəzu-*) > βραχύς;
PIE *d^{h}érs- ~ *d^{h}r̥s- 'dare, be bold' (pf. 3sg. *d^{h}ed^{h}órse > Skt *dad^{h}árṣa*, Goth. *ga-dars*) in *d^{h}érsos 'daring, bravery' > Lesb. θέρσος, *d^{h}r̥sús 'brave, bold' > θρασύς (the latter with -σ- leveled from the former; the former → Att.-Ion. θάρσος by leveling on the latter);
PIE *krétu- ~ *kr̥téw- 'strong' (substantivized in Skt *krátus* 'power') >→ κρατύς;
post-PIE *g^{w}r̥dú- 'slow' (Lith. *gurdùs*) > βραδύς;
PIE *pláth$_2$u- ~ *pl̥th$_2$áw- 'broad' (Lith. *platùs*) → *pl̥th$_2$ús (Skt *pr̥t^{h}ús*) > πλατύς.

In verb paradigms we find αρ before nasal suffixes:

PIE *mr̥-n-h$_2$- 'crush' vel sim. (Skt iptv. *mr̥ṇīhí*) > Hom. mid. μάρνασθαι 'to fight';
PIE *pstr̥-néw- ~ *pstr̥-nu- 'sneeze' (Lat. *sternuere*) > πτάρνυσθαι.

Otherwise the pattern is not clear. We often find αρ ablauting with ερ and ρα ablauting with ρε, strongly suggesting that paradigmatic leveling is in question:

PIE *térp- ~ *tr̥p- 'have enough of' (Skt nt. ptc. as adv. *tr̥pát* 'to satiety') → *τρ̥πέ/ό- > Hom. subj. ταρπώμεθα 'we are refreshed';
PIE *smer- 'to receive a portion' (Lat. *merērī* 'to deserve') > μέρεσθαι; *se-smr̥- > *hε-hμαρ- > ἕμαρται 'it is fated';
pre-Greek *h$_2$mert- 'miss (a mark)' (cf. Hom. νημερτής) in aor. ἁμ̣αρτε͂ν 'to miss, to err' (apparently /h-/ by lexical analogy);
PIE *tres- 'be afraid' (pres. τρε͂ν, Skt 3sg. *trásati*), zero-grade *tr̥s- in adj. *tr̥s-ró-'afraid' > *τραhρο- in pre-Att.-Ion. *τράhρων 'timid' > Hom. τρήρων.

Note that in the last example the development to ρα must have preceded the first compensatory lengthening.

But we also find ρα in the zero grades of roots that contained *er:

PIE *gérb^h- ~ *gr̥b^h- 'cut (into)' (cf. OE *ċeorfan* 'to cut', with full grade thematized) >→ Gk *γραφέ/ó- > γράφε̄ν Hom. 'to scratch, to graze (with a weapon), to engrave', later 'to write';
PIE *dérḱ- ~ *dr̥ḱ- 'look at' (Skt 3pl. *ádr̥śran*) → *dr̥ḱé/ó- > Hom. δρακε̄ν 'to look (at)'.

The latter example is noteworthy because the full grades actually survive in Greek: Hom. pres. δέρκεσθαι, pf. 3sg. δέδορκε. There is also an example with λα reflecting a root for which evidence for the full grade is scanty (cf. *LIV* s.v. **selǵ*):

PIE zero grade *sl̥ǵ- 'let go' (Skt pres. 3sg. *sr̥játi*) > *hlag- in Cret. aor. λαγάσαι, *DGE*179.I.5.

Finally, there are a few notorious examples in which both outcomes are attested, e.g.:

PIE zero-grade *ḱr̥d- 'heart' (Hitt. *kart-*, Lat. *cord-*) in Hom. κραδίη, Ion. καρδίη (e.g. Arkhilokhos 94.3, 114.4, Herodotos 3.35 (twice)), Att. καρδίᾱ;
Hom. κρατερός ~ καρτερός 'strong, etc.';
βραδύς (see above) but βάρδιστοι *Il.* 23.310, 530.

It seems unlikely that the nom. acc. sg. κῆρ 'heart' survived long enough to influence the vocalism of the post-Homeric forms, and I find speculation about the exact meaning and etymology of κρατερός ~ καρτερός (van Beek 2022: 189–236) unprofitable; the most probable hypotheses are that the range of meaning of the latter word was broad and that sporadic metathesis was real.

However, van Beek deserves great credit for tackling a problem that will not go away, namely the anomalous scansion of certain sequences in Homer. Hugo Mühlestein noted that ἀνδροτῆτα (*Il.* 16.857, 22.363, 24.6) has to be scanned with a light first syllable, and that there is a similar problem with ἀνδρεϊφόντης (altered from *ἀνδρο-), νὺξ ἀβρότη (*Il.* 14.78), ἀμφιβρότη, and μή πως ἀβροτάξομεν ἀλλήλοιϊν 'in case we might miss one another' (*Il.* 10.65; Mühlestein 1958: 224 fn. 20, 226 Nachtrag). Wathelet (1966) investigated other cases in which *muta-cum-liquida* fails to 'make position' in Homer, and after eliminating several classes of examples he listed those in which he believed ρV and λV could reasonably reflect *r̥ and *l̥: τραπέσθαι, τράπεζα, δράκων and the related aorist δρακε̄ν, θρόνος, βροτός and its derivatives, κράνεια, κράτος and its word-family, and Πλάταια (leaving aside some more doubtful cases). One can quibble about individual examples, but it seems clear that this is a widespread phenomenon. The question is how to account for it historically.

I have argued above that a late survival of *r̥ in epic Greek is not credible; but what are the other options? Tichy (1981) suggests that these unexpectedly light syllables are not really light; rather, they reflect a stage of the epic tradition in which the shape of the hexameter was not yet fixed, so that heavy syllables could occur in places in which we might not have expected them. But the premise on which this explanation is based is *purely hypothetical*: we have no other evidence that there was ever such a stage of the epic tradition and no rigorous way of reconstructing it (see the discussion of van Beek 2022: 49–54). Van Beek is right to prefer to work with the hexameter as we have it. What we need is a version of his analysis that does not posit implausible behavior on the part of native speakers.

The question we need to ask is this: in an oral poetic tradition, how long could inherited formulas whose shape had been altered so as to disrupt the structure of the verse survive without being regularized? To answer that question we need to look at other traditions of oral poetry. The Serbo-Croatian tradition is not recorded over a long period of time, but the Old English (OE) tradition is; what can we learn from it?

The metrical structure of OE verse is complex, but there is also another organizing principle, namely the alliteration of the initial consonants of stressed words in fixed patterns (Sievers 1893). As it happens, the inherited word-initial velars *k and (fricative) *g were palatalized before front vowels early in the prehistory of OE. That sound change must have occurred before the diphthongization of front vowels by initial palatals in the West Saxon dialect, which in turn occurred before i-umlaut, which in turn occurred before the regular syncope of high vowels, which in turn occurred before three-consonant shortening—and the last can be dated to the first half of the 7th century (Ringe and Taylor 2014: 281–4, 304). It seems that palatalization must have occurred well back in the 6th century at the latest. Yet palatal and velar consonants continue to alliterate with each other in OE poetry. In the *Battle of Maldon*, which is datable to shortly after 991 because the battle in question occurred in that year, there are examples in lines 76, 100, and 256. It seems clear that anomalies validated by tradition can, under favorable circumstances, persist in an oral poetic tradition for well over four centuries. But if we accept the usual dating of the Homeric poems to the 8th century BC, an anomaly which arose in the 12th or even the 13th century might not yet have been 'ironed out' completely. So far as I can see, that is all that is needed to explain the Mühlestein-Wathelet metrical phenomena.

5.4.1 (iii) Other phonological innovations

This is perhaps the best place to mention two puzzling phenomena concerning vowels in Greek verb inflection.

Two words recorded in Linear B appear to refer to baths: the adjective *re-wo-te-re-jo* is best interpreted as *λεϝότρεjος 'for the bath', while the compound *re-wo-to-ro-ko-wo* is manifestly *λεϝοτροχόϝος 'bath-pourer' (Aura Jorro 1999 s.vv.). But the Homeric word for 'bath' is (pl.) λοετρά, with compound λοετροχόος, and the verb root is consistently λοε- (λόεον 'I bathed (him)' *Od.* 4.252, λοέσσομαι 'I will bathe' *Od.* 6.221, aor. λοέσσαι (etc.; eight times). Evidently there was a metathesis, *λεϝο- > *λοϝε-. The same metathesis appears in aor. στορέσαι 'to spread out', PIE root *sterh$_3$- (see Harðarson 1993: 222), and κορέσαι 'to sate', PIE root *ḱerh$_3$- (p. 218). No such metathesis occurred in *λεϝοντ-, λέων 'lion', γεροντ-, γέρων 'old man', Hom. μέροπες, Att.-Ion. περόνη 'fibula', Att. βελόνη 'needle', etc. It seems more than a little odd that this metathesis occurred only in verb roots ending in the third laryngeal, especially since it was clearly a post-Mycenaean development. No adequate explanation has been suggested (see the inconclusive discussion of Cowgill 1965: 157–9 with references).

Possibly connected with that peculiarity is an anomaly in the root-syllables of four thematic aorists:

aorist	*present*	*root*
θορε̃ν 'leap'	θρώσκε̃ν	*d^herh$_3$- (?; see 3.2.3)
μολε̃ν 'come, go'	βλώσκε̃ν	*melh$_3$- (?)
πορε̃ν 'grant'	—	*perh$_3$-
τορε̃ν 'wound'	τιτρώσκε̃ν	*terh$_3$- (?)

Though three of the four roots have very sparse cognates in other IE languages (see the *LIV* s.vv.), the pattern is clear: in thematic aorists whose root ends in a liquid plus the third laryngeal, the αρ or αλ which we expect as the reflex of *r̥ or *l̥ before a vowel appears instead as ορ or ολ even in dialects in which the o-vocalism is not normal. In this case too there is no generally accepted explanation. Remodeling of an ablaut Rω: *αR to Rω: oR on the model of Rᾱ: αR (Cowgill 1965: 147–8 with references) seems at least possible, but then why was βλη-: βαλε̃ν not remodeled to yield *βελε̃ν?

A post-Mycenaean innovation which appears to be pan-Greek is the change of *κσ to χ when immediately followed by a nasal. Five examples seem reasonably secure:

(post-)PIE *ayḱsmo- 'sharp point' or the like (cf. Lith. *iẽšmas* 'spit (for roasting)' > PGk *αἰκσμᾱ́ 'spear-point' (Myc. acc. pl. *ai-ka-sa-ma*) > αἰχμᾱ́ > Att.-Ion. αἰχμή;

PGk *λύκσνος 'light, lamp' (PIE root *lewk-) > λύχνος;

PGk *τέκσνᾱ 'craft' (PIE root *teḱ- 'fashion, create') > τέχνᾱ > Att.-Ion. τέχνη;

PGk *πλοκσμός 'plait, braid' (PIE root *plek-, cf. pres. πλέκε̃ν) > Hom. πλοχμός;

PGk *ῥωκσμός 'break, cleft' (cf. pres. ῥηγνύναι) > Hom. ῥωχμός.

There are a few other probable or plausible examples.

5.4.2 Early morphological innovations

5.4.2 (i) Innovations in verb morphology

The distribution of Arkadian primary mediopassive -(σ)οι, -τοι, -ντοι, Cyprian *ke-i-to-i* Masson 11.2, Mycenaean (3sg., 3pl.) *-to*[15] vs. -(σ)αι, -ται, -νται (or their subsequent developments) in all other dialects, so far as the relevant endings are attested, was discussed in 4.2.6 (iv); I there suggested that the 'Achaian' endings with -οι are in fact inherited. If that is true, then the -αι of the other dialects, leveled from 1sg. -μαι, must have spread through a dialect continuum, probably at a very early date.

The inherited sigmatic aorist has been extended with 'alphathematic' vowels, active 3sg. -ε in all dialects, otherwise -α(-) in most. Pamphylian, however, presents us with thematic forms instead:

ἐβōλᾱ́σετυ 'he advised' (?) Brixhe 3.8;
κατεϝέρξοδυ 'let them enclose' (?) 3.12;
δᾱμιοργίσōσα 'having been *damiorga*' 17.2–3.

It is unclear whether the Pamphylian sigmatic aorist originally had a stem in -σα- but later interpreted 3sg. -ε as thematic and leveled it through the paradigm; or extended the inherited -σ- with the thematic vowel from the first (cf. Brixhe 1976: 116). Two things at least are clear. One is that the Pamphylian forms have nothing to do with the 'mixed aorists' of Homer, which Roth (1990) convincingly explains as secondary developments, mostly confined to the epic tradition. The other is that, if Pamphylian did choose an alternative vowel for the sigmatic aorist from the start, the divergence happened early, given that we find forms such as *de-ka-sa-to* *δέξατο in Mycenaean.

Also likely to have been early is the spread of the future in -σέε/ο-, of which a few examples occur in Attic-Ionic (e.g. Homeric ἐσσεῖται (thrice), Attic πεσεῖσθαι, πλευσεῖσθαι) to all futures originally in -σε/ο-, apparently throughout the West Greek area (Buck 1955: 115, Ruijgh 2007: 422–3). Still more widespread is the replacement of -σσ- by -ξ- in futures and sigmatic aorists to presents in -ζε/ο-; it is prevalent, though not always consistent, in all dialects except Attic-Ionic,

[15] See Bartoněk (2002: 307–23) for a list of the more or less certain Mycenaean examples of verb forms.

Lesbian, and Pamphylian (Buck 1955: 115–16). However, that particular change seems more likely to have happened independently; there are a few Homeric examples (including the archaic ἀβροτάξομεν *Il.* 10.65), and in Attic-Ionic the reverse change is attested (e.g. in ἁρπάσαι). Thus little can be said about its origins or relative chronology.

Various innovations which probably occurred early are found over substantial discontinuous areas of the Greek Sprachraum. Athematic inflection of contract presents is well attested in Lesbian, Pelasgiote Thessalian, and Arkadian, e.g.:

κάλημι 'I'm calling' Sappho 1.16, ἐ]πόημεν 'we used to make' 24.4, χάλαισι 'they're going slack' Alkaios 208.9, gen. sg. τέχνᾱν τεχνᾱμένω 'one who commits fraud' *DGE* 620.10;[16]

Pelasgiote Thess. [στρατᾱ]γέντος 'while ... was general' *DGE* 578A.1, διετέ]λει εὐεργετές 'continues to be a benefactor' l. 10, γυμνασιαρχέντος *DGE* 590.2, dat. pl. κατοικέντεσσι 'inhabitants' l. 14;

Ark. ἀ̓πυέσθω ὁ ἀδικήμενος τὸν ἀδικέντα 'let the one who is being wronged challenge the one who is doing wrong' *DGE* 656.3–4, ποέντω 'let them make available' l. 10, κεὐορκέντι 'and to the one who keeps his oath' *DGE* 665.17–18.

In addition, Cyprian attests an infinitive *ku-me-re-na-i* *κυμερῆναι 'κυβερνᾶν, to steer' Masson 264.4. The agreement of Arkadian and Cyprian strongly argues that this innovation occurred in those dialects before the Dorian immigration.

A new secondary 3pl. ending -αν replacing old -(ε)ν appears in Cyprian, Arkadian, Boiotian, and Lokrian. The original postconsonantal zero-grade ending *-n̥d > *-ą̄δ > *-α, which appeared at least in the sigmatic aorist, had been remodeled to -αν in all the dialects, presumably after its vowel lost its nasalization and its final consonant was lost (see 4.2.6 (i)); it is the spread of that ending at the expense of other alternants that is in question here. The aorist 3pl. of compounds of 'put', mostly meaning 'dedicate', is especially well attested, e.g.:

Cyprian *ka-te-ti-ja-ne**κατέθιjαν Masson 217.27;
Ark. συνέθεαν 'they have contributed' *DGE* 664.27–8;
Boiot. ἀνέθιαν *DGE* 446.1;
Lokrian ἀνέθεαν *DGE* 359.3.

Once again the agreement of Arkadian and Cyprian argues a common development in those dialects early in the Dark Ages. In Attic-Ionic the ending -αν spread

[16] The situation in Lesbian is certainly more complex. For the poets, see Hamm (1958: 138–44). Hodot (1990: 192–4), in discussing the epigraphical examples, suggests that contractions of vowels (on which, see 7.2.3) ultimately gave rise to athematic inflection in Lesbian.

to the imperfect of 'be', yielding 3sg. *ἦς, 3pl. ἦσαν; the dramatic consequences of that change will be charted in Chapter 6.

Similar, but probably later, is the adjustment of primary 3pl. -ατι, South Greek -ασι, to -αντι and (*)-ανσι > -ᾱσι. The latter is universal in Attic-Ionic but is not certainly attested in Arkadian;[17] it therefore seems unlikely that this change preceded the assibilation of -τι, though it clearly did precede the second compensatory lengthening (see 6.2 and 7.2.1). Unassibilated -αντι appears in various West Greek dialects at different dates, e.g.:

West Argolic ἐπιμεμηνᾱ́καντι *DGE* 91.11;
Rhodian ἐξεστρατεύκαντι *DGE* 288.48;
Phokian ἀνατεθέκαντι *IG* IX-1.66.10.

The same innovation appears in Boiot. -ανθι (e.g. ἀποδεδόανθι *DGE* 526.35), though the aspirate in the ending is of uncertain origin; for a list of Boiotian (and Thessalian) examples and the two hypotheses regarding the aspiration—neither very plausible—see Scarborough (2016: 156–61).

I argued in 4.2.1 (ii) that the distinctive double-nasal-affixed presents of Greek are an innovation, beginning with χανδάνε̄ν 'grasp', λαγχάνε̄ν 'get by lot', and μανθάνε̄ν 'learn', in which the apparent nasal infix was etymologically part of the root. Presents of that type spread slowly but apparently steadily to other verbs throughout the early history of Ancient Greek. Already in Homer λανθάνε̄ν is in competition with λήθε̄ν and πυνθάνεσθαι (*Od.* 2.315, 13.256) with πεύθεσθαι (sixteen times);[18] ἁνδάνε̄ν has apparently ousted ἥδεσθαι (though the latter is well attested in Herodotos and Attic, while ἅδομ(αι) appears in Sappho 95.10), and τυγχάνε̄ν has undergone lexical split from τεύχε̄ν. In later Greek the most important addition to this class was λαμβάνε̄ν, originally 'grasp, seize' but increasingly 'take', encroaching on αἱρε̄ν. In Homer the present of this verb is consistently λάζεσθαι, and the same present appears sporadically in later Greek (e.g. λα]ζόμενος *DGE* 168.4 at Khalkedon, a colony of Megara). It appears remodeled as ἐλάζυτο in l. 316 of the long Homeric hymn to Hermes, and the linguistic reality of such an odd stem is confirmed by Boiotian λάδδουσθη (*DGE* 550[g]); it must owe its -υ- to αἴνυσθαι 'grasp, take' and possibly ἄρνυσθαι 'get, gain', neither of which has any other aspect stem. But λαμβάνε̄ν is the present in most dialects from the 5th century on. Other post-Homeric examples of these presents,

[17] The only secure examples are [ϝο̄]φλε̄́ασι *DGE* 661.1 and ἐσλελοίπασι 657.22. There is a possible ἀ̣π(υδ)ε̣δώκανσ̣ι̣ at *IG* V-2.6.82, but the context is damaged and the form emended; it seems possible that it is really an aorist ἀπέδωκαν. If it really is a perfect 3pl. in -ανσι, it shows an innovation within the history of the subdialect of Tegea, from which ἐσλελοίπασι is also attested.

[18] This distribution argues strongly that πυνθάνεσθαι is an innovation, not a true cognate of nasal-infixed stems in other IE languages (cf. *LIV* s.v. *b^h*eu̯d*^{h}, fn. 3).

such as κατελίμπανεν Sappho 94.2, ἀπυλιμπάνω l. 5, are probably innovations as well.

One consonant-final root-present underwent an interesting development in post-Homeric Greek. I argued in 4.2.1 (i) that δεκ- 'receive' is a present rather than an aorist, largely on the grounds of 3pl. δέχαται *Il.* 12.147, which can hardly be anything else. In later Greek (and to some extent even in Homer) this present has been thematized. In most dialects the result is δέκεσθαι, with an etymologically correct κ, but in Attic it is δέχεσθαι, with the χ of the 3pl. forms leveled through the paradigm.[19] But in this case Attic was repeating an earlier Attic-Ionic development in another paradigm; see 6.3 for further discussion.

5.4.2 (ii) Innovations in nominal morphology

The syntactic merger of the dative and locative cases must have occurred early, but probably not in Proto-Greek. Though only the ending -σι (← loc. pl. *-su, with the vowel leveled from sg. *-i) occurs in the plural,[20] both loc. sg. *-i and dat. sg. *-ey are attested, though not in clearly different functions. The former is the usual consonant-stem dat. sg. ending in 1st-millennium Greek and appears also in Mycenaean as s-stem *-e-i* /-eh-i/ (see the discussions of Hajnal 1995: 227–46, Thompson 1997: 327–9); the latter appears as *-e* in the paradigms of Mycenaean consonant stems (Bartoněk 2002: 225 ff.), as well as in Hom. Δι(ϝ)είφιλος 'friend to Zeus'. It seems unlikely that both singular endings could have survived to be attested if the syntactic merger had occurred in PGk, though of course that cannot be excluded entirely. In the post-Mycenaean dialects there is always only a single case, but more than one set of endings survive. For 'third-declension' nominals the endings are always sg. -ι, pl. -σι, but for the other stems we find sg. -ωι, -ᾱι or -οι, -αι and pl. -οις, -αις or -οισι, -ᾱσι → -αισι (Att.-Ion. -ησι → -ηισι → -αισι). The distribution of alternative endings is complicated. In the singular the short diphthongs appear early in Arkadian, Elean, and Boiotian (where they become -ῡ, i.e. /-ø:/, and -η by regular sound change) and could be old locative endings; elsewhere they appear later and might be the results of phonologically regular shortening of the long diphthongs (Buck 1955: 88). In the plural the longer endings, reflecting old locatives, are characteristic of Attic-Ionic, Lesbian, East Argolic, and Cretan (pp. 86, 88). In all those dialects they are steadily replaced by the shorter endings, reflecting old o-stem instrumentals, except in Lesbian, where the acc. pl. forms ended in -οις, -αις by regular sound change (see 7.2.1) and the retention of the longer dat. pl. forms served to distinguish the two cases.

An innovation which clearly spread through the dialect continuum after the Mycenaean period is the remodeling of the masc. and neut. perfect participle.

[19] Thematic forms with χ in our text of Homer are of course transmission Atticisms (cf. Wackernagel 1916: 23–9).

[20] -οις is the old inst. pl. ending; see 2.3.4 (i) and further below.

The Linear B tablets attest two indisputable neut. nom. pl. forms, *a-ra-ru-wo-a* *ἀραρϝόhα 'fitted' and *te-tu-ko-wo-*a_2 (also *-a*) *τετυχϝόhα 'fashioned, constructed', as well as several probable masc. nom. pl. forms in *-wo-e* (Bartoněk 2002: 331); none exhibits the -τ- of later Greek. Szemerényi (1967b: 7–17) established conclusively that that -τ- has nothing to do with the Skt alternant *-vat-*, nor with Goth. *weitwods* 'witness'; it must have arisen within Greek at some point after the collapse of Mycenaean civilization. Though there are other examples of σ-stems being partly replaced by τ-stems (pp. 20–3), it seems obvious that the other active participles in -ντ- had something to do with this particular case (p. 23); in fact Lesbian, Thessalian, and Boiotian remodeled the suffix to -ϝοντ- (see 5.2.1), and one might have expected the other dialects to do the same. Szemerényi, who worked with proportional analogy, suggested (p. 24) that the parallel between dat. pl. pf. *-ϝόσ-σι and zero-grade pres. (*)-ασ-σι was the 'pivot' of the analogical proportion; but both positive and negative exceptions to proportional analogy are so numerous that it cannot be a realistic model of morphological change (Ringe and Eska 2013: 152–3). Moreover, even if one insists on working with proportions, this one is exceptionally shaky: the dat. pl. is too infrequently heard by native learners to prompt a wholesale morphological change, and it is not even clear that *-σσ- < *-s+s- was not simplified in the prehistory of Greek (see the discussion of Morpurgo Davies 1976). A different line of argument seems more plausible. The nom. sg. masc. in apposition with a subject—especially *ϝειδϝώς 'knowingly, deliberately'—must have been the form most often heard. If a three-year-old had to guess at a stem from that one form, what would the result likely be? An outcome *ϝειδϝότ- is actually reasonable, especially if the native learner already knew that other active participles ended in -ντ-, and that is possibly all that needs to be said.

Similar in its timing and in its effects was the remodeling of the older type of comparative adjectives. Here too Mycenaean attests only stems in *-oh-: masc.-fem. nom. pl. *me-zo-e*, *me-u-jo-e* ~ *me-wi-jo-e*, *ka-zo-e*, *a-ro*$_2$*-e* and neut. nom. pl. *me-zo-*a_2, *me-u-jo-*a_2, *a-ro-a* (Bartoněk 2002: 269–70). Precisely those forms, as well as the masc.-fem. acc. sg. in -α, survive throughout Attic-Ionic, e.g. as Att. μέ̄ζο̄ς[21] and μέ̄ζω. But all other forms are ν-stems, e.g. Att. μέ̄ζων, μέ̄ζονες, and even the surviving σ-stem forms are in competition with the corresponding ν-stem forms. The discussion of Szemerényi (1968b) demolished the supposed connection with Germanic *-iz-an-; this innovation too is confined to Greek. It seems clear that the source of the innovation was ἀμείνων 'better', an old ν-stem adjective which happened to develop a comparative meaning (Seiler 1950: 14,

[21] In Attic also acc. pl.; see Ringe and Eska (2013: 183–4). Forms in -ω occur occasionally in literary Doric—I can find ἥσσω Simonides 581.5, ἀρείω Bakkhylides 9.91, μείζω Pindar *Isthmian* I.63—but not in the Lesbian poets. I have found no epigraphical examples, though a Lakonian ἐλάσσως is listed at Buck (1955: 42).

Szemerényi 1968b: 30). Exactly how -ν- spread to the 'real' comparatives is difficult to reconstruct; once again the construction of analogical proportions does not help much.

Though the masculine ᾱ-stem gen. sg. ending -ᾱο can be reconstructed for Proto-Greek (see 4.3.5 with references), nom. sg. -ᾱς cannot; the more archaic ending -ᾱ is well attested in Boiotian and in the far northwest of Greece, and many examples are comparatively early (Morpurgo 1961: 105–6). The innovative -ᾱς must have spread through the dialect continuum, probably early, though the chronology is not recoverable.

Finally, a dative plural ending -εσσι is widespread: it occurs in Homer (part of the epic dialect's Aiolic component), in Lesbian, Thessalian, Boiotian, Lokrian, Delphian, Elean, Pamphylian, and sporadically elsewhere (Buck 1955: 89). It is striking that most of these dialects constitute a continuous block across northern Greece from the Asia Minor seaboard to Delphi and beyond, and it is at least possible that the new ending arose in one of those dialects and spread gradually to the others at an early date, though it probably arose independently in other, non-contiguous dialects. The origin of this ending has been disputed for more than a century; the best presentations of the alternatives are Morpurgo Davies (1976) (-ες, -εσσι remodeled on -οι, -οισι) and Cassio (2018) (generalization of s-stem -εσ-σι without simplification of the geminate), both with references.

5.4.2 (iii) 'Into'

Somewhat later, to judge from its distribution, was the creation of a new preposition ἐνς 'into'. The inherited system, in which ἐν with the accusative indicated motion but with the dative position (roughly as in Latin), was preserved in Thessalian, Boiotian, the northern West Greek dialects (including Elean), Arkadian, and Cyprian; the new preposition with the accusative appears in Lesbian, Attic-Ionic, the Doric dialects, and Pamphylian (!)—in other words, in dialects which might be expected to have been on the trade routes in the Dark Ages. This is an especially good example of an innovation which probably spread widely by contact between dialects. The new preposition came into existence before the sound changes which affected the cluster νς, and before the raising of ε before nasals in Pamphylian, since the outcome was ἰς in that dialect (Brixhe 3.4, etc.). The -ς is obviously that of ἐξ, but it is not clear that direct lexical analogy was involved; also thinkable is the prior construction of an adverb *ἔνσω parallel to ἔξω, followed by extraction of ἐνς from the former, parallel to ἐξ.

6

The Attic-Ionic dialects

6.1 Introduction

So far as I know, the close relationship between the Attic and Ionic dialects has never been questioned; yet even this obvious group is defined to a considerable extent by innovations which spread through a continuum of dialects in contact. We can say that with some confidence because the chronology of sound changes that affected these dialects is to some extent recoverable, as follows.

6.2 Attic and Ionic sound changes

The defining characteristic of Attic-Ionic is the fronting of inherited ᾱ, e.g.:

PIE acc. *pĺ̥h$_2$mām 'flat hand' (Lat. *palmam*) > *πάλαμᾱν > Hom. παλάμην;

PIE *b^{h}éretām 'the two of them were carrying', with augment *é b^{h}eretām (Skt *áb^{h}aratām*) > ἐφερέτᾱν > Att.-Ion. ἐφερέτην;

PIE *b^{h}āǵ^{h}us 'arm' (*-ah$_2$-?; Skt *bāhús*) > πᾶχυς 'forearm' > Att.-Ion. πῆχυς;

PIE *swáh$_2$dus 'pleasant, sweet' (Skt *svādús*) > ᾱ̔δύς > Att.-Ion. ἡδύς;

PIE *stáh$_2$t '(s)he stood up' (Skt *ást^{h}āt* with augment) > ἔστᾱ (also with augment) > Att.-Ion. ἔστη;

PIE *b^{h}ah$_2$ti 'it shines, it illuminates' (Skt *b^{h}āti*) → '(s)he makes clear' → '(s)he says' (cf. Lat. *fātur*) > φᾱτι > Att.-Ion. φησι;

post-PIE deriv. *b^{h}oh$_2$náh$_2$ 'voice' (cf. Beekes 1972: 129) > φωνᾱ́ > Att.-Ion. φωνή;

PIE *Hyéh$_1$g^{w}ah$_2$ 'strength' vel sim. (Lith. *jėga*) > ἥβᾱ 'youth' > Att.-Ion. ἥβη;

PIE ah$_2$-stem dat. sg. *-ah$_2$-ay (Goth. *-ai*) > -ᾱι > Att.-Ion. -ηι;

PIE *é h$_2$aǵed 'it is said that (s)he was leading/driving' (Skt *ā́jat* '(s)he drove') > ᾱ̓γε '(s)he was leading' > Att.-Ion. ἦγε;

PIE *dm̥h$_2$tós 'built' (for the laryngeal-final root, cf. Toch. B /t^{s}əma-/ 'grow') > *δμᾱτός in νεόδμᾱτος 'new-built' (Pindar *Isthmian* IV.62) > Att.-Ion. νεόδμητος;

PIE *ḱm̥h$_2$tós 'tired' (remodeled in Skt *śāntás* 'resting, quiet') > *κμᾱτός in Hom. h. ἄκμητος 'tireless';

PIE *d^{h}n̥h$_2$tós 'fleeting' (?; Skt *d^{h}ánvat* 'it flows', *LIV* s.v. **d^{h}enh$_2$*) > θνᾱτός 'mortal' > Att.-Ion. θνητός;

The Linguistic Roots of Ancient Greek. Don Ringe, Oxford University Press.
 DOI: 10.1093/9780191989162.003.0006

PIE *t̥lh₂tós 'lifted, liftable' (cf. Lat. *lātus* 'carried, brought') > τλᾱτός 'bearable, endurable' > Att.-Ion. τλητός.

That sound change occurred after the first compensatory lengthening, since ᾱ that the 1CL created were fronted, e.g.:

PIE *h₂áwsōs 'dawn' → *h₂usṓs (Skt *uṣā́s*) > *ἀϝhώς > Dor. ἇϝώς, Hom. ἠώς, Att. ἕως;
pre-Gk *σελάhνᾱ 'moon' (cf. σέλας 'torch') > Dor. σελᾱ́νᾱ, Att.-Ion. σελήνη;
pre-Gk *ναhϝός 'temple' (cf. Hom. ναίε̄ν 'to dwell') > Dor. νᾱϝός, Hom. νηός, Att. νεώς;
PGk *στάλλᾱ 'standing stone' > στᾱ́λᾱ > Att.-Ion. στήλη.

The fronting occurred in Attic, West Ionic (of Oropos and Euboia), Cycladic Ionic (of Keos, Naxos, Delos, Amorgos, etc.), and East Ionic (of the Asia Minor seaboard and the islands immediately offshore).

However, the outcome of the Attic-Ionic fronting was at first not identical with η; it must have been lower, i.e. *ǣ (Vendryès 1920: 65–6). A vowel system including this intermediate *ǣ is directly attested in several early inscriptions in Cycladic Ionic (Vendryès 1920: 65–6, Schwyzer 1923: 364), of which the most extensive is the boustrophedon inscription on the Stele of Nikandre (*DGE* 758, Buck 6). It seems best to give a close transcription of the actual letters (see Jeffery 1991: 291–2 with plate 55: 2):

ΝΙΚΑΝΔΡΗΜΑΝΕΘΕΚΕΝΗΚΗΒΟΛΟΙΙΟΧΕΑΙΡΗΙϘΟΡΗΔΕΙΝΟ
ΔΙΚΗΟΤΟΝΑ□ΣΙΟΕ□ΣΟΧΟΣΑΛΗΟΝΔΕΙΝΟΜΕΝΕΟΣΔΕΚΑΣΙΓΝΕΤΗ
ΦΗΡΑ□ΣΟΔΑΛΟΧΟΣΝ

A more or less standard transcription and interpretation is:

Νῑκάνδρη μ' ἀνέθε̄κεν h̯εκηβόλο̄ι ἰοχεαίρηι,
ϙόρη Δεινο|δίκηο το̄ Ναhσίο̄ ἔhσοχος ἀλ(λ)ήο̄ν,
Δεινομένεος δὲ κασιγνέτη, | Φhράhσο̄ δ' ἄλοχος ν[ῦν].
'Nikandre dedicated me to the arrow-handed shootafar [i.e. Artemis],
daughter of Deinodikes the Naxian, outstanding above (all) others,
sister of Deinomenes, now the wife of Phraxos.'

The letter eta, a box with a crossbar, is used both for the sequence hε and for the η that resulted from the Attic-Ionic fronting (in Νῑκάνδρη, h̯εκηβόλο̄ι, ἰοχεαίρηι, ϙόρη, Δεινοδίκηο, ἀλ(λ)ήο̄ν, κασιγνέτη), but not for inherited η, which is spelled ε̄ (in ἀνέθε̄κεν, κασιγνέ̄τη); that must reflect a difference in pronunciation.[1] On indirect evidence for the existence of *ǣ in early Attic-Ionic, see further below.

[1] Of course the two vowels might conceivably have merged by the time the text was cut; the spellings Δεινοδίκηο and ἀλ(λ)ήο̄ν, in which η and a following o-vowel need to be read as monosyllables, seem

Early in the sequence of Attic-Ionic sound changes the sequence *εǣ contracted to *ǣ. The product of that contraction behaved exactly like inherited *ǣ; for instance, Attic fem. χρῡσῆ 'golden' < *χρῡσέǣ exhibits -ῆ throughout the singular while ἀργυρᾶ 'of silver' < *ἀργυρέǣ exhibits -ᾶ, exactly as expected by Attic retraction (see below). This contraction occurred at least before the loss of intervocalic *ϝ, since hiatuses created by that loss typically remain uncontracted; it cannot be shown that any sound change other than fronting preceded *εǣ > *ǣ.

At some time after the fronting of inherited ᾱ, new ᾱ's arose by the second compensatory lengthening and by the contraction of short α with following e-vowels; the former will be discussed in 7.2.1 (since it is not confined to Attic-Ionic), the latter at the end of this section. Neither of those changes can be placed more precisely in the relative chronology of sound changes because they did not interact crucially with any others. It needs to be emphasized that the structuralist arguments of Szemerényi (1968a: 1341–50) and Samuels (2017) regarding the supposed mutual influence of phonemes in a system are unreliable because they are based on the theories of André Martinet, which have been shown to be untenable (see King 1967, Surendran and Niyogi 2006). Chain shifts do occur, but we do not know what drives them; we have to conclude that functional load does *not* drive them, since we cannot predict when chain shifts will occur and when mergers will occur. Sound changes can be placed in a relative chronology only if they feed or bleed each other.

At some point after the fronting, a sequence *ǣ ... ǣ in successive syllables was dissimilated to *η ... ǣ in Attica and in at least some of the Cyclades (Vendryès, *op. cit.*). For the Attic dialect there are at least three clear examples:

PIE *krásnah$_2$ 'moving water' vel sim. (ON *hrǫnn* 'wave') > *kráhnā > κρᾱ́νᾱ 'spring' (attested in Arkadian and in Doric dialects) > *κρǣ́νǣ > *κρήνǣ > Att. κρήνη;

PGk *parawhā́ 'cheek' (lit. '(thing) beside the ear'; cf. Lesbian voc. μᾶλ]ǫπάραυε 'apple-cheeked' Hamm 1958: 204, and see Peters 1980: 295–7) > *παρᾱϝᾱ́ (cf. Myc. *pa-ra-wa-jo* 'cheek-piece (of a helmet)', gen. εὐπαρᾱ́ου Pindar *Pythian* XII.16) > *παρǣϝǣ́ (cf. Hom. καλλιπάρηος) > *παρηϝǣ́ > *παρηǣ́ > *παρηᾱ́ > παρεᾱ́ (Szemerényi 1968a: 1351; see further the end of this section);[2]

to show that the spelling of this inscription was somewhat archaizing. But the point is the same: *ǣ and η had not merged on Naxos at the time the orthography became semistandardized. Italic *h* in my transcription represents a box without a crossbar, which in this inscription is used with σ to write the cluster spelled ξ in the standard 4th-century Ionic alphabet that we still use.

[2] It is true that this word is spelled with ε only once, in an Attic inscription, while two other epigraphical Attic examples are spelled with ει (see *LSJ* s.v. παρειά); but the Lesbian and Doric forms strongly suggest that the Attic vowel was etymologically ε. I am grateful to Philomen Probert for calling this distribution to my attention.

ἰ̄ρά̄νᾱ 'peace' (attested in Arkadian, Boiotian, and West Greek) > *ἰ̄ρǣνǣ > *ἰ̄ρήνǣ > Att. ἐ̄ρήνη.[3]

Obviously the dissimilation must have occurred before the retraction of *ǣ to ᾱ following ρ in Attic (see below).

For Cycladic Ionic the evidence for dissimilation is provided by the text of Bakkhylides. Like his uncle Simonides, Bakkhylides was born and raised in Iulis on Keos. His native dialect can only have been Ionic, but because he wrote choral lyric poetry, he wrote in literary Doric. Normally he presents us with unshifted Doric ᾱ wherever it is etymologically correct, but there are a few exceptions, notably:

Φήμᾱ Bakkhylides 2.1, acc. φήμᾱν 5.194;
dat. εἰρήν[ᾱι 5.200, εἰ[ρ]ήνᾱι 13.189, nom. εἰρήνᾱ fragm. 4.61.

The most plausible explanation is that the dissimilation occurred also in Kean Ionic, and that *ǣ had not yet merged with η when Bakkhylides was acquiring his native dialect in the years just before 510 BC; the poet regularly replaced his native /ǣ/ with Doric ᾱ, but in the words where dissimilation had occurred the penultimate syllable now contained η, which he did not alter (Tucker 1962: 499). To be sure, various forms of εἰρήνᾱ also occur in Pindar (*Olympian* XIII.7, *Pythian* IX.23, *Nemean* I.69), who was Boiotian. But it is possible that their η was introduced into the text by the Alexandrian grammarians—note that the initial εἰ- must be an Atticism in any case; alternatively, the usage of Bakkhylides might be older than its attestation can tell us, and in that case the shape of this particular word might already have become part of the choral tradition. More difficult to explain is ἰ̄ρ]ήνᾱς in the Louvre Partheneion (Alkman 1.91); if its η is not also a grammarians' fiction, then the shape of 'peace' in any given dialect might not be good evidence for much of anything.

In Attic *ǣ then underwent a split: it was retracted to ᾱ in specific environments; subsequently surviving *ǣ merged with η. Those developments interacted with two other changes, the loss of ϝ and the contraction of εα. Unfortunately there is a non-negligible probability that *all three* changes in question were not single historical events: retraction when a front vowel preceded and retraction

[3] In addition to the forms cited here, there are a number of non-Attic-Ionic forms that exhibit a long e-vowel in the second syllable; Frisk s.v. εἰρήνη therefore suggests that this is a non-Greek word that was borrowed into various dialects independently. I am not convinced. The fact that both gen. sg. ἰ̄ράν[ᾱς and dat. sg. ἰ̄ρείνᾳ are attested in 3rd-century Thessalian inscriptions from Larisa (*DGE* 588.5, 589.5) can only mean that the latter is a superficially Thessalianized Attic koine form (cf. Brixhe 1976: 140 on a similar late Pamphylian name); at least some other late examples are susceptible to the same explanation (Vendryès 1920: 64). Whether Pamphylian ἰρε̄νι (Brixhe 3.7) even means 'peace' is not clear from its fragmentary context. The ἰ̄ρήνᾱ of Bacchylides and Pindar will be explained below. Most surprising is a 2nd-century Cretan phrase καὶ πολέμω χ[ἰ̄]|ρήνᾱς in what appears to be a pure dialect inscription (*DGE* 186.6–7), but it seems possible that the word was borrowed from Cycladic Ionic, as Vendryès suggests.

when ρ preceded need not have occurred at the same time, since the triggers (and therefore the phonetic rationale) for the change were different; ϝ is likely to have been lost between vowels before it was lost when a consonant preceded; and the contraction of vowels is known to have been a lengthy process attended by much synchronic variation, since identical etymological sequences do not always yield identical results. The following discussion will try to work out what can be said for certain about the relative chronology of these developments in Attic. The most important discussions of this problem are Szemerényi (1968a), Gates (1976), Peters (1980: 295–305), and Samuels (2017), all of which provide valuable insights.[4]

The Attic retraction of *ǣ to ᾱ when ρ immediately preceded occurred after dissimilation (see above), but before the loss of *ϝ immediately following a consonant. Two examples demonstrate the latter:

PGk *κόρϝᾱ 'girl' (Myc. *ko-wa*, Ark. dat. Κόρϝᾱι *DGE* 676(1)) > *κόρϝǣ > Ion. κο̄́ρη, Att. *κόρǣ > κόρη;
PGk. *δερϝᾱ 'neck' (accent?; Ark. acc. δερϝᾱν *DGE* 664.14) > *δερϝǣ > Ion. δε̄ρή, Att. *δέρǣ > δέρη.

In both cases *ǣ would have been retracted in Attic if *ϝ had not still been in place when retraction occurred.[5] Examples of retraction triggered by an immediately preceding ρ are numerous; those with cognates in other IE languages include:

PIE *b^hráh$_2$tēr 'brother' (Skt *b^hrā́tā*, Lat. *frāter*, Goth. *broþar*) > *φρǣ́τηρ > Att. φρᾱ́τηρ 'member of a phratry, fellow-clansman';
PIE aor. *drah$_2$- 'run' (Skt iptv. 3sg. *drā́tu*) > *δρǣ- in Att. ἀποδρᾶναι 'to run away';
PIE *ḱr̥h$_2$tós 'mixed' (cf. Skt *ā́-śīrtas* 'mixed', *RV* VIII.2.9) > *κρǣτός in Hom. ἄκρητος, Att. ἄκρᾱτος 'unmixed';
PIE *pr̥h$_2$tós 'sold' (for the laryngeal-final root cf. OIr. *renaid* '(s)he sells') > *πρǣτός > Att. πρᾱτός 'sold';
PIE *h$_1$rud^{h}ráh$_2$ fem. 'red' (Lat. *rubra*) > *ἐρυθρǣ́ > Att. ἐρυθρᾱ́.

Nouns in *-ρǣ > -ρᾱ do not usually have exact cognates outside of Greek, but a few are made to inherited roots and appear to be relatively old, e.g.:

*χήρǣ 'widow' (cf. Lat. *hērēs* 'heir') > Hom., Ion. χήρη, Att. χήρᾱ (masc. χῆρος does not predate the 5th century);

[4] But note that Gates is led astray by failure to recognize dissimilation in παρεᾱ́.

[5] It is therefore surprising that Ion. ἀρή 'prayer, imprecation, curse' < *ἀρϝᾱ́ (cf. Ark. acc. κάταρϝον 'under the curse' *DGE* 654.4–5) appears in Attic as ἀρᾱ́, not 'ἀρή'. Backformation from the verb ἀρᾶσθαι is the most likely explanation (see Schwyzer 1939: 188 fn. 2 with references).

*ἕδρǣ 'seat' (cf. Lat. *sella*) > Hom., Ion. ἕδρη, Att. ἕδρᾱ;
*θέφρǣ 'burnt material, ashes' (cf. Skt *dáhati* '(s)he burns (it)') > Hom. τέφρη, Att. τέφρᾱ;
*ϝρήτρᾱ '(verbal) agreement' (Elean ϝρᾱ́τρᾱ *DGE* 409.1) > *ϝρήτρǣ > Hom. acc. ῥήτρην *Od.* 14.393, Att. ῥήτρᾱ.

On the other hand, retraction immediately following a front vowel must have occurred *after* intervocalic *ϝ was lost; note the following examples:

PIE fem. *néwah$_2$ 'new' (cf. Skt *návā*, Lat. *nova*) > PGk *νέϝᾱ 'new (moon), young' > *νέϝǣ > Ion. νέη, Att. νέᾱ;
PIE *póywah$_2$ 'meadow' (cf. Lith. *píeva*) > PGk *ποίϝᾱ 'grass' > *ποίϝǣ > Ion. ποίη, Att. *ποίᾱ > πόᾱ;
PIE *wah$_2$g- 'split' vel sim. (cf. pres. 3sg. Hitt. *wāki* '(s)he bites', Toch. B *wokotär* 'it splits open') in PGk *ϝέϝᾱγε 'it's broken' (Lesbian ἔᾱγε, Sappho 31.9) > *ϝέϝǣγε > Ion. (*)ἔηγε (ptc. nt. pl. κατεηγότα, Herodotos 7.224.1), Att. κατ-έᾱγε.

Inherited words exhibiting retraction after original front vowels are not as numerous as those after ρ, but note the following:

PIE fem. gen. *syáh$_2$s 'one' (see 2.3.6 (i)) → *smiáh$_2$s > PGk *hμιᾶς > *hμιǣς > Ion. μιῆς, Att. μιᾶς;
PIE *sḱáh$_2$ih$_2$ ~ *sḱh$_2$iáh$_2$- 'shadow, shade' (Skt *c^{h}āyā́*, Toch. B *skiyo*; see Ringe 1996: 18–20) >→ *σκιǣ́ > Hom., Ion. σκιή, Att. σκιᾱ́.

'Cheek' also belongs here:

PGk *parawhā́ > *παρᾱϝᾱ́ > *παρǣϝǣ́ > *παρηϝǣ́ > *παρηǣ́ > Att. *παρηᾱ́ > παρεᾱ́.

Because the above pairwise orderings can be demonstrated, it is possible to posit a unitary relative chronology (cf. Szemerényi 1968a: 1353, Gates 1976: 46):

1) fronting;
2) a) dissimilation,
   b) loss of intervocalic *ϝ;
3) retraction (all environments);
4) loss of postconsonantal *ϝ.

Retraction could have been a single change, so far as the arguments adduced above can tell us. Alternatively, the loss of *ϝ in all positions could have occurred at the same time, in which case the chronology would have to be as follows (Gates 1976: 45):

1) fronting;
2) dissimilation;
3) retraction immediately following ρ;
4) loss of *ϝ;
5) retraction immediately following front vowels.

However, it is perhaps more likely that both retraction and the loss of *ϝ occurred in two historical stages, in which case we have two relative chronologies that diverge toward their ends:

1) fronting;
2) dissimilation;

3a) retraction following ρ;	3b) loss of intervocalic *ϝ;
4a) lost of postconsonantal *ϝ.	4b) retraction following front vowels.

To continue with this line of argument we need further evidence.

That evidence is provided by the contraction of *εα to *ǣ. Unfortunately that was a messy sound change—for instance, it typically did not occur in disyllables (Gates 1976: 47)—but it is at least clear that it preceded the loss of intervocalic *ϝ, since in completely isolated forms like ἐννέα 'nine' loss of *ϝ was not followed by contraction (Gates, *loc. cit.*). Thus our chronology must be:

1) fronting;
2) dissimilation;

3a) retraction following ρ;	3b) *εα > *ǣ;
4a) lost of postconsonantal *ϝ.	4b) loss of intervocalic *ϝ;
	5b) retraction following front vowels.

We thus expect to find εh-stem masc.-fem. acc. sg. and neut. nom.-acc. pl. forms in -ᾱ —and we do: the acc. sg. of ἀκλεής and εὐκλεής always ends in -κλεᾶ in Attic inscriptions (Threatte 1996: 299), and though ὑγιῆ 'sound' is the normal form in both categories in 4th-century Attic inscriptions, ὑγιᾶ also occurs (p. 298).[6] Evidently the ending of εh-stem adjectives without retraction has been leveled into ὑγιῆ. Consequently we might suggest that acc. sg. πλήρη 'full', nom.-acc. μέρη 'parts', etc., are also the result of paradigmatic leveling (so Gates 1976: 49–50). But the fact that there are no byforms in -ᾱ—literally none at all—should give us pause; we will be truer to the facts if we argue that retraction immediately following ρ preceded the contraction *εα > *ǣ. We now have the following relative chronology:

[6] Note that acc. pl. ὑγιᾶς, cited by Gates (1976: 51), is apparently a false reading (Threatte 1996: 299).

1) fronting;
2) dissimilation;
3) retraction following ρ;

4a) lost of postconsonantal *ϝ.

4b) *εα > *ǣ;
5b) loss of intervocalic *ϝ;
6b) retraction following front vowels.

So it appears that retraction was not a single sound change (cf. Peters 1980: 303, who also puts retraction following ρ early and retraction following front vowels late);[7] but in that case *ϝ could have been lost in all positions at more or less the same time. That is more or less the conclusion of Samuels (2017: 97) as well.

An across-the-board merger of *ǣ with η eventually occurred throughout the Attic-Ionic dialect area, and not necessarily at the same time in all the dialects. Can we determine when it occurred in any relevant dialect? I observed above that arguments based on relations between vowels in the vowel space are not cogent. Unfortunately the same must be said of Tucker's assumptions about Greek poets' command of dialects (Tucker 1962: 491). Possibly some did simply attempt to transpose, by rule, the forms of their own dialect into forms appropriate for other dialects, but we must also reckon with the possibility that others were exceptional language learners who were able to acquire unfamiliar dialects with near-native fluency; a well-attested example of such a person is Joseph Wright, the famous 19th-century British philologist. For that reason we cannot assume that *ǣ was still distinct simply because the Attic dramatists, for example, replaced it with Doric ᾱ (mostly) correctly. It seems prudent to remain agnostic about exactly when *ǣ merged with η across the board in any Attic-Ionic dialect.

One more striking sound change is characteristic of Attic-Ionic, and only of that dialect group, namely quantitative metathesis (QM). Peters (1980: 303) and Samuels (2017: 97) order it before retraction following front vowels, but in that case the triggers for QM would have been not only a-vowels and o-vowels, but also *ǣ in 'cheek' (i.e. *παρηǣ́ > *παρεǣ́ > Att. παρεᾱ́). It seems much more natural to order retraction first (thus *παρηǣ́ > Att. *παρηᾱ́ > παρεᾱ́, as above), with only *back* non-high vowels triggering QM. It would follow that in this word QM did not apply in Ionic—and that might actually be true: in Homer the first two syllables are always (nineteen times) spelled παρει- with an ει that can be a (graphic) Atticism for η (*pace* Szemerényi 1967a: 64 fn. 68), and the only other early Ionic example I can find is acc. pl. παρειᾱ́ς at Herodotos 1.134.1. Hom. θηήσαο, θηητήρ, etc. < *θǣϝǣ- (see Kretschmer 1892)—never θεη-—point in the same direction.[8]

If the above is true, QM can be stated as follows:

[7] Peters' chronology is much more elaborate, partly because he reckons with rule reordering. However, it is not clear that rule reordering, as opposed to rule changes of other kinds, can actually occur; see Ringe and Eska (2013: 123–31) for discussion.

[8] It would then follow that post-Homeric Ionic θέη, etc., reflect Attic influence.

*ǣ or η followed by a non-high back vowel is shortened to ε, and the back vowel is lengthened if it is not already long; further, lengthened *ο > ω (not ō).

In some ways this is a puzzling sound change: it did not affect ε̄ (on which, see further below), and it remains unclear why lengthened o should also have been lowered. In any case it affected all the Attic-Ionic dialects at so late a date that it must have spread through the dialect continuum. The Homeric text includes many forms in which QM has not occurred, as well as others in which it has. Note especially the following:

PIE pronominal gen. pl. *-ah₂soHom (Skt *tā́sām* 'of those (fem.)', Lat. *-ārum*) > PGk *-ᾱ́hων (Hom. (Aiolic) τᾱ́ων 'of those') > -ǣ́ων (Naxian ἀλ(λ)ήōν 'of (all) others' *DGE* 758.2—see above) > -έων (Hom. πυλέων '(out) of the gates' *Il.* 7.1) > -ῶν;
PGk masc. ᾱ-stem gen. sg. *-ᾱjo (*-ᾱho?; see 4.3.5) > -ᾱο (preserved unchanged in Boiotian, e.g. Θεδωρίδᾱο *DGE* 447.7, and in Hom. Αἰακίδᾱο, etc.) > -ǣο (Naxian Δεινοδίκηο *DGE* 758.1–2—see above) > Ion. -εω;
PGk gen. *πόληjος 'city's' > πόληος (preserved in Homer) > Att. πόλεως;
PGk acc. sg. *γʷασιλῆϝα, pl. *γʷασιλῆϝας, gen. sg. *γʷασιλῆϝος, pl. *γʷασιλήϝων > *βασιλῆϝα, *-ας, *-ος (Cyprian *pa-si-le-wo-se*; Masson 217.6), *βασιλήϝων > βασιλῆα, -ας, -ος, βασιλήων (all preserved in Homer) > Att. βασιλέᾱ, βασιλέᾱς, βασιλέως, βασιλέων;
post-PIE gen. *nāwós 'ship's' (Skt *nāvás*) > *νǣϝος > νηός (preserved in Homer) > Att. νεώς;
PGk *hjᾱ̃ϝος 'for as long as, until', *τᾱ̃ϝος 'for so long' (cf. Skt *yā́vat* 'as much as', *tā́vat* 'so much') > *hǣ̃ϝος, *τǣ̃ϝος > *ἧος, *τῆος > Ion., Att. ἕως, τέως;
post-PIE *h₂usṓs 'dawn' > *hawhṓs (see 3.5.1, 3.5.2) > PGk *ἀϝϝώς (Lesb. αὔως) > ᾱ̓ϝώς (see 5.2) > Att.-Ion. *hǣώς (Hom. ἠώς with psilosis) > Att. *ἑώς → ἕως;
pre-Gk *ναhϝός 'dwelling' > PGk *ναϝϝός 'temple' (Lesb. acc. ναῦον Sappho 2.1) > *νᾱϝός > *νǣός (Hom. νηός) > Att. νεώς;
PGk *λᾱϝός 'body of troops' (Hom. (Aiolic) λᾱός) > *λǣός 'people' > Att. λεώς.

The ᾱ-stem endings and the adverbs show conclusively that QM occurred in all Attic-Ionic dialects; such forms as gen. sg. βασιλέος, πόλιος, etc., are the products of leveling, not of regular sound change. The fact that numerous forms unaffected by QM occur in Homer can be attributed to the formulaic nature of the poems, at least in part; but it also suggests that QM was a comparatively late change, perhaps as late as ca. 800 BC. It obviously followed the loss of *ϝ, another comparatively recent change from the Homeric point of view.

I noted above that ε̄ did not participate in QM. Instead it was shortened before vowels without further consequences. The clearest example is the aorist of 'pour':

aor. *χέϝhαι 'to pour' > PGk *χέϝϝαι (Hom. Aiolic χεῦαι) > *χε̄ϝαι > *χε̄αι > Att. χέαι, cf. also Hom. 3pl. ἔχεαν.[9]

The same sound change affected *ō, to judge from a relatively isolated example:

*ἀκουhά̄ 'hearing' > PGk *ἀκοϝϝά̄ (Lesb. pl. ἄκουαι Sappho 31.12) > *ἀκōϝά̄ > *ἀκōǣ́ > Ion., Att. ἀκοή.

Examples of this sound change are few simply because not many words were of the right shape to be affected when it occurred. Like QM, it clearly followed the loss of *ϝ.

At least one more distinctive sound change affected all the Attic-Ionic dialects, namely the contraction of short α with following e-vowels. While the result was η in West Greek and Boiotian (Buck 1955: 37),[10] in Attic-Ionic it was ᾱ. Nearly all the examples are furnished by forms of α-contract presents and similar futures, e.g. pres. indic. 2sg. τῑμᾶις, 3sg. τῑμᾶι, 2pl. τῑμᾶτε (α+ε), and the homonymous subjunctive forms (α+η). This too must have been a late change that spread through the dialect continuum, given that uncontracted examples are very frequent in Homer. Vowel contraction in general will be treated in 7.2.3, since it occurred to some extent in all 1st-millennium BC dialects.

A final peculiarity of Attic is that /h-/ appears in various words apparently as a reflex of *ϝ-; see Sturm (2018) for discussion and a possible solution.

6.3 Attic-Ionic morphological innovations

These were few, but at least one was far-reaching.

I noted in 5.4.2 that the innovative secondary 3pl. ending -αν spread to the imperfect of 'be' in Attic-Ionic. The inherited 3sg. was ἦς, preserved in other dialects and actually attested in half a dozen local West Greek dialects, literary Doric (beginning with Alkman 16.1), Lesbian, Boiotian, Arkadian, and probably Cyprian (Masson 1978); the new Attic-Ionic 3pl. was ἦσαν. This development appears to have had two, or perhaps three, further consequences.

The most surprising consequence was the reinterpretation of the old 3pl. ἦεν < PGk *ἦhεν < PIE *é $h_1$send (Skt *ā́san*) as 3sg. That must have been the result of native learners' reinterpretation of the form in some specific syntactic context, but

[9] See the older literature at Schwyzer (1939: 745), who wrongly rejects this explanation. Unfortunately later scholars have mostly followed Schwyzer.

[10] In Arkadian, Cyprian, Lesbian, and Pelasgiote Thessalian indisputable examples are hard to find, because in those dialects contract verbs are inflected athematically (see 5.4.2); I can find no relevant examples in the other Thessalian dialects.

the details are not recoverable; it seems reasonable to suggest that it was possible because the new 3pl. ἦσαν was already being learned. In Homer this change is already complete.

The most far-reaching consequence then followed: -σαν was extracted from ἦσαν as a secondary 3pl. ending, since -σ- was no longer obviously part of the root, and spread to other athematic stems in the Attic-Ionic dialects. In Homer this change is not yet complete: we still find ἔβαν beside ἔβησαν, μίγεν beside μίγησαν, and so on. However, it is complete among the commonest irregular verbs: we find only ἴσαν ~ ἤϊσαν 'they went' and ἴσαν 'they knew'. That is a good reason for suggesting that the ending spread from ἦσαν; another is that spread from sigmatic aorist -σαν—the traditional suggestion—is difficult to motivate, since the -σ- of the latter is obviously a stem suffix. In later Attic-Ionic -σαν has ousted older -(ε)ν in every athematic formation except the optative.

A possible third consequence was the creation of 'movable -ν'. As is well known to beginning students, a functionless -ν can optionally be attached to any 3sg. verb form that ends in -ε and to any ending that ends in -σι (in effect, primary 3pl. endings and dative plurals), as well as ἐστι. Since this too is restricted to Attic-Ionic, it must have started from some specifically Attic-Ionic form, and the new 3sg. ἦεν is the only available candidate. The progression must have been ἦεν → -ε ~ -εν → 3pl. -σι ~ -σιν → dat. pl. -σι ~ -σιν and ἐστι ~ ἐστιν. What is interesting about this innovation is that it never got beyond the variable stage, yet it was not suppressed either; that suggests that there was both a significant social reason to adopt it and an equally significant social reason to reject it, resulting in a variationist compromise.

So far as our evidence goes, all Attic-Ionic dialects participated in a change affecting mediopassive perfect and pluperfect 3pl. forms. After stem-final consonants the endings were -αται and -ατο (with α < *n̥), and those were the only vowel-initial endings; all the other endings in the paradigm began with σ, τ, σθ, or μ. Since labial and velar stops assimilated to following obstruents, it must have been difficult for native learners to guess the identity of an underlying stem-final stop from infrequently heard forms. The result was that in the 3pl. etymological π and β were replaced by φ, while κ and γ were replaced by χ. Homer provides several examples, including τετράφατο 'they kept facing' *Il.* 10.189 (root τρεπ-) and ὀρωρέχαται '(horses) are running flat-out' *Il.* 16.834 (root ὀρεγ-). Posthomeric examples include:

τετράφαται 'they are inclined' Theognis 42 (τρεπ-);
εἰλίχατο 'they were wrapped' Herodotos 7.90 (ἐλικ-);
τετρίφαται 'they exhibit bruises' Herodotos 2.93.3 (τρῑβ-);
τετάχαται '(ships) are drawn up' Thoukydides 3.13.3, ἀντιτετάχαται 'they are deployed against' Xenophon *Anabasis* 4.8.5 (ταγ-).

Unfortunately I can find no epigraphical examples. This change gave rise to divergent developments in the Attic and East Ionic dialects; see Ringe (2016) for further discussion.

A final innovation common to all of Attic-Ionic is completely unrelated to the above. The inherited forms of the 1pl. and 2pl. pronouns were the (PIE stressed) accusatives (see 2.3.6 (iii), 3.5.2, 4.3.6); all the dialects built whole paradigms around them, but the Attic-Ionic nom. and acc. forms were distinctive:

PIE *n̥smé 'us' > *hąhmé > *ἁμμέ (Hom. (Aiolic) ἄμμε) > ᾱ̔μέ (preserved in Doric) > *ἡμέ → ἡμέας, whence nom. ἡμέες (Att. >→ ἡμᾶς, > ἡμεῖς);
PIE *usmé 'you (acc. pl.)' > *huhmé > *ὑμμέ (Lesb. ὔμμε Alkaios 309) > ῡ̔μέ (preserved in Doric) → ῡ̔μέας, whence nom. ῡ̔μέες (Att. >→ ῡ̔μᾶς, > ῡ̔μεῖς).

The other dialects preserve the accusative forms unaltered and simply add -ς to form the nominative, so far as forms are attested (naturally they hardly ever occur in inscriptions).

7
Widely shared later innovations

7.1 Introduction

Each of the attested Greek dialects exhibits numerous distinctive innovations. Those that might have occurred early and can reasonably be adduced as evidence to classify the dialects have been discussed in the preceding two chapters. Many of the remaining innovations are confined to single dialects. Some, however, are shared by various dialects in patterns that cut across the older dialect groups. They are the subject of this chapter.

7.2 Later sound changes

7.2.1 νσ-clusters

All the dialects inherited many examples of the sequence νσ, but the sources of that sequence were not the same in all dialects. The PGk accusative plural forms of vowel stems originally ended in -νς (see 2.3.4 (i)), and in all dialects original *nty and *nts became νσ (see 3.6.3, 3.7); in addition, the ordinals of the decads must have ended in *-κονστός (derived from -κοντα). But the South Greek dialects had also evolved new sequences -νσι < *-ντι (see 5.3.1), and some dialects had created a new preposition ἐνς 'into' (see 5.4.2).

One change affecting these clusters probably occurred in all the dialects: when νσ occurred immediately before a consonant, ν was lost. Since ἐνς was affected (see below), it is likely that this was a comparatively late sound change that spread through the dialect continuum. Relatively isolated words exhibit its effects:

*κενστός 'embroidered' (cf. κεντε͂ν 'to prick; to embroider') > Hom. κεστός;
*κόνσμος 'pricked pattern, decoration, adornment' > κόσμος 'adornment; order'; Cret. acc. κόσμον 'magistrate(s)' *DGE* 177.11–12 with derived verb κοσμέν 'hold public office' in pres. ptc. gen. κοσμίοντος *DGE* 179.I.51–2; Lesb. κεκόσμηται 'has been decorated' Alkaios 140.2.

So do the ordinals of the decads, which end in -κοστός in most dialects. In Lesbian we instead find -κοιστος (e.g. fem. dat. sg. εἰκοίστᾱι '20th' *DGE* 620.39), which might suggest that the loss of ν in this position never occurred in Lesbian; but in that case κόσμος would have to be a loanword. It seems more likely that -ν- was

The Linguistic Roots of Ancient Greek. Don Ringe, Oxford University Press.
 DOI: 10.1093/9780191989162.003.0007

reintroduced into the ordinals from -κοντα at some point before the distinctive Lesbian development of νσ (see below). In Attic the loss of ν in συν- before the clusters -στ- and -ζ- (i.e. -σδ-) remains a productive rule (συστέλλε̄ν, συζευγνύναι, etc.).

When -νς was word-final its ν should have been lost when the next word within the phrase began with a consonant but should have survived when the next word within the phrase began with a vowel, as well as phrase-finally. In the 5th-century Cretan law code from Gortyn the accusative plural forms of the article still exhibit that distribution to some extent,[1] e.g.:

τὸς κᾱδεστὰνς καὶ τὸς μαίτυρανς 'the in-laws and the witnesses' *DGE* 179. III.50–1;
τὸς μὲν υἰύνς 'the sons' IV.39–40;
τὰδ δὲ θυγατέρανς 'the daughters' IV.41–2; but
τὰνς ἐν πόλῑ 'those (houses) in the city' IV.32;
τὸνς ἐλεύθερονς 'the free (children)' VII.7–8;
τὸνσς ἐπιβάλλοντανς 'those next in line (for an inheritance)' VII.9–10.

Otherwise forms in -νς have largely been generalized—further examples will be cited below—but there is still some variation: we read τοῦτος ἔκεν τὰ κρε̄́ματα 'they are to have the possessions' three times early in the fifth column, followed by τοῦτονς ἔκεν τὰ κρε̄́ματα at V.27–8.

Other dialects have leveled these outcomes in one direction or the other. We find only accusative plurals in -ος and -ας in Arkadian, Thessalian, and the Doric of Thera—hence also in Kyrenaian, a colony of the latter:

Ark. hεκοτὸν δαρχμάς *DGE* 654.4, τὰς ὕστερας τρὶς ἀμέρας 654.8–9, τὸς τριᾱκάσιος 654.20–1, τὸς ἔσγονος 657.54;
Thess. τὸς ταγός *DGE* 590.3, τὰς ἐπιστολάς 590.43;
Theran τὸς ἀνδριάντας *DGE* 227.B.12;
Kyrenaian ἔς τε τὸς κοινὸς εὐεργ[έτας] Ῥωμαῖος καὶ ἐς τᾶν πόλιν καὶ [ἐς] τὸς ἰαρές *DGE* 236.4–6; πάς 'all' Buck 115.39; acc. τρίς Buck 115.113.

As the Kyrenaian examples show, the same outcome was generalized in other instances of final -νς; for instance, in Arkadian the athematic participles hιεροθυτές '(what he declares) as hιεροθύτᾱς' *DGE* 654.4 and ἐργώνησας 'having contracted' *DGE* 656.12 likewise lack -ν-. Other dialects generalized *-νς (occasionally with lexical exceptions, e.g. Ionic ἐς).

No further change affected νσ in Cretan, West Argolic (Bartoněk 1971: 119–20), Arkadian, or Thessalian. Typical examples include:

[1] However, some phrase-final -ανς have been remodeled from consonant-stem -ας (cf. μαίτυρανς, θυγατέρανς, ἐπιβάλλοντανς); that is, the ᾱ-stem alternation -ανς ~ -ας has been extended to consonant-stem -ας, especially at phrase-end.

Cret. μαίτυρανς παρε̄́με̄ν δρομέανς ἐλεύθερονς τρίινς ε̄̄ πλίανς[2] 'three or more free witnesses of age shall be present' *DGE* 179.V.52–4, ε̄̄ καταθὲνς ε̄̄ ἐπίσπενσανς 'having either mortgaged or promised (it)' VI.19–20;
West Argolic ἐνς πόλιν *DGE* 83.A.4, ἅ[π]ανσαν B.5–6, τὸνς ϝεξέ́κοντα τέλεονς ὄϝινς B.10, τοῖς θῡ́ονσι B.16;
Ark. subj. 3pl. κελεύωνσι *DGE* 656.15, fem. dat. sg. ἐσδοθένσᾱι 'married off' 657.7, τοῖς πρότερον οἴκοι πολῑτεύονσι 'for those who were previously citizens at home' 657.21; fem. acc. pl. πάνσας 665.A.11;
Thess. fem. dat. sg. πάνσᾱ *DGE* 567.2.

These were clearly 'relic' areas (see immediately below).

Perhaps the most widely shared sound change that cannot be used to define dialect groups is the 'second compensatory lengthening' (2CL). The change is simply stated: in a sequence *Vνσ, the ν was lost and the preceding vowel was lengthened. This change must have spread through the dialect continuum—including the Attic-Ionic dialect continuum, since it followed the fronting of inherited *ᾱ which all Attic-Ionic dialects shared. It failed to reach the areas noted in the preceding paragraph, as well as Lesbian, Theran (and Kyrenaian), and in part Elean, which will be discussed below. Mid vowels lengthened by the 2CL usually became ε̄ and ō in those dialects in which they are distinguished from inherited η and ω. I give Attic examples; other dialects have similar forms (to the extent that they also inherited a form with νσ, see above) except that in a few we find η, ω instead of ε̄, ō:

PGk *ἐhεντι 'they are' (Doric ἐντι) > (*)ἐhενσι (Myc. *e-e-si*) > ε̄̓σι;
PGk *φέροντι 'they carry' (preserved in Doric) > *φέρονσι > φέρōσι;
PGk pf. 3pl. *-ᾳτι > -ατι (e.g. in Aitolian γεγόνατι *IG* IX-1[2].171.6) > -ασι (e.g. in Ark. ἐσλελοίπασι 'they have missed' *DGE* 657.22) → *-ανσι > -ᾱσι, e.g. in δεδίᾱσι 'they are afraid';
PGk acc. pl. *-ονς, *-ανς (preserved in four dialects, see above) > -ōς, -ᾱς;
PGk *πάντς 'all', dat. pl. *πάντσι, fem. *πάντjα > *πάνς, *πάνσι, πάνσα (the last attested in Arkadian and Thessalian, see above) > πᾶς, πᾶσι, πᾶσα;
PGk aor. ptc. *θέντς 'upon putting', dat. pl. *θέντσι, fem. *θέντjα > *θένς, *θένσι, *θένσα > θε̄́ς, θε̄̃σι, θε̄̃σα;
PGk pres. ptc. dat. pl. *-οντσι, fem. *-οντjα > -ονσι (cf. Ark. πολῑτεύονσι, see above), -ονσα (cf. Ark. pl. μίνονσαι 'remaining' *DGE* 657.49–50) > -ōσι, -ōσα, and so all other active and aorist passive participles and other ντ-stem nominals;
finally, *ἐνς 'into' > ε̄̓ς.

[2] Three of the examples in this passage have been remodeled from consonant-stem -ας (and 'three' has been remodeled from *τρίνς), but the point is that -νς survived unchanged (and so was available as a model).

In addition to the dialects in which *νσ underwent no change, there are some that underwent a different development of that cluster. In Lesbian and Kyrenaian (so also presumably in Theran[3]) *Vνσ > Vισ. This outcome is copiously attested in Lesbian poetry; among the dozens of examples in Sappho the following are typical:

acc. pl. σατίναις ὐπ' ἐϋτρόχοις ἆγον αἰμιόνοις 'to the well-running carriages they hitched the mules' Sappho 44.13–14;
3pl. ἀπυκρύπτοισι 'they hide away' 34.2, φαῖσ(ι) 'they say' 16.2, ἐπιρρόμβεισ(ι) '(my ears) ring' 31.11–12;
fem. ptc. pres. ἐθέλοισα 1.24, aor. λίποισα 1.7, ὐπασδεύξαισα 'having yoked' 1.9, pass. ἐπιμνᾱ́σθεισ(α) 'upon being reminded' 96.15–16;
παῖς 'all' 2.6, fem. acc. παῖσαν 31.14;
εἶς 'one' 5.8;
εἰς 'into' 56.2.

Kyrenaian examples are few, partly because in that dialect -ς was generalized at the expense of *-νς word-finally (see above), but the following can be cited:

fem. ptc. pres. acc. ἀνήκοισαν 'promoting, conducive to' *DGE* 237.12, pf. dat. pl. προγεγονοίσαις 237.20, aor. nom. sg. καθᾱ́ραισα Buck 115.87;
fem. ἑκοῖσα 'willing' Buck 115.89.

Only Elean exhibits three different outcomes of this cluster. Word-internally the 2CL seems to have applied, cf.:

pres. ptc. fem. δικά(δ)δōσα *DGE* 412.4, ἀνταποδιδῶσσα 425.17;
fem. acc. πᾶσαν 425.12.

Word-finally there are some early examples of acc. pl. -ος and -ας:

ἐλεύθαρος *DGE* 416.3, ἰαρός 416.4, κα(τ)θυτάς 'dedicated' 418.6, 12,

as well as the defective

(πε)ν(τ)ακάτιας κα δαρχμ(ά)ς *DGE* 411.2–3.

But -αις is also attested early:

[3] I cannot find the Theran παῖσα cited in Buck (1955: 67). Bechtel (1923: 529) cites a fragmentary -ωσα that might reflect the 2CL. Most of the epigraphical material is late and largely in the Attic koine.

ζέκα μναίς κα ... κα(τ)θυταίς *DGE* 409.3–4,] μναίς κ' ἀποτίνο[ι κα](τ)θυταίς 410.4.

In later inscriptions, after word-final rhotacism had occurred, we find -οιρ and -αιρ:

ταὶρ δὲ γενεαίρ 'the descendants' *DGE* 424.1, τοὶρ δὲ ἐπ' ἅ(σ)σιστα 'the next of kin' 424.8–9, καὶ ἄλλοιρ καὶ πλείονερ 'and many others' 425.7–8,

the last with the Northwest Greek or later Attic koine replacement of acc. pl. -ας by -ες. Apparently the outcomes -Vς and *-Vνς were still in competition in prehistoric Elean, somewhat as in Cretan; but it is surprising that the 2CL occurred only word-internally.

7.2.2 Loss of *ϝ

In 6.2 we had occasion to discuss the interaction of the loss of *ϝ and other sound changes in Attic. *ϝ was also lost in most other dialects, often considerably later than in Attic; only in Ionic and in insular Doric (not including Cretan) does the consonant seem to have been lost before the earliest inscriptions. Homeric verse often behaves as if *ϝ were still in place, but in more than a few instances it is ignored, which demonstrates that it had already been lost in the poet's (or poets') speech in the 8th century. It was still in place word-initially in the verse of Sappho and Alkaios. The best brief discussion is perhaps still Buck 1955: 46–52.

In most phonotactic circumstances loss of *ϝ had no consequences, except that it occurred late enough to impede contraction of vowels (see 7.2.3) and a few other changes of vowels in hiatus. However, loss of *ϝ immediately following a consonant triggered lengthening of the vowel *preceding* the consonant in West Argolic (Bartoněk 1971: 120), Cretan, insular Doric, and East Ionic; also in the Ionic of Thasos, to judge from names (cf. Bechtel 1924: 72).[4] This is called the 'third compensatory lengthening' (3CL); in other dialects, including Attic and Lesbian, it did not occur. Its geographical distribution creates a strong presumption that it spread through the dialect continuum. Unsurprisingly, the 3CL of *α in Ionic yields ᾱ (not η). Examples are guaranteed variously by the scansion of metrical texts and by the orthography of some inscriptions. In the following examples, mostly from literary Greek, ει = ē̆ and ου = ō; 'Ionic' without further qualification is literary Ionic:

ϝίσϝος 'equal' (attested in Boiotian, Arkadian, and Cretan) > Hom., Ion. ῑσος; Att., Lesb. ἴσος;

[4] Examples from other Ionic-speaking islands are in hexameter verse and can be Homericizing.

καλϝός 'beautiful' (Boiot. neut. καλϝόν *DGE* 538.1) > Hom., Ion. κᾱλός; Att. καλός, Lesb. κάλος;

δερϝᾱ 'neck' (accent?; Ark. acc. δερϝᾱν *DGE* 664.14) > Hom., Ion. δειρή; Att. δέρη, Lesb. δέρᾱ;

κόρϝᾱ 'girl' (Myc. *ko-wa*, Ark. dat. Κόρϝᾱι *DGE* 676(1)) > Hom., Ion. κούρη, Knidian dat. sg. Κούρᾱι *DGE* 262.1; Att. κόρη, Lesb. κόρᾱ;

(*)κόρϝος 'boy' (Myc. *ko-wo*) > Hom. κοῦρος;

(*)ξένϝος 'guest, host' (cpd. πρόξενϝος 'official host' attested in Korkyraian; Corinthian Ξένϝōν *DGE* 121(2) prob. = Myc. *ke-se-nu-wo*, Aura Jorro 1999 s.v.) > Hom., Ion. ξεῖνος, cf. Cret. acc. pl. πρόξηνονς *DGE* 187.6–7; Att. ξένος;

*ϝόρϝος 'boundary' (probably, cf. Myc. *wo-wo*; Korkyraian ὄρϝος *DGE* 135(2), cf. Ark. acc. εὐθυορϝίᾱν 'in a straight line' 664.14) > Hom., Ion. οὖρος, Theran pl. οὖροι *DGE* 221.1, Cret. ὦρος 206g, West Argolic ὄ̄ρος 83.B.6; Att. ὅρος, Heraklean acc. pl. ὄρως *DGE* 62.53;

(*)φάρϝος 'length of cloth' (Myc. pl. *pa-we-a₂*) > Hom. φᾶρος, Ion. pl. φᾱ́ρε(α) Xenophanes 3.3; Att. φάρος;

*ἀρϝᾱ́ 'prayer, imprecation' (cf. Ark. κάταρϝον 'under the curse') > Hom. ἀ̄ρή; Att. ἀρᾱ́ (see 6.2 with fn. 5), Lesb. gen. sg. ἄρᾱς Sappho 86.5;

*hόλϝος 'whole' (cf. Skt *sárvas*) > Hom., Ion. οὖλος; Att. ὅλος;

*πέρϝᾳτα 'limits' (cf. Skt *párus* 'joint') > Hom., Ion. πείρατα; Att. πέρατα, Lesb. gen. pl. περάτων Alkaios 350.1;

*ἔνϝᾳτος 'ninth' (*ἐνέϝᾳ 'nine', cf. Skt *náva*, Lat. *novem*) > Hom. εἴνατος, Kyrenaian fem. acc. sg. ἠνάτᾱν Buck 115.102, West Argolic dat. sg. ἠνάτᾱι *DGE* 91.3; Att. ἔνατος;

*μόνϝος 'alone' > Hom., Ion. μοῦνος; Att. μόνος, Lesb. fem. μόνᾱ Sappho 168B.4;

*νόσϝος 'disease' > Hom., Ion. νοῦσος; Att. νόσος;

*ὀδϝός 'threshold' > Hom. οὐδός, Kyrenaian dat. ὠδῶι Buck 115.134; Att. ὀδός, East Argolic acc. pl. τὸς ὀδṓς *DGE* 108g 1.49;

pres. *κ^wινϝε/ο- 'pay' (cf. Hom. 3sg. τείνυται, Chantraine 1973: 303 with ref.) > Hom. τῑ́νειν; Att. τίνēν;

pres. *χ^wθινϝε/ο- 'wane' (cf. Skt caus. *kṣiṇóti*) > Hom. φθῑ́νειν; Att. φθίνēν;

pf. *δέδϝοικε '(s)he's afraid' (cf. Skt *dvéṣas* 'hatred') > Hom. δείδοικε; Att. δέδοικε;

pres. *φθανϝε/ο- 'do first' > Hom. φθᾱ́νειν, Att. φθάνēν.

7.2.3 Loss of intervocalic *h and *j; contractions of vowels in hiatus

Since intervocalic *h and *j are still (sometimes) written on the Linear B tablets, it is clear that their loss was a post-Mycenaean change; yet it affected all dialects without exception and without irregularities, so far as we can tell. A large number of hiatuses between vowels resulted.

Vowels in hiatus underwent contraction to some extent in all dialects, but the details are somewhat different in each. The most complete presentation of the facts in detail for individual dialects is still the relevant sections of Bechtel 1921, 1923, 1924, while a good summary is Buck 1955: 37–43. Like the latter, this section does not aim at completeness; I will try to give a reasoned overview of the more important developments.

Vowel contraction appears to have been a series of changes that continued over many generations, no doubt with considerable variation at any given time. The following general principles apply (see also Buck 1955: 43).

1) Because intervocalic *ϝ was lost centuries later than *h and *j, a much greater number of vowel sequences originally separated by *ϝ remain uncontracted, even in Attic-Ionic. Sometimes it can be shown that older hiatuses underwent contraction before the loss of *ϝ; as noted in 6.2, the acc. sg. of ἀκλεής and εὐκλεής always ends in -κλεᾶ in Attic inscriptions (Threatte 1996: 299), so that the development must have been *-κλεϝέα > *-κλεϝǣ̄ > *-κλεǣ̄ > -κλεᾶ.
2) Identical vowels contracted much more readily than unlike vowels. That applies even to hiatuses created by the loss of *ϝ; for instance, pres. inf. *πλέϝεhεν > *πλέϝε̄ν > *πλέε̄ν > πλε̃ν 'to be sailing' in Attic, but 1sg. *πλέϝω > πλέω remains uncontracted.
3) Disyllables often remained uncontracted while longer words underwent contraction. That applies even to the older hiatuses; for instance, θεός 'god' < *θεhός (cf. θέσφατος 'god-spoken') is normally disyllabic, but in names like Att. Θο̄κῡδίδης it does contract.

Leaving aside archaisms in Homer, the dialect that contracted least appears to be Boiotian. In the late 3rd-century inscription detailing the financial dealings between Nikareta and the city of Orkhomenos (*DGE* 523) we find, e.g., gen. sg. Πολυκράτιος (<-εος), τῶ ταμίᾱο 'of the comptroller', gen. pl. τᾶν ὑπερᾱμεριάων τᾶν ἰωσάων 'of the existing payments due', aor. subj. ἀποδώει 'pays', perf. ptc. οὗτα ϝεϝῡκονομειόντων 'having handled these transactions', all with hiatuses of types that contract in at least some other dialects. The sequence least liable to contraction is εο, which contracts to ο̄ only in Attic; εα and οᾱ are also relatively resistant: the former contracts to η in Attic-Ionic and some other dialects (in no obvious pattern) but remains uncontracted in others (Buck 1955: 39), while the latter normally contracts to ω only in Ionic (p. 42). Short α typically contracts with ο or ω to ω, but the contractions of long ᾱ with o-vowels are more variable; in Attic-Ionic ᾱ was fronted to η and then underwent QM (see 6.2), sometimes with further contraction to ω, but in most dialects the contraction product is ᾱ (Buck 1955: 37–8). Otherwise contraction with o-vowels usually yields an o-vowel. The most striking widespread difference involves the contraction of (short) αε̄̆ and αη: as observed in 6.2, these sequences yield ᾱ in Attic-Ionic but η in West Greek and Boiotian, e.g.:

Rhodian θοινῆται 'is consumed at a (sacred) feast' *DGE* 286(1).5 = Att.-Ion. θοινᾶται < *θοινάjεται;
Knidian subj. ἐπερωτῆι 'he inquires' *DGE* 263.49 = Att.-Ion. ἐπερωτᾶι < *ἐπερωτάjηι;
Cretan νῑκήθθō 'let him be convicted' *DGE* 181.15 = Att.-Ion. νῑκά́σθω < *νῑκαjέσθω;
West Argolic νῑκῆν 'to be the victors' *DGE* 85.13 = Att.-Ion. νῑκᾶν < *νῑκάjεhεν;
Lakonian hopῆν 'to see' *DGE* 16.4 = Att.-Ion. ὁρᾶν < *hopάjεhεν;
East Argolic [ὁ]ρῆι 'she sees' *DGE* 109.2 = Att.-Ion. ὁρᾶι < *hopάjει;
Megarian τῑμῆ 'it honors' *DGE* 154.17 = Att.-Ion. τῑμᾶι < *τῑμάjει;
Phokian σῡ]λῆν 'to plunder' *IG* IX-1.120.9–10 = Att.-Ion. σῡλᾶν < *σῡλάjεhεν.

In alphabets with only five vowels this η is of course written with epsilon; for instance, ἐνῑ́κε̄ 'he was victorious' appears repeatedly in *DGE* 12, an early Lakonian inscription, and in *DGE* 363.2, an early Lokrian inscription, the last form listed is written σῡλε̃ν. In Boiotian all long e-vowels merged in a higher mid vowel eventually spelled ει; thus corresponding to the last infinitive adduced above we find Boiotian σουλεῖμεν (de Ridder 1895: 157, 2nd inscription, line 7). Few forms with η appear in literary Greek because the Doric of choral lyric mostly uses the Attic-Ionic forms with ᾱ, but at least we can cite ὁρῆις 'you see' Alkman 1.50, νῑ́κη 'he won' Pindar *Nemean* V.5, and perhaps τί δ' ἐνῑ́κης 'what victory did you win?' from Simonides' thirty-first epigram, if Bergk's emendation is correct.

7.2.4 Long mid vowels

The long vowels that Greek inherited from PIE and which resulted from the loss of laryngeals (see 3.2.1, 3.2.3) appear in Greek as η, ᾱ, and ω. But there were also 'secondary' long mid vowels that reflect four sound changes:

1) the first compensatory lengthening, except in Lesbian and Thessalian (see 5.2);

2) the second compensatory lengthening, except in Lesbian, Thessalian, Arkadian, West Argolic, Cretan, Theran, and Kyrenaian (see 7.2.1);
3) the third compensatory lengthening in West Argolic, Cretan, insular Doric, and East Ionic (see 7.2.2);
4) contraction of ε+ε and of o+o (also often of o+ε; in Attic, also of ε+o).

These new long mid vowels appear as ε̄ and ō, distinct from η and ω, in the West Greek dialects spoken north of the Gulf of Corinth, in Megarian, Isthmian, and East Argolic (Bartoněk 1971: 119), and in the whole Attic-Ionic subgroup. They clearly merge with η and ω in Lesbian, Thessalian, Boiotian, Arkadian, Elean, Lakonian, Heraklean, and Epizephyrian Lokrian; the merger products are spelled differently in Thessalian (ει, ου) and Boiotian (ει, ω), but it is the merger that is structurally important. In several dialects, namely West Argolic (Bartoněk 1971 *loc. cit.*), Cretan, and insular Doric, the situation is more complicated. Of course the merger can be detected only in documents in which the Ionic vowel letters η and ω (or the Attic spellings ει and ου) are used, and from some dialects the evidence is insufficient in any case. For the facts in detail, see Bartoněk (1966: 48–109); Buck (1955: 28–30) gives a useful summary. Ruijgh (2007) discusses in great detail the pattern of outcomes and the changes that gave rise to it (see especially pp. 402–6 on the latter). Here I will briefly exemplify the merger, then consider how it came about.

In Lesbian and Thessalian the only source of the secondary long vowels is contraction; in Arkadian the 1CL is also a source. Pelasgiote Thessalian examples are hard to find, especially because contract verbs are inflected athematically, the thematic infinitive ends in -έμεν, and the o-stem gen. sg. ends in -οι (< -οιο); for examples in the interior of words, in personal names and designations of offices, see Bechtel (1921: 144). The merger with the inherited long vowels in the other dialects listed in this paragraph is exemplified by the following:

Lesb. inf. ἄγην Sappho 1.19, ἴδην 16.18 < *-εhεν, πόησθαι 5.9 < *ποιϝέjεσθαι, κῆν(ο) 'that' < *ἐκέjενο (cf. Att. ἐκεῖ 'there'), cf. inherited ἦλθες 1.8, φιλήσει 1.23, κασί]γνητον 5.2;
similarly gen. μέσσω Sappho 1.12, προσώπω 16.18 < *-oho < PIE *-osyo (see 3.6.3), cf. inherited ὤκεες 1.10, subj. 1sg. πείθω 1.18, δῶρα, δώσει 1.22 (as well as the second vowel of προσώπω);
Thessaliote Thess. ἔχειν *DGE* 567.4, cf. inherited ibid. ἐξείκοντα, gen. είβᾱτᾶ;
similarly gen. τοῦ 567.3, 4, cf. inherited ἔδουκε 567.2;
Ark. φθήρων *DGE* 656.17 < *φθέρjων (see 5.2), φέρην 665.A.17, λαχῆν A.3, cf. inherited ϝρήσῑ A.15, ἧς 656.37;
similarly acc. pl. δ[ι]αβωλευσάμινος *DGE* 665.A.25–6 (cf. Lesb. βόλλᾱ and see 5.2), gen. τῶ ἔργω 656.14, cf. inherited ὤμοσαν 665.C.2, τῶν ἔργων 656.7.

In Boiotian, Elean, Lakonian, and Heraklean the 2CL is also a source of these vowels. Examples include:

> Boiot. εἶμεν 'to be' *DGE* 462.A.3 < *ἕhμεν, fem. acc. ἡρεθεῖσαν 'chosen' A.13 < *-θένσαν, fut. inf. ἐσσεῖμεν A.18 < *-σεhέμεν, cf. inherited gen. μεινός 'month' A.1, aor. pass. subj. κουρωθείει A.11 (uncontracted, *-θη- + *-ηι);
> similarly προβεβωλευμένον *DGE* 462.A.3, acc. pl. εὐχομένως A.8, gen. τῶ τρίτω A.1, cf. inherited gen. pl. ϝετίων 'of years' A.12;
> Elean ἦμεν 'to be' *DGE* 424.7, dat. δηλόμενοι 'wishing' 424.6–7, πάσχην 424.13, cf. inherited θηλυτέρᾱν 424.2–3;
> similarly fem. ἀνταποδιδῶσσα 'repaying' *DGE* 425.17, δᾱμοσιῶμεν 'to confiscate' 424.3, cf. inherited φευγέτω 424.4;
> Lakonian ἧμε[ν *DGE* 53.2, cf. inherited ἀνέσηκε 'dedicated' 54.2;
> similarly acc. pl. προξένως *DGE* 53.2, gen. τῶ πατρός 54.3, cf. inherited γεροντεύων 'while a member of the *gerousia*' 54.2;
> Heraklean ἧμεν *DGE* 62.75–6, aor. pass. καταλῡμακωθῇς 'covered with stones' 62.56–7 < *-θένς, fut. ἐγδικαξῆται 'he shall exact the penalty' 62.129–30 < *-σέhεται, cf. inherited hημίσχοινον 'half a rod' 62.20, συνθήκᾱ 62.94;
> similarly acc. pl. τὼς χώρως, gen. τῶ Διονύσω 62.8, cf. inherited hοκτώ 'eight' 62.34.

There are two ways in which this merger could have happened. The original lengthening and contraction products in all dialects might have been ε̄ and ō, which subsequently merged with η and ω in the dialects in question; alternatively, the lengthening and contraction products in those dialects might have been η and ω from the start. The fact that the merged dialects constitute two large continuous blocks which cut across older dialect boundaries[5] suggests that the merger spread through the dialect continuum, which further suggests the first scenario. The West Argolic, Cretan, insular Doric, and Epizephyrian Lokrian data are also relevant, as follows.

The Cretan data are especially instructive (Ruijgh 2007: 404). Not all Cretan inscriptions use the letter η, but among those that do, the earliest exhibit an interesting pattern of usage (Buck 1955: 29): η is used for the long vowel inherited from Proto-Greek and for the result of the first compensatory lengthening, but the long vowel resulting from the third compensatory lengthening is written ε̄, and the result of contraction is also often written ε̄. Buck 116, from the 6th century, is an example. We find inherited η in μή, aor. subj. κοσμήσει (etc.), and ἄκρηστον 'without official position' (κ for χ, as often on Crete); we also find η from the 1CL in the present infinitives ὀπῆλεν 'to owe' (see 5.2; π for φ) and ἤμε̄ν 'to be'. However, in

[5] That is true even of the Aiolic dialects, since Boiotian underwent the first compensatory lengthening while Thessalian and Lesbian did not.

the only clear instance of contraction, the present infinitive κοσμε̄ν, the long vowel is written ε̄. The distribution is not perfect; we also find inherited η written ε̄ in the optatives δικακσίε̄[6] and κοσμησίε̄, and beside ἤμε̄ν, whose ending was evidently influenced by the thematic infinitive ending before the latter was reduced to -εν, we also find ἤμην. Possibly *η was raised after ι and/or word-finally; more likely the merger was already in progress, so that there was substantial variation. But it does appear that the long mid front vowel which arose latest was at first ε̄, which only later merged with η, the spelling used in most Cretan inscriptions. Of course it does not follow that the same thing *must* have happened in other dialects, but the Cretan data increase the plausibility of such a scenario.

The other Doric islands exhibit inconsistent outcomes of the various lengthenings, and it is not always easy to interpret them historically; see Buck (1955: 29) for a summary of the facts. However, Ruijgh (2007: 403–4) observes that, while Kyrenaian usually exhibits η and ω for the secondary mid vowels, a 5th-century inscription (*SEG* 9.45) listing names includes (gen. sg.) Βωλαγόρᾱ (l. 26), showing that the 1CL yielded lower mid vowels, but numerous o-stem gen. sg. forms in -ō (e.g. Καλλιμάχō l. 9, Λύκō l. 42), showing that contraction at first yielded higher mid vowels. Thus the development of Kyrenaian must have been similar to that of Cretan.

Buck's summary of the Argolic situation (*loc. cit.*) has been made obsolete by the demonstration of Bartoněk (1971) that East Argolic belongs to that majority of dialects which do not exhibit the long vowel merger, while West Argolic must be treated separately. In West Argolic the outcomes of the first and third compensatory lengthenings merged with inherited η and ω, e.g.:

ἀπέστηλαν *DGE* 91.11, ἦμεν 85.10, 90.8, ἠνάτᾱι 91.3, cf. ἀνέθηκε 87, τίθητι 90.15;
βωλᾶς *DGE* 85.16, 91.4, cf. βωμόν 89.9.

Augmented forms of vowel-initial verb stems that one might expect to show contraction typically exhibit η, e.g. ἥσσαντο 'they installed' *DGE* 89.6, ἠργάσσαντο 89.13–14, but that could reflect the spread of the lengthened type inherited from Proto-Greek. The contraction of ο+ο apparently always yields ου, i.e. ō, in o-stem gen. sg. forms, e.g.:

τοῦ συνεδρίου *DGE* 85.4, αὐτοῦ 89.11, τοῦ νᾱοῦ 89.19, τοῦ δᾱ́μου 91.8.

The contraction of ε+ε in verb forms must at first have yielded ε̄, which was then raised to ῑ; there are two examples in an early inscription in the epichoric alphabet and another in a late inscription:

[6] Buck's δικασσίε̄ is a misprint; see the original publication, Van Effenterre and Demargne (1937: 334).

τελῖτō 'let him pay the tariff' *DGE* 83.A.13, ἀφαιρῖσθαι B.6, καλῖσθαι 99.12.

If contraction occurred after the third compensatory lengthening, the lengthening-then-merger hypothesis makes sense: the products of compensatory lengthenings, at first ē̜ and ō̜, merged with the inherited long vowels; the products of subsequent contractions, also ē̜ and ō̜, developed in a different direction.

Finally, there is the situation in Lokrian. In Ozolian Lokrian it is clear from spellings such as εἶμεν *DGE* 366.6 (etc.), acc. pl. πολεμίους 366.11, inf. τρέφειν 366.17 that the new long mid vowels did not merge with the inherited ones; from eastern Lokris there is very little epigraphical material, but the consistent spelling Ὀπούντιοι (e.g. *DGE* 367.1, 368.1) points in the same direction. In the colony of Lokroi Epizephyrioi, however, they did merge with η and ω; in the corpus of Franciscis (1972) we find, for example:

πὰρ τῶ θεῶ 1.1, βωλᾶς 2.7, acc. pl. τώς 4.7, cf. inherited θησαυρῶι 2.1, προαρχόντων 4.1;
ὀφήλει 'owes' 5.12, cf. inherited μηνός 1.4, ποιῆσαι 9.13.

Since the colony was founded early in the 7th century (Jeffery 1991: 284–5), the obvious hypothesis is that the merger occurred after the foundation of the colony but before the date of the surviving inscriptions, which are late enough to exhibit some Attic koine forms (Ringe 1984: 250).

7.2.5 Outcomes of palatalization: σσ ~ ττ

A number of Proto-Greek consonant clusters eventually merged in */tʦ/ or the like (see 3.6.3, 3.7):

a) *k(^{h})y;
b) *t(^{h})+y in all dialects, and *t(^{h})y with no intervening morpheme boundary except in South Greek, where the outcome was instead σ;
c) dental stop + *s intervocalically after a short vowel except in South Greek, where the outcome was σ.

In a few early East Ionic inscriptions the outcome is still spelled with a special letter Ͳ (e.g. *DGE* 701, 707, 744 = Buck 2), implying a pronunciation not otherwise provided for in the Greek alphabets, which shows that the eventual outcomes developed at least partly separately in the various dialects. In most dialects, including East Ionic, the eventual outcome was σσ. In Cretan, Boiotian, West Ionic, and Attic it was ττ. The Cretan development must have been separate, but it is hard to believe that there is no historical connection between the ττ's of the three adjacent dialects, two of which were South Greek while the third was very different.

For examples see 3.6.3 and the dialect handbooks. This is perhaps the most salient innovation that cuts across older dialect boundaries.

7.2.6 Psilosis

So far as we can tell, PGk *h survived only word-initially in the post-Mycenaean dialects. It did not survive in all of them; its loss is referred to as 'psilosis'. Psilosis was regular in Lesbian and East Ionic, and it might have spread from one to the other; but it was also regular in Cretan and Elean (Buck 1955: 53), in which it must have been an independent development. Even where /h-/ survived, it seems to have been variably lost, or lost in some environments, in many dialects; the discussion of Buck (1955: 52–5) is a good summary of the complex situation.

Our East Ionic literary texts typically write the spiritus asper even though it clearly was not present in the originals. For Herodotos that is revealed by the fact that we find ἀπ' and κατ', not ἀφ' and καθ', when the following vowel-initial word is marked with the spiritus asper. For Homer the situation is more baroque, because our text was Atticized at least once in antiquity (see especially Wackernagel 1916 for extensive discussion). The fact that contracted ἥλιος has a spiritus asper, while uncontracted ἠέλιος does not, shows part of what has happened: when the *letters* of a word were the same in the text of Homer as in (probably 6th-century) Attic, the Attic breathings (and, probably, accents) were introduced into the text; when the form was foreign to Attic, it was left alone. But then what are we to make of the fact that ἀφ' and καθ' are ubiquitous in our text of Homer? Did the aspiration on those clitic-final consonants survive for a while even after /h-/ was lost, much as the hiatus survives before French 'h aspiré', or is this just more Atticism? I don't think we know.

7.3 Later morphological changes

7.3.1 Third-person plural imperatives

I argued in 4.2.6 (vi) that active 3pl. iptv. -ντον, preserved in Lesbian and colonial Rhodian and ancestral to Pamphylian -δυ, must be an archaism because of its distribution. The other dialects have modified or replaced this ending in a pattern that cuts across the more obvious isoglosses (Buck 1955: 113–14).

A simple and obvious modification of -ντον was the importation of ω from 3sg. -τω, yielding -ντων. That is the ending familiar from Attic-Ionic; it occurs also in Theran (and Kyrenaian, according to Buck) and in Cretan, as well as in Delphian; there is also a possible example from Elean:

Theran ἀναγραψάντων *DGE* 226.18, θέντων 226.19;
Cretan πρᾱξάντων *DGE* 193.109, ἀγγραψάντων 193.117;
Delphian φερόντων *DGE* 323.B.11, συναγόντων B.23–4;
Elean κ]ριθέντōν *DGE* 418.21.

The isolation of Delphian and Elean from the other dialects that have this ending argues that it is a relative archaism.

The maximally innovative alternative -ντω occurs in all the mainland Doric dialects, as well as in Arkadian and Lokrian; in Boiotian it has been altered to -νθω by a process that is not well understood. Its distribution suggests that it spread through the dialect continuum. But -ντω also occurs in Rhodian and Koan, and it is unclear whether that was a separate innovation or whether the ending spread via the trade routes. The following examples are typical:

Arkadian διαγνόντω *DGE* 656.8;
Lakonian δόντω *DGE* 22.18;
West Argolic ἕντō *DGE* 78.7, παρ]εχόντō 83.1;
East Argolic ἀποσ[τ]ειλάντω *DGE* 104.15;
Megarian ἀναγραψάντω *DGE* 163.19;
Boiotian στᾱσάνθω *DGE* 462.16;
Lokrian ἀποδόντω *DGE* 366.A.7;
Rhodian ἀθρεόντω *DGE* 281.18;
Koan ἰόντω *DGE* 251.A.5.

There are no Cyprian examples of 3pl. imperatives. The only Thessalian example that I can find is ἔστουσαν *DGE* 614.43; like Boiotian ἀποδότωσαν *DGE* 523.100, it is certainly a (superficially naturalized) Attic koine form.

A final active third-person plural imperative form is Ionic ἔστων, identical with the third-person dual. It occurs in Homer at *Od.* 1.273;[7] in East Ionic inscriptions it appears at *DGE* 688.A.21 (from Chios), and in Cycladic Ionic at Buck 7.B.11;[8] Smyth (1894: 590) and Bechtel (1924: 177) cite a Chalkidian example (not in *DGE*).

The distribution of the corresponding mediopassive endings is different and less coherent; they tend to be parallel to the active endings (on which they are modeled), but both final -ν and medial -ν- are somewhat more common. See Buck (1955: 113–14) for the details.

[7] The other Homeric example, at *Il.* 1.338, is ambiguous, since it conjoins a dual and a plural.
[8] Buck's ἔστω is a misprint; see the original publication, Daux (1949: 59).

7.3.2 Subjunctives and optatives

As noted in 4.2.5, the short-voweled subjunctive of athematic stems, especially the sigmatic aorist, is well attested in Homer and continues to be attested in Lesbian, East Ionic, and the southeastern Doric dialects well down into the Classical period. That shows that the long-voweled alternant must have spread to those stems through the dialect continuum at a comparatively recent date.

I have argued in 2.3.3 (i) that secondary endings were original in the subjunctive. As Buck (1955: 119 notes), 2sg. and 3sg. forms with secondary endings typically appear in Arkadian, Elean, Boiotian, and Thessalian, which suggests that they are archaisms that have been eliminated in the other dialects. The Kyrenaian sigmatic aorist 2sg. forms in -ες are a different matter, since in that dialect the corresponding 3sg. ends in -ει (Hoenigswald 1997: 96–7); it seems likely that they are products of restructuring, either by Hoenigswald's scenario (*op. cit.*) or otherwise.

Some dialects have extracted from the subjunctive of thematic stems a rule 'lengthen the stem vowel in the subjunctive', whence such forms as subj. δύνᾱται to indic. δύναται (Buck 1955: 120–1). That is obviously an innovation, but its cross-dialectal pattern is not clear, except that the Doric islands (including Crete) provide a large proportion of the examples.

Also as noted in 4.2.5, the original optative of the sigmatic aorist survives only in Cretan 3sg. δικακσίε̄, κοσμησίε̄ Buck 116.2, 3pl. ϝέρκσιεν *DGE* 175.7. The optative suffix appears to have been remodeled in stages. The oldest stage of the remodeling is preserved in Arkadian ὐνιερο̄́σει 'dedicates' Buck 16.3 and διακωλύσει 'hinders' *DGE* 656.6–7: the optative sign -ι, as in thematic -ο-ι, has been added to the indicative 3sg. of the sigmatic aorist. Of course the result is easily confusable with the future indicative of many verbs, and with the (original) sigmatic aorist subjunctive (in most dialects, though not in Arkadian, which has only the secondary 2sg. and 3sg. endings—see above). The next stage was the addition of -ε to disambiguate the form, yielding the -σ-ειε familiar in Attic-Ionic; from other dialects Buck (1955: 121) cites Lesbian δ]ιαδέξειε 'shows clearly' *IG* XII-2.527.57 and Elean κατιαραύσειε 'brings a charge' *DGE* 409.2. On that specific form were modeled 2sg. -ειας and 3pl. -ειαν; that the 3sg. was the starting point explains why there is no 1sg. '-εια' (a fact which puzzled Buck, *loc. cit.*, and Forbes 1958b: 174). Of course there was an alternative, namely sigmatic aorist -σα-ι- parallel to thematic -ο-ι-; that straightforward innovation is unsurprisingly widespread. Elean ἀδεαλτώhαιε 'defaces, renders illegible' *DGE* 424.12 can only represent a conflation of the two types.[9]

[9] This scenario strikes me as more realistic than that of Forbes (1958b), both because she relies on proportional analogy based on the *passive* aorist, which is unexpected, and because the scenario preferred here offers answers to all the details that puzzled Forbes.

7.3.3 Perfect stems

I noted in 4.2.3 (i) that in active perfects made to roots ending in vowels -κ- at first occurred only in the indicative singular and the subjunctive, and that while such a distribution is still largely visible in Homer, in later Greek it survives only in a few very common perfects, especially ἕστηκε 'is standing upright' and τέθνηκε 'is dead'. To that generalization there are two exceptions in Greek inscriptions.

Boiotian preserves the original distribution of -κ- down through the 2nd century BC at least as well as Homer does. Here is a list of the relatively intact Boiotian active perfects made to vowel-final roots that are known to me (Ringe 1984: 172–86):

ἀντέθεικẹ	καταβεβάων
διεσσείλθεικε	κạ[ταβε]βλειώσᾱς
παρκέκλεικε	ἀποδεδοάνθι, δεδωῶσα ἴη, δεδωῶση
ἐπ]ομώμοκε	πεπιτευόντεσσι
	πεποιόντεισσι
	ϝεϝῡκονομειόντων
	ἀπειλθείοντες
	ἀφειώσᾱς

The distribution is obvious. The only exception, ἐκτεθήκανθι *DGE* 450.6, is an inscription from Aigosthena showing substantial Megarian influence; not only the κ but also the η are Doric rather than Boiotian.

The other exception is Arkadian, and it is early. In *DGE* 661.1 we find [ϝō]φλε̄́ασι 'they owe' beside ϝōφλε̄κόσι 'in the case of those who owe' 661.18; clearly -κ- has already begun to spread, though not to the 3pl. yet. Jeffery (1991: 214) dates it to the middle of the 5th century. In later Arkadian inscriptions -κ- has spread throughout the paradigm to the same extent as in Attic; relevant 4th-century forms are ἀπυδεδωκώς *DGE* 657.44, κατηνθηκότι 657.39, λελαβηκώς 656.14, ἐφθορκώς 656.10–11, and optative ἰγκεχηρήκοι 'has begun' 656.12.

Finally, a word should be said about thematized forms of the perfect. The thematic participles of Lesbian, Thessalian, and Boiotian have been mentioned in 5.2.1, and thematic perfect infinitives and modal forms appear in various dialects. Thematic perfect indicatives are much less common, and it seems worth noting that they appear most often in the extreme southeast of insular Doric (Buck 1955: 118), apparently a local innovation.

8
Syntax

So far as can be determined, Ancient Greek syntax had undergone little change from PIE (on which, see 2.5 above). Innovations have affected all the dialects more or less equally; as Buck remarks, syntactic differences between the dialects are modest and mostly amount to the preservation of archaisms (Buck 1955: 136). The following developments seem worth mentioning.

8.1 Constituent order

The largest scale change in Greek syntax is exceptionally difficult to see in the texts because of the great flexibility of Greek word order. It is clear enough that PIE clauses were underlyingly verb-final; it is equally clear that the Greek of the *New Testament* is underlyingly verb-medial. Obviously a major shift in word order has occurred, but when and how?

Taylor (1990) was able to answer that question by an investigation of Homeric word order; her discussion (pp. 82–95) should be read in its entirety, but the crucial points are easily summarized. It is taken for granted that movement rules do not move two or more constituents together, simply because rules that did would be too difficult for native learners to learn. Given that premise, the fact that Greek noun phrases and even parts of noun phrases can be 'scrambled' extensively becomes a powerful tool for determining the underlying order of constituents in a clause (pp. 86–91). It is commonplace in Homer to find discontinuous noun phrases of which one part precedes the verb and another follows; there are also discontinuous noun phrases of which both parts precede the verb. In a sample including *Iliad* 1 and 2.1–264, Taylor found that if both parts precede the verb one part is always in clause-initial position. Here are her figures for that sample, where # indicates the beginning of the clause and the two X's the two parts of the DP (Taylor 1990: 90 with notes 3 and 4 p. 129):

configuration	*number*	*percentage*	
#X...X...V	15	13%	
#...X...V...X	35	31%	
#X...V...X	62	55%	(N = 112)

There was only one example in which both parts of a discontinuous NP followed the verb. Since at least one part is almost always preverbal, the most economical

The Linguistic Roots of Ancient Greek. Don Ringe, Oxford University Press.
© Don Ringe (2024). DOI: 10.1093/9780191989162.003.0008

analysis is that Homeric Greek is underlyingly verb-final, and that postverbal NP's and parts of NP's result from movement rules. That is corroborated by the behavior of the complements of verbs that take two complements (Taylor 1990: 91–5). A complete survey of finite forms of διδοῦναι 'give' and τιθήμεναι 'put', the two commonest such verbs, yielded the following results (where '+O' indicates part of a complement):

configuration	*number*	*percentage*	
OOV	69	47%	
OVO	46	31%	
OOV+O	15	10%	
VOO	10	7%	
OV+OO	5	3%	
OOV+O+O	1	1%	(N = 146)

Even the raw numbers and percentages strongly suggest a verb-final underlying order. But Taylor proceeds to test the two hypotheses, verb-final and verb-medial, against the above data and corresponding data for the single-object verbs τῑ́ε̄ν 'honor', κτε̄́νε̄ν 'kill', and αἱρε̄ν 'take'. Under the verb-final hypothesis she finds (p. 94):

verb-final hypothesis

number of moves	*pattern*	*2-object*	*verbs*	*1-object*	*verbs*
0	(O)OV	69	47%	111	43%
1	(O)VO	46	31%	93	36%
2	(O)OV+O, VOO	25	17%	55	21%
3 or more	OVO+O, OOV+O+O	6	4%	(NA)	

Under the verb-medial hypothesis Taylor finds (p. 95):

verb-medial hypothesis

number of moves	*pattern*	*2-object*	*verbs*	*1-object*	*verbs*
0	VO(O)	10	7%	93	36%
1	OV(O)	46	31%	111	43%
2	+OV(O), OOV	74	50%	55	21%
3 or more	+OOVO, +O+OVOO	16	11%	(NA)	

Under the verb-final hypothesis the incidence of each pattern decreases monotonically as the number of moves required to attain it increases, both for double-complement and for single-object verbs; under the verb-medial hypothesis the numbers make no sense at all. It follows that the underlying order of constituents in Homeric Greek was verb-final.

Since similar tests reveal that the koine Greek of the *New Testament* was verb-medial (Taylor 1990: 151), the shift must have occurred within the documented history of Ancient Greek. Similar shifts in the documented history of English have been studied intensively, and it is clear that they occur gradually, with the innovative alternative slowly increasing in incidence, generation after generation, at a constant rate, so long as relevant conditions do not change (see especially Kroch 1989 for exemplification and discussion). Taylor makes a strong case that the competition between the two alternatives was well underway in the 5th century, arguing from the position of clitics (Taylor 1990: 153–64).

But what does it mean, in real terms, to say that there is a robust competition between two alternative underlying constituent orders? Readers unfamiliar with generative syntax need to remember that it is **NOT a model of language production**; no one is suggesting that in the production of a sentence the speaker begins with the underlying order and then literally moves constituents around. The coexistence of two underlying orders actually means that native learners cannot figure out which of the two is the basic, unmarked order for statements where no special emphasis is required. Native learners are clearly programmed to find a basic, unmarked constituent order in the language they are learning natively; that is why there is an obvious unmarked order in each of thousands of languages, every one of which has been re-created by its native learners in every generation. Yang (2002: 34–6) suggests a simple model for how native learners might zero in on the correct solution from data which are often ambiguous: in effect, each of the possible hypotheses is penalized for every utterance heard which it cannot account for, and the hypothesis that accrues the smallest number of penalties is eventually adopted by the native learner. Usually one hypothesis wins, but not always; if the learner constantly hears alternatives which simply cannot be predicted from a single underlying configuration, (s)he will posit two. It seems that that was the situation in post-Homeric Ancient Greek for many generations.

8.2 Prohibitions

It is fairly commonplace for IE languages to treat prohibitions, or negative commands, somewhat differently from positive commands. In Spanish, for instance, it is simply ungrammatical to use the sentential negative *no* with an imperative; even to a small child[1] you cannot say **¡No lo haz!*—you must instead use the subjunctive: *¡No lo hagas!* 'Don't do it!' Ancient Greek is no exception, but the details of its grammatical rules might reveal something about its prehistory.

While it is normal to express an imperfective prohibition in Greek—i.e. 'stop Xing' or 'don't (ever) X'—by μή with the present imperative, it is normal to express a perfective prohibition—'don't X (which you were about to do)'—by μή with the aorist *subjunctive* (Smyth 1956: 409–11). In terms of the synchronic grammar of

[1] Using an imperative with almost anyone else is of course rude in Spanish.

Ancient Greek that doesn't make much sense, but it does suggest that at some point in the past the use of a sentential negative with an imperative was not normal; that such a rule survives (even if restructured) only in the aorist can be attributed to the fact that perfective prohibitions are much more typical and are more often heard by native learners.

That surmise is supported by details of the grammars of (at least) Hittite, Tocharian, Vedic, and Latin. In Hittite, which has no subjunctive or optative, the prohibitive negative *lē* is used with the present rather than with the imperative (Hoffner and Melchert 2008: 344). The same is usually true in Tocharian, which does have a subjunctive and optative; in the Tocharian B caravan passes one finds, for instance, *ceṃ parra ptārka; tesa auṣap mā tärkanat* 'let these through; more than that do not let (through)', where *ptārka* is an imperative (clearly marked by its prefix *p-*) while *tärkanat* is the corresponding present 2sg. In Vedic the prohibitive negative *mā́* is used with an *injunctive*, i.e. a secondary indicative with no augment; a typical example is *mā́ na Indra párā vr̥ṇak* 'do not abandon us, Indra!' *RV* VIII.97.7, the corresponding imperative being *vr̥ṅdʰi*. In Latin, as many readers of this book will be aware, *nē* is normally used in prohibitions only with the perfect subjunctive, e.g. *nē crēdiderīs* 'don't believe (it)!', in which the verb form has the inherited perfective sense rather than the innovative anterior sense, much like a Greek aorist subjunctive (though etymologically the Latin form is an optative).

What are we to make of this configuration of facts? Even though Hittite is attested just as early and both it and Tocharian are outliers in the diversification of the IE family, Vedic might hold the key to this puzzle. In principle, an injunctive is temporally and modally unspecified: it marks person, number, aspect, and voice, but not tense or mood (Hoffmann 1967a). It therefore makes sense to use an injunctive with a negative which already clearly marks a prohibition, necessarily for the (possibly immediate) future. What we need to figure out is what this implies for the reconstruction of the PIE verb. In particular, since an injunctive is a form with secondary endings but no augment, does it follow that the augment was part of the inherited verb system?

It does not, for the following reasons. Even the structure of the person-and-number endings shows that the secondary endings were unmarked in PIE (see 2.3.3 (iii)); it should follow that they did not mark past tense but simply failed to mark present tense. The use of prohibitive negative *mḗ with such unmarked forms follows automatically. The fact that its successors are used with the present in Hittite and Tocharian must then reflect a shift in the markedness of inflectional categories. In Indo-Iranian the use of the augment as a past tense marker narrowed the function of the unaugmented form to tenselessness. What happened in Greek and Latin must have been more complex. Gothic actually provides a clue: the phrase *ni ogs þus* 'do not be afraid' (four times) includes an aberrant verb form that can only reflect pre-Gothic *ōgiz < *-es, the expected outcome of an injunctive in Germanic.[2] It seems worth suggesting that in some branches of the family the original construction with a verb form unmarked for tense or mood was replaced by an overtly modal form because the marking of verb forms had shifted, as in Anatolian and Tocharian; the details are likely to have been different in each branch.

8.3 Moods

One function of the PIE subjunctive, the expression of future time, has largely been taken over by the innovative future tense in Greek (though there are Homeric examples in which the use of the subjunctive is still close to that of a future; see Chantraine 1963: 209–10). In main clauses the Greek subjunctive still expresses exhortations or (in the 1sg.) the intention of the speaker. Its use in deliberative questions is much like that of Vedic and is probably inherited; its use with μή to express that the speaker does not want something to happen resembles its use with *néd* (i.e. *ná íd*, where *íd* is emphatic) in Vedic, and although the negative employed is not the same, it seems likely that there is some historical connection between the two constructions.

However, many uses of the Greek subjunctive are not closely paralleled in Indo-Iranian, the only other branch of the family that clearly retains both cognate subjunctives and cognate optatives.[3] In particular, the use of the subjunctive with ἄν (/ κεν/κα, depending on the dialect) in subordinate clauses is clearly a Greek innovation. Most striking is the 'future more vivid' conditional construction, with the subjunctive and ἄν in the conditional clause and the future in the main clause. It looks as though the subjunctive might at first have been used in both clauses, only to be replaced by the future in the main clause once that innovative inflectional category was well established. But even such a construction with the subjunctive in both clauses would have been a Greek innovation.

The Greek optative has remained closer to its ancestral roots, expressing the wishes of the speaker and potential events. But once again its use with ἄν, and most of its uses in subordinate clauses, are Greek innovations. The tendency to use optatives in subordinate clauses dominated by a main clause in a past tense, but subjunctives in those dominated by a non-past tense, is certainly a Greek innovation; there is nothing like it in Vedic, and the Latin sequence-of-tenses rule is different in detail and must be a parallel innovation.

[2] The form is also used in a positive command at *Romans* 11:20 and 13:4, in the former case immediately following a prohibition; it seems reasonable to suggest an extension of the original usage in prohibitions.

[3] The Tocharian subjunctives are largely of different origin; in Italic the PIE subjunctive has become a future tense, while in Celtic the subjunctive and optative seem to have undergone syntactic merger.

Finally, the use of augmented past tenses in contrary-to-fact conditions, typically with ἄν in the main clause, must also be a Greek innovation. In general, using a past tense to represent an unreal situation is a natural development—many languages, including English, use past tenses that way—but it is interesting that a language provided with a rich repertory of categories that could be irrealis has resorted to past indicative forms as well.

8.4 Univerbation

I noted in 2.5 that in all the earliest attested daughters of PIE (and in many others) some adverbs are used as preverbs, and that they were eventually 'univerbated' with their verbs. The process of univerbation can be followed by comparison of the most archaic IE languages. In Hittite only the preverbs *pe-* and *u-*, which have no certain cognates in the non-Anatolian languages, have undergone univerbation with their verbs (Hoffner and Melchert 2008: 296); all the others are separate phonological words. Of the latter, the following have (at least approximate) cognates in Greek:

anda 'into'	cf. ἐν 'in(to)'
āppa 'back'	cf. ἐπί 'on(to)', Myc. *o-pi-*[4]
katta 'down'	= κατά
parā 'out, forth'	= πρό

In Vedic univerbation is rule-governed: it always occurs in subordinate clauses and in nominal forms, but never in main clauses. Several Vedic preverbs have cognates in Greek:

ánu 'along'	cf. ἀνά 'up, along'
ápa 'away, off'	= ἀπό
ápi 'close to, on'	= ἐπί, Myc. *o-pi-*
ab^h*í* 'up to, against'	= ἀμφί 'on both sides of'
úpa 'toward'	= ὑπό
pári 'around'	= περί
prá 'forward'	= πρό
práti 'back'	= πρός 'toward'

In addition, the preposition *upári* 'over, above', which is not used as a preverb, is cognate with Gk ὑπέρ.

The only Greek preverbs not mentioned above are ἀντί 'instead of', διά 'through', ἐξ 'out of', μετά (πεδά) 'with, after', παρά 'beside', and ξύν (σύν) 'with', as well as the clearly innovative ἐς 'into' (see 5.4.2); most have at least approximate cognates

[4] Probably not ἀπο- 'off, away', the meaning of which is completely different.

elsewhere in the IE family, preverbs or prepositions or both (cf. Lat. *ante*, *ex*, *dis-*, Goth. *miþ*, *faúr*, Arm. *yet*; the discussion of Brugmann 1911: 758–930 is still useful). Univerbation seems already to have occurred in Mycenaean Greek and is universal in post-Homeric prose, but the fact that it is still optional in Homer shows that it spread through the dialect continuum.

8.5 Clitics

Homeric Greek preserves 'Wackernagel's Law', the rule placing clitics in second position within the clause, without modification: not only clause clitics, but also indefinite pronouns and unstressed personal pronouns form a clitic chain after a clause-initial constituent (often a single accented word). In later Greek that is still an option, but clitics are also found in other positions. Taylor (1990: 133–64) demonstrates, with numerous examples, that post-Homeric clitics which do not 'float' into second position in the clause are instead positioned within the constituents in which they originate, typically DP or VP.

The order of clitics in a chain seems to be fixed in certain cases but not in others (see the observations of Denniston 1954: lx–lxi). Comparison of one particular collocation across dialects shows that at least some orders must have shifted over time. Attic ἐὰν δέ τις and Ionic ἤν δέ τις exhibit the order 'if' + ἄν + δέ + indefinite; but we find the positions of δέ and ἄν switched in Arkadian (εἰ δ' ἄν ϰις), Lesbian (αἰ δέ κέ τις), and Thessalian (αἰ μά κέ κις), while West Greek instead has αἰ δέ τίς κα and Boiotian shows variation between the last two options (Buck 1955: 140). Obviously no more than one of these orders can be original, to the extent that the order was fixed at all.

8.6 Prepositions

Whether or not PIE had prepositions, all attested stages of Greek do. It is noteworthy that the list of inherited prepositions is identical with that of preverbs; that is similar to the Vedic situation and could be inherited from their last common parent. Differences between the dialects are almost entirely differences of detail (Buck 1955: 106–10); the following seem worth mentioning. The difference in shape between Att.-Ion. πρός, Hom. προτί, Cretan πορτί on the one hand and Arkadian πός, West Greek πότ on the other is actually inherited: the former is cognate with Vedic *práti*, the latter with Avestan *paiti*. The most significant difference in usage is that in Arkadian and Cyprian prepositions which in other dialects govern the genitive normally govern the dative (Buck 1955: 108); because of the isolation of Cyprian in the 1st millennium, that common innovation must go back roughly to the Mycenaean period.

8.7 Reflexives

It seems likely that in PIE reflexives and reciprocals were expressed by the mediopassive voice (see 2.3.1), much like the derived reflexive and reciprocal verbs of Semitic and Algonkian languages. No attested daughter preserves that situation unaltered, however. Mediopassive verbs can still be used reflexively in Tocharian, e.g.:

Toch. B *ārwer yamaṣṣamnte.* 'We have made ourselves ready.'

But it is more usual to use an overt reflexive pronoun, e.g.:

Toch. B *wnolmi tallāñco nāksante ṣañ-añm* 'wretched beings blamed themselves' (cited by Adams 2015: 152).

In Hittite reflexives and reciprocals are still expressed by mediopassives but are also usually marked by the particle *-z(a)*, e.g.:

kinuna=wa[5] *ehu, nu=wa zahhiyauwastati* 'Come now, let us do battle with each other' (Hoffner and Melchert 308: 314).

In Core IE, the 3sg. pronoun *swé- ~ *se- (attested in Hittite as enclitic dat. *=sse* 'to him/her') has been repurposed as a reflexive pronoun, but that development seems to have occurred in the independent prehistories of the branches.

Middle verb forms are no longer used as explicit reflexives in Greek, though some are naturally translated as reflexive, e.g. παρασκευάζεσθαι 'prepare (oneself), get prepared'; the implicit object cannot be modified by another word. The middle voice does survive, however, to express an implicit relation between the object of the verb and the subject. The situation in Vedic is similar, though it evolved independently.

In Homer ἕ ~ ἑ seems to be used both as a reflexive and as an ordinary third-person pronoun, partly with a difference in accent; in subordinate clauses ἑ and μιν seem to be used in much the same way (Chantraine 1963: 153–4). The pronoun αὐτός is emphatic only, not reflexive. In post-Homeric Greek a shift in function has occurred: αὐτόν, etc., is usually used with ἐμέ, σέ, ἕ, etc., when they are reflexive within the same clause, but not when they occur in a subordinate clause (Smyth 1956: 304–6). Thus the development of αὐτός in Ancient Greek is more or less the same as that of *self* in Middle English (Vezzosi 2007).

5 *-wa* is the quotative particle.

9
Lexicon

9.1 Derivational morphology

Most of the PIE stem-forming suffixes and compound types discussed in 2.4 survive in Ancient Greek, some remaining productive; here I will summarize some early Greek innovations, few of which can be dated relative to any other development. Debrunner (1917) and Risch (1974) provide good overviews in detail, while Buck and Petersen (1949) is an exhaustive list of examples of suffixes; all three offer valuable discussion and references.

Two types of compound that are apparently confined to Greek and Indo-Iranian have a verbal first member governing the second (Brugmann 1906: 63–4). In one type the first member is an aspect stem; typical are Rigvedic Skt *Trasádasyus* 'terrifying the enemy' and Hom. ἀρχέκακος 'starting trouble, troublemaker', Τληπόλεμος 'enduring battle'. In the other type the first member ends in *-ti-, e.g. Rigvedic Skt *vītíhotras* 'inviting to the sacrifice', Hom. βωτιάνε̄ρα 'nourishing men', τερψίμβροτος 'delighting mortals'. To judge from their distribution, these types must have arisen toward the eastern end of the Central IE dialect continuum. They remained productive in Greek, especially in coining personal names.

A first member of compounds that appears only in Greek and Indo-Iranian is ἀγα- 'very', e.g. in Hom. ἀγά-ννιφος 'very snowy' (νν < *sn, Aiolism; see 5.2.2), Ἀγαμέμνων 'Very-steadfast'; it is cognate with Avestan *aš-* 'great', e.g. in *aš.bāzāuš* 'with big arms', *aš.miždå* 'bringing great reward', both reflecting *m̥ǵh$_2$-, zero grade of *meǵh$_2$- 'big'.

There is also a derivational suffix peculiar to Greek and Indo-Iranian (Risch 1974: 150–1 with references); it appears in Sanskrit as *-tvaná-* (e.g. *mahitvanám* 'size'; cf. Whitney 1889: 477–8) and in Greek as -σύνᾱ (e.g. Hom. δο̄λοσύνη 'slavery'). Greek adjectives in -συνος are much rarer and usually attested later (Debrunner 1917: 162); they might be secondary developments.

Neuter nouns in *-mn̥ and r/n-stems have lost their original ablaut alternations but acquired a -τ- in their oblique stems; the oblique suffix -ατ- then spread to other neuter nouns denoting body parts (e.g. Hom. ο̃ς, ο̃ατ- 'ear', Att. γόνυ, γόνατ- 'knee'). The source of the -τ- remains unknown; the supposed parallel of Lat. *-men* and *-mentum* is not very helpful, since the longer Latin stem includes a known suffix *-to-.

The Linguistic Roots of Ancient Greek. Don Ringe, Oxford University Press.
 DOI: 10.1093/9780191989162.003.0009

Verbal adjectives in *-tó- remained derived adjectives in Greek; they did not become participles, as they did in Indo-Iranian, Balto-Slavic, Germanic, Celtic, and Italic. But Greek also developed extended verbal adjectives in -τέος; though the origin of the suffix is unclear, the fact that it does not undergo vowel contraction suggests that it was originally *-τέϝος. Surprisingly, these adjectives are almost completely absent from Greek verse, though they are abundant in prose; see Buck and Petersen (1949: 530) for discussion and references.

Agent nouns in -τήρ and -τωρ survive in Greek (δοτήρ, γενέτωρ, etc.), but over time they were replaced by masculine ᾱ-stems in -τᾱς > Att.-Ion. -της; a good brief discussion is Buck and Petersen (1949: 544–6). From that base the formation was broadened to denote male persons connected with an activity or institution; πολῑ́της is an obvious example.

Many of the most characteristic Greek suffixes appear to be purely Greek creations. The most striking is -εύς, -ήϝ-, originally denoting a person having a specific skill or office and already firmly in place in Mycenaean Greek (*ka-ke-u* 'smith', *i-je-re-u* 'priest', *qa-si-re-u* 'baron', or the like, etc.); Torsten Meissner has made a strong case that this suffix entered the language as a component of loanwords (Meissner 2016: 27–8; see 4.3.3 above). Buck and Petersen (1949: 27) discusses the development of this suffix in Greek.

Almost equally puzzling are the noun suffixes ending in -δ-. δεκάδ-, at least, might preserve the original final consonant of *dék̂m̥d, and the suffix can have spread to other numerals, just as ἀλλοδαπός, etc., might preserve the original final consonant of neut. *ályod (Debrunner 1917: 189). But for the most part -άδ- and -ίδ- have no clear antecedents. Nouns with the latter are already fairly numerous in Homer (e.g. ἀσπίς 'shield', ἐλπίς 'hope', δαΐδες 'torches'), and there are at least a few with the former (e.g. νιφάδες 'snowflakes'); both suffixes are productive in later Greek.

Of the suffixes ending in the thematic vowel, -ικός competes with inherited -ιος to form adjectives indicating connection with the base word; -ίσκο- (all genders) and neut. -ιον are productive diminutive suffixes. All three suffixes are inherited, but their distinctive functions are Greek innovations.

There are dialect differences in noun and adjective formation which show that the development of various derivational types was comparatively recent (see especially Buck 1955: 130–5). Two details are striking. Lesbian and Thessalian routinely construct adjectives of material in -ιος, whereas other dialects have -εος or (especially) -ινος; thus we find Lesb. neut. χρῡ́σιον Sappho 1.8 but Hom. χρῡ́σεον, Att. χρῡσοῦν, Thess. λίθιος but Hom. λίθεος, while most post-Homeric dialects have λίθινος, and so on. Lesbian and Thessalian also have patronymic adjectives in -ιος, which is probably an archaism, since *-yo- ~ *-io- was a productive suffix in PIE. Other dialects had an originally patronymic suffix -ίδᾱς (> Att.-Ion. -ίδης), -άδᾱς, possibly an extension of fem. -ίδ-, -άδ- (Debrunner

1917: 192), which eventually lost its patronymic force and became a component of names (Buck and Petersen 1949: 441–2) except in West Argolic (see e.g. *DGE* 89.2–5, 91.3–4). In Boiotian that suffix too has been extended, yielding -ώνδᾱς (with syncope of -ι-), and the new suffix has begun to spread to adjacent areas (Buck 1955: 131).

Of the inherited types of derived present stems (see 4.2.1 (v)), denominative contract verbs continue to be productive throughout the history of Ancient Greek, especially α- and ε-contracts; ο-contracts mostly remain specialized for factitive and instrumental verbs. Also very productive are presents in -εύε̄ν, -αίνε̄ν, -ῡ́νε̄ν, -ίζε̄ν, and -άζε̄ν; all five types are already well developed in Homer (see Risch 1974: 289–307), and their subsequent development is conveniently summarized in Debrunner (1917: 104–40). It is worth noting (though not really surprising) that all these productive formations were originally presents in *-yé/ó-, the last syllable coda of the original base having been resegmented to yield a recognizable suffix. All have acquired regular futures, aorists, and perfects in post-Homeric Greek (and to some extent already in Homer).

9.2 Sources of the Greek lexicon

The Greek lexicon, like every other, includes numerous words that do not have solid etymologies. Examination of the Swadesh hundred-word list[1] for Classical Attic gives an idea of the situation.

Half the words on the list have good cognates with the same meanings in other IE languages and were obviously inherited (though some have been remodeled); I list them here with a cognate each (verbs in the pres. indic. 3sg. for ease of comparison):

all (pl.)	πάντες	TB *poñc*
big	μέγας	Skt neut. *máhi*
bite	δάκνει	Skt causative *daṃśayati*
bone	ὀστõν	Hitt. *hastai*
claw	ὄνυξ	Lat. *unguis*
cloud	νέφος	Skt *nábʰas*
come	προσέρχεται	(see 'go')
dog	κύων	Skt *śvā́*
drink	πῑ́νει	Skt ptc. *pītás*

[1] Morris Swadesh devised this list for anthropological linguists who wanted to assess quickly the probable relationships of previously undiscovered languages. As has long been known, it is not an ideal list for any purpose, but it is at least a list of basic vocabulary items which were selected for very different purposes and is thus free of relevant bias.

ear	ὀ̄̃ς	Lat. *auris*
eat	ἐσθίει	Hitt. *ēz'zi*
egg	ᾠιόν	Lat. *ōvom*
feather	πτερόν	TB pl. *paruwa*
fire	πῦρ	Hitt. *pahhur*
fish	ἰχθῦς	Lith. *žuvìs*
fly	πέτεται	Skt *pátati*
foot	πό̄ς	Skt *pā́t*
give	δίδωσι	Skt *dádāti*
go	ἔρχεται	OIr. iptv. *eirgg*
hand	χέ̄ρ	Hitt. *kissar*
head	κεφαλή	Toch. A *śpāl*
heart	καρδίᾱ	Hitt. *kart-*
horn	κέρας	Lat. *cornū*
hot	θερμός	Arm. *ǰerm*
I	ἐγώ	Lat. *ego*
knee	γόνυ	Hitt. *gēnu*
know	οἶδε	Skt *véda*
lie	κεῖται	Hitt. *kitta*
liver	ἧπαρ	Skt *yákr̥t*
man	ἀνήρ	Skt *nā́*
many	πολλοί	Skt neut. *purū́*
meat	κρέας	Skt *kravís*
mouth	στόμα	Av. *staman-*
name	ὄνομα	Hitt. *lāman*
night	νύξ	Vedic Skt *nák*
one	ἕ̄ς	Hitt. gen. *siēl*
red	ἐρυθρός	Lat. *ruber*
sit	κάθηται	Hitt. *esa*
stand	ἕστηκε	Vedic Skt *tast*^{h}*áu*
star	ἀστήρ	Hitt. *hasterz*
sun	ἥλιος	Vedic Skt *súar*
swim	νήχει	Skt *snā́ti*
tooth	ὀδό̄ς	Skt *dán*
two	δύο	Skt *dvā́*
water	ὕδωρ	Hitt. *wātar*
we	ἡμε͂ς	Skt acc. *asmā́n*
what	τί	Hitt. *kuit*
who	τίς	Hitt. *kuis*
woman	γυνή	Vedic Skt *jánī*
you (sg.)	σύ	Lat. *tū*

Another seventeen words based on inherited roots have undergone various derivational processes and/or shifts of meaning in Greek:

ashes	τέφρᾱ	cf. Skt *dáhati* '(s)he burns (it)'
bird	ὄρνῑς	cf. Hitt. *hāran-* 'eagle'
eye	ὀφθαλμός	cf. TB *ek*
full	πλήρης	cf. Lat. *plēnus*
green	χλωρός	cf. OCS *zelenŭ*
hear	ἀκούει	= Goth. *hauseiþ*, but both < *h_2ḱ-$h_2$ows-iéti '(s)he is sharp-eared'
kill	ἀποκτε̄́νει	cf. Skt *kṣaṇóti* 'destroys'
long	μακρός	= Lat. *macer* 'thin'
mountain	ὄρος	s-stem neut. deriv. of ὄρνυσθαι 'rise'
path	πάτος	cf. Skt *pánt^{h}ās*? —but stressed zero-grade *pn̥̓t- is odd
rain	ῡ̔ετός	cf. TB verb *suwaṃ*
sand	ἄμμος	cf. Hom. ἄμαθος = Middle High German *sambt*; apparently the Attic form has been crossed with ψάμμος (etymology uncertain)
say	λέγει	= Lat. *legit* 'collects; reads'
tail	ὀρᾱ́	orig. collective of *ὄρσος 'arse'
that	ἐκε̄͂νος	deriv. of ἐκεῖ 'there', probably built on *ḱi- ~ *ḱe- 'this'
this	οὗτος	built on the article, details unclear
tree	δένδρον	(< δένδρε(ϝ)ον; deriv. of *dóru 'tree, wood', but details obscure)
white	λευκός	cf. Lat. *lūx* 'light'

But more than thirty of these basic words are unetymologized, or of uncertain etymology:[2]

bark	φλοιός
belly	γαστήρ (*γραστήρ 'eater' implausible on semantic grounds)
black	μέλᾱς
blood	αἷμα
breast	μαστός (connected with Hom. μαζός, but not clear how)
burn (intr.)	κᾱ́εται (< καίεται, root καϝ-)
cold	ψῡχρός (deriv. of ψῡ́χε̄ν 'blow')
die	ἀποθνήισκει (root θαν(α)- ~ θνη-)
dry	ξηρός
earth	γῆ
good	ἀγαθός
grease	δημός
hair	θρίξ
human	ἄνθρωπος
leaf	φύλλον
louse	φθέρ
moon	σελήνη (deriv. of σέλας 'torch')
neck	αὐχήν
new	καινός
nose	ῥίς
not	οὐ (etymology disputed: < *h$_2$óyu̯ 'life', with semantic and syntactic development like French *pas* 'not', orig. 'step' < Lat. *passus*?; see Cowgill 1960)
root	ῥίζα
round	στρογγύλος
see	ὁρᾶι
seed	σπέρμα (deriv. of σπε̄́ρε̄ν 'sow')
skin	χρόᾱ (cf. Hom. χρώς)
sleep	καθεύδει
small	μῑκρός
smoke	καπνός
stone	λίθος
tongue	γλῶττα
yellow	ξανθός

2 I should say here that my standards are stricter than those of many etymological dictionaries. The goal of a traditional etymological dictionary is to find a source for every word, so that uncertain or even barely plausible hypotheses are worth reporting; but that is not easily compatible with scientific historical linguistics, of which the goal is to figure out what is most likely to have happened and reject everything judged insufficiently probable.

It may seem surprising that one-third of the basic vocabulary cannot be accounted for etymologically, but in fact Greek is not out of line with other ancient IE languages in that respect. The IE 'homeland', wherever it was exactly, must have been fairly small; otherwise a unitary PIE would not be reconstructable. Almost every attested IE language was a language of immigrants who must have borrowed words from the (often larger) populations that they encountered in their new homes.

Place names and plant names containing -νθ- and -σσ- (or -ττ-) constitute a clearly recognizable pre-Greek stratum of vocabulary (Schwyzer 1939: 510–11, Buck and Petersen 1949: 444–5). Well-known examples include ἄψινθος, τερέβινθος and (in Attica) Ὑμηττός, Προβάλινθος, (elsewhere) Παρνασσός, Κόρινθος, Ζάκυνθος, Τίρυνς (-νθ-). Discussions of the origins of these suffixes are necessarily speculative. Some other words can be identified as loanwords by their distribution in the ancient Mediterranean; obvious examples are μᾶλον (Att.-Ion. μῆλον) 'apple' (cf. Lat. *mālum*), πράσον 'leek' (cf. Lat. *porrum*), οἶνος 'wine' (cf. Lat. *vīnum*), and probably γάλα, γάλακτ- 'milk' (cf. Lat. *lac, lact-*). The sources for such prehistoric loanwords are typically not identifiable (see Frisk s.vv.). Later loanwords can often be etymologized; for example, it seems clear that χρῡσός is a Northwest Semitic loanword (see Frisk s.v.).

Bibliography

Adams, Douglas Q. (ed.) 1997. *Festschrift for Eric P. Hamp*. Washington, DC: Institute for the Study of Man.

Adams, Douglas Q. 2015. *Tocharian B: A grammar of syntax and word-formation*. Innsbruck: Institut für Sprachen und Literaturen der Universität Innsbruck.

Agbayani, Brian, and Chris Golston. 2010. Phonological movement in Classical Greek. *Language* 86: 133–67

Anthony, David. 2007. *The horse, the wheel, and language*. Princeton: Princeton University Press.

Anthony, David, and Don Ringe. 2015. The Indo-European homeland from linguistic and archaeological perspectives. *Annual Review of Linguistics* 1: 199–219.

Anttila, Raimo. 1969. *Proto-Indo-European Schwebeablaut*. Berkeley: University of California Press (= University of California Publications in Linguistics 58).

Aura Jorro, Francisco. 1999. *Diccionario micénico*. Madrid: Consejo Superior de Investigaciones Científicas.

Bammesberger, Alfred (ed.) 1988. *Die Laryngaltheorie und die Rekonstruktion der indogermanischen Laut- und Formensystems*. Heidelberg: Winter.

Barber, Peter J. 2013. *Sievers' Law and the history of semivowel syllabicity in Indo-European and Ancient Greek*. Oxford: Oxford University Press.

Barton, Charles R. 1993. Greek τέθηπα, etc. *Glotta* 71: 1–9.

Bartoněk, Antonín. 1966. *Development of the long vowel system in Ancient Greek dialects*. Prague: Státní Pedagogické Nakladelství.

Bartoněk, Antonín. 1971. Das Ostargolische in der räumlichen Gliederung Griechenlands. Schmitt-Brandt, Robert (ed.), *Donum indogermanicum. Festgabe für Anton Scherer zum 70. Geburtstag*. Heidelberg: Winter, 118–22.

Bartoněk, Antonín. 2002. *Handbuch des mykenischen Griechisch*. Heidelberg: Winter.

Bechtel, Friedrich. 1921. *Die griechischen Dialekte*. 1. Band. *Der lesbische, thessalische, böotische, arkadische, und kyprische dialect*. Berlin: Weidmann.

Bechtel, Friedrich. 1923. *Die griechischen Dialekte*. 2. Band. *Die westgriechischen Dialekte*. Berlin: Weidmann.

Bechtel, Friedrich. 1924. *Die griechischen Dialekte*. 3. Band. *Der ionische Dialekt*. Berlin: Weidmann.

Beek, Lucien van. 2022. *The reflexes of syllabic liquids in Ancient Greek*. Leiden: Brill.

Beekes, R. S. P. 1969. *The development of the Proto-Indo-European laryngeals in Greek*. The Hague: Mouton.

Beekes, R. S. P. 1972. H_2O. *Die Sprache* 18: 117–31.

Beekes, R. S. P. 2011. *Comparative Indo-European linguistics: An introduction*, 2nd ed. Amsterdam: Benjamins.

Beekes, R. S. P. 2013. *Etymological dictionary of Greek*. Leiden: Brill.

Bendahman, Jadwiga. 1993. *Der reduplizierte Aorist in den indogermanischen Sprachen*. Dissertation, Albert-Ludwigs-Universität zu Freiburg.

Benveniste, Émile. 1937. Hittite *ḫatugi*. Hjelmslev, Louis (ed.), *Mélanges linguistiques offerts à M. Holger Pedersen*. Aarhus: Universitetsforlaget, 496–9.

Benveniste, Émile. 1951. Prétérit et optatif en indo-européen. *Bulletin de la Société Linguistique de Paris* 47: 11–20.
Berg, Nils. 1977. Der Ursprung des altgriechischen aktiven Plusquamperfekts und die Entwicklung der alphathematischen Flexion. *Norsk Tidsskrift for Sprogvidenskap* 31: 205–63.
Berg, Nils, and Fredrik Otto Lindeman. 1992. The etymology of Greek αὖος and Od. 19.327 αὐσταλέος: Homeric metrics and linguistics—a question of priority. *Glotta* 70: 181–95.
Blust, Robert. 1974. A double counter-universal in Kelabit. *University of Hawaii Working Papers in Linguistics* 5: 49–56.
Brandenstein, Wilhelm. 1936. Streifzüge. 1. Die idg. Spiranten *þ* und *ð*. *Glotta* 25: 27–30.
Brixhe, Claude. 1976. *Le dialecte grec de Pamphylie*. Paris: Adrien-Maisonneuve.
Brixhe, Claude. 2004. Phrygian. Woodard, Roger D. (ed.), *The Cambridge encyclopaedia of the world's ancient languages*. Cambridge: Cambridge University Press, 777–88.
Brugmann, Karl. 1897. *Grundriß der vergleichenden Grammatik der indogermanischen Sprachen*, Vol. I, 2nd ed. Straßburg: Trübner.
Brugmann, Karl. 1906. *Grundriß der vergleichenden Grammatik der indogermanischen Sprachen*, Vol. II, Part 1, 2nd ed. Straßburg: Trübner.
Brugmann, Karl. 1911. *Grundriß der vergleichenden Grammatik der indogermanischen Sprachen*, Vol. II, Part 2, 2nd ed. Straßburg: Trübner.
Buck, Carl D. 1925. Epigraphical notes. *Classical Philology* 20: 133–44.
Buck, Carl D. 1955. *The Greek dialects*. Chicago: University of Chicago Press.
Buck, Carl D., and Walter Petersen. 1949. *A reverse index of Greek nouns and adjectives*. Chicago: University of Chicago Press.
Byrd, Andrew M. 2015. *The Indo-European syllable*. Leiden: Brill.
Campbell, David. 1988. *Greek lyric. I. Sappho and Alcaeus*. Cambridge, MA: Harvard University Press.
Cardona, George. 1960. *The Indo-European thematic aorists*. Dissertation, Yale University.
Cardona, George. 1965. Vedic imperatives in *-si*. *Language* 41: 1–18.
Cassio, Albio Cesare. 2018. Notes on the origin and diffusion of the -εσσι datives. Giannakis et al. (eds.) 2018: 189–96.
Chang, Will, Chundra Cathcart, David Hall, and Andrew Garrett. 2015. Ancestry-constrained phylogenetic analysis supports the Indo-European steppe hypothesis. *Language* 91: 194–244.
Chantraine, Pierre. 1925. Les verbes grecs en *-θω. *Mélanges linguistiques offerts à M. J. Vendryes*. Paris: Champion, 93–108.
Chantraine, Pierre. 1927. *Histoire du parfait grec*. Paris: Champion.
Chantraine, Pierre. 1963. *Grammaire homérique*. Tome II. *Syntaxe*. Paris: Klincksieck.
Chantraine, Pierre. 1973. *Grammaire homérique*. Tome I. *Phonétique et morphologie*. 5th printing, revised and corrected. Paris: Klincksieck.
Clackson, James. 2007. *Indo-European linguistics: An introduction*. Cambridge: Cambridge University Press.
Colvin, Stephen. 1999. *Dialect in Aristophanes*. Oxford: Clarendon Press.
Colvin, Stephen. 2007. *A historical Greek reader*. Oxford: Oxford University Press.
Colvin, Stephen. 2014. *A brief history of Ancient Greek*. Chichester: Wiley Blackwell.
Colvin, Stephen. 2016. The modal particle in Greek. *Cambridge Classical Journal* 62: 65–84.
Comrie, Bernard. 1976. *Aspect*. Cambridge: Cambridge University Press.
Cooper, Adam I. 2015. *Reconciling Indo-European syllabification*. Leiden: Brill.
Corbett, Greville G. 2000. *Number*. Cambridge: Cambridge University Press.
Cowgill, Warren. 1960. Greek *ou* and Armenian *oč'*. *Language* 36: 347–50.

Cowgill, Warren. 1965. Evidence in Greek. Winter, Werner (ed.), *Evidence for laryngeals.* The Hague: Mouton, 142–80.
Cowgill, Warren. 1966. Ancient Greek dialectology in the light of Mycenaean. Birnbaum, Henrik, and Jaan Puhvel (eds.), *Ancient Indo-European dialects.* Berkeley: University of California Press, 77–95.
Cowgill, Warren. 1969. On resonant clusters in Ancient Greek. *Meeting handbook, 44th Meeting of the Linguistic Society of America*, pp. 22–6.
Cowgill, Warren. 1974a. More evidence for Indo-Hittite: The tense-aspect systems. Heilmann, Luigi (ed.), *Proceedings of the Eleventh International Congress of Linguists*, Bologna: Mulino, 557–70.
Cowgill, Warren. 1974b. Indo-European languages. *The New Encyclopædia Britannica: Macropædia*, 15th ed., Vol. 9: 431–8.
Cowgill, Warren. 1979. Anatolian *hi*-conjugation and Indo-European perfect: Instalment II. Neu and Meid (eds.) 1979: 25–39.
Cowgill, Warren. 1985a. The personal endings of thematic verbs in Indo-European. Schlerath and Rittner (eds.) 1985: 99–108.
Cowgill, Warren. 1985b. PIE **duu̯o* '2' in Germanic and Celtic, and the nom.-acc. dual of non-neuter *o*-stems. *Münchener Studien zur Sprachwissenschaft* 46: 13–28.
Cowgill, Warren. 1986. Einleitung. Cowgill and Mayrhofer 1986: 9–71.
Cowgill, Warren. 2006a. *The collected writings of Warren Cowgill*, ed. Jared Klein. Ann Arbor: Beech Stave Press.
Cowgill, Warren. 2006b. The personal endings of thematic verbs in Indo-European (longer version). Cowgill 2006a: 535–67.
Cowgill, Warren, and Manfred Mayrhofer. 1986. *Indogermanische Grammatik.* Band I. Heidelberg: Winter.
Daux, Georges. 1949. Un règlement cultuel d'Andros. *Hesperia* 18: 58–72.
De Decker, Filip. 2018. The augment use of ἔειπε and εἶπε in early epic Greek: An evidential marker? *Symbolae Osloenses* 92: 2–56.
de Vaan, Michiel. 2008. *Etymological dictionary of Latin and the other Italic languages.* Leiden: Brill.
Debrunner, Albert. 1917. *Griechische Wortbildungslehre.* Heidelberg: Winter.
Delfs, Lauren C. S. 2006. Evidence for the origin of the augment. Paper read at the 25th East Coast Indo-European Conference, Columbus, OH.
Demiraj, Bardhyl. 1997. *Albanische Etymologien.* Amsterdam: Rodopi.
Denniston, J. D. 1954. *The Greek particles.* Oxford: Clarendon Press.
Dieu, Éric. 2021. Dérivation nominale et innovations accentuelles en grec ancien. Autour de la loi de Wheeler. Blanc, Alain, and Isabelle Boehm (eds.), *Dérivation nominale et innovations dans les langues indo-européennes anciennes.* Lyon: MOM Éditions, 255–74.
Dishington, James. 1976. Functions of the Germanic ē-verbs: A clue to their formal prehistory. *Language* 52: 851–65.
Dubois, Laurent. 1986a. Actualités dialectologiques. *Revue de Philologie* (3ème série) 60: 99–105.
Dubois, Laurent. 1986b. *Recherches sur le dialecte arcadien.* I. *Grammaire.* Louvain-la-Neuve: Cabay.
Dubois, Laurent. 1986c. *Recherches sur le dialecte arcadien.* II. *Corpus dialectal.* Louvain-la-Neuve: Cabay.
Dunnett, R. 1970. Thessalian κις. *Glotta* 48: 88–91.
Eichner, Heiner. 1973. Die Etymologie von heth. *mehur. Münchener Studien zur Sprachwissenschaft* 31: 53–107.

Eska, Joseph F. 1989. *Towards an interpretation of the Hispano-Celtic inscription of Botorrita*. Innsbruck: Institut für Sprachwissenschaft der Universität Innsbruck.

Fellner, Hannes. 2021. No deviation from the party(-ciple) line. Paper presented at the 40th (online) East Coast Indo-European Conference, June 17.

Filos, Panagiotis. The dialectal variety of Epirus. Giannakis et al. (eds.) 2018: 215–47.

Forbes, Kathleen. 1958a. Medial intervocalic -ρσ-, -λσ- in Greek. *Glotta* 36: 235–72.

Forbes, Kathleen. 1958b. The formation of the so-called Aeolic Optative. *Glotta* 37: 165–79.

Forbes, Kathleen. 1958c. The relations of the particle ἄν with κε(ν) κα καν. *Glotta* 37: 179–82.

Forssman, Bernhard. 1969. Nachlese zu ὄσσε. *Münchener Studien zur Sprachwissenschaft* 25: 39–50.

Forssman, Bernhard. 1975. Zur Lautform der lesbischen Lyrik. *Münchener Studien zur Sprachwissenschaft* 33: 15–37.

Forssman, Bernhard. 1980. Ein unbekanntes Lautgesetz in der homerischen Sprache? Mayrhofer, Manfred, Martin Peters, and Oskar E. Pfeiffer (eds.), *Lautgeschichte und Etymologie*. Wiesbaden: Reichert, 180–98.

Fortson, Benjamin W. IV. 2010. *Indo-European language and culture*, 2nd ed. Oxford: Blackwell.

Fortson, Benjamin W. 2012. Latin *-rier* and its Indo-Iranian congeners. *Indogermanische Forschungen* 117: 75–118.

Francis, E. David. 1971. *Greek disyllabic roots: The aorist formations*. Dissertation, Yale University.

Franciscis, Alfonso de. 1972. *Stato e società in Locri Epizefiri*. Naples: Libreria Scientifica Editrice.

Frisk, Hjalmar. 1960–76. *Griechisches etymologisches Wörterbuch*. Heidelberg: Winter.

Gamkrelidze, Tamaz, and Vyacheslav Ivanov. 1973. Sprachtypologie und die Rekonstruktion der gemeinindogermanischen Verschlüsse. *Phonetica* 27: 150–6.

García Ramón, José Luis. 2018. Ancient Greek dialectology: Old and new questions, recent developments. Giannakis et al. (eds.) 2018: 29–106.

García Ramón, José Luis. 2020. Change in grammatical and lexical structures in postclassical Greek: Local dialects and supradialectal tendencies. Rafiyenko, Dariya, and Ilja A. Seržant (eds.), *Postclassical Greek*. Berlin: de Gruyter, 303–36.

Gates, H. Phelps. 1976. On the chronology of the Attic Rückverwandlung. *Glotta* 54: 44–52.

Giannakis, Georgios K., Emilio Crespo, and Panagiotis Filos (eds.) 2018. *Studies in Ancient Greek dialects from central Greece to the Black Sea*. Berlin: de Gruyter.

Gippert, Jost. 2004. Ein Problem der indogermanischen Pronominalflexion. Hyllested et al. (eds.) 2004: 155–65.

Goedegebuure, Petra. 2009. Focus structure and Q-word questions in Hittite. *Linguistics* 47: 945–69.

Goldsmith, John A. 1990. *Autosegmental and metrical phonology*. Oxford: Blackwell.

Grassmann, Hermann. 1996. *Wörterbuch zum Rig-Veda*, 6th ed., corrected and augmented by Maria Kozianka. Wiesbaden: Harrassowitz.

Gray, Russell D., and Quentin D. Atkinson. 2003. Language-tree divergence times support the Anatolian theory of Indo-European origin. *Nature* 426: 435–9.

Guarducci, Margarita. 1950. *Inscriptiones creticae*, Vol. 4. Rome: Libreria dello Stato.

Gunkel, Dieter, Joshua T. Katz, Brent Vine, and Michael Weiss (eds.) 2016. *Sahasram ati srajas: Indo-Iranian and Indo-European studies in honor of Stephanie W. Jamison*. Ann Arbor: Beech Stave Press.

Gunkel, Dieter, Stephanie W. Jamison, Angelo O. Mercado, and Kazuhiko Yoshida (eds.) 2018. *Vina diem celebrent. Studies in linguistics and philology in honor of Brent Vine*. Ann Arbor: Beech Stave Press.

Haak, Wolfgang, Iosif Lazaridis, [...], and David Reich. 2015. Massive migration from the steppe was a source for Indo-European languages in Europe. *Nature* 522: 207–11.

Haas, Otto. 1966. *Die phrygischen Sprachdenkmäler* [= *Linguistique balkanique* X]. Sofia: Académie Bulgare des Sciences

Hackstein, Olav. 1992. Eine weitere griechisch-tocharische Gleichung. Griechisch πτῆξαι und tocharisch B *pyāktsi*. *Glotta* 70: 136–65.

Hackstein, Olav. 1993. Osttocharische Reflexe grundsprachlicher Präsensbildungen von idg. **ĝneh$_3$-* 'erkennen'. Meiser, Gerhard (ed.), *Indogermanica et Italica, Festschrift für Helmut Rix zum 65. Geburtstag*. Innsbruck: Institut für Sprachwissenschaft der Universität Innsbruck, 148–58.

Hackstein, Olav. 1995. *Untersuchungen zu den sigmatischen Präsensstammbildungen des Tocharischen*. Göttingen: Vandenhoeck & Ruprecht.

Hackstein, Olav. 2002a. *Die Sprachform der homerischen Epen*. Wiesbaden: Reichert.

Hackstein, Olav. 2002b. Uridg. *CH.CC > *C.CC. *Historische Sprachforschung* 115: 1–22.

Hackstein, Olav. 2005. Archaismus oder historischer Sprachkontakt. Meiser, Gerhard, and Olav Hackstein (eds.), *Sprachkontakt und Sprachwandel*. Wiesbaden: Reichert, 169–84.

Haegeman, Liliane. 1991. *Introduction to government and binding theory*. Oxford: Blackwell.

Hajnal, Ivo. 1995. *Studien zum mykenischen Kasussystem*. Berlin: de Gruyter.

Hajnal, Ivo. 2007. Die Vorgeschichte der griechischen Dialekte. Ein methodischer Rück- und Ausblick. Hajnal (ed.) 2007: 131–56.

Hajnal, Ivo (ed.) 2007. *Die altgriechischen Dialekte. Wesen und Werden*. Innsbruck: Institut für Sprachwissenschaft der Universität Innsbruck.

Hale, Mark. 1987. *Studies in the comparative syntax of the oldest Indo-Iranian languages*. Dissertation, Harvard University.

Hale, Mark. 1994. Rigvedic prosodic structure. Paper read at the 13th East Coast Indo-European Conference, Austin, TX, May 29.

Hamm, Eva-Maria. 1958. *Grammatik zu Sappho und Alkaios*. Berlin: Akademie-Verlag.

Harðarson, Jón Axel. 1993. *Studien zum urindogermanischen Wurzelaorist*. Innsbruck: Institut für Sprachwissenschaft der Universität Innsbruck.

Harðarson, Jón Axel. 1995. Griechisch *τῆλε*. *Historische Sprachforschung* 108: 205–6.

Harðarson, Jón Axel. 1998. Mit dem Suffix *-eh$_1$- bzw. *-(e)h$_1$-i̯e/o- gebildete Verbalstämme im Indogermanischen. Meid, Wolfgang (ed.), *Sprache und Kultur der Indogermanen*. Innsbruck: Innsbrucker Beiträge zur Sprachwissenschaft, 323–39.

Haug, Dag. 2002. *Les phases d'évolution de la langue épique*. Göttingen: Vandenhoeck & Ruprecht.

Heidermanns, Frank. 1993. *Etymologisches Wörterbuch der germanischen Primäradjektive*. Berlin: de Gruyter.

Heisserer, A. J. 1984. IG XII, 2, 1 (The monetary pact between Mytilene and Phokaia). *Zeitschrift für Papyrologie und Epigraphik* 55: 115–32.

Heubeck, Alfred. 1956. Ἄρτεμις ἰοχέαιρα. *Beiträge zur Namenforschung* 7: 275–79.

Heubeck, Alfred. 1979. Remarks on the sign-doublets *ro$_2$, ra$_2$, ta$_2$*. Risch and Mühlestein (eds.) 1979: 239–57.

Hodot, René. 1990. *Le dialecte éolien d'Asie*. Paris: Recherche sur les Civilisations.

Hodot, René. 2018. Lesbian, in space, in time, and its uses. Giannakis et al. (eds.) 2018: 457–69.

Hoenigswald, Henry M. 1953. PA, ΔΕΔΑΕ, ΔΑΣΥΣ, and the semivowels. *Language* 29: 288–92.

Hoenigswald, Henry M. 1960. *Language change and linguistic reconstruction*. Chicago: University of Chicago Press.

Hoenigswald, Henry M. 1965. A property of 'Grassmann's law' in Indic. *Journal of the American Oriental Society* 85: 59–60.

Hoenigswald, Henry M. 1985. From plain to worse. Ölberg, Hermann, Gernot Schmidt, and Heinz Bothien (eds.), *Sprachwissenschaftliche Forschungen. Festschrift für Johann Knobloch*. Innsbruck: Institut für Sprachwissenschaft der Universität Innsbruck, 167–70.

Hoenigswald, Henry M. 1997. Analogy in Cyrene and elsewhere. Adams (ed.) 1997: 93–8.

Hoffmann, Karl. 1955. Ein grundsprachliches Possessivsuffix. *Münchener Studien zur Sprachwissenschaft* 6: 35–40 [= Hoffmann 1976: 378–83].

Hoffmann, Karl. 1967a. *Der Injunktiv im Veda*. Heidelberg: Winter.

Hoffmann, Karl. 1967b. Der vedische Prekativtyp yeṣam, jeṣma. *Münchener Studien zur Sprachwissenschaft* 20: 25–37 [= Hoffmann 1976: 465–74].

Hoffmann, Karl. 1976. *Aufsätze zur Indoiranistik*. Band 2, ed. J. Narten. Wiesbaden: Reichert.

Hoffmann, Otto. 1900. Zwei neue arkadische Inschriften. *Philologus* 59: 201–5.

Hoffner, Harry A., and H. Craig Melchert. 2008. *A grammar of the Hittite language*. Winona Lake: Eisenbrauns.

Holleaux, Maurice. 1897. Questions épigraphiques. *Revue des Études Grecques* 10: 24–57.

Hollenbaugh, Ian. 2018. Re-evaluating the evidence of the R̥gveda and Homer and its implications for PIE. *Indo-European Linguistics* 6: 1–68.

Hyllested, Adam, Anders R. Jørgensen, Jenny H. Larsson, and Thomas Olander (eds.) 2004. *Per Aspera ad Asteriscos. Studia Indogermanica in honorem Jens Elmegård Rasmussen*. Innsbruck: Innsbrucker Beiträge zur Sprachwissenschaft.

Inscriptiones Graecae. IV. 1902. *Aeginae Pityonesi Cecryphaliae Argolidis*, ed. Maximilian Fraenkel. Berlin: Reimer.

Inscriptiones Graecae. V-2. 1913. *Arcadiae*, ed. Friedrich Hiller von Gaertringen. Berlin: Reimer.

Inscriptiones Graecae. VII. 1892. *Megaridis Oropiae Boeotiae*, ed. Wilhelm Dittenberger. Berlin: Reimer.

Inscriptiones Graecae. IX-1. 1897. *Phocidis Locridis Aetoliae Acarnaniae insularum Maris Ionii*, ed. Wilhelm Dittenberger. Berlin: Reimer.

Inscriptiones Graecae. XII-2. 1899. *Lesbi Nesi Tenedi*, ed. William R. Paton. Berlin: Reimer.

Inscriptiones Graecae. XII-3. 1898. *Insularum Symes ... Cimoli*, ed. Friedrich Hiller von Gaertringen. Berlin: Reimer.

Inscriptiones Graecae, Editio Minor. IX-1. 1932. *Aetoliae*, ed. Günther Klaffenbach. Berlin: Reimer.

Jamison, Stephanie W. 1979. The case of the agent in Indo-European. *Die Sprache* 25: 129–42.

Janko, Richard. 1977. A note on the date of Grassmann's Law in Greek. *Glotta* 55: 1–2.

Janko, Richard. 2018. The Greek dialects in the palatial and post-palatial late Bronze Age. Giannakis et al. (eds.) 2018: 107–29.

Jasanoff, Jay H. 1976. Gr. ἄμφω, lat. ambō et le mot indoeuropéen pour 'l'un et l'autre'. *Bulletin de la Société de Linguistique* 71: 123–31.

Jasanoff, Jay H. 1986. Old Irish *tair* 'come!' *Transactions of the Philological Society* 1986: 132–41.

Jasanoff, Jay H. 1987. Some irregular imperatives in Tocharian. Watkins (ed.) 1987: 92–112.

Jasanoff, Jay H. 1988a. PIE *ĝnē- 'recognize, know'. Bammesberger (ed.) 1988: 227–39.

Jasanoff, Jay H. 1988b. The sigmatic aorist in Tocharian and Indo-European. *Tocharian and Indo-European Studies* 2: 52–76

Jasanoff, Jay H. 1989. Old Irish *bé* 'woman'. *Ériu* 40: 135–41.

Jasanoff, Jay H. 1994. The Brittonic subjunctive and future. Rasmussen, Jens Elmegård, and B. Nielsen (eds.), *In honorem Holger Pedersen*. Wiesbaden: Reichert, 199–220.

Jasanoff, Jay H. 1997. An Italo-Celtic isogloss: The 3pl. mediopassive in *-*ntro*. Adams (ed.) 1997: I: 146–61.

Jasanoff, Jay H. 2002. The nom. sg. of Germanic *n*-stems. Wedel, Alfred, and Hans-Jörg Busch (eds.), *Verba et litteræ: Explorations in Germanic languages and German literature*. Newark, DE: Linguatext, 31–46.

Jasanoff, Jay H. 2003a. *Hittite and the Indo-European verb*. Oxford: Oxford University Press.

Jasanoff, Jay H. 2003b. A new Indo-Hittite isogloss. Paper read at the 22nd East Coast Indo-European Conference, Harvard, June 12.

Jasanoff, Jay H. 2004. Acute vs. circumflex: Some notes on PIE and post-PIE prosodic phonology. Hyllested et al. (eds.) 2004: 247–55.

Jasanoff, Jay H. 2009. *-*bhi*, *-*bhis*, *-*ōis*: Following the trail of the PIE instrumental plural. Rasmussen, Jens Elmegård, and Thomas Olander (eds.), *Internal reconstruction in Indo-European: methods, results, and problems*. Copenhagen: Museum Tusculanum, 137–49.

Jasanoff, Jay H. 2018. Palatable thorns. Gunkel et al. (eds.) 2018: 133–40.

Jasanoff, Jay H., and Joshua Katz. 2017. A revised history of the Greek pluperfect. Hajnal, Ivo, Daniel Kölligan, and Katharina Zisper (eds.), *Miscellanea indogermanica. Festschrift für José Luis García Ramón*. Innsbruck: Institut für Sprachen und Literaturen der Universität Innsbruck, 337–51.

Jatteau, Adèle. 2016. *Le statut phonologique de l' aspiration en grec ancien*. Dissertation, Université Paris 8.

Jeffery, Lilian Hamilton. 1991. *The local scripts of archaic Greece*, revised ed. Oxford: Oxford University Press.

Joseph, Brian. 1982. Oscan *slaagí-*. *Glotta* 60: 112–15.

Katz, Joshua T. 1998. *Topics in Indo-European personal pronouns*. Dissertation, Harvard University.

Katz, Joshua T. 2004. The 'swimming duck' in Greek and Hittite. Penney, John H. W. (ed.), *Indo-European perspectives: Studies in honour of Anna Morpurgo Davies*. Oxford: Oxford University Press, 195–216.

Kellens, Jean. 1984. *Le verbe avestique*. Wiesbaden: Reichert.

Kim, Ronald. 2000a. 'To drink' in Anatolian, Tocharian, and Proto-Indo-European. *Historische Sprachwissenschaft* 113: 151–70.

Kim, Ronald. 2000b. Reexamining the prehistory of Tocharian B 'ewe'. *Tocharian and Indo-European Studies* 9: 37–43.

Kim, Ronald. 2001. Tocharian B *śem* ≈ Latin *vēnit*? Szemerényi's Law and *ē in PIE root aorists. *Münchener Studien zur Sprachwissenschaft* 61: 119–47.

Kim, Ronald. 2003. Uncovering the prehistory of the Tocharian class II preterite. *Historische Sprachforschung* 116: 190–233.

Kim, Ronald. 2007. The Tocharian subjunctive in the light of the h_2e-conjugation model. Nussbaum (ed.) 2007: 185–200.

Kim, Ronald. 2012a. The Indo-European, Anatolian, and Tocharian 'secondary' cases in typological perspective. Cooper, Adam I., Jeremy Rau, and Michael Weiss (eds.), *Multi nominis grammaticus: Studies in Classical and Indo-European linguistics in honor of Alan J. Nussbaum*. Ann Arbor: Beech Stave Press, 121–42.

Kim, Ronald. 2012b. The PIE thematic animate accusative plural revisited. Sukač and Šefčík (eds.) 2012: 144–58.
Kim, Ronald. 2014. A tale of two suffixes: *-h_2-, *-ih_2-, and the evolution of feminine gender in Indo-European. Neri and Schuhmann (eds.) 2014: 115–36.
Kim, Ronald, Norbert Oettinger, Elisabeth Rieken, and Michael Weiss (eds.) 2010. *Ex Anatolia lux: Anatolian and Indo-European studies in honor of H. Craig Melchert.* Ann Arbor: Beech Stave Press
Kimball, Sara. 1987. *H_3 in Anatolian. Cardona, George, and Norman H. Zide (eds.), *Festschrift for Henry Hoenigswald.* Tübingen: Narr, 185–92.
Kimball, Sara. 1988. Analogy, secondary ablaut and *OH2 in Common Greek. Bammesberger (ed.) 1988: 241–56.
Kimball, Sara. 1991. The origin of the Greek κ-perfect. *Glotta* 69: 141–53.
King, Robert D. 1967. Functional load and sound change. *Language* 43: 831–52.
Kiparsky, Paul. 1982. *Explanation in phonology.* Dordrecht: Foris.
Kiparsky, Paul. 1995. The Indo-European origins of Germanic syntax. Battye, Adrian, and Ian Roberts (eds.), *Clause structure and language change.* Oxford: Oxford University Press, 140–69.
Klein, Jared. 1988. Proto-Indo-European *g^wiH_3- 'live' and related problems of laryngeals in Greek. Bammesberger (ed.) 1988: 257–79.
Klingenschmitt, Gert. 1975. Tocharisch und Urindigermanisch. Rix (ed.), 1975: 148–63.
Klingenschmitt, Gert. 1982. *Das altarmenische Verbum.* Wiesbaden: Reichert.
Kloekhorst, Alwin. 2008. *Etymological dictionary of the Hittite inherited lexicon.* Leiden: Brill.
Kostopoulos, Georgios. 2023. The outcome of *-*er/ni̯*- in Greek. *Glotta* 99: 122–53.
Kostopoulos, Georgios. Forthcoming (a). Notes on stop palatalization in Greek. To appear in *Revue de Philologie* 96.
Kostopoulos, Georgios. Forthcoming (b). Vowel lengthening in Attic primary comparatives. To appear in *Harvard Studies in Classical Philology* 113.
Krause, Wolfgang. 1971. *Die Sprache der urnordischen Runeninschriften.* Heidelberg: Winter.
Kretschmer, Paul. 1892. Zum ionisch-attischen Wandel von ᾱ in η. *Zeitschrift für vergleichende Sprachforschung* 31: 285–96.
Kroch, Anthony. 1989. Reflexes of grammar in patterns of language change. *Language Variation and Change* 1: 199–244.
Kuiper, F. B. J. 1947. Traces of laryngeals in Vedic Sanskrit. *India antiqua: A volume of oriental studies presented by his friends and pupils to Jean Philippe Vogel, C.I.E. on the occasion of the fiftieth anniversary of his doctorate.* Leyden: Kern Institute, 198–212.
Kuiper, F. B. J. 1961. Zur kompositionellen Kürzung im Sanskrit. *Die Sprache* 7: 14–31.
Kümmel, Martin Joachim. 1998. Wurzelpräsens neben Wurzelaorist im Indogermanischen. *Historische Sprachforschung* 111: 191–208.
Kümmel, Martin Joachim. 2000. *Das Perfekt im Indoiranischen.* Wiesbaden: Reichert.
Kümmel, Martin Joachim. 2007. *Konsonantenwandel.* Wiesbaden: Reichert.
Kümmel, Martin Joachim. 2012. Typology and reconstruction. Nielsen Whitehead, Benedicte, et al. (eds.), *The sound of Indo-European.* Copenhagen: Museum Tusculanum, 291–329.
Kümmel, Martin Joachim. 2020. The development of the perfect within IE verbal systems: an overview. Crellin, Robert, and Thomas Jügel (eds.), *Perfects in Indo-European languages and beyond.* Amsterdam: Benjamins, 15–47.

Labov, William. 1994. *Principles of linguistic change*, Vol. I: *Internal factors*. Oxford: Blackwell.
Lambert, Pierre-Yves. 2002. *Recueil des inscriptions gauloises*. Vol. II, fasc. 2. *Textes gallo-latin sur instrumentum*. Paris: CNRS.
Lejeune, Michel. 1972. *Phonétique historique du mycénien et du grec ancien*. Paris: Klincksieck.
Liddell, Henry George, and Robert Scott. 1940. *A Greek-English lexicon*, 9th ed., revised by Henry Stuart Jones and Roderick McKenzie. Oxford: Clarendon Press.
Lindeman, Frederik Otto. 1965. La loi de Sievers et le début du mot en indo-européen. *Norsk Tidsskrift for Sprogvidenskap* 20: 38–108.
Lubotsky, Alexander. 1989. Against a Proto-Indo-European phoneme **a*. Vennemann, Theo (ed.), *The new sound of Indo-European* (Berlin: de Gruyter) 53–66.
Lühr, Rosemarie. 1984. Reste der athematischen Konjugation in den germanischen Sprachen. Untermann, Jürgen, and Béla Brogyanyi (eds.), *Das Germanische und die Rekonstruktion der indogermanischen Grundsprache*. Amsterdam: Benjamins, 25–90.
Lundquist, Jesse. 2015. On the accentuation of Vedic -*ti*-abstracts: Evidence for accentual change. *Indo-European Linguistics* 3: 42–72.
Lüttel, Verena. 1981. *Κάς und καί*. Göttingen: Vandenhoeck & Ruprecht.
Macdonell, Arthur Anthony. 1910. *Vedic grammar*. Strassburg: Trübner.
Mair, Victor (ed.) 1998. *The bronze age and early iron age peoples of eastern Central Asia*. Washington: Institute for the Study of Man.
Mallory, James P., and Doublas Q. Adams. 2006. *The Oxford introduction to Proto-Indo-European and the Proto-Indo-European world*. Oxford: Oxford University Press.
Malzahn, Melanie. 2010. *The Tocharian verbal system*. Leiden: Brill.
Masson, Olivier. 1961. *Les inscriptions chypriotes syllabiques*. Paris: Boccard.
Masson, Olivier. 1978. La forme verbale ἦς 'erat' dans les dialectes grecs. *Étrennes de septantaine. Travaux de linguistique et de grammaire comparée offerts à Michel Lejeune par un groupe de ses élèves*. Paris: Klincksieck, 123–8.
Mayrhofer, Manfred. 1982. Über griechische Vokalprothese, Laryngaltheorie und externe Rekonstruktion. Tischler (ed.) 1982: 177–92.
Mayrhofer, Manfred. 1983. Ergebnisse einer Überprüfung des indogermanischen Ansatzes 'Thorn'. *Anzeiger der phil.-hist. Klasse der Österreichischen Akademie der Wissenschaften* 119: 240–55.
Mayrhofer, Manfred. 1986. Lautlehre (segmentale Phonologie des Indogermanischen). Cowgill and Mayrhofer 1986: 73–216.
Mayrhofer, Manfred. 1986–2001. *Etymologisches Wörterbuch des Altindoarischen*. Heidelberg: Winter.
Mayrhofer, Manfred. 1989. Vorgeschichte der iranischen Sprachen; Uriranisch. Schmidt, Rüdiger (ed.), *Compendium linguarum iranicarum*. Wiesbaden: Reichert, 4–24.
Mayrhofer, Manfred, Martin Peters, and Oskar E. Pfeiffer (eds.) 1980. *Lautgeschichte und Etymologie*. Wiesbaden: Reichert
McCone, Kim. 1991. *The Indo-European origins of the Old Irish nasal presents, subjunctives, and futures*. Innsbruck: Institut für Sprachwissenschaft der Universität Innsbruck.
Meid, Wolfgang. 1987. Germanische oder indogermanische Lautverschiebung? Bergmann, Rolf, Heinrich Tiefenbach, and Lothar Voetz (eds.), *Althochdeutsch*, Band I. Heidelberg: Winter, 3–11.
Meier-Brügger, Michael. 2005. Sprachkontakte und Sprachwandel beim Zusammenspiel der altgriechischen Dialekte. Meiser, Gerhard, and Olav Hackstein (eds.), *Sprachkontakt und Sprachwandel*. Wiesbaden: Reichert, 437–44.

Meier-Brügger, Michael. 2010. *Indogermanische Sprachwissenschaft*, 9th ed. Berlin: de Gruyter.

Meissner, Torsten. 2016. Archaeology and the archaeology of the Greek language: on the origin of the Greek nouns in -εύς. Bintliff, John L., and Keith Rutter (eds.), *The archaeology of Greece and Rome: studies in honour of Anthony Snodgrass*. Edinburgh: Edinburgh University Press, 22–30.

Meister, Karl. 1921. *Die homerische Kunstsprache*. Leipzig: Teubner.

Melchert, H. Craig. 1987. PIE velars in Luvian. Watkins (ed.) 1987: 182–204.

Melchert, H. 1994a. *Anatolian historical phonology*. Amsterdam: Rodopi.

Melchert, H. 1994b. The feminine gender in Anatolian. Dunkel, George, et al. (eds.), *Früh-, Mittel-, Spätindogermanisch*. Wiesbaden: Reichert, 231–44.

Melchert, H. 1997a. Denominative verbs in Anatolian. Disterheft, Dorothy, Martin Huld, and John Greppin (eds.), *Studies in honor of Jaan Puhvel. Part one: Ancient languages and philology*. Washington: Institute for the Study of Man, 131–8.

Melchert, H. 1997b. Traces of a PIE aspectual contrast in Anatolian? *Incontri linguistici* 20: 83–92.

Melchert, H. 2003. Hittite nominal stems in *-anzan-*. Tichy, Eva, Dagmar S. Wodtko, and Britta Irslinger (eds.), *Indogermanisches Nomen. Derivation, Flexion und Ablaut*. Bremen: Hempen, 129–39.

Melchert, H. 2009. Local adverbs in Hittite: Synchrony and diachrony. *Language and Linguistics Compass* 3: 607–20.

Melchert, H. 2011. The PIE verb for 'to pour' and medial $^*h_3$ in Anatolian. Jamison, Stephanie W., H. Craig Melchert, and Brent Vine (eds.), *Proceedings of the 22nd Annual UCLA Indo-European Conference*. Bremen: Hempen, 127–32.

Melchert, H. 2012a. Genitive case and possessive adjective in Anatolian. Orioles, V. (ed.), *Per Roberto Gusmani. Linguistica storica e teorica*. Udine: Forum, 273–86.

Melchert, H. 2012b. Luvo-Lycian dorsal stops revisited. Sukač and Šefčik (eds.) 2012: 206–18.

Melchert, H. 2014a. 'Narten formations' versus 'Narten roots'. *Indogermanische Forschungen* 119: 251–8.

Melchert, H. 2014b. PIE **-eh*$_2$ as an 'individualizing' suffix and the feminine gender. Neri and Schuhmann (eds.) 2014: 257–71.

Melchert, H. 2016. The case of the agent in Anatolian and Proto-Indo-European. Gunkel et al. 2016: 239–49.

Melchert, H. Craig, and Norbert Oettinger. 2009. Ablativ und Instrumental im Hethitischen und Indogermanischen. Ein Beitrag zur relativen Chronologie. *Incontri Linguistici* 32: 53–73.

Méndez Dosuna, Julián. 1985. *Los dialectos dorios del noroeste. Gramática y estudio dialectal.* Salamanca: Universidad de Salamanca.

Merlingen, Weriand. 1957. Idg. 'þ' und Verwandtes. Μνήμης χάριν. *Gedenkschrift Paul Kretschmer*. Vienna: Wiener Sprachgesellschaft, 49–61.

Merlingen, Weriand. 1962. Zu idg. 'þ'. *Die Sprache* 8: 74–6.

Miller, D. Gary. 1976. Liquids plus *s* in Ancient Greek. *Glotta* 54: 159–72.

Miller, D. Gary. 1977. Was Grassmann's Law reordered in Greek? *Zeitschrift für vergleichende Sprachforschung* 91: 131–58.

Miller, D. Gary. 2014. *Ancient Greek dialects and early authors*. Berlin: de Gruyter.

Moore, Samuel. 1927. Loss of final *n* in inflectional syllables of Middle English. *Language* 3: 232–59.

Morpurgo, Anna. 1961. Il genitivo maschile in -ας. *Glotta* 39: 93–111.

Morpurgo Davies, Anna. 1968. The treatment of *r̥ and *l̥ in Mycenaean and Arcado-Cyprian. *Atti e Memorie del Primo Congresso Internazionale di Micenologia.* Rome: Ateneo, 791–814.

Morpurgo Davies, Anna. 1976. The -εσσι datives, Aeolic *-ss-*, and the Lesbian poets. Morpurgo Davies and Meid (eds.) 1976: 181–97.

Morpurgo Davies, Anna. 1992. Mycenaean, Arcadian, Cyprian and some questions of method in dialectology. Olivier, Jean-Pierre (ed.), *Mykenaïka.* Paris: Diffusion de Bocard, 415–32.

Morpurgo Davies, Anna, and Wolfgang Meid (eds.) 1976. *Studies in Greek, Italic, and Indo-European linguistics offered to Leonard R. Palmer.* Innsbruck: Institut für Sprachwissenschaft der Universität Innsbruck.

Mottausch, K.-H. 2003. Das thematische Verb im Indogermanischen und seine Verwandten. *Historische Sprachforschung* 116: 1–34.

Mühlestein, Hugo. 1958. Einige mykenische Wörter. *Museum Helveticum* 15: 222–6.

Narten, Johanna. 1964. *Die sigmatischen Aoriste im Veda.* Wiesbaden: Harrassowitz.

Narten, Johanna. 1968. Zum 'proterodynamischen' Wurzelpräsens. Heesterman, J. C., Godard H. Schokker, and V. I. Subramoniam (eds.), *Pratidānam.* The Hague: Mouton, 9–19.

Neri, Sergio. 2003. *I sostantivi in* -u *del gotico.* Innsbruck: Institut für Sprachen und Literaturen der Universität Innsbruck.

Neri, Sergio. 2009. Review of Ringe, Don. *From Proto-Indo-European to Proto-Germanic* (1st ed., 2006), *Kratylos* 54: 1–13.

Neri, Sergio, and Roland Schuhmann (eds.) 2014. *Studies on the collective and feminine in Indo-European from a diachronic and typological perspective.* Leiden: Brill.

Neu, Erich, and Wolfgang Meid (eds.) 1979. *Hethitisch und Indogermanisch.* Innsbruck: Institut für Sprachwissenschaft der Universität Innsbruck.

Newton, G. 2005. The contribution of the Old Irish verbal system to the reconstruction of Proto-Indo-European syntax. *Papers in Linguistics from the University of Manchester* 2005: 95–112.

Nikolaev, Alexander. 2010. Исследования по праиндоевропейской именной морфологии [*Studies in Proto-Indo-European nominal morphology*]. St. Petersburg: Nauka.

Nikolaev, Alexander. 2014. Greek εἰαμενή, Vedic *yávasa-*. *Münchener Studien zur Sprachwissenschaft* 68: 127–39.

Normier, Rudolf. 1980. Tocharisch *ñkät/ñakte* 'Gott'. *Zeitschrift für vergleichende Sprachforschung* 94: 251–81.

Noyer, R. Rolf. 1997. *Features, positions, and affixes in autonomous morphology.* New York: Garland.

Nussbaum, Alan J. 1975. -ī- in Latin denominative derivation. Watkins (ed.) 1975: 116–61.

Nussbaum, Alan J. 1985. The Greek thematic genitive singular—yet again. Paper presented at the 4th East Coast Indo-European Conference, Cornell University.

Nussbaum, Alan J. 1986. *Head and horn in Indo-European.* Berlin: de Gruyter.

Nussbaum, Alan J. 1997. The 'Saussure effect' in Latin and Italic. Lubotsky, Alexander (ed.), *Sound law and analogy.* Amsterdam: Rodopi, 181–203.

Nussbaum, Alan J. (ed.) 2007. *Verba docentī: Studies in historical and Indo-European linguistics presented to Jay H. Jasanoff.* Ann Arbor: Beech Stave Press.

Nussbaum, Alan J. 2010. PIE -Cmn- and Greek τρᾱνής 'clear'. Kim et al. (eds.) 2010: 269–77.

Nussbaum, Alan J. 2014. Feminine, abstract, collective, neuter plural: Some remarks on each (expanded handout). Neri and Schuhmann (eds.) 2014: 273–306.

Oettinger, Norbert. 1979. *Die Stammbildung des hethitischen Verbums*. Nürnberg: Hans Carl.

Olander, Thomas. 2015. *Proto-Slavic inflectional morphology*. Leiden: Brill.

Olander, Thomas. 2019. Indo-European cladistic nomenclature. *Indogermanische Forschungen* 124: 231–44.

Olander, Thomas. Forthcoming. To *b or not to *b: Proto-Indo-European *b in a phylogenetic perspective. To appear in *Historische Sprachforschung*.

Ozoliņš, Kaspars. 2015. *Revisiting Proto-Indo-European Schwebeablaut*. Dissertation, University of California, Los Angeles.

Parker, Holt N. 2008. The linguistic case for the Aiolian migration reconsidered. *Hesperia* 77: 431–64.

Parker, Holt N. 2013. Palatalization of labiovelars in Greek. Cooper, Adam I., Jeremy Rau, and Michael Weiss (eds.), *Multi nominis grammaticus: Studies in Classical and Indo-European linguistics in honor of Alan J. Nussbaum*. Ann Arbor: Beech Stave Press, 214–27.

Peters, Martin. 1976. Attisch *hīēmi*. *Die Sprache* 22: 157–61.

Peters, Martin. 1980. *Untersuchung zur Vertretung der indogermanischen Laryngale im Griechischen*. Vienna: Österreichische Akademie der Wissenschaften.

Peters, Martin. 1991. Ein tocharisches Auslautproblem. *Die Sprache* 34: 242–4.

Peyrot, Michaël. 2013. *The Tocharian subjunctive*. Leiden: Brill.

Pinault, Georges-Jean. 1982. A neglected phonetic law: The reduction of the Indo-European laryngeals in internal syllables before yod. Ahlqvist, Anders (ed.), *Papers from the Fifth International Conference on Historical Linguistics*. Amsterdam: Benjamins, 265–72.

Pinault, Georges-Jean. 2006a. Retour sur le numéral 'un' en tokharien. *Indogermanische Forschungen* 111: 71–97.

Pinault, Georges-Jean. 2006b. Sur l'évolution phonétique *tsk* > *tk* en tokharien commun. *Münchener Studien zur Sprachwissenschaft* 62: 103–56.

Piwowarczyk, Dariusz. 2015. The Proto-Indo-European *-Vts# clusters and the formulation of Szemerényi's Law. *Indogermanische Forschungen* 120: 269–78.

Pokorny, Julius. 1959. *Indogermanisches etymologisches Wörterbuch*. Bern: Francke.

Probert, Philomen. 2006a. *Ancient Greek accentuation*. Oxford: Oxford University Press.

Probert, Philomen. 2006b. Clause boundaries in Old Hittite relative sentences. *Transactions of the Philological Society* 104: 17–83.

Pronk, Tijmen. 2019. Proto-Indo-European. **a*. *Indo-European Linguistics* 7: 122–63.

Radford, Andrew. 2004. *Minimalist syntax*. Cambridge: Cambridge University Press.

Randall, W., and H. Jones. 2015. On the early origins of the Germanic preterite presents. *Transactions of the Philological Society* 113: 137–76.

Rau, Jeremy. 2018. The genetic subgrouping of the Ancient Greek dialects: Achaean. Gunkel et al. (eds.) 2018: 380–9.

Rau, Jeremy. 2022. The Greek dialects in the 2nd millennium BCE. Part II. Paper read at ECIEC 41, Harvard University.

Renfrew, Colin. 1987. *Archaeology and language: The puzzle of Indo-European origins*. London: Jonathan Cape.

Ridder, André de. 1895. Fouilles d'Orchomène. *Bulletin de Correspondance Hellénique* 19: 137–224.

Rieken, Elisabeth. 1999a. *Untersuchungen zur nominalen Stammbildung des Hethitischen*. Wiesbaden: Harrassowitz.

Rieken, Elisabeth. 1999b. Zur Verwendung der Konjunktion *ta* in den hethitischen Texten. *Münchener Studien zur Sprachwissenschaft* 59: 63–88.

Ringe, Don. 1984. *The perfect tenses in Greek inscriptions.* Dissertation, Yale University.
Ringe, Don. 1996. *On the chronology of sound changes in Tocharian*, Vol. 1. New Haven: American Oriental Society.
Ringe, Don. 1997. On the origin of 3pl. imperative -ντον. Adams (ed.) 1997: 129–43.
Ringe, Don. 2000. Tocharian class II presents and subjunctives and the reconstruction of the Proto-Indo-European verb. *Tocharian and Indo-European Studies* 9: 121–42.
Ringe, Don. 2001. Review of Rix et al. 2001. *Diachronica* 18: 184–7.
Ringe, Don. 2002. Tocharian B *ṣp* 'and'. Southern, Mark (ed.), *Indo-European perspectives.* Washington, DC: Institute for the Study of Man, 265–6.
Ringe, Don. 2007. Old Latin *-minō* and 'analogy'. Nussbaum (ed.) 2007: 301–6.
Ringe, Don. 2010. 'Thorn' clusters and Indo-European subgrouping. Kim et al. (eds.) 2010: 330–8.
Ringe, Don. 2012. The *hi*-conjugation as a PIE subjunctive. Hackstein, Olav, and Ronald I. Kim (eds.), *Linguistic developments along the silkroad: Archaism and innovation in Tocharian.* Vienna: Österreichische Akademie der Wissenschaften, 121–40.
Ringe, Don. 2016. Phonological rules and dialect geography in Ancient Greek. Gunkel et al. (eds.) 2016: 378–84.
Ringe, Don. 2017. *From Proto-Indo-European to Proto-Germanic*, 2nd ed. Oxford: Oxford University Press.
Ringe, Don. 2018. The nature of the South Greek dialect group. Byrd, Andrew Miles, Jessica DeLisi, and Mark Wenthe (eds.), *Tavet tat satyam: Studies in honor of Jared S. Klein.* Ann Arbor: Beech Stave, 278–83.
Ringe, Don. 2022. Stative perfects. Scharf, Peter M. (ed.), *Indian linguistic studies in honor of George Cardona*, Vol. II: *Historical linguistics, Vedic, etc.* Providence: The Sanskrit Library, 85–98.
Ringe, Don, and Joseph F. Eska. 2013. *Historical linguistics: Toward a twenty-first century reintegration.* Cambridge: Cambridge University Press.
Ringe, Don, and Ann Taylor. 2014. *The development of Old English.* Oxford: Oxford University Press.
Ringe, Don, Tandy Warnow, and Ann Taylor. 2002. Indo-European and computational cladistics. *Transactions of the Philological Society* 100: 59–129.
Ringe, Don, Tandy Warnow, Ann Taylor, Alexander Michailov, and Libby Levison. 1998. Computational cladistics and the position of Tocharian. Mair (ed.) 1998: 391–414.
Risch, Ernst. 1955. Die Gliederung der griechischen Dialekte in neuer Sicht. *Museum Helveticum* 12: 61–76.
Risch, Ernst. 1962. Das indogermanische Word für 'hundert'. *Indogermanische Forschungen* 67: 129–41.
Risch, Ernst. 1974. *Wortbildung der homerischen Sprache*, 2nd ed. Berlin: de Gruyter.
Risch, Ernst. 1979. Les consonnes palatalisées dans le grec du IIe millénaire et des premiers siècles du Ier millénaire. Risch and Mühlestein (eds.) 1979: 267–81.
Risch, Ernst. 1982. Ein Problem des griechischen Verbalparadigmas. Die verschiedenen Formen der 3. Person Plural. Tischler (ed.) 1982: 321–34.
Risch, Ernst, and Hugo Mühlestein (eds.) 1979. *Colloquium mycenaeum.* Neuchâtel: Faculté des Lettres.
Rix, Helmut. 1970. Anlautender Laryngal vor Liquida oder Nasalis sonans im Griechischen. *Münchener Studien zur Sprachwissenschaft* 27: 79–110.
Rix, Helmut (ed.) 1975. *Flexion und Wortbildung.* Wiesbaden: Reichert.
Rix, Helmut. 1976a. *Historische Grammatik des Griechischen. Laut- und Formenlehre.* Darmstadt: Wissenschaftliche Buchgesellschaft.

Rix, Helmut. 1976b. Die umbrischen Infinitive auf *-fi* und die urindogermanische Infinitivendung *-dʰi̯ōi*. Morpurgo Davies and Meid (eds.) 1976: 319–31.

Rix, Helmut. 1977. Das keltische Verbalsystem auf dem Hintergrund des indo-iranisch-griechischen Rekonstruktionsmodells. Schmidt, Karl Horst (ed.), *Indogermanisch und Keltisch*. Wiesbaden: Reichert, 132–58.

Rix, Helmut, et al. 2001. *Lexikon der indogermanischen Verben*, 2nd ed. Wiesbaden: Reichert.

Ross, Malcolm. 1997. Social networks and kinds of speech-community event. Blench, Roger, and Matthew Spriggs (eds.), *Archaeology and language*, Vol. I: *Theoretical and methodological orientations*. London: Routledge, 209–61.

Ross, Malcolm. 1998. Sequencing and dating linguistic events in Oceania: The linguistics/archaeology interface. Blench, Roger, and Matthew Spriggs (eds.), *Archaeology and language*, Vol. II: *Archaeological data and linguistic hypotheses*. London: Routledge, 141–73.

Roth, Catharine P. 1990. *'Mixed aorists' in Homeric Greek*. New York: Garland.

Rothstein-Dowden, Zachary. 2021. On the numeral *cha* '6' in Middle and New Indo-Aryan. Paper presented at the 40th (online) East Coast Indo-European Conference, June 19.

Ruijgh, Cornelis J. 1968. Les noms en *-won-* (*-āwon-*, *-īwon-*), *-uon-* en grec alphabétique et en mycénien. *Minos* 9: 109–55.

Ruijgh, Cornelis J. 2007. L'évolution des dialectes doriens jusqu'à la koina dorienne. Le système des voyelles longues et la formation du futur. Hajnal (ed.) 2007: 393–447.

Sacconi, Anna. 1974. *Corpus delle iscrizioni in lineare B di Micene*. Rome: Ateneo.

Samuels, Bridget D. 2017. Vocalic shifts in Attic-Ionic Greek. *Papers in Historical Phonology* 2: 88–115.

Scarborough, Matthew Joseph Charles. 2016. *The Aeolic dialects of Ancient Greek: A study in historical dialectology and linguistic classification*. Dissertation, Cambridge University.

Schindler, Jochem. 1967a. Das idg. Wort für 'Erde' und die dentalen Spiranten. *Die Sprache* 13: 191–205.

Schindler, Jochem. 1967b. Tocharische Miszellen. *Indogermanische Forschungen* 72: 239–49.

Schindler, Jochem. 1967c. Zu hethitisch *nekuz*. *Zeitschrift für vergleichende Sprachforschung* 81: 290–303.

Schindler, Jochem. 1972a. L'apophonie des noms-racines indo-européens. *Bulletin de la Société de Linguistique* 67: 31–8.

Schindler, Jochem. 1972b. *Das Wurzelnomen im Arischen und Griechischen*. Dissertation, University of Würzburg.

Schindler, Jochem. 1975a. L'apophonie des thèmes indo-européens en *-r/n*. *Bulletin de la Société de Linguistique* 70: 1–10.

Schindler, Jochem. 1975b. Zum ablaut der neutralen *s*-Stämme des Indogermanischen. Rix (ed.) 1975: 259–67.

Schindler, Jochem. 1976. On the Greek type ἱππεύς. Morpurgo Davies and Meid (eds.) 1976: 349–52.

Schindler, Jochem. 1977a. Diachronic and synchronic remarks on Bartholomae's and Grassmann's Laws. Watkins, Calvert (ed.), Indo-European Studies III. Cambridge, MA: Harvard University Department of Linguistics, 1–28.

Schindler, Jochem. 1977b. Notizien zum Sieversschen Gesetz. *Die Sprache* 23: 56–65.

Schindler, Jochem. 1977c. A thorny problem. *Die Sprache* 23: 25–35.

Schindler, Jochem. 1980. Zur Herkunft der altindischen *cvi*-Bildungen'. Mayrhofer et al. (eds.) 1980: 386–93.

Schlerath, Bernfried, and Veronika Rittner (eds.) 1985. *Grammatische Kategorien. Funktion und Geschichte.* Wiesbaden: Reichert.

Schmidt, Klaus T., and Werner Winter 1992. Die Formen der 1. Singular Aktiv der unerweiterten Präterita in Tocharisch B. *Historische Sprachforschung* 105: 50–6.

Schmitt, Rüdiger. 1981. *Grammatik des Klassisch-Armenischen.* Innsbruck: Institut für Sprachwissenschaft der Universität Innsbruck.

Schrijver, Peter. 2006. Review of Meiser, Gerhard, *Veni vidi vici* (Munich 2003: Beck), *Kratylos* 51: 46–54.

Schulze, Wilhelm. 1936. Griech. ὦμος. *Zeitschrift für vergleichende Sprachforschung* 63: 28.

Schwyzer, Eduard. 1923. *Dialectorum graecarum exempla epigraphica potiora.* Leipzig: Hirzel.

Schwyzer, Eduard. 1939. *Griechische Grammatik.* I. Band. Munich: Beck.

Seebold, Elmar. 1967. Sind got. *nawis* und *sutis* *i*-stämmige Adjektive?, *Beiträge zur Geschichte der deutschen Sprache und Literatur* (Tübingen) 89: 42–53.

Seebold, Elmar. 1972. *Das System der indogermanischen Halbvokale.* Heidelberg: Winter.

Seiler, Hansjakob. 1950. *Die primären griechischen Steigerungsformen.* Hamburg: Hansischer Gildenverlag.

Sievers. Eduard. 1893. *Altgermanische Metrik.* Halle: Niemeyer.

Sihler, Andrew. 1995. *New comparative grammar of Greek and Latin.* Oxford: Oxford University Press.

Skelton, Christina Michelle. 2015. Borrowing, character weighting, and preliminary cluster analysis in a phylogenetic analysis of the Ancient Greek dialects. *Indo-European Linguistics* 3: 84–117.

Skelton, Christina Michelle. 2022. Further thoughts on the reflex of syllabic nasals in Mycenaean Greek. Méndez Dosuna, Julián, Thomas G. Palaima, and C. V. García (eds.), *TA-U-RO-QO-RO: Studies in Mycenaean texts, language, and culture in honor of José Luis Melena Jiménez.* Washington: Center for Hellenic Studies, 221–9.

Smyth, Herbert Weir. 1894. *The sounds and inflections of the Greek dialects: Ionic.* New York: MacMillan.

Smyth, Herbert Weir. 1956. *Greek grammar*, revised by Gordon Messing. Cambridge, MA: Harvard University Press.

Southern, Mark R. V. 1999. *Sub-grammatical survival: Indo-European s-mobile and its regeneration in Germanic.* Washington, DC: Institute for the Study of Man.

Sowa, W. 2007. Anmerkungen zum Verbalsystem des Phrygischen. *Indogermanische Forschungen* 112: 69–95.

Stang, Christian. 1974. Ieur. **swad-/*swād-. Norsk Tidsskrift for Sprogvidenskap* 28: 99–101.

Strunk, Klaus. 1967. *Nasalpräsentien und Aoriste.* Heidelberg: Winter.

Strunk, Klaus. 1985. Flexionskategorien mit akrostatischem Akzent und die sigmatischen Aoriste. Schlerath and Rittner (eds.) 1985: 489–514.

Sturm, Julia. 2018. ἵστωρ and ἑορτή: The (Attic-Ionic) rough-breathing reflex of Greek **u̯*. Goldstein, David M., Stephanie W. Jamison, and Brent Vine (eds.), *Proceedings of the 28th Annual UCLA Indo-European Conference.* Bremen: Hempen, 267–76.

Sukač, Roman, and Ondřej Šefčík (eds.) 2012. *The sound of Indo-European 2.* Munich: Lincom Europa.

Supplementum epigraphicum graecum. 2. 1925, ed. P. Roussel et al. Leiden: Sijthoff.

Supplementum epigraphicum graecum. 9. 1938, ed. J. J. E. Hondius. Leiden: Sijthoff.

Supplementum epigraphicum graecum. 24. 1969, ed. A. G. Woodhead. Leiden: Sijthoff.

Surendran, Dinoj, and Partha Niyogi. 2006. Quantifying the functional load of phonemic oppositions, distinctive features, and suprasegmentals. Thomsen, Ole Nedergaard (ed.),

Competing models of linguistic change: Evolution and beyond. Amsterdam: Benjamins, 43–58.

Szemerényi, Oswald. 1960. *Studies in the Indo-European system of numerals*. Heidelberg: Winter.

Szemerényi, Oswald. 1966a. The development of the *-o-/-ā-* stems in the light of the Mycenaean evidence. *Colloquium on Mycenaean Studies* 4: 217–25.

Szemerényi, Oswald. 1966b. The origin of the Vedic 'imperatives' in *-si*. *Language* 42: 1–6.

Szemerényi, Oswald. 1967a. The history of Attic οὖς and some of its compounds. *Studi Micenei ed Egeo-Anatolici* 3: 47–88.

Szemerényi, Oswald. 1967b. The perfect participle active in Mycenaean and Indo-European. *Studi Micenei ed Egeo-Anatolici* 2: 7–26.

Szemerényi, Oswald. 1968a. The Attic 'Rückverwandlung' or atomism and structuralism in action. *Studien zur Sprachwissenschaft und Kulturkunde, Gedenkschrift für Wilhelm Brandenstein*. Innsbruck: Institut für Vergleichende Sprachwissenschaft der Leopold-Franzens-Universität Innsbruck, 139–57.

Szemerényi, Oswald. 1968b. The Mycenaean and the historical Greek comparative and their Indo-European background. Bartoněk, Antonín (ed.), *Studia mycenaea*. Brno: Universita J. E. Purkyně, 25–36.

Szemerényi, Oswald. 1973. Marked-unmarked and a problem of Latin diachrony. *Transactions of the Philological Society* 1973: 55–74.

Szemerényi, Oswald. 1987. *Scripta minora*, ed. P. Considine and J. T. Hooker. Innsbruck: Institut für Sprachwissenschaft der Universität Innsbruck. [Reprint of all the above articles.]

Szemerényi, Oswald. 1996. *Introduction to Indo-European linguistics*. Oxford: Oxford University Press.

Talbert, Richard J. A., et al. 2000. *Barrington atlas of the Greek and Roman World*. Princeton: Princeton University Press.

Taylor, Ann. 1990. *Clitics and configurationality in Ancient Greek*. Dissertation, University of Pennsylvania.

Te Riele, Gérard-Jean. 1967. Le grand apaisement d'Alipheira. *Revue Archéologique* 1967: 209–24.

Thompson, Rupert J. E. 1997. Dialects in Mycenaean and Mycenaean among the dialects. *Minos* 31–2: 313–33.

Thompson, Rupert J. E. 2008. Mycenaean non-assibilation and its significance for the prehistory of the Greek dialects. Sacconi, Anna, Maurizio del Freo, Louis Godart, and Mario Negri (eds.), *Colloquium Romanum*. Pisa: Fabrizio Serra, 753–65.

Threatte, Leslie. 1980. *The grammar of Attic inscriptions*, Vol. 1: *Phonology*. Berlin: de Gruyter.

Threatte, Leslie. 1996. *The grammar of Attic inscriptions*, Vol. 2: *Morphology*. Berlin: de Gruyter.

Thumb, Albert, and Ernst Kieckers. 1932. *Handbuch der griechischen Dialekte*. I. Teil, 2nd ed. Heidelberg: Winter.

Thumb, Albert, and Anton Scherer. 1959. *Handbuch der griechischen Dialekte*. 2. Teil, 2nd ed. Heidelberg: Winter.

Thurneysen, Rudolf. 1946. *A grammar of Old Irish*. Dublin: Institute for Advanced Studies.

Tichy, Eva. 1981. ἀνδροτῆτα und die Vorgeschichte des daktylischen Hexameters. *Glotta* 59: 28–67.

Tichy, Eva. 2006. *A survey of Proto-Indo-European*. Bremen: Hempen.

Tischler, Johann (ed.) 1982. *Serta indogermanica. Festschrift für Günter Neumann zum 60. Geburtstag*. Innsbruck: Institut für Sprachwissenschaft der Universität Innsbruck.

Trubetzkoy, Nikolai. 1926. Gedanken über den lateinischen a-Konjunktiv. *Festschrift für Paul Kretschmer*. Vienna: Deutscher Verlag für Jugend und Volk, 267–74.

Tucker, Elizabeth. 1981. Greek factitive verbs in -οω, -αινω and -υνω. *Transactions of the Philological Society* 79: 15–34.

Tucker, R. Whitney. 1962. On the dual pronunciation of eta. *Transactions of the American Philological Society* 93: 490–501.

Van Effenterre, Henri, and Pierre Demargne. 1937. Recherches à Dréros. II. Les inscriptions archaïques. *Bulletin de Correspondance Hellénique* 61: 333–48.

Vendryès, Joseph. 1920. Sur les mot attiques qui ont ρη au lieu de ρα. *Mémoires de la Société de Linguistique de Paris* 22: 64–7.

Vezzosi, Letizia. 2007. *Himself*: An overview of its uses in Middle English. Mazzon, Gabriella (ed.), *Studies in Middle English forms and meanings*. Frankfurt: Peter Lang, 239–56.

Vine, Brent. 1988. Review of Tamaz Gamkrelidze and Vyacheslav Ivanov, *Индоевропейский язык и индоевропейцы* (Tbilisi 1984: University of Tbilisi Press). *Language* 64: 396–402.

Vine, Brent. 1999. On 'Cowgill's Law' in Greek. Eichner, Heiner, Hans Christian Luschützky, and Velizar Sadovski (eds.), *Compositiones indogermanicae. In memoriam Jochem Schindler*. Prague: Enigma, 555–600.

Vine, Brent. 2006. On 'Thurneysen-Havet's Law' in Latin and Italic. *Historische Sprachforschung* 119: 211–49.

Wackernagel, Jacob. 1888. Miscellen zur griechischen Grammatik 12. Über die Behandlung von *s* in Verbindung mit *r, l, n, m*. *Zeitschrift für vergleichende Sprachforschung* 29: 124–37.

Wackernagel, Jacob. 1895. Miscellen zur griechischen Grammatik 23. Das Reflexivum. *Zeitschrift für vergleichende Sprachforschung* 33: 2–21.

Wackernagel, Jacob. 1904. Studien zum griechischen Perfectum. *Programm zur akademischen Preis- verteilung*. Göttingen: Universität Göttingen, 3–32. [Reprinted in *Kleine Schriften von Jacob Wackernagel*. 1953. Göttingen: Vandenhoeck und Ruprecht, 1000–21.]

Wackernagel, Jacob. 1916. *Sprachliche Untersuchungen zu Homer*. Göttingen: Vandenhoeck & Ruprecht.

Walkden, George. 2014. *Syntactic reconstruction and Proto-Germanic*. Oxford: Oxford University Press.

Wathelet, Paul. 1966. La coupe syllabique et les liquides voyelles dans la tradition formulaire de l' épopée grecque. Lebrun, Yvan (ed.), *Linguistic Research in Belgium*. Wetteren: Universa, 145–73.

Watkins, Calvert. 1969. *Indogermanische Grammatik*. Band III. *Formenlehre*. Heidelberg: Winter.

Watkins, Calvert (ed.) 1975. *Indo-European Studies II*. Cambridge, MA: Harvard University Department of Linguistics.

Watkins, Calvert. 1987. *Studies in Memory of Warren Cowgill*. Berlin: de Gruyter.

Weiss, Michael. 1993. *Studies in Italic Nominal Morphology*. Dissertation, Cornell University.

Weiss, Michael. 1995. Life everlasting: Latin *iūgis* 'everflowing', Greek ὑγιής 'healthy', Gothic *ajukdūþs* 'eternity' and Avestan *yauuaējī-* 'living forever'. *Münchener Studien zur Sprachwissenschaft* 55: 131–56.

Weiss, Michael. 1996. Greek μυρίος 'countless', Hittite *mūri-* 'bunch (of fruit)'. *Historische Sprachforschung* 109: 199–214.
Weiss, Michael. 2012. Italo-Celtica: Linguistic and cultural points of contact between Italic and Celtic. Jamison, Stephanie W., H. Craig Melchert, and Brent Vine (eds.), *Proceedings of the 23rd Annual UCLA Indo-European Conference*. Bremen: Hempen, 151–73.
Weiss, Michael. 2016. 'Sleep' in Latin and Indo-European: On the non-verbal origin of Latin *sōpiō*. Gunkel et al. (eds.) 2016: 470–85.
Whitney, William Dwight. 1889. *A Sanskrit grammar*. Leipzig: Breitkopf & Härtel.
Willi, Andreas. 1999. Zur Verwendung und Etymologie von griechisch ἐρι-. *Historische Sprachforschung* 112: 86–100.
Willi, Andreas. 2018. *Origins of the Greek verb*. Cambridge: Cambridge University Press.
Winter, Werner. 1962. Die Vertretung indogermanischer Dentale im Tocharischen. *Indogermanische Forschungen* 67: 16–35.
Winter, Werner. 1998. Lexical Archaisms in the Tocharian Languages. Mair (ed.) 1998: 347–57.
Wodtko, Dagmar S., Britta Irslinger, and Carolin Schneider. 2008. *Nomina im indogermanischen Lexikon*. Heidelberg: Winter.
Yakubovich, Ilya. 2009. *Sociolinguistics of the Luvian language*. Leiden: Brill.
Yang, Charles. 2002. *Knowledge and learning in natural language*. Oxford: Oxford University Press.
Zerdin, Jason. 2000. *Studies in the Ancient Greek verbs in* -skō. Dissertation, University of Oxford.

Index

1 Greek

Digamma is alphabetized separately, but the lone qoppa-initial form is listed under kappa; Arkadian ϰ is placed at the end of the alphabet. Forms of each word are normally combined in a single entry, so that some knowledge of Greek grammar is needed to use this index. However, when different dialect forms are spelled with different initial letters or diphthongs, they are listed separately so as to make them easier to find. The citation form of a verb is usually its (present) infinitive if it is referenced in the text, but οἶδα is listed under the pf. indic. 1sg. because of its extensive word-initial ablaut. Derivationally related words are occasionally listed together if citations are very few. Inflectional endings are not routinely listed; see the relevant sections (4.2.6, 4.2.7, 4.2.8, 4.3.1, 4.3.5, 5.3.2 (active infinitives and 1pl.), 5.4.2 (i), (ii), 6.3). Cyprian and Mycenaean forms are listed separately at the end.

ἀ- 'un-' 113
ἁ- 113, 131
-α (acc. sg.) 113
ἀβροτάξομεν 291, 295
ἀβρότη 291
ἀγαθός 341
Ἀγαμέμνων 336
ἀγάννιφος 134, 336
ἄγασθαι 175
ἀγγέλλε̄ν, ἄγγελος 159, 194
ἄγε̄ν 186, 209, 276, ἄγεν 277, ἄγην 278, ἄγει 16, 89, ἄγο̄σι, ἄγονσι, ἄγοντι 272, ἆγε, ἦγε 91, 227, 300, ἆγον, ἀγαγε̄ν, ἀγηοχέναι 209
ἀγέ̄ρε̄ν, ἀγρέσθαι, ἀγέροντο 207, ἀγείρομεν 225, ἀγερ- 289
ἀγήνωρ 93
ἀγκοίνῃισι 161
ἄγκος 89, 245
ἀγκύλη 241
ἀγκύλος 89, 170, 252
ἀγκών 161, 236 (partial paradigm), 246
ἁγνός 19, 107, 251
ἀγ- 'break': ἐᾱγέναι 219, ἔᾱγε 305
ἀγορεύε̄ν, ἀγορή 199
ἀγρός 80, 239, ἄγριος 80
ἄγχε̄ν 127, 128, 186, ἄγξαι 212
ἄγχι, ἆσσον 155
-άδᾱς 337
ἀδεαλτώhαιε 326
ἀδελφεός, ἀδελφός 147
ἀδήν 283
ἀδικέντα, ἀδικήμενος 295
ἅ̄δομαι 296
ἁ̄δύς 91, 133, 300, ἅ̄διον 155
ἀέξειν 95
ἆε̄ραι, ἄερρε 267
ἀ̄ϝώς 95, 245, 267, 301, 308, αὔως 95, 267, 308
-αζε/ο- (pres.) 199, 338
ἄησι 90, 109, 174, ἀήμεναι 174
Ἀθήνησι 256
ἀθρεόντω 325
-αι (aor. opt. 3sg.) 130
-ᾱι, -ῃι (dat. sg.) 91, 300, -ᾶι, -ῆι 169
αἰ 'if' 279, 334
Αἰακίδᾱο 308
αἰδώς 138, 246, αἰδοῖος 138
αἰετός, αἰϝετός 160
αἴθε̄ν 94
αἶθος 239
αἰλότρια 160 fn. 46
αἷμα 341
αἱμιόνοις 315
-αινε/ο- (pres.) 199, 338
αἰνε̄ν, αἶνος 196
αἴνυσθαι 196, 296
αἰπόλος 120
αἱρε̄ν 296, 329, ἡρεθεῖσαν 321
αἰσθάνεσθαι, αἰσθέσθαι 181, 206, ἄϊσθε 181
ἄϊστος 121
αἴσχιον 155
αἰτε̄ν 196
αἰχμᾱ́, αἰχμή 293
ἀκλεής, ἀκλεᾶ 306, 318
ἄκμητος 103, 182, 300
ἄκμων 89, 235 (partial paradigm), 246
ἀκοή, ἄκουαι 309
ἀκόλουθος 113, 147
ἄκος 105

ἀκούε̄ν 90, 104, 109, 157, 158, 193, ἀκούει 90, 340
ἄκρᾱτος, ἄκρητος 103, 251, 300
ἄκρηστον (κ for χ) 321
ἄλγιον 155
ἀλέγω 109, ἀλέγει 186
ἀλέξε̄ν 109, ἀλεξέμεναι 223, ἀλέξει 34, 97, ἄλαλκε 211, 223
ἀλκί 97, 238
Ἄλκιππος 118
ἅλλεσθαι 132, 159, 191, ἆλτο 203
ἄλληκτος 122, 134
ἀλλοδαπός 337
ἄλλος 89, 156, 159, 160 fn. 46, 252, ἄλλο 73, 145, 156, 159, 258, ἄλλοιρ 316, ἀλ(λ)ήο̄ν 301 with fn.1, 308
ἄλοχος 147
ἅλς 132, 238, 249
ἀλυκτοπέδησι 122
ἀλύσκων 185
ἀλφάνε̄ν, ἦλφον 206, ἀλφε̃ν 284
ἀλφός 125, 240
ἁλῶναι, ἁλώμεναι 215
ἅμα 114, 131
ἄμαθος 111, 126, 147, 240, 340
ἆμαρ 91, 288, ἄ̄ματα πάντα 248, 288
ἁμαρτάνε̄ν, ἡμάρτανε 181, 206, ἁμαρτε̃ν 105, 181, 206, 289 (2x), ἄμβροτε, ἀμβ[ρό]την 289
ἀ̔μέ 139, 141, 266, 311, ἄμμε 266, 311, ἀμμέ 266, ἀ̔μές, ἄμμες 259
ἀμείνων 154 fn. 42, 298
ἀμέλγε̄ν 109, 187
ἀ̔μέρᾱ 163, ἀ̔μέρας 313
ἄμμος 340
ἀμνός 239, 282
ἀμόθεν 114, 131
ἀμπεληλεῦθεν 219
ἀμπεπαλών, ἀνέπαλτο 210
ἀμφί 97, 125, 333
ἀμφιβρότη 291
ἀμφίεπον 207
ἀμφιμέμῡκεν 208
(*)ἀμφιφορῆϝες 249
ἄμφω 70, 125, 260, ἀμφοῖν 260
ἄν 280, 332–3, 334
ἀνά 333
ἀναβιῶναι 153
ἀναγραψάντων, ἀγγραψάντων 325, ἀναγραψάντω 325, ἀναγραφῆμεν 276
ἄναλτος 99
ἄναξ 195, 249, ἄνακτ- 195, ἄνα 146, ἄνακτος 146, 249
ἀνασσέμεν 195
-ανε/ο- (pres.) 157, 181
ἀνατέλλε̄ν 271
ἀνατιθέναι: ἀντίθειτι, ἀντίθεντι 272, ἀναθέμεν 277, ἀνθῆναι 276, ἀνέθηκε 204, 322, ἀνέθε̄ 204, ἀνέθε̄κεν 301, ἀνέσηκε 321, ἀνέθεαν, ἀνέθιαν 295, ἀντέθεικε 327, ἀνατεθέκαντι 296
ἀνδάνε̄ν 296
ἀνδριάντας 313
ἀνδροτῆτα 291
ἀνέκραγον 208
ἄνεμος 99, 105, 111
ἀνεψιός 18, 240
ἀνήκοισαν 315
ἀνήρ 97, 109, 235 (partial paradigm), 247, 339, ἀνέρ- 109, ἀνδρός 97
ἄνθος 126, 128, 245
ἄνθρωπος 282, 341
ἄνιπτος 122, 251
ἀνιστάμεν 276
ἀνταποδιδῶσσα 315, 321
ἀντί 89, 129, 273, 333
ἀντίος 252
ἀντιτετάχαται 310
ἄνυδρος 114
ἀνωφελής 105
ἀοσσε̃ν 121, 136, 156
ἅ[π]ανσαν 314
ἅπαξ 113
ἀπελήλυθα 218, 224, ἀπειλθείοντες 219, 327
ἄπελος 109, 245
ἆ̄πε̄ρος 156, 240
ἀπέχειν 276
ἀπεχθάνεσθαι, ἀπεχθέσθαι 181, 207, ἀπεχθάνεαι 181
ἁπλόος, ἁπλο̃ς 113, 131
ἀπό 333 with fn. 4, ἀπ', ἀφ' 324
ἀπόβλητος 103, 282
ἀποδάτταθθαι 169
ἀποδόμεν 277, 278, ἀπυδόμεναι 278, ἀποδώει 318, ἀποδόντω, ἀποδότωσαν 325, ἀποδεδόανθι 296, 327, ἀ̣π(υδ)ε̣δώκανσ̣ι̣ 296 fn. 17, ἀπυδεδωκώς 327
ἀποδρᾶναι 300, ἀποδρᾱ́ς, ἀπέδρᾱ 202
ἀποθνήισκει 341
ἀποκτε̄́νει 340
ἀπολλύναι 179, 271, ἀπόλλυσθαι, ἀπολέσθαι 206, ἀπολώλη 219, 221
ἀπολογίτταστη 169
ἀποπαρδε̃ν 207
ἀποστᾶμεν 276
ἀποσ[τ]ειλάντω 325, ἀπέστελλαν, ἀπυστέλλαντος 267, ἀπέστηλαν 322
ἀποτεινύτω 180
ἀππᾱσάμενος 118
ἀππεισάτου, ἀπυτεισάτω 283

ἀπυκρύπτοισι 315
ἀπυλιμπάνω 44 fn. 40, 297
ἄπυστος 121, 123, 252
ἄρ 287
ἀρᾱ́, ἀρή 304 fn. 5, 317 ἄρᾱς 317
ἀρᾶσθαι 304 fn. 5
ἀραρε̄ν, ἄρμενα 142, ἄρμενος, 142, 203, 208, ἀραρών, ἤραρε 36 fn. 31, 208
ἀργός 79, 97, 250, ἀργι- 97, ἀργίποδες 79
ἀργυρᾶ 302
ἀρείω 5 fn. 19
ἀρήγε̄ν 109
ἀρηΐφατος 251
ἀρήν 246, 290
ἀρῑθμε̄ν, ἀρῑθμός 196
ἄριστον 121
ἄρκτος 21, 97, 116, 239
ἅρμα 142, 144
ἄρνυσθαι 87, 296, ἀρνύμενος 179, ἄροντο 206
ἀρο̃ν 190, ἀρόσαι 212
ἄροτρον 78, 111, 122, 241
ἄρουρα 101, 158
ἅρπαξ, ἅρπαγ- 167, 195
ἁρπάζε̄ν 167, 195, ἁρπάσαι 167, 295
ἄρσην, ἄρρην 246
Ἄρταμις, Ἄρτεμις 274, 280, Ἀρταμίτιος, Ἀρτεμίσιος 274
ἄρτι 273
ἀρτοκόπος 282 fn. 13
ἀρχέκακος 336
-ας (acc.pl.) 114, -ᾱς 315
-ᾶς, -ῆς (gen. sg.) 169
ἄσις 136, 137
ἀσπερχές 147
ἀσπίς 337
ἀστεμφής 147
ἀστήρ, ἀστέρ- 109, 236, 247, 339, ἀστράσι 236
ἄστυ 244
ἄτερ 133
-ατι, -ασι (pf. 3pl.) 114, 129, 314, -ᾱσι 314
-ατο (mp. 2ary 3pl.) 114
ἄττα 20, 89
ἅττα 258
ἀτύζεσθαι 109, 166, ἀτυζόμενος 190
αὐδᾱ́, αὐδή 94, 197
αὔδᾱ (iptv. 2sg.) 197
αὔῃ 'fetch fire' 191
αὐλός 239
αὔξε̄ν, αὐξάνε̄ν 96, αὔξεσθαι 159
αὖος, αὖος 266 fn. 2
αὔριον 143, 151
αὐτάρ 288, 289
ἀϋτμή 142
αὐτός 250, 335, αὐτόν 335, αὐτό 258, αὐτοῦ 322
αὐχήν 341
ἀφαιρῖσθαι 323
ἀφεύε̄ν 142
ἄφθιτον 113, 116, 251, 282
ἀφιέναι 278, ἀφειώσᾱς 327
ἆχήν 94
ἄχθεσθαι 116
ἄχος 245
ἄψινθος 342

βάσσων, βάθιστον 154
βαίνε̄ν 115, 160, 190, 282, ἔβᾱ, ἔβη 202, 282, 283, βῆ, βάτην 202, ἔβαν 202, 310, βάν 144, 202, ἔβησαν 310, βαντ-, βάντες 144, βήσομεν 225
βάλλε̄ν 206, 271, βαλε̄ν 106, 206, 290, βλη-: βαλ- 293
βανᾱ́ 242
βάπτε̄ν 162, 190, 282
βαρύς 79, 96, 253, 282, 290, βαρέος 96 fn. 4
βασιλεύε̄ν 199
βασιλεύς 145, 199, 282, 308 (partial Hom. and Att. paradigm), βασιλέος 308
βάσις 78, 243, 274
βάσκε̄ν 113, 185, 282, βάσκει 124
βέλεμνα 103, 111
βέλλειτει, βεῖλειτη 271
βελόνη 293
Βελφοί, Βελφαίō 283
βίᾱ, βίη 153, 197, 285
βιᾶσθαι 197
βιβᾱ́ς 176
βιός 'bow' 153, 285
βιῶναι 215, 285
βλάβη, βλάπτε̄ν 162, βλάβεν, ἔβλαβεν 215
βλαστάνε̄ν, βλαστε̄ν 181, 206
βλίσσε̄ν 164, βλίττε̄ν 164, 193
βλώσκε̄ν, μολε̄ν 104, 185, 206, 293
βοᾱ́, βοή, βοᾶν 197
βō̃λεσθαι 270, 284, βόλεται, βόλεσθε, ἐβόλοντο, βόληται, βόλητοι 270, ἐβōλᾱ́σετυ 294
βōλή, βωλᾱ́ 270, βόλλᾱ 270, 320, βωλᾶς 322, 323
βουκόλος 120
βοῦς 145, 249, 282, βου- 282, βο(ϝ)- 249, 282
βραδύς 155, 253, 282, 290, 291, βράδιον, βάρδιστοι 155, 291
βραχῑ́ων 155 fn. 43
βραχύς 117, 126, 154, 253, 289, 290, βρόχεα 290, βράσσων 154
βροτός 251, 290, 291
βρωτός 104, 282

Βωλαγόρᾱ 322
βωμόν 322
βωτιάνēρα 336

γάλα, γάλακτος 146, 249, 342
γαμψώνυχες 93
γάνυται 178
γαστήρ 235, 341
γελᾶν 195, γελάσαι 4 fn. 40
γέλως, γελω-ε/ο- 196 fn. 20
γέμēν 117, 186
γενεαίρ (acc. pl.) 316
γένεθλον 147
γένεσις 217, 243, 274
γενέτωρ 78, 89, 103, 111, 247, 337
γένος 78, 89, 117, 135, 234, 239, 245, γένεος 89, 135, 235, 245, γένōς 89, 135, 245
γένυς 244
γεροντεύων 321
γέρρον 241
γέρων 293
γεύεσθαι 188
γῆ 341
γίγνεσθαι, γενέσθαι 184, 206, γέγονε 217, 221, γεγόνατι 114, 314, γεγάᾱσι 217
γιγνώσκēν 44, 105, 185, γνώσκēν 185, γνῶναι 44, ἔγνω 91, 105, 202
γλυκύς, γλυκίων, γλύσσονα 155
γλύφēν 189
γλῶττα 341
γνωτός 105
γόμφος 125, 128, 128 fn. 23, 239
γόνος, γονή 77
γōνōσθαι 197
γόνυ 244, 336, 339, γōνα 197, γόνατ- 336
γράφēν 189, 291, γράφωισι 273
γυμνασιαρχέντος 295
γυμνός 119, 198, 252
γυμνοῦσθαι 198
γυνᾱ́ 119, 242, γυνή 119, 242, 339, γύναι, γυναικ- 242
Γυνόππᾱστος 118

δαήμεναι 136, 208, 215, 278, δέδαε 136, 208
δᾱήρ 247
δαίδαλος, δαιδάλλēν 159
δαΐδες 337
δαιμόνιος 156
δάκνēν 157, 182, 206, δάκνει 338, δακēν 182, 206
δάκρυ 244
δᾱμιοργίσōσα 294
δάμνησι, δάμνατο 177, 223, δαμασ(σ)α- 177, 223, δαμήμεναι 114, δαμᾶι 223
δᾱ́μου 322
δᾱμοσιῶμεν 321
δαπάνη 19, 114, 154, 182, 242
δασύς 137, 253
δατέονται, δατēθθαι, δάσσασθαι ~ δάσασθαι, δάσασσθαι 169
δαυλός 137
δέ 334
δέατ', δέᾱτοι 175
δείδω 217, 221, δείδοικα 221, 317, δέδοικε 317, δείδιμεν 217, δεδίᾱσι 314
δεικνύναι 179, δεῖξαι 36, 211
Δεινοδίκηο 301 with fn. 1, 308
δέκα 113
δεκάδ- 337
δέκεσθαι 175, 199, 297, δέχθαι 175, δέχεσθαι, δέχαται 175, 297, δέκτο 175 with fn. 1
δέκτρια 101
δείληται, δήληται, δήλωνται 271, δηλόμενοι 321
Δελφοί 283
δελφῦς 147, 283
δέμας 103
δεμēν 224
δēν 'to tie' 190
δένδρον 340
δεξιός 21, 252
δεξιτερός 252
δέρēν 186
δερϝᾶν, δēρή, δέρη 304, 317, δέρᾱ 317
δέρκεσθαι 188, 291, δρακēν 207, 291, δέδορκε 218, 291, δεδορκώς 218
δεσπότης 84
δήεις 223
δήϊος, δηϊόων 198
δηκνύμενος (δεικνύμενος) 179
δημός 341
διά 333
δ[ι]αβωλευσάμινος 320
διαγνόντω 325
δ]ιαδέξειε 326
διᾱκάτιαι 273
διακωλῦσει 326
διεμέτρεον 196
διασκιδνᾶσιν 177
δίδαξε 208
δίδη 176
διδόναι 112 fn. 15, 276, διδοῦναι 329, διδόμεν 277, δίδων 278, δίδωτι 91, 129, 176, 272, δίδōτι 272, δίδωσι 91, 112, 176, 272, 339, δίδοντι 272, διδοῦσι 99, δίδοτε 112, δίδοι 129, δōναι, δῶναι 276, δόμεν 276 (2x), δόμεναι 278, δωκ- ~ δο- 203–4, ἔδουκε 320, δός 275, δόντω 325, δεδωῶσα ἴη 220, 327, δεδωῶση 327, δώσει 320
Διειτρέφης 234 fn. 47

Διείφιλος 234
δίενται 175
διεσσεῖλθεικε 219, 327
δίζηαι 167, 176, διζήμενος 167
διηνεκής 110
δικάζε̄ν, δικάσαι 167, 169, δικάξαι 167,
 δικάσασθαι, δικάσσαιεν 169, ἐδικάσαμεν 279,
 δικακσίε̄ 226, 322, 326, δικά(δ)δο̄σα 315
δῑ́νη 285
Διονῡ́σω 321
δῖος 80, 269
δίς 153
δισσός, διττός, δίχα 163
διψῆν, διψᾱ́ων 198
διώρυχ- 163
δοκε̄̃ν 199, 214, δόξαι 214, subj. δόξει 225
δολιχός 106, 250, 253
δόλος 239
δο̄λοσύνη 337
δόρυ 244
δοτήρ 78, 337
ἔδραθε 181, 206
δράκων 291
δραμε̄̃ν 206
δραχ-, δαρχμάς 289, 312, 313, 315
δρομέανς 314
-δυ 324
δύνασθαι 178, δύναται, δύνᾱται 326
δύο 153, 260, 339, δύω 153, 260, δυοῖν 260
δώδεκα 153
δῶρα 320

ἕ 260, 335, ἑ 133, 335
ἔαρ 'blood' 142
ἔαρ 'spring' 143, 248, 288, ἔαρος 248
ἐγδικαξῆται 321
ἐγδόμεν 277
ἐγε̄́ρε̄ν 108, ἐγρέσθαι 104, 108, 206, 218,
 ἐγρήγορε 90, 108, 218, ἐγρηγορώς 218,
 ἐγρηγορέναι 206
ἐγκέκλιται 222
ἔγκτησις 118
ἐγώ 259 (paradigm), 339, ἐμέ 75, 335, ἐμεῖο 258
ἑδ- 'sit' 151
ἔδεθλον 147
ἔδμεναι 89, 174, 278, fut. ἔδεσθαι 224 fn. 43
ἕδος 131, 147, 245
ἕδρᾱ, ἕδρη 305
ἐέργε̄ν 108
ἐέρση 108, 140
ἥσσαντο 'they installed' 322
ἐθέλοισα 315
-ει (pres. indic. 3sg.) 129
-ει (pres. subj. 3sg.) 130
εἰ, ἠ, ἐᾱ́ν, ἤν, εἰκ 280, 334
εἰαμενή 107
-ειας, -ειαν 326
εἰβᾱτᾶ 320
εἴκοσι 273 (2x)
εἰκοίστᾱι 312
εἰνατέρες 107, 247
εἴνατος 317
εἰπε̄̃ν 284, ἔειπε 36, 208
ἑκατόν 113
ἔκβασις 243
ἐκγεγαώς 115, ἐκγεγαυῖα 217
ἐκεῖ 320, 340
ἐκε̄̃νος 340, ἐκε̄̃νο 258
ἐκεχε̄ρίᾱ 147
h̲εκηβόλο̄ι 301
ἐκθέμειν 277
ἐκκόψει (subj.) 225
ἐκλέλαθον 210
ἐκτεθήκανθι 327
ἑκυρᾱ́ 133, 240, 243
ἑκυρός 133, 239
ἑκών 187, ἑκοῖσα 315
ἐλαύνε̄ν, ἐλάσαι 158, ἐλάαν 224
ἐλαφρός 20, 108, 114, 127, 250, 282
ἐλαχύς 20, 108, 114, 117, 121, 127, 253, ἐλάσσων
 121, τοὔλασσον, ἐλάχιστον 154, ἐλάσσως 5 fn.
 19
ἐλέγχε̄ν 108, 187
ἑλε̄̃ν 207, ἑλο̃σι, ἑλόνσι 168
ἔλεος 104
ἐλευθερο̃ν 35
ἐλεύθερος 108, 126, 251, ἐλεύθερονς 313, 314,
 ἐλεύθαρος (acc. pl.) 315
ἐλεύσεσθαι 224, ἤλυθε 36, 91, 126, 204, 224, 227,
 ἦλθες 320, εἰλήλουθα 218, 224
ἑλικ- 163
ἑλισσέμεν, ἑλίττε̄ν 163, εἱλίχατο 310
ἕλκε̄ν 132
ἕλος 131, 245
ἐλπίς 337
ἕ̄μα 139, 142, 151, 247, 266, ἕμματα 266
ἐμός 259
ἕσται 151, εἵατο 114, ἕστο 174
ἐμε̄̃ν 192
ἐμμενέν (fut.) 277, ἐμμενέοισι 273
ἐμός 259
ἐμπίπληθι 176
ἐν 89, 299, 333, ἔνδον 89
ἔ̄ναι 174, 232–3, 276, ἦναι 276, ἦμεν 276 (2x),
 277, 321 (3x), 322, εἶμεν 276 (3x), 277 (2x),
 278, 321, 323, ἔμμεν 277, ἔμμεναι 278, ἤμε̄ν,
 ἤμην 322, ἐ̄μι 139, 151, 266, ἐμμι 139, 266, εἶ
 20, ἐστι 89, 129, 142, 151, 174, 272, 310, ἐ̄σι,

151, 314, ἐντι 314, ἔω 135, εἴην 112, εἴη 38, 138, 226, ἔντō, ἔστων, ἔστουσαν 325, ἦα 136, 151, ἦς 91, 146, 151, 227, 309, 320, ἦεν 309, 310, ἦσαν 309, 310 (3x), ἔσκε 184, ἐόντ-, 108, 135, ἔασσα 100, 108, 114, 135, 164, ἰωσᾱ́ων 318, ἐσσῆται 294, ἐσσεῖμεν 321
ἐνᾱράτιον, ἐνηρόσιον 274
ἔνατος 317
ἐναῦσαι 'kindle' 212
ἐνδεδιωκότα 285
ἐνδελεχής 106
ἐνεγκῆν 110, 205, 209, ἐνηνοχέναι 209
ἐνένῑπε, ἠνῑ́παπε 211
ἕνη καὶ νέᾱ 132, 250
ἐνθῡμήθητι 150
ἐνί 135 fn. 29
ἐνιαυτός, ἐνιαύσιος, ἐνιαυτίᾱ, ἐνιαύτια 274
ἐννέα 306
ἔντερα 241
Ἐνυμακρατίδᾱς 110, 246
ἕξ 133, 299, 333
ἐξάγōδι 273
ἐξξανακάδ(δ)ēν 277
ἐξεικάττιοι 273
ἐξείκοντα 320
ἐξεῖμεν 276, ἐξήμειν 277
ἐξεστρατεύκαντι 296
ἐξίμεν 277
ἔξω 299
ἔοικε, ἔϊκτον, ἐΐκτην 217
ἔορες 133, 135, 247
ἔπειτα 279
ἔπει 207, ἔπēν 187, ἔποντα 132
ἐπελήλυθα 218
ἐπερωτᾶι, ἐπερωτῆι 319
ἕπεσθαι 187, 207, ἕπεται 131, 151, 284, ἕπονται 284, ἕ̄πετο 142, 143, 151, ἕσπετο 151, σπέσθαι 151, 207
ἐπί 89, 93, 100, 333
ἐπιάλμενος 203
ἐπιβάλλοντανς 313 with fn. 1
ἔπιβδαν 122
ἐπιδόμεναι 278
ἐπέκριννε 267
ἐπέλησεν 210
ἐπιμελήθην 278
ἐπιμεμηνᾱ́καντι 296
ἐπιμνᾱ́σθεισα 315
ἐπιπτέσθαι 207
ἐπιρρόμβεισι 273, 315
ἐπίσπενσανς 314
ἐπίστασθαι 175
ἐπιστολάς 313
ἐπιτῡ́φεσθαι, ἐπιτεθῡμμένος 150
ἐπ]ομώμοκε 327
ἔπος 78, 119, 245, 284
ἔππᾱσις 118
ἑπτά 113, 131
ἐπώνυμος 93
ἔρασθαι 175
ἠργάσσαντο 322
ἔργον 78, 241, ἔργω, ἔργων 320
ἐργώνησας 313
ἔρδειν 190, ἔοργε, ἐοργώς 218
ἐρεβεννός 140, ἐρεβεννή 266
ἔρεβος 108, 245, 284
ἐρέεσθαι 'ask', ἐ̄ρέσθαι, Att. ἐρέσθαι 98, ἐρείομεν 98, 108, 175, εἴρεσθαι, εἴρεαι, ἔρειο 98 fn. 7
ἐ̄̃ρει 'says' 17, 31, εἴρω 31 fn. 24, ἐρέω 103, 111
ἐρεῖσες (subj.) 225
ἐρείπēν 108
ἄρēν 'to string' 133
ἐρέπτεσθαι 191, ἐρεπτόμενος 108, 161
ἐρεσσέμεναι 164, 196
ἐρέτης 196
ἐρετμόν 164, 196
ἐρεύγεσθαι 108, 186, 207, ἤρυγεν 207
ἔρευνα, 98 fn. 8, 158, ἐρευνᾶν 158
ἐρέφēν 110 fn. 12
ἐ̄ρήνη, εἰρήνᾱ, εἰρήν[ᾱι, εἰ[ρ]ήνᾱι, 303
ἐρι- 133
ἐρίζēν, ἔρις, ἔριδ- 195
ἕρματα 132
ἕρπēν 132, 187
ἔρρēν 165, 192
ἐρρῡτιασμένος 274
ἐρυθρός 79, 108, 126, 250, 339, ἐρυθρᾱ́ 300
ἔρυσθαι 175, ἐρύσσομεν 225
ἔρχεσθαι 185 fn. 6, ἔρχεται 339
ἐρωή 108, 241
-ες (Kyrenaian aor. subj. 2sg.) 326
ἐ̄ς 314, 333, ἐς 313 (3x), εἰς 315, ἐνς 299, 214 (2x), 313, ἰς 299
ἐ̄̃ς 'one' 339, ἕνς 260 (partial paradigm), εἷς 315, ἕν 113, 131, 260, ἑνός, ἑνί 113, μία 70 fn. 65, 101, 134, 260, 265, μίαν 260, μιᾶς, μιῆς 305, ἴα 70 fn. 65, 153, 260, 264, 265
ἔσγονος 313
ἐσδόμεν 277, ἐσδοθένσᾱι 314
ἐσέρπεν 277
ἐσθίει 339
-εσι (i-, u-stem dat. pl.) 237
ἐσλελοίπασι 272, 296 fn. 17, 314
ἕσπερος 151, 240
ἕσ(σ)ασθαι 'put on (a garment)' 212 fn. 39
-εσσι (dat. pl.) 264, 265, 299
ἑσσō̃σθαι 155
ἔσχατος 123

ἔτι 129, 273
ἔτος 245
εὐ- 143
εὗεν 142, 151, 186, 213,
 εὗσαι 212
-εύε̄ν 337
εὐεργ[έτας] 313
εὐεργετές 295
εὐήνορα 248 fn. 53
εὐθυορϝίᾱν 317
εὐκλεής, εὐκλεᾶ 306, 318
εὐκτά 123, 251
ἐϋκτίμενος 116, 174
εὐμενέοντες 193
εὐορκέντι 295
εὐπαρᾱ́ου 302
εὐρύς 81, 94, 253
ἐΰς 143, 253
-εύς, -ῆος/-έος 198–9, 249–50, 263,
 269, 337
ἐΰτμητος 103, 181
ἐϋτρόχοις 315
εὔτυκτος 123, 251
εὐφραίνε̄ν, εὔφρων 161, 195
εὔχεσθαι 127, εὐχομένως 321
ἔφεπε, ἐπισπε̃ν 207
ἐφεστᾱ́κεον 221
ἔχε̄ν 126, 148, 181, 184, 200, 207, ἔχειν 276, 320,
 ἔχην 276, ἔχεν 277, ἔχο̄σι 272, ἕξε̄ν 148, σχε̃ν
 148, 207
ἐχθαίρε̄ν 161, 194
ἐχθρός 123, 161, 194, 207
ᾄωθε 218
ἕως 'dawn' 95, 140, 151, 245, 267,
 301, 308
ἕως 'until' 308

ϝάναχς, ϝάνακτι 249
ϝαρήν 246, 290
-(ϝ)εντ-, -(ϝ)εσσα, -ϝεττα 164
ϝέξ 133
ϝεξακάτιαι 273
ϝέργον 241
ϝέρκσιεν 326
ϝετίων 321
ϝεχέτο̄ 187
ϝhε (ϝ̔ε), ϝε 133
ϝhεδιέστᾱς 133 fn. 28
ἔϝιδε 205
ϝίσϝος 316
ϝῑ́κατι 100, 114, 273
ϝοίκω 234
ϝεϝῡκονομειόντων 318, 327
-(ϝ)οντ- (pf. ptc.) 264, 265, 298
ϝρᾱ́τρᾱ 300
ϝρήσῑ 320

Ζάκυνθος 274, 342, Ζακύνθιος 274
ζειαί 158
ζε̃ν 143, 158
ζευγνύναι 179, ζευγνύμεναι 278, ζεῦξαι 158
ζεῦγος 158, 245
Ζεύς 145, 166, 237 (paradigm), 249, Ζῆνα 19,
 112, Δι(ϝ)- 249
ζυγόν 53, 112, 158, 241
ζῡ́μη 143, 158
ζώε̄ν 186
ζώνη 143, 158
ζωννύναι 179, ζῶσαι 158
ζωός 100, 186, 252

-ή- (intrans. aor.) 30, 215
ἥβᾱ, ἥβη 107, 241, 282, 283, 300
ἥδεσθαι 296
ἡδύς 91, 133, 253, 300, ἡδεῖα 03B1, ἥδιον 155
-ήϝ- 269
ἠθμός 147
ἦθος 147
ἠϊκανός 142
ἧκα 155
ἥλιος 132, 142, 324, 339, ἠέλιος 132, 142, 324
ἧμαι 139, 141, ἧσται 151, 174, ἥαται (εἵαται)
 136, 142
ἦμαρ 91, 145, 163, 248, 288
ἡμε̃ς 311, 339, ἡμέας 139, 141, 311, ἡμέες, ἡμᾶς
 311
ἡμέρᾱ 151, 163
ἦ (quotative) 146, 174
ἡμι- 90, 131, 167
ἥμισυς, ἥμισσον, εἵμιττον 167
hημίσχοινον 321
ἥμορος 142
ἡνάτᾱν 317, ἡνάτᾱι 317, 322
ἡνία, ἡνίαι 140, 141
ἧπαρ 90, 107, 248, 281, 288, 339, ἥπατος 248,
 ἥπατ- 281
ἤπε̄ρος 156, 240
-ησι (pres. subj. 3sg.) 130
ἥσσων 155, ἧσσω 5 fn. 19
ἦτορ 288
ἡττήθητι 150
ἠώς 95, 140, 141, 142, 245, 267, 301, 308

θαλ-: τέθᾱλεν, τεθηλώς, τεθαλυῖα 219,
 τεθᾱ́λαισι 273
θάμβος 128, 148 fn. 36
θανα- ~ θνη- 341
θάνατος 103, 105

θάπτε̄ν, ταφῆναι 148, 161
θαρσῦνε̄ν 137
Θεδωρίδᾱο 308
θέειον, θεειοῦται 197
θέη 307 fn. 8
-θεν, -θι (adv.) 150
θέναρ 248, 288, θέναρος 248
θε̄νέμεναι 119, 127, 192, 208, 283, θενών 192 fn. 15
θεόδοτος 112, 251
θεός 126, 135, 150, 318, θεῶ 323
θέρεσθαι 127
θερμός 127, 252, 339
θέρος 245, 284
θέρσος, θάρσος 126, 137, 140, 290
θέσις 243
θέσσεσθαι 189, 284
θέσφατος 126, 135, 150, 318
θετός 112, 251
-θη- 150, 215–6, -θητι 150
θήγε̄ν, θᾱ́ξαις, θῶξαι, τέθωκται, τεθωγμένοι 219
θηήσαο 307
θηητήρ 236 fn. 50, 307
θηλυτέρᾱν 321
θήρ 117, 237, 249, θῆρα 237
θησαυρῶι 323
-θι (iptv. 2sg.) 90
θιγγάνε̄ν, θιγε̄ν 128
θνᾱ́σκε̄ν 185, θνήσκε̄ν 104, 185, 206, θνήισκε̄ν, θνείσκω 185 fn. 7, θανε̄ν 104, 168, 185, 206, τέθνηκε 221, 327, τεθνάναι 150, 276
θνᾱτός, θνητός 103, 300
θοινᾶται, θοινῆται 319
Θο̄κῡδίδης 318
θρασύς 126, 137, 253, 290
θρᾱ́ττε̄ν, τετρᾱχ-, τετρήχει 148
θραυσθῆναι 150
θρέπτρα 123
θρίξ 148, 341, τρίχα, τριχός, θριξί 148
θρόμβος 128
θρόνος 291
θρύπτε̄ν, τρυφῆναι 148, 162
θρώσκε̄ν, θορε̄ν 104, 185, 206, 293
θυγάτηρ 111, 126, 235, 247, θυγατέρανς 313 with fn. 1
θῡεν 277, θῡ́ονσι 314, θῡσέοντι 272, τεθυκέναι, τεθύσθαι 148, τυθῆναι 148
θῡμός 102, 126, 148, 239
θύρᾱ 126
θωμός 17, 90, 126, 239

-ια, -ιᾱ- (fem.) 157
ἰαύε̄ν 94, 95, ἀέσαι 108
ἰγκεχηρήκοι 327
-ίδᾱς, -ίδης 337
ἴδην 'catch sight of' 320
ἱδρῶν, ἱδρώων 195–6 with fn. 20
ἱδρώς 133, 195–6
ἰέναι 174, 276, εἶτι 129, 174, 272, εἶσι 93, 174, 272, ἴτε 93, ἴομεν 225, ἴθι 129, 231, ἰόντω 325, ἴσαν, ἤϊσαν 310
ἱερεύε̄ν 199
ἱερεύς 199, 249, 280 fn. 11, ἱερής 263, ἱαρές 313
ἱερῑτεύκατι 272
hιεροθυτές 313
ἱερός, ἱαρός, ῑ̔ρος 94, 280, ἱαρός (acc. pl.) 315
ῑ̔́ετο 'he strove' 175, εἴσατο 213
-ιζε/ο- (pres.) 199, 338
ῑ̔́ζεται 34, ῑ̔́ζεσθαι 184
ῑ̔́ησι 93, 100, 176, ἡκ- ~ ἑ- 100, 106, 176, 203–4
ἰθαρώτεροι 94
ἱκᾱ́νε̄ν 115, 132, 180, 206, ἱκνέεσθαι 113, 132, ἱκνε̄σθαι 180, 206, ἱκέσθαι 180, 206
-ικός, -ιον (dimin.), -ίσκο- 337
ῑ̔́κατι 273
ῑ̔́ληθι, ἔλλαθι 176
ῑ̓λῡ́ς 94
ἱμᾱ́ς, ἱμάντ- 94, 195
ἱμάσσε̄ν 195
ῑ̔με̄́ρε̄ν 194, 267, ῑ̓μέρρην 267
ῑ̔́μερος 194
ἰμφαῖνεν 276
-ιος (patronymic) 264, 337
ῑ̓ός 'arrow' 94, 140
ῑ̓ός 'poison' 100, 135, 143
ῑ̓οχέαιρα 77, 137, 142, 290, ῑ̓οχεαίρηι 301
Ἰππημολγοί 93
ἵππιος 194
ἵππος 118, 151, 194, 239
ῑ̓ρᾱ́νᾱ, ῑ̓ρ]ήνᾱς 303, ῑ̓ρᾱ́ν[ᾱς, ῑ̓ρείνᾳ, ῑ̓ρήνᾱ 303 fn. 3
ἰρε̄νι 303 fn. 3
ῑ̓́ς 249, ῑ̓φι 125, 249
ἴσος, ῑ̓σος 316
ἱστάναι 210, 276, ἵστᾱτι 176, ἵστησι, 34, 176, ἱστᾶσι 34, 99, ἵσταντι 98, 272, ἱσταίη 38, στῆναι 276, ἔστᾱ, ἔστη 91, 112, 146, 202, 300, στῆ, ἔσταν, στάν 202, στᾱσάνθω 325, ἕστηκε 220, 327, 339, ἕστηκας, ἕστατον, ἑστᾶσι, ἑστήκᾱσιν, ἑστήκηι, ἕσταθ', ἕστατον, ἕστατε, ἑστάμεν(αι), ἑσταότος 220, ε̄στήκε̄ 142, 220, plup. ἕσταμεν, ἕστασαν 220
-ιστο- (sup.) 254
ἴσχε̄ν 181, 184, ἰσχάνε̄ν 181
ῑ̓χανάᾳ 94
ἰχθῦς 249, 339

κα 280, 332, 334
κᾱδεστάνς 313

καθαίρε̄ν 194, καθᾱ́ραισα 315
καθαρός 194
καθέρπονσι 272
καθεύδει 341
κάθηται 339
καθιερεύων, κατιαραίων 199, κατιαραύσειε 326
καί 131 with fn. 25, 263
καίε̄ν 161, καίεται, κᾱ́εται 341, ἔκηε 213
καινός 341
κακός 155, 163, κακόν 197, κακίων, κάκιστος 155
κάκου (iptv. 2sg.) 197
καλέσαι 4 fn. 40, ἐκάλεσε 103, κάλημι 295, καλῖσθαι 323
καλϝός, καλός, κᾱλός, κάλος 317, κάλλιον, καλλίονες 155
καλλιπάρηος 302
καλύβη, καλύπτε̄ν 162
κάματος 103, 105
κάμνε̄ν 157, 182, 206, καμε̄ν 182, 206, κέκμηκε 221
καπνός 341
κάπρος 239
κάπτε̄ν 162, 190
καρδίᾱ 137, 249, 291, 339, καρδίη 291
κάρρων 165
κάς 131, 263, 275
κασίγνητος 103, 131, 217, 251, 274, κασί]γνητον 320, κασιγνήτων 274, κατίγνειτος 131, 274, κασιγνḗτη 301
-κάσιοι 273
κατά 233, 333, κατ᾽, καθ᾽ 324
καταβεβάων 327
κα̣[ταβε]βλειώσᾱς 327
κατᾱγνύναι 179, subj. κατάξει 225, κατ-έᾱγε, κατεηγότα 305
καταδαρθάνε̄ν, καταδαρθε̄ν 181, 206
καταείνυσαν 139, 179
καταλῡμακωθής 321
κάταρϝον 304 fn. 5, 317
κατατίθεσθαι, καταθίθεθθαι 152, κατθέμεναι 278
καταθένς 314
κατεδίκασσαν 169
κατεϝέρξοδυ 294
κατεληλύθοντος, κατεληλευθυῖα 218, κατηνθηκότι 327
κατελίμπανεν 297
κατέπηκτο 202 fn. 24
κα(τ)θυτάς, κα(τ)θυταίς (acc. pl.) 316
-κάτιοι 273
κατοικέντεσσι 295
καῦμα 161
κε, κεν 280, 332, 334
κεῖται 117, 174, 339
κέλεσθαι, ἐκέκλετο 209
κέλευθος 113, 147
κελεύωνσι 272, 314
κέλσε̄ν 224
κεντε̄ν 312
κεραμεύς 249
κέρας 245, 339
κέρδιον 155
κε̄́ρε̄ν 117, ἔκερσε 31, κέρσαι 212
κέσκεον 117
κεστός 312
κεύθε̄ν 152
κεφαλή 147, 339
κῆνο 320
κῆρ 'heart' 249, 291
κῆρυξ, κήρῡκ-, κηρῡ́σσε̄ν, κηρῡ́ττε̄ν 163, 195
κίδναται, κεδασα- 177
κῑ́νυντο, κῑνε̄ν 178, 206, κίε 206
κίρνη 177, κεράσαι 117, 177, ἐκέρασε 103, 111
κις 286
κιχήμεναι 150, 176, κιχᾱ́νε̄ν 180
κιχράναι 150, 176, κιχρέτω 176
κῑ́ων 246
κλέεσθαι 188
κλέος 78, 117, 245
κλέπτε̄ν 117, 161, 192, 200, 213, κλέψαι 212, 213
κλητός 103
κλῑ́νε̄ν 180, ἐκέκλιτο 222
κλῦθι 202, 205, κλῦτε, ἔκλυε 205
κλυτοτέχνης 242
κνῆν, κνῆ 190
κοεῖς (2sg.) 200
κόθεν, κοῖος, κόσος, κότε, κότερος, κοῦ, κω, κῶς 283
κοθρασίων 155 fn. 44
κοινός 115, 156, 160, (acc. pl.) 313
κοίρανος 156, 160
κονῑ́ε̄ν 138
κονιορτός 97, 251
κόνις 245
-κοντα̣ 273, 313
κόπτην 278
κορέσαι 293
Κόρϝᾱι, κόϝρη, κόρη 304, 317, κούρη, Κούρᾱι, κόρᾱ 317, ϙόρη 301
κορθύεται, κόρθυς 198
Κόρινθος 274, 342, Κορίνθιος 274
κόρυς, κόρυθ- 164, 195, 274
κορύσσε̄ν 195, κορύσσετο 164
κορυφή, κορυφοῦται 197
-κόσιοι 273
κοσμε̄ν 322, κοσμέν, κοσμίοντος 312, κοσμήσει 322, κοσμησίε̄ 226, 322, 326, κεκόσμηται 312
κόσμος, κόσμον 312
-κοστός, -κοιστος 312

κοῦρος 317
κουρωθείει 321
κραδίη 137, 249, 291
κρᾱ́νᾱ, κρήνη 242, 266, 302, κράννᾱν 266
κράνεια 291
κρατερός 92, 137, 291, καρτερός 137, 291
κρατερώνυχες 92
κράτος 291
κρατύς 154, 164, 253, 290, κρέσσων 154, 164, κρέ̄ττων 164
κρέας 111, 245, 339
κρέμαται 175, κρέμασθαι 177, ἐκρέμω (2sg.) 31
κρημνός 145
κρητήρ 236 fn. 50
κριμνάντων 31, 177, κρεμασα- 177, κρεμαννύναι 271
κρῑ́νε̄ν, κριννόμεναι 180, 267, κρεννέμεν 180, 267, 277, ἔκρῑνε 267, κ]ριθέντο̄ν 325
κροτέοντες 200
κρύβδα, κρυπτός, κρυφηδόν 123
κτε̄́νε̄ν 179, 329, κτε̄νύναι 179, ἔκταμεν 116, ἔκτανε, ἔκτα, κτάσθαι 205
κτε̄́ς, κτεν- 247
κτη- 118 with fn. 18
κῡδαίνε̄ν, κῡδρός, κῦδος, κῡδι- 194
κύκλος 61, 119, 239, κύκλα 61, 119
κυνε̄ν 178
κῡ́ριος 118
κύων 153, 235 (partial paradigm), 246, 338, κυνός 17, 246

λαγάσαι 134, 291
λαγχάνε̄ν 182, 296, λαχε̄ν 182, 206, 210, 276, λαχῆν 276, 320, λελάχωσι, λελάχητε 210, λελόγχασιν 182
λάζεσθαι 121, 167, 207, 284, 296, λα]ζόμενος 296, ἐλάζυτο, λάδδουσθη 296, λαμβάνεν 277, 296, λαβε̄ν 121, 134, 167, 207, 284, λαβεῖν 276, λαβέ 233, λhαβο̄́ν 134, 207, λελαβηκώς 327
λαιός 252
λάκε 208, λεληκώς 208, 219, λέλᾱκα, λελακυῖα 219
λανθάνε̄ν 206, λελάθῃ, λελαθέσθαι 210
λᾱός 308
λέγε̄ν 117, 186, λέγει 340, ἐλέγμην, λέκτο 202 fn. 24, συλλέγε̄ν 186
λειμών, λειμῶν- 236, 246
λείπε̄ν 44, 188, 203, 205, 207, 4 fn. 15, 284, λιπε̄ν 188, 205, 207, 233, λιπέσθαι, λιπών, λιποῦ 233, λίποισα 315, λέλειπται 222
λείχε̄ν 117, 126, 187, λεῖξαι 212
λέκτο, λέχεται 203
λέκτρον 122
λέσχη 123 fn. 20
Λεύκιππος 118
λευκός 340
λέχος 122, 123 fn. 20, 127, 147
λέων 293
λεώς 308
λήγε̄ν 134
λήθε̄ν 181, 210, 296, ἐλήθετο 181, ληθάνει 181, 210
λῆνος 110
λίθεος, λίθινος, λίθιος 337
λίθος 341
λιμήν, λιμέν- 236, 246
λίμνη 236
λιμπάνε̄ν 183
λίναμαι 177
λίσσεσθαι, λιτέσθαι 164, 207
λογίζεσθαι, λογίσασθαι 169
λόεον, λοέσσομαι, λοέσσαι 293
λοετρά, λοετροχόος 293
λοῦσσον 156
λυγρός 250
λύει 189, λύτο, λῦτο 202
λύκος 120, 240
λύχνος 293

μά 334
μαζός 341
μαίνεται 115, 160, 194, μανῆναι 215, μέμονε 36, 115, 217, μέμαμεν, μεμάᾱσι 217, μεμαώς 115, 217
μαίτυρανς 313 with fn. 1, 314
μακών, μεμηκώς 208
μᾶκος, μῆκος 250 fn. 54
μακρός 154, 250, 339, μάσσον 154
μάλα, μᾶλλον, μάλιστα 154
μαλακός, μαλάσσε̄ν, μαλάττε̄ν 163
μᾶλον, μῆλον 241, 249, 342
μᾱλ]ο̣πάραυε 301
μανθάνε̄ν 182, 206, 296, μαθε̄ν 182, 206
μάρνασθαι 177, 290
μαστός 341
μᾱ́τηρ, μήτηρ 235, 247 (partial paradigm), μῆτερ 235 fn. 48
Μhεγαρεύς 135 fn. 29
μεγάροισι 135 fn. 29
μέγας 135 fn. 29, 253, 338, μέγα 111, μεγάλο- 254, μhε[ι]άλα 135 fn. 29, μέζων 154, 166, μέ̄ζων 166, 298, μέ̄ζονες, μέ̄ζο̄ς, μέ̄ζω 298, μείζω 5 fn. 19
μέθυ 126, 244
μείδησε 134
μελαίνετο 195
μελάνοσσος 156
μέλᾱς, μέλαν- 195, 341

μέλι 146, 249, μέλιτ- 164, 249
μενε̄ν (fut.) 223, ἔμε̄νε 03B5, μίνονσαι 314
-μενο- 42 fn. 38
μέρεσθαι 134, 290, ῞ε̄μαρται 134, 161, 222, 290, ἔμμορε, ῾ε̄μαρμένον, ἐμμόρμενον 289
μέροπες 293
μέρη 306
μεσαμβρίη 145
μέσος 156, 165, 252, 275, μέσσος, μέττος 165, 275, μέσσω 320
μετά 333
μετασπών 207
μέτρον 196
μή 321, 330, 332
μῆλον 'small domestic animal' 241
μήν 140, 238 (partial paradigm), 246, με̄́ς (μείς) 145, 238, 246, μηνός 145, 267, 323, μῆννος 145, 267, μειννός 267, μεινός 321
μηνίε̄ν, μῆνις 198
μῆτις 243
μήτρως 244
μιαίνε̄ν, μιαρός 194
μῑκρός 135 with fn. 29, 341
μίμνει 31, μίμνε̄ν 184
μιμνήσκε̄ν, μνήσκεται 186
μιν 260
μίσγε̄ν 124, 184, μίκτο 202, μιγῆναι 124, 215, 233, μίγεν 144, 310, μίγησαν 310, μιγε̄́ς 233, μιγέντες 144, μειγ- 184, μειχθῆναι 215
μισθός 126, 240
μναίς (acc. pl.) 316
μνᾶσθαι 186 fn. 8
μνηστῆρες 236 fn. 50
μόνος, μόνᾱ, μοῦνος 317
μόρος, μοῖρα 161
Μροχο̄́ 289
μῡθε̄̃σθαι, μῦθος 196
μυῖα 138
μῡκώμεναι, μύκον, μεμῡ́κει 208
μῦς 102, 238, 249

νᾱϝός, νηός 267, 301, 308 ναῦος 267, ναῦον 308, νεώς 138, 267, 301, 308, νᾱοῦ 322
ναίε̄ν 138
ναῦς, νᾱός 244, νηός, νεώς 244, 308
ναυτίλος, ναυτίλλεσθαι 159
νᾱ́χε̄ν, νήχε̄ν 134, νήχει 339
νεᾶν 35, 197, 198
νέονται 135
νείφε̄ν 127, 134, 187, 284
νέμε̄ν 186
νεόδμᾱτος, νεόδμητος 103, 300
νέος 197, 250, νέον 112, νέᾱ, νέη 305
νεότης 79
νεῦμα 78, 114, 247
νεῦρον 134, 145
νεφέλᾱ, νεφέλη 125, 242
νέφος 125, 245, 338, νέφεος 14
νεφρός 127, 239, 282
νήγρετος 104
νήκεστος 105
νηκούστησε 104
νηλεές 104
νῆμα 247
νημερτής 105, 289
νῆν 134, 190, νῆι 17, 90
νηνεμίη 105
νῆσσα, νῆττα 111, 164, 243
νίζε̄ν 121, 166, 190, νίψαι 121, 282
νῑ́κᾱ, νῑ́κη 93, 100
νῑκᾶν 242, 319, νῑκῆν 319, νῑκο̄̃ντι 272, νῑκᾱ́σθω, νῑκήθθο̄, νῑ́κη, ἐνῑ́κε̄, ἐνῑ́κης 319
Νῑκάνδρη 301
-νῑ́κης 242
νιν 260
νῑ́σοντο, νῑσόμενον 184
νίφα 127, 134, 248, 282
νιφάδες 337
νοε̄̃ν, νόος 196
νόσος, νοῦσος 317
-ντι 129
-ντον (iptv. 3pl.) 145, 324, -ντων 324, -ντω 324
-νῡ- ~ -νυ- (pres.) 179
νύξ 119, 237, 238, 249, 339, νύκτα 113, 237, νυκτός 237, 238, νύκτας 114, νυκτ- 249
νυός 134, 135, 240

-ξαι (aor.) 263
ξανθός 341
Ξένϝο̄ν 317
ξένος, ξεῖνος 317
ξηρός 341
ξύν 115, 156, 333
ξῡνός 115, 156

ὁ, ᾱ̔, ἡ 131, 257 (paradigm), 280, τό 145, 257 (paradigm), το̄̃, τοῖο 138, τοῦ 320, 322 (3x), τῶ 320, 321, 323, τοί (τῡ́), ταί (τή), οἱ (οἰ), αἱ (αἰ) 280, τόνς, τός, τάνς, τάς 313, τώς 321, 323, τοίρ, ταίρ (acc. pl.) 316, τᾱ́ων 308, τᾶν 318
-ο̄, -οιο (gen. sg.) 138
ὀβελοί, ὀβελλός, ὀβολός, ὀδελός 284
ὄγκος 89, 239
ὄγμος 16, 89
ὀδός, ὀδο̄́ς 'threshold' 317
ὀδο̄́ς 237, 238, 249, 339, ὀδόντα 237, ὀδόντος 237, 238, ὀδόντ- 109, 249, ἔδοντες 109
ὄζε̄ν 166

ὄζις 286
ὄζος 89, 239
-οι (pres., aor. opt. 3sg.) 130
οἴᾱξ 94
οἶδα 216, οἶσθα 90, 121, 216, οἶδε 36, 216, 339, ἴδμεν 216, ἴσαν 310, εἰδῶ (partial paradigm) 217, εἰδῇ 216, εἴδομεν 38, 225, εἴδετε 225, ἴσθι 121, 126, 216, εἰδέναι 276, ἴδμεναι 279, εἰδώς 216, ἰδυῖα 101, 138, 216
οἴκοι 130
οἴμη, οἶμος, οἶμος 143 fn. 35
οἴνη 70
οἶνος 342
οἶος 70, 252
ὄϊς 89, 243, ὄϊν 112, ὄϝινς 314
-οις (inst. pl.) 145, -οῖς 169
οἴσε̄ν 224
ὄκα 279
ὀκτακατίᾱς 273
ὀκτώ 21, hοκτώ 321
ὀλίγος 154
ὀλισθάνε̄ν, ὀλισθε̄ν 181 with fn. 4, 206, ὄλισθε 181
ὅλος 132, 317
ὀμείχε̄ν 109, 126, 186
ὀμίχλη 109, 127, 241
ὄμμασι 281
ὀμνύναι 179, ὄμνῡν 278, ὠμόσαμες 279, ὤμοσαν 320, subj. ὀμόσοντι 225
ὁμός 90, 131, 250
ὀμφαλός 97, 125
ὀμφή 78, 127, 128, 147, 242, 282, 283
ὄναρ 109, 156, 248, ὄνε̄ρος 109, 156
ὄνειδος 109
ὀνίνησι 176
ὄνομα 110, 236, 246, 339, ὄνυμα 110, 120
ὀνομαίνε̄ν 99, 114, 160, 193
ὄνοσαι 175
-οντ- (thematic ptc.), -ōσα 164, 314, -ονσα 164, -ōσι 314
ὄνυ 263
ὄνυξ 92, 109, 117, 119, 249, 338
ὄπα 'voice' 118, 238, 248, 281, ὀπός 238
ὀπῑπεύε̄ν 100
ὀπίσω 165, 275
ὅπλα, ὥπλεον 196
Ὀπούντιοι 323
ὀππάτεσσι 281
ὀ̄ρᾱ́, ὀ̄ρή 141, 142, 340
ὁρᾶν, hορῆν, [ὁ]ρῆι, ὁρῆις 319, ὁρᾶι 319, 341
ὀ̄ρανός 142
ὀρέγε̄ν 109, 187, ὀρέξαι 122, 212, ὤρεξαν 227, ὀρωρέχαται 310
ὀ̄ρε̄ν 141, 142, 200
ὀρθός 168
ὅρμος 132
ὄρνῑς 89, 340
ὄρνυται 179, ὄρνυσθαι 97, 340, ὦρτο 202, 205, ὤρετο 205 with fn. 28, ὄρηται, ὄροιτο 205
ὄρος 'mountain' 340
ὀρός 'whey' 133
ὅρος 'boundary' 151, 317, ὅρϝος, ὀ̄ρος 317
ὄροφος 110 fn. 12
ὄρρος 89, 140, 239
ὀρσοπῡ́γιον 140
ὀρύσσε̄ν, ὀρύττε̄ν 163
ὀρφανός 125
ὄρχις 243
ὅς 107
ὀ̄ς 'ear' 140, 142, 245, 336, 339, ὀ̄ατος (οὔατος) 170, 245, 336, ὠτός 170, 245
-ōς (acc. pl.) 314
ὅσος, ὅσσος, ὅσσος, ὅττος 165, 275
ὄσσα 121
ὄσσε 100, 121, 248
ὄσσεσθαι 121
ὀστέον, ὀστο̄ν 89, 338
-ότ- ~ -υίᾱ- (pf. ptc.) 265
ὅτε, ὅτα 279
ὄτῑμι 257–8
οὐ 341, οὐκ 120
οὐδενόσωρος 93
οὐδός 'threshold' 317
οὖθαρ 248, 288, οὔθατος 248
οὔκις 286
οὔκω, οὔκως 283
οὖλος 'whole' 317
οὖρος, οὖροι 317
οὗτος 340, τοῦτονς, τοῦτος 313
ὀφέ̄λε̄ν, ὀφέ̄λε̄ν, ὀφέλλε̄ν 271, ὀπῆλεν 321, ὀφήλει 323, [ϝō]φλέασι 114, 296 fn. 17, 327, ϝōφλε̄κόσι 327
ὄφελος 105
ὀφθαλμός 121, 281, 340
ὄφις 127, 243, 285
ὄφρα 149
ὀφρῦς 102, 109, 125, 249, ὀφρύος 102
ὀχέεσθαι 'drive' 199
ὀχέων, ὀχέεσκον 'endure' 200, ὀχέειν 'cling to' 200 fn. 23
ὄψεσθαι 224
ὀϝέοι 286

πᾱ- 118
παϊδ- 167, παισί 168
παίζε̄ν 167
παλάμη 105, 242, παλάμην 112, 300
πανᾱγόρσῑ 289

πανσυδί, παν]σεϝδί 163
παρά 333
παρασκευάζεσθαι 335
παρεᾱ́ 302, 307 (2x), παρειᾱ́ς 307
παρέχειν 276, 277, παρ]εχόντō 325
παρθενοπῑ́πα 100
παρθένος: φαρθένō 152
παρίμεν 276
παρκέκλεικε 327
Παρνασσός 342
πᾶς 314, πάς 313, παῖς 315, παντ- 164, πάντες 144, 253, 338, πᾶσι 168, 314, πάνσι 168, πᾶσα 164, 314, πάνσα 164, πάνσᾱ, πάνσας 314, παῖσα 315 fn. 3, παῖσαν 315, πᾶσαν 315
πάσσε̄ν, πάττε̄ν 164, 191, 281, πάσαι 212
πάσχε̄ν 123, 185, 206, 224, πάσχην 276, 321, παθε̃ν 185, 206, 224, πάθην 278, πέπονθα 123, 218, 224, πέπονθας 123, πέπασθε 123, 218, πεπαθυίῃ 218
πατήρ 90, 111, 169, 235 (paradigm), 247
πάτος 340
πάτριος 80
πάτρως 244
πάχνη, παχνοῦται 197
παχύς 149, 154, 253, παχύτερος, πάσσων 149, πάσσονα 154
πᾶχυς, πῆχυς 91, 146, 244, 300, πᾶχυν, πῆχυν 112
πεδά 333
πεδίον 11
πέδον 241
πεζός 18, 156, 166
πείθε̄ν 207, 211, πείθω 320, πείθεσθαι 148, 186, 210–11, πιθέσθαι 148, 207, 211, πεπιθε̃ν 211, πεῖσαι, 148, πείσε̄ν, πεποιθέναι 148, 211 fn. 34, πέποιθε, ἐπέπιθμεν 217
πειθώ 244
πεινῆν, πεινήμεναι, πειναᾱ́ων 198
Πεισήνωρ 93
Πεισι-, Πειhι- 168
πέκε̄ν 117
πέλει 188, 4 fn. 11, πέλεται 188 with fn. 11, 283, πλε/ο- 188 fn. 11, 206, ἔπλετο 206
πέλεκυς 244
Πελοπόννησος, Πέλοπος νῆσος 271
πεμπάζεσθαι 195, πεμπάσσεται 195 fn. 19
πεμπάς, πεμπάδ- 195
πεμπεβόηα, πέμπτος 283
πενθερός 147
(πε)ν(τ)ακάτιας 315
πέντε 283
πέος 135
περαίνε̄ν, πε̄ραίνε̄ν 193, πειρήναντε, πεπείρανται 193 fn. 16
πε̃ραρ 193, 248, 288, πε̃ρατα 193, 248, πείρατα, πέρατα, περάτων 317
πέρδεσθαι 186, 207
περί 333
περιδώμεθον 227
περιτελλόμενος 188, 271, 283
περνᾱ́ς, περνάμενα 177, 186, περασα- 177
περόνη 293
πέρυσι 129, 273
περυσινός 273
πέσσε̄ν, πέττε̄ν 120, 192, πέψαι 120, 212, 282
πέσσυρες, πέτταρες 168, 283
πέτεσθαι 186, 207, πέτεται 339, πτέσθαι 241
πετρο- 283
πεύθεσθαι 149, 188, 296, πυθέσθαι 149, 207, πεύσεσθαι 149
πηγνύναι 179, παγῆναι 35, πέπηγεν 219, πεπᾱ́γαισιν 219, 273
πήλοι 283
πικρός 250
πίλναται, πελασα- 177
πιμπλη- ~ πιμπλα- 176, πίμπλεισιν 273, πλῆτο 202
πῑ́νει 338, πιε̃ν, πῖθι 203, 205, πῑ́εσθαι 224
πιπρᾱ́σκε̄ν 186
πῑ́πτε̄ν, πῖπτε, πῖπτον 184, πεσε̃σθαι 294
πίσσα, πίττα 163
πίστις 274
πιστός 121, 123, 251
πεπιτευόντεσσι 327
πιτνᾱ́ς, πίτναντο, πετασα- 177
πιφαυσκέμεν, φάε 207
πῑ́ων 100, 253, πῑ́ε̄ρα 100, 253
Πλάταια 96 fn. 4, 100, 290
πλατάνιστος 19, 114, 154
πλᾱτίος, πλᾱτίον, πλᾱ́σιον, πλησίος, πλησίον 274
πλατύς 90, 96, 253, 290, πλατέος 96 fn. 4, πλατεῖα 100
πλείονερ 316, πλίανς 314, πλεῖστος 92, 96 fn. 4
πλέκε̄ν 117, 293
πλε̃ν 187, 318, πλέω 318, πλεῦσαι 212, πλευσε̃σθαι 294
πλήμνη 145
πλήρης 340, πλήρη 306
πλοῖον 160
πλοῦτος, πλούτιος, πλούσιος 274
πλοχμός 293
πλώε̄ν 190
πόᾱ, ποίη 305
ποθε̃ν 200
πόθος 147, 284
ποί 131 fn. 25

ποιήσει (subj.) 225, ποέντω 295, ἐ]πόημεν 295, πόησθαι 320, ποιῆσαι 323, πεποιόντεισσι 327
ποικῖλλε̄ν, ποικῖλος 159, 194
ποιμαίνε̄ν 193
ποιμήν 92, 193, 235 (partial paradigm), 246
ποινή 242, 283, ποινᾱ́ 283 fn. 14
πολεμίους 323
πολεῖν 'plow' 201
πολε̄ν 'traverse' 201
πόλις 106, 263, πόλῃος 236, 263, 308, πόλῃϊ 236, πόλεως 308, πόλιος 263, 308
πολῑτεύονσι 314
πολῑ́της 337
πόλος 239, 283
Πολυκράτιος 318
πολύς 96, 106, 253, πολλό- 254, πολλοί 160 fn. 47, 339
πορε̄ν 293, πόρε 206
πόρρω 274, πόρσιον 155
πός 'towards' 263, 275 with 5, 334, ποτί, ποί 275, 334
πός 237, 248, 339, πῶς 237 fn. 51, πόδα 113, 237, ποδός 237, ποδ- 248
πόσις 243
πόσος 156, 165, 275, 281
ποταποπῑσάτω 283
ποτᾶσθαι, ποτε̃σθαι 201
πότερος 281
πότνια 101, 243, πότνα 101 fn. 11
ππᾱ-, τὰ ππᾱ́ματα 118
πράσον 137, 241, 249, 342
πρᾱσσέμεν 277, πρήξοισιν (subj.) 225, πρᾱ̄ξάντων 325
πρᾱτός 'sold' 103, 304
πρᾶτος 'first' 263
πρίασθαι 157, ἐπρίατο 101, 281, ἐπρίαντο 101, πρίατο 202
πρό 275 fn. 5, 333
προαρχόντων 323
Προβάλινθος 274, 342, Προβαλῑ́σιος 274
προβεβωλευμένον 321
προγεγονοίσαις 315
προνοήθην 278
πρόξενϝος, πρόξηνονς 317, προξένως 321
προοίμιον 143 fn. 35
πρόστᾱν 278
πρός 93, 263, 275 with fn. 5, 333, 334, προτί 275, 277 fn. 9, 334, πορτί 334
προσέρχεται 338
προσεπῖλνατο 177
πρόσω 165, 275
πρόσωπον 93, προσώπω 320 (2x)
προτίθεισι 273
πτᾱ́σσε̄ν, πτήσσε̄ν 161, 163
πτάρνυσθαι 179, 206, 290, πταρε̄ν 179, 206
πτέρνη 144
πτερόν 241, 339
πτύσσε̄ν, πτύχες 163
πυθμήν 128 fn. 23, 147
πυλέων 308
πύνδαξ 128 fn. 23
πυνθάνεσθαι 183, 296 with fn. 18
πῦρ, πυρός 238, 248, 339
πυρέσσε̄ν, πυρέττε̄ν, πυρέξαι, πυρετός 164
πυρπολέοντας 201
πωλε̄ν 'sell' 201
πωλε̃σθαι 'go around' 201
πωτᾶσθαι 201

ῥα 287
ῥαίνε̄ν, ῥανθείς 161
ῥαπτός, ῥαφή 123
ῥάπτριαι 162
ῥέζε̄ν 'to dye' 190
ῥέζε̄ν 'to sacrifice' 190 fn. 13
ῥε̄ν 134, ῥύη, ῥυῆναι 215
ῥηγνύναι 179, 294, ἔρρωγε 219
ῥητός 103, 251
ῥήτρᾱ, ῥήτρην 305
ῥῑ́γιον 155
ῥῖγος 134, 245
ῥῑγῶν 196 fn. 20
ῥίζα 341
ῥίμφα 108
ῥῑ́πτε̄ν 184
ῥῑ́ς 341
ῥοφε̄ν 134, 200
ῥύπα, ῥυπόω 197
ῥῡ́τιον, ῥῡ́σιον, ῥῡσιάζε̄ν 274
Ῥωμαῖος (acc. pl.) 313
ῥώοντο 104, 190
ῥωχμός 294

σᾶμα, σῆμα 164, 193, 247
σᾱ́μερον, σήμερον 163
σαõν 198
σᾶτες, σῆτες, σᾱ́ετες 163
σατίναις 315
σβεννύναι 179
σέβεσθαι 164, 284, σέβεσθε 200
-σέε̄ν (fut.) 263
σείε̄ν 138, 167
σελᾱ́νᾱ 266, 301, σελήνη 266, 301, 341, σελάννᾱ 266
σέλας 266, 301, 341
σεύεσθαι 163, σεῦται, ἔσσυτο 203, ἔσσυται 222
σημαίνε̄ν 193
-σθε 40 fn. 36, 168

σῑγέν 277
σκαιός 252
σκαπτήρ, σκάφος 123
σκελετός, σκέλλε̄ν, σκληρός 104
σκέλος 245
σκέπτεσθαι 161, 189, 199, σκέψασθαι 212
σκιᾱ́ 242, 305, σκιή 305
ἐσκίδναντο, σκεδασα- 177
σκοπε̄ν 199
σκότιος 156
σκῶρ, σκατός 248
σμερδαλέος, σμερδνός 134
σμῑκρός 135 with fn. 29
σμῡ́χοιτο 135
σοβε̄ν 200
σπένδε̄ν 188
σπε̄́ρε̄ν 341
σπέρμα 114, 341
σπέρχεσθαι 127, 147
σσα 258
-σσαι (aor.) 263
σταγών, στάζε̄ν 166
στᾱ́λᾱ, στήλη 271, 301, στάλλᾱ 271
στάσις 243, 274
στατός 112, 251
σταυρός 92, 240
στέγε̄ν 117, 187
στείχε̄ν 117, 127, 188
στέλλε̄ν 159, 189, ἔστε̄λε 267
στε̃ρα 100
στεῦται 174
στίζε̄ν 166
στόμα 236, 246, 339
στορέσαι 293, ἐστόρεσε 104, ἔστρωτο 222
[στρατᾱ]γέντος 295
στρατηγός 93, στρότᾱγοι 289
στρατός, στρότον 289
στρογγύλος 341
ἐσστροτεύαθη 289
στρωτός 104, 251
σύ 259 (paradigm) 339, σέ 167, 335
συζευγνύναι 313
σῡλᾶν, σῡ]λῆν, σῡλε̃ν, σουλεῖμεν 319
συμμεννάντουν 267
σύν 333, συν- 313
-σύνᾱ, -συνος 336
συναγόντων 324
συναέρραισα 267
συνεδρίου 322
συνέθεαν 295
συνε̄́ρε̄ν 133
σύνες (iptv.) 275
συνθήκᾱ 321
σῦς 132, 249
συστέλλε̄ν 313
σφαγή, σφάζε̄ν 166
σφάλλεσθαι 124
σφαραγεῦντο 124
σφιν 260
σφυρόν 124
σφώ 259
ἔσχων 124
σχίζε̄ν 124

ταγ- 167
ταγός (acc. pl.) 313
ταμίᾱο 318
τάμνε̄ν 157, 181, 206, τεμε̃ν 181, 206
ταναός, τανυ- 114
τάνυται 179
τανύφυλλος 253
ταράσσε̄ν, ταράττε̄ν, ταραχή 163
-τᾶς, -της 337
τάσσε̄ν, τάττε̄ν 166, τετάχαται 310
-τατο- (sup.) 254
τατός 114, 251
ταῦρος 240
τάφος 'astonishment' 128
ταφών, τέθηπεν 148 fn. 36
ταχύς 148, 154, θάσσων 148, 149, θάσσον 154
τε 284
τέγγε̄ν 187, τέγξαι 212
τείνυται 180, 317, τεῖσαι 180, 283
τεῖχος, τοῖχος 147
τεκμαίρεσθαι, τέκμωρ 195
τεκνογόνος 77
τεκταίνεσθαι 195, 214, τεκτήνατο 195 fn. 18, 214
τέκτων 116, 195, 214
τελαμών 103
τελέν 277, τελῑ́τō 323, τέλεον, ἐτέλειον,
τελέσσαι 195
τέλεονς 314
τέλος, τέλε- 'end' 195
τέλσον 140, 283
τέμει 'it encounters', ἔτετμε 208
τέμενος 103, 181
τεός 259
-τέος 337
τερέβινθος 342
τέρετρον 103, 183
τέρμα 247, τέρμων 246
-τερο- (cptv.) 254
τέρπεσθαι 188, 205 fn. 30, ταρπώμεθα 207, 290
τέρσεσθαι 140, τερσῆναι, τερσήμεναι 215
τερψίμβροτος 336
τεταγών 209 fn. 33
τέταρτος 168, τετάρτης, τετόρτᾱυ 289
τετρα- 283

τετραίνε̄ν 103, 112 fn. 15, 183, τέτρηνε 183
τετρακατίαις 273
τετρᾱ́ορος 93
τέτταρες, τέσσερες 168, 261, 283, τέτορες 168, 261, 263, 283, τεσσαρ-, τέτρασιν 261
τεύχε̄ν 149, 187, 207, 296, τεύξε̄ν, τεῦξαι 149, τετευχώς 149, 223, τετυγμένος 223, τετυκεῖν, τετυκέσθαι 211
τέφρᾱ 147, 282, 305, 340
τέχνᾱ, τέχνη 293, τέχνᾱν τεχνᾱμένω 295
τέως 308
τῆλε 53, 283
τήμερον 163
-της, -τα 23
τῆτες 163
τῑ́ε̄ν 329
τιθέναι 150, 276, τιθήμεναι 329, τίθητι 90, 176, 272, 322, τίθησι 90, 112, 176, 272, 273, τίθεντι 98, τιθεῖ, τιθεῖσι 99, τίθετε 112, ἐτίθην 112, θε̄̃ναι 203, 276, θέμεν 277, ἔθεσαν, θήῃ, θείη, θέμεναι, -θείς, ἔθετο 203, θη- ~ θε-, θηκ- 203–4, ἔθηκα 204, 220, ἔθηκε 126, 203, ἔθη 204, θείομεν 225, θές 203, 275, θέντων 325, τεθῆναι 150, θε̄́ς, θε̄̃σι, θε̄̃σα 314
τίκτε̄ν 116, 183, 206, τίκτει 21, τεκε̄̃ν 183, 206, τεκέν 277
τῑμᾱ́, τῑμή 197, 285
τῑμᾱ̃ν 197, τῑμᾱ̃ι 309, 319, τῑμᾱ̃ις, τῑμᾱ̃τε 309, τῑμῆ 319, τῑμᾱθῆμεν 276
τίνε̄ν, τῑ́νε̄ν 180, 285, 317, τεῖσαι 180, 283
τίς 258 (paradigm), 339, τί 145, 258 (paradigm), 285, 339, τέο 138
τις 334, τι 120, 285
Τίρυνς 342
τιτρώσκε̄ν 185, 206, 293, ἔτορε 185, τορε̄̃ν 206, 293
τλᾱ-, ἔτλᾱν, ἔτλη, τλῆ, ἔτλαν 202, τετληότι, τετληότες, τετληυῖα 221
τλᾱτός, τλητός 103, 251, 301
Τληπόλεμος 336
τόρμος 17, 78, 240
τόσος 165, 275
τόφρα 149
τράπεζα 289
τρέμε̄ν 187, 200
τρε̄̃ν 135, 137, 187, 290
τρέπε̄ν 187, 200, 207, τραπε̄̃ν, τρόπην 289, ἔτραπε, ἐτράπετο 207, τραπέσθαι 291, τετράφαται, τετράφατο 310
τρε̄̃ς: τρῖς 260, τρίινς 261, 314, τρίς 313, τρία 101
τρέφε̄ν 123, 148, τρέφειν 323, τρέφεσθαι 128, θρέψαι 148
τρέχε̄ν, ἀποθρέξεσθαι 148
τρήρων 137, 140, 290
τρητός 103, 183
-τρια 101
τριᾱκάσιος (acc. pl.) 273, 313, τριᾱκοσίᾱς, τριᾱκοσίαις 273
τρῑ́βε̄ν: τετρίφαται 310
τριπανᾱγόρσιος 289
τρισχε̄λίο̄ς 266
τρίτω 321
τρομε̄̃ν 200
τροπε̄̃ν 200
τρόχος 77
τροχός 78, 148, 239
τύ 168, 258 (paradigm)
τυγχάνε̄ν 149, 296, τυχε̄̃ν 149, 207, τύχε 207
τύπτε̄ν 191 fn. 14, τυπείς, ἐτύπη 215
τυφλός: θυφλός 152

-ύ- ~ -έϝ- 269
ὑγιής 106, 120, 151, ὑγιῆ, ὑγιᾶ 306 with fn. 6
ὕδρος 240
ὕδωρ 151, 238, 248, 339, ὕδατος 238, 248
ὕ̄ε̄ν 132, 192, ὕ̄ει 151
ὑ̔ετός 340
υἱύς 151, 244, 269 fn. 4, υἱύνς 313
ὑ̔μέ 151, 311, ὔμμε, ὑ̔μέας, ὑ̔μέες, ὑ̔μᾶς, ὑ̔με̄̃ς 311
ὑμέναιος 132 fn. 27
ὑ̄μήν 132 with fn. 27, 151
Ὑμηττός 342
-ῡνε/ο- (pres.) 199, 338
ὑνιερο̄́σει 326
ὑπαρχέμεν 278
ὑπασδεύ̄ξαισα 315
ὑπέρ 151, 333
ὑπερᾱμεριᾱ́ων 318
ὑπό 151, 333
ὑποκλοπέοιτο 200
ὑποκύψει (subj.) 225
ὑπολί̄ζονες 154
ὕπνος 120, 151
ὗς 102, 132, 151, 249
ὑσμῑ́νη 107, 151
ὕστερος 121, 152, 252, ὕστερας 313
ὑφαίνε̄ν 102, 115, 125, 152, 161, 183
ὕψιον 155

φα- ~ φν-: πέφαται 127, 222, 283, πέφνε 150, πεφνέμεν 208, 283
φαγε̄̃ν 206
φαε̄νός, φάεννον 266
φαίνεσθαι, φανῆναι 161
φάναι 174, 232–3, φᾱτι, φησι 91, 125, 174, 272, 300, φᾱσι 273, φαῖσι 273, 315, φάθι 129, πεφάσθω 150

φάρμακον, φαρμάσσε̄ν, φαρμάττε̄ν, φαρμάσσων 194
φάρος, φᾶρος, φᾱ́ρεα 317
φάτις 244, 274
φέβεσθαι 200
πεφιδέσθαι 150
φέρε̄ν 125, 186, 200, 209, 276, φέρην 276, 320, φάρειν 276, φέρεν 277, φέρει 34, φέρο̄σι 314, φέροι 38, 146, φερέτω 146, φερόντων 325, ἔφερε 146, 175 fn. 1, ἔφερον 112, 146, ἐφέρετον, ἐφερέτᾱν, ἐφερέτην 112, 300
φεύγε̄ν 188, 277, φευγέτω 321, φυγε̄ν 125, 207
φήμη 241, Φήμᾱ, φήμᾱν 303
φθάνε̄ν, φθᾱ́νειν 180, 317
φθε̄́ρ 341
φθήρων 320, ἐφθορκώς 327
φθίνε̄ν, φθῑ́νε̄ν 180, 317, φθινύθε̄ν 180, ἔφθιτο 202, 205, ἔφθιεν 205
-φι 55, 125, 150
φῑ́κατι 273
φιλέε̄ν 196, φιλε̄ν, φῑ́λασθαι, φιλῆσαι 214, φιλήσει 320
φιλομμειδής 134
φίλος 155, 196, φιλίων, φῖλτερος, φῖλτατος 155
φλοιός 341
φοβε̄ν 200
φόνος 119, 127
φορβᾱ́, φορβή 282, 283
φορε̄ν 200, φορεῖ 35
φράδμων 167
φράζεσθαι 167, πέφραδε 150
φρᾱ́τηρ 125, 247, 304
φρήν 237 (partial paradigm)
φροίμιον 143 fn. 35
φυγαδεύε̄ν, φυγαδείην 199
φυγή 78, 241
φῡ́ε̄ν, φυίει 269 fn. 4, φῡ́εσθαι 190, ἔφῡ 102, 125, 202, πεφύᾱσι, πεφῡ́κασι, πεφῡ́κηι, πεφυυῖα, πεφῡ́κει 220
φύλαξ, φύλακ- 163, 194
φυλάσσε̄ν 163, 194, 213, φυλάττε̄ν 163, 194, φυλάξαι 213, πεφυλαχέναι, πεφυλάχθαι 150, φεφύλαχσο 152
φύλλον 341
πεφυτευκῆμεν 277
φωνᾱ́, φωνή 91, 169, 300
φώρ, 237, 247, φῶρα 237

χαίρε̄ν 160 (2x), 191, 290, χαρῆναι 160, 215, κεχάροντο 150
χαίτη 127
χάλαισι 295, χαλάσσομεν (subj.) 225
χαλεπός, χαλέπτει 194
χάλκευον 199, χαλκεύς 199, 249
χαμαί 25 with fn. 17, 113, 114, 126, 233
χᾱ́ν 126, 249, χήν 126, 140, 249
χανδάνε̄ν 182, 206, 224, 296, χαδε̄ν 182, 206, 224, χείσεται 182, χε̄́σεσθαι 224, κεχόνδει 182, 224
χαρίεντ- 80
χάσκε̄ν, χανε̄ν 185, 206, κεχηνέναι 150
χέζε̄ν 166
χειμών 246
χειλίων, χέλλιας 126, 140, 266, χειλίᾱς 266
χέλῡς 127, 243
χε̄ν 126, χέε̄ν, aor. χέαι 309, χέε 213, ἔχεαν 309, χύτο 203, χυθῆναι 150, κέχυται 222, fut. χε̄ν 224
χε̄́ρ 126, 140, 147, 238 (partial paradigm), 247, 267, 339, χε̄ρός 247, χέρρες 267
χερνίβα 284
χε̄́ρων (χείρων) 154
χήρᾱ, χήρη, χῆρος 304
χθές 123
χθών 21, 113 (paradigm), 116, 238 (paradigm), 246, χθονί 116
χίμαρος, χίμαιρα 161
χίμετλα 113
χιών 113, 126, 153, 238 (paradigm), 246
χλωρός 104, 340
χόλος, χολο̄σθαι 197
χόρτος 239
ἔχραε 205
χρε̄́μασιν, χρε̄μάτεσσι 277 fn. 7
χρῆσαι 176, κεχρῆσθαι 150
χρόᾱ 341
χρῡσῆ 302, χρῡ́σεον, χρῡσο̄ν, χρῡ́σιον 337
χρῡσήορος 93
χρῡσός 342
χρώς 341
χωρε̄ν 196
χῶρος 196, χώρως 321

ψάλτρια 101
ψάμμος 340
ψῡ́χε̄ν, ψῡχρός 341

ὠδῶι 'threshold' 317
ὠθε̄ν 201, 214, ὦσαι 214
-ῶι (dat. sg.) 169 with fn. 50
ὠιόν 241, 339
ὠκύς 253, ὤκεες 320
ὦλκα 238
ὦμος 140, 142, 145, 239
-ων (thematic ptc. masc. nom. sg.) 254
-ῶν (gen. pl.) 91, 169, (fem. gen. pl.) 308
-ώνδᾱς 338
ὠνε̄σθαι, ὠνῆι 193
ὦνος 142

ὦπα 238, 248, 281
ὥρᾱ 107
ὦρος 'boundary' 317
ϰις 286

Cyprian
a-u-ta-ra- *αὐτάρ 289
a-no-ko-ne *ἄνωγον 221
to-e-na-i *δοέναι, *to-we-na-i* *δοϝέναι 276
e-ke-ne *ἔχε̄ν 276, *e-ke-so-si* *ἔξο(ν)σι 272
e-we-xe *ἔϝεξε 212
i-na-la-li-si-me-na 218
ka-ra-si-ti *γράσθι 175
ka-si-ke-ne-to-se *κασιγνήτο(ν)ς 274
ka-te-ti-ja-ne *κατέθιjαν 295
ka-te-wo-ro-ko-ne *κατήϝοργον 108, 289
ke-i-to-i 294
ku-me-re-na-i *κυμερῆναι 295
o-mo-mo-ko-ne *ὀμώμοκον 218, 221
o-te 279
pa-si-le-wo-se *βασιλῆϝος 308
pe-i-se-i 283
si-se 286
ti-we-i-pi-lo *Διϝείφιλος 234
to-na-i-lo-ne *τōν αἴλōν 160

Mycenaean
a-ke-ra_2*-te* 144
a-mo 144
a-pe-i-si 272
a-pi-po-re-we 249
a-ra-ro-mo-te-me-no 222
a-ra-ru-wo-a 298
a-ro-a,a-ro_2*-e* 298
a-to-po-qo 282 fn. 13
a-to-ro-qo 282
ai-ka-sa-ma 293
de-de-me-no 222
de-me-o-te 224
de-ko-to 175, *de-ka-sa-to* 294
di-do-si 272, *do-so-si* 273, *do-ke* 204
di-u-jo ~ *di-wi-jo* 269
e-e-si 314
e-ke-e 229, 276, *e-ke-qe* 229
e-ko-si 272
e-me 113, 260
e-pi-ko-ru-si-jo,o-pi-ko-ru-si-ja 274
e-ra-se 214
e-re-u-te-ro-se 214
e-u-ke-to 127, 229
i-je-re-ja 267
i-je-re-u 249, 280 fn. 11, 337
i-qo 118
jo-qi 285
ka-ke-u 249, 337
ka-zo-e 155, 163, 298
ke-ka-u-me-no 222
ke-ni-qa 284
ke-ra-me-u 249
ke-se-nu-wo 317
ki-ti-je-si 116, 174, 273
ko-ri-si-jo 274
ko-wa 304, 317, *ko-wo* 317
ma-to-(ro-)pu-ro 289
me-sa-to 165, 275
me-u-jo ~ *me-wi-jo* 154 fn. 42, 269, *me-u-jo-e* ~ *me-wi-jo-e*, *me-u-jo-*a_2 298
me-zo-e,me-zo-a_2 154, 166, 298
no-pe-re-a_2 105
-o-jo (gen. sg.) 138
o-pi 89, 100, 333
o-te 279
o-wo-we 245
pa-si 'says' 272
pa-si 'all' (dat. pl.) 168
pa-we-a_2 136, 317
pe-ma ~ *pe-mo* 114
pe-ru-si-nu-wo 273
-pi 55, 234
po-pi 125
po-qa 282
qa-si-re-u 249, 282, 337
qe-qi-no-me-no, qe-qi-no-to 222, 285
qe-to-ro- 283
qe-to-ro-po-pi 289
qi-ri-ja-to 281
qo-o, qo-u- 282
qo-u-ko-ro 120
ra-pte, ra-pte-re, ra-pi-ti-ra_2 162
re-wo-te-re-jo, re-wo-to-ro-ko-wo 293
te-ke 204
te-tu-ko-wo-a_2 223, 232, 298
to-pe-za 289
to-so 165, 275
tu-ka-ṭạ-ṣị/tu-ka-to-si 289
wa-na-ka 249
wa-tu 244
-wo-e (pf. ptc.) 298
wo-wo 317
wo-ze 190, 289, *wo-ze-e* 276, 289, *wo-zo*, *wo-zo-te*, *wo-zo-me-no* 289
za-ku-si-jo 274
za-we-te 163
ze-so-me-no 158
ze-u-ke-si 158

2 Proto-Indo-European

Reconstructed words identified as 'post-PIE' in the text are included; so are a some labelled 'pre-Greek'. Three Proto-Germanic forms which are especially relevant in context are listed at the end. Alphabetization:
a ā b b^h d d^h e ē ə g g^h g^w g^{wh} ǵ ǵ^h H h$_1$ h$_2$ h$_3$ i ī k k^w ḱ l l̥ m m̥ n n̥ o ō p r r̥ s t u ū w y.
Inflectional endings are not usually listed; see the relevant sections (2.3.3 (iii), 2.3.4 (i), 4.2.6, 4.3.5).

ád 22 fn. 16, 57 with fn. 55
ag^{w}nós 239, 281
-(a)h$_2$- (factitive) 30, 35
-ah$_2$ (fem.) 25, 77
-ah$_2$ay (dat.) 91, 169, 300
-áh$_2$s, -áh$_2$as (gen.) 169
-ah$_2$soHom 308
alb^{h}ós 12, 240
ályos 11, 12, 89, 156, 159, 252, ályod 73, 145, 156, 159, 337
ánh$_2$t- ~ n̥h$_2$t- 111, 164, 243
ár- ~ r̥- 12, 203
ársmn̥ 142
átta 12, 20, 89
awisd^h- 181
awl- 12, áwlos 239
awtós 250
ay- 'give' 12
ay- 'be hot' 12, 94
aydósyo- 138
ayd^h- 12
áyd^{h}os 239
áyerih$_1$dstom 121
ayḱsmo- 293
-ā- (optative) 39
ā́mr̥ 91, 145, 248, 288, ā́mōr 145, 248, 288
ā́peros 156, 240

b^{h}ag- 206
b^{h}ágos 12
b^{h}áh$_2$mah$_2$ 241
b^{h}ah$_2$ti 91, 125, 174, 300
b^{h}áh$_2$ti- ~ b^{h}h$_2$téy- 129, 244
b^{h}āǵ^{h}us 91, 146, 244, 300, b^{h}āǵ^{h}um 112
b^{h}eg^w- 200
b^{h}end^h- 147
b^{h}énǵ^{h}u- ~ b^{h}n̥ǵ^{h}éw-, b^{h}n̥ǵ^{h}ús 149, 253
b^{h}er- 35, 48–9 (paradigm), 76, 200, b^{h}ére/o- 34, 38, 125, 186, b^{h}éreti 129, b^{h}érē/ō-, b^{h}éroy(h$_1$)- 38, b^{h}éroyd, b^{h}éretōd 146, b^{h}érom, é b^{h}érom 112, é b^{h}ered, é b^{h}erond 146, b^{h}éretom, é b^{h}éretom 112, b^{h}éretām, é b^{h}éretām 112, 300
b^{h}éwd^h- ~ b^{h}ud^h- 22, 149, 205, b^{h}ud^{h}é/ó- 205
b^{h}éwg- ~ b^{h}ug- 78, 125, 205, b^{h}ugé/ó- 205
b^{h}eyd- 20
b^{h}eyd^h- 148, b^{h}éyd^{h}e/o- 186, 207, b^{h}eb^{h}óyd^{h}e 217
-b^{h}i 55, 125
b^{h}idstós 20, 121, 251
b^{h}inédst 27
b^{h}ó- 'both' 70
b^{h}oh$_2$náh$_2$ 169, 300
b^{h}oréyeti 27, b^{h}oréye/o- 35
b^{h}ṓr, b^{h}órm̥ 237, 247
b^{h}rag- 12
b^{h}ráh$_2$tēr 125, 247, 304
b^{h}rem- 9 fn. 6
b^{h}ud^h- 'bottom' 147
b^{h}ud^{h}stós 121, 251
b^{h}ugáh$_2$ 78, 241
b^{h}uH- 11, 35, 38, 202, b^{h}úHt 27, 43, 102, 125, b^{h}úHe/o-, b^{h}uH-yéh$_1$- ~ b^{h}uH-ih$_1$- 38
b^{h}uHsyé/ó- 35

dáh$_2$se/o- 223
dáḱru 12, 244
dayh$_2$wḗr 12, 247
dedwóye 27
déh$_1$se/o- 223
deḱ- 9
déḱm̥d 22, 71, 113, 337, dḱṓmd 71
deḱsi- 21, 252, deḱsiwós, deḱsiterós 252
delǵ^h- 9
délh$_1$g^{h}os 106
démh$_2$- 'build' 103, 4 fn. 43, démh$_2$se/o- 224
démh$_2$- 'tame' 114, dm̥náh$_2$ti ~ dm̥nh$_2$- 177, démh$_2$s-, démh$_2$se/o- 223
denḱ- ~ dn̥ḱ- 182
dens- ~ dn̥s- 136, 208
dénsus ~ dn̥séw- 136, 253
dére/o- 186
dérḱ- ~ dr̥ḱ-, dr̥ḱé/ó- 205, 291, dedórḱe ~ dedr̥ḱ- 218
dewh$_2$-, dunáh$_2$- ~ dunh$_2$- 178
deyh$_2$- 175
déyḱ- ~ diḱ- 4 fn. 37, déyḱti, dḗyḱst 44, dḗyḱs- ~ déyḱs- 36, 38, 211, déyḱ-s-e/o-, déyḱ-s-ih$_1$- 38
deywós 15, 60
dēḱnéw- ~ dēḱnu- 179
dh$_1$ié/ó- 'tie' 190
dh$_2$pn̥óm 19, 114, 154, 242

dh₃tós 112, 251
diwyós 79, 269
dl̥h₁gʰós 106, 250
dm̥h₂tós 103, 300
dn̥ǵʰwáh₂- ~ dn̥ǵʰuh₂- 60, 65 (paradigm)
dédoh₃ti 91, 112, 176, dédh₃te 112, dédh₃n̥ti 98
dokéye/o- 199
dólos 239
dóm- ~ dém- 59, dom-, dṓm 23, déms pótis 59, 84
dóru ~ dréw- 60, 63 (paradigm), 244, 340
dráh₂- ~ dr̥h₂- 202, 304
drem- 206
dus- 76
dwey-: dedwóyh₂a 217
dwó, dwóh₁ 70, 260, dwóy(h₁), dwáh₂ih₁ 70
dyéw- ~ diw- 15, 80, 237 (paradigm), dyḗws 145, 166, 249, dyḗm 19, 23, 112, 145, diḗm 19, 112

d(ʰ)ebʰnéwti 30
dʰegʷʰ- 9, 147, 282
dʰ(e)ǵʰem-, ǵʰm- ~ ǵʰm̥- 21, 22, dʰéǵʰōm ~ ǵʰm- 60, 63 (paradigm), 113, 116, dʰéǵʰōm (nom. & acc.) 238, 246, ǵʰmés 238, dʰǵʰém 60, 113, 122, 238, 246, ǵʰmáh₂ ~ ǵʰm̥áh₂ 25, 113, 114, 116, 126, 233
dʰeh₁- 17, 47–8 (paradigm), 126, dʰédʰeh₁- ~ dʰédʰh₁- 34, 38, dʰédʰeh₁e/o-, dʰédʰh₁ih₁- 38, dʰédʰh₁ti 43, 90, 112, 176, dʰédʰh₁te 112, dʰédʰh₁n̥ti 98, dʰédʰēm, é dʰedʰēm 112, dʰéh₁t 43, édʰēm, édʰeh₁s, édʰeh₁t 204
dʰeh₁k- 126, 203–4, édʰeh₁km̥, édʰeh₁ks, édʰeh₁kt 204
dʰéh₁s- ~ dʰh₁s- 126, 135, 150
dʰéh₁snah₂ 150
dʰéh₁ti- ~ dʰh₁téy- 60, 243
dʰenh₂-, dʰn̥h₂ské/ó- 185
dʰénr̥ 248, 288
dʰerh₃- 185, 293, dʰr̥h₃ské/ó- 185
dʰérs- ~ dʰr̥s-, dʰedʰórse 126, 290
dʰérsos 126, 140, 290
dʰérsus ~ dʰr̥séw- 137, 253, dʰr̥sús 126, 137, 253, 290
dʰewb- 9
dʰéwbus ~ dʰubéw- 79
dʰéwgʰ- ~ dʰugʰ- 149, 187, 207, dʰéwgʰe/o- 187
dʰeyǵʰ-, dʰéyǵʰos, dʰóyǵʰos 147
dʰǵʰúHs 249
dʰgʷʰey- ~ dʰgʷʰi- 122, 202, dʰgʷʰinéw- ~ dʰgʷʰinu- 180
dʰh₁snóm 150
dʰh₁tós 112, 251
dʰm̥bʰ- (?) 148, 162
dʰn̥h₂é/ó-, dʰn̥h₂ské/ó- 104
dʰn̥h₂tós 103, 300

dʰoHnáh₂- 61, 66 (paradigm)
dʰóh₁i- ~ dʰʰ₁i- 13
dʰóh₁mos 17, 90, 126, 239
dʰrah₂gʰ- 148
dʰrebʰ- 148
dʰrébʰtrah₂ 123
dʰregʰ- 78, 148
dʰrogʰós 77, 148, 239
dʰrubʰ- 148, 162
dʰr̥h₃ské/ó- 104
dʰubrós 79
dʰugh₂tḗr ~ dʰugtr- 16, 17, 60, 111, 126, 247, dʰugh₂tr̥sú 289
dʰugʰtós 123, 251
dʰuh₂- 78, 148
dʰuh₂mós 78, 102, 126, 148, 239
dʰwór- ~ dʰur- 126
dʰyah₂- 164
dʰyáh₂mn̥ 193, 247
-dʰyo- (inf.) 43
dʰyoh₃gʷ- 9

é- (augment) 29, 226
-e- ~ -o- (thematic vowel) 30, 37, 225
-e- ~ -o- (subjunctive) 28 fn. 21, 33, 37, 225
-ead (abl.) 234
éǵh₂ 74 (paradigm), 259 (paradigm)
eǵʰstrós 123
-éh₁- 30, 35, 144, 215
éḱwos 60, 118, 239
élh₂wr̥ 158
élh₂se/o- 224
-en- (individualizing) 80
én 89
-énd (2ary 3pl.) 144
éndom 89
énteros, éntm̥os 80, énterah₂ 241
éperos 80
epipd- 122
érewr̥ 158
-ero- 80
-es (nom. pl.) 29
-és ~ -os ~ -s (gen.) 29
éti 54 fn. 51
-eti (thematic 1ary 3sg.) 128
-eti (subj. 3sg.) 130
ewgʰ- 127
éwgʰtos 123, 251
éwse/o- 142, 186, éws- ~ ews- 212
éy 73–4 (paradigm)
-ey (dat.) 234, 297
-éye- ~ -éyo- 35
-ē- ~ -ō- 37, 225
éh₂gʷʰti 16

és- 151, ésh₂ar, ésh₂ay 139, 141, ésor 174, ésror, és̥ntoy 136, 142
-ēti (thematic subj. 3sg.) 130
-ēy (loc.) 236

gah₂u-, gh₂n̥u- 178
gem- 117, géme/o- 186
gérbʰ- ~ gr̥bʰ- 189, 291
gérsom 241
gléwbʰ- ~ glubʰ- 189
grés- (grás-?) ~ gr̥s-, gr̥sdʰí 175

gʰan-, gʰn̥-sḱé/ó- 185
gʰay... 127
gʰebʰal- 12, 147
gʰelu- 127, gʰéluh₂(s) 243
gʰend- ~ gʰn̥d-, gʰn̥dé/ó-, gʰegʰónd- 182, gʰéndse/o- 182, 224
gʰórtos 239
gʰrawH- ~ gʰruH-, gʰrawé/ó- 205
gʰrebh₂- 9

gʷah₂- ~ gʷh₂- 182, 202, gʷíǵʷah₂ti, gʷíǵʷh₂- 176, é gʷah₂t 282, gʷh₂ánd 202, 228, gʷh₂óntes, gʷh₂n̥t- 144
gʷelbʰ- 283
gʷélh₁- 103, gʷl̥h₁é/ó- 106
gʷem- 49–50 (paradigm), 182, gʷém- ~ gʷm- 35, 38, gʷm̥sḱéti 15, 27, 43, 113, 185, 282, gʷémeti, gʷémonti, gʷménd, gʷm̥sḱéti, gʷm̥sḱónti, gʷm̥sḱónti 15, gʷm̥yé/ó- 115, 160, 190, 282, gʷémd 15, gʷém-e/o-, gʷm̥-yéh₁- ~ *gʷm-ih₁- 38, gʷegʷóme 43
gʷémti- ~ gʷm̥téy- 60, 78, 243
gʷén, gʷénh₂- ~ gʷnáh₂- 60, 64 (paradigm), 242, 119, gʷenáh₂ 119, 242, gʷnáh₂- 186 fn. 8
gʷh₂bʰié/ó- 162, 190, 282
gʷi(H)- 'bowstring' 285
gʷih₂áh₂- 'force' 153, 285
gʷih₃óh₁- 153, 215, 285
gʷíh₃weti 27, 186
gʷih₃wós 80, 100, 252
gʷl̥h₁tós 103, 282
gʷṓws, gʷów- 145, 249, 282, gʷṓm 145
gʷráh₂us ~ gʷr̥h₂áw- 79, 96, 253, 282, 290
gʷr̥dú- 253, 282, 290
gʷr̥h₃tós 104, 282
gʷyoh₃- 100, 106

gʷʰedʰ- 200, gʷʰédʰye/o- 34, 189, 284
gʷʰen-, gʷʰn̥- 119, 127, 192, 283, gʷʰénti, gʷʰén-ye/o- 208
gʷʰer- 127, gʷʰéros 245, 284
gʷʰn̥tós 251
gʷʰodʰéye/o- 200

gʷʰónos 119, 127
gʷʰr̥mós, gʷʰermós 252

ǵenh₁- 77, 103, 4 fn. 43, ǵiǵénh₁- ~ ǵiǵn̥h₁- 184, ǵn̥h₁yétor, ǵn̥h₁tó, ǵeǵónh₁e 43, 217, 221, ǵeǵn̥h₁wésih₂ 217
ǵénh₁os ~ ǵénh₁es- 59, 78, 89, 117, 235, 245, ǵénh₁esos 89, 135, 235, 245
ǵénh₁ti- ~ ǵn̥h₁téy- 243
ǵénh₁tōr 78, 91, 247
ǵénh₁trih₂ 101
ǵéws- ~ ǵus-, ǵéws-e/o- 188
ǵéwstu- ~ ǵustéw- 60, 63 (paradigm)
ǵénus ~ ǵénu- 244
ǵnoh₃-, ǵn̥h₃sḱé/ó-, ǵn̥nóh₃- ~ ǵn̥nh₃- 43, ǵnóh₃- ~ ǵn̥h₃- 43, 105, 202, ǵn̥h₃sḱéti 27, 185, ǵnóh₃t 91, 105, ǵnēh₃s- 31, ǵnéh₃s- ~ ǵnóh₃s- 43
ǵn̥h₁tós 103, 251
ǵómbʰos 125, 239
ǵónh₁-o-s, ǵonh₁-áh₂-, -ǵonh₁-ó-s 77
ǵónu ~ ǵénu- 244, ǵónu ~ ǵnéw- 60

ǵʰáns- 12, 126, 140, 249
ǵʰdyés 123
ǵʰed- 166
ǵʰíǵʰeh₁- 176
ǵʰélh₃- 104
ǵʰérye/o- 191, ǵʰr̥yé/ó- 160, 191, 290
ǵʰéslom 126, 140, 266
ǵʰésōr 238, 247, ǵʰésr- 126, 140, 238, 247, 267
ǵʰew- 126, ǵʰews- 213, ǵʰéwse/o- 224
ǵʰéymō 246
ǵʰéyōm, ǵʰyém ~ ǵʰiém 113, 126, 246, ǵʰéyōm (nom. & acc.) 238, ǵʰim-és, ǵʰiém 238, ǵʰim- 113, 126, 153
ǵʰl̥h₃rós 104
ǵʰwér 117, 237, 247, ǵʰwérm̥ 237

-Hen- 80
Hiǵnós 107, 251
Hne(n)ḱ- ~ Hn̥ḱ- 110, 205, é Hnéḱt 110, HeHnóḱe ~ HeHnónḱe 110, 4 fn. 29
Hyaǵ- 12
Hyaǵnós 19, 107, 251
Hyéh₁gʷah₂ 107, 241, 282, 300
Hyeh₁ro-, Hyoh₁ro- 107
Hyn̥h₂tḗr, Hyénh₂ter 107, 247
Hyewdʰ- ~ Hyudʰ-, Hyudʰsm- 107
Hyewh₂- 107
Hyéḱʷr̥ ~ Hyéḱʷn- 15, 59, 90, 107, 248, 281, 288
Hyós 73, 107
Hyóti 165, 275

h₁dónts 65 (paradigm), 109, 237, 238, 249,
    h₁dóntm̥ 237, h₁dn̥tés 237, 238, 249h₁es- 45
    (paradigm), h₁és- ~ h₁s- 34, 38, h₁esmi 139,
    266, h₁ési 20, h₁ésti 27, 43, h₁esti 89, 174,
    h₁és-e/o- 38, h₁ésoh₂ 135, h₁s-iéh₁- ~ h₁s-ih₁-
    38, h₁siém̥ 112, h₁siéh₁t 138, 226, h₁s-ónt- ~
    h₁s-n̥t- 108, h₁sónts 68 (paradigm), 135,
    h₁sóntih₂, h₁sn̥tíh₂ 100, 114, 135, 164, é
    h₁esm̥ 136, é h₁est 91, 146, 227, é h₁send 309,
    h₁ské/ó- 184
h₁ésu-, h₁su- 143, 253
h₁ey- 93, h₁éyti 174, h₁éy, h₁idʰí 231, h₁ité, é
    h₁yend 93
h₁éd- ~ h₁éd- 34, 38, 89, h₁édsti, h₁édn̥ti 15,
    h₁éd-e/o-, h₁éd-ih₁- 38
h₁ger- ~ h₁gr-, h₁geh₁góre 90, 108, 206, 218,
    h₁geh₁gr̥- 218
h₁lengʰ- ~ h₁ln̥gʰ- 108, 187, h₁léngʰ-e/o- 187
h₁léngʰus, h₁ln̥gʰús 20, 108, 114, 117, 127, 253,
    h₁léngʷʰios- 121
h₁lengʷʰ- 20
h₁léwdʰeros 35, 108, 126, 251
h₁lewdʰeroyé/ó- 35
h₁léwdʰse/o- 224, h₁ludʰé/ó- 36, h₁ludʰéd 43,
    91, 126, 204, 227, é h₁ludʰed 91, 126, 204, 227,
    h₁eh₁lówdʰ- ~ h₁eh₁ludʰ- 218
h₁léwos 104
h₁ln̥gʷʰrós 20, 108, 114, 127, 250, 282
(h₁)néwn̥ 71
h₁néh₃mn̥ 10, 15, 58, 59, 62 (paradigm), 99, 109,
    246, h₁nóh₃mn- 15, 59, 246
h₁nóh₃mō 58, 62 (paradigm)
h₁n̥h₃mn̥yé/ó- 99, 114, 160, 193
h₁óh₃s 10
h₁régʷos 35, 108, 245, 284, h₁régʷes- 140, 266,
    284
h₁regʷesyé/ó- 35
h₁reh₁- 10
h₁répye/o- 108, 161, 191, h₁r̥pyé/ó- (?) 191
h₁rew-, h₁réwe/o-, h₁r̥wé/ó- 98
h₁rewdʰ- 35
h₁rewg- 108, h₁réwge/o- 186, 207
h₁reyp- 108
h₁roHwáh₂ 108, 241
h₁rudʰéh₁- 35, 38, h₁rudʰ-éh₁-e/o-,
    h₁rudʰ-éh₁-ih₁- 38
h₁rudʰrós 79, 108, 126, 350, h₁rudʰráh₂ 304
-(h₁)se- ~ -(h₁)so- 35, 223
h₁su- 76
h₁sumenesyé/ó- 193
h₁werǵ- 108
h₁wers- 108, 140
h₁wérus ~ h₁uréw- 81, 94, 253
h₁wéryos- ~ h₁uris- 81
h₁widʰéwh₂- ~ h₁widʰwáh₂- 60, 64 (paradigm)

h₁yeh₁- 10, 93, 100, 107, 203–4, h₁íh₁yeh₁ti 93,
    100, 176
h₁yeh₁k- 107, 203

-h₂- (collective) 60, 77, 80
-h₂- (fem.) 61, 66, 80
-h₂a (1sg.) 32
h₂ábʰo(n)- 9 fn. 7
h₂adʰgʰ- 116, 122
h₂áǵʰos 245
h₂áǵeti 16, 27, 43, 89, 186, é h₂aǵed 91, 227, 300
h₂aǵ- 'say', é h₂aǵt 146, 174
h₂áǵrios 80
h₂áǵros 65 (paradigm), 80, 239
h₂ákos 105
h₂ákmō 89, 235, 246, h₂ákmonm̥, h₂ḱ(m)nés
    235, 246
h₂algʷʰ- 206, 284
h₂ándʰos 126, 245
h₂ánǵʰe/o- 127, 186, h₂énǵʰs- ~ h₂ánǵʰs- 212
h₂anh₁- 10
h₂ank- 89
h₂ánkos 89, 245
h₂ánkō 161, 235, 246
h₂ánkulah₂ 241
h₂(a)nkulós 170, 252
(h₂)áns-, (h₂)ansio- 140, 141
h₂ant- 70, 97, h₂ánti, h₂antí 89
h₂(a)ntíos 252
h₂ár- ~ h₂r̥- 'share' 206
h₂árǵu- ~ h₂r̥ǵéw- 79
h₂arh₃- 10, h₂árye/o- 190, h₂érh₃s- ~ h₂árh₃s-
    212
h₂árh₃trom 78, 111, 122, 241
h₂árh₃wr̥ 158
h₂áwh₂os 10
h₂áwis 16, 18, 160, h₂áwy- 160
h₂áwsie/o-/h₂usyé/ó- 191, h₂éws- ~ h₂áws- 212
h₂áwsos 140, 245, h₂áwses-, h₂usíh₁ 20
h₂áwsōs, h₂usós 95, 140, 141, 245, 267, 301, 308
h₂awsr- 143, 151
h₂kestó- 105
h₂ḱh₂owsiéti 16, 18, 90, 104, 109, 340,
    h₂ḱh₂owsié/ó- 157, 158, 193
h₂leg- 109, h₂lége/o- 186
h₂lek- 97, 223, 238, h₂lékse/o- 34, 109, 223,
    h₂lékseti 97
h₂luské/ó- 185
h₂l̥k-´ (noun) 238
h₂melǵ- 109, h₂mélǵ- ~ h₂mélǵ-, h₂mélǵe/o- 187
h₂mert- 181, 289
h₂néḱt, h₂ah₂nóke 44
h₂nér- ~ h₂nr-, 58, 109, h₂nér 97, 109, 235, 247,
    h₂n̥rés 97
h₂n̥tbʰí 97, 125

h₂n̥tbʰóh₁ 125, 260
h₂n̥h₁mós/h₂ónh₁mos 99, 111
h₂óǵmos 16, 89
h₂ónkos 89, 239
h₂óst ~ h₂ást- 59, 89, h₂ostey- 89
h₂ówis ~ h₂áwi- 16 fn. 11, 59, 62 (paradigm), 2 fn. 11, 89, 243, h₂ówim 112
h₂óyu 106, 341
(h₂)ōwióm 18, 241
h₂pélos 109, 245
h₂reh₁g- 109
h₂r̥ǵi- 79
h₂r̥ǵipyós 89
h₂r̥ǵrós 79, 97, 250
h₂r̥néw- ~ h₂r̥nu- 97, 179
h₂r̥sé(n) 246
h₂r̥tkos 14, 97, 116, 239
h₂sewt- 142
h₂stér 61 (paradigm), 109, 236, 247
h₂tug- 109, 166, h₂tugyé/ó- 190
h₂udáh₂ 94
h₂ugsié/ó- 159
h₂wap- 12
h₂wegs- 94
h₂weh₁- 10, h₂wéh₁ti 90, 109, 174
h₂wéh₁n̥tos 144
h₂welk- 238
h₂wes- ~ h₂us- 95, 108, h₂í-h₂us-e/o- 95
h₂wl̥h₁no- 10, 110
h₂wólkm̥ 238
h₂yu-gih₃- 106, 120
h₂yuHn̥táh₂ 79

h₃bʰélos 105
h₃bʰrúHs 102, 109, 125, 249
h₃éǵʷhis ~ h₃óǵʷhi- 16 fn. 11, 127, 243, 285, h₃óǵʷhis 2 fn. 11
(h₃)meyǵʰ- 109, (h₃)méyǵʰe/o- 126, 186
(h₃)migʰláh₂ 109, 127, 241
h₃ner- 109, h₃nḗr 156, h₃ón̥r 248
h₃néryos 156
h₃neyd- 109
h₃nóbʰ-, h₃n̥bʰl̥H- 97, 125
h₃nogʰ-, h₃nogʰw- 109, 117, 119, 249
h₃od- 166
h₃okʷ- ~ h₃kʷ- 'eye' 100, 121, 281, h₃ókʷih₁ 100, 121, 248, h₃ókʷ 238, 248, 281h₃okʷ- ~ h₃kʷ- 'see', h₃okʷye/o- 121, h₃ókʷse/o-, h₃íh₃kʷse/o- 224
h₃ókʷyos 156
h₃omh₃- 10
h₃ór- ~ h₃r̥- 202, h₃r̥néw- ~ h₃r̥nu- 97, 179
h₃órǵʰis ~ h₃r̥ǵʰéy- 243
h₃órō, h₃óron- ~ h₃r̥n- 89
h₃ósdos 16, 89, 239
h₃reǵ- 109, h₃réǵs- ~ h₃réǵs- 122, 212, h₃réǵ- ~ h₃réǵ-, h₃réǵe/o- 187, é h₃reǵsn̥d 227
h₃réǵnih₂ 243
h₃r̥tós 97, 251
h₃slidʰ- 4 fn. 4

-í 233
-i (post-PIE loc.) 234, 297
i/e- 73
-ih₂ ~ -yáh₂- (fem.) 25, 66, 80, 100, 157
-im, -ins (acc.) 18
-im (adv.) 54 fn. 52
-ismo- 81
-isto- 81
ísus, iswós 140
ísugʰesrih₂ 77, 137

kalh₁- 12, 103
kan- 12
kápros 12, 239
karp- 12
kát(a)h₂ 233
káti 130
kátus 12
kaw- 'strike' 12
kawl- 12
kaws- 'burn' 213
k(e)dnáh₂ti ~ k(e)dnh₂- 177
kélse/o- 224
ker- 117, kḗrs- ~ kérs- 212
kes- 8, 117
kh₂pié/ó- 162, 190
klep- 117, 192, klépye/o- 161, 192, klépe/o- (?) 192, klḗps- ~ kléps- 212
kl̥h₁tós 103
knáh₂ye/o- 190
kneyǵʷh-
kokso- 9
kóm 115, 156, 160
kónis ~ kénis- 138, 245
kóros 79
kóryos 79, 156, 160
kowh₁éye/o- 200
krásnah₂ 242, 266, 302
kreḱ- 9
krétus ~ kr̥téw- 253, 290, kr̥tús 154
krétyos- 154, 164
kréwh₂s 111, 245
kréydʰrom 78
krotéye/o- 200
kr̥néy- ~ kr̥ny- 180
ksuróm 241
kwas- 12, 178, kunés- 178
kwath₂- 12

kʷátye/o- 164, 191, 281, kʷáts- ~ kʷáts- 212
kʷe 284
kʷékʷlos 60, 119, 239, kʷekʷlá-h₂- 60, 119
kʷek̑- 9
kʷél- ~ kʷl̥- 188, 201, 206, 283
kʷels- 140, 283
kʷendʰ-, kʷn̥tʰské/ó- 185, kʷekʷóndʰh₂a 218, kʷéndʰse/o- 224
kʷetwóres 71 (paradigm), 168, 283, kʷetwór-, kʷetwr̥- 260
kʷey- 283, kʷinéw- ~ kʷinu- 180, 285
kʷi/e- 73, 258 (paradigm), kʷíd 8, 145, 285, kʷésyo 138
kʷid 74, 285
kʷo- 73, 281
kʷoléye/o- 201 (2x)
kʷólos 239, 281
kʷóteros 281
kʷóti 156, 165, 275, 281, kʷótyos 156
kʷoynáh₂ 242, 283
kʷréyh₂- ~ kʷrih₂- 202, kʷrih₂tó 101, 281, kʷrih₂n̥tó 101
kʷyew- 163, 178

k̑ad- 12
k̑as- 12
k̑el- 35
k̑emh₂-, k̑m̥-né-h₁- ~ k̑m-n̥-h₁- 182
k̑enk- 9
k̑érh₂- ~ k̑r̥h₂- 103, 117, 177, k̑r̥náh₂- 177
k̑érh₂s 245
k̑erh₃- 293
k̑ey- 203, k̑éyor 8, 27, 117, 174, k̑éytor 117, k̑éytoy 117, 174
k̑ér ~ k̑r̥d- 58, 61 (paradigm), 249, 291
k̑i/e- 73, 340
k̑ík̑lh₁se/o- 35
k̑íHō 246
k̑lew- ~ k̑lu- 78, 202
k̑léwos ~ k̑léwes- 59, 77, 78, 117, 245
k̑ley-: k̑l̥néy- ~ k̑l̥ny- 180, k̑ekli- 222
k̑mh₂tós 103, 182, 300
k̑m̥tóm 22, 71, 113
k̑o- 73
k̑remh₂- ~ k̑r̥mh₂- 175, 177, kr̥m̥nh₂- 177
k̑r̥h₂tós 117, 251, 304
k̑wah₂-, k̑uh₂- 118
k̑wón- ~ k̑un-/k̑wn̥- 13, 17–8, 65 (paradigm), k̑wṓ ~ k̑uó, k̑wónm̥ 235, 246, k̑unés 17, 235, 246, k̑wn̥sú 18

labʰ- 12
lad- 12
laywós 12, 252
leb- 9

legʰ- 127, 203, légʰos 127
légʰtrom 122
leg̑- 117, lég̑e/o- 186
lengʰ-, ln̥gʰ-, ln̥gʰé/ó-, lelóngʰ- 182
lewH- ~ luH- 189, 202
leyg̑ʰ- ~ lig̑ʰ-, 117, 126, 187, léyg̑ʰti 117, 126, léyg̑ʰe/o- 187, léyg̑ʰs- ~ léyg̑ʰs- 212
leykʷ- 45–7 (paradigm), linékʷ- ~ linkʷ- 18, 34, 38, linékʷe/o-, linkʷiéh₁- ~ linkʷih₁- 38, linékʷti, linkʷénti 188, léykʷ- ~ likʷ- 188, 205, léykʷe/o- 188, 284, likʷé/ó- 205
léymon- ~ limn- 59–60, 62 (paradigm), léymō, limén(-i) 236, 246, léymonm̥, limnés 236
leys- 31
lowkéyeti 31
lugrós 250
lugtós 122
luktó 27

mah₂tḗr 16, 247
mak̑- 250 fn. 54
mak̑rós 250
málom 241
médʰus 244, médʰu 126, 244
médʰyos 156, 165, 252, 275
még̑ʰ₂- 111, 253, 336, m̥g̑ʰ₂- 336
még̑yos- 154, 166
méh₁lom/mélom 241
méh₁tis 243
melh₃-, ml̥h₃ské/ó- 104, 185, 293
mélid, mlit- 146, 249
men- 'think': mn̥yétor 115, 160, 190, mn̥yétoy 160, 190, memón- ~ memn- 36, 38, memóne 13, 115, 217, memn̥mé 217, memnḗr 13, meméne/o-, memn̥yéh₁- ~ memnih₁- 38, memn̥wós 217, memn̥- 115, mnéh₁- ~ mn̥éh₁- 215
mendʰ- ~ mn̥dʰ-, mn̥dʰé/ó- 182
ménti- ~ mn̥téy- 60, 63 (paradigm)
mértis ~ *mr̥téy- 78
mé 8.2
méh₁n̥s ~ méh₁n̥s- 15, 59, 62 (paradigm), 267, 140, 145, 238, 246, méh₁n̥sm̥, méh₁n̥sos 238
méms ~ méms- 15, 59, 9 fn. 6
-mh₁nó- 42 with fn. 38, 232
mimne/o- 31, 184
misdʰó- 20, 126, 240
misk̑é/ó- 184
mléwHti 19
mlityé/ó- 164, 193
mnah₂- 19, 186, mn̥h₂ské/ó- 186
-mn̥ ~ -mén- 236, 336
-mo- ~ -m̥o- 80
móri ~ mréy- 60, 63 (paradigm)
mrég̑ʰus ~ mr̥g̑ʰéw- 19, 117, 126, 253, 289, 290

mr̥nh₂- 177, 290
mr̥tó 27
mr̥tós 251, 289
múHs/mū́s 249
mus- 138
mustís 14
myewh₁- 19
-m̥ (acc.) 113

nadʰ- 12, 9 fn. 6
náh₂us, n̥h₂wés 244, nāwós 308
nasye/o- 138
nā́sh₁e 15, nás- 12, 15
-né- ~ -n- (infix) 30
nébʰelah₂ 242
nébʰos ~ nébʰes- 59, 65 (paradigm), 125, 245, nébʰesos 14
negʷnós 119, 252
negʷʰrós 127, 282
néme/o- 186
nept- 18
neptiós 18, 2 fn. 12, 240
nésontor, nésontoy 135, nínes- ~ nins- 184
-néw- ~ -nu- 30, 179, 4 fn. 39
new- 78
néwah₂- 35, 38, 197, néwa-h₂-e/o-, néwa-h₂-ih₁- 38
newd- 9 fn. 6
néwios 11, 19
néwmn̥ ~ numén- 78, 114, 247
néwos 11, 35, 197, 250, néwom 112, néwah₂ 305
néwotāts 79
néygʷ- ~ nigʷ- 121, 284, nigʷyé/ó- 121, 166, 190
ni- 93, 100
nigʷtós 251
nisdós 20, 65 (paradigm)
-nó- 80
nókʷt- ~ nékʷt- 59, 61 (paradigm), 119, 238, nókʷts 237, 249, nókʷtm̥ 113, 237, nékʷts 237, nókʷtn̥s 114
n̥- 15, 76, 113
-n̥d (2ary 3pl.) 295
n̥dʰgʷʰitom 77, 113, 116, 251, 282
n̥gʷén 283
-n̥H- (pres.) 157 (2x)
n̥h₁gr- 104
n̥h₁lewés- 104
ń̥h₁sn̥t- 89, 108
n̥h₂kesto- 105
n̥h₂ḱh₂ows- 104
ń̥h₂ltos 99
n̥h₂mertés- 105
n̥h₃bʰelés- 105
ń̥nigʷtos 122
-n̥s (acc.) 114

n̥si- 136
ń̥sl̥h₁gtos 122
n̥smé 139, 141, 266, 311
-n̥ti 114
-n̥to 114
ń̥udros 114
ń̥widstos 121

o- 73
-o-ey (dat. sg.) 91, 169 with fn. 50
-óHom 29, 91, 169
-oh₁ 234
-oh₂ (1sg.) 32, 33
oḱtṓw 21, 71
-omi (1sg.) 32
-ónt- ~ -nt- (ptc.) 42, 232
-ó-oHom 169
op- ~ ep- 'back' 79 with fn. 69, 89, opi- 100
orbʰo- 125
orsáh₂ 141
órsos 89, 141, 239
-os (dat. pl.) 29
ósr̥ ~ ésn- 59
-osyo 320
ówdʰr̥, uHdʰéns 248, 288
oy-, óykos, óynos 70
-oyh₁- ~ -oy- (thematic optative) 17, 37, 39
oysse/o- 224
óywos 70, 252
óḱu- ~ ōḱéw- 253
ómsos 140, 239
-ōys (inst. pl.) 145, 169

pah₂ǵ-: pepóh₂ǵ- ~ pepʰ₂ǵ- 219
páh₂n̥tes (pántes?) 144, 253
páh₂wr̥ ~ pʰ₂uén- 60, páh₂wōr, pʰ₂unés 238, 248
pédom 241
pedyós 18, 2 fn. 12, 156, 166
pekʷ-, pékʷye/o- 120, 192, pékʷe/o- 192, pékʷs- ~ pékʷs- 212, 282
peḱ- 117
péktn̥, pḱténs 247
pelekus 244
pélh₁u- ~ pl̥h₁éw- 253
pénkʷe 71, 283
pérde/o- 186, 207
pérh₃- ~ pr̥h₃- 206, 293
peróm 241
pértus ~ pr̥téw- 78
pérwr̥, pr̥wén- 193, 248, 288
pésos 135, 245
péte/o- 186, 207, pipte/o- 184
p(e)tʰ₂-, p(e)tnh₂- 177
pʰ₂ǵéh₁- 35

ph₂tḗr 16, 22, 65 (paradigm), 80, 90, 111, 129, 169, 235 (paradigm), 247, ph₂tér- ~ ph₂tr- 60
ph₂triós 80
píHwō 100, 253, píHwerih₂ 100, 253
píh₃se/o- 224
pik̂rós 250
plak- 12
pláth₂us ~ pl̥th₂áw- 12, 96, 253, 290, pl̥th₂áwih₂ 100
pleh₁- ~ pl̥h₁- 92, 176, 202, pl̥h₁- 176
pléh₁isto- 92
plek- 117
pléwe/o- 187, pléws- ~ pléws- 212
plóh₃ye/o- 190
plówyom 160
pl̥h₁nós 69 (paradigm)
pl̥h₁ús 96
pl̥h₂mah₂- 61, 66 (paradigm), 105, 242, pl̥h₂mām 112, 300
pl̥nh₂- 'approach' 177
pl̥th₂n̥ós 18, 114, 154
poh₂imén- ~ poh₂imn- 60, poh₂imé(n) 92, 235, 246, poh₂iménm̥, poh₂imnés 235
póh₃tlom 78
póntoh₂- ~ pn̥th₂- 59 with fn. 56
poth₂áye/o- 201
pótis 16 fn. 11, 243
pótnih₂ 101, 243
póyk̂os 159
póywah₂ 242, 305
pṓds 59, 237 with fn. 51, 248, pód- ~ ped- 14, 18, 61 (paradigm), 122, 248, pedés 14, 59, 237, pódm̥ 59, 113, 237
pṓth₂ie/o- 201
prek̂- 22, 34, pr̥sk̂éti 22, pr̥sk̂é/ó- 34, 38, pr̥-sk̂é/ó-, pr̥-sk̂ó-y(h₁)- 38
pró 76
próti, prótyō 165, 275
pr̥Hmós 80
pr̥h₂tós 103, 304
pr̥náh₂ti ~ pr̥nh₂- 177
pr̥sóm 137, 241
pstr̥-néw- ~ pstr̥-nu- 179, 290
pyah₂k̂- 161, 163

-s- (aor.) 31
sah₂giéti 31
sáh₂wl̥ 64 (paradigm), 132, sh₂uéns 64 fn. 61
sáh₂wōl 64 fn. 61
sak- 12
sál- ~ sl̥- 12, 203, sályo/o- 132, 159, 191
sáls 12, 132, 249
sámh₂dʰos 12, 111, 125, 147, 240
sark- 12

sasyóm 12
sáwsos 12, 5 fn. 2
sbʰer- (?) 124
sbʰr̥h₂géye/o- 124
-se- ~ -so- 34, 223
sebʰi 55, 74
sed- 35, 147, sísde/o- 34, 184, sísdeti, sédst 43
sédos 131, 147, 245
seǵʰ- 126, 148, 200, séǵʰe/o- 207, sísǵʰe/o- 184
seh₁- 'sift' 147
seh₁- 78, sish₁e/o- 31
séh₁mn̥ ~ sh₁mén- 60, 64 (paradigm), 78
séh₁mō 64 (paradigm), 78
sék̂ʷe/o- 187, 207, sék̂ʷetor 131, 284, sék̂ʷontor 284, sék̂ʷetoy 131
selk- 132
sélos 131, 245
sem- 70 (paradigm), 260, sḗm, sḗms 260, sém 113, 131, 260, sémih₂, smíh₂ 101, 134, 260, sémih₂m̥, smíh₂m̥, siáh₂- 260, syáh₂s, smiáh₂s 305
sengʷʰ- 78, 147
sénos, sénah₂ 132, 250
sép- ~ sp- 207, sépti, sépe/o- 132, 187
septm̥ 14, 71, 113, 131
ser- 'string' 132, 133, sérye/o- 133
ser- 'flow' 133
-ser- (fem.) 26
sér(i) 133
sérmn̥ 133
sérpe/o- 132, 187
ses- 10
-s-e-si 28 fn. 21
séwH- ~ suH- 'rain' 132, 192
sewyós 11
seyk̂-, sik̂-néw- ~ sik̂-nu- ~ sik̂-n̥w- 115, 132, 180
sēmi- 76, 90, 131, 168
sgʷʰal- (?) 124
sǵʰeyd-, sǵʰinéd- ~ sǵʰind- (?) 124
sǵʰh₂yé/ó- (?) 124
sh₂i-, sh₂iéti 94
siléh₁-, silo- 35
skabʰ- 'scrape' 9, 12
skabʰ- 'prop' 9, 12
skabʰtḗr 123
skaywós 12, 252
skélh₁- 104
skélos 235
skl̥h₁rós 104
sk̂áh₂ih₂ ~ sk̂h₂iáh₂- 242, 305
-sk̂é/ó- 30, 33, 34
slagʷyé/ó- 121, 167, slagʷé/ó- 121, 143, 284
sleh₁g- 134
sĺ̥g- 134, 291

smáḱru 12
smer- 134, 289, sesmr̥- 289
smerd- 134
smewH... 135
smey-, smeyd- 134
sm̥- 113, 131, 147
sm̥H... 'same' 114, 131
sm̥Hó- 'some' 114, 131
sm̥sok^{w}yo- 121, 133
snah$_2$- 134
sneh$_1$- 17, snéh$_1$ye/o- 17, 134, 190, snéh$_1$yeti 90
snéh$_1$mn̥ 247
snéh$_1$wr̥ 134, 145
snéyg^{wh}e/o- 127, 134, 187, 284
snig^{wh}- 127, 134, 281, sníg^{wh}m̥ 248
snusós 60, 134, 135, 240
sn̥tér 133
só 72 (paradigm), 131, 257 (paradigm), 280, sáh$_2$ 131, 280, tósyo 138, tód 145, tóh$_1$ 72 fn. 67, tóy, táh$_2$as 280
sodéye/o- 35
sók- ~ sék- 13
sókr̥, skṓr 248
sók^{w}h$_2$ō 23, sók^{w}h$_2$oy- ~ sk^{w}h$_2$i- 121, 156, sók^{w}yos 156
sólwos 132
somHeyé/ó- 35
somHós 35, 90, 131, 250
sóng^{wh}os, song^{wh}áh$_2$ 78, 127, 147, 242, 282, 283
sórmos 132
sorós 133
spéḱye/o- 161, 190, spéḱyed 27, spḗḱs- ~ spéḱs- 212
spérǵ^h- ~ spr̥ǵ^h- 9, 127
spérmn̥ 114
spoḱéye/o- 199
spónd- ~ spénd-, spénde/o- 188
spr̥d^h- 9
sreb^h- ~ sr̥b^h- 134
srégye/o- 190
sréwe/o- 134
srī́gos 134, 245
srob^{h}éye/o- 134, 200
sr̥b^{h}tós (?) 123
sr̥h$_3$yé/ó- 104, 190
stag- 12, 166
stáh$_2$- ~ sth$_2$- 202, stístah$_2$ti 43, stísth$_2$n̥ti 98, stí-stah$_2$- ~ stí-sth$_2$- 34, 38, stístah$_2$ti 176, stí-stah$_2$-e/o-, stí-sth$_2$-ih$_1$- 38, stáh$_2$t 16, 43, 91, 112, 300, é stah$_3$t 112, 146, stestóh$_2$- ~ stesth$_2$- 220, stestóh$_2$a 27, 43
stáh$_2$ti- ~ sth$_2$téy- 243
stah$_2$urós 92, 240
(s)teg- 117, (s)tége/o- 187
stélye/o- 159, 189
stemb^{h}H- 9, 147
stérh$_3$- 104, 293, stestr̥h$_3$- 222
stérih$_2$ 100
stéwor 174
steyg^h- 9, 117, 127
sth$_2$tós 112, 251, 251
stig- 166
stóh$_3$mn- 246
str̥h$_3$tós 104, 251
-sú 29, 297
su(H)é/ó- 'push' 34
súHs/sū́s 132, 249
suh$_3$nús 14
suh$_3$yús ~ suh$_3$iw- 244
supo 151
swah$_2$d- 12, swáh$_2$dus 91, 133, 253, 300, swah$_2$déwih$_2$ 101
swé 74 (paradigm), 133, 260, 8.2, se- 8.2
sweh$_1$- 147
sweh$_1$d^h-, seswóh$_1$d^{h}e 219
sweḱrúh$_2$ 240, 243
swéḱs 71, 133
swéḱure 14, swéḱuroey 15, swéḱuros 15, 133, 240
swēḱurós 15
swésorm̥ 13, swésores 133, 135, 247
swéyd- ~ swid- 133
-syé- ~ -syó- 35
syúHd^{h}lom 78
syuHmén- 132

tag- 12
-tah$_2$, -étah$_2$ 79
táwros 12, 240
-tāt- 79
teg- 9
teḱ- 9, 21, 116, tétekti, tétḱn̥ti 21, 116, 183
télh$_2$- ~ tl̥h$_2$- 103, 202, 221, tl̥náh$_2$- ~ tl̥nh$_2$- 34, 38, tl̥náh$_2$ti 43, tl̥náh$_2$e/o-, tl̥nh$_2$iéh$_1$- ~ tl̥nh$_2$ih$_1$- 38, télh$_2$t 43, tetólh$_2$- ~ tetl̥h$_2$- 221, tetólh$_2$a 43
témh$_1$- 103, témh$_1$- ~ tm̥h$_1$-, tm̥-né-h$_1$- ~ tm-n̥-h$_1$- 181
ten- 9 fn. 6, tn̥néw- ~ tn̥nw- 34, 38, 179, tn̥-néw-e/o-, tn̥-nu-yéh$_1$- ~ tn̥-nw-ih$_1$- 38
tend- 9 fn. 6
ténge/o- 187, tḗngs- ~ téngs- 212
ténh$_2$us 67 (paradigm), 114, 253, tn̥h$_2$áw- 114, 253
terh$_1$- ~ tr̥h$_1$- 17, 78, 103, 183, téterh$_1$- ~ tétr̥h$_1$-, tr̥néh$_1$- ~ trn̥h$_1$- 183
terh$_3$-, tr̥h$_3$ské/ó- 185, 293
térmn̥ 247
térmō 246

-tero- 80
térp- ~ tr̥p- 205, 290, tr̥pé/ó- 205
ters- 140, tr̥séh_1- 215
tétḱō 22, 116
-ti (adv.) 54 fn. 51
tken- ~ tkn̥- 116
tḱey- 116, tḱéyti 174, tḱiénti 116, 174
tl̥$h_2$tós 103, 251, 301
tm̥$h_1$tós 103, 181
-tm̥o- 80
tn̥tós 114, 251
-tó- 20, 22, 80, 337
tórmos 17, 78, 240
tóti 165, 275
-tōd 145
trem- 200, tréme/o- 187
trep- 200, trép- ~ tr̥p- 187, 207, trépe/o- 187, tr̥pé- 289
tres- ~ tr̥s- 135, 137, 140, 290, trése/o- 135, 187
tréyes 71 (paradigm), 260, tríns 260, trióHom, trisú 18, tríh_2 101
-trih_2 (fem.) 101
tr̥$h_1$tós 103
tr̥sró- 137, 140, 290
túh_2 74 (paradigm), 259 (paradigm), twé 167
tupéh_1- 215
tupyé/ó- 191 fn. 14
tweys-, twéyse/o- 138, 167
tyegʷ- 164, 200, tyégʷe/o- 284

udṓr 151, 238
udrós 240
údsteros 121, 252
uksén- ~ uksn- 60, 65 (paradigm)
-um, -uns (acc.) 18
unébʰ-, ubʰnéH-, ubʰn̥Hyé- 102, 115, 125, 161, 183
upér 151
usmé 151, 311

wah_2g- 305, wewóh_2g- ~ wewh_2g- 219
war- 12
wā́stu ~ wástu- 12, 15, 59, 244
wédōr ~ udnés 58, 60, 238, 248
wedʰh_1- 201
weǵʰ- 50 (paradigm), wéǵʰe/o- 187, wéǵʰeti 44, wḗǵʰs- ~ wéǵʰs- 36, 212, wḗǵʰst 15, 27, 44, wéǵʰsn̥d 15
wekʷ- 36, 78, 208, wéwke/o- 36, 208, 284, wéwked 27, é wewked 208
wékʷos ~ wékʷes- 78, 119, 245, 284
wémh_1- ~ wm̥h_1- 192
-went- 80, -wn̥tih_2 164
wérǵ- 78, wr̥ǵyéti 18, 289, wr̥ǵyé/ó- 34, 190, wewórǵe ~ wewr̥ǵ- 218
wérǵom 15, 60, 65 (paradigm), 78, 241, werǵáh_2 14
werh_1- 17, 103, wérh_1t 43, wérye/o- 17, wéryeti 14, 31, 43, wérye, wéryesi, wéryomos, wéryonti, wéryowos, wéryoyd 14, wéryoh_2 14, 17
wert- 165, wértsti, wewórte 44, wértye/o- 165, 192, wérte/o- 192
wés- 151, wéstor 27, 43, wésto 174, wésn̥to 114
wésmn̥ 139, 142, 247, 266
wesnéw- ~ wesnu- 139, 179
wésperos 151, 240
wésr̥ 143, 248, 288
wétos 245, wétes 163
wewóyke 217
wéyd- ~ wid- 'catch sight of' 35, 205
wéydse/o- 35, 223
wḗyh_1s- ~ wéyh_1s- 213
wḗḱti, wéḱn̥ti 15, 187 fn. 10, wéḱ- ~ uḱ- 187 fn. 10
wḗsus ~ wésu- 15
wih_1- 249
wī́ḱm̥tih_1 71, 100, 113
wīs- ~ wis- 100, 135
wl̥h_3óh_1- 215
wl̥kʷos 14, 120, 240
wódr̥ 58, 60, 248, udén-, wéd-n̥- 60
woǵʰéye/o- 199
worséye/o- 141, 200
worso- 142
-wós- ~ -us- 43, 232
woséyeti 14, 31, 179
wóyd- ~ wid- 36, 38, wóydh_2a 216, wóydsth_2a 90, 121, 216, wóyde 27, 43, 216, widmé 216, wéyde/o- 38, wéydeti 216, widyéh_1- ~ widih_1- 38, widsdʰí 121, 126, 216, wéydwōs, widwésih_2 216, widúsih_2 101, 138, 216
wṓkʷs 119, 237, wókʷm̥ 119, 121, 237, 248, 281, wekʷés 237
wṓsnos 142
wrah_2d- 19, wráh_2d- ~ wr̥h_2d- 58, 61 (paradigm)
wreh_1ǵ-, wewróh_1ǵe 219
wr̥bʰtós (?) 123
wr̥ḗ(n) 246, 290
wr̥$h_1$tós 103, 251

-ye- ~ -yo- (pres.) 34
-yé- ~ -yó- (pres.) 18, 30, 33, 34, 35
-yéh_1- ~ -ih_1- 37, 225
yes- 158, yése/o- 143, 158
yewg- 20, 78, 158
yéwgos 158, 245
yéwos 158

-yo- 156, 337
-yó- (adj.) 14, 18, 79
yoh₃s- 158
-yos- ~ -is- 80
yugóm 60, 65 (paradigm), 78, 112, 158, 241
yugtós 20
yuHs- 158

Proto-Germanic

dēdiz 60 fn. 57
dō- 34 fn. 29
fōt- 237 fn. 51

3 Other Indo-European languages

Note that alphabetization is Roman throughout.

Albanian
mbledh 117

Armenian
anowrǰ 109, 156, 248
arar 36 fn. 31, 208
arb 134
ard 273
aṙnow 97, 179, aṙ 206
asê 146, 174
astł 109
awr 91, 145, 248, 288
ayr 109
-b ~ -w 125
bay 244
berel: eber 175 fn. 1
damban 148, 162
dizanel 128 fn. 24
dowstr 126
ełew 206
erek 108, 245
-ê 129
gaṙn, gaṙin 246, 290
hołm 99, 111
iž 127, 243, 285
jeṙn 140, 267
ǰer 284
ǰerm 127, 252, 339
k^{h}erê 117
lk^{h}anel: elik^h 205
mêg 109
mêz 109
mi 70 fn. 65, 101, 134
now, nowoy 134, 135, 240
orb 125
ows 140 fn. 32
siwn 246
sxalê 124
tesanel: etes 175 fn. 1
-wk^h 55
yet 334
zgenow 139, 179, zgec^{h}aw 4 fn. 39

Avestan
aēuuō 70, 252
aogədā 127, aoxtō 123, 251; pairi.aoɣžā 122 fn. 19
aršā 246
aršō 116, 239
aš-, aš.bāzāuš, aš.miždå 336
-āi (dat.) 91
-å (gen. du.) 55 fn. 53
bāraiia- 200
-biia 56
-biiō, -biš 55
cahiiā 138
caxrəm 119
darəɣō 106, 250
dāiš 36, 211
diβžaidiiāi 122 fn. 19
didąs, dīdaŋ́hē 136
ərənauuataē-ča 97
ərəziš 243
frabdō.drājō 122
gaēsuš 127
haptī 132, 187, 207
iziiā 94
jaδiieiti 147, jaδiieimi 189
jaiṇti 208, -jaɣnaṯ 208 fn. 32
kaēnā 242, 283
maēzaiti 109
maɣnō 119, 252
maziiō 154, 166
mərəzu- 117, 126, 253, 289
naptiiō 18, 240
nāismī 109
niš.hiδaiti 184
-ō (loc. du.) 55 fn. 53
paēma 100
paiti 334
pərətuš 78
rənjištō 121, 253
snāuuarə 145
staman- 339
šaēiti, šiieiṇti 116, 174
tašā 116
uxšiieiti 159
uzārəšuua 202
vacō 237
vaŋri 143, 248, 288
vauuarəza 218
vərəziieiti 34, 190, 289
vohū 63 fn. 60
xratū, xraθβā 63 fn. 60
xšaiieiti 118 fn. 18
xšuuaš 133
x^{v}əṇg 64 fn. 61, 132
yauuaējī- 106, 120
yåŋhaiia- 143, 158
zəmō 116, 126

zīzanənti 117

Early Runic
-u (dat. sg.) 64 fn. 62

Faliscan
fifiqo[n]d 146

French
pas 341

Gaulish
axat, lubijas 39 fn. 34

Gothic
aflinnan 177
agis 245
-ai (dat.) 91, 300
ains 70
aírþakunds 103
akrs 239
amsans 140 fn. 32
anabiudan 149, 188
anasilan 35
andeis 252
asts 89, 239
bai 70
baíran 125, 186
beidan 148, 186, 207, 210
bidjan 147, 189
bindan 147
broþar 125, 304
daug 147
daúhtar 111, 126, 247
-deþs 243
digandin 128, 147
diups 9
doms 90, 126, 239
faúr 334
filu 96 fn. 4, 253
filufaihs 159
gadars 126, 137, 140, 290
gaman 115, 217
ganaitjan 109
ganisan 135
gaqumþs 78, 243
gataíran 186
gatamjan 114
gateihan 212 fn. 37
harjis 156, 160
hauhs, hauhiþa 79
hausjan 109, 157, 158, 193, hauseiþ 90, 340
hlifan 192
hramjiþ 175
ƕaþar 281
ƕis 138
ist 174
-iþ (3sg.) 128
jer 107
junda 79
kaúrus 79, 96, 253, 282
kiusan 188
ligan 122, 127, 192
-m (dat. pl.) 55
man 36, 217
mikils 135 fn. 29
miliþ 193
miþ 334
mizdo 126
namnjan 99, 114, 160, 193
niman 186
-o (gen. pl.) 91
ogs 331
qens 119
riqis 108, 140, 245, 266, 284
sa, so 131, 280, þai, þos 280
saggws 127, 147, 242, 282
saljan 207
siggwan 147
sitan 193
skaban 123
staírno 109
steigan 117, 127, 188
sums 114, 131
sundro 133
swaran 193
swikns 107, 251
taíhun 113
taujan 178
tulgus 106
þana 72 fn. 67
un- 113
wahsjan 95
waírþan 192
wait (1sg.) 216, wait (3sg.) 36, 216
waúrd 103, 251
waúrkjan 190, waúrkeiþ 34
weitwods 298
wisan 108
wulfs 120, 240
wulla 110

Hispano-Celtic
amPiTiśeTi, aśeCaTi, CaPiseTi, -Tus 39 fn. 34

Hittite
Note that *d* is alphabetized with *t* and *g* with *k*.
-a (all.) 53
-ahh- 30
-āi- 30
alpās 125, 240

-ami 32
-an (gen. pl.) 51, 91
anda 333, andan 89
āppa 89, 333, āppan 89
āri 94
armas 98 fn. 6
ārras 89, 140, 239
-as (dat. pl.) 51, 53
-as (gen.) 53
assus 143, 253
attas 20, 89
-e- (stative) 30
esa 174, 339, ēshari 139, 141
ēszi 174
-ezzi 128
ēz'zi 174, 339, adwēni, aztēni 20
hānz, hantī 89
hāras, hāran- 89, 340
harkis 79, 97
harszi 212
hartaggas 97, 116, 239
hastai 89, 338
hasterz 109, 236, 347, 339
hasduēr 89
hatki 116
hatugis 109, 166, 190
hissas 94
hulani 110
hūwanz 109
-i (dat. sg.)
iezzi 93, 106, 176
ishāi, ishiyanzi 34 fn. 30, 94
ispanti ~ sipandi 188
istaman- 246
istuāri 174
īt 231
iukan 53, 78, 241
ganess- 31, ganeszi 44
karpiezzi 9
karszi 31, 117, 212
katta 233, 333
katti- 103, 131
gēnu 60, 339
kēr 249, kart- 291, 339
kēt 54
kī 163
giemi 113, 126
kissar 126, 140, 238, 247, 339
kitta 117, 339
kuaszi, kuassanzi 178
kuēnzi 119, 127, 192
kuis 339, kuit 82 fn. 72, 145, 339
gulszi 140, 283
lahhanzan- 111 fn. 13
lāman 110, 339
lē 331
lilipai 9
linkzi 108, 187
lukkizzi 31
mān 82
mekkis 135 fn. 29
mēyawas 71
milit 146, 193, 249
mimmai 31, 184
natta āra 203, 287
nekumant- 119
nekuz mēhur 119, 237
nēpis 245, nēpisas 14
newahhi 197
nēwas 197, 250
-ni(n)- 30
-nu- 30
pahhur, pahhuenas 238, 248, 339
parā 333
pāsi 31
pe- 333
pēdan 241
sākizzi 31
sakkar 248
sākki, sekkanzi 13
sarhieddu 104, 190
sēr 133
-si (iptv.) 28 fn. 21
sia- 26, 70, siēl 339
-sis 74
sissandu 31
-ske/a- 30
-sse 74, 335
suhhai 132, 192
suwezzi 34 fn. 30
ta 53, 72 fn. 67
dāi, tiyanzi 13
takku 82
damass- 223
tāru 244
dassus 136
tēkan 21, 113, 116, 238, 246, dagān 51, taknā 25, 114
tepnuzzi 30, 178 fn. 2
tēpus 31, 178 fn. 2
teripzi 187, 207
-ttuma 40 fn. 36
tuhhuwais 102
u- 333
ulesta 31
wāki 305
walhzi 215
wassezzi 31

wātar 248, 339, witār 238, 248
wēkzi, wekkanzi 187 fn. 10
wēsta 174
wedand(a) 60
wewakki 34 fn. 29
-z(a) 2 fn. 22, 335

Khotanese
dremäte 206

Latin
abolēre 206
ad 57
advena 242
ager 80, 239
agere 186, agit 16, 89
agnus 239, 282
agricola 242
ait 146, 174
albus 125, 240
aliquid 285
alius 89, 156, 159, 252, aliud 73, 145, 156, 159, 258
altus 99
alvos 239
amb- 97, 125
ambō 70, 125
anas 111, 243
angere 127, 186, ānxisse 212
animus 99 fn. 10
ānsa 140, 141
ante 89, 273, 334
arāre 190
-ārum 308
atavos 22 fn. 16
atta 20, 89
attulat (Old Lat.) 202
auceps 77
audīre 181
auris 339
avis 160
brevis 117, 126, 253, 289
-bus 55
calāre (Old Lat.) 103
caper 239
capere 162, 190
catus, Catō 80
cavēre 200
centum 113
cernere: crēvisse 180 fn. 3
cinis 138, 245
cis 163
clepere (Old Lat.) 117, 192, clepsit 212
cognātus 131
colere 188
cōnsīdere 184, cōnsīdit 34
cōnspicere 161
conventiō 78, 243
coquere 120, 192, coxisse 212, 282
cord- 249, 291
cornū 339
crībrum 78
cum 'with' 115, 156, 160
dacruma (Old Lat.) 244
damnum 114, 154, 242
datus 112, 251
decem 113
decēre 175
dēns, dentem, dentis 237, 249
dēnsus 136, 253
dexter 252
dīcere 211 fn. 37, dīxisse 211
diem 19, 112
dīligere 109, 186
dis- 334
docēre 199
dolus 239
domāre 114
dūrus 106
edere 89, ēst, edunt 34, edim 38
ego 339
en (Old Lat.) 89
equos 239
ērūgere 108, 186, 207
-ēs (acc. pl.) 114
est 89, 174, erō 135, erit 38; (Old Lat.) escit 184, siem 112, siet 138, 226
et 273
ex 123, 334
extrā 123
facere, fēcit 203; (Old Lat.) fēced 126
fāma 241
fānum 126, 150
fātur 91, 125, 174, 300
ferunt 125, feret 38
ferus 237
fēstus 126, 135
fīdere 148, 186, 207, 210, fīsus 121, 251
fierī 190
fingere 128
forēs 126
frāter 125, 247, 304
frīgus 134, 245
fuga 78, 241
fūgit 125, 205
fūmus 78, 102, 126, 239
fūr 247
gemere 117, 186
genetrīx 101

genitor 78, 91, 247
gēns, genti- 243
genū 60, 244
genus 78, 89, 117, 135, 245, generis 89, 135, 245
gignere 184
glūbere 189
gravis 79, 96, 253, 282
haurīre 193, hausisse 212
helvos 104
hērēs 304
herī 123
hic 123
hiems 238, 246, hieme 113, 126
honōs 246
horitur (Old Lat.) 160, 191, 290
hōrnus 107
hortus 239
iacere, iēcit 203, iēcisse 106
iecur 90, 107, 248, 281
illim 2 fn. 52
implēre 92, implēvit 202
in 89
in- 'un-' 113
ingruit (pf.) 205
inguen 283
interior, intimus 80
īre: it 174, ī 231
-it (3sg.) 128
iubēre 107
iūgera 158, 245
iūgis 106, 120
iugum 53, 112, 158, 241
iūs 'broth' 143, 158
iuventa 79
labium 9
lac, lactis 146, 249, 342
laevos 252
lāna 110
lātus 103, 251, 301
legere 117, 186, legit 340
lēvir 247
līber 108, 126, 251
linere: lēvisse 180 fn. 2
lingere, līnxisse 212
linquere 44, 188, līquit 188, 205
locus, loca 61
luere 189, luit (pf.) 202
lūx 340
macer 250, 340
maius 154, 166
mālum 241, 342
māter 235, 247
medius 156, 165, 252, 275
meiere 109, 126, 186
meminit 36, 115, 217
-men, -mentum 336
mēnsis 140, 145, 238, 246, 267
merērī 134, 289
meus 259
mīca 135
miscēre 184
mors, morti- 78
mūs 102, 249
musca 138
nāsus, Nāsō 80
nātus 103, 251
nāvis 244
nē 331
nebrundinēs (dial.) 127
nebula 125, 242
nefrōnēs (dial.) 127, 239, 282
nēmen, nēmine 247
nēre 190
nervos 134, 145
nīvit (Old Lat.) 127, 134, 187 with fn. 9, nivit 197 fn. 9
nix, niv- 127, 134, 282, nivem 248
nōmen 110, 246
nōscere 44, 185, nōvit 91, 202
novāre 35, 197
novem 317
novitās 79
novos 197, 250, novom 112, nova 305
nox, noct- 119, 237, 249, noctem 113, noctēs 114
nūmen 78, 114, 247
ōcior 253
oculus 121
odor 166
orbus 125
orīrī 97, ortus 97, 251
os 89
-osio 57
ovis 89, 243
ōvom 241, 339
palma 105, 242, palmam 112, 300
passus 'pace' 341
pater 90, 111, 235, 247
patrius 80
patruos 244
pecten 247
pectere 117
pēnis 135
pepigisse 219

pēs 237, 248, ped- 156, 166, pedem 237, 248, pedis 14, 237, 248
petere 186, 207
pic- 163
plectere 117
plēnus 340
pluere 187
pōculum 78
pōns 59 fn. 56
porrum 137, 241, 342
portus 78
poscit 22, 34
praeda 182
precēs 22
prehendere 182
quatere 164, 191, 281, quassisse 212
quī 73
quis 73, quid 145, 285
quot 156, 165, 275, 281
rapere 108, 161, 191
regere 109, 187, rēxisse 212
ruber 79, 108, 126, 250, 339, rubra 304
rubēre 34
sāgit, sāgīre 31 with fn. 24
sal 132, 249
salīre 132, 159, 191
sapiat 162
scabere 123
scaevos 252
scelus 245
scindere 124
sella 305
semel 70, 113, 131
sēmen 78
sēmi- 90, 131, 168
septem 113, 131
sequī 187, 207, sequitur 131
serere 'arrange' 132, 133
serit '(s)he sows' 31
serpere 132, 187
serum 133
silēre 35
simplex 113, 131
sistere 210, sistit 176
socer 133, 240
socius 121, 156
sōl 2 fn.61
sōpīre 201
sorbēre 134, 200
specere, speciō (Old Lat.) 189, spexit 212
spernere 124
stagnum 166
statiō 243
sternuere 179, 290
strātus 251
stupēre 215
suāvis 253
sub 151
sūbula 78
suēscere 147, 219
super 151
sūs 102, 132, 249
tangere: tetigisse 209 fn. 33
taurus 240
tegere 117, 187
tentus 114, 251
tenuis 114, 253
terere 103
termen 247
termō 246
tetulit (Old Lat.) 221
texit 2 fn. 15
tingere 187, tīnxisse 212
torrēns 215
tot 165, 275
tremere 187
tū 339
tuos 259
ūber 288
umbilīcus 97, 125
umerus 140 fn. 32
uncus 90, 239
unguis 109, 117, 119, 249, 338
ūnus 70
ūrere 186, ussisse 212
ursus 116, 239
vehere 187
venīre 115, 160, 190, 282
vertitur 165, 192
vesper 151, 240
vetus 245
vēxisse 36, 212
vīdit 205
vīgintī 113
vīnum 342
vīrus 100, 135
vīs 249
vīsere 35, 223
vīvere 186
vīvos 80, 252, 285
vocāre 119
vōx 119, 237

Latvian
drubazas 148, 162

Lithuanian
akmuõ 91, 246
ántis 111
aũlas 239
aušrà 143, 151
bė́ga 200
bū́siu, bū́siąs 35
dẽšimt 113
dubùs 79
dvíejau 55 fn.53
gurdùs 253, 282, 290
iẽšmas 293
ìlgas 106
ir̃ 287
jentė 107
įga 107, 241, 282, 300
kãrias 79, 156
kãras 79
kẽpa 191
knója 190
mélžti 109, mélža 187
miglà 109, 127, 241
minė́ti 215
mirtìs 78
-mus (dat. pl.), -mis (inst. pl.) 55
pèšti 117
piemuõ 92, 235, 246
píeva 305
pìrmas 80
platùs 96, 253, 290
saũsas 266 fn. 2
sẽnas 132, 250
stógas 117
šim̃tas 113
-ų̃ (gen. pl.) 91
-ui (dat.) 169 fn. 50
vasarà 143
ver̃žti 108
viẽšpats 84
vil̃kas 120, 240
vìlnos 110
žuvìs, žuvų̃ 249, 339
žvėrìs 117, 237, 247

Luvian
apin 2 fn. 52
hishiyanti 34 fn. 30
kīsa(i)- 8
kui 8
mallit 193
tūpīti 191 fn. 14
zin 2 fn. 52
ziyar 8, 174

Lycian
adi 204
-e (dat. pl.) 51
kbatra 25
lada 25
tubidi 191 fn. 14
wawa 25
xawa 25, xawã 89, 243

Old Church Slavonic
-a, voc. -o 23
cěna 242, 283
češetŭ 117
deretŭ 186
dlŭgŭ 106, 250
-etŭ 128
grabiti 9
ilŭ 94
krotiti 200
ležitŭ 127, -leže 203
-ma (dat.-inst. du.) 56
mĭgla 109, 127, 241
mĭněti 215
-mŭ (dat. pl.), -mi (inst. tpl.) 55
nebo 125, 245
netĭjĭ 18, 240
oba 70
oko 121, 281, oči 100, 121, 248
otĭcĭ 20
pečetŭ 192
pero 241
pĭstrŭ 250
pletetŭ 117
posteljetŭ 159, 189
postignǫti 188
pǫtĭ 59 fn. 56
prosějati 147
razdražiti 148
rŭdrŭ 79
sěmę 78
sŭnŭ 120
šilo 78
-u (gen.-loc. du.) 55 fn. 53
uxo 140, 245
vědě 216
zelenŭ 104, 340
žely 243
žena 119, 242

Old and Middle English
-a (gen. pl.) 91
ād 239

anga 161, 236, 246
æt 57
bana 127
camb 125, 239
ċeorfan 189, 291
clēofan 189
dǣd 243
dōm 17, 90, 126, 239
draf (ME) 148
duru 126
eald 99
ears 89, 140, 239
fǣmne 92
flōwan 190
folm 105, 242
ġeolu 104
hebban 162, 190
hīeran 104, 109, 157, 158, 193,
hīerþ 90
hwēol ~ hweogol 119, 239
lippa 9
mæġer 250
mǣþ 243
melcan 109, 187
medu 126, 244
mīgan 109, 126
mūs 102, 249
nafela 97, 125
næġl 109, 117, 119, 249
nemnan 99, 114,
160, 193
ōfer 156, 240
rōw 108, 241
sēar 266 fn. 2
seċġ 156
sellan 207
sēoþan 142
slīdan 181 fn. 4
smēocan 134
smeortan 134
snoru 134, 135
spurnan 124
stede 243
stician 166
sum 114, 131
þæt 145, þæs 138
þearm 17, 240
þon 72 fn. 67
un- 114
weorc 241
wer 76

Old and Middle High German

ango 236
anut 111
filu 96 fn. 4
gans 126, 140
gebal 147
gelo 104
jesan 143, 158
lungar 108, 114, 127,
250, 282
nioro 282
nuoen 190
obar 151
redan 200
ringi 108
ruohhen 109
sam(b)t (MHG) 111, 126,
147, 240
sāmo 78
snīwan 127, 134,
187, 284
tenar 248, 288
trebir 148
-u (dat. sg.) 64 fn. 62
ubiri 151
uover (MHG) 156, 240

Old and Middle Irish

*-ā-, *-ase- 39 fn. 34
ad·ella 177
airid 190
arathar 78, 111, 241
arbor 158
at·baill 206
bé 119, ben 242, bein 119,
mná 119, 242
biïd 190
célaid 35
con·sní 190
cuire 79, 156, 160
damnaid 177
droch 78, 148, 239
eirgg 185 fn. 6, 339
éisi 140
giun 244
guidid 34
íar 80
-ib (dat. pl.) 55
il 96 fn. 4
imbliu 97, 125
im·soí 34 fn. 30
lám 105, 242
lenaid 177
lethan 19, 114, 154
luid 36, 91, 126,
204, 227

mí, mís- 145
míl 241
nigid 121, 166, 190
no·daired 185
óen 70
renaid 103,
177, 304
rígain 243
samail 114, 131
seir 124
sniïd 17, 90, 134
tamnaid 103, 181
tánaic 110, 205 fn. 29
tlenaid 34

Old Norse
arðr 111
ál 241
fley 160
gana 185
hafr 239
heyra 109
hrǫnn 242, 266, 302
iðr 241
kjarr 241
kvefja 162, 190, 282
míga 186
mús 102, 249
otr 240
ǫngull 170, 252
raun 98 fn. 8
rífa 108
rœkja 109
sandr 111, 126,
147, 240
setr 131, 245
staurr 92, 240
sundr 133
sýr 102, 132, 249
tafn 114, 154, 242

Old Persian
aiva 70
-anā 72 fn. 67
ǰadiyāmiy 34, 284
kāra 79
xšnāsātiy 44, 185

Old Provençal
sapcha 162

Old Prussian
ains 70
auklipts 117
pintis 59 fn. 56

Old Saxon
dedos 34 fn. 29

Oscan
anams 99 fn. 10
-eí (loc. sg.) 53
heriiad 191
fíísnam 150
slaagím 134

Palaic
hussīnta 191
iska 184
wērti 103

Phrygian
αββερετ, αββερετορ 41 fn. 37
αδδακετ 41 fn. 37, 203, αδδακετορ 41 fn. 37
wen autun 250

Sanskrit
a- 'un' 113
abʰí 333
ad-: átti 174, ádat 38
áhis 16 fn. 11, 127, 243, 285
-ais (inst. pl.) 145
ájati 16, 89, 186, ájanti 272, ā́jat 91, 227, 300
ájras 80, 239
ajryás 80
ákṣitaṃ 113, 116, 251, 282
-ām (gen. pl.) 91
ám̥sas 140 fn. 32
ándʰas 126, 245
ániti 111
ántaras, ántamas 80
ánu 333
anudrás 114
áñcati 89
áṅkas 245
ápa 333
áparas 80
ā́pas 9 fn. 7
ápi 333
ápyas (ápias) 11
árhati 206, 284
-as (acc. pl.) 114
ā́sat- 89
ā́se 139, 141, ā́ste 174, ā́sate 136, 142
asmi 139, 266, ási 20, asti 174, ásti, sánti 34, ásāni
135, ásati 38, syā́m ~ siā́m 112, syā́t 38, 138,
226, sánt- ~ sat- 108, 135, satī́ 100, 114, 135,
164, ā́sam 136, ā́s 91, 146, 227, ā́san 309
ásitas 136
asmā́n 139, 141, 266, 339

ā́śīrtas 103, 117, 177, 251, 304
áśmā 91, 235, 246, áśmānam, áśmanas ~ áśnas 235
áśru 244
āśús 253
áśvas 239
aṣṭáu 21
-ata (3pl.) 114
-ati (thematic 3sg.) 128
-ati (3pl.) 114
ātís 111, 164, 243
ávis 16 fn. 11, 89, 243, ávim 112, ávyas 16 fn. 11
āvís 181
-ayá/ā́- 196
-āyá/ā́- 198 fn. 21
bahús 149, 253, báṃhīyas- 149
bāhús 91, 146, 244, 300, bāhúm 112
bandʰ-, bándʰus 147
budʰ- 22, buddʰás 22, 121, 122, 123, 253, bódʰati 149, 188, budʰánta 205
budʰnás 128 fn. 23, 147
bʰájati 206
bʰárati 34, 125, bháret 38, 146, 186, bháratāt, ábharat 146, ábharam, ábharatam 112, ábharatām 112, 300
bhāti 91, 125, 174, 241, 272, 300
bʰrā́tā 125, 247, 304
bʰrū́s 102, 109, 125, 249
bʰū- 35, bʰavi- 125, ábʰūt 102, 125, 202, bʰúvat, bʰūyā́t 38, babʰū́va 220, bʰaviṣyáti 35
-bʰyas, -bhis 55
-bʰyā́m 56
cakrám 119
cárati 188
catvā́ras 168, 283
ci-: ní cikāya 285
cit 285
cyávate 163, cyávānas 203, cucyuvé 222
cʰāyā́ 242, 305
cʰinátti 124
cʰyati 124
dā-: dádāti 91, 112, 176, 272, 339, dádati 98, dattʰá 112
dabʰ-, dípsati 122 fn. 19, ā́ dabʰnoti 30
dáhati 147, 282, 305, 340
dákṣiṇas 21, 252
daṃśayati 182, 338
dánt- ~ dat- 109, dán 237, 249, 339, dántam, datás 237, 249
dā́ru 244
dās-: ábhi dāsati 223
dáśa 113
dāśnóti 179
dehī́ 147
déhmi 147, dégdʰi, dihánti 128
devā́ 247
deváttas 112
dīdā́ya 175
dīrgʰás 106, 250
diśá-, ádikṣi, ádiṣṭa 211 fn. 37
divyás 79
drā́tu 202, 304
dr̥ś-: ádr̥śran 205, 291, dadárśa 218
dugʰ- 122, dógdʰi 122, 149, 187, 207, dugdʰás 123, 251
duhitā́ 111, 126, 235, 247, duhitŕ̥ṣu 289
dvā́ 339
dvéṣas 317
dyáti 190
dyáus 145, 166, 237, 249, dyā́m ~ diā́m 19, 112, div- 249
dʰā-: dádʰāti 34, 90, 112, 176, 272, dádʰati 34, 98, dʰattʰá 112, dádʰīta 38, ádadʰām 112, ádʰāt 126, 203, hitás 112, 251
dʰánvat 103, 300
dʰr̥ṣ-: dadhárṣa 126, 137, 140, 290
dʰr̥ṣús 253
dʰūmás 78, 102, 126, 148, 239
-dʰva 40 fn. 36, 168
dʰvan-: ádʰvanīt 168
dʰyā- 164
dʰyā́ma 193, 247
-e (ā-stem voc.) 242
édʰas 239
ékas 70
gā-: jígāti 176, ágāt 202, 282
gam- 35, gámat 38, gáccʰati 113, 124, 185, 282
gárbʰas 283
gátis 78
gáus 145, 249, 282, gáv- 282, gā́vas 249
gávyūtis 107
gīrṇás 104, 282
grásate 175
gr̥- 'wake': jāgā́ra 90, 108, 206, 218, jāgr̥vā́n 218
gr̥bʰ-: ágrabʰīt 9
gurús 79, 96, 253, 282, 290
gʰarmás 127
hā-: jáhāti, jíhīte 176
hadati 166
haṃsás 126, 140
hánti 119, 127, 192, 208, hatás 251
háras 245, 284
háryati 191
hástas 126
hemantás 246
hu-: juhóti 126, 203, juhvé 222
hyás 123
i- 31, éti 174, 272, itʰá 93, ihí 231, ā́yan 93

ī́hate 94
ī́kṣate 224
inóti 31
īṣā́ 94
iṣirás 94, 280 fn. 11
íṣuhastas 77, 137
íṣus 94, 140
jámb^{h}āsas 125, 239
jan-: ájījanat 184, jajā́na 217, jātás 103
jánas, janā́ 77
jánas (s-stem) 78, 89, 117, 135, 245, jánasas 89, 135, 245
jánitrī 101
jánī 119, 339, gnā́s 119
jā́nu 244
jīvás 80, 252, 285
jī́vati 186
jmán 89
jñā-: jānā́ti, jñeyā́s 44, jātás 251
jóṣat, joṣati, juṣāṇá- 188
jyā́ 'bowstring' 285
jyā́ 'force' 285
kám 280
katarás 281
káti 156, 165, 275, 281
krátus 253, 290
kravís 111, 245, 339
krīṇā́ti, krītás 101
kṣam- 21, kṣámi 113, 116
kṣaṇóti 179, 339, mā́ kṣaṇiṣṭ^{h}ās 116
kṣáyati 118 fn. 18
kṣéti 116, 174, kṣiyánti 116, 174, 273
kṣid^{h}ī́ 202, kṣiṇóti 317
kṣurám 241
lī-: ní aleṣṭa 31
lināti 177
lunā́ti 189
mā́ 331
mád^{h}us 244, mád^{h}u 126
mád^{h}yas 156, 165, 252, 275
mahánt- 135 fn. 29, máhi 111, 253, 338
māṃsám 140 fn. 32
-mane (inf.) 279
mányate 115, 160, 190, mamanyā́t 38
mā́rjmi 187
mā́s 140, 145, 238, 246, 267
mātā́ 235, 247
matā́, matyā́ 63 fn. 59
meg^{h}ás 109, 127
mé^{h}ati 109, 126, 186
mīḍ^{h}ám 126, 240
mṛṇī^{h}í 177, 290
mṛtás 251, 289
mū́s 102, 249
nā́ 97, 109, 235, 247, 339
nábhas 125, 245, 338
nā́bhis 97, 125
nagnás 119, 252
nagnátā 79
nák, náktam 119, 339
nā́ma 246
násante 135, níṃsate 184
naś-: ā́naṭ 110, 205, ānā́śa 110, ānáṃśa 110, 205 fn. 29
náus 244, nāvás 244, 308
náva 317
návas 250, návam 112, návā 305
návyas (návias) 11
néd (ná íd) 332
nenikté 121, 166, 284, niktás 122, 251
nidānás 109
oh- 122 fn. 19, óhate 123, 127
ójas 96
-os (gen.-loc. du.) 55 fn. 53
óṣati 142, 186
pā-: ápās 31, pītás 338
pácati 120, 192
pánt^{h}ās 340
páñca 283
paraśús 244
pardate 186, 207
pári 333
pā́rṣṇis 144
párus, párvan- 193, 248, 288, 317
parút 129, 273
pásas 135, 245
páśyati 161, 189, 199
pat- 201, pátati 184, 186, 207, 339
pā́t 237, 248, 339, pā́dam 113, 237, 248, padás 237, 248
pátis 16 fn. 11, 243
pátnī 101, 243
pitā́ 90, 111, 235, 247, pitṛ́ṣu 236
pítryas 80
pī́vā 100, 253 pī́varī 100, 253
plávate 187, aploṣṭa 212
prá 333
práti 165, 275, 333, 334
pṛccháti 22, 34, pṛcchā́t 38
pṛt^{h}ús 90, 96, 253, 290, pṛt^{h}ivī́ 100
pur- 106
pūrd^{h}í 206
purupéśas 159
purús 96, 253, purū́ 339
putrávant- 80
rag^{h}ús 20, 108, 114, 117, 127, 253
rájas 108, 140, 245, 284
rajasyáti 35

rā́jñī 243
rajyate 190
rákṣati 34, 97, 109, 223
rā́ṣṭi 187
réḍ^{h}i 117, 126, 187
ric-: riṇákti 34, 44, 188, riñcánti 34, 188, riṇácāva 38
rocáyati 31
rugnás 122
r̥jipyás 79, 89
r̥jrás 79, 97, 250
ŕ̥kṣas 21, 97, 116, 239
r̥ṇóti 97, 179, prá ārta, sám aranta 202
sa- 113, 131, 147
sá, sā́ 131, 280, tásya 138, tát 145, té, tā́s 280, tā́sām 308
sácate 131, 187, 207, 284
sad-: sī́dati 184, sādáyati 35
sádas 131, 147, 245
sadyás 123
sáhas 126
sahásram 126, 140, 266
sáhate 148, 184, 207
sák^{h}ā 121, 156, 244
samás 90, 131, 250
samayáti 35
sánas 132, 250
sápati 132, 187
saptá 113, 132
sáras 131, 245
sárpati 187
sárvas 132, 317
savyás 11
skhalate 124
smáyate 134
snā́ti 134, 339
snā́van- 134
snā́yati 90, 134
snuṣā́ 134, 135, 240
spāśáyasva 199
spr̥háyati 127
sp^{h}uráti 124
sp^{h}ūrjáyant- 124
srávati 134
srid^{h}-: ásrid^{h}ānas 181 fn. 4
sr̥- ‘flow’: sísarti 133, ásarat 203
sr̥játi 134, 291
stambhi- 147
starī́s 100
stáve 174
stig^{h}-, prá stiṅnoti 117, 127, 188
str̥-: tistiré 222, stīrṇás 104
st^{h}ā-: tíṣṭ^{h}ati 176, 210, ást^{h}āt 91, 112, 146, 202, 300, tast^{h}au 220, 339, sthitás 112, 251
st^{h}itís 243
su- 143
súar 2 fn. 61, 132, 339
sumanasyámānas 193
sūnára- 109
suváti 34
sūyávasas 107
svādús 91, 133, 253, 300, svādvī́ 101
svásāras 133, 135, 247
svayám 133
svidyati 133
syáti 34 fn. 30, 94
syū́ma 132
śamnīṣe 182, śāntás 103, 300
śatám 113
śéte 117, 174
śramat 176
śrávas 78, 117, 245
śri-: śiśriye 222
śrud^{h}í 202
śū́ras 118
śvā́ 235, 246, 338, śvā́nam 235, śúnas 17, 235, 246, śvásu 18
śváśuras 133, 240
-ṣáni (inf.) 279
-tá- 22
tákṣā 116
-tama- 254
tanóti 34, 179, tanvánti 34, tanávāvahai 38
tanús 114, 253
tā́ṣṭi 21, 183, tákṣati 21, 116, 183
tā́vat 308
Trasádasyus 336
trásati 135, 137, 140, 187, 290
trī́ 101
tr̥pát 205, 290
tŕ̥ṣyati 140
tujyáte 190
turám 185
-tvaná- 336
tviṣ-: atviṣanta 138, 167
tyájati 164, 200, tyája- 284
ub^{h}-: sám unap, ub^{h}nā́s, aub^{h}nāt 102, 115, 125, 152, 161, 183
ub^{h}áu 70
udā́ 151, 238, 248
udgūrṇas 103, 282, 290
udrás 240
ū́d^{h}ar 248, 288, ū́d^{h}nas 248
ugrás 96
úpa 151, 333
upabdáis 122
upári 151, 333
ūrd^{h}vás 168

ū́rṇā 110
urús 81, 94, 253, várīyas- 81, 253, várīyān 94, váriṣṭʰas 81, 94
uṣā́s 95, 140, 141, 245, 267, 301
úttaras 121, 152, 252
vac-: voca- 284, ávocat 36, 208
vácas 78, 119, 245, 284
vádati 94
vadʰ-: ávadʰīt 201, 208
váʰati 187, ávāṭ 212, vóḍhum 122
vāháyati 199
vā́k 119
vakṣáyati 95
vámiti 192
várṣati 108, 140, varṣáyati 141, 200
vártate 165, 192
vas- 'wear': ávasta 174, ávasata 114
vásati 'stays' 108
vāsáyati 31
vásma 139, 142, 247, 266
vasnayántā 193
vā́stu 244
vaś-: váṣṭi, uśánti 187 fn. 10, uśánt- 187
vā́tas 144
-vatī 164
vā́ti 90, 109, 174
véda (1sg.) 216, véttʰa 90, 121, 216, véda 36, 216, 339, vidmá 216, védati 38, 216, vidyā́t 38, viddʰí 121, 126, 216, vidvā́n 216, vidúṣī 101, 138, 216, vidmáne 279
véṣat 213
vid- 'find': ávidat 205, vittás 121
viṣám 100, 135
vītíhotras 336
vr̥dʰ-, vŕ̥ddʰis 122
vŕ̥kas 120, 240
vr̥trahán- 77
yájadʰva 168
yajñás 19, 107, 251
yákr̥t 90, 107, 248, 281, 339
yás 107
yásyati 158
yát 82
yātár- 107, 247
yávas 158
yávasam 107
yā́vat 308
yójate 158
yúdʰyati 107
yugám 53, 78, 158, 241

Serbo-Croatian
žȇ 117

Slovene
ojȇ 94

Spanish
sepa 162

Tocharian A
āmpi, āmpuk 70
-äṣ 54
kläsmāṃ 224
knānat 44, kñasu, kñasäṣt 31, 44
lyäm 236, 246
-m 55
mar yutkatār 107
-māṃ 43
päklyoṣ 28 fn. 21
päl 109, 245
śanweṃ 244
śpāl 147
śtwar, śtwār 71
ṣya- 70 fn. 65
tām, päṣtāk 204 fn. 27
tsmäṣ 224
want 144
waṣt 244
wṣe 108
yaṣ 93, 106, 204

Tocharian B
antapi 70, 125
ākṣäṃ 174
āntse 140, 239
ārkwi 79
āśäṃ 16, 186
āu 89, 243
ek 156, 281
katnaṃ 177
kälṣäṃ, kälseṃ 224
kälypītsi 117, 161, 192
käryāmtte 101, 202, 281
kele 239, 281
kokale 119
ku, kweṃ 235
kuṣäṃ 126
lac 36, 91, 126, 204, 227
lakle 250
lyam 236, 247
mā 331
-mane 42 fn. 38, 43
māka 135 fn. 29
-me 55

mekwa 109, 117, 119, 249
mit 244
ñem 110, 246
ost 244
parāṃ 186
parwa 241
päklyauṣ 28 fn. 21
pīle 109, 245
plyewsa 212
pokai 146
poñc 144, 253
puwar 238, 248
pyāktsi 161, 163
ratre 79, 108, 126, 250
reksa 212
sälkāte 132
siknaṃ 115, 132
skente 184
skiyo 242, 305
smimane 134
soy 244
spe 151
suwaṃ 132, 192
śaiṃ 186
ścama 147
śtwer 71, 283, śtwāra 71
ṣar 140, 267
ṣñor 134, 145
ṣp 55, 74
tapre 9, 79
tarya 101
tsamṣt 224
tswetär 178
wase 100, 135
wawākau 219, wokotär 305
wässāte 212 fn. 39
wek 119, 237, 248, 281
yente 144
yṣīye 108
/aləskə/e-/ 185
/táka-/, /taká-/ 204 fn. 27
/tˢəma-/ 103, 300

Umbrian
heriest 191
-o, voc. -a 23

Venetic
louderobos 108, 126, 251
vhagsto 203

Welsh
asgwrn 89
chwech 133
eil 11
el 39 fn. 34
ffêr 124
hidl 147
llydan 19, 114, 154
newydd 11
un 70